PRAISE F[illegible]

'Vivid, de[illegible] written.'
Daily Telegraph

'A staggering accomplishment that can't be missed by history buffs and story lovers alike.'
Betterreading.com.au

'A free-flowing biography of a great Australian figure'
John Howard

'Clear and accessible … well-crafted and extensively documented'
Weekend Australian

'Kieza has added hugely to the depth of knowledge about our greatest military general in a book that is timely'
Tim Fischer, *Courier-Mail*

'The author writes with the immediacy of a fine documentary … an easy, informative read, bringing historic personalities to life.'
Ballarat Courier

Award-winning journalist Grantlee Kieza OAM has held senior editorial positions at *The Daily Telegraph*, *The Sunday Telegraph* and *The Courier-Mail*. He is a Walkley Award finalist and the author of sixteen acclaimed books, including the recent bestsellers *Banjo*, *Mrs Kelly*, *Monash*, *Sons of the Southern Cross* and *Bert Hinkler*.

ALSO BY GRANTLEE KIEZA

The Hornet (with Jeff Horn)

Boxing in Australia

Mrs Kelly: The Astonishing Life of Ned Kelly's Mother

Monash: The Soldier Who Shaped Australia

Sons of the Southern Cross

Bert Hinkler: The Most Daring Man in the World

The Retriever (with Keith Schafferius)

A Year to Remember (with Mark Waugh)

Stopping the Clock: Health and Fitness the George Daldry Way (with George Daldry)

Fast and Furious: A Celebration of Cricket's Pace Bowlers

Mark My Words: The Mark Graham Story (with Alan Clarkson and Brian Mossop)

Australian Boxing: The Illustrated History

Fenech: The Official Biography (with Peter Muszkat)

Macquarie

BANJO

GRANTLEE KIEZA

First published in Australia in 2018
This edition published in 2020
by HarperCollins*Publishers* Australia Pty Limited
ABN 36 009 913 517
harpercollins.com.au

HarperCollins*Publishers*
Level 13, 201 Elizabeth Street, Sydney NSW 2000, Australia
Unit D1, 63 Apollo Drive, Rosedale, Auckland 0632, New Zealand
A 53, Sector 57, Noida, UP, India
1 London Bridge Street, London, SE1 9GF, United Kingdom
Bay Adelaide Centre, East Tower, 22 Adelaide Street West, 41st floor, Toronto, Ontario M5H 4E3, Canada
195 Broadway, New York NY 10007, USA

A catalogue record for this book is available
from the National Library of Australia

ISBN 978 0 7333 3591 4 (paperback)
ISBN 978 1 4607 0757 9 (ebook)

Cover design by Lisa White
Cover images: Banjo Paterson by News Ltd; *Watering Gully, Cape Upstart*, Plate no. VII of *Sketches in Australia and the Adjacent Islands*, by Harden S Melville, 1824–1894, courtesy State Library of Victoria
Author photo by Milen Boubbov
Typeset in Bembo Std by Kirby Jones
Printed and bound in Australia by McPherson's Printing Group
The papers used by HarperCollins in the manufacture of this book are a natural, recyclable product made from wood grown in sustainable plantation forests. The fibre source and manufacturing processes meet recognised international environmental standards, and carry certification.

For Mike and Linda Colman, my friends

Barton Paterson Family Tree

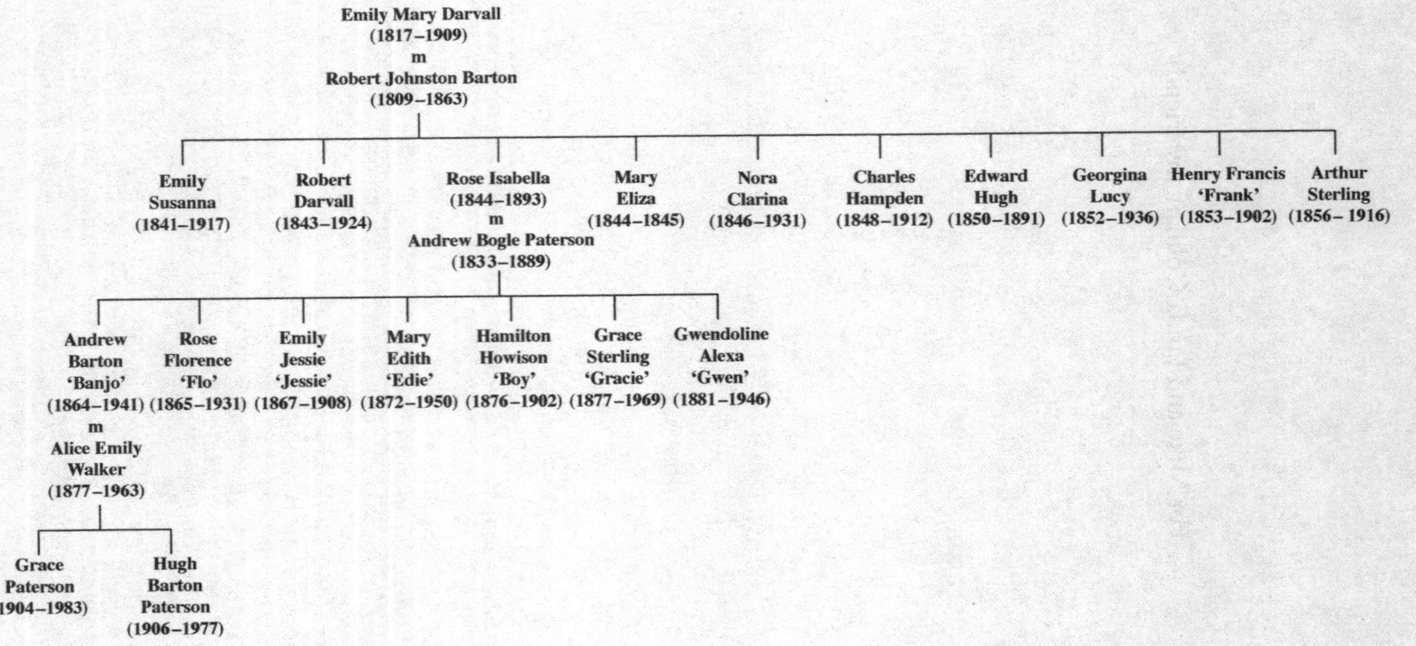

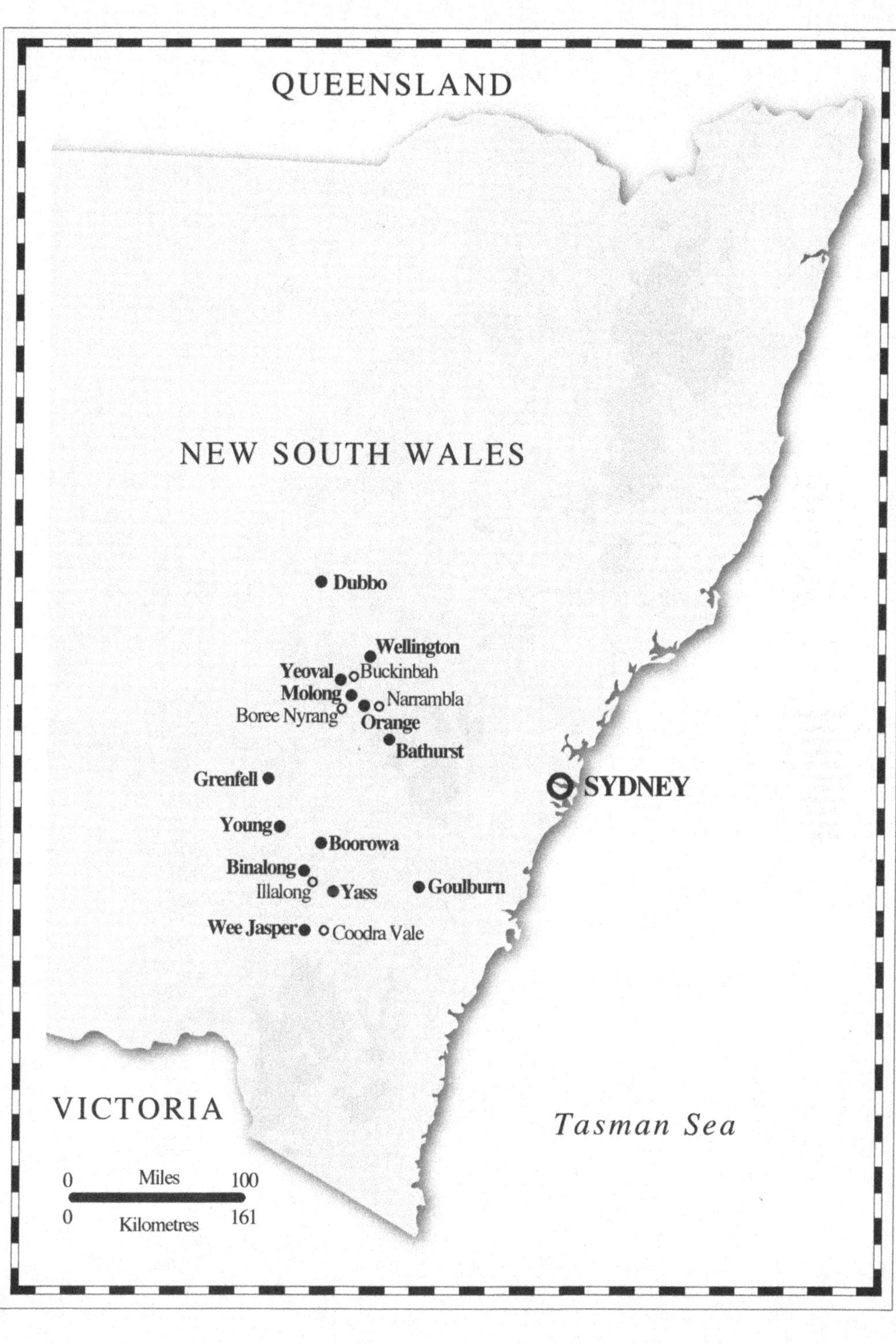
QUEENSLAND
NEW SOUTH WALES
Dubbo
Wellington
Yeoval
Buckinbah
Molong
Narrambla
Boree Nyrang
Orange
Bathurst
Grenfell
SYDNEY
Young
Boorowa
Binalong
Illalong
Yass
Goulburn
Wee Jasper
Coodra Vale
VICTORIA
Tasman Sea
0 Miles 100
0 Kilometres 161

And the bush hath friends to meet him, and their kindly voices greet him
In the murmur of the breezes and the river on its bars,
And he sees the vision splendid of the sunlit plains extended,
And at night the wond'rous glory of the everlasting stars.

BANJO PATERSON, *CLANCY OF THE OVERFLOW*[1]

Prologue

I thought that most of us had a bit of a craving for the free life, the air and the sunshine, and to be done with the boss and the balance sheet.

BANJO PATERSON ON THE INSPIRATION FOR HIS WRITING[2]

Name: PATERSON, ANDREW BARTON
Married or single: Married
Height: Five feet 10½ inches
Weight: 11 stone 10lbs
Chest measurement: 38[3]
Eyesight: Good
Age: 49 years seven months
Occupation: Author

Thus, on 24 September 1915, the handsome, middle-aged but still athletic Andrew Barton 'Banjo' Paterson – writer, editor and battling wheat farmer – applied for a commission in the Remount Unit serving in the Middle East during the First World War. He'd lied about his age – in fact he was fifty-one years and seven months – but his passport to war had always been his horsemanship and, to him, that mattered more than age. In any case he had always been a storyteller, prone to embellishment.

Banjo told the commanding officer that he was an Australian-born British subject and proud of it, that he was a qualified solicitor, and that he was equally qualified for this great job at hand against the enemy, having had considerable experience in the business of war.

In this, he wasn't embellishing. During the Boer War in 1899, he had spent time as a correspondent riding with Lord French's cavalry. More recently, he had reported on the destruction of the *Emden* and had worked a short stint in France as an ambulance driver, having sailed with Australia's First Division from King George Sound off Albany for Egypt on 1 November 1914. It was a huge convoy that stretched for twelve kilometres, made up of thirty-eight troop ships carrying 30,000 Australian and New Zealand soldiers and 7800 Waler horses. A special correspondent embedded with the troops, Banjo wrote in the *Sydney Morning Herald* that 'Sunday, 1 November was a red-letter day in the history of Australia' when the young nation's greatest maritime venture put out to sea, moving 'across the ocean like a large regatta of great steamships … the most wonderful sight that an Australian ever saw'.[4]

BANJO PATERSON LIVED AN EPIC LIFE. As a child he had ridden bareback to a one-room school, following a trail frequented by the bushranger Ben Hall, and was allowed to fire a rifle that was used to kill a bandit. He rode across the Australian bush with Breaker Morant and bounced around the English countryside with Rudyard Kipling. He listened to the bluster of Winston Churchill and saw the brutality of Lord Kitchener. He was a legal advocate for Henry Lawson, his literary rival, and he was a pitch invader at the Sydney Cricket Ground, a tennis ace, a champion jockey and a celebrated polo player. He reported from war zones and had more battles on the sporting field than he could remember. He backed Carbine and Phar Lap, and met the great cricketers, from 'the Demon' Fred Spofforth to Don Bradman. He went to the races in France with the bawdy queen of vaudeville and flirted with the young novelist Stella Miles Franklin.

During his lifetime, Banjo became one of the best-known Australians worldwide. As well as a poet and storyteller, he was a newspaper editor, columnist and highly regarded war correspondent, but it was his fictional heroes – the romanticised bushmen and women, heroic underdogs, tough and independent battlers tackling nature and the establishment head on – that endured, still as vivid and enchanting as they were when they first appeared, somewhere between his memories and imagination. Though he never made a fortune from his writing, he enriched the lives of his readers.

For his two granddaughters he composed marvellous biographical tales of his early days in remote pockets of Australia, in an ode to his family and the country he loved. He left a treasure trove of stories and memories for his nation, and the characters he created would resonate with generations to follow, helping to define the nation's identity and bridging urban life of the twenty-first century with the rural struggles of the nineteenth.

Banjo's works have been sung or recited by artists as diverse as Dame Nellie Melba, Leonard Teale, Chubby Checker, Slim Dusty, The Seekers, Jack Thompson and André Rieu – and countless lesser-known entertainers around Australia. As recently as the winter of 2015, I sat under the starlight beside the Thomson River near Longreach, listening to a local entertainer named John Hawkes sing about the trials and tribulations of life on the great cattle and sheep stations. He sang songs of the bush that – like Banjo's writings more than a hundred years before – rejoiced in the humour and the oddities of a unique world most Australians only know from books and poems. And he sang about a young city solicitor who, in late nineteenth-century Sydney, received a letter from a remote corner of Australia, written in such a meandering script that it could have been put on paper by a 'thumbnail dipped in tar'.[5]

There, beside that languid river in 2015, Banjo's 'Clancy of the Overflow' was as captivating as it had been when he conceived it in 1888,[6] clipping along with its easy rhythm as its author pictured himself on the great plains instead of a 'dingy little office, where a stingy ray of sunlight' struggled between tall buildings all around.[7]

The most memorable of all Banjo's characters is the jolly swagman who camped by a billabong and with nothing but a jumbuck in his tuckerbag confronted the twin powers of money and the law. 'Waltzing Matilda', the ballad of this free spirit who opposed crushing authority, was born from one of Banjo's love affairs, and has become Australia's unofficial national anthem.

The chorus that Banjo and Christina Macpherson jotted down are words of love.

Who'll come a-waltzing Matilda, my darling.
Who'll come a-waltzing Matilda with me.[8]

From the remote, dusty flat country of Central Queensland where these words were composed, 'Waltzing Matilda' became a reminder of

Australian outdoors life, a song synonymous with the nation and its people, even though the vast majority of Australians now live in big cities far from billabongs and shearing sheds. Long after Banjo's death, 'Waltzing Matilda' remains a rallying cry for Australians in times of distress, in times of joy, in times when what Banjo saw as the essence of Australianness – bravery against overwhelming odds – has been sorely needed. It was Australia's song to the world for the Sydney Olympics Opening Ceremony, the victory song for Australia's triumph in the America's Cup, and the first song to be broadcast to earth by astronauts.[9]

Diggers in the caves of Gallipoli and in the trenches on the Western Front sang it to lift their spirits, and during the Second World War it became a song of hope for Australian troops on a suicide mission at the Battle of Muar, and for starving, brutalised nurses as they were loaded onto a truck to become slave labour for the Japanese at Rabaul.[10]

Banjo had sold the rights to 'Waltzing Matilda' for a pittance, but he took comfort in the effect his composition had on other Australians. At the outbreak of the First World War, he heard an impromptu rendition of the song at Sydney's Randwick Racecourse – which had been transformed into an army staging camp[11] – while he was visiting with his friend, the famous artist Daryl Lindsay.[12]

Banjo knew many of the men there that day would never return to their loved ones. He watched these Australian soldiers parading by, heroic like the mountain horsemen he knew, ready for any danger.

The soldiers began singing 'Waltzing Matilda' in chorus.

Once a jolly swagman camped by a billabong
Under the shade of a coolibah tree,
And he sang as he watched and waited till his billy boiled:
'You'll come a-waltzing Matilda, with me ...'

Banjo listened and studied the expressions and bearing of the men. He looked into the eyes of those who would soon be rushing at Germans and Turks under a canopy of bursting shells; who would soon be charging into the ceaseless thresh of machine guns.

As the soldiers continued to sing, Banjo turned to his famous companion. 'Well, Daryl,' he said, with a tear in his eye. 'I only got a fiver for the song, but it's worth a million to me to hear it sung like this.'

Chapter 1

28 OCTOBER 1839, SOUTH ATLANTIC OCEAN, OFF THE COAST OF CAPE SÃO ROQUE, NORTHERN BRAZIL

Cultivated, gentle, kindly spoken, she took up the rough life of the pioneering days … the accidents by flood and field inseparable from station life without ever losing heart

BANJO PATERSON RECALLING HIS GRANDMOTHER EMILY[1]

BANJO PATERSON WAS BORN in the heart of the Australian bush with romance and adventure woven into his soul. His ancestors were dreamers and storytellers, dashing horsemen and sailors who fought pirates and the perils of the deep, and intrepid pioneer women who battled the wilds of nature.

Paterson's earliest memories were of a remote sheep station with its enchanting characters and mysterious wildlife. Australia's most cherished storyteller spent many years listening to the tales of his grandmother, who as a slip of a girl had left country mansions in England and France for life in a largely unpopulated Australian wilderness.

But this story begins on a balmy afternoon off the coast of South America when the deep blue ocean was as smooth as a pond and shining like glass. The winds of change driving the young life of pretty and vivacious Emily Darvall[2] were now becalmed. Emily was a genteel poet with 'large prominent eyes'[3] and the heart for a challenge, and she was sitting with her parents and siblings for an early dinner at the captain's table aboard the *Alfred*, a grand, full-rigged old barque carrying 269 emigrants[4] from the English port of Plymouth to the growing youthful metropolis of Sydney in New

South Wales. The timbers of the 650-tonne ship[5] had creaked and swayed for almost the whole month since it had left England,[6] but now the vessel was travelling at just five knots on the placid waters.

Emily was whip smart and fluent in French and Italian.[7] While she had been working on some verse about her voyage since the ship set sail, she was more interested in a fellow first-class passenger, the dashing Robert Johnston Barton,[8] a tall pious Christian, sensible and amiable, with a luminous smile and polished manners.[9] Emily was a doe-eyed girl with lots of spunk, and her friends called her 'Puss'. She wrote in her diary that 'Mr Barton seems to be a pleasing gentlemanly person',[10] and she was planning on becoming more acquainted with this mysterious stranger.

Then chaos.

'MAN OVERBOARD! MAN OVERBOARD!'

The shriek pierced the serenity on the ship. With a loud clatter, the *Alfred*'s white-haired, red-faced skipper, Captain John Flint,[11] dropped his knife and fork and leapt to his feet.

Another voice bellowed that 'a child has fallen overboard', and Emily's mama gasped in horror that a young life had been swallowed by the briny depths.

Crew and passengers rushed to the vantage point on the top deck, the women holding up the ends of their voluminous skirts to avoid tripping as their feet dashed across the wooden decks. Emily's mad rush was halted as she ran headlong into Mr Barton's broad chest.

The accident did not make her unhappy.

''Tis not a child overboard,' Barton said breathlessly, 'but a sailor in the water.'[12]

Another passenger, Mr Pierman, cut down a lifebuoy from its holding. The stricken crewman was all flailing limbs and cries of panic. Barton took the buoy from Pierman and tossed it overboard, plumb into the outstretched arms of the distressed sailor. With a broad Scottish accent, Captain Flint ordered that a rowing boat be lowered to save the poor wretch. The rescue crew dragged their shipmate into the boat but there was much rude language as he struggled violently with them like a fish out of water. It quickly became clear that the sailor had fallen into the ocean weighed down by a bellyful of rum. When the gibbering wreck was finally dragged back on board, Captain Flint, usually a kindly soul,[13] knew exactly what to do with the drunken sailor.

'Put the damn fool in irons for a day,' he thundered.

Emily had to laugh the next morning when the sailor, now sullen and sheepish, seemed oblivious to the fact that he had been in the water. She thought it 'quite wonderful' that he'd caught the lifebuoy in 'such a state of intoxication'.[14]

EMILY'S FAMILY WAS PROSPEROUS and well connected, and the Darvalls were now on their way to an exciting venture in a new world of opportunity. Great fortunes had been made by clans who had established themselves in India and Canada. Emily's seventeenth-century ancestor Anthony Darvall was a member of the landed gentry in Lincolnshire, and for generations they had had strong ties to a trading powerhouse, the British East India Company. Darvel Bay in north-eastern Borneo was named after Emily's great-grandfather Joseph, and her grandfather Roger Darvall had been on the Council of Madras before retiring to his estate in York.

Emily's papa, Major Edward Darvall,[15] had always been an adventurous man. At sixty-four – an age when most men of his generation were long dead[16] – he was taking on a great new challenge on a distant shore. It was half a century since Arthur Phillip had arrived with his First Fleet of convicts at Port Jackson, New South Wales, and the rapidly growing city of Sydney – with its thirty thousand people,[17] and its mushrooming collection of impressive brick and sandstone buildings around a majestic harbour – promised to be every bit as exciting and exotic as India, where Darvall was born. In 1799 he had been a young officer in the 19th Dragoons at the storming of Seringpatam in India for the Duke of Wellington,[18] when fifty thousand soldiers of the British East India Company battled thirty thousand from the Kingdom of Mysore.[19] He commanded a squadron on King's duty at Windsor Castle before eloping[20] with a sixteen-year-old heiress[21] from a long line of wealthy London merchants. Darvall retired as a major in 1806, and he and his new bride had ten children.[22] Emily was born at their grand home,[23] Nunnington Hall on the River Rye near York, in 1817, christened at the nearby church of St Helen's,[24] and educated at home and by tutors in London, France and Belgium. The Darvalls lived in Brussels from 1822, and in France between 1831 and 1839, in the Chateau de Capecure at the seaside near Boulogne-sur-Mer. They eventually maintained two seaside chateaux there.

In 1839, Major Darvall decided to join the tidal wave of migration to the Great South Land. Emily's older brother John,[25] a graduate of Eton and Trinity College, Oxford, had arrived in Sydney in August. With no news of how he had fared, the next month, Emily – along with her parents, two brothers, two sisters[26] and some servants – set sail on the *Alfred* to join him. At the time Darvall wanted to keep both his chateaux, thinking his family would make another fortune in New South Wales and return to France, but by 1844 both properties were sold. Darvall had a plan to farm land west of Sydney Cove between the Parramatta and Lane Cove Rivers.

Their fellow passenger, the 'gentlemanly' thirty-year-old Robert Barton, planned to go further west – much further. He planned to raise a £20,000 stake for livestock to populate a vast tract of land on the western side of the Blue Mountains. His father, Charles Barton,[27] a lieutenant general and Irish landlord in Fermanagh County[28] who was close to the Prince Regent, later King George IV, had died when Robert was ten. The enterprising lad went to sea aged fifteen, eventually becoming an officer on a ship for the East India Company's merchant fleet as a defence against pirates[29] on voyages to India and China.[30] At twenty-one Robert was eligible to receive the £2500 his father had left him in his will, while his two eldest brothers inherited the general's two Irish properties. Robert lived for a time in Germany and, with a parting gift of about £3000 from his mother, headed for Sydney after resigning from the service aged thirty-one.[31] He brought his officer's sword with him as though he was about to charge into battle.

Robert's uncle Sir Robert Barton had fought with the loyalists in the French Revolution. He'd then taken the 2nd Life Guards to Portugal to join the Duke of Wellington's army in order to drive the French from Spain. Barton's mother's family, the Johnstons, had settled in Bordeaux and were prominent in the wine industry.

BUILT OF TEAK, THE *ALFRED* was sheathed with copper against marine borers. It was home to the Darvalls, Barton and their fellow passengers for four months.

Emily Darvall kept a diary of their voyage and her interactions with Barton. In her old age she would show it to her children and grandchildren, including the impressionable Banjo Paterson. She also wrote the first of her Australian poems, 'Song of Christmas to the Australian Emigrant',[32] while on board.

Early in the voyage, on 19 September 1839, Emily wrote, 'The sun set in beauty, the moon arose and danced upon the waters, the band played, the whole of the inhabitants of our floating home came out on deck and the whole scene became a mass of movement. Hornpipes and reels were performed on all sides and the straw-bonnets of the little emigrant children gleaming in the moonbeams showed that they were not left out in the jubilee.'[33]

On the rainy evening of Monday, 7 October, the stench of rotten potatoes being sorted on the quarter deck soured the journey for a while, and Emily had heard enough of Captain Flint's booming Scottish burr. 'He appears to be very vigilant for his voice is terrific in the night when he generally scolds incessantly as if he had no need of sleep himself, and did not imagine that other people could wish for any.'[34]

A week further into the journey, now off the Ivory Coast, Emily sat down to dinner with her 'Mama and Papa', siblings Fred[35] and Rose,[36] and other first-class passengers Mr Eastmuir, and Mr and Mrs Sillitoe, 'quite respectable shop-keepers of the best class'.[37] Mrs Sillitoe suffered from sea-sickness and remained 'a good deal below', while Mr Barton, who had now been sick for much of the journey, 'stretched on his back and unable to move'[38] suffered from lumbago. His incapacitation, though, gave Robert Barton the opportunity to read some of Emily's verses in the shipboard newsletter she helped produce; he found the verses enchanting.

Robert proved to be an agreeable sort of fellow despite his discomfort, and he was 'much amused' when passengers tied a rope through a porthole to his luggage and startled him by making it dance up and down in his cabin at midnight.[39]

Within two weeks of landing in Sydney, Robert had formed a partnership with Emily's brother Fred and another passenger, Joseph Docker, to buy Boree Nyrang, a sheep run of twenty-four thousand hectares[40] about thirty kilometres west of Orange, between Molong and Cudal.[41]

EMILY'S FATHER PUT DOWN his roots in Sydney, first leasing a farm called Deniston,[42] which eventually became part of the suburb of Denistone. Emily wrote home to a cousin in England to tell her of the beauty of Sydney with its waterways and bays and islands, and that she was so thankful to be in this wondrous new world.

Robert Barton headed west across the foreboding Great Dividing Range and its steep, narrow roads, but with Fred Darvall managing Boree Nyrang for him, he was soon back on the Darvall doorstep courting Emily. Robert and Major Darvall bought out Docker's third share in Boree[43] but it was Robert's interest in Emily that sealed the family alliance. Six months after the *Alfred* arrived in Sydney, the first Lord Bishop of Australia[44] married Robert and Emily at St James' Church in King Street, Sydney.[45] It was a double ceremony, with Emily's younger sister Eliza marrying Henry Kater, who had arrived in Sydney with Durham cattle, 'some long wool sheep, as well as furniture, a carriage, all sorts of luxuries'[46] and six thoroughbred horses to stock Bungarribee, a property near what is now Blacktown.[47] Emily's brother John Bayley Darvall became Solicitor-General of New South Wales and a member of the government's executive council.

Even though Robert Johnston Barton Esq. was appointed a magistrate,[48] the road ahead for the new Mrs Barton looked rocky when her husband took her on the long ride back over the mountains on a horse dray covered by a tarpaulin, which doubled as a home and a receptacle for catching rainwater.[49] The trek, taking several weeks, was slow and exhausting[50] and Boree was a long way in both miles and metier from Nunnington Hall or the salons of Paris and Brussels. Home was a bark hut and the bed a mattress of straw. Robert called it their 'abode in the wilderness'[51] and while the rough frontier shocked Emily's refined sensibilities, there was a lot of love in that little home. Emily was soon pregnant.

From the wilderness she wrote to a cousin, who was living in grandeur in England, that she so looked forward to news from her old friends and relatives but had to admit:

> English letters and papers now give me a strange dreamy sensation like hearing of a world to which I do not belong and, as I sit hour after hour all alone in my hut making little frocks & caps and writing of past, present & future I can hardly persuade myself that I am indeed the same Puss who used to be happy

> in the society of all her kind friends & relations. Sometimes on the hot dreamy days I close my eyes and bring them all around me again and oh the bright dear faces that fill my little room and the groups of smiling friends that come gliding on through the dull green of the silent bush! A change has certainly come over my life but I think not over my heart or my spirits. I am very happy in the ever increasing affection of my dear husband, happy in the prospect of becoming a mother ...[52]

Soon Emily, accompanied by her husband, was crossing the mountains on a return journey to Sydney, awaiting the birth of her first child and wanting to attend to her mother who was at Deniston, dying from cancer of the womb.[53] In a letter home to England, Emily recalled the harrowing scenes at her mother's deathbed.[54] It was 'very distressing',[55] too, she wrote, that her father had quickly become involved with an Irish teenager, Jane McCullough,[56] a dressmaker from Londonderry. Jane was seventeen and Emily's father sixty-six. Still, it proved a happy union. Darvall moved to Ryde, farming hundreds of hectares, planting orchards and building a grand two-storey home called Ryedale after the river that ran by his ancestral home. The old man and the young girl had two children together, and Jane Darvall became a noted philanthropist in Sydney for more than half a century.[57]

Robert and Emily Barton and their new daughter, Emmy,[58] began the long ride back to Boree, hoping for similar prosperity. It was a hard road, though Emily maintained that there was something 'wild and independent' in their 'style of life which makes one forget the loss of a few comforts and luxuries'.[59]

OUT IN THE AUSTRALIAN WILDERNESS, birds did not so much trill, as they did in Yorkshire, but squawk and scream. Poisonous snakes seemed to be everywhere in the hot, dry grass, and there were hostile Aboriginal people and settlers who needed little excuse to attack them, along with bushrangers and drought. There was also the ever-present fear of bushfires and hardly a soul to talk to when her husband was away working.

Emily's brother Horace came to Boree for a time to help when Robert was in Sydney,[60] but dangers for both men and women lurked everywhere. Once, on a visit, Emily's aged father was thrown from his gig and laid up with a fractured ankle, and Emily and her infant daughter barely escaped disaster on the dangerous mountain tracks when a horse pulling their carriage bolted.[61] Then another serious accident occurred on the road from Boree to Molong.[62]

Emily soon realised that not only would she need every ounce of fierce loyalty and determination not to let the harsh land and difficult circumstances conquer her, but also that she had married 'a very bad farmer … absolutely unfitted for such an occupation'.[63] Robert paid twenty-two shillings and sixpence a head for his sheep, 'a very poor lot',[64] and although horses were almost at a prohibitive price, he bought some of the best imported mares and a stallion. A few years later the price of sheep fell to just a tenth of what he'd paid, and his cattle herds were almost valueless.[65]

As Robert began work on a more substantial cottage at Boree Nyrang for his young family, Emily's sacrifices echoed those from the heroes of the George Essex Evans[66] poem 'The Women of the West', who

> … left the vine-wreathed cottage and the mansion on the hill,
> The houses in the busy streets where life is never still,
> The pleasures of the city, and the friends they cherished best:
> For love they faced the wilderness – the Women of the West.[67]

Not long after the newlyweds and their baby arrived at Boree, a Scotsman called John Hood, of Stoneridge, Berwickshire, came to Australia with his son, writing and sketching about his journey across the sunburnt country and its sweeping plains. On 10 November 1841, the Hoods turned up at the Bartons' humble cottage on their remote station and found '… good cheer of every kind, including delicious sauterne and excellent porter. (No man can, prior to experience, duly estimate a glass of London porter on a hot day 16,000 miles from the Thames.) Many thousands of merino sheep bleat on the ranges, and the wool harvest, in all its shapes, was going on. Regularly every morning Mr Barton starts for the washing pool by nine o'clock, and there overlooks the shearers, until the dinner hour.'[68] Hood wrote that, while sheep-shearing time was the most important season of the year in Australia, there had been a drought so great that the whole land looked 'arid sand or red earth ... the clipping struck me as being done in a slovenly way, and with great cruelty to the sheep. Large masses of wool were occasionally left on the pelt, while, in other places pieces of skin and flesh were clipped clean away. They are sheared at so much the score and the shearers, knowing their victims are dumb, and cannot prefer complaints of ill-usage, are regardless of the suffering.'[69]

The wool was pressed into huge bales by assigned convict labour for shipment by bullock teams across the mountains to Sydney's Circular Quay and the mills of Europe. Hood said Robert and Emily represented a 'class of great enterprise and daring'.

Hood followed Robert to watch the local Indigenous people in a corroboree: 'We heard their music, and stole down upon the tribe ... and unobserved, saw them for some time ... The near naked men who dance to this music are painted red, yellow, and white, and display wonderful muscular power, brandishing their war instruments in both hands, boomerangs and waddies; at times stamping and acting as if in combat – then in retreat, then in pursuit. The women, clothed in torn blankets, banging drums made of sheepskin and the noise like humming bees.'[70]

Hood travelled down the Lachlan River to see country that was 'extremely bad', with plains 'as level as if a roller had passed over, but no verdure'.[71] On Christmas Day 1841, he returned to Boree and 'the most delightful draught I ever drank under a broiling sun, a large tumbler of claret'. Hood said Emily was 'one of the most accomplished and agreeable persons I ever met. One almost feels that for her to reside so far in the wild is "wasting her sweetness on the desert air;" but with her lord by her side she does not feel it to be so.'[72] Because of Emily, he said, everything at Boree seemed to run like clockwork.[73]

Emily's first son, Robert Darvall Barton,[74] was born on Boree in 1843 and he later wrote of his mother's many hardships and her strength of character raising children in a remote part of the colony with supplies arriving only once or twice a year, no neighbours within sight, no doctor within almost a hundred kilometres and hardly leaving the property for more than twenty years except for the baptisms of her babies.[75] She would wait anxiously for a postman on horseback riding between Bathurst and Wellington,[76] bringing letters about birth and death from family in Sydney and England, as well as packets of needles and thread. Her passion for painting portraits and watercolours was inspired by the rustic surroundings. Her love of poetry remained despite the dramatic change in her circumstances. She had the hard labours of a farmer's wife, giving birth to ten children[77] over fifteen years, but she still maintained the appearance of English gentility with starched dresses and bonnets. Robert Jr later wrote that while the 'discomforts and troubles that always go with the pioneer' were many, they 'never equalled the troubles and privations that were undergone by the real pioneers, among whom were my parents'.[78]

In 1843, Emily took time from her many chores to write another poem, 'Our First Little Home on the Plains of Boree', which reflects the domestic bliss she strived to maintain with Robert – or 'Robin', the nickname she gave him. It includes the verse:

O, proud are the halls of our own British land,
And fair are the cottages round them that rise;
And oft, in my dreams, on the green hills I stand,
Whence in childhood I gazed on the pale northern skies.
I was blest, I was blest! yet I would not retrace
Even youth's buoyant step on the steep mountain side.
No, my husband, I gaze on thy bright, honest face,
And I love the wild land that has made me thy bride.[79]

The Bartons' family grew with the arrival of twin daughters, Mary Eliza and Rose Isabella,[80] in December 1844. Emily was overjoyed that the babies were strong and healthy: she had been unwell for months, in body and mind, during the pregnancy, weak and full of misery.[81] But Mary was tiny.[82]

Anglican Reverend James William Gunther came over from Mudgee, 175 kilometres away, for a day of christenings at Boree, the first time anyone could recall a clergyman coming to their locality. The woolshed became a makeshift church.

Soon, though, Emily was sharing the greatest heartbreak of bush life with a friend, writing less than a year after the birth of the twins that 'our pretty little gentle Mary' had died. Mary 'fell sick of a teething fever' and expired after twelve days of illness while sleeping in Emily's arms. Her gentle breathing grew fainter and fainter 'and my lovely baby had departed without a struggle ... She was so small and beautiful so like her father.'[83] The grieving young mother took comfort in 'passages of Scripture'[84] and the fact that Rose remained strong even if her life had been threatened in yet another near-fatal accident when a phaeton carriage overturned: 'Poor baby who was taking her turn in the gig was with her nurse thrown over the horse's head & both were much bruised though not seriously hurt ... I trust it may please God, to spare [Rose] to me for she seems now to be dearer than ever.'[85]

IN DECEMBER 1845, the explorers Thomas Mitchell and Edmund Kennedy camped at Boree Creek on their way to exploring North Queensland with what seemed like a small army. Their party included a surgeon, Mitchell's faithful servant, one soldier, two civilians, twenty-three convicts, seventeen horses, three light carts, eight drays, 112 bullocks and 250 sheep. They also had two iron boats, which served additionally as troughs and, on occasions, to carry water for the cattle.[86] It was a dangerous journey, and on a later expedition Kennedy was speared to death at Cape York. Things could be just as precarious around Boree.

Not long after Mitchell and his team set off from Boree, Robert suffered a compound fracture of the leg when thrown out of a gig. Screaming in agony, he was carried home by some of the farm workers, and Emily sent for Dr Samuel Curtis at the military station of Wellington, eighty-five kilometres north. Emily and four-year-old Robert Jr gasped when the doctor, after almost a day's journey, told them the shattered leg should be amputated. Emily would not hear of it. She sent for Dr Richard Machattie of Bathurst, a hundred kilometres east. Between them, they managed to save the leg. But Robert was crippled for life and while at times 'no one could be jollier or more kind-hearted', the injury often made him morose and irritable.[87] Little Robert Jr was only four, but because of his father's gammy leg he was soon tasked with heavy responsibilities helping Emily.[88]

Robert was still lying on a couch waiting for his leg to heal when the Governor of New South Wales, Sir Charles FitzRoy, visited Boree with his cousin Colonel Godfrey Mundy on their way to Wellington. Mundy recalled Robert as an 'English-looking, English-hearted gentleman'.[89] Emily was unable to welcome them as she was about to give birth to her daughter Nora,[90] who quickly stole the attention from Rose.

Emily's youngest sister, Rose Darvall,[91] had married tall, handsome, blue-eyed Englishman Arthur Templer[92] who ran businesses in Wellington. From 1840 he had a flour mill on a property called Narrambla,[93] four kilometres north-east of Orange.

BOREE DEVOURED MONEY SO QUICKLY that Robert and Emily were always short of funds. Their hopes brightened with the prospect of a £10,000 bequest from Robert's maternal uncle, Nathaniel Johnston, an Irish-born Bordeaux wine merchant. Those hopes were shattered, though, when they learnt that Uncle Nathaniel's fortune had been left to a Bordeaux hospital. Robert's mother, Susanna, and her sister contested the will, appealing through their powerful connections to King Louis Philippe of France to intervene. Susanna finally sent Robert and Emily £2000 to help with expenses at their modest home in the middle of nowhere.[94]

The Bartons were then ready to help others. Emily's brother-in-law Henry Kater was facing bankruptcy, having lost his Penrith property, 'land and stock, home, furniture all gone'.[95] Only a loan of £1000 from Emily and Robert stopped the Katers from having to try their luck in the emerging lands around Moreton Bay to the north. Kater opened a successful flour mill of his own at Caleula, about twenty kilometres from Boree, and then a woollen mill.

While their relatives eventually prospered, the Bartons suffered even more financial setbacks. In the 1840s, the market for Australian wool in Britain slumped and the local market for mutton was flooded. One of Robert Jr's earliest recollections was of his father limping down from a new homestead to supervise the killing of his sheep and cattle, and then seeing them boiled down so their fat could be sold as tallow for use in soap and candle making. The sword that Robert Barton had carried so proudly on his ship as an officer of the British East India Company was taken to the stockyard to cut the bullocks' throats. Little Robert Jr had always seen his father as a dashing hero and coveted that sword 'in a small boy's way', but now he 'saw it at last ingloriously covered with rust and dirt lying in the killing yard on the station'.[96]

Things went from bad to worse.

Fifty kilometres east of Boree, Edward Hammond Hargraves, a burly 34-year-old native of Gosport, England, became convinced there were rivers of gold beyond the Blue Mountains; he had recently hauled his 113-kilogram bulk across the golden streams of California with thousands of other prospectors. On 12 February 1851, he and 22-year-old John Lister rode along Lewis Pond Creek, a tributary of the Macquarie River. Near Guyong, a village nestled between Bathurst and Orange, at a spot where Lewis Ponds Creek meets Radigan's Gully, Hargraves said he had an eerie feeling as though he was 'surrounded by gold'. He put some dirt in a tin pan and swilled it around in the creek water. As he washed the dirt away, he found glistening specks at the bottom of the pan. With his blood pressure rising and sweat on his brow, he repeated the process five more times and four times collected little pieces of gold. With Lister dumbstruck, Hargraves shouted, 'This is a memorable day in the history of New South Wales.'[97]

Hargraves named the area Ophir, after a region of vast wealth mentioned in the First Book of Kings in the Bible. Within three months, more than three hundred gold-diggers in the area had tossed in their jobs to stake claims there. The *Bathurst Free Press* reported that rumours of the area around the site being 'one immense goldfield' had produced a 'complete mental madness'[98] in the rush to become rich, and that there appeared 'every probability of a complete social revolution in the course of time'.

Soon Robert and Emily Barton and their children had no one to work their property as the newspapers became 'filled with reports of men going to the goldfields without a shilling and picking up a fortune the next day' – though not much was said of the majority who lost everything searching for instant riches.[99]

BY 1856 EMILY'S FAMILY had grown to nine children and Robert could afford more staff, including Aboriginal maids and stockmen. There was a large Indigenous tribe at Boree, and the children watched many corroborees as guests.

But another tribe from the Yass area came to Boree to make war. Emily hid her children and some of the native girls in a back bedroom as a bloody battle took place around the homestead. 'My father at this time was away in Sydney,' Robert Jr recalled.

> The day before the blacks were attacked, one of the black stockmen reported that he had seen the enemy, in war-paint, camped some miles back, and he got permission to go and inform the other remnants of the tribe, and fetch them down to meet the enemy. However, he never returned, and the few blacks that were camped near the station moved that night to about a hundred yards [90 metres] from the house between the men's huts and the house. The first thing that struck my attention when I walked into the yard was a very big, stout blackfellow lying about a hundred yards away with several spears through him, but still living, because I saw him half sit up and try to pull out the spears … I saw a young black, Charlie by name, rush across the paddock, jump in and out of the sweet-briar hedge of the garden, pursued by a number of his enemies. He ran like a deer across the cultivation paddock and up the pine ridge, which was as far as we could see him, still pursued by the other blacks. About an hour afterwards I saw the pursuing blacks coming back carrying their spears upright, each spear decorated with parts of the human body; they had got poor Charlie, and were carrying his body on their different spears as a memento of victory.[100]

Many of the Indigenous women were marched off as 'prisoners of war'.[101] The next morning one of the men discovered, under a bush near the stables, a possum cloak wrapped like a bundle. Opening it, he was startled to find a young, terrified Indigenous woman with a wrinkled, silent baby. They had lain hidden there together, cramped and cold, for hours without making a move or sound.[102]

One of the local newspapers reported on the incident: 'A party of the Goulburn blacks who have lately been sneaking hereabouts, commenced a murderous onslaught upon the Boree blacks, on the 27th [of November 1850] near Boree Nyrang, the residence of R. J. Barton, Esq., and killed three of them, when, shocking to relate, the savages skinned the body of one of their victims, an old man, and took a portion with them for the purpose of eating it. The Boree blacks are a remarkably quiet tribe.'[103]

The incident was a lesson in the harshness of bush life for the Barton children. Emily did her best to educate them in other ways, imparting to them her love of language: English, French and Italian. She also knew enough Greek and German to teach the rudiments to her children, and once when visiting Boree, the Bishop of Sydney – the 197-centimetre-tall Frederic Barker[104] – craned his grey head around Emily's kitchen door to see her mixing a pudding while teaching Latin to one of her sons.[105] While Rose and Nora and the other girls were educated at home by Emily and a governess, Robert Jr became a boarder at the King's School at Parramatta, crossing the Blue Mountains alone on horseback four times a year from the age of twelve, passing prisoners in chain gangs repairing the narrow road.[106]

THE BARTONS HAD A DIFFICULT relationship with their English neighbours, John and Mary Smith, who had stocked their Molong Run with descendants of the Reverend Samuel Marsden's purebred merino sheep, supplied from King George III's Windsor stud in England. The merinos became the nucleus of Smith's renowned Gamboola stud.

In 1847 Robert Barton had signed the warrant that led to John Smith's arrest for allegedly stealing an iron pot. Smith was acquitted and then failed in two actions against Barton. Eventually, in the harsh environment where every bit of community spirit was needed for survival, the animosity between the families was replaced by a friendship, and the Smiths became in-laws.[107] They also became matchmakers: two Scottish brothers made frequent visits to Gamboola to buy Smith's prized sheep, and along the way met the unmarried Barton girls. They had much in common with the Bartons, not least their shared connections with the East India Company and their difficulties in making a go of their new ventures in an environment totally alien to their former surroundings.

The brothers were John[108] and Andrew Bogle Paterson,[109] and they were lowland Scots from Lanarkshire, descendants of a tall,[110] blond Scandinavian named John Petersen, who had changed his name to Paterson and married a Scottish lass, Christine Haddow.[111] He farmed in Lochlyock, Lanarkshire, until his death in 1682. Banjo Paterson would claim another well-known ancestor in Sir William Paterson,[112] one of the founders of the Bank of England in 1694 and a man who had financed King William III. Sir William was a main driver of the disastrous Darien scheme, an unsuccessful attempt by Scotland to become a major trading nation with a colony called Caledonia in Panama. Thousands of Scots poured their life savings into the scheme only to lose the lot because of 'the malaria and the mosquitoes', according to his version.[113] The financial collapse left Scotland parlous, weakening opposition to the Act of Union with England. Paterson family tradition had it that the investors found Sir William such an admirable character, despite their losses, that they took up a collection and gave him £10,000 to start again. In reality, though, Paterson returned to Edinburgh to a reception of 'abuse and disgust'[114] and fled to London, where he scratched out a living teaching mathematics from his house in Soho.[115] The British government later granted him thousands of pounds for acting as an advocate for their campaign to abolish the Scottish Parliament. Between 1715 and 1720, another of the Patersons[116] brought a 'black Flemish stallion to Scotland' to establish the Lochlyoch stud of Clydesdale draughthorses.[117] Banjo Paterson wrote that the Flemish stallion was named Robin and that it was to the Clydesdale breed what Eclipse – the great eighteenth-century racehorse and sire – was to the thoroughbred.[118] The giants of the equine world were originally known as Lanarkshire horses[119] and sometimes as 'Paterson's Horses'. Between 1750 and 1820, the Lochlyoch mares were in 'very high repute, and Paterson's strain was regarded as the fountain-head of the best blood'.[120]

A few decades later, John and Andrew, trading as Paterson Bros. were young men bent on taming their part of New South Wales. They were the sons of Captain John Paterson, of the East India Company, a dashing athletic hero who excelled in every sport he tried, especially curling. Captain Paterson might have become a Scottish sheep farmer like his father until Napoleon's advances caused volunteers to enlist from across Scotland to fight against the French army. Paterson was appointed first as a lieutenant in an infantry corps and then in the 1st Regiment of Bengal Native Infantry, on its way to India.[121] He became a captain in the East India Company and spent time writing poetry about his adventures.[122] He had the Paterson gift of storytelling and would often relate a story to his children of how, at the storming of a mud fort in India, he engaged a local warlord in a sword fight – but, finding the going tough, he seized his opponent in a bear hug and threw him over the ramparts.[123] The stories filtered down, and years later Banjo Paterson would claim that his grandfather started his service in India as a roughrider and handled 'the rough horses so well that he afterwards obtained his commission'.[124]

Captain Paterson purchased a small Scottish property near Lanark, called Crofton Hill, where he died in 1850. Four sons from two marriages – William, James,[125] John and Andrew – as well as his daughter Jessie[126] all emigrated to Australia soon after.

John and Andrew Paterson gained experience working on a station in the Riverina, then took up a station called Buckinbah at what is now Yeoval, just outside the settlement of Obley, about seventy kilometres north of the Bartons' property. They also had the adjacent run of Curra Creek. They leased the land at four-pence an acre per year. Dingoes were such a threat that the sheep had to be constantly guarded and cattle roamed without fences, often ending up in the possession of neighbours. The brothers also operated Illalong, a property they leased, three hundred kilometres to the south, outside the village of Binalong on the road from Yass. From Andrew's earliest days in New South Wales, he dreamt of building a pastoral empire. In 1854 he had written to the Western Bank[127] in Lanark, Scotland, from 'Illalong, Yass', advising that he had drawn £100 from his account and was now drawing through the bank of Australasia £900 on his late father's estate and a further £800 from his deceased uncle's.[128] In the same letter Andrew's brother James Paterson, who would soon tire of the bush and opt for city life,[129] complained to a Scottish bank manager of the harshness of life in rural Australia, it being '110 [degrees Fahrenheit] in the shade'.[130]

Andrew, he said, had been 'of age' to spend his inheritance for more than six months and needed to raise money quickly because all his capital had been invested in sheep. Stock prices were pitiful, he said, but they were confident of a rise because fires had burnt much of the countryside black and meat was scarce. Yet times were always tough. Robert Barton Jr remembered John Paterson taking 'a number of fat sheep to one of the gold diggings for sale, but as he could not get the price from the butchers which he thought the sheep were worth, he decided to kill them at his camp, and cart them through the town ready dressed, and sell them by the carcass or the quarter to anyone who wanted them at rather a less price than the butchers were asking for their meat.'[131]

IN 1859 THE REVEREND Robert Hansen Mayne, overseeing the parish at the newly built Church of England in Orange,[132] travelled to the Boree homestead to marry John Paterson and the Bartons' eldest daughter, Emmy.[133] John had recently given up his seat after a year as a Member of the Parliament in the NSW Legislative Assembly, representing the seat of Lachlan and Lower Darling. He had found 'the turmoil of political life … distasteful to his inclinations' and did not sit for re-election.[134]

Boree Nyrang was excellent grazing country, but the Bartons continued to struggle to make it pay. Still, they wanted a sense of refinement for their children, the youngest just three. Not long after the wedding, Robert placed a notice in the *Sydney Morning Herald*:

> WANTED, In a family residing in the country, a
> GENTLEMAN, who can combine instruction on
> the pianoforte with the ordinary qualifications of a Tutor.
> Apply by letter to ROBERT J. BARTON, Esq., J.P.,
> Boree Nyrang, Molong.[135]

Emmy left home and travelled down to Illalong with her new husband, but an ill wind blew all around. Seventy kilometres away on the hotbed of the gold diggings at Lambing Flat,[136] miners of European descent staged a number of race riots and protests; eventually they went about beating and scalping Chinese miners. On 30 June 1861, about three thousand of them – marching behind a huge gaudy banner that declared 'Roll Up, Roll Up, No Chinese'[137] – attacked a camp of Chinese workers. One side of the dispute was 'wholly unarmed and defenceless, the other was well supplied with bludgeons, pick-handles, and firearms'.[138] The mob violence baffled 'all description', reported the correspondent for the *Empire* newspaper, who wrote that the victims were rounded up like cattle and savagely beaten: 'I saw several of the Chinese on their knees, with their hands raised towards heaven, begging for mercy; but none was shown to them; all were served alike. Their tents were broken down and burnt, their pockets emptied, and their persons ill-used and beaten with sticks, stones, or whatever came to hand[139] … One Chinaman had an eye gouged out, and several were so severely handled that death will probably ensue.'[140]

Bushrangers thrived.

Robert Barton Jr got to know Ben Hall,[141] and he recalled his uncle Arthur Templer, the miller, 'a fine athlete, of splendid physique', making a citizen's arrest on a highwayman who tried to rob a coach on which he was travelling to Sydney.[142] Press reports said the passengers and driver had been ordered to dismount, 'on pain of having their brains blown out, and that the women on board had commenced shrieking fearing they would be ill-used.[143] One report said: 'Too much credit cannot be given to Mr Templer for his spirited conduct.'[144]

On 15 June 1862, beside some granite boulders near Eugowra, about forty kilometres south-west of Boree Nyrang, a group of bandits including Hall, Johnny Gilbert,[145] Frank 'Darkie' Gardiner, John O'Meally and at least four other accomplices – Harry Manns, Alex Fordyce, John Bow and Dan Charters – carried out the biggest gold heist Australia had seen. With their faces blackened with charcoal and half-hidden by scarves, the robbers forced two bullock teams to block the road. At about 3.30 p.m. they opened fire on a special coach bringing a fortune from the new gold diggings at Forbes towards Orange. The coach driver's hat was shot off and one of the four troopers on guard was hit through the testicles. The bandits rode off with seventy-seven kilograms of gold and £3700 in cash.[146] All the robbers eventually were captured or killed, and young Harry Manns, a minor player in the heist, died an excruciating death from strangulation in Darlinghurst Gaol, the victim of a bungling old hangman.[147]

ANDREW PATERSON HAD FOLLOWED his brother to Australia and now followed him in love. Emily and Robert Barton hosted a second wedding at their home in April 1863.

Robert placed another notice in the *Herald* declaring:

> On the 8th instant, at Boree Nyrang, Molong, by the Rev. R. H. Mayne, of Orange, Andrew [Bogle], fourth son of the late

> Captain John Paterson, of Crofton Hill, Lanarkshire, Scotland, to Rose Isabella, second daughter of Robert Johnstone [sic] Barton.[148]

Rose was just eighteen and Andrew thirty. Rose had always been the plain daughter when compared with her sister Nora, but marriage to this slim, handsome Scotsman with the dark hair and neat spade beard made her blossom. Andrew was gentle and good-natured and worked hard – usually too hard.

While John and Emmy had settled at Illalong, Rose and Andrew began their married life at Buckinbah; Rose journeyed with him across the flat, dusty, hungry plains to a small, isolated granite house beside a creek, a long way from any town. The Paterson brothers had built their cottage in the Scottish dry-stone style without mortar, and it looked like a lonely outcast surrounded by eucalypt trees. The house was tiny compared with Rose's childhood home, not much bigger than the shepherds' huts in the distant paddocks on Boree Nyrang. Not that the Bartons enjoyed their comfortable homestead for much longer.

LESS THAN THREE MONTHS after Rose Paterson's wedding, Boree Nyrang was sold, along with 12,800 sheep and two hundred head of cattle, for just £13,500, much less than Robert's £20,000 original stake more than twenty years before.[149] But the sale was held up, and John Smith, the Bartons' neighbour, eventually purchased a large slice of the land, while the Bartons kept a small run that Robert Jr would manage. Emily and Robert Sr were bound for Gladesville on the Parramatta River in Sydney. He was one of the founders of the Australian Club[150] and planned to spend more time there with a delicious sauterne or excellent porter instead of sweating amid mobs of sheep and myriad blowflies.

Before they could settle into their comfortable retirement, though, Emily was suddenly left a widow.

Robert travelled to Sydney, partly for business but also to see a doctor about a nagging cough he couldn't shake. On 1 October 1863, Dr Alleyne sent Robert to his bed at the Australian Club. He died there three days later of pneumonia, aged fifty-four.[151] Boree Nyrang was so far away that Emily's older brother John Bayley Darvall identified the body and arranged the burial at St Anne's Anglican Church in Ryde before Emily knew about it. She was shattered and went into a deep depression that lasted for months.

Emily soon left their 'First Little Home on the Plains of Boree' and stayed with Rose and Andrew Paterson for a while at Buckinbah[152] as her husband's £16,000 estate was being sorted. Then she headed back to Sydney, where her journey into the wilderness had started. After more than two decades in the Australian bush, the genteel English woman lived the rest of her life in the big city.

ROBERT BARTON JR, now managing a much smaller property for his family, was camping out at Goimbla Station, near Eugowra Rocks, when Ben Hall, Johnny Gilbert and John O'Meally made a raid on the property.[153] The bushrangers set fire to a hay-filled shed and the stables where the station manager David Campbell kept his prize racehorse; it died in the fire.[154]

Campbell, desperate to protect his wife and children, killed O'Meally with a bullet through the neck in a shootout. The other bushrangers fled. Robert Jr rode onto Goimbla the next day and saw O'Meally's corpse. The bushrangers hated Campbell because he had made statements denouncing them and had once informed the police that they had taken the town of Canowindra hostage.

Campbell had received that information from the overseer at Illalong, Thomas William Barnes,[155] an inoffensive Englishman whom the bushrangers had allowed to pass through Canowindra with a mob of sheep so long as he swore not to reveal the gang's whereabouts. Barnes was a small man 'and the least likely to show fight to bushrangers; but, like most new-chums, he was bound to strike trouble'.[156] The bushrangers swore they would get even with Barnes for betraying them.

NOT LONG AFTER HER WEDDING, Rose Paterson fell pregnant, and the story of the gunfight and the fire only reinforced her fears that Buckinbah was too remote and too bereft of medical help for the birth of her first child. So she and Robert, and perhaps her mother, travelled by buggy the hundred arduous kilometres toward Narrambla, the property of Rose's aunt and uncle just outside Orange on the Ophir road.

They took a south-west route from their little stone house, along what was more of a rutted bush track than a road, up and down one taxing hill after another and past the seemingly endless vistas of unfenced paddocks dotted with kangaroos and sheep. To break the journey they most likely stayed with the Smiths at Molong before arriving at Narrambla, with the sight of the broad valley below, the noise of the steam engine grinding grain in Arthur Templer's mill and the smell of smoke from the tall chimney. Sheep grazed on the yellow grass of the low rolling hills around Summer Hill Creek, which downstream met the spot where Hargraves had found gold. The Patersons likely stayed with the Templers in an eight-room timber cottage with a wide veranda, covered in jasmine, honeysuckle and climbing roses,[157] overlooking a postcard view of the Australian bush and Mount Canobolas.[158]

On Wednesday, 17 February 1864, nineteen-year-old Rose Paterson gave birth to her first child. Eight days later, the birth was registered at the Orange courthouse as 'Baby Paterson'. Then on 11 March, as Rose recovered at Narrambla, Reverend Mayne came to the Templer home to christen the new child. Mayne and Rose's brother Robert Barton Jr were the godfathers, and John Smith's eldest daughter, Emily, was the godmother.[159]

The baby was christened Andrew Barton Paterson. His family called him Barty, but one day everyone would call him Banjo.

Chapter 2

1864, BUCKINBAH STATION, FORTY KILOMETRES SOUTH-WEST OF WELLINGTON, NEW SOUTH WALES

My first impressions are of life on a mixed sheep and cattle station ... the mobs of wild horses that went tearing through the timber ... long days spent out shepherding sheep with one of the station lads, days when a motionless sun brooded over a motionless forest till one could almost hear the leaves whispering to each other.

BANJO PATERSON, AS AN OLD MAN, WRITING DOWN HIS EARLIEST MEMORIES FOR HIS GRANDDAUGHTERS[1]

THE BABY PATERSON TOOK his first breaths of Australian bush air at Narrambla, enveloped by the vast Australian sky and surrounded by the country creeks and paddocks that would colour his vivid imagination for the rest of his life. His first three months were spent at his uncle's property as Rose Paterson recovered from the birth; he would spend the next five years at Buckinbah. Soon he had two younger sisters, Flo[2] and Jessie,[3] along with an Aboriginal nurse who kept an adventurous toddler company among the labourers, shepherds and station hands working the land.

Paterson's first home actually comprised three adjoining runs – Buckinbah, Timnie[4] and Curra Creek[5] – forming an immense tract of 86,500 acres (thirty-five thousand hectares). The land consisted of 'splendid box ridges and open appletree flats and small plains, all richly grassed and herbed' and watered by the Little River and Buckinbah Creek, as well as by the Curra and numerous other creeks and their tributaries.'[6]

Marriage was the cornerstone of European settlement of Australia in the nineteenth century, and women like Rose saw themselves as assisting in a noble endeavour to tame the wild land for cultured civilisation. As a homemaker she was engaged in the constant cycle of pregnancy and child rearing – what she referred to as 'the common cause'.[7] This involved mending and making clothes, cleaning, cultivating a flower garden, growing and preserving fruit and vegetables, dressing minor wounds of the body and soul, keeping up the spirits of her husband on the rare occasions he was home, and encouraging her children through the dark times and an uncertain future. She kept an inventory of Buckinbah's stores to sell to travellers: everything from sago to salad oil, pepper and pickles, Lea & Perrins sauce and Liverpool salt, blue serge suits, mohair coats, moleskin trousers and mousetraps.[8] She taught her children reading, writing, arithmetic and music, and a love of God and family. For much of Banjo Paterson's childhood, Rose was both mother and father to him.

From the time he could toddle around it, Paterson was fascinated by the landscape surrounding his first home. Buckinbah Creek would sometimes be dry and other times come down 'a banker'.[9] Paterson remembered a time when a friend of the family was among a party lost off Queensland's Great Barrier Reef when their small schooner went down. A rescue party, including Rose's brother Edward Barton,[10] had gone to provide help in the brig *Maria*. While Edward was away, Barty and his sister Flo sat beside the flooded Buckinbah Creek watching logs float by, 'fascinated by the roar of water'. Every time a log passed with a snake on it, they called the log the 'brig *Maria*' and if it survived the rush of water without being rolled or sucked under, the children said it was a good sign their uncle would return from the voyage with the rescued men aboard. 'It worked too,' Paterson later wrote, 'for the castaways came back without loss of life.'[11]

BUSHRANGERS STILL PREYED on country roads, though their days were numbered. Only a few weeks after Paterson's birth, Frank 'Darkie' Gardiner, the King of the Road, faced court in Sydney.[12]

While Rose and Barty were still at Narrambla, two hundred kilometres to the south near Illalong, Ben Hall and some of his gang were lurking at Emu Flat on the road between Yass and Binalong on the eve of winter.[13] Banjo's eleven-year-old uncle Frank Barton[14] and the Illalong overseer, Tom Barnes, were driving John Paterson's family carriage: 'a funny, cumbersome old English affair, so heavy that it got bogged about twice a week'.[15] But the bushrangers were in no mood for laughter. The bandits rode out from the cover of some trees and pointed a gun at them. It was a cold night, but that was not the only reason Barnes was shaking.

Recognising Barnes as the man who had given information against them to David Campbell, the bushrangers made the diminutive Englishman strip naked and tied him to a tree as young Frank Barton protested as loudly as he could. Barnes shivered and trembled, and while Frank begged them not to kill his friend, Ben Hall sharpened a pocketknife against the wheel of the carriage and said he would slice up his betrayer into little pieces.[16] Then the bushrangers thought better of that idea and, relishing their opportunity, they produced a bullocky's whip. They flogged Barnes across his naked back with such vigour, it looked as though they intended to flog him to death. Barnes cried out in agony but they kept whipping him until the blood ran down his back, and no matter how much Frank pleaded with them, they whipped him some more.[17] Finally, Frank 'begged for his life so eloquently that at last they agreed to let [Barnes] go'. Barnes was in a terrible state as young Frank drove his almost lifeless body in the carriage to Illalong, where blankets were brought out and Barnes was taken in and revived.[18]

In Sydney, Darky Gardiner was sentenced to thirty-two years' hard labour in Darlinghurst Gaol, but a week later Hall, Gilbert and their accomplice James Gordon were involved in a shootout with police while trying to steal racehorses from the appropriately named Bang Bang Hotel at Koorawatha,[19] near Cowra.

Like Gardiner, they were running out of time.

Around the time that Barty Paterson was beginning to totter around Buckinbah on unsteady legs to explore the mysteries and majesties of his bush home, Hall was ambushed by police and Aboriginal trackers at Billabong Creek near Forbes. Thirty bullets were pumped into his back.[20] Eight days later, Johnny Gilbert – responsible for more than six hundred armed hold-ups and the murder of a constable during the robbery on a mail coach near Jugiong –

was shot dead in a gun fight with police at Binalong, seventy kilometres from the goldfields of Lambing Flat. He and his sidekick, John Dunn,[21] had robbed a woolshed at nearby Murrumburrah and were tracked to the home of Dunn's grandfather. Dunn escaped the ensuing gunfight but was hanged in Sydney in 1866. Gilbert was buried on a hill in the police paddock at Binalong. A woman visited the grave for years, placing flowers on it, and there were all sorts of rumours about what unwritten romance had died with the killer.[22]

The violent deaths of those two partners in crime came only a few weeks after 'Mad Dog' Morgan[23] was gunned down in northern Victoria. Morgan went on a crime spree in the Riverina and the South West Slopes districts of New South Wales, killing a station hand and two policemen. Then he held up the Macpherson family and their staff at Peechelba Station near Wangaratta in north-eastern Victoria. One of the station's servants persuaded the big bearded bushranger that she had to tend to the Macphersons' sick ten-month-old daughter, Christina,[24] and Morgan, a mass of wild hair and mania, believed her. In a rare moment of compassion, he let the young woman out of his sight – and, barefoot,[25] she ran to raise the alarm. The next morning Morgan was surrounded by police.

As the men in uniform plotted to capture the cop killer alive, a station hand took aim from thirty metres away and killed him with a bullet in the back.[26] Photographs were taken for postcards as Morgan's body was propped against a wool bale, his hand holding a pistol he had stolen from one of the murdered policemen. Rumours circulated that his scrotum was cut off to make a tobacco pouch.[27] The body was then sewn up in a woolpack[28] and brought into Wangaratta for a post-mortem that was more like a souvenir hunt. Dr Joseph Henry from Benalla stripped the flesh from Morgan's face so that Police Superintendent Francis McCrae Cobham could take the killer's luxuriant beard as a keepsake; it was pegged out on a sheet of bark to dry like a possum skin. Morgan's head was cut off so a plaster cast could be taken and tossed about the room like a football.'[29] The coroner, Dr William Dobbyn, then wrapped the head in hessian, put it in a box and sent it by the Cobb & Co mail coach as a curio to a professor of anatomy at the University of Melbourne.[30]

The baby, Christina Macpherson, was blissfully unaware of the historic events playing out around her. Three decades later and two thousand kilometres away, she would collaborate with Banjo Paterson on his most celebrated work.

THE INFANT PATERSON saw little of his father during this time. Late in 1865,[31] not long after the shooting spree significantly culled the number of bushrangers in New South Wales and Victoria, Banjo's father, Andrew, and uncle John Paterson bought the freehold property of Illalong. With a third partner, an intrepid Englishman named Joseph Wilson Raven,[32] they secured the lease on the 10,500-hectare[33] property Stainburn Downs,[34] twenty-five kilometres from Aramac in Central Queensland. They paid £13 13s a year for the lease and also worked the neighbouring runs: Rider, Medley and Corinda.

Raven was the son a British naval officer, and his grandfather's home was Stainburn Hall in Workington. A man 'of unfailing courtesy and kindly thought',[35] he had started life in Australia driving fat stock to butchers on the Beechworth and Bendigo diggings,[36] and then found work with the Paterson brothers at Illalong. At the time it was principally used as a depot for mustering, until the brothers had numbers of sheep large enough to take across the border for Victorian markets. Raven worked at Illalong for four years before the Patersons made him manager at Buckinbah, where he caught wild horses on the Curra Creek before patiently breaking them in to the saddle and harness.[37] Raven read Sir Thomas Mitchell's glowing description of the country on the Barcoo and Flinders rivers, and decided on purchasing stock and going up there to form his own station. He gave the Paterson brothers notice, but instead they proposed a partnership; Raven set off with four thousand young ewes, a hundred stud ewes, two Rambouillet Merino stud rams, five hundred wethers, two bullock teams, a horse team and thirty thoroughbred horses.

Banjo Paterson would recall that much of his father's time was spent destocking the NSW properties and moving them 1500 kilometres north from the hungry country of Buckinbah to what was then the richer land of Stainburn. Among the many hardships on the journey were battles with Aboriginal people, during which his father's near-sighted cousin, James 'Blenty' Paterson, had his spectacles knocked off his nose by the tip of a boomerang. After '[n] othing went right with the partnership ventures', Andrew had to move the sheep out of the Queensland property because of drought.[38] Andrew Paterson 'tried to take sheep out to some new place, but was caught on flooded country between two rivers, and had to shear them on a sand hill'.[39] Banjo would recall that much of the wool was lost or damaged and what survived brought next to nothing.[40]

Farm life at Buckinbah came with all manner of dangers. In September 1865, a workman was trying to extinguish a fire in a chimney when he slipped off the roof and was impaled on a fence post. Without a hope, two days later he was carted to the Wellington hospital, where – despite the concerted efforts of the much-loved local doctor, Robert Rygate[41] – he died soon after, leaving behind a wife and family in Glasgow.[42]

Rygate spent almost a quarter of a century tending to the sick and injured around Wellington, and he also became well acquainted with the Paterson children. Because of Rose's preoccupation with her young daughters and the endless cycle of work on the remote property, Banjo's upbringing has been described as one of 'benign neglect'.[43] He later wrote of how 'bush families in those days, living miles away from a doctor, had hairs'-breadth escapes from serious injury'.[44]

In his early childhood Banjo's arm was broken, but it was left to heal without aid and somehow the injury went undetected until another fall many years later. As a consequence, his right arm was shorter and weaker than the left; and instead of having the break fixed early on, he had to endure the long painful procedure applied to children with teething problems, which at the time were seen as indicating far deeper ailments. As a toddler he had his gums sliced with a lancet[45] and blisters were created behind his ears in order to facilitate a discharge of poison from his system.[46] His screams were stomach churning, and Rose Paterson's feelings of helplessness and isolation were never more gut-wrenching. She later wrote to her sister Nora to say: 'I cannot forgive either of myself or Dr Rygate for having been such a pair of thoroughbred donkeys as not to have found out that his arm was broken that time we thought he had inflammation of the brain caused by teething, & I took him into Wellington where Dr Rygate saw him 3 times a day for 3 weeks … and never found out that the whole illness must have been caused by accident … It is somewhat strange that no one should have observed the crookedness in the arm in all the years which followed.'[47]

Paterson had a respectful attitude to Australia's first people, but apparently without any evidence Rose looked for a scapegoat and accused Banjo's Aboriginal nurse of being responsible for the broken arm. 'That horrid Black Fanny must've been climbing trees with him or something of that sort,' she claimed, 'and never let on to us for a moment that anything happened to the child.'[48]

Paterson's earliest memories of a fatherless existence at Buckinbah were of the emus, those great flightless birds, skulking up to the stone house to chew on the bridles of the station horses so that many went off to join the mobs of wild brumbies that hurtled through the surrounding timbers. Paterson recalled a stallion 'charging behind as a sort of rear guard'.[49] He also remembered the district doctor driving 'incredible distances through the night to attend confinement cases'.[50]

Rose Paterson, he said, 'was busy from daylight to dark' with household work, and consequently from a young age he sought out the company of his first hero, an old shepherd known as Jerry the Rhymer, 'tall bearded and straight as a sapling, with a rugged face and deeply sunken eyes'. Jerry was a former convict, the other station workers said, who had been sent from the 'old country' for a minor offence he claimed not to have committed, but he had 'done very much worse things which had never been found out'.[51] He was a great storyteller who would tell the young Paterson tales in verse, such as the one about his son's dogs: 'Baldie and Nigger gets bigger and bigger, with eating their muttons like so many gluttons ...'[52]

Paterson recalled that at the time Buckinbah was 'held on lease from the Crown at a few pence per acre and was worth no more'. It was dingo-infested, unfenced country 'where the sheep had to be shepherded and the cattle, 'as the blackboys said, could go "longa bush" and wander afield until they got into somebody else's meat cask or could be mustered and driven away by enterprising people who adopted this cheap method of stocking-up. In these surroundings, I, the immature verse-writer, son of Andrew Paterson, had my first taste of bush life.'[53]

Barty's first job at Buckinbah was as an assistant shepherd to Jerry's son Jim, and he never forgot the long days in the fields, the endless vista of the sky, and a sun that seemed to hang suspended forever as the wind whispered among the leaves of the forests all around. The unfenced country stretched for miles, Paterson remembered, 'with big belts of timber and patches of scrub'.[54] Jim was about twelve but already he could boil a billy, track sheep and ride a horse like a champion; his two dogs obeyed his commands and whistles as they chased and turned the sheep, though they sometimes feigned deafness to peel off and chase a kangaroo rat hiding in the grass or a long-legged emu that invariably left the dogs snapping at air. 'If ever the dogs caught up to an emu,' Jim told young Barty, for Jim knew all about such matters, 'one of them things could turn around and kick a dog's head off, just as easy as you'd knock the head off a thistle.'

Jim was always fearful that his father would beat him if he lost sheep, or let the dingoes attack them, or got mobs mixed up so that precious hours would be wasted to separate them. As the young Barty did his best to help Jim avoid feeling old Jerry's wrath, shepherding gave him his first taste of responsibility. Each morning the boys would let the mob of sheep out of a yard built from saplings as tall as a man and laced with wire to keep out the dingoes.

Sometimes Jim would cut throwing sticks and hurl them at the koalas nestled in the trees. The koalas would cry like babies, and Barty would feel sorry for them, but Jim told his young assistant that it was for the animals' own good, to make them climb towards food in the higher branches; Barty thought the excuse was less than convincing. Jim reckoned the koalas were stronger than 'bullicks [sic]' and that you couldn't hurt them because they were so strong. 'If they was as big as bullicks,' he said, 'then two bears could pull a wagon of wool.' They were almost as strong as wombats, who he said he'd seen dragging three dogs into a burrow.[55]

Barty learnt from a young age that sheep did everything differently from every other animal. They did not thrive on green grass and water but were at their best in the dry western plains, wearing a thick overcoat under a broiling sun, getting water out of a saddle-coloured tank and picking seeds from the dirt; long, healthy grass only gave the sheep worms and fluke.[56] They were also the 'champion passive resisters'[57] of the animal world with a determination to do the wrong thing. The eccentricities of the sheep were matched only by the men who tended them, providing young Barty with a wealth of material for future entertainment.

Jim's great fear of his father was realised on one memorable occasion when the boy took his mind off the job and climbed a sapling to snare a wild silkworm nest. Old Jerry, who was supposed to be supervising the work of the two boys, was instead missing, probably asleep, and two mobs of sheep became so mixed that 'separating them would have been like unscrambling scrambled eggs'. Baldie and Nigger tried to restore order but a hundred dogs could not have sorted out the mess. 'Not a word was heard as we marched the two mobs back to the homestead,' Paterson recalled. 'The sheep put up with it with their usual lack of interest in life. I suppose they thought the sorrow was divided about fifty-fifty between them and their owners, and when a sheep comes out anywhere near square with anybody, he thinks he is doing rather well. They don't expect much.'[58]

Barty was sacked as a shepherd and his job was taken by a visiting swagman with a dog. Old Jerry gave Jim a flogging, the sort of brutal punishment that Jerry knew as a convict but which was alien to Banjo as the son of more tolerant, relaxed parents. For the Paterson children, corporal punishment was rare. Rose had been raised by parents who read the classics, played the piano and painted portraits. Andrew was of a similar mind, and he was also slow to anger; one observer remarked that 'no man had greater or more respectful tolerance for the opinions of others, either in religion or politics',[59] and Rose said her husband was 'so good tempered that it would be a hard matter to offend or quarrel with him'.[60]

Perhaps Banjo Paterson had Jerry the Rhymer in mind years later when he wrote 'The Man from Ironbark' about a bushman who reacts violently to a practical joke played on him by a mischievous barber in the big smoke of Sydney. Ironbark was an early name for Stuart Town, near Buckinbah. When the barber pretends to slice the bushman's throat, the Man from Ironbark knocks him out with a tremendous blow from 'his hairy paw', and then turns the barbershop inside out. He returns to Ironbark to regale the other shearers with his tale of a lucky escape.

Old Jerry was a man of worldly wisdom, which the Paterson family sometimes called upon in times of need. It was a lonely existence out in the bush, and strangers coming to the house were often regarded as only being in the middle of nowhere because they were on the run. Like his brother John, Andrew Paterson was a local police magistrate, and one dark night a police trooper arrived at

Buckinbah wanting him to sign a warrant for the arrest of a man named Howard, one of the station's shepherds. Howard was said to be holding the gold taken from a traveller in a highway robbery nearby. But Andrew had just left for Queensland again, so Rose asked Old Jerry what she should do. He said that Howard 'had more names than the King of England'[61] and he was sure to clear out. In fact, when Jerry's son went to check, the shifty shepherd was already long gone.

At another time, with all the station men away, a 'particularly villainous-looking stranger' arrived at the property. Barty watched as his mother perched in her sitting room pouring lead and shot into the barrel of an old muzzle loader. But she was more suited to the piano than firearms, and having cocked the hammer, she slipped, causing the gun to fire with 'a frightful blast'.[62] The shot brought down a shower of whitewash from the calico ceiling onto her head and sent a bullet flying past a family of possums who lived in the roof. 'The stranger must have heard the shot down in the travellers' hut,' Paterson recalled, 'for he was very civil when he came along in the morning to draw his meat, tea and sugar: "And if you could spare a bit of bread, lady, I'd be glad of it. I ain't much hand at makin' damper."'[63]

ROSE MISSED HER MOTHER, 'Mama' Emily Barton, and her siblings, now scattered around Australia. Many of them were involved in pastoral pursuits, but Mama Barton had now moved with some of her younger children into her Sydney home at Gladesville on the Parramatta River above Looking Glass Bay. She bought it on 9 August 1867 after the money from the sale of Boree Nyrang was settled. The home was constructed in the Victorian Georgian style in about 1857 by master builder John Crotty[64]. It was just off the Great North Road[65] that carried travellers from Sydney to Newcastle via the Hawkesbury River crossing at Wisemans Ferry. Mama's garden occupied more than an acre (0.4 of a hectare) and featured orange trees and an orchard, and there was 'a bathing house at the waterside'.[66] After years of fighting nature, Mama could relax in a home that was a shimmering jewel perched on rocks above a spectacular waterway. She called it Rockend, and over the years it became a safe haven for her children and grandchildren as she became 'the matriarch of the tribe comprising a horde of Darvalls and Bartons, and their families. She was the centre of gravity of tribal affairs, the model and inspiration for their conduct.'[67]

Mama was a prodigious letter writer, sharing her love of language with her older children scattered around the countryside.[68] Rose looked forward to every letter from a woman who also knew the loneliness of frontier life. And although the correspondence reminded Rose of a far more comfortable and civilised life than that of a pioneer, it also gave her much-needed comfort and reassurance. She continued to have very little company at Buckinbah and every reason to be wary of mysterious strangers.

In February 1868, a boy named Francis Evans was raped and murdered while out shepherding his father's flock near Windeyer, seventy kilometres from where Barty was born. When his killer[69] was eventually hanged, the executioner made the drop too long so that the head was torn from the body, the rope having cut through the flesh 'causing a horrid gaping wound, from which the vertebrae protruded, whilst blood spurted forth in streams from the several veins and arteries'.[70]

Then on 17 March 1868, what the papers called 'a series of the most atrocious and bloodthirsty murders' was committed by a disgruntled employee at Conroy's Gap, a place that would later feature in Banjo Paterson's writing and which was not far from the Paterson brothers' property, Illalong. The 'ghastly details' chilled readers throughout Australia, and especially those who lived with small children and absent husbands in remote pockets of the wilderness. The *Yass Courier* reported that:

> … five persons in succession fell victims to the inhuman monster, who was a shepherd, and for the past six months has been in the employ of John Conroy, a squatter, and an elderly man, who is one of those so brutally murdered. The five persons who have been so terribly deprived of life are John Conroy, his wife, a young man named Smith, a shepherd named White, and another shepherd name unknown. The murderer is a ticket-of-leave man, named William Monday[71] or Collins. He is a little, spare, wiry, active-looking person, and he is not at all of a repulsive appearance. At the inquest, held on Thursday, he did not appear

> to be at all concerned at the horrible tragedy in which he had been the principal actor; he was cool, collected, and apparently much more indifferent to the proceedings than the most callous of the spectators. Insanity has been hinted at, but so far as we could judge, and we watched the prisoner narrowly during the investigation, we could discover nothing, either in his manner or appearance, to lead us to suppose him to be insane … [Previously, He] was tried on a charge of murder at Maitland in 1851, and was found guilty of manslaughter. He received a sentence of fifteen years, ten of which he had served, when he received his ticket-of-leave.[72]

To nineteenth-century readers, details of the crime played out like the most disturbing horror novel.

> It seems that during the night of Tuesday, the prisoner rose, and with an axe murdered the shepherd who lay alongside of him. The noise awoke Smith, who slept in the opposite room, and on his rushing in the prisoner stuck him in the abdomen with the blade of sheep-shears, and then struck him several blows with the axe. Conroy then appears to have left his bed, and rushed with merely his shirt and night-cap on to see what was the matter, when he was murdered in a similar manner. Mrs Conroy having also heard the scuffle, rushed from the place where she slept, evidently in an excited state as she had no clothing on except her chemise, when she was struck in the abdomen with the blade of the shears, and then terribly gashed across the head and face with the axe. Thus four victims fell to the axe of the inhuman ruffian; and next morning a fifth was added to the awful pile of disfigured and slaughtered persons.[73]

All the bodies were 'fearfully cut',[74] and Mrs Conroy's leg was broken. The killer made a pile of his victims, intending a huge bonfire the next night, but was arrested before carrying out that part of the plan. He freely confessed and produced the long-handled axe, which still had grey hairs on the bloody blade. From the pile of corpses, he drew out the blood-soaked shirt he'd been wearing when he went on his killing spree.[75] Three months later the killer was hanged at Goulburn

Gaol.[76] He said he'd gone on his rampage because old Conroy had underpaid him.[77]

Rose Paterson did her best to make sure her workers were content; she kept the old muzzle-loader handy just in case.

BANJO PATERSON WOULD IDEALISE rural life as a poet and storyteller, yet his family knew the grim realities of pitting themselves against the elements. There were 20.1 million sheep in Australia in 1860,[78] but over the next decade as the numbers grew dramatically, wool prices began to tumble.[79]

At Stainburn in Central Queensland, a fire that engulfed the countryside for four hundred kilometres around burnt the long dry grass and consumed the stockyards and shepherds' tents. Skirmishes with Aboriginal people prevented carters bringing supplies from the port of Rockhampton 650 kilometres away. Then came the credit squeeze of the late 1860s,[80] when 'all the banks foreclosed on all those over whom they held a mortgage and realised on those who were in a good position'.[81] If that wasn't enough on Andrew Paterson's plate, in 1866 he had to appear in court in Sydney, giving evidence against a man who had forged a £10 cheque in his name.[82]

When Barty was barely five, his father became 'just another of the many pioneers who unsuccessfully threw dice with fate'. To 'meet losses in Queensland',[83] Buckinbah, Illalong and Stainburn Downs had to go. Robert Barton Jr recalled that the Patersons made nothing out of the Queensland property and that 'supporting it ruined them on their stations in New South Wales, and the whole of their properties were sold or foreclosed on'.[84]

The real estate company Richardson & Wrench took out large newspaper advertisements for the NSW properties, asking for a 'Positive Sale to close a partnership'. On offer were:

> The following choice Properties, viz.:
> LOT 1: ILLALONG STATION, LACHLAN DISTRICT, situated 20 miles from YASS, with 8740 Sheep, more or less, and 100 Head of Cattle, more or less.
> LOT 2: BUCKINBAH STATION situated in the Wellington District, 25 miles from Wellington, with 14,114 Sheep, more or less, and 180 Head of very quiet Cattle, more or less

The advertisements declared that: 'RICHARDSON and WRENCH have received instructions from Messrs. Paterson, Brothers, to sell by public auction, at their Rooms, Pitt street, Sydney, on TUESDAY, the 15th June next, at 11 o'clock, The above valuable pastoral properties.'[85]

There were no satisfactory bids on either property on 'the 15th June next, at 11 o'clock', but both were eventually offloaded after private offers.[86] Buckinbah and its associated properties – as well as Andrew Paterson's 14,114 sheep and 180 head of cattle (a mixed herd)[87] – were sold for £5549 to another Scot, Thomas McCulloch,[88] a convict's son who paid roughly 7 shillings a sheep and 40 shillings a head for the cattle.[89] McCulloch leased the land – all thirty-five thousand hectares of it – from the crown for £110 a year.[90]

The wealthy merchant Thomas Laidlaw, aka 'Honest Tom of Yass',[91] secured an even better deal for Illalong, with a lease of just £20 a year.[92] The property was soon transferred to Henry Brown, who had the neighbouring Bendenine property. Stainburn Downs went to the Queensland conglomerate controlled by Alexander MacDonald and Charles Smith.[93] The new owners bought much of the starving flock for six shillings a head, and the Paterson brothers drove the rest to sell in Melbourne, almost two thousand kilometres south.

Removed from ownership of Illalong, the Paterson brothers instead became the managers there for Henry Brown.[94] One of their primary roles during hard times was the boiling down of thousands of sheep for their fat. There were six boilers erected on stone basements at Illalong with small fireplaces underneath for fuel. A visiting journalist noted: 'From 50 to 100 sheep can be accommodated in each boiler, and nine men and boys are employed in the operation. The woolshed is the scene. The sheep are slaughtered by three butchers, skinned, cut up in four pieces and all fat saved … the fat being barrelled under the superintendence of an experienced and practical man, each cask containing seven hundredweight [350 kilograms]. The tongues are being salted and the hams preserved to test the English market.'[95] Amid all the slaughter, though, a journalist saw glimmers of the inherent beauty of the area when he was given an inspection of paintings by Barty's aunt Emmy Paterson. She had made many 'artistic and life-like paintings of Australian birds [from the] beautiful specimens of ornithology [that] existed … within a short distance of Illalong', many of them attracted to the homestead by 'the pretty lake-pond close by the garden fence'.[96]

Young Barty Paterson also saw the beauty in the brutal world of farm life. As his young family packed their possessions at Buckinbah and despondently said goodbye to a failed attempt at building a rural empire from their remote home, he looked all around him at the vistas and characters that coloured his earliest memories.

Some visitors, he reasoned, believed this flat country on the Central Tablelands was 'dull and monotonous'. To him it was anything but, with a charm all of its own: a harsh but exotic place where the countryside could stage 'anything from the desolation of a drought to a sea of waving grasses'.[97] Banjo would always remember how at daybreak, in the dry air above that stone house and the wide paddocks in front of it, there would sometimes be a false dawn when the eastern sky glowed with all the colours and wonder of an opal. As the opalescence faded, it was replaced by a pale silver sky as 'luminous as first-class pearl', which in turn gave way to the rays of the rising sun as the distances all around became visible, the silver of the myall trees stark against the almost-black foliage of the belah, the bronze of the young leaves on the apple trees and the tall stiff pines. And across the wide, unique landscape were animals like those that Noah forgot, inhabiting:

A land, as far as the eye can see, where the waving grasses grow
Or the plains are blackened and burnt and bare, where the false mirages go
Like shifting symbols of hope deferred – land where you never know.

Land of plenty or land of want, where the grey Companions dance,
Feast or famine, or hope or fear, and in all things land of chance,
Where Nature pampers or Nature slays, in her ruthless red, romance.[98]

Kangaroos and emus were everywhere. 'Quaint, uncanny creatures,' Paterson called them, 'moving silently through that grey light like the creatures of a dream.'[99]

Chapter 3

1869, ILLALONG STATION, THIRTY-FIVE KILOMETRES NORTH-WEST OF YASS, NEW SOUTH WALES

There were swimming pools in the creek 10 feet deep and half a mile long, horses to ride, and the tides of life surged round us. The gold escort from Lambing Flat, too, came by twice a week, with a mounted trooper riding in front with his rifle at the ready and another armed trooper on the box with the coachman.

BANJO PATERSON RECALLING AN ACTIVE, ADVENTUROUS CHILDHOOD[1]

ILLALONG, WHICH HE LATER described as 'the family mountain station near Yass',[2] offered five-year-old Barty Paterson many opportunities and adventures in partnership with his seven-year-old cousin Jack. But in the winter of 1869 it was an unhappy 300-kilometre journey for the family down from Buckinbah to their new home on the Southern Tablelands of New South Wales.

They drove across the mountains, stopping at the village of Little Hartley for the christening of Jessie, who 'had never before been in the hands of a Minister of Religion'.[3] Then they creaked on in their carriage further south to Illalong, set in hilly and wet land first opened up by the explorer Hamilton Hume who now lived in Cooma Cottage[4] at nearby Yass. 'Some of the hills were very steep and rough with big patches of scrub where the kangaroos lay about in the shade during the heat of the day, just like shearers having a smoke during a spell,' Paterson wrote later in life.[5] The roads were 'quite unmade', and when one track 'got so cut up that a wagon would sink down to its axles, the bullockies would try a new track'. The highway became 'a labyrinth of tracks, half a mile wide, with here and there an excavation where a wagon had been dug out'. When, as often happened, a wagon got stuck in a creek bed, the bullockies would hitch two teams of bullocks to it and then – as one of the bullockies said – 'either the wagon or the bed of the creek had to come'.[6]

A few months after Andrew and Rose brought the Patersons to Illalong, the area was swamped by a disastrous flood that destroyed the new iron bridge on the Yass River.[7] 'When you get anything in Australia,' Paterson once remarked, 'you get too much of it.'[8] After many days of deluge, Illalong Creek flooded and the mass of water took a short cut across the horse paddock. Towards evening it entered Emmy Paterson's kitchen, and the two Paterson families took refuge in an old cottage up the hill. The cottage was used as a store, and the Patersons spent a 'weird and awful night' among the rock salt and bags of smelly potatoes. The next day they were taken to Bendenine Station, where Henry Brown, the Paterson brothers' new boss, made them comfortable while the accumulated silt and water was being bailed out of the Illalong homestead.[9] The children had a fine time but their visit ended in disgrace after they discovered a turtle – 'species "Stinking Jim"' – which they placed in Bendenine's water supply, thinking they had done a great deed. Henry Brown, however, 'entirely disagreed'.[10]

For Rose, the sale of Andrew's herds and flocks had been particularly distressing. She had seen her father beaten down by the uncertainty of life in the Australian bush, and now her husband and children were suffering the same reversal of fortune. Andrew had gone from the owner of three immense properties to a hired servant on what was once his own land. At Illalong, Rose constantly fretted about their future. As well as the emotional, economic, physical and mental hardships she faced with her husband, she also had to endure pregnancies and childbirth in another remote corner of the Australian bush, miles away by horse-drawn buggy from the nearest doctors and nurses. She was tasked with caring for and educating the children, listening to their night-time prayers, and making sure they were washed and clean for dinner, that they minded their manners and that they behaved. It was probably only half in jest that before long she complained to her beautiful sister Nora – now enjoying far more affluent circumstances as the wife of a wealthy and much older politician and pastoralist[11] – that she was trapped 'in monotonous torpidity in this poor old prison of a habitation'.[12]

While Illalong continued to fuel Barty's imagination, he would come to regard it as 'an unlucky place – enough to break anyone's heart'.[13] His family were involved in constant squabbles with local squatters over waterways,[14] and young Barty saw the difficulties many families like his own had in dealing with the vagaries of the seasons and the viciousness of the banks.

Illalong was a bush paradise with jasmine flowers and roses. The air was laden with perfume, and no swagman was ever turned away hungry. It was a good life with lots of sport, a racehorse now and then, and dainty ladies visiting. And yet, so many families on the land were just one season from disaster.

Illalong and the adjoining property Kunjong represented an area of 21,760 acres (8800 hectares) of 'choice grazing country, principally consisting of box and she-oak ridges, abundantly supplied with water from the Illalong and Kunjong Creeks and Cumbramurra River and its tributaries'.[15] Even though Barty reckoned the land was 'poor country'[16] compared with Buckinbah, there was a large garden, reputed to be one of the best in the district,[17] with all manner of English trees and plants: white cedars, cypress, holly, hawthorn and a 'glorious avenue of acacias'.[18] The orchard was repaired after the flood, and soon it was full of figs, walnuts, mulberries, cherries, grapes, apples and peaches. The fruit never seemed to run out and was a magnet for all sorts of birdlife: bower birds, little silver-eyes, leatherheads and parrots with their pincer-like jaws that ripped apart the peaches. The Patersons also had a pet white cockatoo named Uncle who learnt to mimic the voice of Barty's father and would call out for 'Rose' at all times of the day. Uncle progressed to calling for the farm dogs by name. He would walk the clothesline like a man on a tightrope, unloosening the pegs so that, one by one, each item of clothing dropped into the dirt. Then he learnt how to take out the screws holding down the galvanised iron on the roof. Barty's father, gentle soul that he was, said Uncle was more a blessing than a curse because he gave the family so much to talk about.

John and Emmy Paterson lived with their four children, including an aloof daughter nicknamed Madam,[19] in a modest cottage of seven rooms that included a storeroom, detached kitchen, nursery and pantry. Andrew, Rose and their three children made their home in the four-room overseer's cottage,[20] a dilapidated bark shack. The arrangement was only brief. Despite the financial hardships of the Paterson brothers, John retained the appearance of a prosperous country gentleman, well regarded in his district as a former Member of Parliament and still a hard-working magistrate on the Binalong bench, hearing minor cases. He occasionally wrote humorous columns for the *Yass Courier* and lectured at the Yass Mechanics' Institute, delivering one memorable discourse on Scottish eccentricities.[21]

But on 9 August 1871, when Barty was seven years old, his uncle rode off the seven kilometres to Binalong to conduct some business in town before returning to Illalong in the afternoon.[22] According to the *Yass Courier*,

> [He] proceeded about his affairs as usual but shortly after retiring he was seized with what was supposed to be cramp in the region of the heart, and Mrs. [Emmy] Paterson at once despatched a messenger into the deep hollow[23] of Yass for Dr. Campbell. The party sent, however, had not got out of sight of lllalong when Mr. Paterson expired. The cause of death is supposed to have been an effusion of blood on the chest. The deceased was only 40 years of age. Mr. Paterson for very many years has resided at lllalong, and was a most esteemed neighbour and active and painstaking magistrate. The deceased leaves a wife and young family behind. Since the intimation of Mr. Paterson's death reaching town all places of business have been partially closed, and will continue to be so until after the funeral takes place.[24]

Emmy organised to have John buried in the St Clement's Anglican churchyard at Yass[25] and then took her three youngest children to live with her mother, Emily Barton, beside the Parramatta River at Rockend. Emmy's days as a battling pioneer were over. Jack, her oldest boy, stayed at Illalong to keep Barty company.

ALTHOUGH HER LANDSCAPE had changed, Rose felt that she still saw nothing of her husband because he was always away.[26] He was in 'delicate health' for much of the time, but still a workaholic, 'knocking about a great deal' despite his fatigue.[27] He eased the pain of his constant lumbago with alcohol and the opium-based medication laudanum, and when he was home he drank at Binalong's Swan Inn, a low-slung building made from rammed earth and hand-hewn hard woods.[28] His reliance on self-medication created tension between husband and wife, and he could be as irascible as the Charles Dickens villain Quilp.[29] The Paterson family were well versed in Dickens from the time Barty could first remember; his father had bought him the complete set of Dickens and Walter Scott novels, and while Rose is said to have protested about 'such extravagance', Andrew replied, 'My dear, I have given them an education.'[30]

After John Paterson's death and the farewells to his widow and children, Rose moved her family into Illalong's homestead, a grand word for a home Paterson would recall as 'an old-fashioned cottage, built of slabs covered with plaster, whitewashed till it shone in the sun'.[31] The roof had originally been bark; when the bark crumbled, workers were sent out with axes to strip some more. They would cut a seam down the side of a tree and then peel it as a bark cylinder before flattening and drying it in the sun.

When a roof of galvanised iron was eventually placed over the bark, wild ducks flying through the moonlight would sometimes mistake the shining metal for a sheet of water and would land on it with an almighty thump, waking the household and terrifying Rose, who often slept alone. Paterson recalled that 'the ducks were quite ashamed of themselves at having made such a mistake'.[32] They were not the only thing to go bump in the night around the tumbledown house. The noise of landing birds competed with the nocturnal cries of the local quoll population and the disturbing squawks of the mopoke owls. Then there was the frequent clatter of possums scampering along the ridgepole of the roof or sliding down the galvanised iron with their claws struggling to gain traction.

Andrew Paterson was away from home when everyone in the house was shaken from sleep by their introduction to the demonic screech of the powerful owl, the largest and noisiest nocturnal bird on the continent. As Rose and the children fretted in the dark over these 'dreadful sounds', which they feared came from a banshee, 'a great grey bird on noiseless wings'[33] drifted over their heads and glided into what seemed an eternal darkness.

Rose had a brief respite from childbearing, but not too brief. Her daughter Edie[34] was born in 1872 and before long was 'all that the fondest hopes could have pictured: a nice fat little brown-headed brown-eyed cherub, as good as gold … I never lost an hour's sleep with her at night & scarcely ever heard her voice in the day time except in playful gurglings and coos & though I cant quite say that her last month has been equally peaceful, still she has not been so bad as any of the others were under the same circumstances.'[35]

Eventually there were seven children, though there would be twelve years between Barty and his nearest brother Hamilton 'Boy' Paterson,[36] so for a long time cousin Jack was Barty's best mate.

Despite being surrounded by her children and farm workers, Rose craved the company of her female relatives. The whimsical correspondence she conducted with her sister Nora in light of the many perils and privations of bush life would have an important influence on her son's later writings, her optimism and good humour flavouring his tales of rural characters and their adventures. Rose knew about the comfortable life her mother was leading at Rockend with Emmy and others of her family, and it was in a state of loneliness and frustration that she wrote to Nora in 1873 to complain:

> I am in a state of semi-starvation for want of news. We might as well be on a desert island as here for all we know of the doings of the rest of the world or even of our own family. Now that Mama has so many of us in different places to write to, we cannot complain if we do only get treated to a scant scrawl once a fortnight from her especially as her hand seems to continue so shaky and as for the boys & all the other members of our corresponding staff, the cares & business & pleasures of this world occupy them so much that they never have half an hour to spare for we poor exiles (existing) not living … Now you ought to have plenty of time for letter writing & plenty of materials. So 'Pity the sorrows of the forlorn & shipwrecked sister' & please write me a nice long letter straight off before you forget it … I will set you an example by filling you a good big sheet of paper to wade through so that if you pay back in quantity I shall call it a 'red letter day' when I receive your answer.[37]

Not that there wasn't a steady stream of visitors to Illalong. Every spring a flow of itinerant working men headed past the station on their way to the western shearing sheds. Most were mounted but some were on foot, and it was always these weary footsloggers who had 'a habit of helping themselves to any quiet horses they could catch in a paddock at night'. Banjo would recall that when he was about six years old an 'overlander' arrived at Illalong, claiming he had just delivered some cattle. He came into the station leading a horse so knocked about that it could barely stagger. With the men of the station absent and Rose preoccupied with her new baby, the stranger offered to sell the pony to Barty and Jack for five shillings to cover his coach fare to Yass. Somehow the boys raked together the five bob and bought the tired old nag, nursing it back to health with 'handfuls of herbage'[38] lush from recent rains. When Andrew returned home, he told the boys that he didn't mind them buying the horse but he could tell from the brand that it had been stolen from Queensland. Andrew wrote to the station owner, who replied that the boys could keep their new pet. It was duly broken in by an Aboriginal boy and sold for £5, making the two young horse traders a handsome profit.[39]

The experience with this thieving stranger gave weight to Rose's warning that Barty was not to go anywhere near the bullockies, 'who were supposed to be up to stratagems and spoils, especially in the way of stealing horses'.[40] 'But a lonely child will go anywhere for company,' Banjo recalled, 'and I found that they travelled with their families, dogs, and sometimes even fowls. These latter gentry after fossicking about the camp for worms and grasshoppers, would hop up into the wagon as soon as the bullocks were yoked, making for their crate where a little food awaited them. They hurried too!'

One of the bullockies gave young Barty a demonstration with a whip, 'cutting great furrows in the bark of a white gum tree'. When Barty said that with the force of the whip it was no wonder the bullocks pulled, the bullocky remarked feelingly: 'Sonny, if I done that to them bullocks I'd want shooting. Every bullock knows his name, and when I speak to him he's into the yoke. Many a night I've dug up a panel of a squatter's paddock and slipped 'em in, and I've been back there before daylight to slip 'em out and put the panel up agen. So long as they'll stick to me I'll stick to them.'[41]

BARTY WAS SOON DEEMED old enough to ride alongside Jack to the one-room Binalong Public School.[42] In those days Binalong was a two-pub town 'famous for the fact that the bushranger Gilbert was buried in the police paddock.[43] His grave and the house where he had been shot were the 'two show places of the town'.[44] The Swan Inn provided staging facilities for Cobb & Co coaches on their five-day journey between Sydney and Melbourne, and there was the gold escort from Lambing Flat, protected by heavily armed guards. Young Barty hoped that the escort would be bailed up outside Illalong one day, just for some excitement,[45] and he reckoned there were plenty of locals who would have had a crack at the gold if not for the armed guards.[46]

At school Barty sat on a hard wooden bench alongside youngsters who told him they were relatives of the bushranger lying in the police paddock grave. They may have had imaginations to match Barty's, since Gilbert was a Canadian who had grown up down in the south of Australia, in Victoria. Still, Binalong had been a 'great bushranging district' until recently, and the relatives of the hanged bandit John Dunn were all around. Men like Barty's father regarded the bushrangers as a scourge, but to the bush workers who had nothing they were coloured with heroism. Half of Australia's rural working population was of Irish extraction and their folk singing would season Paterson's later writings. On warm summer evenings the workers of Illalong would sit out on the woodheap and, to the accompaniment of a concertina, sing about desperadoes such as 'The Wild Colonial Boy' and 'Dunn, Gilbert and Ben Hall'.[47]

> Come! all ye lads of loyalty, and listen to my tale,
> A story of bushranging days, I will to you unveil,
> 'Tis of those gallant heroes, God bless them, one and all.
> And we'll sit and sing, God save the King, Dunn, Gilbert and
> Ben Hall.[48]

Paterson would save many of the old bush songs and preserve them for future use.[49] The Irish ballads he recalled in later times were a 'mixture of Irish wit and Irish pathos',[50] and the full effect could only be brought out by a good singer. The individualism of the heroes in those folk ballads would one day infuse characters such as the Man from Snowy River and, further along, the Australian Digger.

Rose wrote that Jack and Barty were 'growing to be smart boys': 'They get their own ponies in every morning at daylight, saddle them themselves & start off to school quite independently after breakfast. They take sandwiches for lunch, turn their ponies into Mr Futter's paddock for the day & catch them again in the afternoon & come home at 6 o'clock in time for tea.'[51]

Jack Paterson said it was at Binalong that his cousin 'first got his education – both literal and equestrian'.[52] Barty had to catch his fourteen-hand pony for the ride to school almost every day for two years, in all manner of weather. On warm summer mornings the dry grass made for 'slippery walking', but there were the 'wonderful glories of a bush sunrise'.[53] In winter hoarfrost lay on the ground like snow.[54] The horse, chestnut and white, was a mix of Arab stallion and Timor pony, and had cost £2 10s, 'a fair price in those days'.[55] Barty would go out to fetch his horse and ride it bareback to the house before breakfast. After eating, he would ride off to start school at 9.30am, going up a big hill where Ben Hall had once stuck up his uncle and everybody else who came along 'lest they should warn the mail coach of his presence'; one woman galloped off when Hall's back was turned and defied him to make her return. 'I often wondered,' Paterson reminisced, 'whether I would have the nerve to do it if the same thing ever happened to me.'[56] Paterson later reflected on life at a country school by remarking, 'I think Australian boys who have never been at school in the bush have lost something for which town life can never compensate'.[57]

Rose thought Barty's schoolmaster, '[George] Moore … spare, gaunt, and Irish by descent',[58] was a 'very painstaking man', giving Barty and cousin Jack 'a better foundation in English & arithmetic than they would be likely to get in a more fashionable school.'

A few years after leaving Binalong Public School, Barty could remember nothing of the curriculum except the 'handers … which formed, for the boys at any rate, the one absorbing interest of the day'.[59] 'Handers' were cane strokes that Mr Moore delivered on the palm of the hand and that were doled out with dreaded rapidity 'according to the offence': 'Not being able to answer a question, one on each hand; late at school, two on each hand; telling lies, three on each hand, etc etc.'[60] Binalong endured a cold climate, and the bite in the air exacerbated the burning bite of the cane on frosty mornings. The children had 'wild theories that if you put resin on the palm of your hand, the cane would split into a thousand pieces and cut the master's hand severely, but none of us had ever seen resin, so one's dreams of revenge were never realised'.[61]

Barty soon learnt that his stern schoolmaster was a surprise packet outside the classroom: his extracurricular activities extended to chasing down kangaroos with his team of dogs and breeding fighting roosters. The boy imagined that in an earlier time, Moore may have been an Irish Fenian rebel, as some of his schoolmates had parents sent out to Australia from the Emerald Isle for 'similar festivities'.[62] Only a few years earlier a wild Irishman named Henry O'Farrell had put a bullet into the back of Queen Victoria's son, Prince Alfred, at Clontarf Beach in Sydney.[63]

It was not unusual for the schoolmaster's class to follow him on long summer afternoons to watch the kangaroo hunts. And even though cockfighting was illegal, 'the elite of the school, the poundkeeper's son and the blacksmith's boy, would be allowed as a favour to stop after school and watch a "go-in" between two cocks with-out the steel spurs, as part of their training for more serious business'.[64] Micky Tracey, son of the livestock poundkeeper, told Barty that he had sneaked up on old Moore and O'Mara, the local Irish police trooper – who between them 'represented law, literature and the Government' – and had seen them pit 'fighting game cocks *agin* each other, and the cocks with steel spurs on'.[65] One day the class was hushed with anticipation as the sergeant of police from Yass, 'a little spitfire of a man about five feet nothing'[66] arrived at the school in plain clothes and 'in a natty little trap with a pair of ponies'.[67] The students jumped to the conclusion that he had heard of this cockfighting business, and that the schoolmaster would be led away in handcuffs: 'While the sergeant was inside with the teacher we children swarmed all over his buggy, and there in a neat lattice-lined box under the seat we found a gamecock, clipped and looking for fight! The gamecock was rather surprised to see us in charge of his caravan, but not nearly so astonished as we were to see HIM. It was our – or, at any rate, my – first introduction to the ways of the world and to those who go about in sheep's clothing, but are inwardly ravening wolves.'[68]

Apart from his odd sporting activities, Banjo recalled, there 'was little fault to find with our teacher. Poor man, he was almost daily confronted by irate mothers, real rough sorts, whose children he had whipped, and who threatened to bring "the old man" down to deal with him if it ever happened again'.[69] Paterson recalled Moore's assailants as 'fierce snorting old Irishwomen' who came to the school to give 'the Master some first-class Billingsgate for having laid on the "handers" too forcibly, or too frequently, on the hardened palm of her particular Patsy or Denny[70] ... We used to sit with open mouth and bulging eyes, while the dreaded pedagogue cowered before the shrill and fluent abuse of these ladies. They always had the last word, in fact the last hundred or more words, as their threats and taunts used to be distinctly audible as they faded away down the dusty hill.'[71]

The schoolmaster was called upon to show his own fighting qualities in the arrest of Big Kerrigan, a Herculean railway navvy and the biggest, drunkest man Barty had ever seen. When Barty was eight years old, work began on the railway line from Goulburn to Yass that would connect Sydney to Melbourne; all around Binalong there was 'nothing but torn earth and navvies' camps, and blasts going off, and the clang of temporary rails. Fettlers, gangers, dobbin [draughthorse] drivers and construction men' all swarmed into the little town.[72] Not only did the railway bring the newspaper every day, instead of it arriving once a week by mail coach, but the navvies were followed by all manner of entertainments: 'Cornish wrastlers',[73] English bareknuckle boxers, music hall singers and dancing troupes. And grog – rivers of it. On payday Friday, 'not Monte Carlo itself had anything on [Binalong] when it came to drink and gambling'.[74] The navvies didn't consider themselves properly drunk until they had lost all control of speech and movement. Bearing bottles, they would stagger and stumble along the road until they fell 'gloriously' into the dust. Barty trained his pony to jump over them as though they were logs on the track,[75] ignoring the danger to all concerned if a navvy was to rise while the horse was in flight.

Big Kerrigan was another matter altogether. He was said to be the champion 'wrastler' of a dozen railway camps and able to lift an anvil above his head. But after drinking his wages all through Friday night and the weekend, he presented a fearful sight the following

Monday, armed with an axe and swinging it about as the demon drink urged him to create mayhem. Constable O'Mara, who was said to have arrested several bushrangers single-handedly – and who had been involved in the hunt for Gilbert around Binalong[76] – called at the schoolhouse to gain Moore's assistance in subduing the offender before he harmed himself or the innocent townsfolk.

'To our dismay, the teacher showed every sign of being a conscientious objector,' Barty recalled, 'telling O'Mara: "'Tis your job to arrest drunks. Tis my job to teach the childerrun. Ye've been carrying that revolver a long time, let us see do you know how to use it."'[77]

Eventually O'Mara was able to cajole the hesitant schoolteacher into action. Knowing Barty was the son of a bush magistrate, Moore grabbed him by the hand and – with the other children following like a pack of hounds ready to chase down a kangaroo – marched off to do battle with the giant. They found the 'poor crazed mammoth'[78] in a big clump of trees beside a creek. He had 'foam on his lips and stark terror in his eyes' as he swung the axe at imaginary pursuers while bellowing, to no one in particular, 'they're after me, they're after me'. Luckily O'Mara was a 'Master of Arts' when it came to dealing with drunks, and he managed to talk the ferocious beast around, persuading him to accompany the two men to the police station. There a nip of brandy proved to be a perfect anaesthetic, and while in a coma he was chained to a post. The crisis was averted, though Kerrigan occasionally woke at intervals during the night, roaring like a volcano and setting off a chorus of the local dogs, fowls, turkeys and 'Kiley's bull in his paddock across the road'.[79] The incident caused Paterson to detest anyone who sold alcohol to someone already intoxicated.

Despite shrinking back initially, the old schoolmaster was forever a hero to the young Barty. 'It was my fate, in later years, to meet many great men – Lord Roberts, Lord French, Rudyard Kipling and Winston Churchill. Would any of them have done any better?'[80]

MEN LIKE BIG KERRIGAN kept Rose Paterson's nerves on a knife edge while the local area was filled with railway workers. Andrew was still rarely home, and in his place strange men often appeared at her doorstep looking for work. In exchange for cutting firewood or similar chores they were paid in meat, flour, sugar and tea. Rose found friends and some security in the Futter family – 'very nice neighbours', she called them[81] – and would sometimes take Barty to visit. Binalong grew to a small collection of buildings, and before long there were five hotels[82] full of rowdy itinerant workers, but only one store. It was run by the local postmaster, the genial and kindly Laurence Dargan from Tipperary, who lived in the town for seventy years.[83]

Because their parents 'had but little time to spare'[84] – like most of the parents in the district – the Paterson girls, Flo and Jessie, looked after the storekeeping at Illalong even though they were only eight and six years of age. They sold goods to all manner of travellers, from dandies with Oxford accents to other foreigners who couldn't speak a word of English. The girls had the authority to dole out old boots with a little tobacco if they saw a customer's toes peeping out from his boots, and many a weary traveller had their blistered feet massaged by infant fingers using 'liberal dabs of ointment'.[85] Just about every visitor to Illalong had a story to tell and Barty filed them away to mix with his fertile imagination for future use.

Rose complained many times to Nora about the isolation and the dangers of being virtually a sole parent, miles from help. By a flickering lamp, in the deathly quiet of her bush home, huddled under a black canopy that stretched across the heavens, Rose wrote that:

> Andrew is away tonight … There are such numbers of Navvys camped quite close here that I feel rather nervous at being quite without protectors, at night particularly as I feel sure that if a man were to walk into the room now while I am writing I should be so petrified with fear that I should not be able to utter a single sound … I feel sure that the navvies are in the garden every night (indeed one of them turned Kings evidence and told Barty so) but as long as they come no nearer I shall not interfere with them.[86]

It was about this time that young Barty made the acquaintance of the former convict Edmund Galley,[87] who in 1836 at the Devon Summer Assizes in England was sentenced to death for murder.[88] Galley later proved that he was at Dartford Fair on the day of the killing, but he was not exonerated: his death sentence was merely commuted to transportation for life in New South Wales. He had been in the colony for more than thirty-five years as assigned labour, working as much as he could to receive a pardon and some way of apology, when Barty was sent out in a spring cart to take him his weekly rations: 'ten pounds of flour, ten pounds of meat, some sugar, and some tea'.[89]

The Paterson children were enveloped in the smells of the goods in their new farm store, the tang of brand-new elastic-sided boots and saddles, greenhide whips, and black plug tobacco so full of nicotine that the plugs stuck together and had to be pried apart with a chisel.[90] There were butcher's knives and sugar 'so slightly removed from molasses that it was full of black sticky lumps',[91] along with meat, flour, tea, a few blankets, a few rolls of cotton cloth, pickles, jams, sauces, and bottles of the liniment Farmer's Friend[92] and Painkiller.

Barty first met Galley when the youngster drove out in his ration cart past the Bullock Hill and up Kuryong Creek, through unfenced country until he saw the bark roof and slab walls of Galley's hut. Galley was always on the lookout for the cart, and as soon as the boy and the rations came into sight the old 'lifer' – already past his sixtieth birthday – left his sheep and came trotting down to meet the youngster. 'He was a little, hard, wiry Englishman, perhaps a provincial of some sort, though I have no recollection of his using any dialect,' Paterson recalled. 'On my first visit he looked hard at me to see whether I could by any possibility be the man who committed the murder for which he had been sentenced to death. This was his obsession.'[93]

'Will you come in and have some tea? You're not afraid of me, are ye?' Galley asked. Barty knew nothing about Galley except that he was an ex-convict, but told him he 'was not a bit afraid'. 'This seemed to indicate a lack of appreciation of his importance, so he came out with his story, all of a rush.'

'I'm sent out for life,' Galley explained, 'sent out for a murder I never done. There's lots would be afraid of me, I know the man that done it, though I never knew his right name. 'Twas a man they called the Kentish Hero. He got lagged for something else afterwards and he's out here somewhere now, and someday I'll find him.'[94]

'Old Edmund', as Barty called him, was always absent without leave when out shepherding, always on the lookout for the Kentish

Hero, scrutinising any visitors to his hut closely in case they might be the mysterious villain. He accused 'all sorts and conditions of men, including a clergyman'.[95] Such was Old Edmund's obsession that the Patersons' overseer, Charles Brigstocke, Barty's hero because of the way he was 'always riding incredible distances on outlaw horses',[96] was frequently called upon to saddle up in the middle of the night to round up sheep that Galley had abandoned in his quixotic pursuit of justice.

Later on, Barty would take Galley's rations to a new hut 'which he shared with a man named Howard,[97] who had a wife and some half-dozen children'.

> This mixed ménage seemed to get along well and Galley must have welcomed the change from solitude; but, one day, there arrived at the homestead a rider on a sweating horse to say that Howard had been found dead at the foot of a tree with his skull crushed in and nothing to show how it happened. Rumour ran rife round the scattered huts and homesteads that Galley and Howard had had a quarrel and that this was the result. By the time that the story had got a good start people had already invented the cause of the quarrel and added all sorts of picturesque details. The Yass police were called in; and, with Galley's record at his back, things might have gone hard with him, only that the police puzzled out the explanation. Howard had been ringbarking a tree when he was killed. A large branch of dead timber was found lying alongside his body. Marks on the tree-trunk showed that this branch had been leaning against the tree and that the vibration caused by the ringbarking had made it slip off the tree-trunk, killing Howard with a glancing blow as it fell. Some of Howard's hair was found on the butt of the branch.[98]

The *Yass Courier* reported that Howard was another of Henry Brown's workers and that a 'magisterial inquiry held at Kuriong on 5 February 1874 by Mr. John S. Futter, J.P.' concluded that 'his death was probably instantaneous, as when his body was discovered it was found that his neck was broken. The body must have been out for nearly three weeks, when found very little flesh was left on the bones. He was missed from home but little notice was taken of his absence as he was in the habit of occasionally leaving home and remaining away for a month and more at a time'.[99]

Old Galley wasted no time moving in with Howard's widow, Jane, a New Zealand-born woman thirty-two years his junior.[100] They were married at Illalong on 11 June 1875[101] and the first of their three children was born less than four months later.[102]

Eventually the House of Commons approved a pardon for the old man[103] after testimonials about his character were offered by Barty's father as well as Henry Brown, and the wealthy and influential Walter Friend, Brown's brother-in-law. All were local magistrates.[104] Galley was also given £1000 as some sort of compensation for a life 'completely ruined',[105] and Barty's father was made trustee:[106] 'This started all sorts of trouble, for all Edmund's "friends" descended on him like crows on a carcass, selling him horses, traps, sideboards (he lived in a mud-floored hut) and enough liquor to wash out the memory of the past. Of course my father had to put his foot down on this, for neither the man's money nor his life would have lasted a month if the boom had been allowed to continue.'[107]

BARTY'S MOTHER FREQUENTLY wrote letters about the tribulations of life in the Australian bush, sometimes about the dangers of pregnancy – 'the common cause', she called it – and of the high infant mortality rate that had claimed Rose's twin sister and so many bush babies. When Barty was nine years old, Rose wrote to Nora from Illalong that: 'I have heard from Mamma in her hurried bulletins something of your and Georgie's (another younger sister) sufferings (from the common cause). However the worst of your time must be over now I think, so you ought to be picking up, enjoying yr meals & growing fat and correspondingly jolly.'[108]

Rose encouraged Nora to always use a doctor for childbirth rather than just a midwife, and suggested she smuggle a bottle of chloroform into her room to ease her pain and 'use it like scent on your pocket handkerchief without inhaling it pure. I am sure there is no danger in it and a good deal of relief.'[109] She went on to write about the death of Amelia,[110] wife of local hero David Campbell who had shot the bushranger O'Meally at Goimbla Station. Amelia had died on their new property Cunningham Plains in 1870, four days after giving birth to twin daughters.[111] Two years later Campbell had married

Louise Powell[112] and now, in 1873, Louise was pregnant with a son. Having babies in the bush seemed an endless occupation for so many rural wives, and it was tough. Rose told Nora:

> Mrs DH Campbell is a fellow sufferer of yours ... though she has been very sick and miserable & still looked very white when I spent 4 days there a fortnight ago, she is in quite good spirits again now & seems to think very little of what is before her. She will stay at the Plains for the affair & doesn't wish to send for a Dr but of course with his late wife's fate before his mind, David will at least insist on sending for the 'Young' Dr [Barnett] 12 miles distant. I don't know why I tell you all this except that it is consoling to know that one is not the only bearer of a secret sorrow – when in your position.[113]

Banjo Paterson remembered David Campbell as a 'two gun man of the Wild West type': fair-haired, shy, courteous and softly spoken; a champion who left it to others to relate the tale of how he had gunned down Ben Hall's sidekick when the 'miserable murderin' hounds'[114] came to attack his family at Goimbla.

Barty and Jack were invited to stay at nearby Cunningham Plains with Campbell, Louise and three children from his first marriage. Not only did the wide-eyed boys get to talk to a real-life hero, but they were also allowed to take pot shots at wild turkeys with the rifle that had killed a bushranger.[115]

Campbell ran Cunningham Plains for the Salting family. It was a huge property, extending from near Binalong to the vicinity of Cootamundra seventy kilometres away. The fine homestead was located near Murrumburrah and was said to be the first in the district to be built with walls made from soil rammed between moulds.

Campbell told Barty and Jack that O'Meally and the other bushrangers had torched his stables at Goimbla, and by the light of the flames had begun shooting at the house from the cover of a fence. Campbell was well armed and returned their fire as fast as his wife loaded and handed him the rifles. The fence gave good cover to the gunmen, but at last Campbell got his chance when O'Meally's head appeared over the top. When O'Meally dropped dead, the robbers fled – but it was said that they first yanked some valuable rings off his fingers.[116] Campbell's two young sons had been asleep in one of the rooms, and bullets were found embedded in a wall just above their beds. Campbell showed Barty and Jack the silver coffee urn[117] presented to the late Mrs Campbell for her pluck in exposing herself to gunfire by rushing across to the store for a further supply of ammunition.[118] There was also a letter of support signed by ninety-three locals from the Forbes district, including squatter Thomas Alexander Browne,[119] who would later find fame as the novelist Rolf Boldrewood.

While Paterson's poem 'How Gilbert Died' was something of a homage to his time at Binalong, a later poem, 'In the Stable', was more darkly influenced by his meeting with Campbell. It reflects the dangerous reality of life on the frontier with bushrangers who would threaten women and kill a horse for a lark. They were a scourge on the community, Paterson wrote, until 'Gilbert was shot by the troopers, Hall was betrayed by his friend, / Campbell disposed of O'Meally, bringing the lot to an end.'[120]

Campbell told the Paterson boys that bushrangers were a mongrel mob.

Barty and Jack's interaction with the man who won a shootout with bandits was a thrilling experience for the youngsters. For weeks after their visit to Cunningham Plains, the boys played out the dramatic shootout while Flo or Jessie took turns to play Mrs Campbell, reloading the rifles and then running to get more bullets. The gunshot sound effects were made by beating on a kerosene tin.[121]

Soon, though, Barty found an activity that was even more exciting than his pretend shootouts with bushrangers. It was a pastime that would captivate him for the rest of his life and provide fodder for some of Australia's most memorable verse.

Chapter 4

JANUARY 1873, BOGOLONG, NEW SOUTH WALES

A man who speculated largely told me that he could put ten thousand pounds into a speculation without a tremor, but if he put a pound on a horse he could hardly hold his glasses steady enough to watch the race.

BANJO PATERSON ON THE THRILL OF BACKING A RACEHORSE[1]

THE WAY BANJO RECALLED IT, his introduction to horseracing began on the New Year's holiday when he was eight years old. His father was away, yet again, and the station roustabout – having filled the water barrel, cut the wood and fed the fowls – was free to go to the Bogolong races thirteen kilometres away. 'He suggested that I should go with him, and my mother agreed, though I would not have had a hundred-to-one chance of getting leave from my father. Picture us then, a youth of eighteen and a boy of eight setting out to take part in the sport of kings! Bogolong [now called Bookham] was a township on the main southern road, and consisted of two pubs half a mile apart, with nothing in between.' When Barty asked the roustabout what had happened to the rest of the town, he replied, 'This is all they is. One pub to ketch the coves coming from Yass and the other to ketch the coves from Jugiong.'[2]

Barty's cousin Jack recalled that in the 'good years of the 1870s'[3] there was no end of sport on the stations, and most properties 'kept a racehorse now and then'. Andrew Paterson had one at Illalong called The Banjo which Barty would ride.[4] Barty liked that name, 'The Banjo'.

'Old-timers would never forget the comic-opera bush race meetings. These were not run on the lines of the Australian Jockey

Club, but were delightfully casual. A course of sorts was cleared in the scrub, and as it was not fenced it was quite possible for a horse to pull off and join the throng at the "next time round".'[5]

The Bogolong racetrack was about eight hundred metres out of the town, unfenced, with no grandstand, and mostly laid out through a scrub of gum trees and stringybarks. The Bogolong Town Plate over one mile (1600 metres) was the feature race, and there were to be three heats to decide the winner.

Only a few weeks earlier, as many as fifty thousand people[6] had packed into the Flemington track in Melbourne to see The Quack win a fourth Melbourne Cup for his trainer John Tait, a pugnacious Scot who had earned a reputation for 'serving good straight whisky and good straight rights'[7] at pubs not far from Barty's birthplace.[8]

Bogolong was a world away from the Melbourne Cup. The racehorses there were tied to saplings, as were hundreds of other horses ridden by wild men from the Murrumbidgee Mountains who had all brought their dogs. Some of the men had come down from Lobs Hole,[9] which was on the track to the Kiandra diggings and regarded as a place so steep that young Barty was told 'the horses wore all the hair off their tails sliding down the mountains'.[10] There was probably a man from Snowy River or two as well, from the sort of 'rough country where a rider sometimes shuts his eyes while his horse works around a slippery sliding with a thousand feet drop below him'.[11]

Barty had cantered over to the racetrack on a pony with a child's saddle. After arriving he started to take in the sights and sounds of the big day, and glanced back to check on the welfare of his horse. He saw a 'Murrumbidgee mountaineer about seven feet high' taking the saddle off his pony and putting it on a racehorse that was a starter in a heat. Running over to him, Barty managed to gasp out, 'That's my saddle.'

'Right-oh, son,' the saddle-borrower replied, 'I won't hurt it. It's just the very thing the doctor ordered. It's ketch weights, and this is the lightest saddle here so I took it before anybody else got it.' The mountain man pointed to his mount and said, 'This is Pardon, and after he wins this heat you come to me and I'll stand you a bottle of ginger beer.'[12] Barty could hardly contain his excitement over the prospect of some lolly water.

When the great race began, he watched transfixed as Pardon lay behind the leaders until they went out of sight behind the stringybark scrub; he watched them come into sight again, with Pardon still lying third; and then the crowning moment as the horse drew away in the straight and won comfortably. There was then delirious joy when, in the second heat, Pardon led the field all the way, so that there was no need to run a third.

Barty found the ginger beer a disappointment as it was 'bitter, luke-warm stuff with hops in it', but what did he care? His new friend assured him that Pardon could not have won without the saddle. It had made all the difference.[13]

Candidates for Parliament always made the bush-race meetings 'their opportunity for delivering a torrent of eloquence', usually with promises about delivering a load of blue metal for road-making where it would be "handy like".'[14] After the speeches, Barty and the Illalong roustabout had thirteen kilometres of riding to get home, so they decided to leave '... before things got really lively ... But before we departed two men had an argument about a bet and each made a run to pull a stirrup-iron out of his saddle. My old friend the sergeant of police from Yass had no objection to a fight, but he drew the line at stirrup-irons! He and the mounted trooper handcuffed first one man and then the other with their arms round saplings, a performance which I had never seen before and have never seen since.'[15]

Paterson later varied the details about the origins of his poem 'Pardon the Son of Reprieve',[16] but it was the colour and the rhythm of his experience that mattered most. Racing would remain one of the great passions of his life, from riding bush nags to watching the mighty Phar Lap.

ROSE PATERSON HAD INHERITED from her mother, Mama Barton, a love for music and a gift for storytelling, and she in turn passed it on to her son Barty: from an early age Barty's storytelling would win him a sizeable audience, first at the Binalong school where he mingled with 'bush youngsters from huts and selections and homesteads far and near'.[17]

Children of the bush were an inventive bunch – they had to be, given the vagaries of rural life – but for some reason their adaptability stopped at the classroom and they became a 'curious lot' with 'an absolute want of originality'.[18] There was only ever one excuse for being late for school: 'Father sent me after 'orses', and Paterson recollected whimsically on the stock thefts in the area that since many of the parents were 'largely engaged in looking after horses, mostly other people's …' the excuse was more than probable. But they didn't 'garnish' their excuses 'with a Sir, or anything of that sort', and with constant repetition the excuse wore thin on Mr Moore. Barty reckoned the other boys were 'too lazy or too stupid to invent anything to replace it'.[19]

Barty and Jack were given special dispensation to arrive late since they lived so far out of town, and having what he termed 'a particularly vigorous and cultivated imagination', Barty supplied each of his classmates with a different excuse: one was to have forgotten his book and gone back for it, another was to have been deceived by the sun rising late since 'not one in fifty had a clock in their house', another was to have been sent on an errand to the store and been delayed by the clerk. Barty thought they were first-rate excuses, but when the time came and Mr Moore demanded of one conspirator, 'What makes you late, Ryan?', Ryan gasped, his eyes rolled, his jaw dropped and he spluttered, 'Father sent me after 'orses.' One by one as the other boys were questioned about their lack of punctuality, they panicked and fell back on their old refrain, and each took two cuts of the cane on each hand.

Barty despaired. 'I gave them up after that,' he said, 'my inventive talent was wasted upon such people.'[20]

The children of the railway workers were a different story, showing Barty a cleverness and cunning that he could only admire. 'When the railway came to the town the children of the navvies came to the school and how they did wake it up! Sharp, cunning little imps, they had travelled and shifted about all over the colony.'[21] The railway children had strategies to escape the cane such as the Binalong children had never dreamt of. 'They had a fluency in excuse,' Paterson remembered, 'and a fertility in falsehood which we could admire but never emulate.' Sometimes their fathers, the navvies working alongside Big Kerrigan and Cornish Jack, went on prolonged drinking bouts that would result in a 'disease known to science … as delirium tremens', but in the vocabulary of Binalong better known as 'the horrors' or 'the jumps'. 'The townsfolk shortened up even this brief nomenclature – they used simply to say that so-and-so "had 'em" or "had got 'em".'[22]

At home Rose doted on her son, and he was the man of the house during his father's long absences. Rose also found adult company in the letters to Nora. While Rose had been born into the landed gentry of the Barton dynasty, Andrew Paterson's financial woes had seen her circumstances diminished. The discomfort was heightened by the fact that Nora had married into money and was living the life of a young pastoral queen. On 18 December 1872, Nora had married Thomas Lodge Murray-Prior, an aristocratic widower and notorious womaniser who claimed to be descended from the Emperor Charlemagne.[23] He was fifty-three and Nora, who had trained as one of the 'Florence Nightingale' nurses at the Sydney Infirmary,[24] had just turned twenty-six.

Murray-Prior's first wife had borne him twelve children, including the writer Rosa Praed.[25] Nora would bear him eight more. Murray-Prior was the son of a commander at Waterloo and had travelled north with the explorer Ludwig Leichhardt in 1843, becoming one of the earliest squatters in the country north of the Tweed River. He was one of the leaders in a massacre of Aboriginal people in the Burnett region, west of Maryborough, that saw as many as five hundred Indigenous men, women and children killed in retaliation for the murder of eleven settlers.[26] By the time he married Nora, Murray-Prior was a life member of Queensland's Legislative Council and postmaster general. During parliamentary sessions, he and Nora and their children lived in splendour at Brisbane's Kangaroo Point, but their main residence was Maroon, a lush station in the picturesque Border Ranges south of Boonah.

For Rose there was no longer the luxury of governesses, which she had known as a child, only 'overpowering heaps of mending ever accumulating & nobody but me to do it'.[27] Rose was often frustrated by Andrew's absences from family gatherings.[28] The properties he managed were so big that it took more than a day to ride around them[29] and the work was relentless: supervising the maintenance of fences and outbuildings, organising the shearing of the sheep and the overall care for the stock, taking off with his '"footrotters" … a new & delightful title given to men who are employed in dressing the sheep's feet'.[30] Early in the Paterson's time at Illalong, Nora's husband had offered to find Andrew a post office appointment in Queensland, though only on a quarter of the salary Henry Brown paid him. The money was too light on, and an office workplace was not for Rose's husband.

> A large station managership or working partnership might tempt us to your side of the world but not a Post Office appointment on 50 pounds per annum unless things get worse with us instead of better [which] heaven forbid.[31]

Rose lived in fear, though, that the post office job might become a necessity if things went from bad to worse at Illalong. There was always the chance that Henry Brown could terminate Andrew's employment and the Patersons would have to get off the land that Andrew had once owned. Her fear occasionally bordered on paranoia, and she told Nora that she suspected spies were everywhere.

> Andrew & Mr Brown have always been on very good terms; Andrew is so good-tempered that it would be a hard matter to offend or quarrel with him, & so hard-working & steady & sensible that it would be a hard matter to find fault with him … Please do not speak as if we were discontented or say anything that the B's might not like to hear repeated: they have an extraordinary faculty for finding out whatever is said about them, even going the length of listening at keyholes! I have been told, & I know for a fact that they question servants and people of the lowest possible character to find out what we, & others say and do … Anyway, burn this & remember that Mr B. will be in Brisbane soon, & anything you may say may come round to him if you're not careful.[32]

Barty and Jack had a much more favourable impression of Henry Brown. Jack thought him to be a fine 'old squire', and said he and his wife Annie[33] 'were beloved of all who knew them … His smiling face was like John Bull of the picture-books. He wore a grey "bell-topper" hat, which infuriated the magpies in the nesting season. They always tried to spear holes in it with their bills. Oh, but he was good to us boys, and gave us ponies; and … when we were washed out by the big flood on the next station, he took in the family for weeks – until the place could be bailed out.'[34]

The Browns lived in comfort on Bendenine Station, with its 'delightful old homestead, pleasant garden and orchard and gaudy peacocks'.[35] That was the focus of Henry's land holdings. Illalong was the poor cousin, according to Rose. 'This being not the head station & no money ever spent in making the slightest repair to house or garden you can imagine what a dreary wreck it looks from outside,' Rose complained, adding that 'the blighted fruit trees' were spreading 'their mouldy branches to make a screen to keep out any brighter view there might be from outside & from our front windows'.[36] She told Nora that Illalong 'seems to me to grow bleaker, baggier & colder, as it certainly grows rottener & older every winter.'[37]

The Patersons had outgrown their home at Illalong and another house, built from red-box gum slabs,[38] was transported from the property of a selector who had sold out to Henry Brown. The house was put onto rollers by a bullocky and a bush carpenter, and moved to its new foundations by a team of beasts – led by two named Rodney and Spot. The house came floating across the paddocks and through the bush swaying 'like a ship at sea, but holding together'.[39]

Illalong, though, continued to slide into disrepair.

ROSE ENCOURAGED HER first-born son's education, not just from the tattered classics in the primitive library but from all the sights, sounds and experiences around him. There were the wild ducks nesting close to the house; the mother duck covered her eggs with down from her breast and then later led her ducklings to the creek for their first swim, 'one of the prettiest sights in Nature'.[40] Cousins, both boys and girls, who came to Illalong for Christmas holidays helped Barty and Jack with their explorations as they went out on foot and sometimes on horseback across the hilly paddocks, getting to know all the birds and animals of Illalong. There was a wedge-tailed eagle[41] that the children called The MacPherson because its hooked nose and fierce eyes reminded them of the picture of a Scottish chieftain they had seen in one of Illalong's books.[42] When a wedge-tailed chick, MacPherson Junior, was found injured and brought to the house as a pet, a Muscovy duck named Mr Wattles made the mistake of waddling too close to the tethered predator. He became a tasty lunch. Barty recalled that Mr Wattles was not popular in the farmyard and his death was not mourned by anyone.

Under the roof of Illalong's veranda were swallows with their mud nests, depositing droppings that coated the veranda floor like sticky white paint. Rather than cruelly smash the nests of the little birds or kill them, as some farmers might, the Patersons placed planks beneath the nests to catch the droppings so that everyone was happy, especially the birds.

Out in the fields, spur-winged plovers wheeled and dived at intruders to protect their young. Magpies took meat from the hands of the children, and the gaunt grey curlews were forever wailing like banshees. Parakeets flashed past 'like green and gold projectiles' shrieking a greeting as they went.[43]

Crows did not hold a similar affection for Barty. They had 'more brains than most birds'[44] and that only made it easier for them to be 'detestable villains'.[45]

Barty regarded the little finches, the blue-caps, as 'the most delicate and dainty of All Australian birds', and they would come to the very door of Rose Paterson's kitchen to beg for tiny scraps of meat.[46] There were snakes, too, 'moving as silently as water flowing over the ground',[47] but their presence was always detected by the 'noisy miners', the 'soldier birds' of the bush, who sounded the alarm without fail. These feathered fighters were 'fierce-eyed little grey ruffians', darting at the snakes from above and pecking at their heads, keeping the feet of little children safe.

In the creek was Old Man Platypus, who would come ashore to brush his fur or sun himself like a gentleman, and there was also the water rat – Oily Gammon, they called him – as slippery as an eel, disappearing under the water when he was being watched only to appear in some other place among the weeds, resplendent in his shiny hide that looked like a black satin coat and white cravat. All attempts to catch him with pieces of crawfish failed as he outwitted the children and stole the food from the traps. 'These were the harmless people of the bush,' Paterson later relayed to his granddaughters, lamenting that soon enough they would 'be almost exterminated by poisoned rabbit baits and by foxes'.[48]

In his bush home, surrounded by wildlife and family, Barty could never be morose for long, and this state of mind stayed with Paterson throughout his life. His mother's sense of fun and irony, given her declining fortunes, flavoured his writings from his earliest verses. All he ever needed to charm an audience was to remember the people and places of the bush, and as an old man he would disarm critics by admitting he never 'aimed very high; in fact I never "aimed" anywhere but just wrote of the little things I knew about'.[49]

Adventures were everywhere, and often Barty and Jack were left to their own devices. On one week of school holidays their uncle Frank Barton, survivor of the Ben Hall incident, and Sid Blaxland[50] – a grandson of the explorer Gregory Blaxland – decided on some duck shooting at Illalong. When they left their gunpowder flasks lying about, Barty and Jack seized upon the treasure. They poured the black powder onto a sheet of paper, and Jack threw lit matches at the target as Barty leant in for a close look. 'A lightning like sheet of flame shot up from the powder and I had my eyebrows burnt off, my hair singed, my face blackened and my eyes temporarily closed.'[51] Briefly blinded, he was led home by Jack – 'two nice objects to confront a harassed housewife and one can imagine the relief when it was found that my injuries were only superficial.'[52]

It was a loving household even if once when the boys were out late hunting and failed to return until well after dark, they were 'cuffed firmly' and sent to bed after a meal of 'cold mutton salted with tears'.[53] Such punishment was rare, though danger was ever-present – even among the foodstuffs of the store.

The cook presiding over Illalong's travellers hut once took out some arsenic to lay baits for the quolls hanging around the fowls. He put the packet of arsenic on the shelf above the hot fireplace alongside a packet of baking powder. There were three travellers in the hut and, hurriedly mixing them a damper bread, the cook used the arsenic instead of the baking powder, and poisoned all three of the travellers and himself. Poor old Mr Brigstocke had to ride at full speed more than thirty kilometres into Yass in the middle of the night to rouse the doctor from his bed. Fortunately, the cook had used so much arsenic that the stomachs of all the victims rudely eliminated the contents. But for a while it was a toss-up.[54]

Paterson no doubt recalled the absent-minded cook when he wrote 'Johnson's Antidote' many years later.

Barty's life at Illalong was never 'monotonous or bare of adventure'.[55]

THERE WERE SO MANY other characters and adventures around Illalong that fuelled Barty's imagination.

An Aboriginal family lived in a hut made from three saplings and bark, with a small fire constantly glowing in front of their abode. The head of the household wore a brass plate around his neck proclaiming that he was Billy Budgeree, King of the Lachlan, and Barty always thought it unfair that his wife did not have her own plaque announcing her as 'Queen Sally of the Lachlan'.[56] Their stick-thin daughter was Nora. All three had been given their Anglicised names by Baptist missionaries, and Nora described her christening ceremony of full immersion as 'Close up that fella drown himself.'[57] Their only bedding seemed to be a tattered old possum rug, a flourbag and a government blanket, and on cold nights they would lie down with their three dogs to stay warm. Still it gave the Paterson children a thrill to 'think that we were meeting royalty face to face' and they would beg cold mutton for them from the cook and hint to Barty's father 'that he might spare a fig of tobacco from the store for Billy's insatiable pipe'.[58] Andrew Paterson was reluctant to reward Billy with alcohol, even though the laws governing the supply to Aboriginal people were not stringently enforced at that time.

Among Billy's possessions were a tomahawk to shape boomerangs, a spear and its launching stick called a woomera, and a piece of limestone that Billy reckoned could induce rain anywhere at any time – though the young Barty noticed that Billy only chanted an incantation over it when clouds were about and that the incantation usually involved a request for another blanket from 'Old Mr Paterson'.[59] On one memorable occasion, after Billy trotted out the limestone, it rained seventy-five millimetres in one night, Illalong Creek coming down 'a banker', the frogs in chorus, the water rats showing off their shiny black coats, the wild ducks and turkeys moving in from all the nearby districts that seemed to have missed the nourishing downpour.

The rain was not always so welcome. In the wet seasons 'sheep suffered terribly from footrot and fluky liver' and 'there were patches of clay substratum that would bog a duck'.[60] Barty's mother could only despair that 'This part of the country never suffers much from want of rain but much more from too much.' In fact, she wrote to her sister: 'We ... have had such a dose of rain since the drought broke up that I am present ardently longing for another drought as soon as possible.'[61]

Still, King Billy's fame spread far and wide as a man with uncanny powers: 'Billy had been looked upon as a cadging old nuisance at the neighbouring stations and his dogs were in even less favour than himself. Now he was told that he could come along and bring his dogs any time that he liked. They could not afford to overlook a rainmaker of his class.'[62]

Billy was rewarded with sugar, flour, tobacco and mutton, but within two days it was all gone, and aggrieved that he had not been properly rewarded for his miraculous feat, the King of the Lachlan was 'very little inclined to put himself out for anybody'[63] after that. When the Paterson children badgered Billy for a spear-throwing demonstration he told Sally to do it, before the assignment was passed on to skinny little Nora. Her feeble attempt went less than ten metres but left the spear protruding half a centimetre into Barty's leg. He ran crying and screaming to Rose, the weapon still hanging from his calf. There was no thought of sending to Binalong for a doctor, though, because worse accidents happened to station workers every day, from mishaps with horses, axes and waterways.

The mishap was not big news, but Paterson later heard it was briefly discussed by two station hands on a nearby property. One of them felt that somebody was badly at fault in allowing a woman to throw a spear when children were about. It could have had disastrous consequences, he said. The spear might have hit a horse.

In any case, Rose had a ready supply of Farmer's Friend and Holloway's Ointment to repair the damage to her son. Her handkerchief dried Barty's tears but his wound was not the only health concern to trouble her family.

Rose was convinced that her husband's cousin James 'Blenty' Paterson[64] was 'trying so hard' to break his own neck,[65] so frequent were his disastrous accidents. The bespectacled farmer was short-sighted and fond of a drink, and Rose told Nora that on one occasion Blenty fell from his horse while he was cantering in the dark; he was left unconscious at the side of the road for seven hours with two broken ribs until a Good Samaritan arrived. His wounds had hardly healed when he was riding in a buggy with Ned Dunn, the brother of the hanged bushranger John Dunn. A harness broke and the horses tore off. Blenty leapt for safety but Dunn, 'with a heroism' worthy of a man with a better family connection, stuck his leg out to try to stop the horses – only for the leg to be caught in the spokes of a wheel. The leg was shattered and Dunn was thrown on the roadside while the horses made off with the £40 buggy, smashing it to pieces as it ricocheted off trees.[66] 'Blenty (always a philosopher) walked to a shepherd's hut & got his dinner & then made arrangements for sending Dunn home to his friends and getting a Dr for him.'[67]

At another time Blenty was riding across a decaying wooden bridge on the road to Yass when his horse fell through rotted timber. Somehow Blenty survived. He would become the model for Banjo Paterson's blundering yokels.

ROSE CONTINUED TO FIGHT a losing battle to keep the house in order for her husband and children. Andrew's drinking and self-medication for his bad back caused tension in their relationship when he was at home, but she was ever loyal and never harsh in writing about him to her relatives.

The work on a rapidly deteriorating home was constant. 'I have kept preservingly at work inside with fresh paper, lime, tacks and calico,' Rose told Nora, 'so that the interior is not so bad except the kitchen & the veranda which connects house & kitchen. This last is almost shingleless & the bricks are half of them out in the kitchen floor.'[68]

The house became so dilapidated that Rose had trouble finding domestic servants of the standard she expected. 'The kitchen & servants quarters are so rough & tumbledown that we can't hope to keep servants here except such as being brought up in bush huts & whose ways are correspondingly rough and dirty… & we have to pay tremendous wages even to these'.[69] When workers were found it was tough to retain them, and years later Rose eventually complained with her wry sense of pathos: 'We have very great trouble getting people <u>who will do any work at all</u> … I find Madame using a dirty sausage machine, kneading bread in a trough with the dough of <u>centuries</u> … & pouring the milk unstrained into the jugs out of a dirty bucket … one can't box the ears of a dignified married woman, who has 'notice' on the tip of her tongue to give if found fault with.'[70]

Other workers in the field were more industrious. There was Henry Ward, who according to Jack Paterson was 'a remarkable identity who lived and died in the service of Illalong'.[71] He was an exceptionally strong man of the 'stocky, thick-set English type'; he walked all over the run, and if he wanted to go to Yass he walked thirty-two kilometres each way rather than go by train. He was never actually known to ride or use any vehicle, declaring that he 'would have no truck with horses'. The Patersons heard that he had been in an accident in his youth that had prejudiced him against horses for life.[72]

A pair of lean and athletic brothers, Jim and Jack Donnelly were mainstays of the station and idols of the Illalong children. Their faces were suntanned dark brown, and they moved quickly and with purpose, always ready to leap onto some fast young horse to solve some urgent crisis. Even when they were just harnessing up Rose, the old white cart mare, the Donnellys looked ready for any emergency. They could sing and dance too, each taking turns to make their feet rattle like 'castanets to the accompaniment of the mouth organ played by his brother'.[73] The Paterson children would sit on the woodheap, in still summer evenings, listening to the brothers sing love songs about sailing off to their sweethearts in Baltimore. Neither of the brothers had ever seen a large boat or had the foggiest idea of where Baltimore might be, but that only made them more charming. Four-year-old Jessie Paterson confessed to her father that she was in love with Jim Donnelly, while Barty Paterson, growing up surrounded by the rhythm and sentiments of Irish folk music, was already forming a view that 'isolation in the bush made individuals of men'.[74]

The brothers taught Barty much about farm animals and how even the Patersons' old blind black Aberdeen Angus cow had certain senses that people did not – how cattle could smell water twenty miles away. Jack Donnelly was the boundary rider in charge of the ewe paddocks, bringing in the sheep to be shorn, sometimes in great heat with the weary dogs limping behind, 'lamed by the thorns and spiny burrs'.[75] On one occasion he told the children that twenty lambs had been born one night, and fifteen had been unclaimed by their mothers. Barty and the other youngsters decided to rescue the newborns from certain death and volunteered to forgo their own daily drink of milk to feed their new pets. Jack brought the lambs over in the cart, and the children gathered the few tins of condensed milk from Illalong's store. They mixed the milk with warm water and castor oil, and prepared feeding bottles, the same as Barty's mother used for her own babies. Then began the arduous task of feeding the squirming, wriggling contortionists unused to human hands, and before long the young pets were sucking at the fingers of their saviours hoping for more milk.

In the months ahead, the children felt a warm glow of satisfaction when those lambs ran out of a passing mob of sheep and tried to suckle their fingers again.[76]

A SHEPHERD WHO CALLED HIMSELF John Wilberforce Morley, 'reputed to be an Oxford man who had come down in the world',[77] was another of Barty's great teachers, telling him tales about his shaggy-coated, big-footed Russian dog, Peter the Great, who had a fringe of hair that almost blinded him, was 'nearly the size of a pony' and could eat a horse.[78] Morley was always shooting kangaroos, wallabies, eagles and crows to keep the mutt sated, and once even fed him an echidna after he'd taken out all the spikes.

Morley eventually returned to England with the dog, but not before he gave the children repeated renditions, worthy of a Shakespearean theatre, about Peter the Great ripping the throat from a wild cattle dog they had found mauling a sheep.[79]

Barty's first real introduction to the working dogs of Illalong came when he was a small boy and would go out into the paddocks with an old labourer accompanied by what the elderly man called his 'Smiffield Collies'.[80] They were like their master – big, rough and hairy. The shepherd was illiterate, had never been on a train and had survived more fights at mining camps than he could remember. His dogs had no tails and were forever tearing apart animals they cornered.

Later, the Paterson children would take their own dog, a Scotch collie, whenever they went hunting for possums or kangaroo rats, or down to the creeks to look for the little freshwater lobsters that Barty called crawfish. On those excursions, each child had four feet of twine with a piece of raw meat to dip into the water; as each crawfish took the bait it was hauled out, goggling eyes and all, while the children grabbed hold of it behind its madly waving claws.[81]

Barty had an everlasting affection for the land around him and the animals he encountered, even the ones he hunted. The district teemed with game birds: mostly ducks, quails and bronze-wing pigeons, attracted by the seed in the property's huge masses of blue thistle. The pigeons made 'splendid pies'.[82]

Horses were always Barty's favourite farm animal, even though his right arm gave him considerable grief. It was when he had a fall from a horse, not long after arriving at Illalong, that investigation of the damage revealed the break from his infancy. At one time doctors thought they should remove his whole thumb down to the wrist, and although a later operation saved the thumb, his right arm was shorter than the left and there was significant muscle damage.[83] Sir Edward Knox,[84] who became chairman of the Colonial Sugar Company and the Commercial Banking Company, remembered that even in middle age Banjo had trouble with the arm and developed a quirky, cramped action in stuffing tobacco in his pipe.[85]

Barty told his family years later that the injury to his arm gave him a very light hand on the rein and this, together with his ability to 'stick on' a horse, made him a much accomplished rider'.[86] Sticking on a horse in the bush, though, could be a deadly pursuit and not everyone was able to ride like him. At Binalong, a colt ran away with one of Barty's schoolfriends, throwing the boy with terrific force among big trees and killing him. Paterson remembered that the boy's people 'were Irish folk and the intense, bitter sadness of their grief was something terrible.'

ALL TOO SOON, ILLALONG would be a distant memory for Barty Paterson.

His adoring mother wrote that he was a clever boy who 'ought to have a profession which will need more head than hands'.[87] He was about to move to Sydney, where nobody in his new circle of friends ever had the 'horrors' or the 'jumps'; none of them were ever sent after 'orses; nobody wore spurs in school; most of the boys learnt dancing, and some could play the piano.[88]

It was a more civilised, sanitised world.

But Paterson's soul would always long for the wide open spaces.

And his heart would always be among the people and the places of the bush.

Chapter 5

1874, ROCKEND, A COTTAGE ON THE PARRAMATTA RIVER AT GLADESVILLE, SYDNEY

... Emily Mary Barton found time to write some very good verse (published privately) and whatever of ability the present 'Banjo' Paterson may have was undoubtedly inherited from her.

BANJO PATERSON RECALLING HIS GRANDMOTHER EMILY[1]

BARTY WAS TEN YEARS OLD when his parents sent him and his cousin Jack to stay with Rose's mother, Emily Barton, in Sydney. The children all called her Mama. Jack was reunited with his mother, Emmy Paterson, who had been living there with his young sisters since the sudden death of her husband at Illalong.

The boys were to receive a big city education, and Paterson later remembered that 'a new world opened before me ... up to the time of my arrival in Sydney, my experiences of life had been limited to contacts with the unsophisticated children of Nature'.[2] The youngster was swapping his home among the gum trees for what he would one day describe as the 'dusty, dirty city', its 'foetid air and gritty'[3] three hundred kilometres north-east along the rail line being built through Illalong. The Binalong school, and the likes of Big Kerrigan and Cornish Jack, and the campfire singalongs, and the cousins of the bushrangers perched next to him in Mr Moore's classroom – all of these would be mere memories until he saw their like again on the next school holidays.

Rose wanted her son to make the most of his inventive mind and expansive imagination. The first train to Binalong was still two years away,[4] and so Barty travelled by horse to Goulburn and then boarded the train to clickety-clack through the lush green pastures around the Southern Highland towns of Bundanoon, Moss Vale[5] and Mittagong.

Around the time that the locomotive was chugging towards Sydney's Central Station – and a new world of experiences and adventures for the boys – a new order of Australian literature was gathering steam with the publication of the groundbreaking novel *His Natural Life*[6] by the highly strung and frequently broke Marcus Clarke.[7] The novel, which would later be known as *For the Term of His Natural Life*, was originally serialised over twenty-seven monthly instalments in *The Australian Journal*. Clarke was the editor there when the first instalment was published in February 1870. The periodical was produced by Clarson, Massina & Co from 1865[8] and promised its audience that 'the ablest COLONIAL pens of the day will be engaged on our staff'.[9] Its pages featured such well-known local writers as Adam Lindsay Gordon and Henry Kendall, but Alfred Massina[10] wanted a regular hook for his readers. He and his business partner William Clarson 'hit upon'[11] the young Marcus Clarke to boost circulation and appointed him editor. 'He ran it for a month,' Massina recalled, 'during which time the circulation dropped from 12,000 to 4,000. If he had run it for another month it would have been dead.'[12] It was Massina and Clarson, though, who funded Clarke's trip to Tasmania to research his masterwork about the escaped convict Rufus Dawes.

'Clarke came to me one day and said, "Massina, I want £50." "Oh," I said, "you've had enough out of me. What more do you want?" "£50," replied Clarke, "I can write a story for your journal. I am going to Tasmania to write up the criminal record and I'll do the story for £100."'

'We jumped at it,' Massina said. 'Now, Clarke was going to write that story in twelve monthly sections. At first, he wrote enough for two months, then enough for one month, and got down to very little. In fact, we had once to put it in pica type instead of brevier, to swell out the size of that month's contribution. But on one occasion he had nothing ready, and we had to go to press with an apology to our readers. Finally, we had to lock him in a room to get another written.'

The book, released in 1874, had a profound effect on Australian readers and Australian literature. Paterson would later say of Clarke that he had 'local colour to hand in abundance and used it lavishly. The horrors of the convict system gave him new colour, new characters, and new and awful surroundings. He daubed the misery on in great lumps, laid it on with a trowel, poured it out of a bucket.'[13] Before long many other Australian writers, led by Rolf Boldrewood, would emulate Clarke's work. Australian books by Australian authors would boom in popularity just as Banjo Paterson was finding his voice.

First, though, the Paterson boys had to find their feet in Sydney. They were bound for Sydney Grammar.

Barty and Jack spent a short time settling in at what Barty called 'an old dame's school in a suburb of Sydney ... a nice quiet institution where we were all young gentlemen, and had to wear good clothes instead of hob-nailed boots and moleskins in which my late schoolmates invariably appeared. Also we were ruled by moral 'suasion instead of "handers".'[14] Barty and Jack joined the preparatory school at Sydney Grammar in January 1875. Jack's mother Emmy, still living at Rockend, went on record as his guardian. Barty was a faster learner than his older cousin; in April he was placed in the remove class, while Jack stayed in the lower school.

At home in Gladesville, Mama Barton began teaching the boys French and introduced them to her favourite authors: Thomas Carlyle, John Ruskin and Algernon Swinburne. Her home and circle of friends fostered an environment of intellectualism. She also introduced the boys to her poetry, some of which she had penned on board the *Alfred* as it ferried her and the handsome Captain Barton to the Australian frontier almost thirty-five years earlier. At the start of that voyage, from which she would never return, she had written in her diary:

> Morning again and through the opened port
> Darts the first crimson ray: waking, I bless
> The first return of light: and rising, hail
> The glistening waters and the lovely shore,
> The wooded hill and mast-concealed isle,
> The shining page which Nature to our eyes
> From her vast book of beauty here presents.
> Does the bright sun sprinkle one watery path
> With yellow spangles but to lure us on
> From England, home and friends?[15]

This gentle, softly spoken but stoic woman also told Barty stories of her pioneering days, of the droughts and flooding rains, of the corroborees and the warring Aboriginal people, of the great mobs of sheep and cattle, and of the squatters who went bust.

Mama's home, Rockend, was much different from the slab house at Illalong and the rough life Barty had known. His new home was perched on a picturesque rise above the Parramatta River at Gladesville, near Hunters Hill, one of Sydney's more fashionable areas. Just across the water was Looking Glass Point, named by the colony's first governor, Arthur Phillip, after he astonished a local Aboriginal man with a looking glass just after the arrival of the First Fleet.[16] There were no bridges, but a punt to the city berthed at the bottom of Mama's garden, and her carriage was always at the ready in the driveway. Her neighbours and friends included many of Sydney's elite families, and Barty was introduced to a world of wealth, privilege and education. Sydney's high society came to Mama's garden parties, which meant that children of well-connected family's became Barty's playmates.

At Ryedale, there was Jane Darvall, the wealthy widow of Mama's father, Major Darvall. The explorer Gregory Blaxland lived at Brush Farm above Ryde in 'a sort of eagle's eyrie, whence he could see the Blue Mountains which he had conquered'.[17] Nearby were the families of Judge Windeyer,[18] Dr Le Gay Brereton and some of the wealthy Murray-Priors. One neighbour, Teddy Betts[19] – grandson of the pioneering Samuel Marsden, 'the flogging parson' – was the assistant superintendent of the Hospital for the Insane,[20] just a few hundred metres up the hill from Rockend. Betts became mayor of Ryde and Hunters Hill. He was also an outstanding amateur jockey in race meetings across Australia, treasurer of the Sydney Turf Club (up the river at Rosehill), and a committee member of the Australian Jockey Club and the Sydney Hunt Club. He furthered Barty's interest in thoroughbreds and sport in general – Barty became his protégé. Betts was a progressive doctor who tried hard to destigmatise the Hospital for the Insane, wanting it known more for parties than padded cells. He fostered social interaction as therapy for patients and organised regular dances, which friends and benefactors such as the Patersons and Bartons were welcome to attend.

As a boy in the bush, Barty had read newspaper reports about Australia's best cricketers. He followed their progress with 'rapt admiration',[21] though 'not even the most optimistic of us ever believed that they would ever be able to play England on level terms'.[22] When Barty first arrived at Rockend, his head was 'crammed with facts about cricketers',[23] but within a few years he was actually shaking hands with the mythical figures at hospital functions where Teddy Betts entertained them on 'cold roast suckling pig and all the beer they wanted'.[24] Barty met the big-hitting George Bonnor,[25] who like him was from the Bathurst-Orange Region and was a 'very picturesque personality ... He was about six feet two (187cm) high, a beautifully built man who could run a hundred yards in ten and a quarter seconds.'[26] Barty saw the Test bowler Joey Palmer[27] spinning the ball viciously on luxuriant grass in a charity match at the hospital, and he watched the mighty all-rounder Tom Garrett sinking a long beer after every twenty runs on a very hot day, then refusing to bowl and only fielding if allowed to stand under the shade of a tree.[28] Garrett told Barty that he'd had such a good time on Australia's first Test tour of England that he had spent two years paying off the trip. George Giffen,[29] the heroic South Australian all-rounder, played at Gladesville too, hitting the bowlers all over the field and finally smashing one ball so far it was never found again. This was entertaining cricket for the small, appreciative crowd, but not everyone cheered. Teddy Betts warned Giffen that the hospital's wicketkeeper, sour at the batsman's performance, had been incarcerated for 'homicidal mania and I saw him reach over to pull a stump out of the ground'.[30]

TO BARTY'S DELIGHT, even the big, bustling city had plenty of the great outdoors, and the Paterson boys spent as much time as they could on the Parramatta River, 'an estuary by the sea',[31] drifting by the settlements along its banks, such as Putney, Chiswick, Henley, Greenwich, Woolwich and Mortlake – names harking back to the old country of the residents.

Barty and Jack bought a decrepit boat, 'mostly held together by tar'. As a way of brightening up the colour scheme, they painted the floor white over the tar: 'This was not entirely satisfactory, as the tar turned the paint to a sort of unwholesome muddy colour, which refused to dry; so then we had to buy caustic soda to remove both tar and paint and begin all over again. When we got her finished she was a fine fishing boat, for there was generally as much water inside as out, which kept our fish fresh till we got them home.'[32]

Barty and Jack travelled to Sydney Grammar in style. The days of riding bareback to a bush school on frosty mornings were over. Instead, dressed in ties and jackets, they travelled by steam ferry, often accompanied by their young uncle Frank Barton, who lived with them and was a promising lawyer. They left the jetty near Rockend each morning to cruise along one of the world's most spectacular waterways to the wharf at King Street, Sydney. From there they made their way up the crowded thoroughfares of the city: King Street, across Clarence, George and Elizabeth, and through Hyde Park, and finally to the sandstone grandeur of Grammar's main building on College Street.

One of Sydney's Great Public Schools, Grammar had been founded twenty years earlier by an act of Parliament after Sir Henry Parkes,[33] the father of Australian Federation, tabled a petition from citizens who wanted a nursery for the fledgling University of Sydney. The school opened in 1857 in buildings used by the university. When Barty started there, French-born Englishman Albert Weigall,[34] an Oxford graduate, was seven years into a mammoth 45-year term as headmaster and had been steadily building up attendance from thirty-nine boys and five masters when he took over in 1867.[35] A devout Anglican, Weigall worked hard to foster a sense of camaraderie among the boys along with a strong loyalty to the school. He encouraged sport, introduced school colours and a uniform cap, and instituted a prefect system.

A year after Barty was enrolled in 1874, Weigall supported the publication of the first *Sydneian* magazine for school news. The first edition declared, 'This magazine is published as a record of school life and an exponent of public opinion … In recording the doings of the school, the object of the Editors will be to exhibit the mental and physical aspects of school life in their proper relations and, in imitation of the wisest of the states of antiquity, to hit the golden mean between athletic idiocy and intellectual priggishness.'[36]

For the time being, Barty was more interested in 'athletic idiocy' than anything intellectual, but Grammar had a grand scholastic tradition. Alumni included Edmund Barton, the young barrister who would become Australia's first prime minister; John Springthorpe, a prominent Melbourne doctor; and Sir Edward Knox, the business bigwig who gave his name to Grammar's school prizes. Barty's schoolmates included Harry Chauvel,[37] a fellow bush boy who went on to become one of Australia's most respected military commanders and leader of the First World War desert forces in such campaigns as the charge on Beersheba. Like young Barty, Chauvel was a horseracing enthusiast and flirted with the idea of one day becoming a jockey.[38]

Barty was a bright student, but in later years he preferred to remember the games and adventures of his youth rather than any hard study. Because of his gammy right arm, he learnt to ride and play tennis with his left hand;[39] he was a keen cricketer, playing at Grammar and at Illalong when he was home on holidays, where he could also ride his horses as hard and fast as they would go.

Barty put his head down long enough in 1875, aged eleven, to share Grammar's Junior Knox Prize[40] as dux of the junior school with George Rich,[41] later a High Court judge. Barty remarked later, 'If I had paid as much attention to my lessons as to fish and rabbits, I too, might have been a Judge of the High Court. There is a lot of luck in these things!'[42]

The award ceremony was held on a hot summer's afternoon on 16 December 1875, in a large classroom festooned with flags and evergreens, and with prominent supporters of the school in attendance. Barty received his award from one of the great jurists of the colony, Sir Alfred Stephen,[43] the 73-year-old former chief justice and now lieutenant governor. On the stage surrounding Barty was another of the leading lights of the day: the ancient Scotsman John Dunmore Lang,[44] Presbyterian Dean of Sydney and an ardent campaigner for an Australian republic. Judge Windeyer and Edward Knox sat nearby.[45] As well as the honour, Barty received £5 and an impressively bound set of books by William Makepeace Thackeray.[46] The headmaster told Barty that he should feel honoured to receive his prize from the famous judge who was deserving of honour himself,[47] but Barty was more interested in the approaching Christmas holidays. He was always keen to get back to the fish and rabbits and all the other wildlife on Illalong.

DESPITE ROSE'S MOST ARDENT WISHES, life at Illalong was nothing like the serenity of Rockend. It rained too much, it rained too little, and while the navvies were finally moving on there were often dangerous-looking drifters tramping by. As always, trouble lurked everywhere. Rose told Nora of a time when Andrew was:

> … training a gem of a horse for me and one morning suddenly and without notice the gem commenced bucking furiously and threw Andrew into an upturned hencoop. I was the alarmed spectator and thought from appearances that he must have been dreadfully hurt but to my relief he got up again alright except for some nasty bruises, the wretch of a horse having danced a war dance over him and trodden on his leg in 2 places. He had been previously suffering from influenza and was in a low spirited wretched state, but strange to say the excitement and the shaking did him a world of good.[48]

Rose now had three young daughters, but in her isolation she craved more mature company and was always glad when her oldest child came home on vacation.

In August 1875 she rode into Binalong with Barty to see 'our very nice neighbours the Futters',[49] a family also desperate for company. Rose's sister Emmy travelled down from Rockend to look after Flo Futter while Mrs Futter was in Wagga Wagga about to give birth.

Rose lived in hope that her family might be able to save enough money so that Andrew could resign his management position and take up a property of his own. There was a glimmer of hope when Andrew's sister Jessie Morgan informed them that their rich uncle Hamilton Howison had died in Scotland: '… whether he has had the kindness to remember … us is an anxious question … I confess I shall feel somewhat as if a sail [which] seemed to promise rescue from a desert island had passed away if Providence has not put a touch of natural feeling into old Hammy's heart at the last.'[50]

Soon she was able to write that old Hammy had come through and the family would not be reduced to 'serfdom and beggary':[51]

> My dearest Nora, At last you may congratulate us on a providential rescue (for me at all events) from a prospect of life-

> long & hopeless misery & bondage, [which] would certainly have ended in melancholy mania for me before long if Heaven had not sent a direct answer to my appeal in the shape of substantial assistance … Uncle Hammy has left to each of the three families – John's Andrew's and Jessie's – a sum of £3000.[52]

Rose explained that the £3000 would remain in the hands of trustees for the children until the death of the parents, but the parents would receive interest on the sum, which she supposed to be a little more than £100 per annum. It was not quite enough, she said, 'to carry us out of a land of bondage straight, but enough to make bondage much more bearable for the present'. She remained optimistic that the time would come when Andrew would see 'the advisability of either striking out for himself again or getting some more congenial employment'.[53] Still suspicious to the point of paranoia about her husband's employers, the Browns, she said that Andrew running his own station would make her feel happier 'than I do under the smothering influence of the low-bred, whispering, slandering, suspicious snobs who have poisoned the whole atmosphere of our formerly friendly simple-minded neighbourhood'.[54]

Rose had been hoping to find a cheap and cheerful governess to help her look after the children, and she received some aid after her husband's cousin Blenty Paterson married a Scots girl, Mary Wilson,[55] who assisted her with housework at Illalong. But she was after someone elderly enough 'not to set the Browns whispering in their usual fashion'. A German governess whom Rose called 'Frau Persicker' was just what she was looking for, and she positively gloated over the value for money in the old German woman, who promised 'to be quite a gem. She can teach French, German & English, music & drawing, is to sew & mend stockings & to make beds or puddings when required & is only to get £30 per annum.'[56]

While Rose missed Barty terribly, the other children kept her from having much time to brood. 'Our youngsters are all thriving,' Rose told her sister, 'Mary [Edie] is the finest specimen of the bunch. She is growing very amusing. She was found today holding a book up close to the cat's face & saying 'Weed Putty'. Flo is very fond of books and sometimes reads aloud [to] herself the most eloquent flow of gibberish ever heard at the top of her voice for an hour at a stretch.'[57]

Barty probably looked forward to school holidays more than any of the other boys at Grammar, and his visits home to the bush were the highlights of each year – even though they occasionally ended in tears. Flo and Jessie were always melancholy when he left them and went back to school.[58]

Over the Christmas vacation of 1876, Barty broke his right arm in the same place as before, and having his arm in splints for weeks 'spoilt his holiday very much'. Rose hoped that the resulting treatment might straighten the limb but saw no real improvement when the splints were removed in January 1877.[59]

When not riding with Rose, Barty went camping and shooting with cousins and friends along the Murrumbidgee. Sometimes he would invite schoolmates from Grammar to come down with him,[60] and sometimes they would ride up into the snowy country as well, yarning with the mountain men and admiring their wiry ponies.

THE BUSH DID NOT HAVE a monopoly on heroes, though, and back in Sydney Barty and Jack were intrigued by the ironmen of the water: the scullers, rowing like pistons on the championship course right in front of Emily Barton's doorstep. Twenty-five to thirty men could be seen on any fine morning cutting through the water like torpedoes,[61] and to the Paterson cousins the scullers were as mighty as gladiators. 'Beginning with [William] Hickey and [Michael] Rush, on down through Ned Trickett and Elias Laycock, to [Bill] Beach and [Ned] Hanlan, [Jim] Stanbury and [John] Maclean, last and greatest of them all, Harry Searle – we knew every man of them, and could tell them by their styles at three-quarters of a mile distance … Elias Laycock could eat a dozen eggs for breakfast; Maclean, an axe-man from the northern rivers, could take an axe in either hand, and fell any tree without stopping for rest … These great scullers were mostly young country men reared on home-grown food.'[62]

Harry Searle[63] had such an astonishing chest development that there were rumours he had an extra rib on either side of his body. Paterson remembered him as 'a flaxen-haired giant'[64] who featured in an odd incident at a dance given at Teddy Betts's Hospital for the Insane.

> These dances were for the amusement of the patients, and all visitors were expected to dance with them. A lady from Sydney, no less than a daughter of Sir William Windeyer, Judge of the Supreme Court, was very good-natured about it all, and after trotting several of the patients out she invited Searle to have a turn. On coming back to her chaperon she said 'What a pity that fine young man is mad. He talked quite sensibly until all of a sudden he said that he was the champion sculler of the world. I got away from him as soon as I could!'[65]

In 1875, Barty and Jack both contributed more than £1 each towards a new boat for the Grammar School,[66] and the next year – when Barty was twelve – they were thrilled when Ned Trickett,[67] the son of a convict from the nearby harbourside suburb of Greenwich, became Australia's first world champion in any sport. Trickett travelled to England to beat Joseph Saddler[68] by four lengths in a race along a stretch of the Thames that measured four miles and 374 yards.[69] The tall and lanky[70] Trickett was heavily sponsored by Sydney businessmen and called his boat *Young Australia*. His victory before a huge crowd and against the odds[71] ushered in a golden era for Australian scullers.

Barty described Trickett as a 'long-armed quarryman' and said of his world title triumph: 'The contest was rather one-sided, for the English people were too busy with other things and had to work too hard for their money to waste much of it on paying the expenses of boat rowers. They bethought themselves that they had a rowing champion of some sort, a man past his prime. Him they threw into the front of the forlorn hope, but while he did his best, he was rather easily beaten.'[72]

Trickett collected £400 in stakes money for the victory, and he received 'a most enthusiastic reception' on his arrival home to Sydney at the end of 1876 with 'between 25,000 and 30,000 persons assembled on the quay. Several bands of music were present, and the firemen, with torches, had their engines out. The horses were unharnessed from the dray in which Trickett sat, and men drew it to Punch's Hotel.'[73]

Trickett was eventually beaten by the Canadian champion Ned Hanlan.[74]

To Barty, it became a matter of national importance that Australia should find a man to beat Hanlan. From riverside farms, from axemen's camps in the North Coast timber country, from shipyards and fishing fleets, potential champions flocked to the Parramatta River – but 'none stood the test'.[75]

Then, as Barty remembered it, Dr George Fortescue, a leading surgeon at Prince Alfred Hospital in Sydney, was asked to examine the blacksmith Bill Beach[76] who hailed from the South Coast town of Dapto. Beach – sometimes known as Gipsy Beach – was an Englishman by birth, with what Paterson remembered as 'the face of Bismarck, the man of blood and iron' and with a frame 'knotted with muscles built up by years of swinging the sledge hammer'.[77] Beach was only a novice sculler, but Barty recalled that Dr Fortescue said that of all the thousands of men whom he had examined in his life, 'he had never seen such a perfect physical specimen. "This man," he said, "will beat that little Canadian (Hanlan)". He backed his opinion with his money, too, helping Beach to get boats and a trainer.'[78]

Beach beat Hanlan for the world title on the Parramatta River[79] and then trounced him again in two more races, and so 'started such an orgy of sculling as never was seen in the world before …'[80]

SYDNEY IN THE MID-1870s was 'growing like a mushroom', Paterson remembered; 'new railways were mooted every day'.[81] Not long before Barty's birth, the population of Sydney was ninety-five thousand as the city lagged behind its southern rival Melbourne, which was still riding the euphoria of the gold rushes. Now, though, Sydney was a surging metropolis with a population nudging a quarter of a million and expanding by fifteen thousand people a year,[82] the 'overflow of bricks and mortar spreading like a lava-flood' over all the hills and valleys around Sydney's waterways.[83] The new post office in Martin Place, built from local sandstone, was a magnificent example of the Victorian Italian Renaissance style, and the newly completed clock tower on Sydney's Town Hall in George Street would dominate the city's skyline for decades. There were expansive parklands, but already the narrow streets were clogged and the hustle and bustle gathered even more pace when the steam trams, complete with double-decker carriages and their hissing, spitting engines, gradually overtook the horse trams and hansom cabs that had left their exhaust material in steaming piles of dung along the crowded streets.

On Saturday nights, when Barty was taken down the river and into the city for a special treat, the boy from the bush gasped at the mass of people crowding along George and Pitt Streets, the main thoroughfares. Thousands of gaslights shone on their faces and on the gaudy advertising hoardings for the rows of shops and open-air markets. Street musicians played fiddles and concertinas, and uniformed policemen kept an eye on the young larrikins and other unsavoury coves who formed various gangs called 'pushes'.

IN THE SAME YEAR that Ned Trickett gave Australia its first world sporting champion, Rose Paterson gave Barty a baby brother: Hamilton Howison Paterson, named in honour of the dear departed Uncle Hammy. The *Sydney Morning Herald* reported simply under the heading 'Births': 'PATERSON—Sept. 5, Gladesville, Mrs. A. B. Paterson, of a son.'[84]

To ensure there were no complications from a bush birth, Rose had gone to stay with her mother and Barty at Rockend. Only a few months earlier Rose's sister Nora had lost her baby Emmeline Murray-Prior at just nine months. Infant mortality rates in the 1870s remained high; for many women, the difficulties of pregnancy and the pain of childbirth were followed by the grief of a lost child.

Rose urged Nora to come down with her daughter Meta to Illalong, as rundown as it was, so the young girl could make friends with her cousins. 'Even the flavour of a little bush roughness,' she said, 'would have a good effect in changing the current of your thoughts.'[85]

For women on isolated properties such as Illalong, childbirth was hard labour and often dangerous. Births required careful preparation: deciding when to leave home, and assessing the fitness of the expectant mother to travel, the safety of roads and the availability of the nearest doctor. Arrangements had to be made for someone to care for the children left home. And then there were the financial considerations. In 1879, the minimum fee for a standard confinement was three guineas (£3 3s) or about three weeks' wages for a labourer; a caesarean delivery could cost as much as a hundred guineas[86] or two years' pay. Most rural battlers couldn't afford medical assistance and used midwives or 'gamps' instead.

For the birth of her second son, Rose left her other children in the care of Andrew and Frau Persicker,[87] and put herself in her mother's care. After the privations of Illalong, Rockend with its magnificent vistas and Mama's circle of cultured, wealthy friends must have made Rose feel as though she were in paradise. As it was she could not find a suitable midwife around Binalong 'and Dr Campbell positively declined to recommend me one from Yass. So I made a rush [to Sydney] at the last minute … & then we found that nurse hunting even down here is not always a successful game … I had to write to Yass to get the address of Mrs Curran, the Yass nurse who attended me last time at Illalong, but who has taken to Sydney practice lately … I engaged her & we have got on very well together.'[88] One advantage of having a baby away from home, she confessed, was that despite 'long continued weakness', back on the farm not long after a birth it always seemed 'everybody considers one quite fit for the everyday work of life'.[89] In her absence Frau Persicker was 'turning up trumps' and teaching the other children 'well & systematically & keeping them tidy and respectable', while the other servants and farm workers 'have been all that could be desired'.[90]

Rose was a diligent and devoted mother who found her pregnancies difficult and feared for the health of each little one. She once confessed after a birth in the country that 'I have always a very paralysing time of it through being such a bad nurse myself & having chiefly to depend on cow's milk [which] is not always wholesome in these parts where the cows eat all sorts of rank herbage after rain'.[91] She admitted that she was not always pleasant company when she was pregnant, and with a touch of wit that she passed on to Barty, feared that her bad moods might be contagious when Barty's younger brother finally arrived on 5 September 1876.

> I have a private dread that he [Hamilton Howison] may turn out a young murderer on our hands if you take his temper from mine, as it was, during most of the time of the first few months of his being thought of. I am sure I could have roasted some people at slow fires with great relish! However, so far the youngster has shown nothing but placidity & good temper & as far as looks go, I have a notion that he will be the best-looking of the family someday, tho as yet, puffy eyelids and 'red gum' make it difficult

> to foresee the future Adonis in the present chrysalis encased in flannel and diaper.[92]

Her fears of a potential murderer were unfounded. Young Hamilton, known as Boy to the family, had a huge shock in store for his loved ones, but as an infant back at Illalong he became 'the Prince of babies for amiability & fat'.

IN 1878, BARTY AND JACK sat for the Junior Examinations as a prelude to possible entrance to the University of Sydney.

The *Australian Town and Country Journal* printed their results among those for hundreds of other boys across Australia. 'Paterson, Andrew Barton', aged fourteen, from Sydney Grammar School, secured a 'High' for English (no surprise there), a 'Low' for French – despite his grandmother's tutoring – and 'High' for Latin and arithmetic. Jack or 'Paterson, John Edward', aged sixteen, fared much worse, with 'Low' for both English and Latin. He then suffered having the results in the paper for all of the colony to see.[93]

Barty still spent more time hitting the sporting fields than he did the textbooks. He sometimes visited the Albert Ground, which had been built on swampy land at Redfern[94] in the year he was born, and which had a grandstand and a pavilion around three sides of the playing surface. A row of trees had been planted by English cricket players who had come to Australia in the summer of 1863 to '64. The ground was also used for amateur athletics 'patronized by the best people',[95] and it was the home ground of Australia's demon bowler Fred Spofforth,[96] who was still able to extract alarming lift and bounce there despite the soft couch grass on the cricket pitch. Other great players to feature there included Dave and Ned Gregory, the peerless wicketkeeper Jack Blackham, Billy Murdoch and Charley Bannerman.[97] In 1877 in Melbourne, Bannerman faced the first ball ever bowled in Test cricket, scored the first run in Test cricket and made the first Test century.[98] When Barty was thirteen, the Albert Ground was closed and redeveloped, and major cricket matches moved to the Garrison Ground at Moore Park. It was also called the Civil and Military Ground and then the Association Ground, before finally being renamed the Sydney Cricket Ground.

'Many a Saturday afternoon'[99] Barty paid his shilling and sat at the hill there to watch the cricket. Just short of his fifteenth birthday, he was among a crowd of ten thousand[100] when the infamous riot broke out during a match between an English invitational team – under the young and dashing Lord Harris[101] – and a NSW side that included the greats of the day: Spofforth, Murdoch, Bannerman, Hugh Massie and 'Handsome' Dave Gregory, the first captain of Australia. It was one of the most inflammatory incidents in cricket history, and Paterson later wrote that it made 'the bodyline controversy of later years look like a goodwill gesture'.[102]

Gregory's 1878 Australian team had just returned home from England, where the cocky locals – still regarded as convict colonials by many of the upperclass English supporters – beat the home side in less than a day at Lord's. The Harris XI was out to restore the English upper hand on their tour Down Under.

But Australia won the first match at the Melbourne Cricket Ground in January, with the demon Spofforth taking thirteen wickets, including the first ever Test hat-trick. New South Wales then beat Harris's tourists in Sydney with a rematch commencing on Friday, 7 February 1879.

Each side was allowed to select an umpire. New South Wales chose prominent cricket official and budding prime minister Edmund Barton, a very distant relative of Barty's.[103] The Englishmen chose 22-year-old Carlton Australian rules footballer George Coulthard,[104] on the recommendation of the Melbourne Cricket Club where Coulthard was a promising bowler. The young sportsman was an extraordinary character who two years earlier had survived a frenzied shark attack while on a fishing trip in Sydney Harbour. He faced similar ferocity at the cricket, as gambling – and its associated restless crowds – was common at matches in the 1870s. New South Wales was heavily backed to beat the Englishmen. Open betting took place in the pavilion despite placards declaring that gambling was banned,[105] and punters were quick to boo and blaspheme if things did not go their way. Rowdiness was the order of the day.

There was controversy during the Lord Harris innings when he edged a ball to Billy Murdoch, the wicketkeeper, but Coulthard ruled him not out. Journalists covering the game said it was 'a mistake'.[106] Spofforth tore up the wicket with his boots in his delivery stride, while off-spinner Edwin Evans, sending them down from the other end, pitched nearly every ball into the furrows.

England lost 7/34 to be all out for 267.

The match recommenced at noon the next day, Saturday, 8 February, and ten thousand in attendance, including Barty Paterson and the Governor of New South Wales, Sir Hercules Robinson,[107] saw New South Wales collapse to be all out for 177. Under the rules at the time, New South Wales had to follow on because they were more than 80 runs in arrears. The opening partnership between Murdoch and Alick Bannerman put on just 19 when Murdoch was given run out by Coulthard for 10 in what Barty reckoned 'was a very close decision'.[108] The fact that the umpire was a Victorian only fed the suspicions of the crowd during a time of great intercolonial rivalry. The jeering of the decision started a chorus among gamblers in the stands, with 'one well-known betting man' inciting the crowd to work themselves 'into a state of violent excitement'.[109] There were cries of 'Not out!' and 'Go back to the playing field, Murdoch!' – and some rather more rude.

'Handsome' Dave Gregory refused to send out a new batsman, and as the crowd continued to hoot, Lord Harris walked towards the pavilion and met 'Handsome' Dave at the gate, where the NSW skipper asked Harris to change his umpire. ('Handsome' Dave was later accused of trying to fan the dispute for his advantage.) Harris refused, telling him that his fielders at point and cover had both had a good view of the run-out and said it was a fair decision. Edmund Barton said it was out too.

But the NSW captain wouldn't budge. As the two men argued, the angry crowd – led by larrikins – continued to jeer. One of the English professionals called out to the noisier patrons that they were nothing but the 'sons of convicts'.[110]

And it was on. A larrikin mob jumped the fence and charged at the Englishmen. Barty was sitting by the picket fence, just below where the scoreboard later stood. He couldn't tell from there whether Murdoch was out or not, but everyone was hooting and jeering. 'A chap sitting near me said, "Come on, boys, We can't stand this", and he jumped in over the pickets. His feet had hardly touched the ground when there were 1000 men over the fence all running to the centre of the ground.'[111] Before long there were two thousand led by 'hundreds of roughs who took possession of the wickets. The English team soon found themselves in the centre of a surging, gesticulating, and shouting mob, and one rowdy struck Lord Harris across the body with a whip or stick.'[112] England's opening batsman, 'Monkey' Hornby,[113] a champion at cricket and rugby and a boxing enthusiast, sorted the assailant out, though his shirt was ripped in the process.

Paterson remembered that 'The Englishmen thought they were going to be murdered and some of them got round the umpire and the others pulled the stumps out of the ground to defend their lives. I remember seeing a big Yorkshireman named Ulyett[114] waving a stump at the crowd, so I sidestepped him. I was only a boy.'[115]

Cricket officials and ground staff hurried to the assistance of the English team, and more blows were exchanged. The small body of police present were too late to get to the centre of the ground and found it difficult to fight their way through the angry crowd, but eventually the English players were escorted into the pavilion. Lord Harris's assailant was locked up in one of the committee rooms. A bell rang to clear the ground, but it was some time before the excitement subsided.

When the crowd saw that umpire Coulthard was not being replaced, some of the louts rushed the ground again. Harris and Gregory argued about having another umpire, but the majority of the Englishmen refused to concede and all hope of resuming play was abandoned.

When the game finally got back under way two days later, New South Wales were all out for 49 and England won by a landslide.

The riot was portrayed by the media as a disgrace that left 'a large majority of the public deeply humiliated'. 'Such a display of unbridled rowdyism, perpetrated as it was in the presence of his Excellency the Governor, Lady Robinson, and party, and a large number of the prominent citizens of Sydney, and directed against the English players who are at present our guests, will probably remain as a blot upon the colony for some years to come.'[116]

Barty agreed, saying it gave Australia a bad name in England for a long time.[117] His interest in cricket never wavered, though, and he could later say that he had seen the best Australia produced for more than sixty years from Bannerman to Bradman. He always had a soft spot for the greats of his boyhood, including the prince of wicketkeepers, Jack Blackham, and his 'battle scarred fingers twisted like an eagle's claws' from standing up to the wickets to take Spofforth's fastest deliveries.

Dave Gregory, Paterson recalled, was 'black-bearded, high-shouldered, remarkably like the English captain [W.G.] Grace and with a good deal of Grace's invincible self-confidence … Spofforth the demon bowler, six feet of wire and whipcord.'

> I have seen Spofforth on more than one occasion break a stump, and if he had bowled bodyline he would have exterminated the opposition. Charley Bannerman … not a tall man … would cut ball after ball to the fence without giving a chance. Poor old Charley – there should be a statue to him on every cricket ground in Australia: but he never looked after his money and when the crowd had done with him I have seen him holding a bag for a kindly bookmaker at Randwick … the idol of thousands, making money for cricket but none for himself … His brother [Alick] Bannerman was the very reverse of Charley; he would take no risks in batting nor any risks with his money … He was a dyed-in-the-wool stonewaller, or rather we thought he was until an English player named [William] Scotton came along and made four runs in two hours. I don't know why we let him live.[118]

The Lord Harris Riot coincided with Ned Kelly's raid on the NSW town of Jerilderie, six hundred kilometres to the south-west, that same weekend. Kelly's gang bailed up the small country town and, dressed as policemen, took £2000 from the Bank of New South Wales. Kelly, who had shot three policemen a few months earlier, also delivered his 'Jerilderie Letter': a long statement claiming police persecution. The raid was a daring crime, so gobsmackingly audacious that it fuelled a degree of public support for the bold bandits.

That same month under the byline 'B—', *The Sydneian* published an article entitled 'Bushrangers'.[119]

'Now that the deeds of the Kellys are attracting so much attention', the student author wrote, 'I think that a few stories about the old bushrangers could not fail to prove interesting to my readers.' 'B' went on to relate some of the tales he had heard from David Campbell and his family members about Ben Hall, and how despite the mythology around armed criminals roaming the wilds of Australia, the country policemen were the real heroes of the day and the gunmen just treacherous cowards. 'Bushrangers' was 750 words pieced together with invention and fragments of memory, but it had excitement and drama and intrigue, and it celebrated the heroes of the bush and a way of life that was already starting to disappear. 'B' was just fifteen but he was finding his voice.

There remained all sorts of distractions at Grammar. A pastime called 'wallarooing' was popular between classes. Boys would target a victim, push him to the ground, stuff his mouth with grass, rip off his boots and throw them away, and then stamp on the victim's hat until it was flat as a plate. It seemed like fun at the time, though no one could remember wallarooing Hubert Murray, the 1877 school captain who went on become England's amateur heavyweight boxing champion and long-time Lieutenant Governor of Papua. Barty recalled a fight between two doctors' sons that lasted a whole lunchtime, carried over for a couple of hours after school, restarted the next morning and finished just before school began – mainly because one of the boys' fists was injured. He also remembered how he and his classmates would catch large flies and tie scarlet thread to their feet, and thus create an imitation wasp to terrify their teachers. Another student stunk up the classroom by pouring foul-smelling wattle beans across the floor, while another set a wastepaper basket over a door as a booby trap. A future solicitor dodged a caning to 'live a bandit life in boilers and empty cases on the wharves for several days'.

Still, in between the larks, a great writing career was off and racing and Barty had many more stories to come.

Chapter 6

18 DECEMBER 1879, SYDNEY GRAMMAR SCHOOL

I suppose I've done pretty well everything that one has to learn to be in the bush, such as riding after cattle, felling trees, yarding sheep, shearing, and all the rest of it. But I soon saw there wasn't a livelihood to be gained in the bush. Everyone who goes in for farming right out comes to grief sooner or later. At the best it is only a continual struggle.

BANJO PATERSON ON HIS CAREER CHOICES[1]

THE BUSH WAS CALLING for fifteen-year-old Barty, but he had to attend one important function before he caught the train down to see Rose, Andrew and his five siblings: Flo, Jessie, Edie, Boy and the new sister, Gracie.[2] Here on another hot summer's day in Sydney, as the school prepared to break for the Christmas holidays of 1879, Grammar was rewarding him for his elastic mind.

After taking first-class honours in English[3] and an award for the Classics, Barty was called onto the stage at a presentation ceremony. The long line of prize winners[4] included Harry Chauvel and the future High Court justice Albert Piddington.[5] Sir Alfred Stephen presented the awards again. The old judge was seventy-seven and, though slowing up considerably, he was still occasionally taking the office of acting governor,[6] still overseeing work on Hyde Park near his home and basking in the success as vice-president[7] of the commission for the recently opened Sydney International Exhibition,[8] built on six hectares that are now part of the Royal Botanic Garden.

Henry Kendall,[9] the pre-eminent Australian poet of the day, wrote the cantata and the hymn of praise for the exhibition, winning a prize of 100 guineas from the *Sydney Morning Herald* for the best poem about the event.[10]

Central to the exhibition was a magnificent wooden Garden Palace, complete with a 65-metre high dome[11] and the first hydraulic elevator in Sydney. Barty was an enthusiastic visitor – and three years later[12] he was stunned when a spectacular fire reduced the great palace to a charred skeleton.

Barty's uncle Frank Barton, now on his way to a high-powered civil service and legal career,[13] was encouraging his young protégé to follow him into the law. Barty did not have a huge inheritance coming, and a legal career offered him a comfortable life. Frank also took his young nephew to Sydney's Royal Agricultural Society's shows, held at Prince Alfred Park beside Central Station before the venue was changed in 1882 to ten hectares of sandy scrub at Moore Park[14] that became the Sydney Showground. Agricultural shows, both the big city events and the bush ones, fascinated Barty for his whole life.

SYDNEY GRAMMAR INTRODUCED its prefect system in 1878,[15] but despite his scholastic abilities Barty wasn't part of the leadership group in 1879. Perhaps the masters believed he lacked ambition – as he was wont to say throughout his life – or perhaps he spent too much time in class daydreaming about the bush. Or perhaps, by his own admission, he spent too many valuable hours skylarking. He once confessed that in Form 3A:

> … two of us, who sat in the second row from the back, established a vendetta against two boys who sat in the second row from the front. While the Master was writing on the blackboard and had his back turned to the class, one of us would glide silently out of the seat, drop on all fours and crawl round the desks up behind the unsuspecting foe. Then for a brief and glorious instant he would rear himself up behind them, hit each of them an awful blow on the head with his open hand, of course making as little noise as possible, and then glide back as silently as he came … Of course this was great fun for the rest of the class, and they used to watch the stalking with keen interest.[16]

Though Barty seemed more interested in a good time than great marks, the writing career of Grammar's star reporter 'B' was also making an impression among his fellow students. 'B' followed his essay on Australian bushrangers from the February 1879 issue with three reports and a poem[17] in the bumper August offering that sold for sixpence. 'Going to See the Governor' read like an entrée to a comedic Banjo Paterson poem: 'Together with two friends I formed one of a numerous but hardly select assemblage, who escorted the [school] band down to the wharf, where his Excellency was to land … It was rather dull waiting; but seeing some boys fall into the water, and one policeman kick a dog, which immediately bit the next policeman, somewhat enlivened the time.'[18]

'B' also wrote of the country around Illalong in a tale of his holiday spent on the banks of the Murrumbidgee, shooting ducks, turtles and a platypus.[19] There is the hint that he was mixing fact with fiction, and while the account would have shocked readers of a later age it went down well at the time. The piece involves plenty of excitement that harks of the flying horses from Snowy River. 'Travelling over the Murrumbidgee Ranges is no joke,' 'B' told his audience. 'In some places we used to fasten a sapling to the buggy to act as a brake going down some of the steepest places.'[20]

In the September issue he wrote of the fun he and his mates had shooting cranes and pelicans on the Parramatta River.[21] These were clearly different times, and a decade later Banjo admitted in *The Sydneian* that his tale was imaginary and argued that storytellers have a licence for invention to shock their readers.[22]

DURING THE SCHOOL HOLIDAYS OF 1879, Barty found his mother frazzled after the birth of her sixth child and still living in hope that Andrew Paterson would one day be able to own his own property again. Her new daughter, Gracie, had proved a handful because of Rose's difficulties feeding her. The potentially lethal condition mastitis (known then as milk fever, it involves blocked and infected milk ducts) was a constant fear for new mothers.

Rose and Andrew rarely had time to socialise. A ball that they had attended at the Mechanics Institute in Young, where they acted 'larky' in 'their old age',[23] seemed an eternity ago; Rose was then between pregnancies, and Andrew had hitched up the buggy for a

92-mile (150-kilometre) round trip to the kind of festivity that was all too rare for them.

Before long, Rose was delighted that Barty's little sister was a 'splendid child … not only in face & form but in mind and understanding': 'She has more sense in her little hard nut than four ordinary 2 year olds roll'd into one & she has such an expressive face & such pretty manners that she is a born Queen of Hearts … Everyone knows her for miles around, & when I was in the butchers in Binalong getting some suet last week, he volunteer'd his impromptu opinion thus 'My Word Mrs Paterson that's a lovely child, that last one of yours'. I have thought more of the butcher's discrimination & taste ever since, & mean to get some more suet tomorrow!'[24]

Frau Persicker had by now handed in her notice, with her place taken by a 'Miss Powell' who was willing to work for even less than the old German woman. 'Miss Powell is a very inferior order of being as a teacher,' Rose complained, 'but she is good temper'd & will nurse the Baby if required – & takes whole charge of Hamilton & her screw is [a] very small £25. So on the whole she suits us better than a more accomplished person.'[25]

AFTER YEARS IN THE DOLDRUMS, Australia's rural economy was on the rise. At Christmas time in 1879, there was great excitement throughout the colonies as the SS *Strathleven*, a steamer normally used for the Atlantic trade, left Melbourne for England with a shipment of more than five hundred frozen sheep and cattle carcasses, as well as a large supply of butter in kegs.[26] The French had been experimenting for several years with shipping frozen meat from South America, and Australian pastoralists saw the new technologies as opening up whole new markets for them in Europe. The days of station owners having to boil down their starving livestock for tallow, as Robert Barton had once been forced to do, were slowly disappearing. Visitors taken on board the *Strathleven*'s giant freezer as it readied for departure on a wharf at Williamstown found themselves in utter darkness, and in an Arctic atmosphere. Their feet slipped on the icy boards, 'and as they groped for something by which to maintain their equilibrium, they could feel nothing but pendant carcasses chilly to the touch, or upright posts covered with a thick layer of hoar frost'.[27] The *Strathleven* left Melbourne on 6 December 1879 and arrived in London, with its cargo still in excellent condition, on 2 February 1880.[28]

At home Barty's mother went to great lengths to make visitors welcome with fresh meat. The visitors were many: nieces, nephews and cousins from throughout Australia, along with schoolmates of Barty and Jack from Grammar. Once when Rose's sister Nora and family were heading for Melbourne on the train after visiting their mother and Barty at Rockend, Rose pulled out all stops in celebration. She was disappointed when the trip was delayed. 'We have been killing our ducks & turkeys all this week & last,' she wrote, 'with the laudable intention of having ... "a good feed" for you when you should make your appearance, instead of which we have had to eat them ourselves in sadness & gloom ... [Y]ou had better make haste ... or ... you will come in for tough salt mutton instead of ducks & peas.'[29]

Sometimes Barty had to do it tough on his visits, as he did for the Easter holidays of 1880 when he was 'rather glum at finding only fish for breakfast' after having had to walk the seven kilometres from Binalong Station to Illalong. There was such a crowd on the train for the holidays that he could only get standing room in the guard's van, alongside a load of salt fish as his travelling companion. On that warm autumn journey it 'did not smell very fragrant', and after three hundred kilometres riding next to the fish he told his mother he was in no mood to eat some.[30]

While the voyage of the *Strathleven* was revolutionary, another revolution was taking place and changing the lives of Australians – particularly those in far-flung corners of this vast continent. The first issue of a bold new weekly magazine, *The Bulletin*, appeared on newsstands for the first time on Saturday, 31 January 1880. It cost four pence, and all three thousand copies soon sold. Before long it was selling eighty thousand copies a week and was known as 'the Bushman's Bible'. It was a publication that unified a large part of the populace with a collective nationalist voice when the continent was still composed of disparate colonies, often suspicious of each other. The first issue featured eight pages and infinite promises that the journal would be 'unsurpassed in the vigour, freshness and geniality of its literary contributions'. 'Excellence is the passport to success in colonial life,' the first front-page editorial declared, '[and] to this end the services of the best men of the realms of pen and pencil in the colony have been secured.'[31]

The feature article for the debut issue was a vivid account of the hanging at Darlinghurst Gaol of the Wantabadgery bushrangers, Captain Moonlite and Thomas Rogan, and an interview with the man who broke their necks. Robert Howard, the colony's hangman, had been known as 'Nosey Bob' for years, ever since a horse kick to the face had left him horribly disfigured.[32] The report was penned by oddball publisher Jules François Archibald, who had been born John Feltham Archibald[33] in Geelong twenty-four years earlier but fancied a far more bohemian handle. 'Racially,' Paterson wrote later in less politically correct times, 'Archibald looked like a Jew. He had the hawk nose, the open eye, and the quick movement of the Oriental people; physically he was a fairly strong and well-set-up man of medium size, long in the arms, untidy in dress, wearing a moustache and pointed beard.'[34] Archibald was also a powerhouse of jingoism. Paterson wrote:

> He was about the first Australian to 'call' the English bluff. In pursuance of his policy of cheering for the underdog, he asserted that an Australian lawyer, or doctor, or inventor, or singer, or actor was every bit as good as any importation.[35]

The Bulletin saw itself as a 'journalistic javelin'[36] and shouted with an Australian nationalist voice, a voice that grew louder and louder among white workers across the Australian landscape. From the perspective of these workers, it was the little man's champion in the fight against banks, bureaucracies and absentee landlords. Its encouragement of nationalist – even xenophobic – sentiments remained influential for decades, and in a different political and social clime its writers and cartoonists regularly mocked Aboriginal people, British, Chinese, Japanese, Indians and 'Hebrews', even though Archibald would marry the daughter[37] of a Jewish merchant. The public couldn't get enough of it, and Barty Paterson would soon ride *The Bulletin*'s popularity to all points of Australia.

BY THE TIME HE WAS SIXTEEN, Barty was a handsome, athletic young man with dark aquiline features and a bright wit. His crooked arm still gave him trouble, and he was a flop in one of his last cricket games at the school; he turned out for a team of twenty-two against Grammar's First XI the day after his birthday on 18 February on a 'rather damp'[38] ground. Barty came in to bat at No. 19 and was out caught without scoring. Still, the 28 made by the XXII was one more than the First XI could muster.[39]

On Barty's Easter break in 1880, Rose wrote that 'he has grown a good deal in the last 6 months & is on the turn for improving his looks. [He] brought his hair into better subjection than formerly. His fate is still wavering in the balance as to whether he shall matriculate & leave school next June & be articled to a lawyer or whether he shall try for a scholarship & if he gets one, go through a University career, & start in the world with B.A. following A.B.P.' Now in his final year at Grammar, he had 'plenty of good sense'. Rose was grateful that he had 'no desire for fast ways & fast companions. So I think we may fairly hope for a good future for him.'[40]

Visits home always gave Barty inspiration, especially the sight of wild mountain horses on the run. He would remember how stallions would establish themselves up in the hills with a few mares in the spring and then come on down to the common paddocks where horses roamed free around country towns. The stallion would drive off any mares that were there and add them to his harem, and likely kill any geldings that wanted to go with them because 'the stallion is a very good imitation of a pirate king when he gets the chance to run things his own way'.[41] Sometimes when riding through the bush, Barty would catch sight of a mob of wild horses and off they would go 'full split' into rocky country where only the Man from Snowy River and his ilk had any chance of catching them. Barty had heard many stories of the pioneering days of his parents when wild horses got to be as great a plague as the rabbits of a later time, and were trapped in pens and shot like vermin. Killing such proud, noble animals seemed a dreadful thing to do, he lamented, but the farmers believed that if they didn't get rid of the wild horses, the wild horses would soon get rid of them.[42] The shooting days were 'pretty well done when I came into the business', Paterson wrote many years later, but he and his mates would still run wild mountain horses into yards with the mistaken idea of breaking them in and making some money out of them.

> Half a dozen of us would go out and we would ride half a dozen good horses blind getting the mob in. Then the crack riders among us would pick out a horse each and start to break it in. By the time it had kicked every dog in the place, or those that it had missed it had kicked others twice for; by the time that it had broken every bridle and rolled in every saddle on the place and by the time that every rider had been run against at least one tree in every paddock, then it was saleable at about thirty bob if anyone could be found fool enough to buy it.[43]

Trying to break in wild old horses, he said, was an almost impossible task, like teaching an old cannibal to be a vegetarian, though he knew of some good horses that had once been wild brumbies up near the summit of Kosciuszko.

In June 1880, Barty came back down to Illalong to ride in a buggy with his mother and baby Gracie. They went on a long journey visiting the local stations as his mother travelled north to Orange. The Patersons were already good friends with David Campbell and his family, but they forged close ties with other station owners and workers in their district. It was a cold ride in the depths of winter, one that Rose said would have been far more pleasant in the spring, but one they 'nevertheless enjoyed very much'.[44] They visited the Beaumonts at Marengo, the George Campbells at Jerula and the Crowther family at the Pring property, and they stopped at Toogong, where Rose's friend Mrs Jago spared no pains to make her guests comfortable. From Orange, Rose and the children took the train to Sydney to stay at Rockend.

Barty could still be a handful for Rose, though, and she told him she didn't like him being pert to his elders, especially his mother. When she returned to Illalong she resolved to send him two shillings and sixpence to buy a book about a well-behaved boy [nothing of Mark Twain's though] – 'with which to improve his mind'.[45] Rose had always championed her easygoing husband, but when it came to disciplining their oldest son, she said Andrew was far too lax 'in allowing smartness & not rebuking rudeness and sauciness'.[46]

IN THE FIRST THREE MONTHS OF 1880, typhoid claimed seventeen lives in Sydney,[47] and in May that year it claimed the wife and four children of a Parramatta policeman.[48] Sydney was a rapidly expanding metropolis, but in many places sanitary conditions were still archaic despite public warnings to clean up horse manure from the streets, to boil water and milk, and to use covered bins for garbage.

Typhoid spread all the way to Rockend, where Barty's cousin Jack came down with fever, lethargy and abdominal pain. Rockend was placed into quarantine while Barty was sent to stay with Emily Barton's friend Mrs Edith Blaxland at her grand home Cleves, at Kissing Point on the Parramatta River in Putney.[49] The families were close, and many of the holidaying Bartons and Patersons stayed at Cleves when Rockend had no vacancies. Mrs Blaxland's brother was Teddy Betts, and her husband Herbert Blaxland[50] was the medical superintendent for the Hospital for the Insane. She knew enough about medicine to order that Barty not go within fifty yards (forty-five metres) of Rockend until the quarantine order was lifted; while he agreed to abide by those rules, he was frustrated that his preparation for exams at Grammar had been interrupted. Grammar decided to stagger the school attendances as a precaution against a typhoid epidemic, and during the crisis Barty only went to school two days a week and missed the November Senior Public Examination in 1880. As he sat around waiting for the coast to clear, he couldn't resist getting an update on his cousin's condition – Mrs Blaxland caught the pair yarning over the back fence. She told Rose back at Illalong of her son's dangerous disobedience. He was leading a 'desultory' life, Rose said, and she was furious and worried about what Mrs Blaxland would think of the Patersons' 'code of honour'. She had already chipped Barty about his impertinence, and now she sat down to write to her headstrong son and give him 'a good blowing up'.[51]

She could give him a clip over the ears soon enough, when he came down to Illalong for the Christmas holidays. She was looking forward to his company even though he was sometimes proving to be hard work. Andrew had been made the returning officer for the electorate of Burrowa,[52] and if he wasn't already spending too much time away from home it was going to get worse. She told her mother that Andrew was suffering from his annual 'spring attack' of an illness.

He was nowhere near as sick as his boss Henry Brown, though. The wealthy squatter had left his properties shortly before Christmas for a visit to Ferncliff, his Sydney home in Hunters Hill, not far from Rockend. At the time he 'seemed in most excellent health and spirits, and separated from his friends in his usual happy and joyous manner'.[53] But his bronchitis worsened, and he died on 1 January 1881[54] aged just fifty-three.

Andrew Paterson now had no boss, and Rose feared that soon the Paterson family would have no home. Would a new owner give them their marching orders?

They would have a long and anxious wait to find out. Brown's will had been written twelve years earlier and stipulated that all of his considerable properties – including more than twenty-six thousand hectares he owned around Yass and Binalong – should be sold, with his wife to receive a quarter and most of the rest going to the family of his friend Sir George Wigram Allen,[55] a philanthropist who at the time was Speaker of the NSW Legislative Assembly. Rose contemplated Andrew taking a well-paid position as a police magistrate so that he would be done at last with long hours in the saddle and long days away from home. If that didn't work out, she had a plan where they could buy the rundown Illalong homestead off the Brown estate and a few acres around it to raise sheep, horses and poultry. She saw a market in selling eggs and fattened turkeys. She wanted Barty to bring down from Sydney 'a well authenticated clutch of Dorking eggs' to improve her stock at Illalong and then sell off a coop full of her inferior birds in Sydney for Christmas dinners. 'I might turn a penny by fowls,' she told Nora, 'if I can get a good connection & get my name up for good ones.'[56]

Barty's 'Uncle Tye' – Robert Barton Jr – had provided £50[57] for the teenager to return to school in 1881,[58] so he could either sit the matriculation exam or try for a scholarship to university. When Barty visited Illalong for the Christmas holidays, he talked to his parents about what the future held. Andrew decided to travel with him to Sydney, to use whatever contacts and family connections the Patersons and Bartons had to map out a career path in the law for his bright boy. Andrew hoped to gain him a place in a solicitor's office where he could learn on the job.

On 11 February 1881, Rose wrote to Nora to say that her husband and oldest son were on the train to Sydney. Andrew was off to speak to the executors of Henry Brown's will, in order to see if the family could remain at Illalong, while Barty was off 'to seek his fortune, or have it sought for him'. 'Andrew is going to hawk him about among the swell solicitors till he finds an amiable firm willing to give him his indentures gratis,' Rose said. 'Should the Sydney solicitors all be so stony-hearted as to charge the full premium for admittance, £250, there is a more moderate man in Goulburn, a Mr Davidson, whose premium is only £50, with whom we may place him.'[59] Davidson was 'a gentleman & a rising lawyer' and promised to look after her boy. She and Andrew already had digs in Goulburn where he could stay for a guinea a week. Rose was pretty sure that if Barty could land a job in Sydney, her sister Emmy would let him board at Mama's again; Mama, Frank Barton and Emmy's children said they were all 'wild to get him back'.[60]

While father and son were away in Sydney, Rose was at her wits' end over the latest drought scorching southern New South Wales. She was stuck there for the foreseeable future because of the bad luck Andrew had suffered, and while she dreamt of a home in England or closer to the lush pastures of the NSW coast she had to put up with the fickle climate. Before long the cows were suffering 'from excessive heat together with inferior grass & water' and there was nothing but 'hot winds day after day, till the leaves on the fruit trees [looked] like a bush fire had passed under or through them'.[61] When rains finally came the old homestead became so damp and full of mildew that Rose and the children wished they were back in drought.[62]

Barty was now seventeen and his days at Grammar were over; of course, like so many old boys he would maintain strong connections there. The school had nurtured his talent even though he had not always given the lessons his full attention. In later years he would declare that the school offered a fair go for all, with no favours to anyone, regardless of class and creed. It was only after he left that he realised the benefits of having attended the school. Wherever he went in Sydney, even decades down the track, he would meet old classmates working in law offices, government offices, sometimes tailors' shops. Sydney Grammar, he said, was a place where 'if a boy liked to work he "got on", and if he didn't, he got a certain amount of information forced into his head whether he liked it or no'.[63]

Barty's job search with his father was derailed temporarily when Barty went down with the same fever and malaise as Jack a few months earlier. Mama Barton recognised the symptoms immediately and remembered that awful day, almost forty years before, when she had held baby Mary on her knee and listened as her tiny daughter's breathing grew softer and finally silent. She put Barty to bed. He was diagnosed with a severe case of typhoid on 23 April 1881.

Rose rushed up to Rockend to help nurse him back to health. Barty was so sick that he spent a month in quarantine and was forbidden to travel the three hundred kilometres to Illalong. On 22 May 1881, Rose was able to report that he had come through the worst of it and would go home with his sister Flo in the June holidays. He did, and Rose was relieved that there was 'no deafness or mental weakness as a result of the fever'. He was eating well but still pale and thin, and he had a long way to go until he made a full recovery.[64]

Barty's hopes of sitting for the Senior Public Examination on 7 June at the University of Sydney had been ruined. In order to qualify to become an articled clerk, he would have to either sit the Senior Public Exam the following November or wait until the next matriculation in June 1882. Or find a benefactor. Years later Paterson would write that he 'had a try for a bursary at the University, but missed it by about a mile and half'.[65] He was being characteristically modest.

AT ILLALONG, IN THE MIDDLE OF 1881, Rose was now thirty-six and feeling a hundred. She was pregnant with her seventh child. Barty spent most of his time in Sydney, and she fretted over what the future held for him given his illness and the way it had affected his vital exams.

Money at home was tight, as always, but having put Barty through Grammar, Rose was now doing her best to have her older girls receive the best education the family could afford. Her three oldest daughters – Flo, Jessie and Edie – rode into Binalong twice a week after hours to receive lessons in arithmetic from the public school teacher Mr Creagh. Rose wrote, 'Flo's music is better than that of 9 governess's out of 10 & we shall never get one at our salary who could teach either of them anything, so it is more comfortable to let Flo teach Jessie & Jessie [teach] Edie, till the happy time comes when we can afford to send them both off to school.'[66] Rose believed that 'a good & sound education bestowed upon a child of good disposition & average intelligence' was as 'good an investment as one could make ... Therefore educate, educate, educate is my advice.'[67] Without education, Rose said later, society produced a 'helpless & useless lot of consumers (& not producers) of means' and inflicted 'irreparable injury on your offspring & another on society & the worst of all on yourself'.[68]

Flo spent two months in Yass with a family friend, Mrs Alexandra Yates, of Thantalla Station, and was able to attend a boarding school at Creek Cottage in Meehan Street started by Maria and Harriet Allman. The school offered an education for £2 a term to day pupils over the age of eight. Flo was given lessons in dancing, music, calisthenics and painting, and Rose told Nora, 'I think she has had more advantages in the way of education than we ever had.'[69] She was sent off to the Sydney Ladies College on Macquarie Street, 'the foremost training institute in the colony for ladies',[70] and the 69-year-old headmistress, Miss Mary Ann Flower,[71] wrote 'enthusiastically' to Rose about 'Flo's talents and virtues'. Rose supposed the 'gushing old body' wrote 'in the same strain to all parents. I only hope she behaves as such, that is, in the same loving style as she writes.'[72]

Rose considered herself fortunate that unlike so many mothers of the time, including her own, she had not had to deal with infant mortality. All her children had grown up healthy, and, to the best of her ability, happy as well. Andrew's health was not robust, though. He had all sorts of aches and pains from the hard physical work of the land, and had long been treating his injuries with homemade remedies based on opium and alcohol. Rose had started to refer to him, with only a hint of sarcasm, as an 'old cripple'.[73]

Just before Henry Brown's death, Andrew's boss had promised to raise his salary to £400 a year starting in 1881, but it was only a verbal agreement – like the promise of £50 for Barty to become an articled clerk – and Rose knew it was not legally binding on the executors of his will.[74] Now, not only might her family miss out on a much-needed pay rise, but with her seventh child just weeks away Rose began to agonise over the prospect of the family home being sold from underneath them. Mrs Brown's brothers Walter[75] and Owen Friend[76] showed a keen interest in the property. They ran the York Street business of their father, a prominent Sydney ironmonger and hardware merchant.[77] Walter, who had known Andrew for years and was a local justice of the peace, was on his way[78] to becoming chairman of the Australian Joint Stock Bank.[79] But Rose had an 'instinctive distrust of them'. She explained to Nora that while they were civil to Andrew, she feared that when it came time to wind up the estate and they had no further need of his services, the Patersons would be shown the door. She even feared that the Friends would take their horses, buggies and furniture, since Andrew had no proof that they were the Patersons' private property and not part of Brown's estate.[80]

From September 1881, large newspaper-display advertisements were regularly placed in Sydney and Melbourne calling for buyers for the 'MAGNIFICENT FREEHOLD and PASTORAL ESTATE, known as BENDENINE, and comprising the following well-known properties, viz: BENDENINE, EAST GALONG, ILLALONG, KURIONG, DUNDERALLIGO, and CURIANGA'.[81]

The sales pitch said that improvements to the property were first class, and there was a comfortable ten-room homestead on Bendenine with a detached kitchen and servants' room. Illalong only had a 'dwelling house' of eight rooms, but the selling agents weren't going to talk that up too much since it was nothing like the house at Bendenine. Still, it was home to Rose and her family, and she hoped that she could continue living there for the foreseeable future, her husband having spent more than a decade working around the clock running the property.

Two of Rose's cousins, Henry and Ned Kater,[82] who had wide-ranging pastoral and business connections, expressed an interest in buying the properties but decided not to proceed. They could help out Rose in another way, though. Their youngest sister Alice Kater[83] was about to marry a rising young star of the legal world named Herbert Salwey,[84] who was in partnership in a Sydney firm with another lawyer, Staunton Spain.[85] Rose and Andrew had little money, but there was always the power of what she called the 'bush squattocracy'[86] – she was well connected through the families of

Kater, Barton, Paterson and Darvall, and friends like the Blaxlands and the Betts.

Keen to help out relatives of his charming fiancée, Salwey was happy to give Barty a start, even though the teenager didn't have his matriculation certificate. Salwey soon sent a letter to Illalong containing 'Articles of Agreement' between Herbert Salwey of Sydney and Andrew Bogle Paterson, father, and Andrew Barton Paterson, son. Barty would learn the ways of the law on the job, and Salwey went even further to help the lanky youngster: he waived, in a sense, Barty's premium of £100 due on the signing of the articles, changing it into an advance payment for young Paterson's work over the next five years. The two A. B. Patersons then rode together the thirty-five kilometres to Burrowa, where solicitor Harold O'Brien witnessed their signatures. Then, Judge Windeyer and another Supreme Court Justice, William Montagu Manning, signed the documents on 19 August 1881, allowing Barty to begin work for Salwey as an articled clerk.

ADDING TO THE DISCOMFORT of her pregnancy, Rose was suffering from rheumatism, worsened by the winter draughts and chills coming off the Snowy Mountains. The cold snaked through the cracks in the old walls and made Andrew's lumbago even more painful.

At least they could breathe a little easier when Illalong and the whole Bendenine parcel of properties was broken up and sold. Henry Brown's widow[87] took her share of the property but would pass away at Hunters Hill within a few months, joining her husband in an early death. The remainder of the property was bought by Mrs Brown's brothers, the Friends, at what Rose said 'was a very low rate' due to the 'dry weather & general depression'.

Walter and Owen Friend soon opened the purse strings, showing themselves to be 'large-hearted and liberal', and funding improvements to the house at Illalong with 'a large supply of timber, wall paper and calico for the refurbishing of this old ruin'. They also promised Andrew a contract for five years at £500 per annum, including travel expenses and money for telegrams and postage. It was much better, Rose said, than a trip to the 'Back Blocks' with a new baby,[88] and she was delighted that Barty had 'entered on his professional studies'.[89]

As Rose's confinement neared, her friend Mrs Yates offered a helping hand financially but Rose was too proud to accept,[90] even though she was worn down with a 'roasted out body'.[91] She did, however, take up her wealthy friend's offer to stay with her at the Royal Hotel in Yass. The hospitality was nothing to write home about, though. 'Johnny', the Chinese cook, refused to prepare any of the simple dishes that Rose requested, and his chicken was too tough for her brittle teeth, so she made do with porridge. She was embarrassed by her family's circumstances and said that the generosity of Mrs Yates was 'not the sort of kindness one generally meets with in rich people, especially where poor people (who can make no return) are concerned'.[92]

Rose delivered a healthy baby girl on the morning of Christmas Eve 1881 but it was a painful breech delivery with the baby 'dragged into this wicked world (feet first)'.[93] Every day after the birth, Dr Harding – the new medical man in town[94] and 'a nice gentlemanly old man'[95] at that – came to chat with her about politics and paintings and current events in the news. He also had a good chat to her about 'women's rights'.

At thirty-seven and after seven babies, it was time for Rose to retire from the 'common cause', though she still thought about having one more 'big boy'. Rose and Andrew named the new baby Gwendoline Alexa[96] – Alexa after Mrs Yates, who became the baby's godmother. Rose stayed with Mrs Yates for sixteen days before returning to Illalong. After all the pain and debilitation of the difficult birth, Rose's strength and tenacity were tested to the limit when little Gwen started displaying all the symptoms of typhoid. Then Rose was afraid she would have to wean the girl too early after she developed mastitis, telling Nora that she had 'caught cold in one breast' and it threatened an abscess.

Gwen was a 'queenly child', Rose said, with the nose, mouth and chin of the Bartons and the 'strong & fine' eyes of a Paterson. A month after the event, she had 'not cried for half an hour since she has been born', showing 'serenity through all the changes from cows' milk, preserved milk & Mother's milk, pipe bottle, flat bottle & spoon'.[97] Rose hoped that Gwen had inherited the 'Barton digestion' rather than the delicate stomach of the Patersons.

Rose had given birth to her last baby almost eighteen years after the first. Her life was no easier than when she and Andrew had ridden in the buggy all the way down from Buckinbah to Narrambla for Barty's birth in 1864. Despite far more difficult circumstances than those into which she herself had been born – despite the heat, the flies, the floods, the dangers and the isolation – she had shown unwavering loyalty to her husband and done her best over the years to give her children a chance at a good future. As she held the small wrinkled bundle of new life in her arms at Illalong and rocked Gwen to sleep, she could rest easy for a while knowing that the family would continue to have a roof over their heads in their bush surrounds and that in Sydney her eldest son was on the first rung of a ladder to success.

Barty was a bright boy who had inherited a dry whimsical attitude to life from Rose and her mother. The classroom combined with the wide open spaces of Australia had given him a special type of education. Now, Rose's pride and joy was about to start work in the office of a big city lawyer. She loved to hear all about his adventures and his progress, and she was sure that A. B. Paterson would have many more stories to tell.

Chapter 7

JUNE 1882, THE OFFICE OF SPAIN AND SALWEY, SOLICITORS, EXCHANGE BUILDING, BRIDGE STREET, SYDNEY

He made people think. Breaking away from traditions, holding no shams sacred, he was one of the first to make the Australian believe in himself. To that extent he rendered a service to his country, and this good at any rate lives after him.

BANJO PATERSON ON *THE BULLETIN* PUBLISHER J. F. ARCHIBALD[1]

BARTY WAS NOW EIGHTEEN, the same age as his mother had been when she married Andrew Paterson at her father's house on Boree Nyrang. He had none of Rose's cares and responsibilities, though, and as a good-looking teenager with wealthy connections in a vibrant city, he made the most of his seemingly endless possibilities. Cousin Jack had left school to become a clerk with the NSW Railways, and for a time, Barty and his chums lived in a shack of their own – like a college fraternity house – along the river. They charged about the foreshore looking for a good time in a dilapidated horse-drawn buggy powered by the fastest gallopers they could locate.[2]

The early 1880s were fast times in Sydney. An explosion in subdivisions and land sales continued the massive surge in population as new suburbs bloomed. Tram, horse-bus, train and ferry services were extended.

Tales of uniquely Australia stories were becoming increasingly popular with the expanding populace following the publication of Marcus Clarke's *Natural Life*, along with the real-life capture and execution of bushrangers such as Captain Moonlite and especially Ned Kelly, whose final shootout in a suit of armour in June 1880 was reported around the world. One of Australia's most prominent journalists was enthralled by the thought of 'bushrangers clad in armour, attacking a train and standing a siege of many hours'. He called it 'more wonderful than the wildest dreams of fancy indulged in by the authors of boys' novels'.[3]

The Australian public was eager for more outlaw tales, real or imagined. On 1 July 1882, a weekly magazine, *The Sydney Mail and New South Wales Advertiser,* began a serialisation of a novel written by Thomas Alexander Browne, under his pen name Rolf Boldrewood. Browne's imagination had been stirred by his neighbour David Campbell's shooting of John O'Meally, and he was now married to Campbell's cousin, Margaret. He was also now the police magistrate and mining warden at Dubbo.[4] Under the headline 'Fiction', the first instalment of Boldrewood's Australian classic in the *Sydney Mail* begins:

> Robbery Under Arms.
>
> Chapter I.
>
> My name's Dick Marston, Sydney-side native. I'm twenty-nine years old, six feet in my stocking-soles, and thirteen stone weight.[5] Pretty strong and active with it, so they say. I don't want to blow – not here, any road – but it takes a good man to put me on my back, or stand up to me with the gloves, or the naked mauleys. I can ride anything – anything that ever was lapped in horsehide – swim like a musk-duck, and track like a Myall blackfellow. Most things that a man can do, I'm up to, and that's all about it. As I lift myself now, I can feel the muscle swell on my arm like a cricket ball, in spite of the – well, in spite of everything.[6]

Despite his strength and vigour, Dick Marston curses the day he was born, cries like a child and beats his head against the stone floor. Strong as a bullock and full of life, he is about to face the hangman for committing robbery under arms.

The serialisation played out until August 1883, and Boldrewood's novel was then published in book form. His epic tale highlighted how petty crimes led to major ones for Marston, while hard work led to a happy, successful life for his childhood friend who became a wealthy landowner and magistrate like many of the men Barty had grown up around. At Illalong, Rose Paterson thought Boldrewood such a good novel writer that she said the government should have made him concentrate just on that and not 'suck the public treasury'.[7]

Robbery Under Arms further whetted the appetite of Australian readers for poetry and prose with a distinct Australian flavour: stories that celebrated and illuminated a people in a land far removed from the subject of most reading matter from Great Britain.

Barty already had reams of stories revolving around his head from his days in the bush, but he was hearing plenty of wild tales in his new job as well. From the office of Spain and Salwey at the Exchange Building in Bridge Street,[8] Paterson began to learn more of the world.

> 'We did a lot of shipping business and one of my first jobs was to go out and gather evidence for the defence of a captain who was prosecuted for not showing a riding-light over the stern while at anchor,' he related. 'Evidence! It was too easy. The captain had seen the boatswain put out the riding-light. The boatswain remembered that riding-light well, as he had nearly fallen overboard while fixing it. The chief officer had been strolling about the deck and had noticed the reflection of the riding-light on the water. I chuckled to think how small the opposition would feel when we unloosed our battery of testimony. Then the sea-lawyer who was on the Bench, without whys or wherefores, and without summing-up, found the captain guilty and fined him a fiver! I walked away from the court with the captain, and was just starting to speak a piece about this awful iniquity when he said: "Oh, well, I didn't know you had to have a riding light. They'd drive a man mad with their regulations in these &*$! places." An unnerving experience, but it taught me that a case at law is like a battle: If you listen to the accounts of the two sides you can never believe that they are talking about the same fight.'[9]

In England, Rosa Praed – the stepdaughter of Barty's aunt Nora Murray-Prior – was building a reputation as a literary force with the publication of *An Australian Heroine.*[10] She would go on to produce another forty-four books over four decades, more than half of them dealing with Australian life.[11] Her success and her tales of battlers standing up to the Australian frontier gave Barty pause to reflect on his many mirrored experiences. Henry Kendall's poetry was also a hit around Australia, and his third collection of verses, *Songs from the Mountains,*[12] was proving to be outstandingly popular.

Barty's right arm continued to give him grief, and he broke it again in 1882. The doctors told him there was a chance of the arm becoming 'both longer & stronger after the knitting has taken place', and he had hopes that the break this time might turn out to be 'a matter of congratulation' in the end.[13] It wasn't. He used calipers for a few months but then threw them away.

At Illalong, Rose's travails continued. In September one of the new owners of the Bendenine properties, Walter Friend, and his wife, Mary,[14] came calling on Rose and the family. They stayed a night and part of the day, and Rose began to warm to them. She enjoyed their company far more than she had that of the Browns. She'd always been suspicious of the widow Brown and found her snobbish.

Rose had to raise her large family in the wake of Andrew's absences and ill health, and the constant nagging malaise of now being long-time boarders on a property they had once owned. But the pain was not just to her pride. On Wednesday, 9 December 1882 in Yass she had eight teeth removed by a touring dentist who had advertised that he would be performing extractions with the aid of chloroform. Having all her bottom teeth replaced with a set of crude 'falsies' would save the family the further expense of ongoing dental treatment. Rose was willing to take a bullet for the team, as always – ready to put up with the agonies and risks of primitive dental surgery, suspect hygiene and unreliable sedation. Before riding down the thirty-five kilometres from Illalong to the makeshift surgery in Yass, she complained that her 'stumps' were in such a bad way that she was now reduced to eating only sago and soup, and was sorely in need of 'fresh grinders'. 'I am quite without teeth in the lower jaw,' she told Nora after the extractions, '& have only 5 in the upper so my eating is a matter of consideration … I took chloroform & did not feel the first 6 stumps a bit.' The last two extractions, though, fuelled her nightmares for many years.

She was in no mood for misbehaving children and with good nature told Nora that she would take no prisoners if Nora's mischievous daughter Meta[15] came to visit the Patersons at Illalong, stipulating 'for full permission to whack her if she is naughty! Or to otherwise suppress her.'[16] She'd already had enough of brats after one visitor brought her unruly brood to visit and had the temerity to criticise Rose's loose rein on Barty's baby brother Hamilton 'Boy' Paterson. 'I have just had a visit of nine days from Mrs Davies and 7 of the naughtiest children I ever saw … I should go wild (or bring them into subjection) in a week if I had such a quarrelsome bad-tempered lot to deal with. The most amusing part of the thing was that Mrs D. was quite solicitous & compassionate about 'Boy's' "unfortunate temper" when she has 7 – each one ten times worse than he.'[17] When Barty's nineteen-year-old cousin Annie Morgan[18] came to stay at Illalong in 1882, Rose despaired that she was 'the most indolent girl I have seen for a long time, very different in that respect from her poor mother' and hoped that the teenager's new stepmother would 'teach her the pleasures of active employment'.[19] Despite her indolence, or perhaps because of it, Barty's cousin lived to be 102.[20] Rose always found the Grammar boys and Barty's other friends from along the Parramatta River to be far more industrious when they came down to the farm to holiday, remarking that they were all 'nice gentlemanly lads & pleased to be in the bush even tho there is no amusement to offer them beyond making them useful at running in horses'.[21]

Rose made the most of life in the country, and to entertain her own brood would often turn her 'youngsters out to graze in the vineyard for a treat'. They would carry off a large dish of grapes to make jelly and that would keep them quiet for days.[22] But she also pitied the lot of women – much like herself – who had to rely on their menfolk for support or who were trapped in unhappy marriages. Rose had certainly come down in the world financially from the days when the Darvalls and Bartons were landed gentry, but she loved Andrew and saw them fighting adversity together, even if she still had to endure long stretches of 'grass widowhood'.[23] It pained her to know that her sister Nora, though married to a wealthy man, had to endure his womanising, and that Nora's stepdaughter Rosa Praed had married a bounder.

Two of Rose's friends, Mr and Mrs Crace, from a station just outside Queanbeyan, had travelled to England with Rosa and her husband Campbell Praed, who had given up his cattle run, Monte Christo, on Curtis Island near Gladstone. It was there that Rosa had spent two 'lonely, miserable years'[24] in 'terrifying hardship',[25] before moving with her husband as he started a new venture in the brewing trade in Northamptonshire.[26] The Craces told Rose that they pitied 'Mrs Praed' very much, and implied that she was a neglected and bullied wife. 'Alas!' Rose said. 'That the days of chivalry should have so completely passed away that delicate and sensitive women should so often be called upon to play the role of such to conceited & self-indulgent "lords" so call'd, but in reality mean tyrants! … not that I have personally much to complain of at the hands of my Lord and Master. It is mostly other people's experiences which arouse my fire.'[27] Even if Rosa Praed had to write under the byline Mrs Campbell Praed, Rose knew she had 'the talent and power to make a name (& I suppose money) independently of her inferior "superior"'.[28] Which is what she did.

But even at Narrambla, the home where Barty Paterson was born, Rose had seen a proud woman ground down by the men around her. Her aunt Rose Templer, the former Rose Darvall, had greater financial hardships than the family at Illalong, and Rose Paterson blamed Arthur Templer's financial mismanagement, asking Nora: 'Is it not melancholy to think of what a life of perpetual anxiety about money matters poor Aunt Rose's has been, all through the doings of the menfolk with whom her lot has been cast in different ways – useless husband, useless son & mad, & improvident sins in each: it is enough to make one turn "American woman's righter".'[29] She warned Nora not to name any of her children 'Rose', because it was a most unlucky name.

BARTY WAS WORKING HARD under the tutelage of Herbert Salwey, as the legal firm was making a solid reputation in shipping and commercial cases.[30] There was the Port Jackson Steamboat Company fighting for a compensation before Judge Windeyer,[31] another compensation case involving work on railway cuttings,[32] and a wrongful dismissal case for a sea captain.[33] Barty's mentor was his uncle Frank, and at Salwey's office he studied Real Property and

Commercial Law. In November 1883, he placed fourteenth out of sixteen for the solicitor's intermediate examination. He was no legal genius but he was on his way to a promising legal career.

Halfway through 1884, Barty's sister Flo, now eighteen, was about to marry Edwin Lumsdaine,[34] a successful solicitor with dreams of entering the clergy. Andrew and Rose would soon travel to the wedding at the Christ Church in Gladesville,[35] where the groom's father, Reverend William Lumsdaine, was the Anglican rector.[36]

Barty was in demand too. Fanny Kater, whose sister Alice was now married to Salwey, convinced Barty's boss to give him an extra week's holiday, so he could escort her to a local shindig near Illalong, the Cunningham ball. But Fanny took leave, and Barty took the train to Binalong alone. His father met him at the station, wearing a dress suit. Since he was conveniently all dressed up, he suggested they head straight to the races after breakfast in town. The two Andrew Patersons had one great hobby, horses, and Fanny Kater knew how much going to the races with his father meant to Barty. Father and son were both grateful for Fanny's 'little lark'.[37]

Not that Barty saw a joke in everything. He was growing increasingly interested in the views espoused by *The Bulletin*, which was continuing to encourage white Australians to stand on their own two feet and see themselves as their own people and not subjects of a throne thousands of miles away. Australia's emerging novelists focused on the unique identity of homegrown Australians, and Melbourne's National Gallery Art School, opened in 1867, was championing the study of Australia and its people through the eyes of independent Australians. While Aboriginal rights were further eroded and the Board of the Protection of Aborigines was given power to break up Indigenous families in forced assimilation, trade unions were demanding a fairer go for workers and increasingly gaining power with strike action and socialist support from rural workers, especially shearers and labourers. The white women's suffragette movement was also gaining traction, with one of the key drivers in Sydney being Mary Windeyer, wife of the famous judge and vice-chancellor of the University of Sydney. The university had just started admitting female students.[38]

As the railway lines spun a web across Australia, wool fuelled the economy and the various colonies accelerated towards self-sufficiency. The first government-run telephone exchange opened at Sydney's General Post Office in 1882 – almost, it seemed, as a signal for Australians to speak up. Barty Paterson began clearing his throat and putting his thoughts down on paper.

AT AROUND THE SAME TIME that Barty was planning the trip to the Binalong races with his father, a British army general, Charles 'Chinese' Gordon,[39] was starting a race for his life in the Sudan. Gordon was a veteran of British campaigns in Crimea and China, and had been sent to Khartoum to organise the evacuation of Egyptian soldiers and civilians in the face of a rebellion against British-backed Egyptian control. He had first gone to Sudan a decade earlier in the service of Ismail the Magnificent,[40] the Khedive – or viceroy – of Egypt for the Ottoman Empire. Gordon later became Governor-General of Sudan before returning to Europe in 1880. In 1884 he was back in north Africa and fighting a revolt against British influence and harsh taxes. The Sudan rebellion was led by a Shi'ite Muslim religious cleric, Muhammad Ahmad,[41] who had proclaimed a jihad against Egypt and who had vowed to purify Islam by clearing the Sudan of Christians. Ahmad's followers saw him as a Messianic figure known as 'The Guided One' or 'Mahdi'. In Khartoum, as he readied to fight the rebels, Gordon had about eight thousand soldiers armed with Remington .43 calibre rifles from America, and a huge ammunition dump containing millions of rounds. He also had food to last six months. El Mahdi's forces grew like rolling storm clouds, though, and the telegraph lines between Khartoum and Cairo were cut on 15 March 1884, severing communication between Gordon and help. By the end of the year, the soldiers and civilians still in Khartoum were starving to death – and they had eaten all the horses, donkeys, cats and dogs. Gordon told the civilians that anyone who wished to leave Khartoum, even to join El Mahdi's army, was free to do so. Thousands immediately left[42] and El Mahdi's forces kept advancing. The religious fundamentalist believed he would soon head a worldwide caliphate when all would 'bow before him'.[43] Gordon's struggles played out in the international media as the British left him to fend for himself.

On 26 January 1885, Khartoum was finally overrun, and ten thousand defenders and civilians were killed. It is said that Gordon, seeing himself as a Christian martyr, put on a ceremonial gold-braided blue uniform and a red fez, and went out to face the enemy with a revolver in one hand and a sword in the other. He was soon chopped down by the hordes and his head cut off for display. His death sickened the English-speaking world. In Sydney, Barty read:

> General Charles George Gordon, whose death at Khartoum is announced this morning, was a man who, combining the qualities of the soldier, the statesman, and the philanthropist in a high degree, occupied a singular position as the representative of his Government in situations where great issues depended on the skill and disposition of those who had to deal with them. With all his achievements, he was remarkably self-denying and free from personal ambition … His story indeed is the story of a swordless conqueror; of a true disciple of the Divine Master, who laid down His life for humanity; of a complete Christian in thought, word, and deed.[44]

Barty wasn't so sure about all that imperialist propaganda and even less impressed by the departure of 750 troops, toting six cannons, two field guns, two Gardener machine guns and two Gatling machine guns, from Sydney's Victoria Barracks to bolster an avenging British Army.[45] A special NSW Cabinet meeting on 12 February 1885 had decided to offer five hundred infantrymen, plus two batteries of field artillery, to go after Gordon's killers. It was a controversial move as the decision was made without full Parliamentary sanction. There was great fanfare, though, as the local men marched off to battle on 3 March 1885. The *Illustrated Sydney News* reported:

> THE departure of the little army from our shores to the aid of the mother country is, perhaps, not a great deal in view of the tens of thousands she has under command; but is a very significant mark of the loyalty we bear, and indicates that if the old country really was in danger, she has wealthy colonies who are ever ready to buckle on the armour and do their share of the fighting. From early morning, on the 3rd of March, the Victorian Barracks presented a scene of activity and excitement – soldiers, volunteers, and friends thronged the place. Those destined for the Soudan,

> were in the highest spirits, and those who remained behind were fired with such military ardour, that, if one 'Soudan man' had remained behind, a hundred were ready on the spot to fill the vacancy. Pathetic scenes were there in abundance, as wives, mothers, sisters, and sweethearts took a last farewell.[46]

Barty was not caught up in the patriotic fervour, despite coming from a long line of British military figures. For Australians to be kowtowing to British demands made him retch – as a young iconoclast he believed that sending Australians to fight in a foreign war was an abomination. The newspaper reports, combined with the weekly Australia-first editorials of *The Bulletin*, made him a very angry young man. He thought the Australian troops were facing a fate as grim as the 2200 two-tooth ewes his father had just sold for the Friend brothers.[47] Andrew had sent in a few verses to *The Bulletin* over the years[48] and by the time the Sydney contingent sailed for north Africa, Barty – now a 21-year-old articled clerk – had already sent in a few of his own, starting with what he called an anonymously written account of a 'glove fight'.[49] He was reading a lot of the decadent, defiant poetry of Englishman Algernon Swinburne[50] at the time – a man he regarded as a degenerate human like Lord Byron, but one who wrote 'wonderful poetry'.[51] Now was his chance to thumb his nose at authority, too.

The thought of Australians dying in a British war in Africa caused him to blast out a poem of four rough verses as an outlet for his angst. He saw the conflict through the eyes of El Mahdi, in his mind a freedom fighter faced with foreign invaders. To Barty, Australians were now 'in arms against the freeman's right', striking 'a blow for tyranny and wrong' and blindly supporting 'England's degenerate generals' as they tried to keep a puppet ruler of the Turks in power. Barty bashed out his opposition with as much vitriol as he could summon, and sent if off to *The Bulletin*. He knew it was a risky move, especially for a young man trying to make his way in the law, so he signed his protest 'El Mahdi'.

It was a long way from his best work – it was closer to his worst – but the anti-establishment tone was exactly what Jules Archibald and *The Bulletin* were looking for to kick the hornet's nest again. *The Bulletin* published it on page four of its 28 February 1885 issue.

A few days later, the soldiers heading to the Sudan marched down College Street past Barty's old school and towards Circular Quay. Tens of thousands of supporters massed across the road in Hyde Park, throwing floral tributes at the troops and displaying placards with mottos that declared 'For England, Home, and Gordon' and 'Well done, N.S.W.' It was an emotional goodbye from Sydney, and 'more than one brave fellow's voice grew husky as he took a farewell embrace of some loved friend'.[52] Newspapers said the send-off was a 'demonstration which surpassed in its tumultuous enthusiasm anything of the kind that had ever taken place in Australia'.[53]

The Bulletin took a different tack. Barty's first poem for the magazine coincided with its front-page editorial, which declared that even Gordon 'the soldier-martyr' would groan as the colony of New South Wales made such a 'fearful mistake' sending troops to avenge his death. Archibald and his staff told readers across the Australian colonies: 'The idea of vengeance for Gordon belongs to the barbaric age, to the days of the Crusades, when swarms of Christian men, smitten with a shameful enthusiasm, which they imagined to be virtuous and noble, flocked to the Syrian deserts to slaughter Saracens for the love of Christ. When we see and hear around us the cries of wrath and the shouts of devotion – the marshalling of fighting men and the embarkation of the machinery of destruction – it seems as though we were back in the dark ages ...'[54]

The 'little army from our shores'[55] suffered six deaths from the Sudan invasion, the result of typhoid and dysentery rather than battle, and returned to Sydney on 23 June.

MONEY CONCERNS WERE STILL paramount for Rose and Andrew Paterson at Illalong, but they now also had the stress of dealing with the teenage angst of Banjo's sister Jessie. At seventeen, she had become the family's problem child. Rose had hoped that Jessie would follow older sister Flo to Miss Flower's Finishing School, but Jessie was visiting Rose's sister Nora at the mountainous Murray-Prior station, Maroon, near Beaudesert in southern Queensland – and she was causing trouble. She had no plans to go to finishing school and no plans to subject herself to her mother's control. Rose didn't have the money to travel north to deal with Jessie or bring her home. So she wrote a stern letter to her, telling her that unless she promised 'obedience & amiability at home for the future' she had better find somewhere else to live.[56] It was just another load on the mind of a hardworking bush housewife already with enough strife on her plate.

Barty relaxed for a while ... by watching dogs tear each other apart. He and his cousin Edward Darvall invested in a fighting dog and took it to the wilds of seaside Cronulla to take on all comers.[57] A decade later Paterson wrote about his experiences for *The Bulletin*, changing the location to 'out Botany way'; the short story ran next to an advertisement for Nestle's Food, billed as being beneficial 'as a Diet in severe cases of Typhoid'. Barty remarked that while dogfighting had become illegal it was still organised by 'gentlemen who follow the occupation of slaughterers'. Bull terriers, he said, were 'the gladiators of the canine race'.[58]

> One dog was on the ground when we arrived. He had come out in a hansom cab with his trainer, and was a white bull terrier, weighing about forty pounds, 'trained to the hour', with the muscles standing out all over him ... He knew as well as any human being that there was sport afoot, and he looked about eagerly and wickedly to see what he could get his teeth into ... The trainer and dog got out of the cab, and we followed ... About a hundred people were at the ringside, and in the far corner, in the arms of his trainer, was the other dog, a brindle.
>
> It was wonderful to see the two dogs when they caught sight of each other. The white dog came up to the ring straining at his leash, nearly dragging his trainer off his feet in his efforts to get at the enemy. At intervals he emitted a hoarse roar of challenge and defiance. The brindled dog never uttered a sound. He fixed his eyes on his adversary with a look of intense hunger, of absolute yearning for combat.[59]

The stakes were said to be £10 a side. After some talk, the dogs were carried to the centre of the ring by their seconds and put on the ground.

> Like a flash of lightning they dashed at each other, and the fight began ... Bred and trained to fight, carefully exercised and

> dieted for weeks beforehand, they come to the fray exulting in their strength and each determined to win ... Now and again one dog got a grip of the other's foot and chewed savagely, and the spectators danced with excitement. The moment the dogs released hold of each other they were snatched up by their seconds and carried to their corners, and a minute's time was allowed, in which their mouths were washed out and a cloth rubbed over their bodies ... The brindled dog's condition was not so good as the other's, and he used to lie on his stomach between the rounds to rest himself, and it several times looked as if he would not cross the ring when his turn came. But as soon as time was called, he would start to his feet and come limping slowly across glaring steadily at the other dog; then, as he got nearer, he would quicken his pace and at last make a savage rush, and in a moment they would be locked in combat. So they battled on for fifty-six minutes till the white dog (who was apparently having all the best of it), on being called on to cross the ring, only went halfway across and stood there growling savagely till a minute had elapsed, and so he lost the fight. No doubt it was a brutal exhibition. But it was not cruel to the animals in the same sense that pigeon shooting or hare hunting is cruel. The dogs are born fighters, anxious and eager to fight, desiring nothing better. Whatever limited intelligence they have is all directed to this one consuming passion.[60]

BARTY KNEW THE STRUGGLES of his mother and had been deeply affected by the battles of so many people like her in the bush; by seeing wealthy squatters grow richer from the work of the men like his father who toiled hard for them out in the fields with sheep and cows. As well as conducting his legal work, Barty was making a serious study of history and economics, and as a young idealist believed 'it was up to me to set the world right'.[61] He started work on an 11,000-word treatise called 'Australia for the Australians – a Political Pamphlet Showing the Necessity for Land Reform Combined with Protection'.[62] His writing was serious and solemn, not at all what would be expected from the young tearaway hooning around the streets in his old carriage near his grandmother's house with as much horsepower as he could find in the stables.

He started his political manifesto by declaring: 'It is of the greatest importance to every man amongst us, that he should have some clear idea of what position he occupies in relation to other people, and that he should understand what it is that fixes his prospects, and circumstances in life.'[63] He wrote that he feared that big business and the banks would soon make Australia's rural workers as hard done by as Irish tenant farmers, and there would be 'plenty of good landlord shooting then'.[64] The Irish struggles in Australia were often in his thoughts, as many of his later characters would attest: Clancy and Kiley, Mulligan's Mare, Father Riley's Horse, Tommy Corrigan and Gilhooley's Estate.

The young zealot thundered:

> Let those who do not see the necessity for any change or questioning of the present arrangement of affairs take a night walk round the poorer quarters of any of our large colonial cities, and they will see such things as they will never forget. They will see vice and sin and misery in full development. They will see poor people herding in wretched little shanties, the tiny stuffy rooms fairly reeking like ovens with the heat of our tropical summer. I, the writer of this book, at one time proposed, in search of novelty, to go and live for a space in one of the lower class lodging houses in Sydney, to see what life was like under that aspect. I had 'roughed it' in the bush a good deal. I had camped out with very little shelter and very little food. I had lived with the stockmen in their huts, on their fare, so I was not likely to be dainty; but after one night's experience of that lodging I dared not try a second. To the frightful discomfort was added the serious danger of disease from the filthy surroundings and the unhealthy atmosphere. I fled. And yet what I, a strong man, dared not undertake for a week, women and children have to go through from year's end to year's end. And there were places compared with which the one I tried was a paradise.
>
> Some say of course that all this misery is the fault of the people themselves; in some cases it is. There are people who would be hard up, no matter what chances they got; but there are a great many who, try as they may, cannot make any comfortable kind of a living. Do you, reader, believe that it is an inevitable law that

in a wealthy country like this we must have so much poverty? Do you not think there must be something wrong somewhere? Of course people are much worse off in the older countries. God grant that we never will reach the awful state in which the poorer classes of England and the Continent now are. Are we not going in the same direction? That is the question which we have to consider. The same trouble is showing itself here which has come up everywhere. Instead of the position of the working people improving at the same rate as the various appliances for getting a living are improved and perfected, we find a woeful deficiency. The improvement in productive power has been like the speed of a racehorse, while the improvement in the position of the people who ought to be benefited thereby has been like the speed of the mud turtle – if indeed any progress has been made at all.

We who have no pressing cares, look with indifference on the hardships of poverty-stricken people; but it may be our turn next. It is a matter we should look into. The accepted theory to explain all this is one which was started by a clergyman named Malthus.[65] He said that people had to slave day and night, and women and little children had to suffer hunger and want because the earth would not produce enough to support its population. He said that just in the same way if a man kept on breeding sheep he would in time overstock his run, so we human creatures tend to increase and multiply so rapidly that we would overstock the earth, were it not that our numbers are kept down by starvation, disease, dirt, misery, and all the evil consequences which follow on and spring from poverty.[66]

Barty highlighted the inequity in Australian society, with rich fat cats in Sydney making fortunes from property and the unfairness of the old rule of 'fee simple' that granted huge areas of Crown lands to the wealthy while poor farmers struggled to get a start. The rich got richer, he argued, while the poor funded their lifestyle: 'To whom does the finest house in Sydney belong? It belongs to a man who inherited a huge fortune made solely out of the rise and rents of real estate near Sydney: a man who counts his fortune by hundreds and thousands, and spends most of his time in England. He never did a day's work in his life, and yet can have every luxury while hundreds of his fellow countrymen have to toil and pinch and contrive to get a living.'[67]

More than half a century later, Paterson said just the thought of that youthful bluster made him blush,[68] though he and his father and so many other characters of his boyhood knew only too well the unfairness of a land grant system that made many absent landlord speculators wealthy on the toil of lowly paid workers.

Barty sent his creation to *The Bulletin*, whose banner proclaimed 'Australia for Australians'. He had high hopes for his political manifesto – but it 'fell as flat as the great inland desert'.[69]

While he reorganised and reshaped his ideas for publication at a later date, Paterson sent in another poem to *The Bulletin*, this time under the pseudonym that would stick until the present day. He was afraid that if Jules Archibald and his staff identified the poem's author as the same writer of the political pamphlet it would make its way to the bin unread.[70] Paterson had signed some of his schoolboy efforts as 'B', and he thought about calling himself 'Cincinnatus'[71] in honour of the flamboyant American Cincinnatus Miller,[72] the 'Poet of the Sierras'. But for his new and controversial poem, 'The Bush Fire', Paterson signed himself as 'The Banjo', not after the musical instrument – because he had never held one in his life[73] – but after the 'so-called racehorse'[74] his father had had on Illalong when Paterson was a boy.

'The Banjo' sent in twenty-five six-line verses about Ireland's demand for Home Rule from England. With all his boyish zeal he compared a deliberately lit fire on a tinder-dry Australian property to Irish anger as British Prime Minister William Gladstone (Billy Gladstone in the verses) tries to battle the flames with the Home Rule Bill (the equivalent of a bough from a blue gum tree), while a wise colonial observer (the cornstalk kid) tells Billy that there is no use in fighting the fire unless he catches the people responsible for it. The moral, Banjo told his readers, was that Gladstone had to treat the anger of the Irish rather than try to beat out the flames with his laws.

Banjo well knew the plight of the poor Irish battler in Australia. Working in the law, where he saw merciless bank managers trying to squeeze every skerrick from the working man when they often had no skerricks left, he could feel their angst against oppression.

Back at Illalong, Banjo's father continued managing the Friend brothers' new properties, and he also worked in various official capacities on the Land Board[75] and as a justice of the peace. He took a close interest in local political matters and was a frequent writer of letters to newspapers on the state of his community. He had immense pride when – a few weeks after 'The Banjo's' debut in *The Bulletin* – Andrew Barton Paterson was admitted as a solicitor on 28 August 1886.[76] Rose, proud of her son's achievement, told Barty's sisters at Illalong, 'Now remember girls, Barty's opinion is worth six and eight-pence.'[77]

But the Patersons had another reason to celebrate. Jules Archibald was impressed with the few verses he had read from the youngster – though not so much with the pamphlet. The poems were rough, but there was something bright and dazzling and new in what he was reading. On 22 August 1886 he had written to the budding young lawyer to say Banjo's copy was 'on the average clear enough to be dreamt of by good sober printers in holy dreams of heaven'. 'Will you drop in and see me at your earliest convenience, as I would like to have a long talk with you about a lot of things. I shall be glad to have from you any topical verses which may come into your head and you would do me a great favour by trying your hand at writing for us weekly some short snappy paragraphs – two, three or four lines each, no more ...'[78]

Archibald told Paterson that *The Bulletin* aimed at being an 'Australasian' publication that would appeal to the man in the city or up at Cape York or down at Cape Otway, and that the publication's policy was to 'howl for the undermost dog'.

'By the way,' Archibald added, 'you would help me greatly by contributing from time to time some perky comments on social affairs – paragraphs containing a little good nature and a little ginger.'[79] That was just the way Rose Paterson composed her letters.

Banjo called *The Bulletin* the 'most unsatisfied paper in Australia',[80] as it represented the great bulk of Australians who, he believed, were crying out for a better deal. He recalled that 'in the eyes of all "right-thinking people" – a class which its editor held in sincere detestation', *The Bulletin* 'was a scurrilous rag, certain to do a great amount of harm; in the eyes of the ordinary, heedless, unthinking man in the street, it was a very good comic paper; to such few iconoclasts, uplifters, and regenerators of society as then existed, it represented a new gospel'.[81]

Banjo went over to see Archibald in his office at 24 Pitt Street. The busy thoroughfare was as far from the lowing cattle and the singing stockmen of Barty's childhood as he could imagine. Smoke billowed from nearby factories and there was gutter language of children fighting, the noise and commotion of tram bells clanging, hoofs clattering and iron-rimmed carriage wheels crunching the road surfaces. Banjo strode down Pitt Street to a small, shabby brick building hidden away among ship chandleries, fish shops and wool stores. As the smell of the fish wafted down from a narrow alleyway, men in overalls rolled great bales of wool, perhaps from the backs of sheep shorn at Illalong or Buckinbah, along the cobblestones.

Banjo climbed 'a narrow and never dusted flight of stairs into a narrow and equally undusted passage, with hardly room for two men to walk abreast'.[82] Off this passage there were two or three little cubicles of rooms, furnished with a table and a chair, 'dust illimitable, piles of newspapers all about the floor, and its walls decorated with ink stains and newspaper illustrations'.[83] In the first cubicle Barty saw a sallow young man 'who with feverish haste was writing paragraphs'. It was Wilfred Blacket,[84] *The Bulletin*'s subeditor, and later a King's Counsel barrister. Without even looking up from his desk, Blacket indicated with a jerk of his thumb that the editor's cubicle was the next one over.

Barty walked past walls decorated with caricatures of Henry Parkes and Queen Victoria, and Chinese coolies with exaggerated eyes and teeth, and stood before a door marked 'Mr. Archibald, Editor'. On the door was pinned a spirited drawing of a man lying flat out in a street with a dagger through him, and the caption read: 'Archie, this is what will happen to you if you don't use my drawing about the policeman!' It cheered up Banjo because to him it meant the office was 'a free and easy place'.[85]

Inside, Archibald was hard at work shaping the next edition of the magazine from his rolltop desk, cutting and coaxing the paragraphs before him to further fuel *The Bulletin*'s growth as a national institution. Paterson met a bearded and bespectacled Archibald 'peering at a world which was all wrong … not that he ever put forward any concrete scheme for setting it right; he diagnosed the diseases, and left others to find the cure.'[86]

Archibald was a remarkable man who looked much older than his thirty years. *The Bulletin* had now been running for six years and was one of the great success stories in Australian publishing. Archibald would be remembered as 'a grand companion, a conversationalist of sparkling wit',[87] the cooker of sublime chicken casserole, and an editor who described himself as a 'soler and heeler of paragraphs'.[88] He would pounce on a piece of verse with potential and polish it clandestinely for weeks. He favoured poetry with a musical lilt, 'something a commercial traveller in a red cummerbund' could recite at smoke nights. He looked for verses that had swing in every line, and usually when he sent poems to the printers he had massaged every single line. 'He was an anti-cleric, a republican, a devotee of French art and literature … He even arranged his genealogy so that his mother was a French Jewess and his father a Scots Irishman.'[89]

In fact, Archibald had been born into an Irish-Catholic family, the son of a police sergeant. At fourteen he was apprenticed in the print works of the *Warrnambool Examiner*; he delivered morning papers before work and practised his shorthand in the evenings. At eighteen he left for Melbourne, cocksure he would soon become editor of *The Argus*, but ended up as a compositor on *The Herald* and then a reporter on the now-defunct Melbourne *Daily Telegraph*. He took a job as a clerk in a Queensland engineering firm and toured remote goldmines of north Queensland before John Haynes,[90] a journalist with Sydney's *Evening News*, found him a clerk's job on the paper. Archibald soon became a reporter there, and in 1879 he and Haynes, with about £140 in savings between them, bought a small case of battered display type, put a deposit on a second-hand press and rented the ramshackle Scandinavian Hall at 107 Castlereagh Street where they used packing cases for a desk and counter. They worked around the clock selling advertising[91] for their new magazine.

In their first issue of *The Bulletin*, they declared: 'The public eye rejects as uninteresting more than half of what is printed in the publications of the day. It is only the other half which will be found in the "BULLETIN".'[92]

Archibald had married Rosa Frankenstein at the end of 1885,[93] but *The Bulletin* remained the great love of his life. By the time he met

Banjo Paterson in 1886, he had bought out his other partners, Haynes and *The Bulletin*'s editor, William Henry Traill.[94] He believed Banjo had a way with words that Australians would love. In that cluttered office in Pitt Street, the pair spoke for just ten minutes. After offering him seven shillings and sixpence a poem, Archibald told Paterson he would like him to try some more verse. He asked, did 'The Banjo' know anything about the bush? Paterson told him that he had been reared there.

'All right,' Archibald said, 'have a go at the bush. Have a go at anything that strikes you. Don't write anything like other people if you can help it. Let's see what you can do.'[95]

Chapter 8

OCTOBER 1886, OFFICE OF THE BULLETIN MAGAZINE, 24 PITT STREET, SYDNEY

Henry Lawson was a man of remarkable insight in some things and of extraordinary simplicity in others. We were both looking for the same reef, if you get what I mean; but I had done my prospecting on horseback with my meals cooked for me, while Lawson had done his prospecting on foot …

BANJO PATERSON ON THE HUMBLE BEGINNINGS OF HIS GREAT LITERARY CONTEMPORARY[1]

BANJO WAS ON THE MOVE. Upwards in his literary career and downtown in his legal work.

In the *Bulletin* office on Pitt Street, Jules Archibald placed the next work of 'The Banjo' on page nine of the Saturday, 30 October 1886 edition. The cover price was now sixpence, and readers received eighteen pages of nationalist fervour, racist insults and caustic political commentary – as well as The Banjo's preview of Australia's greatest horserace, which was to be run three days later.

Banjo called the poem 'A Dream of the Melbourne Cup' and modestly subtitled it 'A Long Way After Gordon', indicating that while he hoped to emulate the late, great poet Adam Lindsay Gordon[2] there was still a long way for him to go. Archibald scrawled across Banjo's manuscript: 'Doggerel. Fun in the idea. Might be remodelled.'[3] Still, the livewire publisher ran it as Banjo cast his eye over the actual field to run that year. The work hinted at the excitement Banjo would create in later verses about fast horses and daring riders. It played on old prejudices too, the hero betting with 'a Hebrew money-lender' at a million to five. Archibald noted on Banjo's submission that he liked this bit.

Three days after publication, as many as 120,000 people were at Flemington to see the chestnut favourite, Trident,[4] and the big brown outsider, Arsenal, a battler from Sydney with just two wins to his name, locked together as they rounded the turn into the home straight[5] leaving Hales behind. Six hundred metres from the finish line, Trident appeared to forge ahead; but Arsenal was with him, and then amid tremendous uproar Trident started to lag less than a hundred metres from home. Two other horses, Trenton and Silvermine, passed him, but Arsenal could not be overtaken and stormed home in a huge boilover.[6]

While the celebrations were uproarious among those in New South Wales who had managed to back the colony's new hero at 25 to 1, there were celebrations of a different kind in Banjo's workplace. Earlier in the day, Herbert Salwey announced he had formed a new partnership with well-known lawyers Donnelly Fisher[7] and Henry Ralfe as 'Fisher, Ralfe and Salwey – Solicitors, Attorneys and Proctors'.[8] Fisher was a well-connected man about town, and the grandson of the explorer and statesman William Charles Wentworth.[9] The firm would soon employ Walter Macansh,[10] who would go on to marry Barty's cousin Hester Paterson,[11] Jack's little sister; the Reverend Lumsdaine performed the ceremony at Christ's Church near to Hester's home at Rockend.[12]

The firm's new office was on the corner of Pitt and Bond Streets – just around the corner from the *Bulletin* headquarters, where Banjo was starting to make a name for himself as a 'versifier'.[13]

Banjo enjoyed writing much more than he did spending month after month composing letters of demand for Fisher, Ralfe and Salwey, trying to 'screw money out of people who had not got it'.[14] He eventually became a managing clerk for the firm, doing legal work 'for three banks in the depression which preceded the dreary days when the banks themselves had to shut'.[15] Writing became his outlet for that frustration at making the lot of the little Aussie battler even worse. He was not a diligent lawyer; he had the easygoing nature of his father and no great desire to be a high-profile legal mind like his grandmother's brother John Bayley Darvall, or even his uncle Frank. Every chance he could get, he was back at Illalong or taking trips to see relatives on stations in other parts of rural Australia, testing his light hand on the rein and his ability to stick on a horse. Many times he followed men into the mountains, watching riders in rough country as they shut their eyes while the horse worked around a slippery siding with a 'thousand feet drop below him'[16] when 'any slip was death'.[17] Writing allowed Banjo to transport himself to those places and those experiences, even though every day there was only a desk and legal pad before him.

Archibald wrote to Banjo to say:

> I want you to remember that Australia is a big place, and I want you to write stuff that will appeal not only to Sydney people, but that will be of interest to the pearler up at Thursday Island and the farmer down in Victoria. On all public questions the press are apt to sing in chorus. If you go to a concert you may hear a man sing a discord which is put there by the composer, and that discord catches the ear over the voices of the chorus. Well, don't be afraid to sing the discord. Even if you are wrong, you will have drawn attention to what you want to say, and you may be right. In my experience the man who sings the discord is generally right nowadays. For the same reason, do not be afraid to cheer for the underdog in a fight. You will have all the cheering to yourself, for one thing, and the underdog may come out on top.[18]

This resonated with Banjo at a time when he felt that 'all right-thinking people got their ideas, their boots, their shirts, their titles, their jobs, their political, moral, and religious standards from England. It was looked upon as "blow" and bad taste for an Australian to talk of anything that Australians had done. We were patronised by imported Governors, insulted by imported globetrotting snobs, exploited by imported actors and singers, mostly worn-out and incompetent. These people rode rough-shod over us, and we meekly submitted.'[19]

Banjo resolved to write Australian stories for Australians, to cheer for the battler, to present the people and the places he knew in a heroic light.

For the special 1886 Christmas edition of *The Bulletin*, he followed his Melbourne Cup preview with the cheerful 'The Mylora

Elopement' and established an alliterative rhythm in the opening lines:

By the winding Wollondilly where the weeping willows weep,
And the shepherd, with his billy, half awake and half asleep,
Folds his fleecy flocks that linger homewards in the setting sun,
Lived my hero, Jim the Ringer, 'cocky' on Mylora Run.

Jimmy loved the super's daughter, Miss Amelia Jane McGrath.
Long and earnestly he sought her, but he feared her stern papa;
And Amelia loved him truly – but the course of love, if true,
Never yet ran smooth or duly, as I think it ought to do.[20]

There are echoes of flying hoofs and mountain ponies that would crop up again later:

The sound of a whip comes faint and far,
A rattle of hoofs, and here they are,
In all their tameless pride.
The fleet wild horses snort with fear,
And wheel and break as the yard draws near.
Now, Jim the Ringer, ride!
Wheel 'em! wheel 'em! Whoa back there, whoa!
And the foam-flakes fly like the driven snow,
As under the whip the horses go
Adown the mountain side.

Jules Archibald thought the poem 'Rough but humorous',[21] and Banjo told him he had plenty more where that came from. Archibald took the red pen to every writer whose work came through the door, and invariably sharpened and shaped it to his vision of what Australians wanted. Banjo found the whole atmosphere at *The Bulletin* to be inspiring and far more stimulating than his day job. At *The Bulletin* he felt he was surrounded by genius – especially by men such as Archibald and the two leading artists for the magazine at the time, Livingston 'Hop' Hopkins[22] and Phil May,[23] whom Banjo regarded as celebrities of the day. Both had started their illustrious tenures at the publication after the then editor William Traill, a man Banjo called 'a large expansive person',[24] had gone on a recruiting drive, hiring Hopkins in America in 1883 and May in England in 1886.

Banjo said as artists they were as 'unalike as possible in every way'.

> 'Hopkins was of the large, somnolent type; but give him an idea for a comic picture and he would make three jokes grow where only one grew before. May was a bundle of nerves and vitality, wearing himself out before his time.'[25]

Hopkins was a dignified man with a puritanical streak, tasked with drawing the weekly political cartoon. May was the life of the party, a true eccentric, who was nonplussed by anything outside of the urban bohemian environment in which he thrived. Even a trip to the cafes and hotels of the Blue Mountains, just outside Sydney's outer suburbs, was considered 'a wild adventure in strange territory'.[26]

May was at *The Bulletin* only for three years but produced about eight hundred illustrations[27] of his quirky take on life and current events, before returning to England to become one of the leading cartoonists for *Punch*. Banjo remembered him as 'an extraordinarily skinny man, with a face like a gargoyle' who always spent much more than he earned. 'He was a self-taught artist, a self-taught actor; could give a Shakespearian reading as well as most dramatic artists, and could dance a bit if required.' When he returned to London 'he knew everybody in the artistic, literary and theatrical world, and his Sunday evenings at St John's Wood gathered together the brightest and best of the Bohemians'.[28]

With Archibald's guidance and the confidence that came from seeing his work read by a huge audience, Banjo was on a roll with his writing. Two months into 1887, he had two pieces published on the same day. He penned an acerbic commentary on the way the wealthy racing industry disregarded as mere flotsam the youngsters tasked with trying to hold on to half a tonne of flying horseflesh. He began 'Only a Jockey' with a newswire in which the death of a youngster riding the 1886 Newmarket and Oakleigh Plate winner is seen as being of little consequence relation to that of the health of the horse. Banjo reproduced the brief report above the poem: 'Richard Bennison, a jockey, aged 14, while riding William Tell in his training, was thrown and killed. The horse is luckily uninjured.'[29]

The Australian literary scene was abuzz[30] with the arrival in 1886 of a self-published detective novel, *The Mystery of a Hansom Cab*, by British-born Fergus Hume,[31] a Melbourne barrister's clerk. The novel inspired English doctor Arthur Conan Doyle to create his own detective, Sherlock Holmes, for a novel called 'A Study in Scarlet', a modest performer at the time compared with Hume's international bestseller, the most successful mystery novel of the Victorian era.

Even though Hume gave away the British and American rights to his novel for just £50, he was still making a lot more money from his writing than Banjo Paterson. Banjo's work was appearing regularly in *The Bulletin*, but poets were paid a pittance – Banjo still needed his day job in order to stay afloat.

So he kept on working as a sort of desk-bound debt collector for the big banks. No one was immune from his demands, even the former long-serving premier of New South Wales, Sir John Robertson,[32] an ancient-looking politician with the long white beard of a Biblical prophet. Despite his fame, Robertson could yarn with anyone and was a man after Banjo's heart: thirty-five years earlier he had fathered the *Robertson Land Acts*, which sought to open up Crown land and break the monopoly of the squatters. Like Banjo's father and grandfather, Robertson had also 'had a rough ride over the financial rocks'.[33]

Banjo was asked to write a 'nice firm letter' to the old man demanding payment of an outstanding debt. Robertson was a man of action and strode into the office of Fisher, Ralfe and Salwey to demand satisfaction. He looked around the office through old rheumy eyes and thundered: 'Who's looking after the affairs of this English, Scottish, Continental, Japanese, Australian ... bank?' Banjo nervously replied that he was the man in question. 'Well, you tell them not to write me any more damned silly letters,'[34] he announced before striding out of the office as majestically as his old legs would allow.

Robertson's confederate Sir Henry Parkes[35] – another white-bearded statesman with a mane of silvery hair who had spent years in the premier's chair – was also a frequent visitor to Fisher, Ralfe and Salwey, 'always full of dignity, in a frock coat and a tall hat, to discuss his pecuniary complications'. Banjo remembered seeing him at a dinner when the waiter poured him a glass of champagne and made to move off with the bottle. 'Leave that bottle,' Parkes ordered the waiter, 'I'll finish that and probably another one after it.' Banjo could only wryly observe that Sir Henry always got the temperance vote.[36]

Sir Henry would feature in Banjo's next piece for *The Bulletin*, 'The Deficit Demon',[37] in which he was lampooned as 'Sir 'Enry the Fishfag', while the recently deposed NSW premier Sir Patrick Jennings was 'Sir Patrick the Portly'.

In Banjo's next effort, 'Our Mat', he imagined the stories behind the humble doormats that were being made by prisoners at Darlinghurst Gaol in the shadow of the flogging triangle and the gallows that had recently been used to hang four of the Mount Rennie rapists.[38]

SYDNEY HAD ALL MANNER of distractions for Banjo. Over the years he was a keen rower on the Parramatta River for the Sydney Rowing Club[39] at Abbotsford, across the river from Rockend, and at Balmain[40] closer to the city. His debilitated right arm contributed to him finishing third out of three starters in the Sydney Rowing Club's maiden double sculls of 1884,[41] but he remained a fan of the sport all his life. He was already an amateur jockey of some renown and he rode well with the Sydney Hunt Club. He played tennis at the Hunters Hill Club[42] and earned a reputation for being ambidextrous, often playing left-handed.[43] The sporting newspaper *The Referee* called him a 'front rank player in New South Wales'.

Banjo eventually became treasurer of the Sydney Lawn Tennis Club, locking horns with Phil Sheridan, the secretary at the Sydney Cricket Ground, and Ned Gregory, the ground manager and brother of Handsome Dave, the former Test cricket captain. Both men were against tennis being played on the SCG, with Sheridan calling it a 'sissified game' that wouldn't last a year when the popularity waned. Still, the popularity of tennis shot ahead 'like a bushfire' to the dismay of the diehards. The annual Sydney tournament was played on the turf wicket of the SCG. Banjo reckoned it was a coup, since Ned Gregory 'never took much notice of anyone's opinion but his own'.[44]

THERE WAS A LOT OF HOSTILITY in the air in Sydney during 1887. It was around the fiftieth anniversary of Queen Victoria's reign, during an electric atmosphere of fervent nationalism opposed to rigid conservative forces, that Banjo first crossed paths with Henry Lawson,[45] his great literary rival for the next three decades.

Lawson was a twenty-year-old tortured genius hidden inside an impoverished house painter. He was trying to make a living in the big city while trying to have his voice heard against men and women of much greater learning. He had been born into poverty during a fierce winter on the Emu Creek gold-diggings at Grenfell, 120 kilometres north-west of the Paterson home at Illalong. His father, Niels (Peter) Larsen,[46] was a well-educated Norwegian quartermaster who had jumped ship in Melbourne in 1855 on a fruitless search for gold. Eleven years later at Mudgee, Peter had married the precocious Louisa Albury,[47] a frustrated teenager who had been prevented from taking a teaching job at the local school because she had to care for her younger siblings on the farm. Louisa knew she could do better and chafed at the lot of women denied professional opportunities. The Larsens anglicised their surname to Lawson, and Henry was born in a tent on the goldfields near the Grenfell cemetery at a time when diggers were tunnelling under coffins searching for gold.[48] For six years the family moved around in perpetual disappointment following the gold trail, before settling on a sixteen-hectare selection at Pipeclay,[49] just north of Mudgee. Henry was a lonely child. His father was a talented musician and his mother a great spinner of bush stories, but Peter was often away from home working as Louisa took in sewing, sold dairy produce and fattened cattle. Despite the presence of younger siblings, Henry was introverted and reclusive.[50]

Lawson first attended the bark-slab school at Eurunderee[51] when he was nine, but soon suffered an ear infection that left him with partial deafness. The condition made him even more self-conscious, a situation exacerbated by watching his parents' marriage fall apart. By the age of fourteen he was substantially deaf. He had just three years of schooling all told, but at the Mudgee Catholic school he studied poetry, pored over the novels of Charles Dickens, and devoured *For the Term of His Natural Life* and the serialised *Robbery Under Arms*. From the age of thirteen, Henry worked with his father as a builder around Mudgee and nearby at Rylstone, and then at Mount Victoria in the Blue Mountains. At sixteen, with the Lawsons' marriage having dissolved, Henry joined his mother in Sydney, staying with her and his sister Gertrude and brother Peter in Marrickville, and then in Phillip Street and Clarence Street in the city. He became apprenticed as a coach-painter among a 'rough crowd' at Hudson Bros Ltd at Clyde[52] near Parramatta, and undertook night-class study towards matriculation. But his workmates taunted him and twice he failed the university public examinations. He couldn't hear most of the questions and 'failed in everything, save English history and English composition'. For a time he worked at the Redfern railyards, and one day he painted some beams that he found out had been used on the gallows to hang the Mount Rennie rapists. Lawson always had the longing for 'something better – something higher, something different' but felt 'more or less the hollow hopelessness of attempting to rise higher': 'I was painfully shy and extremely sensitive – sensitive about my deafness, my lack of education, my surroundings, my clothes, slimness, and paleness, my "h's," handwriting, grammar, pronunciation (made worse by deafness) – everything almost. I was terribly shy of strange girls, and if a girl I knew took any notice of me, I would reckon that she was either pitying me or laughing at me.'[53]

As he walked through the early morning darkness to catch the train to work, the faces in the street began to haunt him – the faces, and the 'wretched rag-covered forms on the benches, and under them, and on the grass'. He would look with sympathy at the homeless on rainy mornings sleeping under the verandas around the old Central Markets, and under the eaves of the sheds on Circular Quay. One morning he saw a bundle of old rags and bones 'that had been a woman' struggle up from the wet grass in the park, and 'staggering, try to drink from an empty bottle'. Many times Henry went without work, and he knew what it was like to be down in front of the *Sydney Morning Herald* office at 4 a.m. during bitterly cold winters; to be 'one of the haggard group striking matches' as they ran their eyes down the 'Wanted' columns on the damp sheets posted outside the building. He knew what it was to tramp long distances and be one of a hopeless crowd of job applicants turned away; what it was to drift about the streets in shabby and patched clothes, and feel 'furtive and criminal-like'.[54]

Like Banjo, Lawson wanted to be a regular writer for *The Bulletin*. The hostility surrounding Queen Victoria's jubilee in 1887 presented Lawson with a perfect opportunity to showcase his work.

LAWSON HAD NONE OF THE ADVANTAGES that Banjo enjoyed in Sydney, and he had to scrape and scrap and slave for everything.

Even though Banjo had written the eleven-thousand-word socialist war cry 'Australia for the Australians', and even though his parents had suffered a serious reversal of fortune, Banjo was still a young man leading a privileged life. He had powerful connections, and a grandmother whose home was a meeting place for many of Sydney's rich, famous and influential. He had much greater ambitions than his father, still struggling as a hired hand with a large family at Illalong. Banjo's old school tie was valuable currency: many of his former Grammar schoolmates were making their way in legal circles and willing to give him a leg up. George Rich and Albert Piddington were on their way to becoming High Court judges, and two other school chums, Philip Whistler Street[55] and his older brother John,[56] were rising fast as the latest members of a political and legal dynasty. Their father was a member of the NSW Legislative Assembly, and their late mother[57] a granddaughter of the heroic William Lawson, who had first crossed the Blue Mountains with Blaxland and Wentworth. The Streets lived close to Rockend and also visited Jane Darvall, widow of Banjo's grandfather, at Ryedale.

But Banjo was growing tired of screwing money out of battlers on behalf of big banks. Not all of Henry Salwey's practices were above board, either. He would soon be struck off as a solicitor for fraud and false swearing over a deal for 'certain land situated near Bondi, and known as "Dover Heights"'.[58] So Banjo and John Street got to talking. Maybe someday, the two young lawyers could pool their talents and go into business together.

SYDNEY'S MONARCHISTS SWOONED at the fact that Queen Victoria would be celebrating fifty years of her reign on 20 June 1887. But their festivities were being planned against a backdrop of rising Republican sentiment. The jubilee coincided with the upcoming centenary of the First Fleet bringing European settlers to Australia on 26 January 1788, and *The Bulletin* continued to fan the flames of those who wanted an Australia only for white Australians. The 1880s marked the first time that Australian-born Europeans outnumbered the immigrant population, and the spirit of independence was infectious.

On 3 June 1887, a boisterous public meeting was held at Sydney Town Hall. Mayor A. J. Riley,[59] a wealthy draper, had organised the gathering to discuss ways of celebrating the jubilee. But the meeting was composed largely of people who called themselves democrats and were strongly opposed to any celebration. A plan to stage a feast and fete for children at Sydney's Exhibition Building and grounds in Prince Alfred Park was squashed, and a 'large majority' supported an amendment that declared: 'That, in the opinion of this meeting, the proposal to impress upon the children of the colony the value of the Jubilee year of a Sovereign is unwise and calculated to injure the democratic spirit of the country.' Riley called for three cheers for the Queen, but the only response he received was a few hurrahs, accompanied by hissing and hooting.[60] Humiliated, the mayor called another meeting on 10 June 1887 by invitation only to keep out the Republican riffraff. Special invitation cards were printed, which the naysayers were able to forge. As Premier Henry Parkes watched helplessly from the stage of Sydney Town Hall, the gatecrashers created mayhem and police had to be called in to disperse the crowd.[61]

Henry Lawson was caught up in the Republican movement. His mother, Louisa, had many radical friends and they fired in him a burning pride for Australia. Louisa had seen her poetry, inspired by the death of an infant daughter, published in the *Mudgee Independent*;[62] with the money she had saved from sewing and washing and taking in boarders, she was preparing to print her first issue of a small, struggling newspaper she had purchased called *The Republican*. Louisa surrounded herself with others of a like mind, and Henry would soon help to write and edit the copy. He also sent a poem to *The Bulletin* under the byline 'H.A.L.' – Henry Archibald Lawson. The poem was rough and needed work.

Meanwhile, on 15 June a third meeting about the jubilee was held, this time at the Exhibition Building in Prince Alfred Park. Henry Parkes sought to erase the 'terrible stain'[63] of disloyalty arising from the Town Hall uproar. This time there was a much bigger police presence, and volunteers from the military and local football clubs, as well as a smattering of prizefighters loyal to the Queen who were on hand to deal with troublemakers. Some of them came armed with their overcoats buttoned up to their chins, 'strong sticks in their hands, and slouch hats on their heads'.[64] The public meeting was said to be the largest ever in Sydney, with a crowd of twelve thousand. Among the fifty-two politicians and dignitaries on the platform were Parkes, Mayor Riley and Edmund Barton, who until recently had been Speaker of the NSW Legislative Assembly. Mayor Riley held up a 'vast roll of paper' signed by fifteen thousand people who had declared their loyalty, and Parkes then submitted the resolution to 'remove from the colony the stigma of disloyalty'. The resolution was put to the massive crowd by semaphore and carried, though there were a few hundred dissenters. After the overwhelming vote, the meeting 'became thoroughly disorganised'. The crowd kept being pushed forward onto the platform by those outside trying to get in, and 'a number of exciting hand-to-hand combats took place between the occupants of the platform and those who were endeavouring to get a place on it'.[65]

On 18 June, just three days later, in the 'Correspondence' section of *The Bulletin*, Jules Archibald sent a note to his hopeful recruit: 'H.A.L.: The first four lines are the best. Try again.'[66]

Lawson was painting houses at the time and making ends meet, just, with odd jobs. He remembered trudging home through a storm at Hyde Park near Banjo's old school one night after working late on a job at Paddington. There was rain and wind, and fallen branches and the sickly glow of gaslights on the wet asphalt. There were poles and scaffolding about in preparation for the jubilee celebrations.[67] He thought about the colonies being beholden to a monarch far, far away and started rolling words around in his head for a poem he would call 'Sons of the South', about a brotherhood among the Australian population and a rejection of British rule. He had to write or burst.[68]

Archibald had seized on the discord in Sydney over the jubilee. In his magazine on 2 July 1887, he said the issue was about 'Royalty versus Republicanism':

> Let there be no mistaking the issue! The recent Sydney troubles have been between the people of Australia and Imperial Officialdom; between the Native Australian of Republican instincts

> and tendencies and the imported Royalist. It is the old question of Freetrade versus Protection – Home Rule versus foreign domination, and the traitors to the cause of the colonies have been paid, if not with Imperial gold, with at least Imperial titles.[69]

The magazine saw itself as 'The National Australian newspaper',[70] even though Australia was not yet a nation. It promised to fight for Australians but only those it deemed to be truly Australian – and there were specific guidelines under its scale. In the same issue Archibald defended the change of *The Bulletin*'s banner from 'Australia for Australians' to 'Australia for the White Man'.

> By the term Australian we mean not those who have been merely born in Australia. All white men who come to these shores – with a clean record – and who can leave behind them the memory of the class-distinction and the religious differences of the old world; all men who place the happiness, the prosperity, the advancement of their adopted country before the interests of Imperialism, are Australian. In this regard all men who leave the tyrant-ridden lands of Europe for freedom of speech and right of personal liberty are Australians before they set foot on the ship which brings them hither. Those ... who leave their fatherland because they cannot swallow the worm-eaten lie of the divine right of kings to murder peasants, are Australian by instinct – Australian and Republican are synonymous.[71]

The editorial went on to explain that 'No nigger, no Chinaman, no laksar, no kanaka, no purveyor of cheap coloured labour is an Australian.'[72] So there – that was the mood of the time.

By lamplight Henry wrote down the verses to his Republican call to arms. With a quickening pulse, he took them personally to the *Bulletin*'s office in Pitt Street while on his way home from another house-painting job after dusk. He intended to slip his poem surreptitiously into the letterbox, but a cleaning woman, broom in hand, opened the door suddenly and gave him a start. He thrust 'the screed'[73] into her hand and scurried away.

After his earlier rejections he did not have the courage to go near *The Bulletin* office again, but instead would lie awake at night, and get up very early and slip down to the nearest newsagent to have a peep at the magazine. He rarely had a spare sixpence to buy a copy.

In the issue of 23 July 1887, Archibald ran two lines in the 'Correspondence' column: 'H.A.L. Will publish your "Sons of the South". You have good grit.'[74] In the same issue on the facing page, Archibald ran a Phil May cartoon of a well-to-do black man elegantly dressed in a top hat, tails and cane; the caption read, 'From the Zoo – Things we see when we come out without our gun.'[75]

The *Republican* newspaper allowed Lawson to vent his spleen, calling for Australia to reject 'landlordism, the title worship, the class distinctions and privileges, the oppression of the poor, the monarchy, and all the dust covered customs that England has humped out of the middle ages where she properly belongs'.[76] But *The Bulletin* had a circulation exponentially greater than Mrs Lawson's little journal, despite the passion of mother and son for the cause, and each week Lawson would continue his fruitless missions to see his work in Jules Archibald's magazine until the wasted walks made him 'sick with disappointment'.

Finally, this shy, nervous young man, who only asserted himself through paper and ink, plucked up the courage to climb the same stairs that Banjo had mounted a year before, to knock on the same door which Banjo had tapped. Lawson was invited in to Archibald's office to see a small, intense bespectacled man, copy in one hand, pen in the other, shaping the way thousands of Australians thought.

Archibald seemed surprised to finally meet H.A.L. He encouraged the youngster and told him that the poem was on hold for a special edition. He gave him some writing tips; told him 'not to strain after effect', to 'avoid anti-climax' and to, 'blot out every word you can do without.'[77]

After tinkering with Lawson's copy and changing the title to a more dramatic, more topical 'A Song of the Republic', Archibald ran it in a prominent spot on page five of the 1 October issue. Forget about H.A.L. – the byline was 'Henry Lawson', and though the man himself was self-conscious and skinny and plagued by self-doubt, Lawson's words roared from the pages of the magazine. He no longer had any need to slink in and out of a newsagent's in disappointment.

A SONG OF THE REPUBLIC

Sons of the South, awake! arise!
Sons of the South, and do.
Banish from under your bonny skies
Those old-world errors and wrongs and lies.
Making a hell in a Paradise
That belongs to your sons and you.

Sons of the South, make choice between
(Sons of the South, choose true),
The Land of Morn and the Land of E'en,
The Old Dead Tree and the Young Tree Green,
The Land that belongs to the lord and the Queen,
And the Land that belongs to you.[78]

With that one work, Henry Lawson had arrived as a poet of renown. 'I was in print,' he said, '... in a journal I had worshipped and devoured every inch of for years. I felt strong and proud enough to clean pigsties if need be, for a living for the rest of my natural life – providing the *Bulletin* went on publishing the poetry.'[79] While his regular work involved varnishing an old hearse, *The Bulletin* was breathing life into a great writing career. Lawson needed the money much more than Banjo, and he always remembered receiving his first cheque as a writer – £1 7s – from *The Bulletin*. He was painting at Mount Victoria at the time, earning 8 shillings a day.[80]

Two months later, Archibald ran Henry's 'The Wreck of the Derry Castle' with a commentary that shaved three years off his age but gave him the sort of praise that most aspiring Australian writers could only dream of: 'In publishing the subjoined verses we take pleasure in stating that the writer thereof is a boy of 17 years, a young Australian, who has as yet had an imperfect education and is earning his living under some difficulties as a housepainter, a youth whose poetic genius here speaks eloquently for itself.'[81]

The Bulletin was reaching its peak of popularity. It mounted a campaign to change the celebration of the centenary of the First Fleet's arrival from 26 January to 3 December, the date of the Eureka Stockade rebellion against British authority. 'Australia began her political history as a crouching serf kept in subjection by the whip of a ruffian gaoler,' the magazine roared, 'and her progress, so far, consists merely in a change of masters … the loud-mouthed tyrant has given place to the suave hireling in uniform.'[82] It said that rather than commemorate 'the day we were lagged', the thing to really celebrate was 'the day that Australia set her teeth in the face of the British Lion'.[83] The campaign for a change of date didn't work, but the popularity of the magazine among rural Australia and the working classes continued to rise.

Lawson and Banjo would become the most celebrated of all the writers featured in the magazine over the next century and then some, including C. J. Dennis, Mary Gilmore, Dorothy Mackellar, Ethel Turner, Breaker Morant, Will Ogilvie, Vance Palmer, Steele Rudd, Katherine Susannah Prichard, and more recently future Liberal prime ministers Tony Abbott and Malcolm Turnbull.

The two bush bards saw Australia from different perspectives. The artist Norman Lindsay, who knew them both, said Banjo compacted in himself the best of the Australian ego, the rugged outdoorsman who regarded 'life as a high adventure in action, even to the risk of a broken neck'. Lawson's Australia reflected his own demons, his own sadness 'sodden with self-pity … that of the underdog'.[84]

Over the years, they often yarned about their inspiration. Lawson told Banjo once that 'I can catch ideas anywhere, but I can't always make 'em go in harness. Simple stuff is the best. One day I picked up a pair of pants and found they had a hole in the stern and I wrote, "You've got to face your troubles when your pants begin to go". That hit them where they lived, for most of them had to face their troubles in life.'

Although they were never great friends, Lawson and Banjo knew each other well, and Banjo would even go on to represent Lawson in legal matters, including acting on his behalf in contract negotiations with the publisher Angus & Robertson.[85]

Sitting in his solicitor's office in Sydney, Banjo envied the seemingly free and easy life of the western drovers.

State Library of Victoria H92.160/137

Clancy of the Overflow

I had written him a letter which I had, for want of better
  Knowledge, sent to where I met him down the Lachlan, years ago,
He was shearing when I knew him, so I sent the letter to him,
  Just 'on spec', addressed as follows, 'Clancy, of The Overflow'.

And an answer came directed in a writing unexpected,
  (And I think the same was written with a thumb-nail dipped in tar)
'Twas his shearing mate who wrote it, and verbatim I will quote it:
  'Clancy's gone to Queensland droving, and we don't know where he are.'

In my wild erratic fancy visions come to me of Clancy
  Gone a-droving 'down the Cooper' where the Western drovers go;
As the stock are slowly stringing, Clancy rides behind them singing,
  For the drover's life has pleasures that the townsfolk never know.

And the bush hath friends to meet him, and their kindly voices greet him
  In the murmur of the breezes and the river on its bars,
And he sees the vision splendid of the sunlit plains extended,
  And at night the wond'rous glory of the everlasting stars.

I am sitting in my dingy little office, where a stingy
  Ray of sunlight struggles feebly down between the houses tall,
And the foetid air and gritty of the dusty, dirty city
  Through the open window floating, spreads its foulness over all

And in place of lowing cattle, I can hear the fiendish rattle
  Of the tramways and the 'buses making hurry down the street,
And the language uninviting of the gutter children fighting,
  Comes fitfully and faintly through the ceaseless tramp of feet.

And the hurrying people daunt me, and their pallid faces haunt me
  As they shoulder one another in their rush and nervous haste,
With their eager eyes and greedy, and their stunted forms and weedy,
  For townsfolk have no time to grow, they have no time to waste.

And I somehow rather fancy that I'd like to change with Clancy,
  Like to take a turn at droving where the seasons come and go,
While he faced the round eternal of the cash-book and the journal –
  But I doubt he'd suit the office, Clancy, of 'The Overflow'.

Chapter 9

APRIL 1888, THE DINGY LITTLE OFFICE OF STREET & PATERSON, ATTORNEYS, SOLICITORS AND PROCTORS, 105 PITT STREET, SYDNEY

Clancy of the Overflow ... This ballad had its being from a lawyer's letter which I had to write to a gentleman in the bush who had not paid his debts.

BANJO PATERSON EXPLAINING THE INSPIRATION FOR ONE OF HIS MOST CELEBRATED POEMS[1]

ON 2 APRIL 1888, 24-year-old Banjo Paterson and his former schoolmate John Street announced they had entered into a partnership and would open a legal practice as Street & Paterson at 105 Pitt Street.[2] Soon they were advertising for an office boy[3] and eyeing an even better office in the Waltham Building in Bond Street,[4] a short, narrow street connecting Pitt and George streets. It was close to the *Bulletin* office. Banjo rented a flat at 13 Bond Street, almost opposite his new office, and he decorated it with reminders of his time at Illalong, stuffed birds and Rose's possum-skin rugs.[5]

Street & Paterson set off to chart their own course at a time of stormy waters in the Australian economy. A great depression was just around the corner, as businesses and banks went belly up. Banjo would recall that before long he 'saw bank booms, land booms, silver booms, Northern Territory booms, and they all had one thing in common – they always burst. My partner and I had banked some money for a client in the Bank of New Zealand, and we were told that "she was sure to shut." We shifted the money into another bank and the New Zealand concern weathered the storm, while the bank into which we had put the money folded up like a blanket!'[6]

Business and a busy personal life kept Banjo preoccupied, and he had only two poems published in *The Bulletin* in 1888: the indifferent 'Uncle Bill',[7] and the far more evocative and memorable 'Old Pardon, the Son of Reprieve' about Angel Harrison and his black gelding, which recalled Banjo's trip to the Bogolong bush racetrack as an eight-year-old.

Paterson was a myth-maker, not a historian, and he played with audiences. Sydney journalists who worked with him in later years said his knowledge of the racing industry was 'phenomenal': he could cite the breeding of any horse they nominated going back three generations.[8] The real Reprieve and Pardon were actually sisters.[9] Pardon was best known for winning the 1877 VRC Oaks,[10] while Reprieve went neck and neck with Dagworth in a dead heat for the 1873 AJC Plate over three miles at Randwick.[11] To anyone who knew racing, the story of 'Old Pardon, the Son of Reprieve', had them scratching their heads as to whether the horse was real or imagined. Readers would get to meet owner Angel Harrison again in a few years.

The publication of 'Old Pardon' came in *The Bulletin*'s final, bumper issue of 1888, and as Banjo Paterson readied to enjoy Christmas he had many reasons to be glad. 'Pardon' was the first of the big bush ballads that would become synonymous with his writing, and it appeared as the magazine entered a golden age of popularity and reach.

Banjo had another reason to celebrate. John Street had introduced him to Street's 25-year-old cousin, Sarah Ann Riley,[12] from Melbourne; Street's father's second marriage was to Sarah's aunt.[13] Sarah was the pretty daughter of the elderly James Riley, for many years the inspector of stock in Geelong, and she lived with her parents at their home, Llandillo, in the Melbourne suburb of Moreland. Her father had been in Australia for half a century and was of a 'kindly genial disposition, and made numerous friends'.[14] Two of her brothers[15] had gone to the outback to make their fortune on the land, and they now ran the 100,000-hectare[16] station Vindex near Winton in partnership with a wealthy Melbourne family, the Chirnsides.[17]

Sarah had been a student at the prestigious St Kilda school Oberwyl,[18] which was opened by the Swiss art patron Madame Elise Pfund, the subject of one of Tom Roberts' most celebrated portraits.

The school quickly gained a reputation for its elegance and French culture.[19] At school Sarah's best friend was Christina Macpherson, who as a little girl had been a central figure caught up in the shooting of bushranger Dan Morgan outside Wangaratta. In Sydney, Sarah's charm meant she quickly became firm friends with Banjo's family, especially Mama Barton at Rockend, who reckoned the pretty young lass was quite a catch and that her grandson, as clever as he was, was punching well above his weight.

Mama wrote to Banjo's aunt Nora, then holidaying in Switzerland – as the wives of rich graziers could – that 'Barty's fiancé Sara [sic] Riley has been staying with us, & does credit to his taste; she is an exceptionally nice girl, well connected and well educated. I sometimes wonder that she should not have look'd higher, but his talent goes a long way, and also makes his worldly prospects pretty secure. He is in partnership with a son of our old neighbour John Street, who is a cousin of hers.'[20] Not long after, Banjo wrote:

Oh, I love you, sweet, for your locks of brown
And the blush on your cheek that lies –
But I love you most for the kindly heart
That I see in your sweet blue eyes.
For the eyes are signs of the soul within,
Of the heart that is leal and true,
And mine own sweetheart, I shall love you still,
Just as long as your eyes are blue.[21]

ROSE PATERSON HAD NO OPPORTUNITY to holiday in Switzerland like her rich sister – there was barely enough in the coffers for her and the children to visit Rockend occasionally to see her mother and Banjo. But Banjo's sister Flo was certainly moving up in the world. Her husband Edwin Lumsdaine's legal business was booming, and together they were building a grand waterfront house in Wharf Road, Gladesville. Edwin, a pious man who still yearned to enter the clergy, had a small chapel built within the house, and from the property he and Flo could wave across the water towards Mama at Rockend.[22]

It was a different story for others in Rose's family. On 6 August 1888 she had written to Nora fretting about the prospects of their youngest sister Georgie, who, after years of trying to make a living with her much older husband[23] in Queensland, had moved with him and their children to England. They were met there with a bleak house and a 'miserable screw' of £200 a year 'out of which to find house rent, food and clothing for a year'.[24]

At least the rains had come to Illalong, and everything was tinged with green. 'Three Tasmanian rams are having a stable built for them & even we have had some improvements made in our dwelling house,' Rose said. Her children still at home were blooming, 'especially my blue-eyed Gwendoline, who is my show child'.[25] She assured Nora that both she and Banjo's father were keeping well.

Unfortunately, that was not really true. Rose's eyesight was starting to fail, and Andrew not only was using increasing quantities of laudanum to take the edge off his lumbago but also had recently survived a bout of serious illness.[26]

Mama Barton saw Illalong as a place of deep turmoil and stress. In October 1888, Rose underwent an operation 'necessary to her future well-being',[27] and Mama despaired that her daughter was 'only too impatient to get home again to the worries which are the main cause of all her trouble'. But Andrew was in an even poorer state of health, Mama told Nora in a letter, adding that his 'habits' made his continued employment at Illalong 'a very doubtful affair'.[28] He was drinking heavily now and using even more sedatives.

WHILE SARAH AND BANJO TALKED about marriage, and his future appeared to mirror that of his learned friends with wives, children and well-paid work in the offices and courts of the big city, Banjo was not ready to settle down just yet. He had a lot of work to do and a plan to see as much of Australia as he could. In 1889, while he was working to build up his legal business, he had thirteen poems and a short story published in *The Bulletin*, including some of the best verses of his life.

He also witnessed the birth of 'Australia for the Australians' as a political pamphlet for publishers Gordon & Gotch. In its somewhat dismissive review of Banjo's youthful manifesto, the *Sydney Morning Herald* said 'Mr Paterson' was 'an enthusiast in his subject' and had traced 'most of the social evil and the poverty that exists among us to bad land laws and a free market'.[29]

The Bulletin ran Banjo's 'The Corner Man',[30] about the end singer in 'a nigger minstrel show', in its 26 January 1889 edition. It was followed two weeks later by 'The Sausage Candidate',[31] about a shifty politician rorting his expenses as the NSW colonial election took place.

Soon Banjo was echoing the chagrin of at least one colonial newspaper that the Premier George Dibbs,[32] about to be ousted by Sir Henry Parkes for another term, had appointed eight of his favourites to the NSW Legislative Council. Banjo could only agree with one paper that declared: 'It will only be expressing the opinion of every constitutionalist when we say that the Government have committed a grave blunder – if indeed their action might not be described in stronger-terms – in exercising such powers, when they know that a vote of want-of-confidence is hanging over their heads.' One of the eight was Banjo's second cousin Henry Kater, who had helped him get a start with Herbert Salwey. But the relationship had soured – and Banjo, in all his youthful rage, submitted 'Who is Kater Anyhow?',[33] suggesting his uncle only got the position because he had married Mary Eliza, the daughter of the former premier William Forster. Banjo's father was a harsh critic of the dysfunctional political system of the time, and Banjo's words were weapons. Rather sheepishly, though, Banjo submitted the attack under the byline of John Street's first two initials, 'J. W.'

Why, oh why was Kater lifted
From the darkness, where he drifted
All unknown, and raised to honour,
Side by side with Dick O'Connor,[34]
In the Council, free from row?
Who is Kater, anyhow?

Banjo was already becoming disenchanted with legal work and the confines of cramped city offices, but like his mother he could find wry humour in just about any situation and weave a story around his disappointments. However, there was no bright side to the months ahead.

ANDREW PATERSON HAD BEEN AILING for some considerable time, but on 30 May 1889 he rode off to Burrowa,[35] forty kilometres away, for a day's business. He returned in a distressed state and went straight to bed. Rose had nursed him back to health before, when he had had similar episodes, and did not send for medical help in Yass. A doctor had given Andrew more laudanum for his pain. On 6 June, Andrew felt weak and took some of the laudanum, as was his custom. A sound sleep followed, but his health was much poorer than he or Rose had believed.

With his wife of twenty-five years watching on helplessly, Andrew fell into a comatose state on the morning of 7 June and never woke again. He was just fifty-six, and Rose was now a widow with young children and no home. The top young medical man in Yass, Dr Philip Thornton Thane,[36] was called in to give evidence at an inquest at Illalong the next day and testified that Andrew's heart was 'very much enfeebled', and that he had suffered from 'fatty degeneration of that organ'. The post-mortem decided that the cause of death was an 'overdose of opium (laudanum), the weak state of the septum being accentuated by continued heavy drinking'.[37]

Two days after he died Andrew was buried in the Binalong cemetery. There were dozens of mourners, and the pall-bearers included the postmaster Laurence Dargan. The service was performed by the Reverend Samuel Thornton Dickinson. Andrew's local newspaper paid tribute to a life of hard toil and public service:

> He was a very capable magistrate, and the oldest in the Burrowa district; was the first returning-officer for the Burrowa electorate, and was appointed to a seat on the first Licensing Bench under the Licensing Act, of 1882. Four years ago he was appointed a member of the Local Land Board, which office he continued to hold up to the time of his death, and was held in unqualified confidence and great esteem by all classes. He was well read, and possessed good literary ability. Intelligently observant in politics, he frequently expressed his undisguised contempt of the present abandoned and insipient state of New South Wales politics, and of the screed of politicians who of late years have monopolised the political arena; but no man had greater or more respectful tolerance for the opinions of others, either in religion or politics.[38]

Andrew had worked himself to an early death, beaten down by circumstance and the fickle nature of the seasons and surrounds of rural Australia. Rose had a headstone erected with an engraving of white cedar twigs like the ones from Illalong and a line from the Psalms: 'He giveth his beloved sleep.' She left out the first part of the verse that says it is in vain 'for you to rise up early, to sit up late, to eat the bread of sorrows'.[39] That had been the story of Andrew's life. Banjo and the rest of the Paterson family knew that Andrew had earned his rest.

Rose had lost her soulmate. She had borne Andrew seven children and stayed with him through sickness and health, good seasons and poor. She was starting to suffer from heart palpitations and succumbed to fainting fits. Now there was no way she could stay at her house of the past twenty years, despite having worked around the clock to make it a home. With tears and regret, she packed up her youngest children – Edie, Gracie and Gwen – and, like her mother and sister in their widowhoods before her, moved back to Gladesville. Her youngest son, Hamilton (Boy) Paterson, left school early and soon headed for the goldfields of Coolgardie in Western Australia. Aunt Nora said Rose's illness would cause the postponement of Barty's plans to marry Sarah Riley.[40]

BANJO TOOK A HIATUS from writing to sort out his family's personal affairs. He could see that Rose's health was poor: she was only in her mid-forties but the privations of her life had taken their toll. Mama Barton was now in her early seventies with a full house at Rockend. Banjo eventually found his mother and siblings a cottage nearby and became the breadwinner for them all. The extra money he made writing for *The Bulletin* helped with the costs. He followed Archibald's advice to remember that Australia was a big place.

'Tar and Feathers',[41] which appeared in the magazine in September 1889, is a comic take on a country circus at Narrabri, New South Wales, and was complete with Hop Hopkins illustrations. In the same issue, a few of the pink pages further back, 'How M'Ginnis Went Missing' told the story of a man with a bottle in his hand who disappeared when the mighty Murray was in flood at Tallangatta just over the Victorian border.

The words poured out of Banjo's pen. As he sat in his city office, his thoughts would always drift back to Illalong and the mountains and the rivers beyond, of camping trips along the Murrumbidgee, of riding with his father in places where there was no noise of traffic and no foul factory smells.

Not that the bush was a paradise. 'Hughey's Dog' was a grotesque short story about the brutality of station life with butchered sheep and a mad Dutch cook – 'a half-witted chap who occasionally went religion-mad' – who feared that as 'soon as dem stars gets togedder de vorld vill be purnt up'.[42] The mad Dutchman takes his revenge on a dog that bites him, before going off to 'preach to the beeples'.[43]

Then, the galloping doggerel of 'Mulligan's Mare',[44] which ran next to *The Bulletin*'s advertisements for Josephson's Ointment and Anglo Scandinavian Condensed Milk, offered sage advice for racegoers:

> And whether you're lucky or whether you lose,
> Keep clear of the cards and keep clear of the booze,
> And fortune in season will answer your prayer
> And send you a flyer like Mulligan's mare.[45]

Banjo was saving his best for last, though, and Archibald decided to showcase his emerging 'twin deities of Australian literature'[46] in the Christmas issue of the magazine on 21 December 1889. He ran two of Henry Lawson's poems, 'The Roaring Days'[47] and 'The Legend of Mammon Castle',[48] on the same day as *Australian Town and Country Journal* ran three others: 'The Teams',[49] 'Brighten's Sister-in-Law'[50] and 'Mount Bukaroo'.[51]

Archibald featured four pieces by Banjo. 'An Idyll of Dandaloo'[52] is another fast-paced romp, continuing Banjo's theme of shenanigans at country race meetings like Bogolong. 'The Scapegoat',[53] which took out all of page fifteen, was lavishly illustrated with Hop's pen. It pokes fun at Judeo-Christian religious customs, in the manner of Lord Byron's 'Don Juan', and was sensationally provocative in conservative times.

Banjo explained that the Jews were instructed to find a sacrificial goat, confess their sins on it and lead it into the wilderness to die of thirst as an atonement for the collective wrongs of the people. Except the goat of this poem unrepentantly doubles back and causes mayhem for his tormentors.

'Song of the Future'[54] is a naive hymn to a better and fairer land – despite the fact it was appearing in *The Bulletin*'s pages, which screamed of overt racism and mocked just about anyone who wasn't white Anglo-Saxon.

Tucked away on page seventeen of that Christmas 1889 issue was Banjo's last poem for the year. It appeared almost as an afterthought, buried under an illustrated short story by Francis Adams[55] called 'Flowers for the Dead'. But Banjo's poem is immediately arresting from the fast tempo of its opening lines, which bound along with the infectious rhythm of a cantering horse. It celebrates the great Australian outdoors and the fortunate few who rode the wide open spaces; who lived for the free life, bolstered by the bush air and the sunshine. Those lucky ones who were done with the boss and the balance sheet.[56]

The poem had its genesis in a letter of demand from Street & Paterson to a drover Banjo had met down in the Lachlan River area some years earlier. The letter was sent from a dusty, dingy office in a noisy, crowded city to a man unfettered by the bonds of urban life. One of the drover's mates sent a letter back with handwriting so appalling it looked as if it had been composed with a thumbnail dipped in tar. The drover's mate told the big city lawyers that the man in question had gone to Queensland droving, 'and we don't know where he *are*'. Banjo was hooked by the fractured grammar and the idea of a man roaming free, unconcerned about what was happening in the offices being choked by foetid air.

'So there it was,' Banjo recalled fondly, 'the idea, the suggestion of the drover's life, the metre, and the exact words for a couple of lines of verse, all delivered by Her Majesty's mail at a cost of a postage stamp.'[57]

Banjo was always modest and even self-deprecating about his writing ability. When suggestions were made about how Rudyard Kipling and Adam Lindsay Gordon had found their inspiration, he replied that 'lacking the ability to write anything like either of those masters, I had to imitate the gentleman who was sentenced to ten years' hard labour and told the Judge that he would never live to do it: whereupon his Honor very kindly told him, "Do as much of it as you can." I had to write what I could. I never aimed very high; in fact, I never "aimed" anywhere, but just wrote of the little things I knew about.'[58] Banjo had received in the mail a hook on which to hang not just the best verses he had composed to that point, but also perhaps his most beautiful and evocative homage to the land he loved. He poured his heart into every line of his ode to the Australian bush and its bushmen.

BANJO EARNED JUST 13 shillings and sixpence[59] for 'Clancy of the Overflow',[60] but it soon became a priceless treasure of Australian literature. More than anyone before him, Banjo had made the Australian stockman and drover – the equivalent of the American wild west cowboy – a hero for all Australians: a laconic, free spirit who lived a romantic life, beholden to nothing except the natural world around him. It was an unrealistic vision in so many ways. Banjo, and more so his father, had known just how tough life was in the great Australian outdoors – but every day that Banjo and thousands of city workers like him turned up in their offices, the 'vision splendid of the sunlit plains extended' was a shining hope for something better than their world.[61]

The poem won immediate praise. In his literary column in the Melbourne-based newspaper *The Australasian,* Rolf Boldrewood wrote in an article titled 'Old Stockriders': 'I may stop here to state that "Clancy of the Overflow," quoted by a writer who signs himself "Banjo," which appeared lately, is, in my opinion, the best bush-ballad since [Adam Lindsay] Gordon. It has the true ring of spur and snaffle, combined with poetic treatment – a conjunction not so easy of attainment as might be supposed.'[62] A month later, Archibald replied in *The Bulletin*: 'We have – much pleasure in informing Mr. "Boldrewood" that "Clancy of the Overflow" was not merely "quoted" but was originally written by "The Banjo" (a modest young man of Sydney) and author, by the way, of "Old Pardon, the Son of Reprieve" for [the] last Christmas number of *The Bulletin*.'[63]

'Clancy' and 'Old Pardon' were included, along with Henry Lawson's 'Faces in the Street' and 'His Father's Mate', in a *Bulletin* compendium, 'Golden Shanty – a collection of Australian stories and sketches in prose and verse',[64] to celebrate the magazine's tenth birthday. The Sydney *Daily Telegraph*'s reviewer said 'Old Pardon' was a 'swinging horse-ballad and that the same poet, who uses the singular pseudonym "The Banjo" in "Clancy of the Overflow" has, however, touched an infinitely higher note and produced a poem which breathes the very spirit of the happy vagabondage of a drover's life at its freest and happiest'.[65]

Banjo always maintained that Clancy was based on a composite of characters he had met throughout his twenty-four years; he stipulated that the 'Overflow' was not intended to refer to any particular run and was just used 'as a typical name'.[66] Yet within a few years of the poem appearing, Irish-born Thomas Gerald Clancy,[67] who called himself a 'bottle-stopper' from County Cork, claimed that he was the 'party'[68] Banjo had used as the subject. He even had a will signed by A. B. Paterson, solicitor.[69]

In 1910, Thomas Clancy was living in Melbourne's North Carlton when he told the *Advocate* newspaper that he had been born in 1835 and arrived in Melbourne as a six-year-old. He remembered Elizabeth Street as a broken gully where bullock teams were often bogged, and he had celebrated mass in a stonemasons shed as the St Francis's church was being built. He went to work as a newsboy on Melbourne's first paper, John Fawkner's *Patriot*,[70] and then became a shepherd at a boiling-down works on the Yarra.[71] He said he was among the crowd that farewelled Burke and Wills when they left on their ill-fated expedition into the interior.[72] He worked on properties across eastern Australia and kept extensive diaries of his travels when he would move huge mobs of cattle or sheep, numbering up to fifteen thousand at a time. His entry for 29 September 1882 places him with a mob of sheep on the Lachlan River, where the narrator of 'Clancy of the Overflow' says he knew Clancy 'years ago'.[73]

He was in Rockhampton with his family early in 1898, planning to join the Klondike gold rush in Alaska, when he got yarning in a pub with J. D. Gillespie, the shorthand instructor at the local technical college. They got to talking about the name 'Clancy', and old Tom told Gillespie about how he was the subject of the poem – and that he, in fact, had written a response to Banjo in verse. He recited it to Gillespie, who wrote it down in shorthand.

Clancy never made it to the Klondike. He and his family moved to Gippsland instead, but on the way he stopped in Sydney to meet Banjo for the first time and to have his will signed. Eight years later – after having lost all trace of Mr Clancy and wondering whether he was still in the land of the living – J. D. Gillespie sent Clancy's verses to a Sydney newspaper.

Speaking in 1910, Thomas Clancy reckoned the reply to Banjo that first appeared in *Freeman's Journal* was a more accurate reflection of the bush life he knew. It contained these verses:

Tired of life upon the stations,
With their wretched, scanty rations,
I took a sudden notion
That a droving I would go;
Then a roving fancy took me,
Which has never since forsook me,
And decided me to travel,
And leave the Overflow.

And my path I've often wended
Over drought-scourged plains extended,
where phantom lakes and forests
Forever come and go;
And the stock in hundreds dying,
Along the road are lying,
To count among the 'pleasures'
That townsfolk never know[74]

But old Tom Clancy had company in the race to claim he was the subject of the famous verses. In 1949 when the noted journalist A. H. Chisholm[75] was compiling a new edition of the *Australian Encyclopaedia* for Angus & Robertson, he was swamped by phone calls and letters from other men claiming to be the singing drover. 'Another big section of opinion held that Clancy was Thomas Michael [Macnamara], who was born at Tumut, but best known in the Wagga district. He also was droving all over the middle of the State. He had a brother-in-law, Jim Troy, who, the [Macnamara] protagonists claimed, was the original of Paterson's "Man From Snowy River".'[76]

Callers identified three Overflow stations. One was on the Barcoo River in Central Queensland, and two others were in Central New South Wales, one near the town of Nymagee and the other near Warren. Tom Clancy said he knew the Overflow station near Nymagee well; he had never actually worked there, but had been on a neighbouring property and said he had once had the job of droving a 'tremendous herd' from the Overflow.[77] His brother John Clancy, who spent most of his life as a teacher, did work at the Overflow, though, and his descendants have long claimed that *he* was really the model for Paterson's character. John is said to have always carried a copy of Banjo's poem in his pocket, as though that somehow proved the point.[78] John's grandson, the Reverend Eric Clancy, wrote to Paterson in 1934 to seek evidence for his relative's role in the Australian classic, but he received a handwritten letter from Banjo on an Australian Club letterhead that said, 'The character of Clancy was a type and not an individual.'[79]

Through 1888 and 1889, Street & Paterson defended clients being pursued for money through court action,[80] but Banjo saw in Clancy the archetype of a man who was free to enjoy the great outdoors in all its splendour. Perhaps Banjo was also writing of his own dearly departed father, lying in the little Binalong bush cemetery at the opposite end of town to Johnny Gilbert's grave in the old police paddock. Andrew Paterson had waged a lifelong battle to make a go of things in the country, even when it might have been far easier for him to create a life in the city among the hurrying people.

After all, the drover's life had pleasures that the townsfolk never knew.

Chapter 10

LATE IN 1889, TOM GROGGIN STATION, NEAR CORRYONG IN THE FOOTHILLS OF THE SNOWY MOUNTAINS

To make any sort of job of it I had to create a character, to imagine a man who would ride better than anybody else, and where would he come from except from the Snowy? And what sort of horse would he ride except a half thoroughbred mountain pony?

BANJO PATERSON EXPLAINING THE ORIGINS OF HIS POEM 'THE MAN FROM SNOWY RIVER'[1]

AS BANJO AND HIS FAMILY enjoyed the enthusiastic reception and critical acclaim bestowed on 'Clancy', the artist Tom Roberts was putting the finishing touches on what would become another iconic showpiece of Australian rustic life. Like the verses of 'Clancy', Roberts' painting *Shearing the Rams* displays manly Australian rural workers in their heroic glow. They are sweating away in rolled-up shirtsleeves in a timber shed, as they go to work with blade shears producing Australia's most important export, wool. The painting celebrates the long hours of toil in remote areas that helped to expand the nation's wealth.

Roberts modelled his painting on a shearing shed at the 24,000-hectare Brocklesby sheep station near Corowa, in the Riverina area of New South Wales, which he had first visited to attend a family wedding. He spent two years there capturing the light and the atmosphere, committing the hard toil of bush life to oil and canvas at a time when shearers were Australian folk heroes.

Like Banjo's 'Clancy of the Overflow', *Shearing the Rams* looks at bush life through a rose-tinted lens. It conveniently ignores the powder keg of tension rumbling between the shearers and the wealthy station owners, who were trying to slash their pay and sully their working conditions. The Australasian Shearers' Union had been formed at Fern's Hotel in Ballarat in 1886,[2] and the Queensland Shearers' Union was established in Blackall the next year.[3] Soon those unions claimed to represent thirty thousand[4] men standing up for a fairer go against the money and power of the pastoralists, who were forming their own organisation for a looming fight. At the annual conference of the Australian Shearers' Union in Bourke, New South Wales, in February 1890, members resolved not to work alongside non-union shearers.[5] By May 1890, when Roberts unveiled *Shearing the Rams* at his studio in the Grosvenor Chambers on Melbourne's Collins Street, shearers were walking off the job at Jondaryan near Oakey on Queensland's Darling Downs,[6] while wharf labourers in Rockhampton were refusing to load bales of wool that had been shorn by non-union 'scab' labour.[7]

Shearing the Rams was painted during a great wave of nationalistic art produced by the emerging Heidelberg School, formed by Roberts and a group of Melbourne-based impressionists who depicted rural life and the bush, glorifying Australia and promoting a sense of nationalism for the colonies in a way that could have been orchestrated by J. F. Archibald. Frederick McCubbin had just finished *Down on His Luck*, which depicts a dejected swagman sitting by a campfire wondering where it all went wrong. Arthur Streeton's *The Selector's Hut (Whelan on the Log)* depicts the noble pioneer spirit of a selector resting from his labours in front of the type of rough bush shelter that was home to Banjo early in his life. The penniless artist Charles Conder had caught syphilis from his landlady while paying his rent with sexual favours, but in the meantime had painted *Under the Southern Sun*, illustrating the scorching sunlight and desolation of an Australian drought.

At the same time that Roberts displayed his great work for the first time in Melbourne, Banjo had just finished another of his masterpieces.

A free, compulsory and secular education in all the colonies brought more readers for the emerging stable of Australian writers being promoted through *The Bulletin.* That educated audience was thirsting for stories about their surroundings and their homegrown heroes. Soon the bushman replaced the goldfields digger as the natural cultural hero, the model for the Australian attitude to life. Everything Australian suddenly became worth writing about: the slums, the outback, the diggings, the seaside, the selections, the stock routes, the wheat fields. In place of English fields and their daffodils, Australian writers now set their laconic heroes and anecdotes against a backdrop of droughts and floods, dry creek beds and raging mountain torrents, and that seemingly limitless blue canvas that stretched across the sky. Castles and fortresses and old London town gave way to the shearing sheds and the stations and the outback homesteads as the setting for Australia's most cherished literature. The bush ballad, heir to the bush songs Banjo had listened to around the woodheap at Illalong, was coming into its inheritance.

Good-tempered humour and loyal mateship, the qualities with which Rose Paterson had infused her son, were being woven into the fabric of the Australian ethos. With the death of his father, holidays at Illalong were now a thing of the past for Banjo, but his love for the bush lived on and he hungered to see as much of it as he could. Marriage to Sarah Riley would have to wait.

IN HIS SUMMER VACATION OF 1889, Banjo shook off the shackles of city life to stay with wealthy friends Peter[8] and Walter[9] Mitchell on their property, Bringenbrong Station, in the high country that borders the Murray River. Their father, Tom Mitchell,[10] had first come to the Snowy Mountains in 1845,[11] and the brothers had inherited Bringenbrong and the nearby stations that their father had acquired. They had built strong reputations throughout Australia for the breeding of fat black Aberdeen cattle and thoroughbred horses,[12] and they would go on to breed the racehorse Trafalgar, winner of the Sydney Cup.[13] Bringenbrong Station became one of the finest properties in New South Wales, and the mountain country around it was an untamed frontier that was always spectacular, always dangerous.

Banjo remembered that Bringenbrong was within a day and a half's ride of the summit of Kosciuszko, Australia's highest mountain, and the brothers often made camping trips there with packhorses. The journey started down in the Murray Valley: 'where the melted snow water ran clear over beds of sparkling pebbles. On the trip up, through the Murray Gates, the Leatherbarrel, and Tom Groggin, tourist traffic was so infrequent that the wallaroos would sit on the rocks and hardly bother to get out of the road as the cavalcade went by. Dingoes followed the expedition for miles, possibly hoping that something edible would be dropped from the pack-horses; and lyre-birds were as thick as fowls in a barnyard.'[14]

The Mitchell brothers seemed as impressive as the countryside, and Banjo was taken with not only their ideas about improving their thoroughbred horses, a subject close to his heart, but also their dream of bettering the physique of the human race. Banjo remembered Peter Mitchell as a man who had been in the bush all his life and had 'thought out a lot of things for himself, as bushmen do … He told me one day he had a scheme for improving the breed of Australia. He said you can improve horses and cattle: why should not you improve men.'[15] Thirty years later Peter left £178,478 in his will for the establishment of various self-improvement competitions to enhance the strength of the white race[16] because 'he was always keenly interested in the development of a vigorous manhood' as a way of alleviating 'the aggregate of human misery and suffering around the globe'.[17]

The Mitchells invited Banjo to Bringenbrong to show him the magnificent ride to the roof of Australia where even in summer there was often a carpet of snow. Up there among an other-worldly windswept landscape dominated by jagged peaks, Banjo could imagine wild horses charging around, nostrils flared, manes swaying in the cold wind. He could visualise the horses plunging down terrible descents and then bolting up the side of what looked like rugged battlements, racing over rocks and then, with a thunder of hoofs, bursting through the clouds of fog that cover the high country with a ghostly translucence.

As their horses carefully paced towards the 2228-metre summit of Kosciuszko, the wealthy brothers told Banjo about the loner who was the overseer on Tom Groggin Station,[18] an aloof and abrupt little mountain man, wiry as a jockey, with a white spade beard. He lived alone in a remote hut made of logs and slabs with a shingle roof. The rough shelter was shrouded in snow for half the year, and its occupant only ventured down from the high places with a packhorse now and then to gather supplies that would sustain him for weeks. He would ride into Corryong on the Victorian side of the Murray or Khancoban on the NSW side and often stop for a whisky or three since he was fond of a drink. He was a local legend after a ride down treacherous ravines and mountain sides that made veteran mountain horsemen shudder.

His name was Jack Riley.[19] He was closing in on his fiftieth birthday, and he had been in Australia for thirty-five years, arriving from Ireland as an illiterate teenager whose parents were both dead. It was said that he had spent most of his life in the high country after coming first to Omeo in search of gold. For a time he lived with his sister Ann and her husband Joseph Jones, a shepherd, who once beat a charge of threatening to kill her,[20] was fined for assaulting her and fined for not sending their three children to school.[21] The story around the high country was that Jack had set up shop as a tailor on the diggings opposite Omeo's Golden Age Hotel[22] before moving on to the mountain diggings across the NSW border at Kiandra.[23] There were also stories that his prospecting had been interrupted by a two-year stretch in Parramatta Gaol for horse stealing, but that Jack had taken the blame for a wayward brother-in-law.[24] Jack had returned to the mountains as a brumby hunter and horsebreaker,[25] and five years before Banjo's holiday to climb Kosciuszko, Jack had become the overseer at the 8000-hectare Tom Groggin for the owner John Pierce.[26] Over the summer months he would keep the cattle fed on the high-country grass and herbs, and then drive them down the mountains to the warmer paddocks before winter set in. Almost the whole time, he lived alone and saw few visitors. To the Mitchell brothers, Jack Riley's reputation was almost mythical, such was the fantastic story of the wild ride he'd made to capture a valuable stallion that had joined the wild bush horses. It was said that as a small man he was like a feather on horseback, and John Pierce called him the best bush rider he ever saw.[27]

Banjo and the Mitchells arrived at Riley's remote cabin beside the Snowy River, surrounded by steep precipices on all sides. They took a bottle of whisky with them into the primitive structure, and by the flickering light of the cooking fire, as the contents of the bottle disappeared, the white-bearded Riley told them about his wild rides.[28]

The countryside of this land beside the Snowy River was nothing like the boggy green expanse of County Mayo that Riley had known as a child. In fact, Banjo thought the hills of the Snowy region were twice as steep and twice as rough as anywhere else in Australia, the surface so rocky that the horses' hoofs struck firelight with every stride. The mountain sides were treacherous and dangerous. Any slip was death.

'See here, now,' Riley said, for he always prefaced any statement with that phrase.[29] He told his visitors how a few years earlier he had joined a party of stockmen trying to recapture a thoroughbred stallion that had joined a wild mob of horses.

It had happened on the Leatherbarrel Mountain, on the track to Kosciuszko from Tom Groggin. The horse had defeated every attempt to catch him, although all of the other horses in the mob had been rounded up. The horse had become something of a legend, 'as elusive as smoke, as defiant as lightning'.[30] His capture became a matter of pride, 'a needed balm' for the local stockmen who felt humiliated at being outwitted and outrun by a rival with more legs and more smarts than the human pursuers. A council of war was held, and a campaign devised to trap the outlaw horse. The men built a yard across tracks near a creek that the horse habitually crossed. The riders tracked their magnificent prey to high on a ridge. They spread out with a plan to swoop upon him from many angles and chase him into their makeshift stockyard. But the chase had only just begun. The great racehorse surveyed his attackers one by one, then – like a Melbourne Cup favourite – he broke into a furious gallop and hurtled down a perilous slope that no rider had ever braved.

He flashed down the cliff face in an instant and weaved through the thick timber and the scrub, dodging the wombat holes, wild scrub and loose shale. But Jack Riley pulled his hat over his ears, and with a wild yell charged after the outlaw while his friends gasped for breath. Riley vanished from sight in a flurry of heels and a shower of dirt.

Hardly one of his comrades expected him to survive. Forlornly, they made their way down the steep slopes to the trapyard across the creek trail. When they arrived on their horses, the riders sat slack-jawed with amazement.

There before them in the pen was the runaway racehorse, foaming with sweat and short of breath. Jack Riley was trotting back up the slope to meet his friends. The lash of the branches, the menace of boulders, the clawing brush had threatened to kill him at any moment of his chase, but he told his mates that he had loved every moment of the desperate ride.

'See here, now,' Riley said, 'I went so fast down the slope the wind got in me eyes and the tears blinded me.'[31] Unable to see, he had galloped full blast straight past the yard into which his quarry had careered headlong, and he was unaware of the capture until his breeze-tortured eyes had cleared.

Other locals remembered the tale of Riley, on a bald-faced bay, chasing station horses that had 'gone wild' through venomous scrub country littered with fallen timber. He followed the escapees like a bloodhound and ran them single-handed till they were cowed and beaten. When John Pierce and the other Groggin stockmen arrived on the scene, they found that Riley's legs were covered with blood. But it was the bay horse, not Riley, that had a piece of timber protruding from its shoulder. 'See here, now,' said Riley, examining the injury, 'I was wondering what made her falter as we came through the timber patch up there ...'[32]

AFTER SPENDING A NIGHT at Jack Riley's hut, Banjo and the Mitchell brothers rode on higher the next day, passing through the low-hanging clouds that wafted around Kosciuszko. They stopped with their horses at the summit to survey the panorama of the rocky peaks and the Snowy River below. Then they returned to Tom Groggin via Mount Pilot, and headed back to Bringenbrong.

When Banjo came home to Sydney, he had enough material for a ballad that would outlive him, his children and his grandchildren.

Henry Lawson's growing reputation as a short-story writer inspired Banjo to replicate the form. Just two weeks after 'Clancy of the Overflow' appeared, *The Bulletin* ran Banjo's comic tale of how he accidentally shot a short, fat, squat, bald-headed police officer 'with a keen instinct for whisky, and an unlimited capacity for taking things "easy"; he would have been a tall man had Providence not turned round so much of his legs to make his feet'.[33] Banjo's 'How I Shot the Policeman' had echoes of Edward Dyson's 'The Tiredest

Man',[34] another poem about a policeman that had run in *The Bulletin* two weeks earlier and dealt with a man whose 'chronic weariness' was his 'strongest characteristic': '… for 20-odd years he fluttered feebly about his beat, dragging his feet after him with a painful effort, lurking in the shadows hooked to convenient projections, sleeping in unfrequented places, leaning hopelessly in out of the way corners and hanging dejectedly over railings and horse-troughs, and growing more and more fatigued as the years rolled by'.

Then, on 22 March 1890, Banjo's 'Our New Horse' had its first run. It was another Banjo bush farce about some likely lads on a station passing off a dud racehorse to a city buyer, only to have an unsuspecting agent buy the nag back on their behalf for 50 quid more than they'd received:

And life has grown dull on the station,
The boys are all silent and slow;
Their work is a daily vexation,
And sport is unknown to them now.
Whenever they think how they stranded,
They squeal just like guinea-pigs squeal;
They bit their own hook, and were landed
With fifty pounds loss on the deal.[35]

But that horse ballad was just an entree for Banjo's big hit of 1890. From his trip to the snow country, he fashioned a story to 'describe the cleaning-up of the wild horses'[36] around Illalong when he was a boy. Banjo reckoned that conditions around Binalong were 'rough enough for most people, but not nearly as rough as they had it on the Snowy'.[37] With his idea for a great horse ballad in mind, Banjo had searched for a hero. Based on the stories he had heard at Jack Riley's hut and around the campfires on various trips, he created a character that typified the brave Australian battler taking on the elements, the lone horseman standing up to everything that nature and fear could throw at him.

At Rockend at night, listening to the stories his mother and grandmother told about their lives in remote corners of the colony, Banjo wrote his great ballad with the galloping rhythm of alternating lines of seven and five iambic feet. He told the story of a valuable racehorse, foaled by the broodmare Regret, which had bolted from the station to join a mob of wild brumbies. All the best riders of the district had come together to bring it home, including two of Banjo's characters from previous works: Clancy of the Overflow and the white-haired Angel Harrison, introduced two years earlier in 'Old Pardon, the Son of Reprieve'. Even though Clancy had learnt to ride while droving on the flat country, 'no better rider ever held the reins';[38] he was up for the challenge in the steep hills and deadly ravines. But the hero of this poem would be 'a stripling on a small and weedy beast',[39] a character very similar to a younger version of the jockey-sized Jack Riley. The stripling was riding a galloper 'like a racehorse undersized, with a touch of Timor pony'. Banjo knew Timor ponies well; he had ridden one to school at Illalong every morning and recalled that in the Yass district, 'a gentleman had a stud of Timor ponies, beautiful little animals, and when the diggings broke out in Victoria he took the whole lot over and sold them to the diggers at big prices. The diggers used them for racing, but great numbers of them got away and made their way home again to their native district, where they ran wild. These ponies and their descendants were well worth yarding, but they had such speed and endurance that any man who could yard them thoroughly earned his reward.'[40]

Banjo's new poem was a tale of cracking stockwhips and daring swoops through deep, dark gorges, the noise of thundering hoofs echoing across cliffs and crags as the wild horses and their pursuers raced upward until the hunted were totally spent and the young stripling's pony was ' blood from hip to shoulder from the spur'.[41]

And he ran them single-handed till their sides were white with foam.
He followed like a bloodhound on their track,
Till they halted cowed and beaten, then he turned their heads for home,
And alone and unassisted brought them back.[42]

To Paterson, the rider who got through the chase from end to end was a hero, as was his horse.[43]

'The Man from Snowy River' appeared on page thirteen of the 26 April 1890 issue of *The Bulletin* above an advertisement for 'Scott's Emulsion of Cod Liver Oil'. Banjo would make some subtle changes to his work over the next few years as he tinkered with the rhythm, but the death-defying charge at the poem's heart remains the same, and the courage, horsemanship and doggedness of the stripling as he hurtled down the mountain side 'while the others stood and watched in very fear' was a key in the development of a national ethos. Not only was *The Bulletin* a champion for the little Aussie battler, but at the same time Banjo had created a hero for every Australian underdog striving to prove themselves – and for a collection of colonies eager to impress the world.

Banjo knew he was making a myth, and he knew that parts of the ballad didn't ring true, but it didn't matter. This was a piece of impressionism, just like *Shearing the Rams.* The real mare Regret had never given birth to a colt, as Banjo knew all too well. It was, as one critic observed, as though he was telling anyone who knew the Australian Stud Book that the poem was pure make-believe.[44] Even if a colt 'got' away from a mountain station, Banjo knew it was unlikely to join a mob of wild horses, since wild stallions were prone to kill any perceived threats around their mares.[45] And the prospect of the exhausted horses turning their docile heads for home with just one man controlling them doesn't ring true; they were always herded into yards in pincer movements. In a piece for the *Sydney Morning Herald*, Banjo explained the real nature of yarding wild horses: stockmen tried to wheel them away from the rocky places into more open country, or else rush them into a trapyard.

> The wild horses are a great nuisance to stock owners, because valuable animals constantly stray away and join them, and nothing but desperate riding and great good fortune will get them back. Very often the owner sells his right, title, and interest in an escaped animal for a few pounds, and the buyer will probably break down three or four good horses trying to yard his purchase. Sometimes a reward is offered, and then all the young colonials in the district will be after the mob, in season and out of season, riding their horses' heads off, their only tactics being to 'go at them from the jump', and try and run them down. This is very good fun while it lasts; but the usual result is that, after a desperately run ten miles or so across rough country, the pursuer's horse knocks up, and he has to walk home and carry his saddle. Sometimes, by a dashing

> bit of riding, he may 'cut out' the horse he wants from the mob, or fate may kindly enable him to wheel the whole lot into the jaws of a trap yard, in which case he fills the whole district with his brag for months to come. But to 'run horses' properly four or five splendidly mounted men are required; they must know the country well, and must know in what direction the mob will run, and when to let them go and when to wheel them ...[46]

Despite the rollicking nature of 'The Man from Snowy River', the poem created little attention in the middle of 1890. Banjo remained a 'modest'[47] and anonymous young solicitor, better known for his tennis prowess than his poems. A couple of weeks after *The Bulletin* ran 'The Man from Snowy River', he was running opponents ragged in the Intercolonial Lawn Tennis Tournament on the grass of what would become the Sydney Cricket Ground.[48]

It was not yet in Banjo's professional interest to show himself as the author of *The Bulletin*'s work, given the fact he was still making his way in a very conservative profession while writing for a radical publication. Not that he had any great love for legal work, as he showed in his next poem for *The Bulletin*, 'The Hypnotist':

> 'I am a barrister, wigged and gowned;
> Of stately presence and look profound.
> Listen awhile till I show you round.
> When courts are sitting and work is flush
> I hurry about in a frantic rush.
> I take your brief and I look to see
> That the same is marked with a thumping fee;
> But just as your case is drawing near
> I bob serenely and disappear.
> And away in another court I lurk
> While a junior barrister does your work;
> And I ask my fee with a courtly grace,
> Although I never came near the case.
> The loss means ruin to you, maybe,
> But nevertheless I must have my fee!
> For the lawyer laughs in his cruel sport
> While his clients march to the Bankrupt Court.'[49]

Banjo stuck another barb firmly into greedy lawyers with his next work, 'Gilhooley's Estate',[50] in which a high-priced wigged barrister is called in despite Gilhooley's widow declaring:

'My childer have little to ait:
Just keep the expenses as low as you can'.

From the Barristers' Court there's a mighty hurrah
Arises both early and late:
It's only the whoop of the Junior Bar
Dividing Gilhooley's Estate.[51]

WHILE BANJO WAS COMPOSING ODES to the country he loved, parts of it were beginning to disintegrate. The unrest in the shearing sheds and on the loading docks was being mirrored in the coalmines. A detachment of eighty-six soldiers from the permanent artillery and seventy-five police had been needed to break up rioters at the New Lambton Colliery in Newcastle on 18 September 1888.[52] More soldiers were needed a week later to protect labourers called in to work the nearby West Wallsend Colliery after miners downed tools.[53]

Two years later, an Australia-wide strike led by the Mercantile Marine Officers' Association involved 28,500 seamen as well as wharf labourers, gas stockers and coalminers who refused to dig coal for non-union-operated vessels. In Melbourne, on 30 August 1890 – a week after *The Bulletin* ran 'Gilhooley's Estate' – Lieutenant-Colonel Tom Price told his men of the Victorian Mounted Rifles how to deal with crowd unrest at a public meeting in Flinders Park scheduled to host fifty thousand[54] strike supporters the next night. 'You will each be supplied with forty rounds of ammunition, leaden bullets,' he said, 'and if the order is given to fire, don't let me see any rifle pointed in the air; fire low and lay them out so that the duty will not have to be performed again.'[55] Mercifully the ammunition was not used. The platform for the speakers at the strike rally was decorated with a copy of the Eureka Flag that the Ballarat miners had used in their brief bloody battle with police and troopers in 1854.

Banjo celebrated a more convivial Australia with 'Those Names';[56] he created a comical scene as 'shearers sat in the firelight, hearty and hale and strong', yarning and telling tall tales – with the ringer (the champion shearer of the shed), the novice, the tarboy (who was responsible for applying antiseptic tar to the wounds of sheep cut in the shearing process), the cook and his assistant, the 'slushy', the sweeper (who swept the board), the picker-up (who collected the fleece from the shearing-shed floor) and the penner (whose job was to keep the sheep pens full for the shearers). They got to recalling exotic place names they'd encountered: Adjintoothbong, Nimitybelle, Conargo, Wheeo, Bongongolong …

> Then the shearers all sat silent till a man in the corner rose;
> Said he, 'I've travelled a-plenty but never heard names like those.
> Out in the western districts, out on the Castlereagh
> Most of the names are easy – short for a man to say.
>
> 'You've heard of Mungrybambone and the Gundabluey pine,
> Quobbotha, Girilambone, and Terramungamine,
> Quambone, Eunonyhareenyha, Wee Waa, and Buntijo –'
> But the rest of the shearers stopped him:
> 'For the sake of your jaw, go slow,
> If you reckon those names are short ones out where such names prevail,
> Just try and remember some long ones before you begin the tale.'
> And the man from the western district, though never a word
> he said,
> Just winked with his dexter eyelid, and then he retired to bed.[57]

As *The Bulletin*'s pages reported the escalating tensions between Australia's shearers and the rich men who employed them, Banjo's 'The Maori Pig Market'[58] recalled a visit to New Zealand where the local people and the Irish were 'fighting like sin'.[59]

LIKE THE REST OF AUSTRALIA, Banjo thrilled to the Australian performances of the New Zealand stallion Carbine. In 1889 Banjo had been trackside to see some of Carbine's great wins at Randwick Racecourse, where the big bay took out the Sydney Cup, the All Aged Stakes and the AJC Plate. The next year Carbine won all three races again, and as 1890 neared to a close he topped those efforts with an astonishing run in the Melbourne Cup. Under the handicap system, Carbine carried an extraordinary sixty-six kilograms, twenty-four kilograms more than the second-placed horse, Highborn,[60] and he conquered the biggest field that had ever been assembled with thirty-eight runners.[61] His time was a race record. The newspapers were ecstatic, saying the winner of the most valuable handicap race ever run in the world was the greatest horse yet seen in Australasia.[62]

> Long before the champion had reached the winning post, the spectators burst into wild expressions of delight and admiration, as it could be seen some distance from the post that Carbine would have to fall down to lose.[63]

Horses were not just instruments of sport in 1890, they were the lifeblood of everyday Australian life. Banjo revelled in the success of the great champion, although he would later write that Carbine, 'whom all Australians so proudly claim, was bred and reared in the cool climate of New Zealand; and his sire was an imported English horse and his dam an imported English mare'.[64]

Carbine's victories came as Banjo's celebrations of horses and horsemen were finding huge audiences. His year had started with his excitement over the stories of Jack Riley and the other men from Snowy River, and at the end of 1890 all of Australia was talking about another mighty horseman and his mount's memorable dash.

But working life in Australia was increasingly tough for the man on the land. 'On Kiley's Run',[65] published in *The Bulletin*'s 1890 Christmas edition, portrays the heartbreak and despair of station life that Banjo had seen through the weary eyes and vain toil of his father. Kiley's life of struggle proves pointless as a new owner takes control.

Decades later, Banjo recalled that rather than just reflecting the life on the Kiley property near Binalong, 'On Kiley's Run' reflects the loss of an Australian way of life when authorities tore apart leased properties – supposedly to spread out ownership of the land, but invariably just shifting more land to those who already had plenty. He said the poem was 'the story of a station or rather of a lot of stations rolled into one'.

> The bona-fide settlers were referred to in speeches as the 'sturdy yeomanry, the country's pride' but in course of time almost all these bona-fide settlers sold their blocks to the station-owners and moved on to fresh fields and pastures new, leaving things exactly as they were when they started except that the station had become a vast freehold instead of a vast leasehold. Paddocking came in instead of shepherding; the few remaining mobs of wild horses were run down and impounded; and boundary-riders who could not afford to indulge in flashness took the places of the cattle hands. Thus passed the principal picturesque feature of Australian station life.[66]

Likewise, 'The Story of Conroy's Gap'[67] – which appeared a few pages further back in the Christmas edition – recalls the people and places of Banjo's youth in a tragic love story involving a horse thief, a shy bush girl and a horse called the Swagman, very much like the mount of the Man from Snowy River.

Banjo had finished 1890 with a flourish – but the highlight of his year, some might say his career, had come with 'The Man from Snowy River' in April. It spawned a bestselling book, a film in Banjo's lifetime,[68] another far more successful international film long after his death,[69] a television series and arena spectaculars.

As 'The Man from Snowy River' grew in popularity, so did the number of contenders to rival Jack Riley as the model for the superhuman rider. Riley always remained the favourite, but others had their champions who claimed Banjo had heard their story as well. Over the years, Paterson's friend Lachie Cochran of Adaminaby, 'Hellfire' Jack Clarke of the Monaro district, George Hedger of Numbla Vale, Jim Spencer of Jindabyne and Jim Troy from Wagga were all put forward as being the real Man from Snowy River.

Tom Macnamara, who reckoned he was Clancy in the poem, said Troy was definitely the 'Man'. 'I well remember the ride as if it took place yesterday,' Macnamara told the *Courier-Mail* in 1938 when he was living in Brisbane at the age of ninety.

> From Troy's place near Wagga, you could see the hills in the direction of Tumut. Our adventure was not down [Kosciuszko's] side, as Paterson sang. Banjo shifted the mountain into our

> country to make the tale poetic. Three fine horses broke away from Troy's place, including the £1000 colt from Old Regret, and they joined the wild horses in the hills. The horsemen who rode that day were Tom Troy, my cousin, Andy Macnamara, Jim Troy, and myself. When Jim joined us on little Mungo, long-bearded Tom, who sat on Yellow Clarence, laughed at Jim and his weedy animal. Then I took Jim's part. As Banjo truly says, 'Only Clancy stood his friend,' and I added, 'I think we ought to let him come.' Andy Macnamara rode Roan Clarence, and I had a Lintot horse. We started after the colts, up hills and through gullies, but the wild horses took fright as we approached. 'You can say good-bye to the mob,' yelled Tom Troy. But Jim and Mungo went on. Later, Jim had the mob moving towards us. Tom told me to get on the next hill and wheel the mob to the right, but they beat us. Jim stuck to them, and ran them, as the poem says, 'single-handed till their sides were white with foam.'[70]

Charlie McKeahnie had his supporters for the title role, too. He was a bold young rider famous throughout the mountains for chasing a brumby stallion for twenty-five kilometres until the wild horse missed its footing and fell to its death.[71] That ride was the subject of a Barcroft Boake[72] poem in *The Bulletin*[73] that appeared between Banjo's publication of 'The Man from Snowy River' and 'How Wild Horses Are Yarded'. According to *The Age* newspaper, 'On their deaths most of the mountain horsemen in turn were proclaimed in various journals as Paterson's hero … Thus the claims proceeded in bewildering succession. The Man from Snowy River died many deaths.'[74]

IT WAS SAID AROUND Corryong and Khancoban that no one knew the mountains like Jack Riley. After Banjo's visit he lived out the rest of his life alone in his little hut on Tom Groggin. Even though Jack preferred solitude, he was 'better known than probably any other man in the mountains',[75] and was ready to help the increasing number of hikers and riders passing through – especially if they brought whisky or rum to share as he told them the story of how he was the Man from Snowy River.

Once when a party of visitors came to Tom Groggin during a spate of treacherous weather, Jack offered to guide them to Kosciuszko. They told him there was no need because they had a good compass, an instrument Jack said was no match for local knowledge. Fog and clouds descended on their route for two days and afterwards the same party of bedraggled walkers returned to Groggin in a pitiful, bewildered state. Old Jack never said a word. He gave them a feed and a drink of tea and, catching his horse, led them out over the mountains and put them on the track for home. One of the tourists offered Jack five shillings, but Jack refused to take it. Riding to the top of Kosciuszko so many times had made him familiar with the mountain's capricious moods, and if he warned a tourist that it was a bad day to try the ascent, the warning was worth a lot more than five shillings.[76]

Advancing years and the rough, lonely life began to tell on Jack, though. In 1911 he thought he was dying and asked friends to find him a priest. Father Patrick Hartigan[77] – who published bush verse under the name John O'Brien – was summoned all the way from Albury, 130 kilometres away, where he was the Diocesan Inspector of Schools. Hartigan set off in his eight-horsepower Renault car with two oil lamps in front, but no doors or windscreens. It took him two days over hills and mountains where there was often no road and there were often almost perpendicular descents.[78]

Old Jack had made something of a recovery by the time Hartigan arrived, and they got yarning about Banjo's famous poem. Hartigan was 'astonished' to find that Jack 'was by no means pleased with Banjo's version of the story'. 'We often had to do that sort of thing, and had tougher "goes" than that,' Jack told him, with more than a touch of annoyance. 'I was taking a party up to Kossy, and was telling them about it, and one of them put it in a book; but he brings in the names of a lot of men who weren't there at all. There was nobody named Clancy …'[79]

Three years later in the depths of winter, Jack suffered a heart attack. Five bushmen set out from Tom Groggin in the snow on 14 July 1914 to bring the helpless and half-conscious old man eighty kilometres down the steep gorges to Corryong, using an improvised stretcher. The men took turns holding the stretcher handles, but the track rendered it too difficult to use, so old Jack's limp form was lifted into a saddle and strapped in. The lightest of his mates sat behind him to hold him in place, and two of the other men walked beside the horse to make sure Jack didn't slip off. Snow fell on their cold grey faces. They spent a dark, freezing night in a deserted miner's hut, their grave expressions illuminated only by a flickering fire they made to keep Jack warm. By now he was barely breathing. He rallied a little during the night and spoke a few words to his mates. Then suddenly he swayed in his seat, his heart stopped and he was gone. Surrounded by great, silent trees covered with snow and rain gently falling on the roof of the hut, his friends put a blanket over Jack's face.[80]

He was taken into town and his body laid out at the Corryong Coffee Palace. Then he was buried in a quiet corner of the local cemetery, with a view of the grand mountains beyond. Over the next few days, newspaper eulogies described Jack as the original Man from Snowy River,[81] but naysayers were everywhere. A writer calling himself 'An Old Hand on Monaro' wrote to the *Corryong Courier* to ask:

> How many are there who claim to have been the one who inspired those lines? About half a dozen have died, and dozens are still living who claim this distinction. Like heroes in romance, I think 'The Man from Snowy River' was a myth. But if anyone was entitled to that distinction it was not Riley, for in his young days there were men on the Snowy River who could lose Jack in rough country, and he never could ride a buckjumper. There are numbers who can vouch for what I assert is true. I do not wish to detract anything from his horsemanship, but Riley at fifty years was a better rider than at twenty-five, strange as this may seem, but it is correct, for riding is a game that most men fail at quickly, but Riley living for over thirty years in the roughest country in the States of New South Wales and Victoria, kept up his pace, and during his last twenty years it would have been safe to say that there was not a man his age in either State who could have paced him in rough country ... My knowledge of Riley goes back nearly half a century ... He must have been possessed of a cast-iron constitution, for during the last 38 or 40 years he lived often in solitude in the roughest country in Australia, and lived on the

> roughest of fare …Had he liked to live in comfort he had offers of friends in Khancoban, at the head of the Murray, who would have cared for him; he also had relatives in Omeo.[82]

Still, Walter Mitchell's son Tom[83] – a Cambridge-educated barrister and ski champion who became a prisoner of war of the Japanese at Changi and then a prominent Victorian Country Party politician – had heard the stories many times of his father's ride to Kosciuszko with Banjo Paterson and their meeting with Jack. Tom said he was at a party in Sydney once when he asked Banjo, 'Who really was the Man from Snowy River?' According to Tom, Banjo replied that the character was largely imaginary but 'woven around Jack Riley'.[84] In 1947, Tom had a headstone placed over Riley's grave in Corryong Cemetery declaring him to be 'The Man from Snowy River' – though maybe this act had as much to do with promoting the town of Corryong and local tourism as anything else.

In 1935, Tom had married Elyne Chauvel,[85] daughter of Banjo's old schoolmate Harry Chauvel. She knew a lot about horses and wrote classic children's novels, including *The Silver Brumby.* Late in her life, she remained convinced that the Man from Snowy River was a 'composite character'.[86]

That was in line with what Banjo himself wrote back in 1938, when he said *men* from Snowy River had 'turned up from all the mountain districts – men who did exactly the same ride, and could give you chapter and verse for every hill they descended and every creek they crossed. It was no small satisfaction to find that there really had been a Man from Snowy River – more than one of them.'[87]

Banjo wrote of wild mountain horses seeing their chance for freedom and charging beneath the stockwhip with a sharp and sudden dash. National Library of Australia PIC/10555/27

The Man from Snowy River

There was movement at the station, for the word had passed around
  That the colt from old Regret had got away,
And had joined the wild bush horses – he was worth a thousand pound,
  So all the cracks had gathered to the fray.
All the tried and noted riders from the stations near and far
  Had mustered at the homestead overnight,
For the bushmen love hard riding where the wild bush horses are,
  And the stock-horse snuffs the battle with delight.

There was Harrison, who made his pile when Pardon won the cup,
  The old man with his hair as white as snow;
But few could ride beside him when his blood was fairly up –
  He would go wherever horse and man could go.
And Clancy of the Overflow came down to lend a hand,
  No better horseman ever held the reins;
For never horse could throw him while the saddle-girths would stand,
  He learnt to ride while droving on the plains.

And one was there, a stripling on a small and weedy beast,
  He was something like a racehorse undersized,

With a touch of Timor pony – three parts thoroughbred at least –
  And such as are by mountain horsemen prized.
He was hard and tough and wiry – just the sort that won't say die –
  There was courage in his quick impatient tread;
And he bore the badge of gameness in his bright and fiery eye,
  And the proud and lofty carriage of his head.

But still so slight and weedy, one would doubt his power to stay,
  And the old man said, 'That horse will never do
For a long and tiring gallop – lad, you'd better stop away,
  Those hills are far too rough for such as you.'
So he waited sad and wistful – only Clancy stood his friend –
  'I think we ought to let him come,' he said;
'I warrant he'll be with us when he's wanted at the end,
  For both his horse and he are mountain bred.

'He hails from Snowy River, up by Kosciusko's side,
  Where the hills are twice as steep and twice as rough,
Where a horse's hoofs strike firelight from the flint stones every stride,
  The man that holds his own is good enough.
And the Snowy River riders on the mountains make their home,
  Where the river runs those giant hills between;
I have seen full many horsemen since I first commenced to roam,
  But nowhere yet such horsemen have I seen.'

So he went – they found the horses by the big mimosa clump –
  They raced away towards the mountain's brow,
And the old man gave his orders, 'Boys, go at them from the jump,
  No use to try for fancy riding now.
And, Clancy, you must wheel them, try and wheel them to the right.
  Ride boldly, lad, and never fear the spills,
For never yet was rider that could keep the mob in sight,
  If once they gain the shelter of those hills.'

So Clancy rode to wheel them – he was racing on the wing
  Where the best and boldest riders take their place,

And he raced his stock-horse past them, and he made the ranges ring
  With the stockwhip, as he met them face to face.
Then they halted for a moment, while he swung the dreaded lash,
  But they saw their well-loved mountain full in view,
And they charged beneath the stockwhip with a sharp and sudden dash,
  And off into the mountain scrub they flew.

Then fast the horsemen followed, where the gorges deep and black
  Resounded to the thunder of their tread,
And the stockwhips woke the echoes, and they fiercely answered back
  From cliffs and crags that beetled overhead.
And upward, ever upward, the wild horses held their way,
  Where mountain ash and kurrajong grew wide;
And the old man muttered fiercely, 'We may bid the mob good day,
  NO man can hold them down the other side.'

When they reached the mountain's summit, even Clancy took a pull,
  It well might make the boldest hold their breath,
The wild hop scrub grew thickly, and the hidden ground was full
  Of wombat holes, and any slip was death.
But the man from Snowy River let the pony have his head,
  And he swung his stockwhip round and gave a cheer,
And he raced him down the mountain like a torrent down its bed,
  While the others stood and watched in very fear.

He sent the flint stones flying, but the pony kept his feet,
  He cleared the fallen timber in his stride,
And the man from Snowy River never shifted in his seat –
  It was grand to see that mountain horseman ride.
Through the stringy barks and saplings, on the rough and broken ground,
  Down the hillside at a racing pace he went;
And he never drew the bridle till he landed safe and sound,
  At the bottom of that terrible descent.

He was right among the horses as they climbed the further hill,
  And the watchers on the mountain standing mute,

Saw him ply the stockwhip fiercely, he was right among them still,
  As he raced across the clearing in pursuit.
Then they lost him for a moment, where two mountain gullies met
  In the ranges, but a final glimpse reveals
On a dim and distant hillside the wild horses racing yet,
  With the man from Snowy River at their heels.

And he ran them single-handed till their sides were white with foam.
  He followed like a bloodhound on their track,
Till they halted cowed and beaten, then he turned their heads for home,
  And alone and unassisted brought them back.
But his hardy mountain pony he could scarcely raise a trot,
  He was blood from hip to shoulder from the spur;
But his pluck was still undaunted, and his courage fiery hot,
  For never yet was mountain horse a cur.

And down by Kosciusko, where the pine-clad ridges raise
  Their torn and rugged battlements on high,
Where the air is clear as crystal, and the white stars fairly blaze
  At midnight in the cold and frosty sky,
And where around the Overflow the reedbeds sweep and sway
  To the breezes, and the rolling plains are wide,
The man from Snowy River is a household word to-day,
  And the stockmen tell the story of his ride.

Chapter 11

8 OCTOBER 1891, DARLINGHURST COURT OF GENERAL AND QUARTER SESSIONS, SYDNEY

I ... woke up to the fact that I was becoming known as a writer of verse, and from that time forth I seem to have 'caught on' with Australian readers everywhere. I often receive letters of congratulation from men out back who have read my pieces. You see, I understand them and their lives, and they know it.

BANJO PATERSON ON HIS NEW-FOUND FAME[1]

AT TWENTY-SEVEN YEARS OLD, Andrew Barton Paterson was still virtually anonymous in Australian literature. But his *Bulletin* pseudonym 'The Banjo' was winning friends and influencing people right across the colonies. He was revelling in the accolades, even if only his friends and family knew he was the author of some of the magazine's most celebrated works. Often he would receive gifts from appreciative but 'perfectly unknown donors, probably bushmen' who simply addressed their offerings to 'The Banjo, Sydney'.[2]

While he only made pocket money as a poet, he enjoyed the trappings of being a well-paid lawyer in a big city, surrounded by rich and influential friends and family. He was 'a very handsome young man'[3] and although engaged to Sarah Riley 'was very popular with the young ladies'.[4] He was seeing Sarah more than ever; her aunt Anna Maria Street became a widow in March 1891, and Sarah became a regular visitor to her home in Elizabeth Bay.

Throughout 1891 Banjo still found time to make monthly contributions to *The Bulletin*, even though he and John Street were kept busy with their successful legal business. Times were becoming increasingly tough, though, for those not so well heeled. Australia had entered a great depression.

The gold rushes of the 1850s had created tremendous wealth in Australia, though there had been periods of boom and bust, and a great drought in the early 1860s across the eastern colonies and South Australia. Sydney and Melbourne had become great cities to rival the capitals of Europe and to rival each other in prosperity. Two million people had visited Melbourne's 1888 Centennial International Exhibition, a showcase of the city's economic might. Many of Victoria's richest families had made their fortunes on vast grazing runs, but increases in land taxes and the freeing up of the countryside for smaller settlers forced many of the great squatter barons to look towards the newly opened expanses in Central Queensland. As the Australian colonies experienced boom times in the 1880s, Banjo knew there would eventually be a bust.[5] Rapidly escalating property prices, especially in Melbourne, could only end in a bubble and tears, and falling returns for wool were about to create chaos. It was always the battler who suffered the worst.

Although his legal work gave him an enviable lifestyle, Banjo had long grown weary of it – he hated chasing money from people under pressure. And he hated representing creeps. But in the middle of 1891, the firm of Street & Paterson was retained by the family of a convicted child molester, William Benjamin Burnett: a man described as being of 'weak intellect' with a 'hereditary tendency to insanity'.[6] A few months earlier, Burnett had been sentenced to three years in jail for 'defiling' a girl under the age of fourteen at the Petersham Congregational Sunday School picnic at Chowder Bay, on the northern side of Sydney's harbour. The judge considered sentencing Burnett to a flogging as well, before deciding otherwise, and said it would have been better for the little girl to have met a wild animal rather than the prisoner.[7]

Burnett was only in the cold, damp cells at Berrima Gaol for five months when his poor health persuaded authorities to move him to the warmer climes of Parramatta Gaol.[8] In June 1891, Burnett's relatives and friends hired Street & Paterson to petition the government for Burnett's early release because he was coughing up blood and suffering chest pains from his heart condition. Although he was still a young man at twenty-three, it seemed he was not long for this world.

At the time, Banjo had been thinking about following his uncle John Paterson into politics, and it was rumoured in *The Bulletin* that he would stand for the electorate of Yass Plains 'in the democratic interest', but he changed his mind. The case of William Benjamin Burnett took up much of his time.

On 14 July 1891, Burnett was released 'as is usual in cases where prisoners are reported to be suffering from disease likely to prove shortly fatal, or to be seriously aggravated by further incarceration'.[9] Street & Paterson had done their job.

Burnett was out for less than a month when he molested three more children. At his subsequent trial, Street and Banjo instructed Burnett's barrister and mounted a defence based on insanity. They claimed that Burnett could not distinguish between right and wrong, and that he had three uncles who were certifiable 'lunatics'.[10] The argument didn't impress the judge, and Burnett was eventually sentenced to ten years in prison; he accepted the new sentence with 'the greatest indifference'.[11]

Banjo would rather have been riding with the men from Snowy River than representing lowlifes and banks, but he escaped from the disagreeable cases and characters of the courtroom by writing and playing sport. During the early 1890s he competed in some amateur athletic events: he ran the half mile,[12] became a tennis champion and then administrator at a young age, and rode with the Sydney Hunt Club. He also became an amateur rider with the Sydney Turf Club at Rosehill.[13] Over time he grew prouder of the triumphs he had on horseback than of anything he'd written.[14]

THE DEPRESSION WORSENED. Nearly a dozen major banks were about to close and British investment in Australia dried up.[15] As manufacturing industries went bust, unemployment became contagious. In the bush, one foreclosure after another saw more and more small properties merge into bigger properties for the wealthy. Thousands of Australians became homeless; they picked up swags with all their possessions and tramped the bush roads, begging to work for food. Industrial action flared as cheap labour from China and the South Sea Islands was shipped in to take the jobs of local men.

Paterson empathised with his fellow bushmen.

The Bulletin thrived in this atmosphere of angst and fear. The working man had toiled hard helping rich bosses get richer, but now the field worker and the factory hand, the stockman and the labourer were being left by the wayside as rich men rode high.

Banjo and John Street managed to stay afloat, while Banjo was able to indulge in a new, expensive hobby. When a cavalry officer came out from England and started a polo club, Banjo and his wealthy young friends 'took to the game like ducks to water'.[16] 'This polo business,' he said, 'brought us in touch with some of the upper circles – a great change after the little bush school, the game-cocks, and the days when I looked upon the sergeant of police as the greatest man in the world.'[17] Banjo had morphed from the angry young man writing political pamphlets against the big city elites to a polo-playing pillar of society, hobnobbing with the key legal figures of Sydney and planning to marry a girl with wealthy connections. Mama Barton now owned four impressive rental properties around Rockend.

Banjo became a key figure[18] in the Sydney polo set. In the middle of 1891, he started playing the game at the highest level alongside military men and wealthy young friends, including newspaper heir Charles Burton Fairfax. Every Tuesday afternoon[19] Banjo would saddle up for the new Sydney Club at the Agricultural Showground in Moore Park.[20] He named his beautiful grey horse Snowy[21] in honour of what had become his best-known poem. Banjo's sister Edie described her brother of the early 1890s as being:

> ... about five feet ten inches in height, of very athletic build. He was an expert horseman and played polo and was an outstanding tennis player, a fairly good boxer and rifle-shot. His hair was dark and his eyes were brown, but not very dark and were very keen and clear with a penetrating look. His nose was slightly aquiline and the darkness of his complexion depended on whether he was working outdoors or indoors. He had a moustache for a short time – rather short than drooping. As a rule he spoke quickly. He was not unduly spare, though muscular and quite well-covered. He danced beautifully.[22]

Banjo's first work of 1891 for *The Bulletin* was a short story, 'The Downfall of Mulligan's',[23] about a group of sporting swindlers from the bush who are turned inside out by a card-sharp priest. He followed it soon after with another piece of prose about 'Greenhide Billy', the biggest liar in the Clarence River district of New South Wales. The story ran above an ad for Pear's Soap, and it told the story of a blowhard who claimed to have 'seen bigger droughts, better country, fatter cattle, faster horses, and cleverer dogs than any other man on the Clarence'.[24] But one night when the rain was on the roof, and the river was rising with a moaning sound, and the men were gathered round the fire in the hut smoking and staring at the coals, Billy turned himself loose and gave the men 'his masterpiece'.[25]

Billy wove a tale about how, single-handed, he had halted a stampede of a thousand head of cattle – 'wild mountain-bred wretches' – through wild scrub after his mate went to sleep under a log. The story was more bull than a rodeo, and Billy's audience knew it.

The poem 'Come-by-Chance' was followed by 'In the Droving Days'. It tells of Banjo finding a broken-down old drover's horse and buying it at auction out of pity, for fear it would end up being flogged and starved towing a hawker's cart:

And the old grey horse was knocked down to me.
And now he's wandering, fat and sleek,
On the lucerne flats by the Homestead Creek;
I dare not ride him for fear he'd fall,
But he does a journey to beat them all,
For though he scarcely a trot can raise,
He can take me back to the droving days.[26]

'The Flying Gang: A Railway Song' races along at a gallop, telling the story of the railway men called out on emergencies along the line:

'Twas a chosen band that was kept at hand
In case of an urgent need,
Was it south or north we were started forth,
And away at our utmost speed.

If word reached town that a bridge was down,
The imperious summons rang –
'Come out with the pilot engine sharp,
And away with the flying gang.'[27]

'The Lost Drink'[28] has echoes of Banjo's boyhood brush with Big Kerrigan, and 'An Evening in Dandaloo' shows the comic horrors of the demon drink at the scene of an all-in brawl:

Jack Macpherson seized a bucket,
Every head he saw he struck it –
Struck in earnest, too;
And a man from Lower Wattle,
Whom a shearer tried to throttle,
Hit out freely with a bottle,
There in Dandaloo.

Skin and hair were flying thickly,
When a light was fetched, and quickly
Brought a fact to view –
On the scene of the diversion
Every single, solid person
Come along to help Macpherson –
All were Dandaloo!

When the list of slain was tabled,
Some were drunk and some disabled,
Still we found it true.
In the darkness and the smother
We'd been belting one another;
Jack Macpherson bashed his brother
There in Dandaloo.[29]

'History of a Jackaroo in Five Letters'[30] is another comically grim portrait of outback life for the unwary. It begins with an Englishman coming to a sheep station for experience after paying a £500 fee for the education.

No. 1 Letter from Joscelyn de Greene, of Wiltshire, England, to college friend

Dear Gus,

The Governor has fixed things up for me at last. I am not to go to India, but to Australia. It seems the Governor met some old Australian swell named Moneygrub at a dinner in the City. He has thousands of acres of land and herds of sheep, and I am to go out and learn the business of sheep raising. Of course it is not quite the same as going to India; but some really decent people do go out to Australia sometimes, I am told, and I expect it won't be so bad … I have been going in for gun and revolver practice so as to be able to hold my own against the savages and the serpents in the woods of Australia. Mr Moneygrub says there isn't much fighting with the savages nowadays; but, he says, the Union shearers will give me all the fight I want. What is a Union shearer, I wonder? … I am only to pay a premium of £500 for the experience …

Joscelyn de Greene.

No. 2 Letter from Moneygrub and Co., London, to the manager of the company's Drybone station, Paroo River, Australia

Dear Sir,

We beg to advise you of having made arrangements to take a young gentleman named Greene as colonial experiencer, and he will be consigned to you by the next boat. His premium is £500, and you will please deal with him in the usual way. Let us know when you have vacancies for any more colonial experiencers, as several are now asking about it, and the premiums are forthcoming. You are on no account to employ Union shearers this year; and you must cut expenses as low as you can. Would it not be feasible to work the station with the colonial experience men and Chinese labour? &c., &c., &c.

No. 3 Letter from Mr Robert Saltbush, of Frying Pan station, to a friend

Dear Billy,
Those fellows over at Drybone station have been at it again. You know it joins us, and old Moneygrub, who lives in London, sends out an English bloke every now and again to be a jackaroo. He gets £500 premium for each one, and the manager puts the jackaroo to boundary ride a tremendous great paddock at the back of the run, and he gives him a week's rations and tells him never to go through a gate, because so long as he only gets lost in the paddock he can always be found somehow, but if he gets out of the paddock, Lord knows whether he'd ever be seen again.

No. 4 Letter from Sandy Macgregor, manager of Drybone station, to Messrs Moneygrub & Co., London

Dear Sirs,
I regret to have to inform you that the young gentleman, Mr Greene, whom you sent out, has seen fit to leave his employment and go away to the township. No doubt he found the work somewhat rougher than he had been used to, but if young gentlemen are sent out here to get experience they must expect to rough it like other bushmen.

No. 5 Extract from evidence of Senior Constable Rafferty, taken at an inquest before Lushington, P.M. for the North-east by South Paroo district, and a jury

I am a senior constable, stationed at Walloopna beyant. On the 5th instant, I received information that a man was in the horrors at Flanagan's hotel. I went down and saw the man, whom I recognise as the deceased. He was in the horrors: he was very bad. He had taken all his clothes off, and was hiding in a fowl house to get away from the devils which were after him. I went to arrest him, but he avoided me, and escaped over a paling fence on to the Queensland side of the border, where I had no power to arrest him. He was foaming at the mouth and acting like a madman. He had been on the spree for several days. From enquiries made, I believe his name to be Greene, and that he

> had lately left the employment of Mr Macgregor, at Drybone. He was found dead on the roadside by the carriers coming into Walloopna. He had evidently wandered away from the township, and died from the effects of the sun and the drink.[31]

'Victor Second'[32] recalls another bush horseracing meeting in uproarious detail: 'Buckatowndown Races. Red-hot day, everything dusty, everybody drunk and blasphemous. All the betting at Buckatowndown was double-event. You had to win the money first and fight the man for it afterwards. The start for our race, the Town Plate, was delayed for a quarter of an hour, because the starter flatly refused to leave a fight of which he was an interested spectator. Every horse, as he did his preliminary gallop, had a string of dogs after him, and the clerk of the course came full cry after the dogs with a whip.'[33]

Banjo followed with his love poem for Sara Riley: 'As Long as Your Eyes Are Blue'. His next poem that year, 'Been There Before', tells the story of an out-of-towner who gets the better of the sharpies in Walgett. 'A Mountain Station',[34] written several years before, revealed Banjo's long-held dream to one day be a station owner like his father had been before misfortune struck, even if the country was rough and hard to work.

'The Cast-iron Canvasser'[35] is a work of pure comic genius about the activities of book publishers Sloper and Dodge, who sold their volumes to country folk on time payment by using persistent door-to-door salesmen – or 'canvassers'.

Sloper 'was a long, sanctimonious individual, very religious and very bald – beastly, awfully bald'. Dodge was a little, fat American, with bristly black hair and beard, and quick, beady eyes. He was eternally smoking a reeking black pipe, swallowing the smoke and then puffing it out through his nose in great whiffs, like a locomotive on a steep grade. Anybody walking into one of those whiffs incautiously was likely to get paralysed because the tobacco was so strong.

Sloper and Dodge had put a lot of money into the business – 'all they had, in fact' – but the public had revolted against them and their salesmen. Then an apparent saviour arrived: 'an inventor, a genius ... who offered to supply the firm with a patent cast-iron canvasser'. When wound up, this automaton would walk about, talk by means of a phonograph, collect orders, and stand any amount of wear and tear, even violent attacks. If this could indeed be done, Sloper and Dodge were saved.

The genius had built into the cast-iron canvasser a number of self-defence features. The canvasser's head and body were full of concealed springs, and if anybody hit him in the face, or in the pit of the stomach ('the favourite place to hit canvassers'), a strong spring was released and the automaton threw a right-hand punch that could knock any opponent into the middle of next week. The blow was so fast, the genius said, that the great defensive boxer of the time 'Young Griffo' couldn't dodge it, and the toughest heavyweight boxer of the era, 'Paddy' Slavin, couldn't stand against it.[36] No man would ever hit the canvasser twice. And he was dog-proof too: his legs were padded with tar and oakum, and if a dog took a bite out of him, the genius said it would 'take that dog the rest of his life to pick his teeth clean'. The phonograph could be charged for a hundred thousand times,[37] meaning the automaton could bail up the householder and talk non-stop for hours. There was no escape – that was until a malfunction made things go hilariously, horribly wrong.

Banjo was in a happy place at his desk, retreating into a fantasy world in which he could see humour in the little slices of life even though much of Australia was struggling during the economic downturn. Nothing made Banjo happier, though, than to be on a fast horse – as he showed in 'The Ace, from Snowy River',[38] later known as 'The Open Steeplechase':

> I had ridden over hurdles up the country once or twice,
> By the side of Snowy River with a horse they called 'The Ace'.
> And we brought him down to Sydney, and our rider Jimmy Rice,
> Got a fall and broke his shoulder, so they nabbed me in a trice –
> Me, that never wore the colours, for the Open Steeplechase.[39]

Sport was taking up most of Banjo's leisure time when he wasn't composing poetry or prose. While delegates from around the colonies met at Sydney Town Hall for the 1891 Constitutional Convention to discuss a federated Australian nation, Banjo was busy as honorary treasurer of the Lawn Tennis Association of New

South Wales.[40] He was busily organising the annual tournament against Victoria on Sydney's main cricket ground, but he still had plenty of time to practise his serve and volley. An *Illustrated Sydney News* reporter was impressed, declaring, 'One of the most improved players in the Sydney Club is A. B. Paterson, the hon. Treasurer.' His game was better than what it had been last season, the reporter said, 'and shows promise of further improvement'.[41] Two weeks later, the newspaper reported that 'A. B. Paterson is playing a sterling game. He has done a great deal of practice this season, and it has had a highly beneficial effect. He uses both hands equally well, and it is apt to make a man weary and annoyed trying to pass him from the back of the court.'[42]

Banjo won some and lost some during the big intercolonial tournament, but his organisational work won the praise of Sydney's *Daily Telegraph*, which reported: 'It would be impossible to say too much in praise of the committee of the Sydney Club with regard to the management of the tournament'.[43] All of Banjo's arrangements 'were without fault or flaw', and ran 'on day after day ... with extreme smoothness'. A cold luncheon kept the crowd happy, and Mr Quong Tart's tearoom in the Queen Victoria Building supplied patrons with 'his best Foochow'.[44]

HENRY LAWSON DIDN'T PLAY MUCH TENNIS. His lifestyle was quite different from Banjo's. Lawson's deafness had not been alleviated, despite treatment at the Victorian Eye and Ear Hospital, but his writing had grown more strident with his mother's urging.

In 1888, Louisa Lawson had started a successful magazine, *The Dawn*, announcing that it would fight the good fight for women and agitate for their suffrage. On 31 December 1888, Louisa had inherited £1103 from her estranged husband, Peter, which helped *The Dawn* to rise so that soon she was employing ten women, including female printers.

Henry still could not make a living from his creative work, although he was writing beautifully. He had followed 'Faces in the Street' with the memorable 'Andy's Gone with Cattle',[45] for the *Australian Town and Country Journal*:

Our Andy's gone to battle now
'Gainst Drought, the red marauder;
Our Andy's gone with cattle now
Across the Queensland border.

He's left us in dejection now;
Our hearts with him are roving.
It's dull on this selection now –
Since Andy went a-droving.[46]

Then in 1889 he wrote 'Eureka!'[47] for Jules Archibald – and for the union shearers – as a tribute to the spirit of rebellion shown during the stockade on the Ballarat goldfields, and as a follow-up to an earlier work, 'The Flag of the Southern Cross'.[48] He spent a few months in 1890 working as a tradesman in Albany, Western Australia, a boom town after the arrival of the Great Southern Railway from Perth. He also wrote to the Virginia-born editor of the *Albany Observer*, asking if he could contribute some poetry and telling him: 'You will no doubt perceive that I have not had the advantages of a good education, but if I could only raise myself from the cursed drudgery of day labour, I would soon make up for that.'[49]

In 1891 Gresley Lukin[50] – the former editor of the *Brisbane Courier* and its weekly offshoot the *Queenslander* – offered him a job in Brisbane. Lukin knew Lawson's mother from her work on *The Dawn* and offered Henry 'the first, the last and the only chance I got in journalism'. Lukin paid Henry £2 a week to write the 'Country Crumbs' column for a weekly newspaper, *The Boomerang*,[51] which Lukin hoped would rival *The Bulletin* in popularity as a voice of the worker.

Having travelled to all points of the Australian compass, Lawson arrived in Brisbane at a time of great upheaval in the colonies and especially in Queensland. Lukin had bought *The Boomerang* from an odd little agitator named Billy Lane,[52] a small, delicate-looking English-born journalist with a club foot, gold-rimmed spectacles, a drooping moustache and a fighting instinct for the working class. The 29-year-old Lane, who appeared much older, had learnt the craft of journalism on the American newspaper the *Detroit Free Press*, and after arriving in Queensland he became a union agitator. In 1890 he was appointed the first editor of *The Worker*, which was financed by the Australian Labour Federation and other Queensland labour bodies. Lane also offered to publish Lawson's poetry in his socialist paper, as Queensland teetered towards what many feared would be a civil war.

Trouble in the shearing sheds of Australia had been simmering for several years. There had been bitter strikes and walkouts as men downed tools and refused to work alongside low-paid Chinese labour brought in by the pastoralists. The shearers had opened 1891 by landing their first heavy blow of what became a great strike at Logan Downs, near the town of Clermont. The station was part of the great expanse of Australia controlled by George Fairbairn, a Scottish shepherd made good, and his sons, George Jr and Charles. The Fairbairns had three million sheep and millions of hectares among their twenty-eight properties.[53] On 5 January 1891, George Taylor, an organiser for the Queensland shearers' Central District Union, led a walkout by two hundred shearers and labourers. They formed a camp on the banks of Wolfgang Creek as *The Bulletin* and thousands of other shearers voiced their support. On 1 February 1891, a 'strike committee' in Barcaldine, having met under the branches of the town's mighty ghost gum, declared that 'the Queensland bush is to be a battleground whereon is to be decided whether capitalism can crush Australian unionism altogether into the dust'.[54]

'Fellow unionists,' the committee declared, 'we call upon you all, individually and unitedly, to pull the unions through this fight, let the cost be what it may. If our unions go down we are totally enslaved … the squatters expect the Queensland bush unions will fight hard, but they do not know how hard.'[55]

Telegraph lines were cut, and the shearers began lighting fires in the tinder-dry grasses across Central Queensland. They torched millions of hectares, including an almost forty-kilometre stretch between the Jericho and Alice train stations.[56] The Rockhampton and Mount Morgan corps of mounted infantry rode the train to Clermont, where two hundred armed men were rallying behind Julian Stuart,[57] a 24-year-old former schoolteacher who would one day write for *The Worker* and *The Bulletin*.

On the balmy summer evening of 20 February 1891, as the sun set over the Brisbane River, sixty soldiers from Queensland's permanent artillery marched up the gangway onto the steamer *Burwah*, ready for what the *Brisbane Courier* called an 'industrial Armageddon'.[58] The soldiers were bound for Rockhampton and then a train to the colony's broiling centre. Each soldier carried a Martini-Henry rifle, and together they had not only a state-of-the-art cannon that fired 4.5-kilogram shells but also the newest weapon of mass destruction, an American-made Gatling machine gun – the infamous 'slaughter machine' – with six barrels spitting out up to nine hundred bullets a minute.[59] Before long there were 1400 soldiers and fifty-eight armed constables in Central Queensland with their trigger fingers itching. The reinforcements brought with them the British-built Nordenfeldt machine gun.[60] At Emerald, shearers had seized large quantities of gunpowder and ammunition, and the *Courier* warned that they intended 'extreme violence'.[61] At armed camps around the big stations where millions of sheep grazed, shearers burnt effigies of the Queensland premier, Sir Samuel Griffith, and then continued to burn the countryside as well as fences, woolsheds, bales of wool and sometimes sheep. At Clermont Railway Station police drew their swords as shearers attacked a group of squatters. There were riots at Barcaldine, Capella and Clermont, where shearers threatened to scalp non-union workers. At Minerva, soldiers drove off unionists with bayonets when a train arrived with 'scab' labourers.[62] Shearers even tried to derail a train by placing a log across the tracks.[63]

In Charters Towers, 21-year-old firebrand journalist Frederick Vosper, who had no intention of standing up to bayonets himself, urged others to fight to the death, declaring that the shearers needed 'revolution throughout Australasia'. 'If your oppressors will not listen to reason, let them feel cold lead and steel,' he wrote. 'Better to see the last member of this hateful (Queensland) government butchered than to see one jot or one tittle of the sacred rights of the people lost.'[64]

But the government had the military muscle to put down all rebellions. On 7 April 1891, Julian Stuart and five other prisoners were taken in chains and under heavy guard by special train from Clermont to the Barcaldine police station. There they were surrounded by a military outfit comprising five hundred men: mounted troops and field artillery, infantrymen with fixed bayonets, Scottish pipers and drummers, and a brass band. A few shearers bellowed out 'scab protectors' as the soldiers marched the prisoners along Ash and Oak streets – but, just in case the unionists were thinking of causing a ruckus, the military stationed the ambulance corps at the rear. It let everyone know that any resistance was futile and that any opposition would end in a bloodbath.[65]

Fourteen men were eventually committed for trial on charges of conspiracy, and the trials began at the Rockhampton Supreme Court on 1 May 1891. Billy Lane watched through his round spectacles from the press table, though many believed he should have been in the dock over his writings in *The Worker*, urging the shearers to fight 'tyranny' with everything they had.[66] In Queensland's Legislative Assembly, Lane's writings were described as 'incendiary' and he was called 'an arch fiend ... who stands behind the men, driving them on'.[67]

On the same day that the trials began in Rockhampton, Barcaldine hosted a May Day labour parade to celebrate the eight-hour day won by Australian unionists in the aftermath of the Eureka Stockade rebellion. There were 1340 shearers and their families taking part; they carried banners for the Australian Labour Federation, and the shearers' and carriers' unions, and 'Young Australia' and the Eureka rebellion flag of the Southern Cross featured prominently.[68]

Despite the arrests, Billy Lane and Henry Lawson used the pages of *The Worker* to encourage the Queensland rebels to maintain the rage. In *Freedom on the Wallaby*[69] – 'Wallaby' being a term meaning 'to carry a swag' – Lawson drew on the memory of Eureka and the Southern Cross banner:

> So we must fly a rebel flag,
> As others did before us,
> And we must sing a rebel song
> And join in rebel chorus.
> We'll make the tyrants feel the sting
> O' those that they would throttle;
> They needn't say the fault is ours
> If blood should stain the wattle![70]

A Queensland politician, Frederick Brentnall, read out parts of that poem in the Queensland Legislative Council on 15 July 1891, during a 'Vote of Thanks' to the lawmen who had broken up the Barcaldine strike camp. There were calls in the chamber for Lawson's arrest for sedition, but he was ready to take on all comers and gave Brentnall a lashing with 'The Vote of Thanks Debate'.[71]

> The other night in Parliament you quoted something true,
> Where truth is very seldom heard except from one or two.
> You know that when the people rise the other side must fall,
> And you are on the other side, and that explains it all.
> You hate the Cause by instinct, the instinct of your class.
> And fear the reformation that shall surely come to pass;
> Your nest is feathered by the 'laws' which you of course defend,
> Your daily bread is buttered on the upper crust, my friend.[72]

Eventually more than twenty leaders of the strike were sent to prison – for conspiracy, rioting or sedition – on the fearsome St Helena Island in Moreton Bay, with three years' imprisonment the most common sentence. On 15 June 1891 the strike was officially called off, and eventually most of the shearers went back to work grudgingly.[73]

Their efforts did not go unrewarded, though. According to Australian Labor Party folklore, an early version of the new Queensland Labor Party Manifesto[74] was read out under the great ghost gum in Barcaldine, which was named the Tree of Knowledge, and Queensland ushered in the world's first labour government in 1899, under Andrew Dawson[75] – even if it was in power for just a week.

Although the great strike was over, frequent skirmishes still broke out, and the ill will between the haves and have-nots would inspire Banjo's most famous work.

NOT THAT THE DEPRESSION or the violent confrontations in outback Queensland had much effect on Banjo at the time. Life was good and he was revelling in his sporting prowess.

In November 1891, he was one of the stars on show when the Sydney Polo Club threw open the invitation to 'a large gathering of ladies' to watch practice and enjoy afternoon tea in one of the Moore Park rooms on the Agricultural Society's grounds. The spectators included the club patron – the NSW Governor Victor Child Villiers,

7th Earl of Jersey – and some of Sydney's most influential families.[76] The club had about seventy members, of whom twenty-five were players. In January Banjo and his clubmates caught the train to Scone, three hundred kilometres north of Sydney, to play polo against the landed gentry in that picturesque part of the colony. Banjo played well and in the final quarter 'got the ball out of a hustle, and took it up the field to within a foot of the goal, when the Scone full-back just managed to tip it to the side and save the goal'.[77] The locals eventually won, but it was a spirited match that lasted two hours, and the players all worked up an appetite for a convivial dinner at Scone's Golden Fleece Hotel.[78]

Banjo was moving in the highest circles in the continent. Two weeks later at Rosehill Racecourse,[79] he was locked in a race with George Goschen,[80] secretary to the governor and the son and heir to Viscount Goschen, England's Chancellor of the Exchequer. The poet and the aristocrat were among five entries in the Polo Stick Race, in which riders took the ball three hundred yards round a post and back in front of the grandstand. Banjo rode as hard as the Man from Snowy River but finished runner-up, eight seconds behind Goschen's winning time of two minutes twenty seconds.[81] By now Banjo was a regular guest at Government House; he had a team of polo ponies with the pick of them being Snowy and a horse called Pegasus, which he kept stabled near Rockend.[82]

Henry Lawson did not play polo and could not afford a pony. His luck ran out again. Despite Gresley Lukin announcing that his *Boomerang* was a raging success,[83] it was struggling from the first issue in the tough economic climate. Henry was let go in September 1891. Depressed, he returned to Sydney and looked for odd jobs while writing what he could for *The Bulletin*, including his tale of woe in 'The Shame of Going Back':[84]

When you've come to make a fortune and you haven't made your salt,
And the reason of your failure isn't anybody's fault –
When you haven't got a billet, and the times are very slack,
There is nothing that can spur you like the shame of going back;
Crawling home with empty pockets,
Going back hard-up;
Oh! it's then you learn the meaning of humiliation's cup.[85]

Lawson was well aware of the success Banjo was having and the name he was making as an advocate for a country life – a life that had been nothing but hard toil for Henry since he could remember. Banjo was creating timeless Australian heroes, but Lawson had heard more than enough of cracking whips, flying horses and loveable rogues.

He wanted to tell *Bulletin* readers what the bush was really like. So he challenged Banjo to a duel.

Banjo had been riding high and writing superbly, but now he faced the toughest fight of his life.

Chapter 12

27 APRIL 1892, ROSEHILL RACECOURSE, SYDNEY

So, no doubt, the bush is wretched if you judge it by the groan
Of the sad and soulful poet with a graveyard of his own.

BANJO TAKING A SHOT AT THE MELANCHOLY WRITINGS OF HENRY LAWSON[1]

BANJO RECKONED it was Henry Lawson's idea. A battle between the two best-known poets in Australia putting forth their views on bush life.

As an old man, in his reminisces for the *Sydney Morning Herald*, Banjo wrote:

> … one day [Lawson] suggested that we should write against each other, he putting the bush from his point of view, and I putting it from mine. 'We ought to do pretty well out of it,' he said. 'We ought to be able to get in three or four sets of verses each before they stop us.' This suited me all right, for we were working on space, and the pay was very small – in fact, I remember getting exactly thirteen and sixpence for writing 'Clancy of the Overflow': – so we slam-banged away at each other for weeks and weeks; not until they stopped us, but until we ran out of material.[2]

By 1892, Banjo and Lawson were literary celebrities, and Banjo was creating the template of the Australian bush hero as a national identity. Archibald welcomed the idea for what became known as the *Bulletin* Debate as a way to stir controversy and spark further interest in his magazine around the colonies over the merits and miseries of the bush. What really was the true Australia? Was bush life in the colonies really like the romantic idyll of fearless horsemen and visions splendid as described by 'The Banjo'? Or was the endless Australian landscape as cruel and unforgiving as Lawson claimed in his stark prose?

Lawson had been the people's champion in his strident campaigning for the rights of the shearers in the Great Strike. While he and Banjo were portrayed as representing opposite camps, Banjo had shown time and time again that he was on the side of the battler, too; his father had worn himself out from hard work, and his mother now looked and felt much older than her late forties because of the privations of her isolated rural life.

But Banjo had now firmly changed his writing style from protest to escapism, and his bush ballads were mostly fantasies. Rather than tramping anywhere with his swag or riding in the caboose on the train, he was now very much an establishment man, having followed the example of his grandfather Robert Barton as a member of the Australian Club in Macquarie Street in February 1892. Henry Kater – whom Banjo had lampooned anonymously only a few years before – sponsored Banjo's membership into the exclusive Sydney establishment, while the Minister for Public Instruction, Frank Suttor,[3] the long-time member for the seat of Bathurst, supported Banjo's inclusion. It was 30 guineas to join and then an annual membership fee of 12 guineas. Banjo soon regarded the club and its plush furnishings as his home – and he did so for the rest of his life, enjoying the expansive views of the Botanic Garden and Sydney Harbour.

Henry Lawson was not a member. Nor was he part of the hoopla when the *Australian Star* newspaper reported that Banjo, in his mauve and straw colours, scored 'a very brilliant goal' for the Sydney Polo Club in their victory over Muswellbrook at Rosehill Racecourse on 27 April 1892. Banjo's disabled right arm appeared not to handicap his polo playing. The match was played in delightful weather on soft ground, and 'a good number of sport-loving folk patronised the special train timed to leave Redfern at 1.25 p.m.' Banjo was now very popular with female admirers, and the paper reported that 'Amongst the onlookers were a great many ladies, and it is easily to be seen that polo will be a favourite game amongst the gentler sex.'[4] With Banjo tearing around the field on his horse Snowy, Sydney was eventually declared the champion polo team of New South Wales.

Henry Lawson was no fan of sports. His earnings from poetry could hardly buy peanuts, while Australia revered its sporting heroes and Banjo made gods out of working men. Lawson complained:

In the land where sport is sacred, where the lab'rer is a god,
You must pander to the people, make a hero of a clod!
...
To be buried as a pauper; to be shoved beneath the sod –
While the brainless man of muscle has the burial of a god.[5]

Banjo cantered on, unconcerned by Lawson's woes. He was largely aloof when it came to befriending other poets and writers of the *Bulletin* circle, preferring the men of action he met at the racetrack and on the polo ground. But he did seek out advice from two other *Bulletin* contributors, A. W. Jose[6] along with the much older John Farrell,[7] who had been a partner in a brewery at Goulburn and then was briefly[8] the editor of Sydney's *Daily Telegraph*. Even though the pressure of running the newspaper had become too much for Farrell, he had continued as the *Telegraph*'s leader-writer. He wrote extensively in support of the tax reform ideas of the American journalist Henry George, whose book *Progress and Poverty*[9] had sold three million copies worldwide, probably more than any other American book until that time. In 1889 Farrell had formed the Single-Tax League, and Banjo became a member.

Lawson and Banjo continued to be the luminaries of Australian poetry, but others were striving for some of the stardust.

Will Ogilvie[10] was a young Scot who came to Australia in 1889 and stayed for twelve years, working as a drover, horse-breaker and roustabout. He fell in love with Australian women and was in awe of the horses, and the first of his two volumes of verse was named after his poem 'Fair Girls and Gray Horses'.[11]

Ballarat-born Edward Dyson[12] wrote many of his ballads about the mines but looked further to the far horizons of the bush and the outback plains.

And there was E. J. (Ted) Brady,[13] five years younger than Banjo but a good friend during their early *Bulletin* days. Brady worked as a tallyclerk on the wharves at Woolloomooloo, and he wrote of ships and sailors in the same way that Banjo wrote of the bush and bushmen. He worked for the labour weekly, *Australian Workman*, and once shamelessly stole Lawson's poem 'The Cambaroora Star' from *The Boomerang* and passed it off as his own work. Lawson confronted Brady in his office, and after the initial shock of being caught red-handed, Brady became a great supporter of the forlorn versifier with the skeletal frame, hangdog expression and droopy moustache.

Barcroft Boake[14] was close on Banjo's heels when it came to ballads about horsemen, as he showed in 'On the Range':[15] 'Stride for stride, lengthened wide, for the green timber belt, / The fastest half-mile ever done on the plain.'[16]

Banjo and the *Bulletin* staff well knew just how harsh life could be for the man on the land, and they saw it in Boake's life story. The 26-year-old aspiring writer returned from a stint as a surveyor around Wagga in a state of depression. On 2 May 1892 he left his father's house at Croydon and hanged himself from the bough of a tree with a stockwhip in scrub at Long Bay, Middle Harbour.[17] His body was in a terrible state when found eight days later.

BANJO HAD WRITTEN A SHORT STORY, 'The Tug-of-War',[18] for *The Bulletin* about a two-week international sporting event at Darlinghurst Hall[19] featuring strong men from around the world: Norway, Italy, Russia, Ireland, the West Indies, Australia and many points between. He followed it with the poem 'The Pannikin Poet'[20] but was just warming up for Lawson's opening salvo in the skirmish between the two writers.

It started with 'Borderland'[21] on 9 July 1892. While A. W. Jose said that the 'Bulletin's two chief bards were usually on the edge of animosity',[22] the two treated their rivalry as a good-natured contest that could make them a few quid.

The sunny plains, Lawson wrote in 'Borderland', were really 'burning wastes of barren soil and sand with their everlasting fences' stretching out across Australia. There was desolation and desert everywhere, a 'luny bullock' staring with reddened eyes, a 'sun-dried shepherd' dragging behind his crawling sheep enveloped in clouds of dust. There were treacherous tracks; dark and evil-looking gullies;

dull, dumb flats and stony rises; lizards and snakes. It was either heat and dust or destructive floods:

I am back from up the country – up the country where I went
Seeking for the Southern poets' land whereon to pitch my tent;
I have left a lot of broken idols out along the track,
Burnt a lot of fancy verses – and I'm glad that I am back –
…
I believe the Southern poets' dream will not be realised
Till the plains are irrigated and the land is humanised.
I intend to stay at present – as I said before – in town
Drinking beer and lemon-squashes – taking baths and cooling down.[23]

Lawson did not name Paterson in 'Borderland', only making reference to 'Southern poets', but Banjo publicly made the battle a personal one with 'In Defence of the Bush (On Reading Henry Lawson's "Borderland")'[24] in *The Bulletin* two weeks later:

So you're back from up the country, Mister Lawson, where you went,
And you're cursing all the business in a bitter discontent;
Well, we grieve to disappoint you, and it makes us sad to hear
That it wasn't cool and shady – and there wasn't plenty beer,
And the loony bullock snorted when you first came into view;
Well, you know it's not so often that he sees a swell like you;
And the roads were hot and dusty, and the plains were burnt
 and brown,
And no doubt you're better suited drinking lemon-squash in town.
…
You had better stick to Sydney and make merry with the 'push',
For the bush will never suit you, and you'll never suit the bush.[25]

Banjo even had a shot at Lawson over the melancholy of one of his rival's best-known poems: 'And the women of the homesteads and the men you chanced to meet – / Were their faces sour and saddened like the "faces in the street".'[26]

The battle became a literary sensation around Australia, but Banjo's retort looked puerile – especially when in the same issue of *The Bulletin*, a few pages back, Archibald published the Lawson masterpiece

'The Drover's Wife'[27] about a 'gaunt sun-browned bushwoman' missing her ever-absent husband and caring for her four 'ragged, dried-up-looking children' while battling a poisonous black snake that lurked under the cracks of her rough slab floor.[28] The drover's wife is surrounded by her frightened brood as she tries to outwit the snake and thinks about all her battles.[29]

Lawson could have been telling the story of Rose Paterson's marriage. Banjo never wrote of his mother's pains and privations, nor of his father's demons, preferring to gloss over the harsh realities of his mother's time in isolation at Buckinbah and Illalong, and his father's demise. He concealed his family background, while Lawson used his own misfortune as a vast canvas.

On 6 August 1892, Archibald ran Lawson's 'In Answer to "Banjo" and Otherwise'.[30] Lawson rained rhyming blows all over Banjo's reputation, before extending the hand of friendship after his final fusillade and some instructions on the true spirit of their friendly debate. The venomous tirade was later sarcastically renamed 'The City Bushman':

Then we had to wring our blueys which were rotting in the swags,
And we saw the sugar leaking through the bottoms of the bags,
And we couldn't raise a chorus, for the toothache and the cramp,
While we spent the hours of darkness draining puddles round the camp.
Would you like to change with Clancy, go a-droving? tell us true,
For we rather think that Clancy would be glad to change with you,
. . .
Did you ever guard the cattle when the night was inky black
And it rained, and icy water trickled gently down your back.
Till your saddle-weary backbone started aching at the roots
And you almost heard the croaking of the bullfrog in your boots?
. . .
Did you fight the drought and pleuro when the 'seasons' were asleep,
Felling sheoaks all the morning for a flock of starving sheep,
Drinking mud instead of water – climbing trees and lopping boughs
For the broken-hearted bullocks and the dry and dusty cows?
. . .
But you'll find it very jolly with the cuff-and-collar push,
And the city seems to suit you, while you rave about the bush.[31]

Lawson slipped in the boot again with the 'Grog- An'- Grumble Steeplechase', poking fun at the image and characters of Banjo's 'Open Steeplechase':

'Twixt the coastline and the border lay the town of Grog-an'-Grumble
In the days before the bushman was a dull an' heartless drudge,
An' they say the local meeting was a drunken rough-and-tumble,
Which was ended pretty often by an inquest on the judge.[32]

Banjo must have felt surrounded as Lawson and other poets mocked him and his work. He struck back again with 'In Answer to Various Bards',[33] scoffing at the melancholy of a poet 'with a graveyard of his own'.[34] He is said to have developed the idea after seeing an early draft of Lawson's 'Poet of the Tomb'.

Well, I've waited mighty patient while they all came rolling in,
Mister Lawson, Mister Dyson, and the others of their kin,
With their dreadful, dismal stories of the Overlander's camp,
How his fire is always smoky, and his boots are always damp;
And they paint it so terrific it would fill one's soul with gloom,
But you know they're fond of writing about 'corpses' and 'the tomb'.
So, before they curse the bushland they should let their fancy range,
And take something for their livers, and be cheerful for a change.

Now, for instance, Mr. Lawson – well, of course, we almost cried
At the sorrowful description how his 'little 'Arvie' died,
And we lachrymosed in silence when 'His Father's Mate' was slain;
Then he went and killed the father, and we had to weep again.
Ben Duggan and Jack Denver, too, he caused them to expire,
And he went and cooked the gander of Jack Dunn, of Nevertire;
So, no doubt, the bush is wretched if you judge it by the groan
Of the sad and soulful poet with a graveyard of his own.
...
But that ends it, Mr. Lawson, and it's time to say good-bye,
We must agree to differ in all friendship, you and I.[35]

A week later Lawson's 'The Poets of the Tomb'[36] appeared, answering the charge that he specialised in writing about 'corpses' by declaring:

The world has had enough of bards who wish that they were dead,
'Tis time the people passed a law to knock 'em on the head,
For 'twould be lovely if their friends could grant the rest they crave –
Those bards of 'tears' and 'vanished hopes', those poets of the grave.[37]

By then Lawson was beginning an epic outback adventure, his first real foray into the wide Australian wilderness of red earth and frying heat at the back of Bourke, walking in the baking shoes of the bushmen he wrote about. If anyone was drinking lemon squashes that summer it was Banjo.

A few weeks later, in the Christmas 1892 edition of *The Bulletin*, Archibald published Banjo's comic 'The Man from Ironbark'[38] about the befuddled bushman running amok in a Sydney barber shop. Archibald was so impressed with what many still regard as Banjo's most humorous work that *The Bulletin* took out its entire front page with illustrations. When Lawson wrote a parody of the poem for *The Bulletin*, Archibald refused to run it, so instead Lawson sold 'The Man from Waterloo (With Kind Regards to Banjo)' to *The Truth*.[39] Waterloo is a Sydney suburb.

Two years later, Banjo had one last go in 'A Voice from the Town':[40]

I thought, in the days of the droving,
Of steps I might hope to retrace,
To be done with the bush and the roving
And settle once more in my place.
With a heart that was well nigh to breaking,
In the long, lonely rides on the plain,
I thought of the pleasure of taking
The hand of a lady again.

I am back into civilisation,
Once more in the stir and the strife,
But the old joys have lost their sensation –
The light has gone out of my life;
The men of my time they have married,
Made fortunes or gone to the wall;
Too long from the scene I have tarried,
And, somehow, I'm out of it all.[41]

A writer of the time remarked, '"Barty" Paterson, as he is familiarly called, although the singer of bush delights, is a thorough town man in appearance, thin-faced and clean shaven, always to be seen at Government House balls, Town Hall concerts and fashionable first nights, with a great hobby for polo. Of the two Sydney verse men, Paterson and Lawson, some epigramist smartly said that Lawson praised the town and lived in the bush, while Paterson praised the bush and lived in the town.'[42]

Years later Banjo remarked, 'I think that Lawson put his case better than I did, but I had the better case, so that honours (or dishonours) were fairly equal. An undignified affair, but it was a case of "root hog or die."' He added: 'To show how a poet can be without honour (or profit) in his own country, I remember Lawson's wife telling me that she was quite happy because Henry was "working" again. "What's he working at," I asked, "prose or verse?" "Oh, no," she said. "I don't mean writing, I mean working. He's gone back to his trade as a house painter."'[43]

Henry Lawson's widow reckoned that was bunkum. Banjo might have been a first-rate storyteller, but she knew that like so many great storytellers he was a master of invention. She was irate over what she claimed were fabrications about her late husband. Immediately upon reading Banjo's recollections about Lawson, with whom she had a rocky relationship, Bertha Lawson wrote to the *Herald*'s editor to complain:

> My husband never returned to his trade during our married life, with the exception of one day and a half in Western Australia, an incident Mr Patterson [sic] knows nothing of. The story of the duel between 'The City and the Bush' is also without foundation of fact. Henry Lawson did not meet Banjo Patterson [sic] until Patterson [sic] and verse appeared.[44]

Through all their jousting, Banjo and Lawson remained respectful colleagues – if not friends – and were quick to help with suggestions for each other's work.

On 3 September 1895, Angus & Robertson wrote a memorandum to Banjo to say: 'Lawson suggests as "The Story of Conroy's Gap" is widely known as "Conroy's Gap", "The Story of" ought to be dropped. It would look better from a compositor's point of view I think too.' Banjo wrote across it: 'All right. This suits me. – A.B. Paterson.' [45]

Over the next few years, Banjo helped Lawson free of charge with his contractual arrangements and copyright issues.

Lawson was a troubled man, plagued by depression and alcohol dependence – but even though he and Banjo were publicly rivals, Banjo had his back. On 15 July 1899, Banjo wrote to George Robertson of Angus & Robertson saying 'I think you are too critical as to the quality of his last pieces. What I read were distinctly good: you were very set on getting his work and now that you have got it at your own price you don't like it!'[46]

The next day Paterson scribbled another memo to Robertson, saying: 'Lawson submits the enclosed for your perusal and would be glad to get an advance of say £5. – A.B.P.' On the back of the note, Paterson scrawled in pencil: 'This may suit you to pay a fiver in advance. If not, say so. – A.B.P.'

Lawson himself rarely mentioned the contest again, but a decade and a half later, in Sydney's *The Newsletter*, he penned 'In the Height of Fashion':[47]

I like your book, Mr. Lawson,
'Clancy of the Overflow'
Better far than Mr. Banjo's –
'When Your Pants Begin to Go.'
No I am no longer snarling,
Long ago we had our row –
Don't be angry Banjo, darling,
Though I'm fashionable now.[48]

BANJO TOOK WHATEVER OPPORTUNITY he could – on vacation and at weekends – to get back into the country, whether it was longer trips into the outback or short excursions into the Blue Mountains. On one memorable occasion he went as far west as the Darling River, where he saw a steamboat that reminded him of the stories of Mark Twain. Steamboats thrived on the Darling and the Murray before the trains cut out the river trade.

From a young age Banjo had a wanderlust, and his sights were set way beyond New South Wales. Before he knew it he would be travelling the world, reporting on fascinating places and extraordinary characters – and sometimes deadly action.

For the time being, though, he was sharing rooms in Wharf Road across the water from Rockend where his mother was slowly dying.

At just twenty-five, Rose Paterson had seen her home taken from her in 1869. She would never again own a home, and had been relying in recent years on the charity of her mother and Banjo's comfortable wage to put a roof over her head. She lived at Rockend and another cottage with her youngest daughters, but her health was in rapid decline. Almost from her first day of marriage Rose had suffered from the stress of loneliness in the vast Australian bush and the constant battle to make ends meet under threat of financial ruin. Her body had been ravaged by the cycle of pregnancy and child rearing; of a poor, unbalanced diet; of hard toil; of infrequent and inadequate medical attention; of having half her teeth ripped out because it was cheaper than repair. There was the worry of feeding and educating the children, the fears over their scrapes with injury and despair.

Then her husband had just up and died of a drug overdose, leaving her with no money and nowhere for her and her brood to live. She had suffered a physical and psychological breakdown. From the time she had moved back to Sydney, she had suffered kidney and heart problems and succumbed to frequent fainting spells. After two decades of scrimping and scrounging, Rose had returned to a far more refined way of life among educated, genteel folk. But her poor health meant that she hardly had a chance to enjoy the garden parties and grand vistas of Gladesville.

Dr Quaife was a regular at Rockend and treated Rose for her many maladies. She died suddenly on 24 February 1893. She was only forty-eight, but the years of stress and disappointment had taken their toll. Banjo thought she was older.

He arranged her funeral. She would not lie next to her husband in the lonely bush cemetery at Binalong, near the property where she had spent most of her adult life battling the forces of nature and the ill winds of financial hardship with a 'roasted out body'.[49] Instead she was laid to rest near the Darvalls and Bartons in the St Anne's churchyard at Ryde, not far from Rockend.

Her death notice in the *Sydney Morning Herald* read simply: 'PATERSON.—February 24, at her residence, Theta, Gladesville, Rose Isabella Paterson, widow of late Andrew Bogle Paterson, of Illalong, Yass, aged 49 years [sic].'[50]

Her gravestone bears this inscription:

'God is Love'
Rose Isabella Paterson
3rd daughter of
Robert and Emily Barton
Born 30th Decr 1844
Fell asleep 24th Feb 1893

Even though the bush had not been kind to Rose, there was a lot of good nature evident in the ginger of her writings and always a wry smile in the way she could find humour during the darkest of times.

Banjo had jousted with Henry Lawson over the romantic vision of the bush, but he knew as well as his literary rival that there were many women like 'The Drover's Wife' battling to keep their families afloat.

The *Bulletin* Debate had come and gone, and though Banjo never went so far as George Essex Evans in his tribute to 'The Women of the West', he was probably thinking of his own mother in her narrow grave when he wrote 'Under the Shadow of Kiley's Hill', recalling hard times on Boree Nyrang:

Gone is the garden they kept with care;
Left to decay at its own sweet will,
Fruit trees and flower beds eaten bare,
Cattle and sheep where the roses were,
Under the shadow of Kiley's Hill.

Where are the children that throve and grew
In the old homestead in days gone by?
One is away on the far Barcoo
Watching his cattle the long year through,
Watching them starve in the droughts and die.
. . .

What of the parents? That unkept mound
Shows where they slumber united still;
Rough is their grave, but they sleep as sound
Out on the range as on holy ground,
Under the shadow of Kiley's Hill.[51]

Chapter 13

6 MAY 1893, POLO GROUND IN COOMA, NEW SOUTH WALES

From what I saw of Morant I find it hard to believe that he killed anybody for gain. Reckless ne'er-do-well he was, but one finds it very difficult to think of him as a murderer.

BANJO PATERSON ON HIS RIVAL HORSEMAN BREAKER MORANT[1]

AS THE STEAM LOCOMOTIVE carried Banjo and his well-heeled friends south to Cooma for a weekend lark playing polo, Banjo could only have imagined the hardships Henry Lawson was enduring in the wilds of western New South Wales, the borderland where Burke and Wills had floundered and perished. Lawson was doing it tougher than ever, and Banjo was having the time of his life.

A story went that Banjo said he couldn't marry Sarah Riley because he couldn't afford it. But there were more than a few raised eyebrows over the fact that he *could* play a game enjoyed by only the wealthiest men in Sydney.

A year earlier, Banjo had been in Goulburn to see the local champions in a polo match against 'the roughies' from Cooma on the banks of the Wollondilly.[2] Banjo reckoned he must have had the 'gift of prophecy', because he wrote 'a jingle' called 'The Geebung Polo Club'[3] – which, in his words, 'outlasted much better work'.[4] On returning to Sydney, Banjo arranged for his teammates to play the Cooma boys. He and three pals travelled down on 5 May 1893. On arrival at Cooma Station, the visitors were taken on a four-horse dray to their lodgings. Their polo ponies had come down on an earlier train and were in good order, 'very comfortably stabled in big loose boxes'.[5] A 'great concourse of people' turned out on a bracing Saturday, 6 May 1893, to see a 'closely contested'[6] encounter on the Cooma Club's lumpy ground at the back of the railway station.[7] Banjo would later write that the four men in his team were the best to ever represent Sydney.[8]

A local paper gave the game away and said the 31-year-old lawyer was the man who was 'The Banjo' of *The Bulletin* and that he had played brilliantly alongside Tom Watson, the starter for the Australian Jockey Club. 'Both these gentlemen were splendidly mounted.'[9] For two quarters of the game Banjo was on 'the handsome grey pony Snowy, reputed to be one of the fastest and best ponies in Sydney, and winner of [the] champion prize at [the] last Sydney exhibition. The way in which Snowy followed the ball and left his pursuers behind was a treat to witness.'[10] Banjo remembered the Cooma team as 'real wild men with cabbage-tree hats, and skin-tight pants, their hats held on by a strap under their noses'.[11] Even though the ground was damp and slow[12] the match was thoroughly enjoyable, with Banjo's men winning 2–1, and Ted Litchfield and Zouch Moriarty impressing for the locals.[13]

The post-match dinner at Rolfe's Prince of Wales Hotel was a great success. More than forty people came to celebrate the match, and they were entertained with singing to the accompaniment of piano and violin. Local grazier Granville Ryrie,[14] later a knighted army major-general, gave an exhibition of whistling.[15] Banjo was asked to recite 'The Man from Snowy River', 'the hit number of the period',[16] but instead he served up his new composition 'The Geebung Polo Club': an appropriate entertainment about the rough-and-ready bush battlers, 'long and wiry natives of the rugged mountainside',[17] who took on the wealthy city swells – 'The Cuff and Collar Team' – in a game so fierce that one spectator's leg was broken just from watching, and all the players on the field were killed as the rival teams clubbed each other down. They finally continued their rivalry as ghosts 'on misty moonlit evenings, while the dingoes howl around'.[18] Banjo's poem went down splendidly with the Cooma crowd, who reckoned he had recited 'rollicking verses in his best colonial style'.[19]

The poem first appeared in print in the 1893 issue of the illustrated annual *The Antipodean,* which had debuted a year earlier under the ownership of the London publishers Chatto & Windus, in collaboration with George Robertson,[20] a Scottish-born publisher from Melbourne. Robertson was the namesake of but unrelated to the British-born Sydney publisher[21] whose partnership with David Mackenzie Angus[22] was instrumental in making Banjo Paterson a household name in Australia.

On the way home from Cooma, Banjo and his buddies stopped in Goulburn to play the locals. Banjo scored three goals in succession in Sydney's comprehensive victory, his fast ponies being 'of great service for riding off and hustling'.[23]

Banjo would later write that polo had its origins with the 'hill tribes in the north of India'[24] and that in England 'no better training for riding, coolness, and dash could be found for a young officer'.[25] 'It is a pity that in Australia the military forces are hardly able, as a rule, to afford the expense of the game,' he wrote. 'Indeed, all over the colonies it is the factor of expense which has kept the game confined to a select few, and hindered its growth.'[26]

The expense was not a worry for Banjo. In polo he combined the excitement of riding like the Man from Snowy River with mingling among the upper levels of society and the beautiful women who dwelt there.

WHILE BANJO WAS OFF CAROUSING and showing the wild men of Cooma how to ride an expensive horse, Henry Lawson was back working as a house painter. This time he was living in the dusty heat of far-flung Bourke, eight hundred kilometres north-west of Sydney on the south bank of the Darling River.

When he and Banjo had started their joust over the identity of the real Australia, Lawson was a man of many sorrows and was drinking heavily to drown them, stumbling from one bar to another in Sydney's Rocks area, then a rough waterside slum. He was living with his Aunt Emma in a cottage in North Sydney, but she saw less of him than the many barmaids who greeted him every morning.

Ted Brady, who had once pinched Lawson's poem 'The Cambaroora Star', was now doing his best to make it up to his friend, though Lawson seemed to be in a perpetual downward spiral. Brady recalled that at the time he was living in a ground-floor room of an umbrella repair shop in Regent Street, Redfern, 'writing hard'[27] – mostly for Archibald and the hard-drinking John Norton,[28] who was editor of the racy *Truth*. Brady wasn't making a fortune and was 'postponing the turkey and champagne for future occasions'.[29] Brady wrote later:

> I do not know where Henry was living but he arrived at my caravanserai on an early morning in one of his blackest moods. We walked down to the old *Bulletin* office in Pitt Street, and went upstairs to the old editor's office. Archibald, keeping his hand on the copy he was revising, screwed partly round in his chair, and regarded us with what I thought was an uncivil eye. Henry found occasion to go downstairs about something. Still keeping his hand on the [manuscript] before him, Archibald suddenly wheeled right round and asked me to sit down. Then this kindly, black bearded fatherly arbiter of a hundred Australian literary ambitions demanded: 'What's the matter with Lawson?'[30]

Brady stalled for time to think of an appropriate response. Hesitantly, he said, 'He's all right.'

'No, he is not all right,' said Archibald, who seemed to have a fatherly interest in his wayward star. 'He is coming here in the morning with tobacco juice running down his jaw, smelling of stale beer, and he has begun to write about "The Rocks". The next thing he will be known as "the Poet of the Rocks"; and ...'

'Look!' Brady cried, seized by inspiration. 'If he got away to the bush he would be all right.'

Archibald turned back in his chair and regarded the manuscript. That wasn't such a bad idea. Though Lawson wrote movingly of bush characters, Archibald wondered just how much of Australia's interior he had seen beyond Grenfell and Mudgee. 'Why doesn't he go back to the bush?' Archibald demanded of Brady over his shoulder.

'No money,' Brady ventured.[31]

Archibald could fix that, though he was not about to make Lawson wealthy even if 'The Drover's Wife' was being lauded as a piece of literary brilliance. Still, fresh air and new horizons could perhaps quell the demons tormenting his sad star of the Sydney literary scene – it might also produce more winning articles to lift *Bulletin* sales. Archibald gave Lawson £5 in spending money and a one-way ticket to Bourke worth £4.[32]

Before leaving Sydney, Lawson sent a poem, 'A Stranger on the Darling',[34] to Bourke's *Western Herald* under the pseudonym Joe Swallow. He hoped to gain some journalism work in the western town but he packed his paintbrushes just in case.

Two of the *Bulletin* staff, including A. G. Stephens[33] – editor of *The Bulletin*'s 'Red Page' of literary gossip and reviews – escorted him to Redfern Station. Their brief was to make sure the deaf, shy and brooding wastrel got on board. Lawson left Sydney in a cloud of steam and smoke and under a cloud of suspicion about his future. Bourke offered him a new start with a population of more than three thousand, about two hundred businesses,[35] wide streets and brick buildings with iron roofs that reflected a dazzling sun. It could also be a launching point from which to explore the outback even further west.

Bourke represented the end of the railway line from Sydney. It was the largest inland port in Australia, where drays delivered huge loads of wool to be carried on barges down the Darling River. And it was a staunch union town with unwavering support for the striking shearers of a year before, so Lawson knew he would meet men of a kindred spirit there.

It seems the *Bulletin* Debate with Banjo was paramount in Lawson's mind as the train rattled and rocked along the line. He arrived at Bourke late on the afternoon of 21 September 1892,[36] after a journey of thirty-six hours, and promptly wrote to his Aunt Emma with a degree of justification: 'The bush between here and Bathurst is horrible. I was right, and Banjo wrong.'[37]

Lawson had an argument with a shearer about how many sheep could be shorn in a day, and met one braggart so full of bluster that he convinced Lawson that all bushmen were liars.

Lawson took a room at the Great Western Hotel – and if Archibald and Brady had hoped the outback heat would dry up Lawson's drinking, they were wrong. He gave Bourke the nickname 'Comeanaveadrink', as among its wide and welcoming streets were nineteen pubs. He told his aunt that he had a problem and these establishments were not helping him overcome it. 'I'm an awful fool,' he wrote to her, explaining that he had hardly unpacked his swag when some Great Western barmaids 'as cunning as the devil' sent him to bed 'boozed'. He promised that he had learnt his lesson and knew that to escape the demon drink 'I must take to the bush as soon as I can'.[38]

Lawson wrote some political poems for the *Western Herald*, one of two local papers in town. The union men made him feel like a true comrade, and he formed some strong friendships in the town – particularly with Donald Macdonell,[39] a shearer who would soon become secretary of the Bourke branch of the Amalgamated Shearers' Union of Australasia and later the Member for Cobar in the NSW Legislative Assembly.

There was still little money in poetry, though, and not much more in painting. Archibald's £5 was soon gone.

Banjo, meanwhile, was playing polo at Rosehill racecourse. He entertained large crowds of desirable young women with his daring athleticism in games on 7 October 1892[40] and then fifteen days later.[41] Archibald would soon publish Banjo's 'The Boss of the "Admiral Lynch"'[42] about war in South America, and 'A Bushman's Song' about the nomadic life of a rural worker on the hunt for a job when work kept going to cheap imported labour.

Six weeks after Lawson arrived in Bourke, Archibald published his short story 'In a Dry Season',[43] which ends with 'P.S. Never tackle the bush without a good mate. With one you can do anything and go anywhere.'[44] The hard-drinking and destitute 25-year-old found a good mate that November in eighteen-year-old Victorian Jim Gordon,[45] another battler who had gone outback looking for work and money. According to Gordon, who later found success as a writer under the pseudonym Jim Grahame, these two hard-up strangers felt an immediate rapport when they met in Mitchell Street, the main thoroughfare of Bourke.

'I was lonely, and somewhat frightened and home-sick,' Gordon recalled, 'and he was alone, pacing the footpath up one side and down the other.'[46] Lawson was living rough after his funds had dried up. When Gordon spoke to him, Lawson 'looked up suddenly and had on his face the look of one who was embarrassed at being caught daydreaming'.[47] Gordon did not know the identity of this odd man who 'seemed different to all the others', but he accepted Lawson's invitation to join 'a couple of us camped in a place just across the billabong'. The next day Lawson got a job as a house painter and landed Gordon work with the same contractor, but the youngster was sacked within two weeks because his efforts were not up to scratch. The pair then decided to look for jobs elsewhere.

Lawson put his paintbrushes away, joined the General Labourers' Union, and on 24 November 1892 set off with Gordon under a blazing summer sun for sixty kilometres of hard slog south-west. They tramped along a dusty track beside the winding Darling River until they finally reached Toorale Station and the confluence of the Warrego. Along the way they scavenged for cast-off boots at a deserted surveyors' camp.

It was almost the end of the shearing season but the two young mates earned a small wage at Toorale, working briefly as roustabouts. They picked up the fleeces from the shearing-shed floor and helped to load the great bales onto the river boats for transport down the Darling and the Murray, all the way to Adelaide. At night under the creaking tin roof, as the other men joked and yarned about their work, Lawson was withdrawn, isolated by his deafness and agitated by the enforced sobriety among station workers. Gordon saw Lawson as 'a man apart, having little in common with those whom he worked with' and 'moody most of the evenings'. As a rule Lawson would lie on his bunk from teatime until the lights were out, 'talking very little and gazing at the cobwebby corrugated-iron roof'.[48] For a man in poor health and with a drinking problem and depression, the bush was even worse than Lawson had imagined. 'A shearing shed,' he observed later, 'is perhaps the most degrading hell on the face of this earth.'[49]

When the shearing finished in mid-December, Lawson and Gordon trudged back wearily to Bourke for Christmas. But a few days later they set out again, with their swags and water bottles and wide, battered hats – this time to Hungerford, which straddled the remote border of Queensland. The walk took them on more than two hundred kilometres of a meandering odyssey across some of the driest and most unforgiving country on earth. They hoped to find work at stations along the way, but all they found was a ceaseless sun baking their heads and the hot earth burning the soles of their tattered boots.

While Banjo was prospecting for material while seated on horseback, Lawson was fossicking on foot.[50] A. G. Stephens likened Lawson's journey to that of 'a damned soul swagging it through purgatory'.[51]

On and on, Lawson and Gordon trudged like the explorers Burke and Wills stumbling to their doom. 'Time means tucker,' Lawson wrote in his poem 'Out Back', 'and tramp you must.'[52] Occasionally

Lawson and Gordon met other swagmen looking for food and shelter, or bullockies driving their teams across the rough, rutted tracks, cursing the red dust and the heat and the flies and the heat and the flies and the flies and the heat. And the dust. And the meanness of station owners who told them to keep walking. 'You have no idea of the horrors of the country out here,' Lawson told his aunt. 'Men tramp and live like dogs.'[53] They survived on cornmeal flatbread called 'Johnnycakes' and 'cadged a bit of meat here and there at miserable stations'.[54]

At night, Lawson and Gordon took comfort in the cooler weather. They camped under the black canopy, gazing at the 'wond'rous glory of the everlasting stars' but wishing they were in a town with a roof over their heads. Lawson complained to Aunt Emma that it had been two months since he had slept in a proper bed: 'The physical hardship was bad enough, but the sense of degradation was worse.'[55]

It took them more than two weeks to reach Hungerford, and they found it underwhelming. They didn't even see the town until they were 'quite close to it', the reflection of the sun bouncing off 'two or three white-washed galvanized-iron roofs' rising out of the mulga.[56]

As soon as he arrived in Hungerford, Lawson wrote to his aunt to say that he was 'a beaten man'[57] and that he was ready to leave the next day – 17 January 1893 – for Bourke but would go 'off the track to try to get a few weeks work on a Warrego station'.[58] He promised to 'find the means of getting back to Sydney – never to face the bush again'.[59] 'My boots were worn out and I was in rags when I arrived here,' he told Aunt Emma, 'you should have seen the last hat I wore. I find that I've tramped more than 300 miles since I left here last. That's all I ever intend to do with a swag.'[60]

On the return journey to Bourke, Lawson and Gordon were given a hand by William 'Baldy' Davis, the owner of Kerribee Station, who supplied them with as much food as they could carry and added a pound note for good luck. The two worn-out travellers plodded into Bourke in February, Lawson to resume his work as a painter – sometimes painting inside the Great Western bar – and Jim to wander off for more station work.

In June 1893 Lawson finally boarded a train back to Sydney with a free pass to oversee 'five trucks of cattle',[61] having walked in worn-out shoes through what he called the 'Out Back' hell like so many of the men he wrote about – 'the poor, hopeless, half-starved wretches who carry swags through it and look in vain for work – and ask in vain for tucker very often'.[62] Banjo was still celebrating the Sydney polo team's triumph over Cooma and Goulburn, and getting ready for a busy lawn tennis season.[63] Lawson returned to Sydney still a drunk, still depressed and still broke. But Lawson had 'escaped'[64] the bush and was now rich in experience. Archibald's £5 investment would pay handsome dividends in Lawson's work for years to come, as he had had experiences that Banjo never knew.

He also had a postcard from a man Banjo would get to know very well.

It was while he was at Bourke that Lawson had received a Christmas card from another of *The Bulletin*'s versifiers, a bush poet infamous as a rogue around north Queensland and western New South Wales. The card was sent from Walgett and written in doggerel. It congratulated Lawson for his victory over Banjo in the *Bulletin* Debate, and it reached Lawson via the *Bulletin* office in Sydney after he had returned from Hungerford. It was sent by a wild horseman, 'handsome adventurer'[65] and bush poet named Harry 'Breaker' Morant.[66]

ROSE PATERSON'S BROTHER Arthur Barton had warned Banjo all about 'The Breaker'.

Uncle Arthur knew that Morant was a conman – but a charming one nonetheless. The Breaker wrote for *The Bulletin*, but Uncle Arthur doubted most of his stories and he warned Banjo not to fall prey:

> There is a man going down from here to Sydney, and he says he is going to call on you. His name is Morant. He says he is the son of an English Admiral, and he has good manners, and education. He can do anything better than most people; can write verses; break in horses; trap dingoes, yard scrub cattle; dance, run, fight, drink, and borrow money; *anything except work*. I don't know what is the matter with the chap. He seems to be brimming over with flashness, for he will do any dare-devil thing so long as there is a crowd to watch him. He jumped a horse over a stiff three-rail fence one dark night by the light of two matches which he had placed on the posts![67]

Although he told everyone he was an admiral's son, The Breaker's real name was Edwin Henry Murrant, and his parents were the master and matron of a workhouse at Bridgewater in Somerset, where he was born ten months after Banjo's birth at Narrambla. On 1 April 1883, The Breaker arrived in Townsville. His self-confidence was infectious.

From Townsville, the new arrival headed for Charters Towers, a town made wealthy by goldmining. He charmed his way into the pockets of his new acquaintances, inviting himself to jobs on stations and borrowing money. At the nearby Fanning Downs Station he met 21-year-old Daisy May O'Dwyer,[68] an immigrant from Tipperary who became better known as Daisy May Bates, the esteemed welfare worker and anthropologist. On 13 March 1884 they were married in Charters Towers. Murrant described himself as a 'Gentleman' on the church register, explaining that he didn't have to work for a living and that any money loaned to him would soon be repaid when his remittances arrived from England. He promised Reverend Barlow a £5 note for performing the ceremony as soon as his remittance came to hand – but subsequent enquiries by the local newspaper in Charters Towers 'proved that even Curates sometimes make bad debts'.[69]

A month after the wedding Murrant beat a charge of stealing pigs, but he and Daisy, 'the latter now pretty well understanding the character of her husband',[70] decided to separate. The Breaker first used the name Harry Harbord Morant on a cheque that bounced, and Daisy was left to return his unpaid gifts.

'Morant' drifted about Queensland doing odd jobs, working for a while on a newspaper in Hughenden and creating a legend around himself as a horse-breaker. He would boast that he knew every country pub and hospital, since broken bones were an occupational hazard. He headed south-west to Winton, telling everyone there and in future travels that he was the son of Admiral Sir George Digby Morant and that he had studied at the Royal Naval College. He was a convincing speaker who could mix in any circles, and he was a fine bush poet whose first work for *The Bulletin* was 'A Night Thought'.[71] He claimed it was written on a Warrego sand ridge on 8 August 1891, and he signed it 'The Breaker'.

When Banjo was in his late thirties, he recalled that his first meeting with Morant was at a hunt; the self-assured Englishman was riding a livery stable horse. 'He rode so well,' Banjo remembered, 'that the delighted livery-stable keeper was induced to not only postpone payment for the hire of the moke, but actually to lend Morant £2 …'[72]

As an old man Banjo changed the story and wrote that he had actually first met The Breaker in the office of Street & Paterson, when the infamous horseman had followed close behind Arthur Barton's cautionary letter to the Waltham Building.

The Breaker buttered up Banjo, talking about hunting in England and riding in the bush. Then at 3 p.m. he looked at his watch.

> 'By Jove,' he said, 'I've enjoyed myself so much talking to you that I forgot I had to cash a cheque. And now the banks will be shut. Perhaps you could cash a cheque for me for a fiver. I've got to pay some bills and I've run myself clean out of money.[73]

Morant was a smooth operator, and 'almost unwillingly' Banjo replied that he did not have any cash on him; he suggested that The Breaker should let his creditors wait till the banks opened in the morning. Morant 'dismissed the matter with a wave of his hand, and neither then nor at any other time did he bear any malice for the refusal'.[74]

ON 26 APRIL 1894, Banjo rode an old black gelding called The Ace in the Point to Point Steeplechase at Canterbury, a race promoted by the Sydney Hunt Club. The course 'was about two miles, across fairly big fences, and a nasty-looking water-jump had to be crossed twice'. The Ace slipped at the first fence with Banjo coming a 'cropper', his bung arm having been damaged so many times in falls since childhood. Banjo was immediately remounted and went after the leaders, catching them.

Four months later, one of Australia's great sporting heroes, the jockey Tommy Corrigan, died from a fall in the Caulfield Grand National Steeplechase on 11 August 1894. Corrigan was the battler's friend, 'a merry hearted little Irishman' who won fortunes for punters during a time of great economic difficulty in Australia.

Banjo rushed into print, eulogising Corrigan as one of the great heroes of Australia:

You talk of riders on the flat, of nerve and pluck and pace,
Not one in fifty has the nerve to ride a steeplechase.
It's right enough while horses pull and take their fences strong,
To rush a flier to the front and bring the field along;
But what about the last half-mile, with horses blown and beat –
When every jump means all you know to keep him on his feet?

When any slip means sudden death – with wife and child to keep –
It needs some nerve to draw the whip and flog him at the leap –
But Corrigan would ride them out, by danger undismayed,
He never flinched at fence or wall, he never was afraid;
With easy seat and nerve of steel, light hand and smiling face,
He held the rushing horses back, and made the sluggards race.[75]

'Tommy Corrigan' was written among some of Banjo's most enduring work. His writing had now captured the attention of book publishers, and it was becoming more and more popular with *Bulletin* readers.

For the 1894 Christmas edition of *The Bulletin*, he wrote 'Saltbush Bill',[76] the humorous tale of a hardy drover who dragged out a fist fight with a squatter's jackaroo for as long as he could, so his mob of hungry sheep could have a good feed on the squatter's grass.

HENRY LAWSON HAD GONE to start afresh in New Zealand but ended up unemployed in Wellington, freezing cold instead of frying hot. Sometimes he slept rough in large earthen pipes that were due to be laid for drainage in the city. He was not exactly a great advertisement for writing as a career. His former boss at *The Boomerang*, Gresley Lukin, who had become a leading reporter on the *Evening Post*, found Lawson some work, but he was still struggling for a feed and to pay his bar bills.

Soon, though, his mother would help him publish a one-shilling collection of his works, *Short Stories in Prose and Verse*,[77] in time for Christmas 1894. The book could be purchased through *The Dawn* or *The Worker*. He prefaced the book by declaring: 'This is an attempt to publish in Australia, a collection of sketches and stories at a time when everything Australian, in the shape of a book, must bear the imprint of a London publishing firm before our critics will condescend to notice it …'[78]

The plains of Boree Nyrang as they are today, almost 180 years after Banjo Paterson's grandparents arrived there. *Grantlee Kieza*

Above: Banjo's grandmother Emily Barton (née Darvall) was a major influence on his writing. *City of Ryde*

Above left: Banjo's grandfather Robert Barton.

Left: Banjo's great-grandfather Major Edward Darvall, who brought his family to Australia in search of pastoral fortune.

Banjo's mother, Rose Paterson. Her witty letters reflecting the joys and setbacks of bush life had a major bearing on Banjo's writing. *Paterson family photo*

Banjo's father, Andrew Bogle Paterson, knew all too well the hardships of life in the saddle. *Paterson family photo*

Andrew Barton (Banjo) Paterson (left) and cousin Jack Paterson were boyhood chums while growing up on the property known as Illalong. *Paterson family photos*

Rockend Cottage, Banjo's home at Gladesville in Sydney, where he lived with his grandmother Emily Barton. It is now a fashionable restaurant. *Sardaka (CC BY 3.0)*

Banjo (standing sixth from right with hand on heart) at a gathering of the Sydney Hunt Club at Rouse Hill on 18 July 1895. Banjo rode a horse called Gossip on the day.

Banjo at a meeting of the Sydney Hunt Club, where his outstanding horsemanship won him many admirers and trophies. *Paterson family photo*

Jockey Tommy Corrigan as he looked in 1894 when he was the best-known rider in Australia. His death in a race fall inspired Banjo's moving eulogy. *National Library of Australia 136087388*

Banjo Paterson, drawn by Walter Syer, after coming second in the six-kilometre Sydney Hunt Club Steeplechase from Blacktown to Prospect, west of Sydney, on 26 October 1895. *State Library of New South Wales P2/275*

Banjo Paterson pictured circa 1890, at the height of his fame after the publication of 'Clancy' and 'Snowy River'. *National Library of Australia 136524579*

The Boer farmers were skilled horsemen and fierce opponents of the British and Empire forces. Working as a war correspondent, Banjo gained enormous respect for these fighting farmers, who reminded him of battlers from the Australian bush. *Australian War Memorial P07379.064*

A studio portrait of Private Harry 'Breaker' Morant, just before he left for South Africa with the 2nd Mounted Rifles from South Australia to join the British fight against the Boers. *Australian War Memorial A05311*

A caricature of Lord Kitchener from a French pro-Boer magazine, criticising his scorched earth policy. Banjo was appalled at the brutal war Kitchener waged on the Boer women and children and the establishment of deadly concentration camps. *Alamy*

Phil May, the brilliant *Bulletin* cartoonist who amazed Banjo with his devil-may-care lifestyle.

An 1894 self-portrait of Livingston 'Hop' Hopkins, another of the revered *Bulletin* cartoonists. *National Gallery of Victoria P7-1973*

A bullocky and his team traversing the rugged New South Wales bush. Men and teams like this had a big influence on Banjo's storytelling. *National Library of Australia 163374872*

Banjo was well acquainted with woolsheds like this one and the struggles of the man on the land when wool was Australia's chief export. *State Library of South Australia PRG 280/1/43/204*

Christina Macpherson, who co-wrote 'Waltzing Matilda' near Winton in Central Queensland amid great scandal. *National Library of Australia 224075340*

Sarah Riley, Banjo's long-time fiancée, pictured in later years. Their relationship ended after Banjo's collaboration with Christina Macpherson, Sarah's childhood friend.

A swagman with his pack in the Yass region of New South Wales near Illalong, Banjo's childhood home. Banjo's mother was always afraid of strangers arriving at the doorstep of her remote farmhouse but their ceaseless tramp – their 'waltzing Matilda' – inspired Banjo's most famous work. *National Library of Australia 153094677*

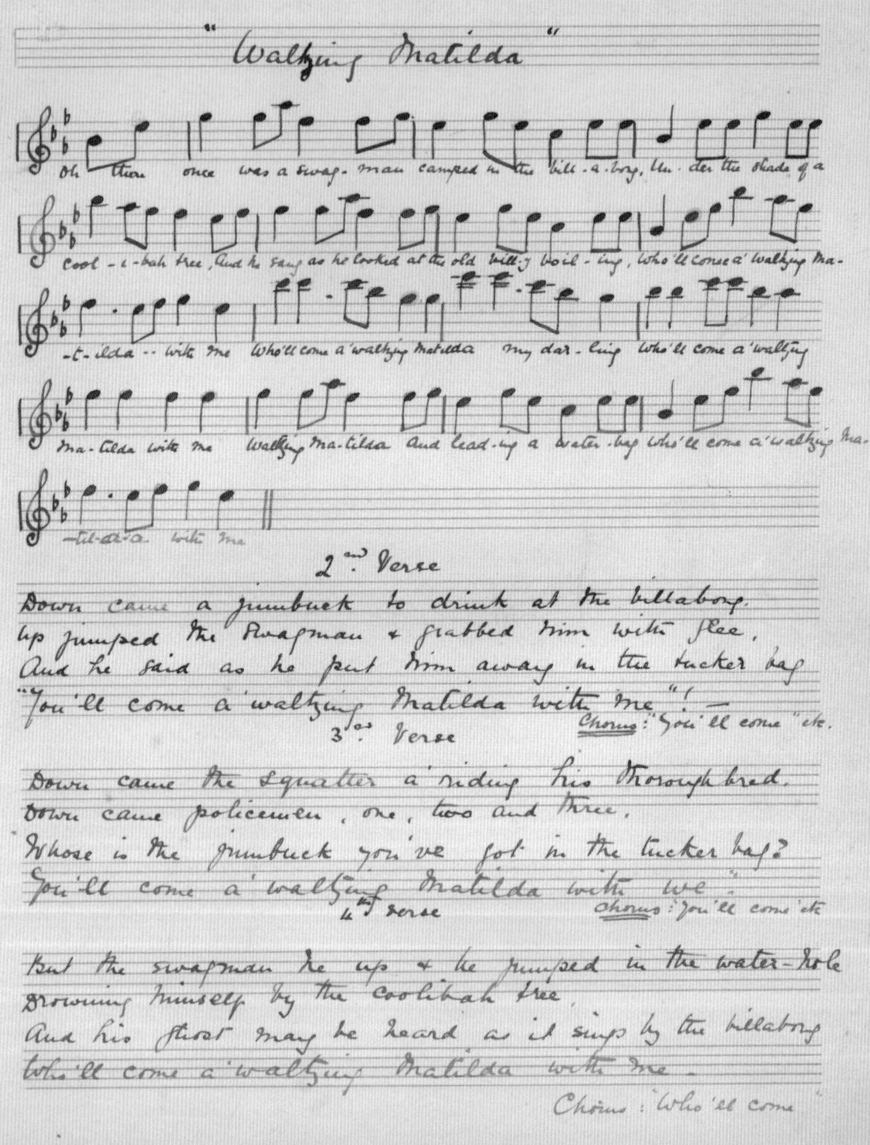

2nd Verse

Down came a jumbuck to drink at the billabong,
Up jumped the swagman & grabbed him with glee,
And he said as he put him away in the tucker bag
"You'll come a' waltzing Matilda with me"! —
Chorus: "You'll come" etc.

3rd Verse

Down came the Squatter a'riding his thoroughbred.
Down came policemen, one, two and three,
"Whose is the jumbuck you've got in the tucker bag?
You'll come a' waltzing Matilda with me."
Chorus: You'll come etc

4th Verse

But the swagman he up & he jumped in the water-hole
Drowning himself by the coolibah tree,
And his ghost may be heard as it sings by the billabong
"Who'll come a' waltzing Matilda with me."
Chorus: "Who'll come"

Christina Macpherson's draft of 'Waltzing Matilda'. *National Library of Australia MS 10086*

The start of the 1905 Dunlop Motor Reliability Trial at Sydney Town Hall. Banjo experienced a wild ride all the way to Melbourne in an Australian-built twenty-horsepower Innes that belonged to his friend Colonel John McLean Arnott. *State Library of Victoria H2013.117/7*

The young author Miles Franklin sought advice from Banjo and was flattered by his attentions. *State Library of New South Wales P1/597*

Banjo Paterson, right, smoking a pipe, regularly travelled the Australian bush with biscuit baron Colonel John McLean Arnott (left) and their friend and driver Thomas Leslie Griffin (centre).
National Library of Australia 136499876

Lady Dudley, also known as Rachel Ward, was considered one of the great beauties of the age, and she had a lasting effect on Banjo.

Bulletin publisher J. F. Archibald (left) was a mentor to both Banjo and Henry Lawson (right). *National Library of Australia 146528688*

Banjo Paterson with wife, Alice, and daughter, Grace, in 1906, photographed by artist Lionel Lindsay.
State Library of New South Wales ON 186 226-227

George Lambert's sketch of Major A. B. 'Banjo' Paterson while he served as an officer in the Middle East during the First World War. *Australian War Memorial ART02780*

Banjo's image was used on a series of postage stamps for The Bush Ballads series in 2014 that coincided with the 150th anniversary of his birth. Here the young solicitor daydreams about the world of Clancy of the Overflow. *Artists: Jamie and Leanne Tufrey; ©Australian Postal Corporation 2014*

Banjo's portrait in oils was painted in 1927 by Agnes Noyes Goodsir. He looked a weary man by the time he was in his early sixties. *State Library of New South Wales 840606*

Banjo (second from left) at the track with renowned pastoralist and horse trainer Hunter White (left) in 1930. *National Library of Australia 162398614*

The publisher Angus & Robertson was becoming interested in Lawson's work, and perhaps he felt that he had gone ahead of Banjo in their rivalry – though Banjo was having too much fun to notice.

On 27 October 1894, Banjo took three of his best horses to the Sydney Polo Club's well-attended sports day at Kensington, which was regarded as a 'comic race meeting'[79] for Sydney's bright young things.

Two months later at Sydney's Randwick racecourse, Banjo rode the old bay gelding Albert in a disaster-strewn steeplechase over two and a half miles. There were nine starters and almost as many falls. Albert had nearly been handicapped out of the event. With a whopping twelve stone seven pounds (seventy-nine kilograms) he hit the fence on the hill but was 'splendidly recovered by Mr Paterson', according to a racing writer at the event. Two of the horses fell at the final hurdle and The Ace refused the jump, leaving The Joker to canter home for the first prize of two hundred sovereigns. Banjo and 'old Albert who had been plodding along hopelessly in the rear' struggled home to 'secure second money' of fifty sovereigns.[80]

In the new year Banjo became the secretary of the NSW Polo Association.[81]

Then on 18 May 1895, Banjo and his mate Breaker Morant, who was visiting from Bourke, travelled out to Belmore with a large gathering of the Sydney Hunt Club. They were to trial a new pack of hounds, sent down from Brisbane.

Breaker Morant was just one of the many bold personalities Banjo would meet. In fact, at the age of thirty-one he already had a lifetime of stories to draw upon.

George Robertson wanted Angus & Robertson to be in business with Australia's best-known versifier. The identity of 'The Banjo' was an open secret in Sydney's legal and sporting circles, but he remained largely anonymous in the wider community. That was about to change. Robertson had a plan to make Banjo Paterson the most famous man in Australia.

Banjo saw many swagmen throughout his life, humping all their belongings from station to station begging to work for food. Picture: State Library of South Australia B21537

Waltzing Matilda

Oh! there once was a swagman camped in the Billabong,
Under the shade of a Coolabah tree;
And he sang as he looked at his old billy boiling,
'Who'll come a-waltzing Matilda with me.'

Who'll come a-waltzing Matilda, my darling,
Who'll come a-waltzing Matilda with me?
Waltzing Matilda and leading a water-bag –
Who'll come a-waltzing Matilda with me?

Down came a jumbuck to drink at the water-hole,
Up jumped the swagman and grabbed him in glee;
And he sang as he put him away in his tucker-bag,
'You'll come a-waltzing Matilda with me!'

Down came the Squatter a-riding his thorough-bred;
  Down came Policemen – one, two, and three.
'Whose is the jumbuck you've got in the tucker-bag?
  You'll come a-waltzing Matilda with me.'

But the swagman, he up and he jumped in the water-hole,
  Drowning himself by the Coolabah tree;
And his ghost may be heard as it sings in the Billabong,
  'Who'll come a-waltzing Matilda with me?'

Chapter 14

1895, DAGWORTH STATION, 130 KILOMETRES NORTH-WEST OF WINTON, QUEENSLAND

While resting for lunch, or while changing horses on our four-in-hand journeys, Miss Macpherson … used to play a little Scottish tune on a zither and I put words to the tune and called it 'Waltzing Matilda'. Not a very great literary achievement perhaps, but it has been sung in many parts of the world.

BANJO PATERSON EXPLAINING THE ORIGINS OF HIS MOST CELEBRATED WORK[1]

STREET & PATERSON was a successful law firm, but by his early thirties Banjo was starting to seriously question his career choices.

In 1894 he had jotted down his ideas for a prose sketch based on what his family believed was an actual incident. A widow towing two children behind her arrived at his office, 'somewhat breathless with the unaccustomed exercise of toiling up the stairs', and she started to explain her errand before she had quite recovered her breath. Consequently, she gasped a little in her speech:

> 'Are you the – ah – lawyer?' she said.
>
> I admitted that I was a lawyer; perhaps not the lawyer of the century, but still up to ordinary market expectations.
>
> 'Well,' she said, 'my 'usban' died a' Friday week and Fitzpatrick said to come an' see you an' see what we ought to do about sellin' the land.'
>
> 'Oh,' I said, 'what did your husband's estate consist of?'

> 'Estate,' she said, wonderingly, 'he hadn't no estate. Just a free selection up on Kuryong Creek was all he had. It was on Kiley's Run, you know. We thought Kiley'd buy us out when we selected, but after me 'usband finished his time, old Kiley went broke – got busted in the drought – and now the bank has the station.'

With bush people, Banjo wrote, 'no distinction is ever drawn between one bank and another. They look upon banks as public enemies, like bailiffs and book-canvassers.'[2]

Banjo took his little sketch no further, but soon after, Archibald published 'The Man Who Was Away':[3]

> The widow sought the lawyer's room with children three in tow,
> She told the lawyer man her tale in tones of deepest woe.
> Said she, 'My husband took to drink for pains in his inside,
> And never drew a sober breath from then until he died.
>
> 'He never drew a sober breath, he died without a will,
> And I must sell the bit of land the childer's mouths to fill.
> There's some is grown and gone away, but some is childer yet,
> And times is very bad indeed – a livin's hard to get.[4]

A year earlier Banjo had highlighted the plight of bush families at the mercy of the banks he sometimes represented, in 'Reconstruction: From a Farmer's Point of View':[5]

> So, the bank has bust its boiler! And in six or seven year
> It will pay me all my money back – of course!
> But the horse will perish waiting while the grass is germinating,
> And I reckon I'll be something like the horse.
>
> There's the ploughing to be finished and the ploughmen want their pay,
> And I'd like to wire the fence and sink a tank;
> But I own I'm fairly beat how I'm going to make ends meet
> With my money in a reconstructed bank.
>
> 'It's a safe and sure investment!' But it's one I can't afford,
> For I've got to meet my bills and pay the rent,

And the cash I had provided (so these meetings have decided)
Shall be collared by the bank at three per cent.[6]

Disillusioned with the law, Banjo was all ears when he and George Robertson got to talking in the Sydney offices of Angus & Robertson.

At 89 Castlereagh Street, David Angus and George Robertson had built an impressive publishing business from humble beginnings. The 35-year-old Robertson, born in Essex of Scottish parents, was a big and powerfully built man, with black hair, a black beard and dark brown eyes.[7] His father, a Unitarian minister, had died when Robertson was seven, and the boy's mother had moved back to Scotland. As Robertson yarned with Paterson, his speech flavoured with the faintest trace of a Scottish accent,[8] he was enjoying the success of thirteen years' hard work since he had started stacking shelves at a Sydney bookshop just four days after arriving in Australia. In January 1886 Robertson had invested his savings of £15 with fellow Scot David Angus to create a business that became known as 'the biggest bookshop in the world'.[9]

Robertson was an outdoors man with a family weekender in Blackheath in the Blue Mountains, and Banjo's poems and tales of the great Australian outdoors intrigued him. Robertson planned two books: a collection of the old Australian bush songs, before they were forgotten, and a compilation of Banjo's best work.

Lawson was also working out an agreement for his collection of short stories *While the Billy Boils*[10] and his book of poems *In the Days When the World Was Wide and Other Verses.*[11]

Of the work he and Lawson compiled, Banjo would later say:

> Our 'ruined rhymes' are not likely to last long, but if there is any hope at all of survival it comes from the fact that such writers as Lawson and myself had the advantage of writing in a new country. In all museums throughout the world one may see plaster casts of the footprints of weird animals, footprints preserved for posterity, not because the animals were particularly good of their sort, but because they had the luck to walk on the lava while it was cooling. There is just a faint hope that something of the same sort may happen to us.[12]

For the old bush songs, Banjo began by writing to friends and colleagues in the literary sphere – among them Lawson, Ted Dyson, Peter Airey[13] and D. H. Souter[14] – asking if they could contribute any morsels. He also began writing extra poems for a compilation of his best work; it was to be called *The Man from Snowy River*, built around his best-known verses to date. Among the forty-eight works featured would be six new creations, including 'Jim Carew', about an English rogue, most likely modelled on Banjo's hunting companion Breaker Morant:

> Born of a thoroughbred English race,
> Well proportioned and closely knit,
> Neat of figure and handsome face,
> Always ready and always fit,
> Hard and wiry of limb and thew,
> That was the ne'er-do-well Jim Carew.[15]

WHILE BANJO AND BREAKER were riding to hounds, Banjo's grandmother Emily Barton was writing about how a young lass in her social circle, Alice Emily Walker[16] from a grazier's family in Tenterfield, was having trouble warding off a suitor.[17]

Alice was a 'sweet, gentle person'[18] and 'a most intelligent and well-read woman'.[19] At eighteen, Alice was now in Sydney for her coming-of-age celebrations overseen by her fabulously wealthy uncle James Thomas Walker, a 54-year-old financier from Edinburgh keen to have a seat in the first Australian Parliament. At a reception at Paddington Town Hall on Tuesday, 17 September 1895, Alice was resplendent in white silk and white lace decorated with white lilies,[20] and a day later she was at the Kensington Racecourse with her uncle and cousin among a sea of dignitaries to see the Sydney Polo Club's gymkhana where 'Mr A. B. Paterson' and two members of the Queensland Polo Club 'distinguished themselves much by their riding'.[21] Soon after there was a charity ball at Sydney Town Hall[22] and then the coming-out party on 1 October 1895 at Rosemont, James Walker's lavish home in Woollahra.[23] Among the floral decorations on the broad verandas and the myriad Chinese lanterns across the manicured lawns were two hundred dignitaries and guests, most of them unmarried. Banjo Paterson, dashing horseman and high-profile lawyer, was in his element.[24] Each man had the chance to dance with all the ladies.[25]

As Banjo was enjoying the hospitality of Alice Walker's wealthy uncle, his fiancée Sarah Riley was soaking up the sun in the Queensland outback. She was with her old schoolfriend Christina Macpherson,[26] now a shy and bespectacled 31-year-old spinster whom everyone called 'Chris'.

Sarah had been visiting her aunt in Sydney when she'd accepted the invitation to visit her brother Fred at Winton, Central Queensland. Fred was now running Vindex Station following the death of their brother James. Sarah went home to Melbourne and then travelled north on the steamer *Wodonga*. Her arrival in Rockhampton in May 1895 warranted a few lines in the social pages of the *Brisbane Courier*[27] and she spent a few days there before taking the train to Longreach, seven hundred kilometres west. After a hot and exhausting coach ride of 180 kilometres north-west through the dry, dull red country with its stunted mulga trees, Sarah was a hit at the Winton Races, looking 'very neat' in her 'gray rillettes costume' and sailor hat.[28] She was already well known in the area, having been the governess for the Morrison family who had the sprawling station Ayrshire Downs.

Sarah stayed with Fred and his new wife, Marie, in a colonial bungalow called Aloha in Vindex Street, Winton. A month after Sarah's arrival there, Chris Macpherson also left Melbourne on the *Wodonga*, along with her father, Ewen,[29] and her sister Jean,[30] who was planning to marry Sam McCall McCowan, the manager of Kynuna Station.[31] Chris was joining her four brothers[32] who ran Dagworth Station,[33] a massive holding of more than a hundred thousand hectares on the Diamantina River, about 130 kilometres north-west of Winton. The Macphersons were still mourning the death of their mother,[34] and Chris would occasionally pluck out a marching tune called 'Thou Bonnie Wood of Craigielea'[35] on an autoharp or zither to brighten the mood. She had heard the tune played by the Garrison Artillery Band at a steeplechase meeting in Warrnambool, Victoria, in the last week of April 1894. Chris was something of a drawing-room pianist and couldn't get the tune out of her head.

ON 19 OCTOBER 1895, just two weeks after he had attended Alice Walker's coming-out party, Banjo was celebrating the publication of his first book, *The Man from Snowy River and Other Verses.*[36] Robertson had been a severe critic, demanding only the best and rejecting works that he regarded as inferior, such as 'El Mahdi' and 'The Ballad of G. R. Dibbs'. The resulting compilation would outsell the work of any other Australian poet.

Rolf Boldrewood, who had previously given his stamp of approval to 'Clancy of the Overflow', provided the preface and some purple prose:

> It is not so easy to write ballads descriptive of the bushland of Australia as on light consideration would appear. Reasonably good verse on the subject has been supplied in sufficient quantity. But the maker of folksongs for our newborn nation requires a somewhat rare combination of gifts and experiences. Dowered with the poet's heart, he must yet have passed his 'wander-jaehre' [apprenticeship] amid the stern solitude of the Austral waste – must have ridden the race in the back-block township, guided the reckless stock-horse adown the mountain spur, and followed the night-long moving, spectral-seeming herd 'in the droving days' ... In my opinion this collection comprises the best bush ballads written since the death of [Adam] Lindsay Gordon.[37]

Robertson sent hundreds of review copies to newspapers throughout Australia and even to great overseas literary figures such as Rudyard Kipling.

The reception was euphoric. The first edition sold out in the first week, 2350 copies were gone in six weeks, seven thousand within a year – huge sales for the times. More than a hundred thousand copies would eventually leave the shelves.

Banjo awoke one morning and was famous around Australia. Women adored him even more than before and in much greater numbers. Florence Earle Hooper, an early biographer, recalled that she had met 'old ladies who in their girlhood were thrilled to be introduced to the famous young man'.[38] A week after publication, A. G. Stephens wrote in *The Bulletin* that '... it is stirring manly stuff that one rejoices to read and remember: ... "The Banjo" rides and wins his steeplechasing and then, one may believe, sits down with a still tingling pulse and conveys the tingling to the pulses of his readers ...'[39]

Soon after that endorsement, the magazine informed readers that 'The Banjo's book was issued by Angus & Robertson on October 19th. By the first week in November the publishers had sold the entire edition, handed the author his share of the profits, squared all accounts, and were lying low for another record-breaker.'[40] Banjo was still concerned about how his book would be received in England and expressed his fears to his Aunt Nora, telling her, 'I am very anxious about it, as the reviews there will make such a lot of difference.'[41]

He need not have worried.

The London *Times* said Banjo at his best compared 'not unfavourably with the author of "Barrack Room Ballads" [Rudyard Kipling]',[42] and the *Glasgow Herald* described the ballads, especially 'the racing ones', as 'full of such go that the mere reading makes the blood tingle'.[43] Kipling, writing on 10 December 1895 from his American home in Dummerston, Vermont, told Robertson:

> Some of Mr Paterson's verse I read (and enjoyed) in last year's Xmas Bulletin – 'The Amateur Rider', 'The Two Devines' and best of all, to my thinking, 'Saltbush Bill'. 'The Travelling Post Office' is new and catching to me and I like it, as do I like all the descriptions of droving, shearing and tramping … I want Mr Paterson to write more and more about the man who is born and bred on the land – to say what he does and what he thinks of things and how he manages his affairs: all without any moral reflections run in. People will always do their own reflecting if you put a straight tale before them. 'A Bushman's Song' to take an instance makes one think five times as much as 'A Voice from the Town'. 'Till I drink artesian water from a thousand feet below' is good and real and that is the kind of thing most folks want to know more about. I hope you will not be offended with this and will give my best salutations to Mr Paterson and tell him to do it again… . Wishing him good luck and you good sales.[44]

Banjo's portraits of noble frontiersmen – such as the brave rider from Snowy River and Clancy from the Overflow – hit the mark with readers, but Banjo wanted to maximise sales. In October 1895 he sent to his publishers a list of his friends who, he felt sure, would buy the book. If the second edition 'hung fire', he could 'scare up a lot more purchases, I think'. He had ideas for sales promotion that included a card 'stuck in booksellers' windows' with the title of the book 'Now on Sale'.

Already the legends about Banjo were growing taller than the tales he related of daring mountain riders, outback drovers and feisty shearers. A biographical note for Banjo's book in the Melbourne *Review of Reviews* – written by 'a well-informed correspondent', most likely George Robertson – claimed that in his boyhood Banjo would visit his father's property in Queensland 'delighting to turn out along with the station hands and take a share in the mustering, drafting, branding, washing, and shearing during the day, and at night steal off to the men's huts to hear them tell regal lies of "back-block" adventures, of desperate rides and wonderful feats on road and racecourse, until he became imbued with the very spirit of the bush and thoroughly acquainted with what may be termed the "back-block vernacular".'[45] Not bad for a boy who was just five when the Queensland property was sold.

THE ENORMOUS SUCCESS of 'The Man From Snowy River' – poem and book – would eventually be eclipsed by a ballad Banjo wrote after joining Sarah Riley and Chris Macpherson at Dagworth Station.[46]

Banjo's Aunt Nora had visited Rockend around that time, and on 2 October 1895 she wrote to her eldest daughter, Meta, that rumours were doing the rounds that Banjo was no longer engaged to Sarah but to a 'Miss Alice Cape, a nice, Roman Catholic, very musical young lady'. 'But he has not said a word about it to his relations,' Nora explained, 'and perhaps all the world is drawing conclusions from mistaken premises – Bartie has so many lady friends ...'[47] Banjo was apparently looking for even more lady friends when he travelled north.

This was at a time when western Queensland was again aflame with trouble. Although the Great Strike had ended in 1891, the price of wool had plummeted. As the pastoralists sought to cut wages, shearers went on strike again. Once more there were violent confrontations and assaults on 'scab labour' at railheads.

The tension erupted at Tolarno Station, all four hundred thousand hectares of it around the Darling River at Menindee in western New

South Wales. In 1894, Benjamin Chaffey became the new owner of Tolarno after the collapse of the Union Bank of Australia had forced out the long-time owners, the Reid family.[48] Union shearers were using intimidation and blockades along the railway lines as part of their fight for better wages. In an effort to keep his woolshed running, Chaffey sent the £5000 paddle steamer *Rodney*, one of the finest boats on the Darling River, to collect fifty non-union shearers from Echuca. It was always going to end in tears. Just before 4 a.m. on 26 August 1894, armed men with masks or smears of river mud on their faces rushed onto the boat like ants[49] while it was moored to an island in the river at Moorara Station (forty-five kilometres downstream from Tolarno). The invaders chased the hired labourers into the water and looted the vessel, then doused it in kerosene and set it alight.[50] The *Rodney* burnt for six hours as the masked men hooted and gave three cheers. Then the boat finally collapsed into itself and sank. This is the only recorded act of piracy on inland waterways in Australia.

The shearers sent out warnings that other vessels would burn and that 'scabs' would be badly hurt or worse if they tried to break the blockade again.[51] The following night, police shot and wounded two union shearers[52] as the men attacked imported labourers and the officers protecting them at the Grassmere woolshed, on Nettalie Station near Wilcannia, east of Broken Hill.[53]

A few days later the trouble exploded on the Macphersons' Dagworth Station after months of violence around Winton. Shots were fired, and sheds, woolstores and pastures were set alight.[54] At Dagworth, Chris Macpherson's older brother Robert – or 'Bob Mac' as most in the area knew him – had eighty thousand sheep ready for the shears.[55] Strike action had delayed the work and Bob, heavily in debt, was desperate. His shed had stands for forty shearers and he organised for the sheep to be shorn by non-union labour working for lower wages. Before the shearing began, he was ready for the inevitable backlash. The woolshed on the neighbouring Ayrshire Downs[56] had recently been torched, along with six others in western Queensland, and the Macphersons had Senior Constable Michael Daly on standby at Dagworth, armed with a carbine, a revolver and fifty-nine rounds of ammunition.[57] They had about twenty men as back-up.

Just after midnight on 2 September 1894, a day before the shearing was due to begin, sixteen union men – said to be led by local agitators John Tierney[58] and Samuel Hoffmeister[59] – took matters into their own hands. They assembled on the Four Mile Billabong on the Diamantina River, about seven kilometres from the township of Kynuna. In darkness they rode their horses along the dry Diamantina riverbed to Dagworth. The senior constable and Dagworth's overseer, Weldon Tomlin, guarded the shed. The night sky threated rain and 140 weaner lambs were taken under cover. Like silent predators, the unionists navigated the dry riverbed on their horses and crept to within fifty metres of the woolshed. A dozen shots rang out. Three bullets burst through a cottage where three of the Macpherson brothers – Bob, Jack and Gideon – were sleeping alongside two other workers. Bob and Jack had been at Peechelba along with their little sister Chris when the bushranger Mad Dan Morgan was gunned down, and they were ready for a fight. One of the attacking unionists called out, 'Hold your hands up you bastards or die', but the Macphersons fired back as the union men took cover in a dry creek bed. Muzzle flashes and the thunderclaps of rifles erupted on the plains for about twenty minutes.

Then one of the attackers sneaked up under covering fire, and with matches and kerosene set fire to the woolshed. Bob Mac tried to save the lambs and some of his valuable wool bales but was beaten back by gunfire from the creek. The constable and the station hands kept blasting into the darkness.

When the shed was beyond saving, the unionists retreated to their horses. With rain masking their movements, they galloped back along the Diamantina riverbed towards their camp. The shearing shed was destroyed and most of the lambs burnt alive.

The Macphersons spent the next few hours cleaning up the carnage and putting the rest of the dying lambs out of their misery.

'It may be interesting to state,' noted one newspaper, 'that the brothers Macpherson, who own Dagworth station, are not the sort of men who would have given the incendiaries much quarter, or would be likely to hesitate in following them up. They are splendid bushmen, excellent horsemen, and hardly know what fear is.'[60]

At first light Bob Mac and Constable Daly gave chase. Though the rain obscured the tracks of the arsonists, open gates showed they were heading back towards Kynuna. Macpherson and Daly rode thirty kilometres into Kynuna to get help from Constables Austin Cafferty and Robert Dyer, and were told that one of the union leaders, Samuel Hoffmeister, had shot himself beside the Four Mile Billabong outside town. Bob Mac and the three policemen went out there to investigate: 'Down came the Squatter a-riding his thoroughbred; and Down came Policemen – one, two, and three.'[61] The dead man had a Martini sporting rifle beside him and sixty-eight rounds of ammunition along with a .380 revolver and twenty-one cartridges. It appeared that he had shot himself in the head with the revolver.[62]

On 4 September 1894, the *Brisbane Courier* reported: 'Information has been received at Winton that a man named Hoffmeister, a prominent unionist, was found dead about two miles from Kynuna. The local impression is that he was one of the attacking mob at Dagworth and was wounded there. There were seven unionists with Hoffmeister when he died. These assert that he committed suicide.'[63] At a magisterial inquiry, 'Frenchy' Hoffmeister's comrades said that he seemed 'barmy' before killing himself. His death certificate listed him as a German, born in Berlin in 1862, but some of the locals in the 'wild west'[64] said he was 'the son of an old South African Boer who pursued the vocation of a carrier in the Springsure district'. Frenchy always carried firearms and always advocated violence in dealing with 'scabs'.[65] It was surmised that he had shot himself because of the trouble he was in over the arson, but his death was cloaked in mystery.

WHEN BANJO TRAVELLED NORTH to be reunited with Sarah, he arrived at Dagworth on a coach pulled by four horses.[66] Melbourne money was everywhere. Chirnside and Riley were at Vindex, the Macphersons had Dagworth, and many other wealthy Victorian families – Knox, Ramsay, Bell and Fairbairn – dominated the landscape. Squatter kings made 'royal progresses to each other's stations'.[67]

During a recent drought, the Chirnside and Riley workers had been forced to slit the throats of five thousand starving sheep. But recent rains and bore water had transformed the land with beautiful blue grass and Mitchell grass, carpeting the plains 'with the sheep all fat and the buyers all busy'.[68] At Dagworth, Banjo went riding with Bob Mac and sometimes the other Macpherson brothers, and they told him the story of Frenchy Hoffmeister's death beside the billabong, and how Bob and the policemen had ridden up to the body. Banjo also heard about George Hamlyn Pope, who on 17 September 1891 had drowned in the scour hole on Dagworth where the wool was washed.[69] There was a story, too, of a swagman who had killed a sheep near one of the waterholes on the Diamantina and drowned while trying to escape.

In fact, Chris Macpherson would recall that Banjo and Bob Mac went riding together on Dagworth one day and came upon a billabong where the skin of a freshly killed sheep was 'all that was left by a swagman'.[70] In western Queensland, she said, there were 'always numbers of men travelling about the country, some riding, & some on foot & they are usually given rations at the various stations that they come to but in Queensland the distances are so great they help themselves without asking'.[71] The locals, she said, called sheep 'jumbucks'.

The phrase 'Waltzing Matilda' – popularised by Germans on the goldfields – had also caught Banjo's imagination. According to popular stories, Bob Mac hosted a party at Dagworth that Banjo, Sarah and Chris Macpherson all attended, and Banjo is said to have heard a station overseer tell Macpherson that earlier in the day he had seen a swagman 'waltzing Matilda' down by the Diamantina. The expression 'auf der walz' meant 'to go tramping', while 'Matilda' was the name given to a coat that kept swagmen warm just as the battle maidens had warmed Teutonic soldiers in medieval times.

Two years earlier Henry Lawson had scoffed at the notion that 'waltzing Matilda' was a fair dinkum Australian expression, in his *Bulletin* article 'Some Popular Australian Mistakes': 'A swag is not generally referred to as a "bluey" or "matilda", it is *called* a swag. No bushman thinks of "going on the wallaby" or "walking Matilda" or "padding the hoof": he goes on the track – when forced to it.'[72] Still, Banjo liked the way 'Waltzing Matilda' rolled off the tongue.

As the Dagworth house guests sat under wide verandas, marvelling at the vision splendid of the Queensland plains before them and listening to the muted cries of the bush all around, Chris Macpherson remembered the marching tune she'd heard at Warrnambool. It had such a rousing lilt, and she thought she might play it to entertain the guests. She played it by ear on a zither owned by the station bookkeeper, John Tait Wilson, then absent on leave.[73] Banjo's handsome face creased into a wide smile as she plucked out the tune.

Banjo was a good-looking man, and as good a horseman as any in the land. The writer Henry Lamond[74] was a ten-year-old boy at the time, the son of a local police inspector, and he remembered Banjo as 'tall, tanned, wrinkled, well-balanced on his feet, lithe and active'.[75] Chris was shy and dowdy and vulnerable, still broken-hearted over the loss of her mother. Banjo asked her the name of the tune, but Chris didn't know it. No matter, he said; he could write some lines to fit, and together they could make beautiful music. As the two sat there, locking eyes, Banjo looked down at his pad to write:

> Oh there once was a swagman camped in the billabong,[76]
> Under the shade of a Coolibah tree,
> And he sang as he looked at the old billy boiling,
> 'Who'll come a waltzing Matilda with me?'[77]

It had an infectious rhythm. The Paterson–Macpherson combination was working well, and Banjo was so charming. The co-writers continued to work on the tune, getting closer and closer. A second verse followed:

> Down came a jumbuck to drink at the waterhole,
> Up jumped the swagman and grabbed him in glee,
> And he sang as he put him away in the tucker-bag,
> You'll come a waltzing Matilda with me.[78]

Banjo thought it went well, and he gradually worked up the rest of the verses about the swagman who steals the sheep and then, surrounded by the policemen, dives into the water and drowns himself rather than surrender. It's a romantic tale of the battler defying his oppressors any way he can, but the words have a romantic tone on a whole other level too.

The chorus that Banjo and Chris jotted down are also words of love:

Who'll come a-waltzing Matilda, my darling.
Who'll come a-waltzing Matilda with me.[79]

What Banjo was really saying to Chris Macpherson was 'Who'll come *walking beside me and keep me warm at night*, my darling, / Who'll come *walking beside me and keep me warm at night*.' Banjo and Chris had created something special.

The party of house guests later journeyed by carriage to Aloha, the home of Sarah Riley's brother in Winton, where there was a piano. 'Waltzing Matilda' was polished some more. Nearby, at a station called Oondooroo owned by the wealthy Ramsay family, the Dagworth guests watched a demonstration of firefighting equipment that involved a steel mat hung from a pole towed by horses with leather leggings.[80] Later around the station piano as Chris played the tune, Herbert Ramsay,[81] who had a fine baritone voice, sang 'Waltzing Matilda' while dressed in a swagman's costume for effect. Chris wrote out two manuscripts of the words and music,[82] and before long the song was being performed at the North Gregory Hotel in Winton and the Kynuna Hotel. In a short time, everyone in the district was singing it,[83] and eventually it spread across Australia like wildfire.

BANJO'S ENGAGEMENT TO SARAH RILEY – like the swagman – was dead in the water. For all the years that she had known him he'd been a popular ladies' man, but enough was enough. His attention to Chris Macpherson may have been totally innocent, but according to her relatives he was given his marching orders. Sarah left to live in England and Scotland for most of her life, and did not return to Australia until 1930.

In later years Chris's grand-niece Dianna Baillieu, who knew Chris as an elderly spinster, said that Banjo's behaviour at Dagworth was 'caddish' and claimed the Macpherson brothers told him to 'never to darken their doorstep again'.[84] 'It was just part of the family history; the broken romance with Sarah and the fact that it was over him making passes at Chris,' said Dianna, whose son Ted became the Premier of Victoria. Dianna said that Christina never got over her affection for Banjo and what happened at Dagworth – he was the only real love of her life. Chris never married, and as Dianna said, 'It was very much a class society and a very small social society, where everybody knew each other, even though there was great distances, gossip would go around. It simply wasn't the thing to break off engagements and it certainly wasn't the done thing to get off with your fiancée's best friend.'[85] Dianna also recalled that Chris was 'a very sweet aunt … [and] rather a shy little lady in a lot of ways … [Banjo] was obviously a lady's man and he not only sort of cast an eye upon, a flirty eye upon Aunty Chris, and she'd been so lonely and innocent, it's no wonder she sort of fell for him. He was obviously a very, very attractive man.'[86]

Sarah's niece Ethel Vivienne Riley, who also knew Chris Macpherson, was adamant that Banjo behaved badly and didn't let his wandering eye stop at Chris. She wrote: 'The reason Aunt Sarah did not marry Barty Paterson was: He flirted with the Sewing Mistress on Dagworth Station.'[87]

Banjo returned to Sydney and the fame that his book was creating. Sarah stayed in Queensland visiting the wealthy pastoralist families, though her friendship with Chris Macpherson never really healed. On 11 March she left Rockhampton on the *Arawatta* for Sydney then Melbourne, and eventually headed to London for a while. Chris stayed for the wedding of her sister Jean in April 1896. Like Chris, Sarah remained broken-hearted and never married.

Chris claimed that Banjo corresponded with her for some time over the song they had written,[88] even though in later years his memory of her faded and he believed that she, and not her sister, had married into the wealthy McCall McCowan family.[89] Banjo rarely spoke of his collaboration with Chris again, though women were always a powerful influence on this particularly masculine writer. He later told Vince Kelly, who worked with him as a Sydney journalist in the 1920s, that he had a greater affection for the ballad than for almost all his other verses,[90] but he had unhappy memories about its composition – and the end of his long romance with the delightful Sarah and her eyes of blue.

'Waltzing Matilda' remained a popular tune in western Queensland. Two years after Banjo and Chris wrote the song, Herbert Ramsay performed it for Lord Lamington, then Governor of Queensland, when the dignitary visited Winton and was entertained at a banquet at the Post Office Hotel.[91] The words to 'Waltzing

Matilda' were first published in the *Hughenden Observer* in 1902,[92] and in 1903 Banjo sold the text without music along with some other odds and ends of verse ('old junk', he called it) for £5 to Angus & Robertson.[93]

The company on-sold the musical rights of the verses to the Sydney tea merchants Inglis & Co. who marketed the popular Billy tea brand and saw the song as an ideal brand partner. Mrs Marie Cowan, the wife of the manager for Inglis & Co. and a gifted amateur musician, set the words to music, perhaps basing her version on a 1901 tune whose copyright was held by Harry Nathan. She tinkered with Banjo's words a little to make them fit her tune, and her version is the one best known today. The first editions of the song, as published by Inglis & Co., in 1903, stated that the music was 'arranged' by Marie Cowan but in later editions the word was changed to 'composed'; the lyrics were attributed to A. B. Paterson, 'author of *The Man from Snowy River*'. Inglis included the sheet music in packets of Billy tea as a free gift to customers, marrying what was becoming Australia's national song with 'Australia's national drink'.[94] Mrs Cowan's husband is said to have recalled that Paterson told him he was very happy about the song, and that 'Mrs Cowan has done a good job, good luck to her'.[95]

The intense marketing campaign further increased the popularity of 'Waltzing Matilda', as did its inclusion in a 1911 collection called *The Australasian Students' Song Book* (edited and published by a committee of Sydney University students), and its inclusion in the 1934 bestselling travel book *Cobbers* (by English composer and writer Dr Thomas Wood). They all pushed 'Waltzing Matilda' into the national consciousness. Shortly before her death, Chris Macpherson wrote to Dr Wood outlining the details of how she and Banjo had worked on the song together at Dagworth.[96]

By the time of the Second World War, when diggers sang the song in battle, 'Waltzing Matilda' had become Australia's unofficial national anthem. In 1966, the author Clement Semmler wrote that 'Waltzing Matilda' '... is learned at school and sung with pleasure, and becomes the one song that adults sing, as a group, naturally and unselfconsciously. The words satisfy a certain instinct for nationalism: every Australian knows what "waltzing Matilda", "jumbuck", "tucker-bag" and "billabong" mean, so that the song is almost a password in foreign countries. And the elements of "fair go", of the little man against the big man, of anti-authority, of bravado and of the setting of the outback give the song that added appeal to the average Australian conscious of his colonial beginnings.'[97]

In the mid-1890s, Banjo couldn't have imagined that the song he had just co-written would have such an illustrious fate. He had returned to Sydney to a legal practice he no longer enjoyed and an even busier social life. As a handsome and famous young poet, he was a favourite at Government House and had no shortage of female admirers at the many banquets and balls he attended. But Banjo was ready to saddle up for some more adventures. His friend Breaker Morant was about to become a cornerstone of the North Richmond Polo Club.[98]

Banjo recalled that Morant was asked to ride a buckjumper at a charity gymkhana, at the Sydney Agricultural Ground, that drew five thousand spectators. Morant borrowed ten pounds from the organising committee to pay the expenses for a grey buckjumper he planned to bring down from Dubbo by rail. People flocked to the gymkhana to see Morant ride, but the man who owned the buckjumper knew Morant well and believed that if he loaned him the horse he might never see it again. Instead Morant brought a horse to the show that knew no more about buckjumping 'than it knew about the Einstein theory'. The animal's performance at the gymkhana was such a 'flop' that the committee squealed about their ten pounds. One newspaper reported The Breaker's performance as 'a fiasco, the horse absolutely refusing to buck', while another described how Morant caused the crowd to collapse with 'roars of laughter'. Banjo said that The Breaker – dirty rotten scoundrel that he was – simply brushed off the ignominy. He said that he was called away suddenly to Queensland, to inspect a station and handed over the pony as a gift to a boy whose family had lent him money. It was a touching scene until the pony's rightful owner arrived and said he had paid Morant a couple of pounds to quieten it for a little girl.

Banjo helped save the day at the gymkhana by winning the Race for Ladies and Gentlemen. Despite The Breaker's devious nature, he and Banjo were bonded by their love of horses, and in this loveable rogue Banjo saw the same sort of dash and daring that he saw in himself – that he saw in Jack Riley and the Man from Snowy River.

Chapter 15

LATE IN 1898, NORTHERN TERRITORY

Such is life in a buffalo camp – about the last remaining relic of the old wild days. It is life as it was in the beginning of things. Risk and roughness there no doubt are. Sometimes the horses are killed by charging buffaloes and the riders seriously hurt … But it is a rare experience to anyone who is not afraid of roughing it a little.

Banjo Paterson on the thrill of hunting wild buffalo from horseback in the Northern Territory[1]

BANJO WAS NOT QUITE thirty-two when the weekly Melbourne magazine *Table Talk*[2] published the first major interview with Australia's literary sensation. The magazine had been founded during Melbourne's boom a decade earlier, and it sent the young playwright and actor Bernard Espinasse[3] to profile a man they regarded as a great artist: a writer whose works were 'the most valuable contribution to purely Australian literature yet made'.[4]

Banjo's ears were still tingling from the cheering he'd received[5] when he strode onto the stage at Sydney's Criterion Theatre a few weeks earlier in December 1895 after the success of the comic opera *Club Life*, which he had written with the composer Ernest Truman.[6] It was almost as exhilarating as Alice Walker's coming-out party.

Writing for *Table Talk*, Bernard Espinasse was a fan:

> … there is at the present moment assuredly no name better known throughout the length and breadth of Australia than that of 'Banjo'. In the lonely shepherd's hut on far northern 'runs' around the drovers' fires, 'where the Overlanders camp' and at

> the afternoon teas of fashionable Toorakians and Potts Pointers alike, his verses have been read and discussed. The world of the drover and the shearer, of the rough rider and the man of the bush is the world of his work, and he has drawn pictures of their feelings and modes of life with a rugged truthfulness that no one has hitherto equalled, and the secret of his success is that what he writes he knows. As was said of Adam Lindsay Gordon, he has ridden the race he describes.

On arriving at the Waltham Building and entering the office of Street & Paterson, Espinasse realised that in 'Clancy', Banjo had painted his working environment accurately: inside 'the prosaic four walls of a lawyer's office, in the very heart of busy Sydney, amid the ceaseless din', '... from 9 a.m. till 6 p.m. daily the author of *The Man from Snowy River* is a busy solicitor, and it is only when the closing of the office door permits him to forsake the devious paths of law for that more romantic road'. For inspiration, one of Banjo's office walls was decorated with a magnificent watercolour painted by Frank Mahony, depicting a mob of wild horses.[7] It occupied pride of place, and Banjo told Espinasse that he had already spent 'a good deal of money on paintings by local artists' and that he intended to 'add very considerably to his present art gallery'.

Espinasse said he found Banjo surrounded by 'legal weapons'. His library contained books that had been written in the mid-1700s, and he had eclectic tastes. Some of Darwin's *On the Origin of Species* was cheek by jowl with Sterne's *Sentimental Journey*, first published in 1768 and resplendent in a rare old binding and with the quaint black lettering of a bygone age. A very rare copy of *The History and Adventures of an Atom,* written in 1769 and long out of print, was wedged between two volumes of *The Bulletin*'s compendium *A Golden Shanty*.

Paterson told Espinasse that he was a moderate smoker, almost a non-drinker, and had a fancy for dogs: 'I began to write for the Sydney *Bulletin* about eight years ago. My first contribution was an account of a glove fight! After that I sent in some sentimental verses, which were printed, somewhat to my surprise. After that I began to pay more attention to writing, but always as a pastime ... I wrote *Clancy of the Overflow* and *Pardon, the Son of Reprieve*, and woke up to the fact that I was becoming known as a writer of verse, and from that time forth I seem to have "caught on" with Australian readers everywhere.'[8]

He showed Espinasse his bush souvenirs: the possum skin rugs his mother had sewn and others that were sent to him, 'sufficient to completely carpet his room'. He proudly took out from a drawer a magnificent snow-white plume, recently sent to him anonymously. 'This is the plume of the white crane,' Banjo said with enthusiasm, 'and is, I believe, exceedingly rare. I don't think anyone possesses one like it.' Banjo's suntanned face shone with delight. 'I'm going to have it mounted.' He also showed off a number of cups and racing trophies scattered about his shelves, and said that more would be coming soon. He told his interviewer about his athletic background and that he had won a number of steeplechases as an amateur rider; he said he was prouder of those triumphs than about anything he'd written. He was especially fond of polo, and his love for it came through in 'The Geebung Polo Club'.

> I am very particular about my work. It is not enough for me that a line scans correctly, or that it even contains a thought, it must satisfy me. And sometimes a verse takes a lot of re-arranging before it does satisfy me … I don't know that I'm wholly satisfied with any of my work. I always think I can do better. My bush pieces I think are the best I've done.[9]

He explained the origin of his pen-name and talked about his new book.

> 'Banjo' was the name of a horse I once rode. I was at a loss for a signature for my first contribution, not wishing to put my own name, and Banjo being in my mind at the time, I just slapped that down, and, somehow, it stuck to me … Eh! my book? Oh! well, it was the *Bulletin* made me publish, and I've done very well out of it. I owe a great deal to Archibald.[10]

Banjo frankly acknowledged that he seldom read verse, and that when he did he preferred the simplest forms of poetry. Espinasse remarked, 'Involved phrases and obscure ideas, however finely expressed, do not commend themselves to him.' His favourite poets were Tennyson and Longfellow, but he told Espinasse: 'I am not a poet, I am a versifier.'[11]

AUSTRALIANS SAW BANJO AS A POET, though, and he was very much their favourite. A month after *Table Talk* published its lengthy interview, newspapers reported that *The Man from Snowy River* had beaten the sales record for an Australian book with more than 4500 copies sold in Australasia in less than four months: 'This, though the price of the book is 5 shillings. Banjo is likely to think book-making better than lawyering at this rate.'[12]

Banjo had drawn up the agreements for Henry Lawson's two books with Angus & Robertson, but over the next few months Lawson would become even more despondent than usual as Banjo's books galloped off the shelves while his seemed to be glued there. After returning from a visit to Perth, Lawson asked Banjo, 'Do you know who's buying my book?' Before Banjo could reply, Lawson told him, 'Your friends of the capitalist class. Mine have declared me bogus for showing up some good points in a squatter.'[13]

Banjo rented a cottage in Gladesville for his sisters Grace, now nineteen, and Gwen, fifteen, while he shared an apartment in the city with Irving Kent, a polo player from the Queensland wool town of Jondaryan. They had a Japanese valet to wait on them.

Lawson was doing it a lot tougher, even though Banjo managed to extract £5 from *The Bulletin* in June 1899 for some of Henry's work. In 1896, Lawson had married Bertha Bredt,[14] daughter of feminist Bertha McNamara. Soon after, though, he became infatuated with a young bookkeeper and artist's model, Hannah Thornburn,[15] and dedicated some of his poetry to her.

> There was never a church that could marry,
> For never a court could divorce
> In the season of Hannah and Harry,
> When the love of my life ran its course.[16]

Henry's new wife went to the offices of *The Bulletin* and asked Archibald for two tickets to New Zealand, and for letters of introduction to people who might help Henry find work. In 1897, Lawson tried to make a living for them as a teacher in a country school on the South Island of New Zealand. It didn't last, and soon he was back in Sydney. He spent time being treated for alcoholism in late 1898, and before long he had four mouths to feed[17] on a meagre, uncertain income.

Not so for Banjo. Even though his dalliance at Dagworth had proved a disaster, he was moving on and trying to make every post a winner.

Two months after Banjo's interview appeared in *Table Talk*, he and Breaker Morant raced in the Hunters Steeplechase at Rosehill. Morant had a heavy fall on Queen Mab, but battered and bruised 'made a good showing for a mile and a-half'.[18]

Throughout the first half of 1896 Banjo was too busy basking in his success to do much writing, but on 16 May the Rosehill Races card used 'Out of Sight', one of the poems Robertson had rejected for Banjo's book, and in July the *Sydney Mail* ran 'Mulga Bill's Bicycle',[19] Banjo's comic take on what he viewed as a sad state of affairs that saw bikes replacing horses at many shearing sheds.

> 'Twas Mulga Bill, from Eaglehawk, that caught the cycling craze;
> He turned away the good old horse that served him many days;
> He dressed himself in cycling clothes, resplendent to be seen;
> He hurried off to town and bought a shining new machine;
> And as he wheeled it through the door, with air of lordly pride,
> The grinning shop assistant said, 'Excuse me, can you ride?'

Mulga Bill had ridden many a wild beast, but none so vicious as a bicycle with a demented mind of its own.

Banjo was selling his work to the highest bidder. On 8 July 1896, he wrote to the editor of the *Australian Town and Country Journal* to say that Angus & Robertson had shown him a proof of that magazine's Christmas supplement and that he was quite prepared to write some verses for it. 'How much do you want?' he asked. 'And when do you want it? I would like to turn out something fairly good and if so I suppose you will give me a fair price. Yours truly A.B. Paterson.'[20] The result was 'Pioneers',[21] a poem that could have been written about his grandparents.

Banjo began contributing to journals and magazines that appeared suddenly and then often disappeared just as quickly. *The Antipodean* ran for two years, and Banjo contributed 'Saltbush Bill's Second Fight',[22] with illustrations by Frank Mahony, and 'Ballad of the Calliope',[23] about the bravery of a ship's crew caught in a cyclone in Apia harbour. Banjo was joint editor, with George Essex Evans, of the February 1898 issue. He wrote an article on polo for *Australian Magazine*, remarking that 'those who have the money to purchase first-class horses cannot ride them, and those who can ride them have not the money'.[24]

BUT BANJO WAS SICK of his dingy little office, even if it did have the possum rugs and the Mahony watercolour, and even if being a successful lawyer kept him in sharp suits. He was consumed by wanderlust and itching to see as much of Australia's north as he could.

Breaker Morant's notoriety as a horseman could only inspire Banjo to pursue the adventurous life. At the Hawkesbury Show in 1897, The Breaker jumped on Dargin's Grey, a devilish horse that had slung off riders across the colony, and 'without any ado', took out the prize for best display of horsemanship at the event.

Banjo also preferred the saddle to the chair and desk, and he spent a good part of 1897 travelling through Queensland, catching up with various Bartons scattered across the vast colony while doing his best to avoid the Rileys and Macphersons. Rockhampton, he said, was called 'the city of sin, sweat and sorrow', but 160 kilometres inland from there was the basin of the Dawson and Nogoa rivers where he had once seen the country flooded over thirteen kilometres. The bullock teams had been bogged for a week, and all the men had had to eat was koala and mushrooms.[25]

On his return in 1898 he took to socialising with the artist Tom Roberts and his wife, Lillie at their studio. This was in Sydney's Vickery's Chambers, 76 Pitt Street, where Lillie had created a pleasant place for friends to meet on Thursday afternoons. The couple had two rooms beside the studios of fellow artists Hall Thorpe and Sid Long. Banjo and The Breaker were often there.[26]

Towards the end of 1898, Banjo – now close to thirty-five – was gifted an opportunity that he had been desiring for years: a tour of the Northern Territory. He was commissioned by the Eastern and Australian Steamship Company to contribute an article to its tourist guide on the types of big-game sport available in the Territory, including buffalo-shooting and alligator-hunting. He couldn't wait to pack his suitcase and his gun, saying later that this time in the north was among the most exciting of his life.

South Australia held sway over the Northern Territory – but although the state had put in the Overland Telegraph to Darwin, the vast arid area remained a conundrum and money drain.

It was the buffalo-shooting in the Territory that really stirred Banjo's passion and blood, and he wrote a breathtaking piece for the *Sydney Mail* – superbly illustrated by George Lambert[27] – explaining that he had gone to Darwin 'per s.s. Guthrie to make the closer acquaintance of these formidable animals, and to see what sport buffalo shooting could afford'.[28] The Indian buffalo of the Northern Territory, he said, were ungainly, savage-looking brutes, having a dull, bluish-coloured hide and enormous horns. Their hides had a market value of fifteen shillings.

> At first the shooting was done on foot, but this was found too slow, too unprofitable, and too dangerous, and soon some of the dashing cattle men of the Territory took the matter up in earnest and started shooting from horseback, which is the plan that now prevails ... Even if mortally wounded, a buffalo will usually struggle on for half a mile or so before he drops, and in the long jungle grass the skinners could not find the carcase. So that it became evident, if the shooters wished to get a living at the business, they had to be prepared to race right alongside the buffalo and shoot downwards into the loins alongside the spine. This particular part of the animal can only be reached from above, as the high hips and croup protect the loins from any bullet fired from behind. Thus there was evolved the present method of buffalo shooting, where the shooter, holding the carbine in one hand like a pistol, races right alongside the buffalo and fires at full gallop, taking his chance of the animal wheeling and attacking him either before or after he fires.[29]

Hunting buffalo on horseback with locals Ben Martin and Walter Rees[30] gave Banjo a rush of adrenaline the likes of which he had never experienced before. The shooters were, as a rule, 'men who had been stockmen – bold, fearless riders, with any amount of nerve; men who undertook the riding of unbroken horses, and the management of vindictive wild cattle, as a regular part of their lives'.

Banjo was just a novice buffalo hunter, but he bagged several bulls in the death-defying hunt and told the *Northern Territory Times and Gazette* that 'the sport was splendid, far exceeding' his expectations.[31] He played tennis, too, against some of the locals in Darwin and he taught them a few tricks.[32]

Banjo saw the north as a great goldmine of potential that was untapped. Darwin was so close to Asian markets, but there were no freezing works and hardly any livestock trade.

When Banjo left the Territory on 28 October 1898, he returned to the office of Street & Paterson with two pairs of enormous buffalo horns as souvenirs.[33] Legal pads and letters of demand no longer had any hold on him. He was a restless rover looking for action.

Angus & Robertson commissioned him to write an introductory memoir for a new edition of Marcus Clarke's *For the Term of His Natural Life*, and in his preface to the 1899 edition he drew parallels between Marcus Clarke and himself: their lack of satisfaction, the untimely death of their fathers, the battling circumstances in which they were born and their restless natures. He wrote some fine poems including 'Father Riley's Horse',[34] which resurrected the idea of a phantom rider.

The 1898 referendums surrounding the question of a federated Australia inspired Banjo's wry commentary. 'Johnny Riley's Cow: A Ballad of Federation'[35] highlighted the absurdity of colonial borders separating people already united as Australians, as Johnny's cow cost him heavily in fines every time it splashed into the Murray River.

A FAR DEADLIER GAME was taking place in South Africa, where tensions between Dutch and British settlers over land, diamonds and gold had been bubbling for more than a hundred years – with frequent eruptions. President Paul Kruger had been steadily building up the military might in Transvaal, importing the latest cannons and machine guns as well as thirty-seven thousand new Mauser rifles and more than forty million bullets. Most of the Boers were members of civilian militias but also men of the land; most were expert horsemen and crack shots. They were resilient and skilled bushmen, and war seemed imminent as the Boers looked to expel the British.

On 10 July 1899, Queensland offered Queen Victoria 250 mounted troops and a machine-gun section if the Boers attacked.[36] New South Wales offered troops soon after, then South Australia – where Harry Morant was headed – then Victoria, New Zealand and Western Australia. On 4 October 1899, all one hundred men in a regiment of the NSW Lancers, then training in England, volunteered.[37]

In early September, President Kruger ordered commandos to the Natal border. On 9 October 1899, he gave the British government forty-eight hours to withdraw all their troops from the borders of both the Transvaal and the Orange Free State, or the Boers would be at war with England.

Two days later, on 11 October, war was declared and the Boers began savage guerrilla attacks on British positions. Banjo couldn't wait to get among the thick of the action in South Africa. As an angry young man he had once ridiculed the NSW government for getting involved in the Sudan, but his tune had changed completely. Just a week after the Boers declared war on the British, Banjo sorted out his arrangements so he could sail from Sydney with the First Contingent of NSW Lancers. The Breaker was enlisting with the Second Contingent of the South Australian Mounted Rifles at Adelaide.[38] Banjo had envied his baby brother, Hamilton, who had pursued a life of adventure and had gone to the diggings in Coolgardie, Western Australia, to find his fortune or his fate.

Through his polo connections, Banjo was well acquainted with the Fairfax family, owners of the *Sydney Morning Herald*. Just a few days after the declaration of war, Banjo had marched into the *Herald* office and told Sir James Fairfax that he would like to write letters from the front: 'descriptive letters',[39] unlike the brief cables that carried news of the day. Banjo offered to go to South Africa at his own expense on trial for a month, which was as long as his finances would hold out, given the expenses of the city flat and the polo ponies, as well as his young sisters who still relied on his income. Instead Fairfax gave him £100, while friends gave Banjo two horses. Within a week all arrangements for the trip were in place.

Banjo only had one good arm but was happy to be included in the fighting force as a correspondent for the *Sydney Morning Herald* and the *Sydney Mail*, its weekly offshoot. He would soon be advised that he was reporting for *The Argus* as well, as that newspaper's correspondent Donald McDonald[40] was trapped in the siege of Ladysmith.[41]

Banjo celebrated the start of this new adventure at the Australian Club, where he souvenired a mat to protect his saddle horse in its stall on the long voyage across the Indian Ocean. He left a note at the club instructing the secretary to buy a replacement. He said he would reimburse him when he returned – and if he didn't make it back, he was sure his life insurance would cover it.

On 28 October 1899, forty Lancers and eight-six men of the Army Medical Corps marched in the heavy rain through Sydney to board the *Kent* bound for Cape Town.[42]

Banjo busied himself stalling three horses,[43] his favourite being a tough black thoroughbred gelding about fifteen hands in height. Another was a gift from Tom Watson, the starter for the Australian Jockey Club. There were 182 horses on board and it would take a long time for them to get their sea legs.

The *Kent* sailed on the morning of 30 October to great fanfare from boats on the harbour and onlookers on shore, the loudest cheers coming from a steamer load of newsboys. For the first time Australia was sending a combined fighting force to aid the Empire.

As a sportsman Banjo had always played rough. He had hunted pelicans on the Parramatta River as a boy, been ringside for boxing and dogfights, ridden with hounds and survived falls and violent collisions at polo.

Now Australia's greatest writer was about to experience what he would see as the worst kind of blood sport.

Chapter 16

29 MARCH 1900, OUTSIDE BLOEMFONTEIN, SOUTH AFRICA

... met Kitchener. As far as mobility of expression goes, you could put Kitchener's face on the body of the Sphinx, and nobody would know the difference. He has the aloof air and the fixed expression of a golf champion.

BANJO PATERSON'S THOUGHTS ON ONE OF HISTORY'S GREAT MILITARY FIGURES[1]

ON THE DAY BANJO SAILED for South Africa on the *Kent*, the *Sydney Mail* ran his portrait. The paper told readers that they could depend on vivid descriptive matter from his pen and that his bush experience would be of the greatest service to him in campaigning.

> His name is well known in Australia in consequence of the wonderful success of his book of verses, and his description of buffalo shooting which appeared in our columns was widely copied into English newspapers ... Mr. Paterson takes over letters of introduction to Cecil Rhodes and others in authority, so that he expects to be enabled to see whatever is to be seen. In addition to his literary capacities Mr. Paterson is well-known as an amateur steeplechase rider and as a judge of horses at the Sydney show. He takes with him a complete photographic outfit, and during the war will forward pictures to accompany his reports.[2]

The *Sydney Morning Herald* predicted that 'so capable a writer and so experienced a bushman' would 'graphically depict the events in which our men at the front may take part'.[3]

Owing to the hurried preparations for the *Kent*'s departure, a lot of loose horses had to be taken on board, and during the first day stalls were erected for them. On the trip down the harbour the horses skated about on the slippery decks in imminent danger of falling, and men had to be at their heads all the way.

Doubts had been freely expressed in Sydney as to whether the pine fittings of the *Kent* would be strong enough to stand a heavy sea. 'They are being strengthened now,' Banjo told his readers early in the journey, 'and it is to be hoped will be found sufficient; if not we may have a repetition of the Mounted Rifles' experience when going to England, when they had their horses down in heaps, kicking and maiming each other, and many were lost.'[4]

The men of the medical corps practised their rifle-shooting at a box towed over the stern, and then with revolvers at bottles thrown overboard. For a long time no one hit a bottle, and Banjo reckoned some of the shooters even missed the Indian Ocean.[5]

He had heard that by all accounts the Boers were only part human. He asked an ambulance orderly – a retired sergeant-major of British infantry – whether the Boers would fire on the ambulances. The orderly said, 'Of course, they'll fire on the hambulances. They 'ave no respect for the 'elpless. They've even been known to fire on the cavalry.'[6] Banjo could only laugh. This war business seemed like a lark.

Conditions on the voyage across the Great Australian Bight to Albany in Western Australia were catastrophic. If the skipper had not reduced the speed to just two knots, the decks would have been swept with water. One horse had perished, wild eyed and screaming with terror, and most of the other horses – mainly police mounts donated by the NSW government – were so weary and worried by the wind, wet and cold that they couldn't stand much more. Banjo believed it was outrageous that no one had thought to provide slings to make the horses more comfortable, though all the officers were granted a bottle of beer every time they sat down to dinner, as well as half a tin of salmon per meal.[7]

Most of the young volunteers were fighting among themselves before fighting any of the Boers. The army medical men came aboard a day earlier than anyone else and barricaded themselves in a square of the ship; they closed two doors of access to other parts of the ship, commandeered all the hammocks they could lay their hands on, and sat tight. A squadron of cursing Lancers fought and struggled in the alleyways, and traffic was congested. The machine-gun section wanted an acre of deck for their drills, and the signallers wanted the same area. All stores were below decks and could be accessed only by one of the three great powers: the chief officer, the boatswain and the carpenter. Consequently, everybody followed the chief officer, the boatswain and the carpenter about like lost lambs. Thus the men readied themselves to brave the Indian Ocean, 'toiling, rejoicing, and borrowing gear and equipment – generally without the knowledge or consent of the lender'.[8]

BANJO WAS OFF ON THE ADVENTURE of his life, but he still had weighty financial matters on his mind. And he was still working his way through the ideas, the plots and even the title for the novel that became *An Outback Marriage*. He wrote to George Robertson while on board:

> c/- Troopship Kent,
> off Albany, W.A.
> 5 November 1899
>
> I think a good name for my book would be 'An Heiress from the Never Never'. It is rather like Bret Harte but not a bad fault I think, and gives an idea of locality, etc ... This is written in a very heavy sea ... with horses all over the deck.[9]

Banjo had sent Robertson most of the book three months earlier, telling him: 'It is not all typed but I send it on as I want to let you see it and you can easily read the sense of it. There are heaps of alterations to be made, but we will discuss these later on. You might think over some names for it – "Red Mick and His Relations", "A Mountain Station", "In No Man's Land", "The Finding of Considine", and so on ... I fear the love-making is very flat and there is too much fight and drink all through it. Still I hope to please a large section of the public and if we do that the critics won't break our hearts.'[10] A few days later Banjo asked for the manuscript to be returned, saying that his *Bulletin* colleague John Farrell would have a look at it before he started on altering it. 'I was working at a new scheme last night – I am afraid to put any reliance on [A.W.] Jose's opinion as he is a hopelessly bad judge where humour is concerned – at least that is my opinion. A lot of the stuff that he wants isn't exactly the stuff that will appeal to the same public who bought *Snowy River.* Anyhow it will be more satisfactory to get another reader's opinion as I am very frightened that a lot of weak points have been overlooked by Jose.'[11]

In September Banjo wrote to Robertson and returned the manuscript, saying that he had shortened it and rewritten a good part of it 'on the lines suggested by Jose'. He asked for an advance, telling his publisher: 'If I go to South Africa I will want the money.'[12]

AS THE *KENT* STEAMED OUT OF ALBANY, a pilot vessel took it through the King George Sound very gingerly, while the troops bound for war all stood on the bridge deck, watching. Slowly the vessel slipped through, and the *Kent* finally dropped the pilot and was away at full speed to the open sea. Leaving the lights of Albany blazing behind under a faint moonlight, Banjo and the troops settled down for the 'long twenty days' steaming across to Africa'.[13]

The *Kent* worked her way round the dreaded 'Leuwin, the Cape of Storms'. It was a fine calm day, but a great rolling swell caused the terrified horses to again slip and slide in their stalls.[14] All hands set briskly to work taking down the rails between the horses, sweeping out the stalls, clearing up the deck, and throwing the litter overboard. The forage was brought up from below decks as the horses leant out over double doors and grabbed at the bags with their teeth. The feed was mixed into mashes in huge tubs while the horses keep up a volley of applause, pawing at the floor with their front feet. At feed time every horse's head was thrust out, clutching at the men's clothing, and a regular pandemonium began as the animals trampled the ground, rattling their boxes and biting at each other.

Men went through drills every day on board, practising their rifle volleys, while the medical corps was kept busy dealing with an epidemic of influenza and, at any given time, several men with lung or throat troubles who required watching. The ship's surgeon, Major Tom Fiaschi,[15] treated the men with a concoction of rum and quinine. But when the quinine ran out it was mostly rum – and it proved exceedingly popular.

Banjo took notes and used a makeshift darkroom below deck to develop the photographs he was taking on the voyage. He took a shot of the men gathered around a cockfight between drills on board, and he snapped a photograph of the place where a terrified horse had died leaping from its stall on a hatchway and landing on the ship's ventilator.

There was another taste of severe weather when it poured rain all day long. The decks were wet and streaming, soaked fodder was lying about, and horses slid around again, their heads hanging down and the water running off their ears. The medical men practised sutures on a dead horse and experimented with operations on its innards.[16] Most of the horses were fortunate to survive the ordeal.

The *Kent* pressed on, plugging her way steadily over the blue waters of the Indian Ocean, 'looking as puny and insignificant in that waste of water as an ant travelling over the Old Man Plain'.[17]

On approaching the South African coast near Port Elizabeth on 29 November,[18] Banjo thought the shore looked very much like Bondi Beach but without the houses gathered about.[19] The next morning they steamed into the town, full of vim over their part in defending the Empire. But Banjo was left flattened by news that the 130 Australians on board were but a drop in the ocean compared with the thousands of British troops who had already landed in South Africa and the thirty thousand who were coming close behind. 'The Kangaroo began to think that he was not such a very large animal after all,' Banjo wrote.[20]

The men spent an hour on shore before heading west around the Cape of Good Hope to Cape Town. Apart from the 'flat-tipped eminence of Table Mountain',[21] Banjo reckoned it was 'very like Adelaide, only that it is built on a steep hill'. 'The cabmen drive little Rasuto ponies, wiry little things,' he said, 'that shamble up and down the hills at a great rate.'[22]

Banjo felt that he was still 'as green as grass in the ways of the world',[23] and the British soldiers treated him and the rest of the contingent with disdain. That was until they learnt that the newly arrived Australians were from the same regiment of NSW Lancers who had travelled from London a month earlier and 'made a successful debut' in a battle at Graspan.[24] 'We were no longer outsiders,' Banjo wrote, 'no longer a handful of Australian refugees crawling along the coast in a disconsolate tramp steamer; we were of the brotherhood, and could hold up our heads with the best. The kangaroo was himself again!'[25]

IN CAPE TOWN, BANJO MET his first Boer prisoner: a doctor with an English degree, who could make a fifty break at billiards. In contrast to the war propaganda, the prisoner was 'not long and wild and hairy' but 'refined and educated'.[26]

'Apparently these Boers are at any rate partially civilized,' Banjo wrote. 'He says that, if the Boers catch our hospital orderlies with rifles in the ambulances, they will be entitled to shoot them. He evidently looks on us as less civilized than his own people – the poor fish. He got hurt in some way during a raid and the British are only keeping him till he is fit to go back.'[27] The Boers were not savages, Banjo said, and any talk along those lines was nonsense. They were having the best of the fighting too, because they fired until the last moment before retreating, losing positions but saving the lives of their men.

Banjo also met his first 'world-wide celebrity, for our country is a bit off the beaten track for celebrities'.[28] It was Sir Alfred Milner,[29] the Governor of Cape Colony and a contender to become Australia's first governor-general. Banjo became a favourite of this 'long dark wiry man, with a somewhat high-strung temperament'. He knew Milner had been a pressman, so 'nothing ought to rattle him'.[30] Banjo asked Milner if he could get to the front as a correspondent with the Australian troops, and Milner jokingly remarked that there would soon be more correspondents than fighting men at the front. Still, he gave Banjo a letter to the chief press censor suggesting that the Australians ought to have a man of their own to report the exploits of their soldiers.[31]

Milner also asked Banjo to take two ladies, the Duchess of Westminster and Lady Charles Bentinck, to a jackal hunt led by a pack of English hounds. When Banjo said he was without a horse, as his three had been sent on with the troops, Milner replied that 'an Australian could always get a horse'; the term 'Australian horse-thief' had become a popular catchphrase among the British in South Africa because of the reputation that the larrikin Australians had made from the moment they arrived. Accepting the challenge, Banjo went looking. After drawing a blank at a dozen places, he found that the groom in charge of the British officers' horses had been in Australia and had actually looked after a horse Banjo had ridden in a race.

After bribing him to borrow one of the Argentine horses specially imported to South Africa, Banjo soon arrived at the hunt wearing a pair of English-made buckskin breeches and mounted on a splendid hunter ready to impress the 'young and attractive women' who were both 'beautifully turned out ... Both carried whisky and water in hunting-flasks and they both smoked cigarettes ... I realized that they looked upon me as the Wild Colonial Boy, the bronco buster from the Barcoo, and I determined to act up to it. It seemed a pity to disappoint them.'[32] Banjo listened to them gossip about the various members of the British High Command and was shocked to learn that one army chief wore a corset and rouge.[33] He came to the conclusion that British military appointments were 'like the Order of the Garter – there was no damned merit about them', that 'everything in England was run by aristocratic cliques' and that the aristocrats fought 'like cats over the big jobs'.

The hunt ended with the jackal cornered by the salivating dogs and going to ground. 'The ladies sat and smoked without blinking an eyelid while a Dutch farmer, under the impression that he was airing his English, used the most frightful language while digging the animal out.'[34] Banjo himself was prone to use language that seems frightful today, though was commonplace at the end of the nineteenth century, so that throughout his South African experience Australian readers were repeatedly told of 'a shambling, bandy-legged flat footed old nigger', 'another similar nigger', 'large niggers', 'small black boys' and 'as fine a specimen of a nigger as one could wish to meet'.[35]

Banjo sent back his first Boer War poem, 'The Reveille', for the *Sydney Mail.* The poem is so jingoistic and trite, it's hard to imagine it was penned by the man who had already written so many Australian classics.

Trumpets of the Lancer Corps,
Sound a loud reveille;
Sound it over Sydney shore,
Send the message far and wide
Down the Richmond River side –
Boot and saddle, mount and ride,
Sound a loud reveille.[36]

Banjo's best work of this period came in his newspaper reports of the war, and then thirty-five years later in his 'Happy Dispatches' recollections.[37]

He had been in Cape Town only a day when he received his pass as a war correspondent from 'a polite military official, who informed me in a bland voice of the pains and penalties I would undergo if I misbehaved myself in any way'.[38] Banjo was introduced to Major Douglas Haig[39] from General French's staff. The British soldiers told Banjo that 'Haig carried French's brains' and that French would be lost without him.[40] Banjo wrote:

> Luckily for me, Haig had been in Australia, where I had seen him play polo. After examining my credentials, he said: 'Now, look here. I ought to send you round to army headquarters and let them decide whether you are to stay or not, but I'll let you stop here on this understanding. Everything you write has to be censored by me. If you try to send anything away that isn't censored, then you'll be sent away. You've got to play the game. You mustn't go anywhere, or do anything, without getting the proper permission. Sometimes the wires are crowded; then each correspondent is allowed to send so many words and no more. One man sent a message in the morning and another message in the afternoon; but we found it out and he has been sent away. Don't try to be too clever, and you'll get along all right.'

Haig explained the duties and powers of a war correspondent by saying: 'You can come out with the staff and see anything that's going on. If you want any information, come to me and I'll tell you – if I have time. Don't worry the General. He's not at his best with correspondents any time, and he might say something you didn't like. Let him alone and he'll let you alone. We're going out in the morning and you can come along if you like.'[41]

Reporting on the war was a dangerous job. The Boers were expert marksmen. On the evening of 4 December 1899, Banjo and the *Kent* contingent boarded a slow train for the front. The horses were taken in narrow carriages that barely held them; for two days, as the train rattled along the narrow gauge railway, the horses tried to kick their boxes to pieces. The days were as hot as Bourke and the nights as cold as Kosciuszko.[42] Springboks were bounding about, but Banjo thought they were very 'over-rated'. After all the reports of their majesty, he had imagined he would see an animal the size of a calf leaping like a steeplechaser – when the reality was, the springboks were not much bigger than a hare. Seeing 'these little grey shadows pottering along over the veldt was a great come-down from what we expected'.[43]

THE TRAIN ARRIVED AT NAAUWPOORT,[44] 'a frightful place – just a lot of small galvanised iron houses and a dust storm'.[45] Sometimes mule wagons, with the drivers unable to see a metre in front of them because of the dust, would crash into each other. General John French,[46] who had survived divorce and adultery scandals during his recent time in India, was in charge of the British troops. Banjo wrote that French's 'troubles through life had been mostly female and financial'[47] and that French 'took all things as they came, especially women'.[48] French inspected the battered Australian horses and granted them a day's respite.

Banjo decided to follow two other war correspondents to the fighting at Colesberg, fifty-five kilometres north, leaving camp with a saddle horse and a packhorse. He camped with New Zealand troops and the next day rode with them to Arundel, halfway to Colesberg. The New Zealanders pushed on across a wide plain, and pulled up under a steep hill and dismounted to reconnoitre. In a few minutes, a mighty roar sounded from a big hill about 2400 metres away. A seven-pound cannon shell burst between the men.

Their hurried search with binoculars found that dozens of Boer were assembled on the big hill, and no doubt hundreds more were in hiding. Shells crashed down with 'nasty screaming',[49] and sand erupted all around as the Boers opened fire with their new Mauser rifles. Banjo huddled among the rocks of a small hill until the Lancers located the exact position of the Boer cannons – they simply charged towards them until the firing recommenced. Having found the positions, the men retreated to their camp and enjoyed 'quite a good meal'.[50] One horse was shot, another broke its leg and a third ran away. A staff sergeant had a severe fall but was not seriously hurt.

At Arundel on 8 December 1899, Banjo found the Boers defending a big hill a few miles from the British camp.

> It was only a small skirmish that was going on, but quite exciting enough for beginners such as ourselves … The battleground was a great big plain (called veldt in this country) with a circle of irregular hills round it. These hills are very rugged and stony, and are called kops if of a great size and kopje (pronounced coppy) if small. All Africa so far as we have seen it is either veldt or kopje … No better fighting ground for cavalry could be found than the veldt, and no worse ground for them could be found than the kopje.[51]

The action would soon become much more brutal. And every soldier was soon 'as dirty as a badger with the dust'. One night a storm flooded the tents and stained everything with muddy water. 'We have no time to think of appearances,' Banjo explained. 'I have averaged 14 hours a day in the saddle since I came here. We thought we were being put in a little quiet out-of-the-way corner, where we could do no harm; but ever since we came here we can have a fight any hour of the day that we happen to want it, and it is supposed that a really big battle must be fought before we take Colesberg.'[52]

Early in his South African adventure, Banjo was present at the taking of a Boer homestead, the owner having been arrested as a sympathiser with the enemy. Banjo was given the use of the stable for his horses. It was, he said, absurdly like an Australian homestead in every way. 'Sheep-yards, horse-yards, cultivation paddocks – everything reminds one of Australia. There is a spring here of lovely water and a grand garden. The troops keep great discipline. The crops are untouched in the fields, the sheep go out with their shepherd through the middle of the camp.'[53]

Lord Roberts[54] arrived in Cape Town on 11 January 1900 to take charge of the campaign, with Herbert Kitchener[55] as his chief of staff. Roberts had replaced Victoria Cross recipient Redvers Buller,[56] who was sent off to a subordinate role in Natal. Roberts had a plan to capture Bloemfontein, capital of the Orange Free State.

Two days later, *The Leader* began the serialisation of Banjo's book – with the first title, *In No Man's Land* – and it would run until May.

Banjo returned briefly to Cape Town in order to interview the author and anti-war campaigner Olive Schreiner,[57] whose brother,

William, was the Cape Colony prime minister. After six weeks of blazing days and freezing nights, spent in tents where the dust storms coated everything with a dull-red powder, wondering how close he could get to the enemy without being shot dead, Banjo felt he was entering another world in the salubrious suburb of Newlands with its grand avenues and splendid trees that grew 'most luxuriantly – sunflowers, box-hedges, roses, and all manner of grasses flourishing everywhere'.[58] To Banjo, the suburb looked like Sydney's Botanic Garden would if a few grand homes had been built there. Schreiner was a 'little woman, small in stature, but of very strong physique, broad and powerful; her face olive-complexioned, with bright, restless eyes, and a quick mobile mouth. She spoke fluently and with tremendous energy, her thoughts emphasised by a sharp, uplifted finger.[59] There were more people in South Africa against the war than for it, she said.

> You Australians and New Zealanders and Canadians, I cannot understand it at all, why you come here light heartedly to shoot down other colonists of whom you know nothing – it is terrible. Such fine men too – fine fellows. I went to Green Point, and saw your men in camp; oh, they were fine men – and to think that they are going out to kill and be killed, just to please the capitalists! It is terrible – such men to come and fight against those fighting for their liberty and their country. You people – you are all volunteers! Why have you come? ... You say that England was at war, and you wished to show the world that when the mother country got into a war the colonies were prepared to take their place beside her! Yes, but you ought to ask, you ought to make inquiries before you come over. You Australians do not understand. This is a capitalists' war! They want to get control of the Rand and the mines ... it will be a war of extermination ... There will be no end. The Boers are fighting for life or death, and they have no idea of giving in.[60]

Banjo replied by writing that the South African campaign seemed like an unwinnable war. Even if the British prevailed it would still take a large and permanent force to maintain order, and there would be constant trouble from a disaffected people. If the Boers scattered and broke to the mountains, they would be 'practically unreachable'. The English people, Banjo wrote, were too humane to care about reprisals; they would never resort to destroying homesteads 'and leaving their wives and children without shelter'.[61]

WHILE BANJO WAS HAVING his first taste of war, Breaker Morant was preparing to ride into the conflict from Paringa Station, a sprawling cattle property on the Murray River near Renmark, about 260 kilometres north-east of Adelaide.

The Breaker had spent sixteen years in the eastern colonies, and perhaps he had finally worn out his welcome with too many bad debts. He was as daring as ever in his new surroundings, though – he rode his horse into the upstairs bar of the new Renmark Hotel.[62] His storytelling grew new legs.

Australians were caught up in patriotic fervour and The Breaker saw a war in South Africa as a free passage home to England. He set off from Renmark on Boxing Day 1899 for Morgan, the railhead for Adelaide, to enlist with five other members of the Renmark Defence Rifle Club. The *South Australian Register* reporters lapped up everything Breaker told them and listed his particulars as 'Morant, Harry Harbord, journalist, Renmark, son of Vice-Admiral Morant, of [United Services] Club. London, S.W. Served in West Somerset Yeomanry and Cavalry. Born at Devon. England, December 9. 1870. Known as "The Breaker," of the Sydney "Bulletin", for which paper he has written verse for ten years. He is a member of the Sydney Hunt Club. Single.'

The Breaker continued to claim that he was an admiral's son, and he knocked off six years from his age. He passed the medical exam, shooting test and riding trial. Within a couple of weeks of enlisting, he was not only a lance corporal but also the star player in a polo match on 20 January 1900 between the Adelaide Polo Club and some of the soldiers headed for war, who gave themselves the Banjo-inspired nickname of 'the Geebungs'. Breaker sailed for South Africa on 26 January 1900 aboard the *Surrey.*

WHILE MORANT WAS STILL crossing the Indian Ocean, William John Lambie,[63] a distinguished reporter from *The Age*, was trying to flee Boer bullets near Jasfontein in Natal Province. Born in

Argyllshire, Scotland, the forty-year-old had come to Australia aged just two, when his Presbyterian minister father took an appointment with the church in Victoria.

Lambie had worked for newspapers in Victoria, New South Wales and Tasmania. Writing for the *Sydney Morning Herald*, he was one of three special correspondents for Sydney newspapers when General Charles Gordon was killed in Khartoum in early 1885.

Lambie went on to cover the uprising against German forces in the Samoan Islands and in 1899 set off to cover the Boer War for *The Age*. He was with a patrol of Tasmanian troopers near Jasfontein on 9 February 1900. The troops were ambushed, surrounded by forty Boers, but Lambie and fellow reporter Alfred 'Smiler' Hales, an Australian writing for the London *Daily News*, ignored calls to surrender and bolted on their horses.

'A rain of lead whistled around us,' Hales recalled. 'We were racing by this time, Lambie's big chestnut mare had gained a length on my little veldt pony, and we were not more than a hundred yards away from the Mauser rifles that had closed in on us.

'All at once I saw my comrade throw his hands up with a spasmodic gesture. He rose in his stirrups, and fairly bounded out of his saddle, and as he spun round in the air I saw the red blood on the white face, and I knew that death had come to him sudden and sharp.'[64]

Hales was wounded before being captured by the Boers, who treated his wounds and buried Lambie. The kindly Boer commander admonished Hales when he discovered the pair were correspondents, not combatants: 'Sir, you dress exactly like two British officers; you ride out with a fighting party, you try to ride off at a gallop under the very muzzles of our rifles when we tell you to surrender. You can blame no one but yourselves for this day's work.'[65]

Lambie was the first Australian to die in the war in South Africa, and the first Australian war correspondent to be killed in action. Seven out of sixty reporters covering the Boer war died from bullet wounds or fever in the first six months of fighting.

ON 17 FEBRUARY, BANJO'S unit joined with General French's forces at the Modder River on their agonising four-day march to relieve the city of Kimberley,[66] which had been besieged by the Boers for four months. There was 'terrific heat',[67] though at the start it 'was a magnificent sight, the convoy being seven miles [12 kilometres] long, with 3500 mules in wagons and 4000 oxen and 15,000 troops of all sorts, marching across the vast plains'.[68]

Banjo saw horses dying of cold and of suffocation from the dust, and soldiers dropping, delirious with fever. There was no feed for the horses since the Boers had burnt the grass, and smoke added to the misery of the dust and the heat. In time thousands of horses would perish in the war, dropping dead on the road to be picked over by vultures or often by starving black Africans who leapt upon the carcases as they fell, stripping them of flesh as quickly as possible and leaving nothing for the birds.[69] It was impossible to send messages out of Kimberley, so Banjo made a bold dash on his black colt to the Modder River and got his report away – scooping all other correspondents and making headlines in the London *Times* and other international newspapers: 'The heat was awful, and the men and horses suffered terribly. The Scots Greys are a well-mounted regiment, but their big English horses suffered much, and the lean, leathery [Australian] Walers had a long way the best of it. As for the gun horses, they were dropping in their harness, and every here and there along the line a pistol shot told where some good horse was being despatched to put him out of misery. Still on, on, was the cry, and the pace was kept up until even the cavalry horses began to fall.'[70]

At Kimberley, Banjo met Cecil Rhodes,[71] the politician who had made much of his fortune from the diamond mines around the town. At the onset of the siege Rhodes had gone to Kimberley with the goal of pressuring the British into sending a massed force to defend it and protect his business interests. He had used his fortune to provide water and refrigeration facilities, as well as constructing fortifications, manufacturing an armoured train, and building a cannon called the Long Cecil that could fire a shell 7600 metres. Banjo introduced himself to Rhodes and later wrote that the strain had obviously told on the giant of colonisation – he was 'very much older looking than one would imagine from portraits. The town must have surrendered but for him'.[72]

Banjo's fearless reporting attracted the attention of Rudyard Kipling's friend Howell Gwynne,[73] the chief Reuters representative in South Africa and later editor of the London *Morning Post*.[74]

Gwynne appointed Banjo as an extra stringer for Reuters, to report especially on the actions involving Australians and New Zealanders.

On 27 February 1900, in the Battle of Paardeberg near Kimberley, Lord Roberts forced the surrender of Boer general Piet Cronje[75] and more than four thousand men, 'as motley a crew as man ever saw … Their clothes ranged from the most tattered moleskin and Crimean wear to really first-class English cut clothes.' Banjo studied Cronje closely: 'a square-set, farmer-like man, with dark eyebrows and a short beard, was dressed in the outer costume of a long black frock coat, light trousers, tan boots, and a slouch hat'.[76] Lord Roberts, the conquering hero, Banjo said, was 'a very small, grizzled old man – they say he is seventy – but he sits his horse like a youngster. Though he is studiously polite to everybody, he has broken several generals already, so the brass hats and the red-collared popinjays of staff officers are wondering, when they go to bed at night, whether their jobs will be gone in the morning.'[77]

AFTER THAT VICTORY, the taking of Bloemfontein on 13 March 1900 was 'ridiculously easy'.[78] The Boers headed for the hills, leaving the town unprotected. Banjo and two other war correspondents wanted to make history as the first of the invaders into Bloemfontein; unsure whether they might suffer bullet wounds or capture, they raised their whips and galloped as fast as they could for more than a kilometre. Banjo was mounted on his favourite horse, a six-year-old black colt by the well-performed racehorse Myles-na-Coppaleen from a New Zealand mare by Ringleader. The horse not only had survived French's death march by eating anything that he could bite,[79] but had also proved himself much faster than the mounts of the other two pressmen.

Banjo reached Bloemfontein first, and once in the town the reporters slowed to a walk. They were warmly welcomed by the townsfolk, 'who all shook hands with us and hoorayed as though they liked having their town captured. The fact is that the Boer – the man we are fighting – is not a townsman at all. In these towns the names of the shops and the trades are all in English … and the townsfolk of Bloemfontein are 80 per cent English – at any rate they are nearly 100 per cent English tonight, as the Dutch element has run away.'[80] Banjo and his comrades guided the mayor out to see

Lord Roberts and surrender the town.[81] The weather even turned spectacular, as though celebrating the British victory. 'Think of the best possible Australian day, sunny and clear, with a brisk invigorating breeze blowing, followed by a cool calm night,' Banjo wrote, 'that is South African weather day after day. The Boers are giving up their arms in hundreds at the Government buildings. Big sturdy bearded men riding in on their marvellous African ponies, and solemnly depositing their well-beloved rifles at the door, and solemnly riding away again.'[82]

Banjo rented a room in Bloemfontein. Two weeks later, he finally met Rudyard Kipling, who was making a hurried visit to the war. Kipling remembered reading Banjo's *Man from Snowy River*. Banjo found it hard to believe that this small 'square figured man with the thick black eyebrows and the round glasses was the creator of Mowgli, the jungle boy … and of *The Man who would be King*'[83] as there was 'nothing of the dreamer about him'. 'Met Kipling,' Banjo wrote. 'He is a little, square-built, sturdy man of about forty. His face is well enough known to everybody from his numerous portraits; but no portrait gives any hint of the quick, nervous energy of the man. His talk is a gabble, a chatter, a constant jumping from one point to another.'[84] He seemed more like a fast-talking businessman 'than a literary celebrity'.[85] Kipling's time living in America had flavoured his speech too, and he was forever saying 'yep' instead of 'yes'.[86]

Three days later, on 28 March 1900, Banjo sat next to Kipling at a correspondents' dinner in honour of Lord Roberts. Twenty-four guests attended the function at Bloemfontein's railway station, which had the largest room in town and the best cook in the colony. Banjo and the dignitaries were treated to tomato soup, boiled salmon, fricassee of chicken, braised oxtail, roast sirloin of beef, roast turkey, salad, potatoes, French beans, pudding, blancmange, jellies, and oysters wrapped in bacon, as well as cheese and coffee.[87] Among the guests were Alfred Milner, Roberts, his private secretary and aide-de-camp Colonel Neville Chamberlain[88] (who is said to have invented the game of snooker in India, and should not be confused with Britain's future prime minister of the same name), and General Hector 'Fighting Mac' MacDonald,[89] who committed suicide not long after – 'one of the world's great soldiers gone wrong'.[90] MacDonald had risen through the ranks from a private. 'He yarned away about the Australians at a great rate, and obviously thinks our troops are as good as any for the work here.'[91]

Sitting next to Kipling, Banjo was amazed by the English writer's 'cock-sureness'.

> Then I remembered that he had been for years on the editorial staff of a big Indian newspaper. Once a man has been privileged to use the editorial 'we' he feels that the world is out of joint, and that he is born to set it right ... Kipling is two men – a sort of Dr Jekyll and Mr Hyde ... It was most fascinating. He yarned away about shoes and ships and sealing-wax and cabbages and kings; interested in everything; asking questions about everything; jumping from one subject to another ... His training as a journalist may have made him a bit of an adviser-general to the world at large, but it taught him to talk to anybody and to listen to anybody, for the sake of whatever story they might have to tell. You could have dumped Kipling down in a splitter's camp in the back-blocks of Australia and he would have been quite at home; and would have gone away, leaving the impression that he was a decent sort of bloke that asked a lot of questions.[92]

Banjo asked Kipling for a souvenir of their meeting, and on the dinner menu Kipling scribbled extracts from two of his poems: 'The Long Trail', Banjo's favourite, and 'The Flowers'. The menu remained one of Banjo's most prized possessions for all his life.[93]

Around the same time, Banjo also met the stony-faced Lord Kitchener, whose staff said, according to Banjo, 'that he is all right when you know him, but you've got to know him first. They say that he has some humour concealed about him, and that he is a collector and is fond of literature.'[94]

Banjo also met the mercurial Winston Churchill, who was working as a war correspondent for London's *Morning Post*.[95] Banjo regarded Churchill as 'the most curious combination of ability and swagger'. He drank a big bottle of beer for breakfast every morning and had the audacity to frequently confront General French, which Banjo reckoned was 'about equal to earning the V.C. twice over'.[96] Churchill was a man to be 'feared if not liked'. He was a graduate of the Royal Military Academy Sandhurst, and while he had done some soldiering he was unpopular with his superiors. He had 'such a strong personality', Banjo explained, 'that the army were prepared to bet that he would either get into jail or become Prime Minister'.[97] Churchill told Banjo 'This correspondent job is nothing to me; but I mean to get into parliament through it … I am going to plaster the *Morning Post* with cables about our correspondent, Mr Winston Churchill, driving an armoured train, or pointing out to Lord Roberts where the enemy is. When I go up for parliament again, I'll fly in.'[98] When the British finally arrived at Johannesburg, Churchill was riding a bicycle.[99]

Breaker Morant had arrived with the South Australian contingent in Cape Town on 23 February 1900, and he was soon promoted to sergeant. He spent the next nine months carrying dispatches to Prieska, a town on the Orange River.

IN APRIL, BACK IN AUSTRALIA, while Banjo was still enjoying the hospitality of Bloemfontein, Bertha Lawson was encouraging Henry Lawson to take his young family for a total change of scene. She hoped it would allow him to turn a corner in his life and to find his place in the international literary arena – it would also keep him away from the artist's model Hannah Thornburn. On 20 April 1900, Lawson set sail for London with Bertha, their infant son, Jim, and their daughter, Bertha Jr, who was just two months old. Things looked promising: Lawson was represented by J. B. Pinker, a leading literary agent in England, and had written his four Joe Wilson stories – among his very best.

William Blackwood published two new Lawson collections in two years: *Joe Wilson and His Mates* (1901) and *Children of the Bush* (1902). But the Lawson marriage was imploding because of Henry's drinking and the stresses associated with caring for small children in an alien environment.

An Australian woman, Edith Dean, had invited the Lawsons to her home in Harpenden in leafy Hertfordshire so she could help look after them. Edith was the widow of the poet Francis Adams[100] and had handed him the revolver so he could kill himself when he was riddled with sickness; she was now married to the painter Frankland Dean. On 18 October 1900, Edith wrote to J. F. Archibald that 'Three weeks ago my husband and I left for a holiday leaving a servant here. On our return we find Mrs Lawson in the County Lunatic Asylum and Lawson in lodgings with *my* servant and the children in London – and their home sold up.'[101]

From May 1901 Bertha spent three more months in Bethlem Royal Hospital as a mental patient. The hospital is better known today as 'Bedlam'. Lawson then lived with Mrs Dean's former servant Lizzie Humphrey and his daughter in a three-roomed flat at Clovelly Mansions on London's Gray's Inn Road. Lawson's son Jim was staying with Mrs Brandt, a family friend in the Surrey village of Shepperton on the Thames. Lawson wrote a three-part story, *The Triangles of Life*,[102] in which a domestic servant, 'Lizzie Higgins', appears in a crucial role, and Lawson used the same address in the story at which he lived with Lizzie Humphrey.

The Lawson marriage never recovered, and really neither did Henry. He later wrote sombrely of 'That wild run to London / That wrecked and ruined me'[103] and of 'Days in London like a nightmare.'[104]

WHILE STILL AT BLOEMFONTEIN, Banjo reported on how General de Wet[105] had taken the local water supply and destroyed the pumping station, while also capturing three hundred men and snaring seventy loaded supply wagons.[106] Banjo rode with an ambulance corps into the middle of a Boer commando unit and interviewed a fifteen-year-old lad who declared he would fight 'Till the last Afrikander is dead.'

'If there is only he and I left,' the boy said, touching the man next him, 'we will fight till we are both killed. Then you will have the land. Till then, No!'[107]

The British had the numbers and they marched north, taking Johannesburg on 31 May 1900 and Pretoria on 6 June. Banjo's black colt carried on tirelessly, 'weary hungry and footsore as he was'.[108] The day before the victory at Johannesburg, Banjo travelled with a dispatch rider from Lord French's force on the west of the city to Lord Roberts's force on the east. They arrived at about 3 a.m. Roberts was sleeping on a little stretcher in a back room but came out in his nightshirt to look at them. 'He doesn't spare himself, seventy years and all as he is,' Banjo wrote. 'The dispatch officer introduced me as an Australian correspondent; and the old man, standing there in his night-shirt, with the weight of the campaign on his shoulders, found time to ask me how the Australians with French were getting on. "When I first saw the Australians," Roberts said, "I thought they were too untrained to be of much use. But the work I have given them to do is the best proof of what I think of them now.'"[109]

The attack on Pretoria began on 2 June 1900 and involved a Boer ambush. Banjo was thrust into a world even more deadly than the slopes of Kosciuszko.

> As we went on the gorges got deeper and deeper, and often the whole force was pushing along a narrow road with a steep hill on either side strewn with great rocky boulders.
>
> The advance squadron was hunting the Boers in front of it, and just as we got to the very narrowest and rockiest part of the road the force pressed very close on the Boers' heels. They turned and hid themselves in the rocks and thorn bushes, and when the advanced scouts came round a bend in the road they found themselves right in a Boer trap. Two of the scouts were shot dead, and some more fell severely wounded. General Potter, who commands the 1st Cavalry Brigade, was close behind the squadron, and General French, who was in charge of the whole force, was just behind him. The two generals, with their respective staffs, halted on the road when the firing started ahead, but before long the bullets began to come whizzing through the trees right among the staff horses, and just over the packed mass of horsemen and guns that were crowding and jostling along the road … a horse or two got hit, and I for one felt thoroughly sure that I was looking on at what would in future be known as 'French's great disaster'. We were like rats in a trap, and if the Boers had advanced they could have shot the whole lot of us, but luckily they contented themselves with driving the advance squadron back. I left the road and took to the rocks, and was retiring as fast as possible, the pony slipping and stumbling over the boulders, when suddenly a bullet struck a rock alongside and ricocheted off, and came whizzing, and hit me in the ribs, almost hard enough to knock me off the horse. I let his head loose then, and he went over boulders and stones as if they were so much sand, skipping from rock to rock like a goat. They say that

> a frightened rider makes a frightened horse, and certainly this pony appeared to know that he was expected to travel fast. A few seconds got us over a hill and into comparative safely, and the guns were pushed forward one by one and opened fire, six guns working at once at 1200 yards range, while one pom-pom barked and clattered like a mad thing, and the Maxim rattled away as fast as it could be loaded. The echoes in the gorge were very great, and all the firing created a most extraordinary din ...[110]

Banjo thought those victories might have spelt an end to the war, but Boer resistance continued in the rugged countryside. Six days later, fourteen thousand men – including some of French's cavalry and the mounted infantry under General Ian Hamilton[111] – went hunting to bring down General Louis Botha and his four thousand troops in a battle at nearby Diamond Hill.[112] Banjo wrote, 'It was then that [the NSW regiment] lost two brave young officers, Harriott[113] and Drage.[114] Both these men – Harriott was little more than a boy – had shown bravery out of the common ... Harriott was struck with an expanding bullet in the thigh, and came to the ground with a shattered leg. Poor boy, his sufferings were awful, but nothing could be done for him, as there were no means of getting him down that rocky precipice under such fire.'[115]

General de Wet was still creating havoc, too, capturing trainloads of supplies and ammunition.[116] Although he had only fifteen months of schooling and had never seen the sea, the Boers regarded him as another Napoleon.[117]

Before long, Banjo's reports home dripped with tears as Roberts[118] and then Kitchener enforced a scorched-earth policy, torching homes and crops, poisoning wells, salting the earth and slaughtering livestock. Banjo saw 'women and children turned, homeless and crying, out on the open veldt'. It made him want to be home and done with the war.[119] 'On the Trek'[120] told one story:

> When the dash and the excitement and the novelty are dead,
> And you've seen a load of wounded once or twice,
> Or you've watched your old mate dying – with the vultures overhead,
> Well, you wonder if the war is worth the price.[121]

There was another story, too, as the British established more than a hundred concentration camps across South Africa. More than twenty-five thousand Boer prisoners were sent overseas to Colombo or St Helena. The vast majority of Boers in the concentration camps were women and children left behind; more than twenty-six thousand of them died from starvation and disease.

So it was that at the end of July 1900, Banjo had seen enough misery. He rode across the border into Basutoland and, with a policeman as guide and interpreter, visited a kraal on the Caledon River, remarking that after so long immersed in war it was a 'most wonderful relief to drive through the Basuto country'. The Basutos had stayed out of the conflict but their possible involvement had been a matter of great interest:

> From reading the reports one got the idea that there were about ten thousand raging savages rushing up and down along the border, dressed in war paint and feathers … only waiting an excuse to hurl themselves over the border and wade in blood. After General Hunter had captured Prinsloo, on the Basuto border, I came through Basutoland to have a look at those warlike people.[122]

The Basuto horses were a cross between Arab steeds and Shetland ponies.[123] One of Banjo's horses had fallen ill in Bloemfontein and another was sold to Prince Francis of Teck,[124] who was serving as a major in the Transvaal and was the brother of England's future Queen Mary. Banjo sold his black colt in Basutoland[125] as he could find no room for him on the boat home to Australia. He would soon pen an ode to all those horses that had carried their riders through hard times in the South African campaign.[126]

Banjo wrote at least nineteen poems during his nine months in South Africa, but his journalism continued to be his most captivating work during this time, such as this description of the cruellest of all blood sports: a manhunt with artillery.

> It is grey dawn. The stars are growing pale in the cold frosty sky, and away to the east a faint cheerless white light begins to spread over the plain. Away on all sides spread the dimly seen stretch

of veldt, in some places reaching to the limit of human sight, in others terminating abruptly in some towering rooky mound called a kopje … With a rush and a clatter and a swing, the guns fly past behind the madly straining horses, while the drivers ply their whips, and the men on the limbers with clenched teeth hold to their seats as the guns rock and sway with the pace they are making. 'Action Front,' and round come the trained horses like machinery, and like lightning the men uncouple the limber and place the gun in position. The range is calculated and the order goes: 'At three thousand. Fuse fourteen. Ready. Fire number one gun!' And with an exulting scream, like a living thing released from prison, away goes the shell across to the little knot of galloping men. An absolute silence prevails as the shell whizzes away out of hearing, and then 'bang' it has burst right over the little dust cloud that is travelling across the plain. It is a splendid shot, and a buzz of congratulation arises, and a wild feeling of exultation wakes in every man's breast. This is something like sport, this shooting at human game with cannon over three thousand yards of country.

'Hooray! Give 'em another.'[127]

Chapter 17

21 SEPTEMBER 1900, SYDNEY TOWN HALL

In the front of our brave old army! Whoop!
the farmhouse blazes bright.
And their women weep and their children die –
how dare they presume to fight
BANJO PATERSON ON THE BOER WAR [1]

BANJO LEFT SOUTH AFRICA a changed man, the horrors of war clouding his visions of Empire and Australia's ties to England. He had left Basutoland and travelled from Harrismith in the eastern Transvaal to Ladysmith, and then on to Durban. There he jumped off the train and climbed aboard the *Wilcannia*, one of the Blue Anchor Line's fast steamers operated by Danish-born Wilhelm Lund and his sons. The ship carried Banjo and a detachment of thirty invalided soldiers, mostly suffering enteric fever,[2] to Adelaide, where it docked on 7 September. Banjo immediately contacted the *Sydney Morning Herald* to report that 'notwithstanding the many hardships' he had endured in South Africa, he had suffered no ill health during the campaign and 'enjoyed to the utmost the work which necessarily falls to the lot of a war correspondent'.[3]

On the following day he left by train for Melbourne and then Sydney, where he was welcomed by a large gathering of friends and family[4] at Redfern Station on 11 September. He told a reporter that he had ridden some five thousand kilometres on his black colt as he followed the Australian troops, and witnessed some of 'the most dramatic incidents of the war'. He planned to give a series of lectures on his experiences.[5]

Banjo thought that with the fall of Johannesburg and Pretoria, the British presence would just be a police action. But the fighting would continue for two more years as the war became mainly a guerrilla conflict against British mounted troops. About sixteen thousand Australians took part in the war, including a small number who fought on the Boer side. The casualty list eventually included 282 who died in action or from wounds sustained in battle, while 286 died from disease and another thirty-eight from accident or unknown causes.[6] Another forty-three were listed as missing in action, and 735 were badly wounded. South Africa's rural economy was devastated by Kitchener's scorched-earth policy and the salting of the earth that made farmland useless. Concentration camps devastated the population. Destitute Boers and black Africans swelled the ranks of the urban poor.

Banjo was eventually moved to write a response in parody to the jingoism of the British press and its propaganda surrounding the war, especially against Boer leader Paul Kruger,[7] or Oom Paul (Uncle Paul) as he was widely known, whose family had been victims of the concentration camps. Banjo wrote that Britain's Colonial Secretary Joseph Chamberlain[8] was a 'Birmingham Judas'[9] who had led Australia into the war and had no way of getting it out.

And first let us shriek the unstinted abuse that the Tory Press prefer
De Wet is a madman, and Steyn is a liar, and Kruger a pitiful cur!
(Though I think if Oom Paul – as old as he is – were to walk down the
    Strand with his gun
A lot of these heroes would hide in the sewers or take to their heels and
    run!
For Paul he has fought like a man in his day, but now that he's feeble
    and weak
And tired, and lonely, and old and grey, of course it's quite safe to
    shriek!)

And next let us join in the bloodthirsty shriek, Hooray for Lord
    Kitchener's 'bag'!
For the fireman's torch and the hangman's cord – they are hung on the
    English Flag![10]

Six days after Banjo arrived home to Sydney, Queen Victoria made her 17 September 1900 proclamation from the Court at Balmoral, that 'on and after the first day of January, One thousand nine hundred and one, the people of New South Wales, Victoria, South Australia, Queensland, Tasmania, and Western Australia shall be united in a Federal Commonwealth under the name of the Commonwealth of Australia'.[11] While Banjo said he swore allegiance to the British Empire, he had seen enough Australians die in South Africa to know that they wanted 'Our Own Flag'[12] and that the Southern Cross was what truly represented them. He wrote: 'We shall carry our own flag up to the front / When we go to the wars again.'[13]

THE LEGAL OFFICE PARTNERSHIP with John William Street officially lasted for another year, but Banjo was done with the law. He had seen too much in South Africa to keep quiet, and there was money to be made and crowds to entertain with stories as thrilling as any he had ever written. He had plans to follow the NSW contingent to China in order to witness the suppression of the Boxer Rebellion against British colonialism. But that would have to wait until he was done with his lecture commitments, which were heavily promoted by the *Sydney Morning Herald*, revelling in the fame of its correspondent.

Just ten days after arriving home, Banjo spoke to a full house of two thousand at Sydney's Centennial Hall inside the Town Hall. When he stepped onto the platform, suave in evening dress even though he had gained a few kilograms in South Africa, he was 'painfully nervous'[14] in front of the packed crowd, especially after they gave him a 'hearty outburst of applause'.[15] Banjo gradually calmed his anxiety and 'settled into a comfortable conversational attitude'. He began to chat 'easily and in colloquial style of his experiences and observations, drawing his matter from what was an almost inexhaustible storehouse'. 'His gestures are few and he indulges in no elocutionary effects,' the *Herald* reported, 'but tells his story in a very simple style, relying on the intelligence of his audience to appreciate the good points, whether they be part of the description of pathetic scenes or included in the narration of humorous incidents.'[16] Banjo spoke for an hour and a half, and showed lantern slides from the photographs he had taken. Some of them displayed the NSW

Medical Corps at work; he said they were men who deserved the greatest praise.

He reminded his audience that the Australians, being mounted troops, were used for quick movements, so were not subjected to the 'cutting up' that the regular infantry so often suffered. Nevertheless, he said, their work was equally dangerous and probably much more skilful. 'It speaks very well for the Australian soldiers that, after the gruelling they had at the Modder and Colesberg, General French included every Australian he could get in a force of 5000 picked men which he required for special service, and where the best cavalry were needed he took the New South Wales Lancers among them.'

He was whole-souled in admiration of Lord Roberts – but not of Kitchener, who had paid a visit to the hospital at Bloemfontein, looking for a friend. 'He walked through, but never said a word to anyone nor made any inquiry about the wounded. He walked out of the place, and blamed the sentry for not turning out the guard for him … Kitchener is disliked in the British Army for that kind of conduct.'[17] Banjo recalled that Kitchener had launched a suicidal attack on General Cronje's forces near Paardeberg, in which 1100 men were killed or wounded. Kitchener personally ordered a small group of exhausted NSW riflemen, under Captain John Antill,[18] to attack an entrenched kopje, even though Antill said his men and horses had been starving for two days. The riflemen bravely held the Boers off for several hours until Kitchener 'sent 3,000 men to help them in a task which he had asked 100 men to do before breakfast'.[19]

Banjo won over many listeners, including the critics from the racy *Truth* newspaper. They derided most of the war correspondents-turned-lecturers, including Duncan MacDonald, as those 'peregrinating pressmen [who] chase the nimble shilling by posing on public platforms, waving the jingo flag, and curdling the blood of audiences with graphic accounts of the horrors of war. Australia has had her full share of this infliction.'[20] But Banjo's lectures were not like that. According to *Truth* he did not rave over successes of the British, nor belittle the Boers.

> We got from 'Banjo' some little truth of the awful bungling in the war against the Boers which, up to date, has caused the British nearly 70,000 casualties, and is likely to cost them a lot

> more yet. Hence, when it became known that he intended taking to the lecture platform, many people were glad, feeling sure that Mr. Paterson … would shed a lurid light on the doings of the campaign. Many were glad of this; many more were exceedingly sorry … He had the most fatal faculty of telling the truth. Though this was warmly welcomed by many, it was resented by most, and 'a frost,' began to be writ large over the enterprise. Fancy a man, in this jingo-cursed age, being found honest enough and brave enough to say that he had a poor opinion of the English Tommy, and believed him very much inferior to both the Scotch and Irish. Yet 'Banjo' said it, and said considerably more. He described Kitchener as a bully, A BRUTE, AND A BLUNDERER … There is much he says that is unpalatable, but we must accept it. He is removing misconceptions, refuting calumnies, telling the plain unvarnished truth … 'Banjo,' here's to you![21]

In later years Banjo reckoned that General French could well have failed, and that some other general would have been put in charge of the British Army in France in the First World War had it not been for 'having the cool clearheaded [Douglas] Haig[22] at his elbow'.[23] 'French would take one look at a position and say: "I think we'll go up here, Douglas." But Haig would say: "I think that's the centre of their position, sir. Suppose we send a patrol up these hills on the right, and get the beggars to shoot a bit? Then we'll know where they are."'[24] Haig had the capacity to take infinite pains, Banjo told his audiences. 'His instructions were always clear and distinct, and he meant them to be obeyed. As to his appearance, everybody has seen thousands of photos of Haig. Probably no man in the world ever got so much publicity. A very square-chinned man, with a broad forehead, he might have made a great public-school teacher, or a great judge. He gave the impression of being a very earnest man, who took things seriously …'[25]

Following his lecture debut, Banjo returned to the same venue the next night. The audience was graced this time by the presence of NSW Governor William Lygon, the 7th Earl Beauchamp.[26] Four months earlier, the *Sydney Morning Herald* had published Banjo's report – taken from the Bloemfontein *Friend* newspaper – on the death of the governor's brother, Edward Lygon, from the

3rd Grenadier Guards.[27] Banjo gave four more lectures at the hall, telling his audience that Roberts put most of his trust in generals Ian Hamilton, John French, Archibald Hunter[28] and Robert Baden-Powell.[29]

But somehow Kitchener had taken over.[30]

Banjo believed England had employed the wrong tactics in South Africa – that on the vast, level, treeless veldts, five or six thousand mounted Australians were worth ten to fifteen thousand infantry.[31] He said the greatest qualities needed for the troops were 'mobility, dash and intelligence, and in all these qualities the Australian and New Zealand regiments without exception proved their excellence. It must never be forgotten that the Australians were accustomed all their lives to finding their way in the open, to noticing what was taking place around them, and to relying on themselves at a pinch; the English "Tommies" were drilled and trained to obey orders, and there their ideas stopped. It was not that the Australians were any braver than the English, but that the latter were less intelligent and had less practical outdoor experience.' He said the NSW Lancers could not have been better mounted. They had police horses that were the best available. The English cavalry horses, much more solidly bred, were better weight-carriers; they could bear 115 kilograms on their backs, weights that bowed the backs of the more lightly framed Australian horses.

Banjo wrote later that he was appalled by the treatment of the horses. On a hard day's march, the mounts were given a meagre meal at dawn: a handful of hard, uncrushed Indian corn. Then they stood saddled with forty kilograms of equipment often into the blazing noon, while their riders waited for orders. After a little maize or raw oats at midday, they were galloped or cantered most of the afternoon over rocky hills, then often tied together all night. They were frequently left for forty-eight hours with their saddles on, and no opportunity to rest after that. Eventually there was the sorry spectacle of a long, drawn-out string of weak and weary horses plodding hopelessly across the veldt, unable to gallop.[32] According to Banjo:

> The fact is that all well-bred horses were too delicate to stand starvation, sickness and mismanagement. They became sick,

> refused their food, and, of course, soon died. The English horses fared no better than ours, and, indeed, it would have taken a lot of iron horses to stand the vicious mishandling to which the poor four-footed servants of the Army were subjected. Good horse, or bad horse, right type or wrong type, the ill-treatment and hardships they had to undergo brought them all to one level … It was not the severity of the work they had to do which killed them; but it was the wretched conditions under which they did their work. If our horses could have been kept free from sickness, and have been properly fed, they could have done all the Army work with the greatest of ease. As it was, they died like flies …[33]

Banjo headed to Parramatta where he gave two more lectures alongside the commander of the NSW Lancers, Lieutenant Colonel James Burns,[34] the businessman behind the trading business Burns, Philp & Co. In October 1900 Banjo appeared in Newcastle, then followed that with appearances in Melbourne, Launceston and Hobart. On 30 October 1900, he wrote to George Robertson from Launceston to say, 'I am in very miserable health since I came back, can't get enough exercise. The days I should have to myself I have to wait in to see interviewers. I think as soon as this tour is over I will be off to China or else buy a pig-farm in the country and never move off it … The lecturing is not so bad but the lonely travelling is awful. Anyhow the money is good which is the main thing.'[35] He lost the weight he had gained in South Africa but made another £300 by touring throughout Queensland[36] early in 1901.

By then Australia was a sovereign nation with a new sovereign. Queen Victoria died on 22 January 1901. Her funeral was one of the largest gatherings of royalty ever to take place, sixty-four years after the burial of the previous monarch, William IV. The Queen wore a white dress and her wedding veil as her sons Edward and Arthur and her eldest grandson Kaiser Wilhelm II lifted her into her coffin. The new king was crowned Edward VII. Australia's prime minister was Edmund Barton, the old cricket umpire.

BREAKER MORANT HAD distinguished himself for a few weeks as a dispatch rider in South Africa. He carried reports through dangerous territory for the London *Daily Telegraph*'s war correspondent Bennet Burleigh,[37] who in earlier years had been a pirate and Confederate spy.

The Breaker started telling people he planned to move into some of the conquered land in the Transvaal and put down his roots, and he was paid out handsomely for his war service. But in October 1900, after eight months in South Africa, he took up the opportunity of a free passage to England.

There, Morant visited his young friend Lieutenant Percy Frederick Hunt,[38] who was also on leave. It was even claimed that he and Hunt had become engaged to a pair of Devon girls. But after a long holiday of hunting and playing polo, The Breaker found that his cash reserves were gone. Unable to borrow more, he followed Hunt back to the Boer War.

Hunt was about to be made a captain in a new unit composed mostly of volunteers. They would be used for counterinsurgency against the Boer guerrilla fighters in the northern Transvaal. The unit of about 350 men[39] was formed on 21 February 1901 by an Australian lawyer, Major Robert Lenehan, who had once had The Breaker ride a horse for him in Sydney, and knew all about his pluck and dash. Lenehan advertised for men who could ride and shoot. A week after recruiting began, Peter Handcock,[40] a blacksmith from Bathurst, was commissioned into the unit as a veterinary lieutenant. The Breaker was commissioned on 1 April 1901 under the command of Captain Hunt. The regiment was called the Bushveldt Carbineers.

HENRY LAWSON WAS FIGHTING his own wars at the Gray's Inn Road flat that he now shared with Lizzie Humphrey and his daughter. He wrote to George Robertson to tell him he'd been an invalid for six months.[41] Bertha's stay in hospital was costing him three guineas a week[42] and Lawson needed to stay busy to pay the bills.

William Blackwood was publishing another collection of his stories and sketches, *The Country I Come From*,[43] and Lawson was writing the preface to a new novel, *My Brilliant Career*,[44] by a sassy young woman named Stella Miles Franklin.[45] Lawson told Robertson that 'the truth and vividness of the work was startling even to me'.[46] Robertson wasn't as enthusiastic, but Lawson had convinced William Blackwood to publish it.

When Miles Franklin had first written to Lawson, seeking assistance with her writing from the literary icon, she'd remarked that 'unless one has swell influence one might as well try to sell an elderly cow for a young racehorse'.[47] Not realising that Miles Franklin was a twenty-year-old woman, Lawson had responded with: 'Mr M Franklin, Dear Sir ...' He told 'Mr Franklin' that he had enjoyed 'his' work and called it 'the first great Australian novel'. He asked for details of Mr Franklin's career.[48]

BACK IN SYDNEY AFTER THE END of his lecture tour, Banjo briefly flirted with standing for the seats of Boorowa and Braidwood. Boorowa was held by the author and cavalry officer Kenneth Mackay,[49] whose 1895 novel, *The Yellow Wave*,[50] speculated on a Chinese invasion of Australia orchestrated by the Russians. Banjo had the backing of Frank Suttor, who was now vice president of the NSW Parliament's Executive Council. Banjo caught the train down from Sydney to attend a political meeting at Burrowa and 'dealt with a variety of political questions and was very well received.[51]

But eventually Banjo decided to leave politics to the professionals. Having already had such a taste of adventure, he was ravenous for more.

The artist Norman Lindsay[52] began working for *The Bulletin* in 1901, with his brother Lionel[53] starting to contribute works a couple of years later. Norman created in words a portrait of Banjo that was not altogether flattering and perhaps not entirely accurate. (He had also created definitely inaccurate and unflattering *Bulletin* caricatures of comic Aboriginal and Jewish people, the latter invariably portrayed as 'old-clothes dealers with hooked noses'.)[54] Norman called Banjo 'sardonic' and an 'aristocrat',[55] and said that while the writer Steele Rudd[56] was a typical Aussie bush battler, Banjo was very much from the 'squattocracy'.[57] 'He preferred to consort with men of action. Wherever there was a war or a revolution, or any other state of human conflict he was first in the ring ... He spoke slowly, with a slight drawl, which had a saturnine inflection. Saturnine is another definitive label which must be added to his portrait. Every line in his dark-textured face defined it.'[58]

He said Banjo did not mix with artists or writers, and that the darkness of his skin was due to the affliction of 'bile'. Others said his permanent suntan was due to swarthy Scottish ancestors and a love for the great outdoors, and that it was untrue he was not a great mixer; they pointed to the fact that he had helped Henry Lawson for free and was one of the organisers of the Victor Daley[59] Testimonial Fund[60] to help the dying poet and journalist. *The Truth* called Banjo 'a decent, genial fellow, who has never merited the ill-will of a single man' and 'a keen follower of healthy outdoor sports'.[61]

ON 13 JULY 1901, the *Sydney Morning Herald* ran Banjo's thoughts on 'Our Federal Army and Its Cost',[62] in which he explained why the training of officers was the key to military success.

He was then given approval by Sir James Fairfax for a project he had been planning for months: a tour of Asia and Russia to report on the world's trouble spots for the *Sydney Morning Herald.* As Japan and Russia threatened each other with war, on 27 July 1901 the *Herald* informed readers that Banjo, together with his photographic equipment, would travel to the Far East on the China Navigation Company's steamer *Changsha.* He would visit China and Japan, and then take the Trans-Siberian Railway to St Petersburg. In the event of war breaking out, Banjo would be on hand to act for the *Herald* 'as occasion may require'.[63]

Banjo was soon telling readers that the Far East was really the part of the world that should concern Australia the most. 'It can do us most harm and least good; and we surely should be interested in knowing what our next door neighbours are doing … for only eight days' steam from our Northern Territory there lies the great seething cauldron of the East.'[64]

AS BANJO TRAVELLED NORTH FIRST-CLASS, Breaker Morant was out on the veldt applying what he called 'Rule .303' – the calibre of the British rifles – as he orchestrated a killing spree. He had become 'like a man demented',[65] according to his comrade George Witton.[66]

On 2 July 1901, six Boer prisoners had been shot in the Spelonken area of the northern Transvaal, about 130 kilometres east of Fort Edward, the base for the Bushveldt Carbineers near Pietersburg.[67] Kitchener asked for an investigation by an Australian intelligence officer, Major Ramon de Bertodano,[68] a former student at St Paul's

College at the University of Sydney who had worked briefly as a solicitor in Bulawayo.

On 5 August 1901, Morant's friend and commanding officer Percy Hunt was killed when hunting Boer commander Barend Viljoen. Hunt and seventeen of the Bushveldt Carbineers attacked Viljoen and his men at a farmhouse at Duival's Kloof – but Hunt had underestimated the strength of his opponents. His men were outnumbered, and he, his sergeant and a Lobedu warrior fighting for them were killed in the battle that also claimed the life of Barend Viljoen, Viljoen's brother and another Boer.

Morant went looking for revenge, ordering every available man out on patrol. Morant soon learnt that Hunt had been shot in the chest and had been heard moaning in pain as the Carbineers were driven back by Boer gunfire. Hunt's naked body was found lying in a gutter, mutilated; his neck had been broken, his face had been kicked in with what Morant was told were hobnailed boots, and his genitals had been slashed.[69] Morant did not see the body, though, as Hunt had already been buried. The bodies of Viljoen and his comrades had also been mutilated, and there has been speculation since that it was actually the work of Lobedu witchdoctors in keeping with their traditional warfare practices. Still, according to Witton, Morant blamed the Boers and 'vowed there and then that he would give no quarter and take no prisoners'.[70]

A few days later, after a gunfight, Morant captured a Boer named Floris Visser who was wounded in the heel. Visser spent two days as Morant's prisoner. According to Witton, Morant examined and questioned him, and found in his possession articles of clothing: a tunic called a 'British Warm' and a pair of trousers that he identified as the property of the late Captain Hunt. He told Witton he would have Visser shot. 'This man,' Morant said, 'has been concerned in the murder of Captain Hunt; he has been captured wearing British uniform, and I have got orders direct from headquarters not to take prisoners, while only the other day Lord Kitchener sent out a proclamation to the effect that all Boers captured wearing khaki were to be summarily shot.'

Witton asked Morant to leave him 'out of it altogether, as I did not know anything about the orders, I had been such a short time there.' Morant then walked away, and ordered his sergeant-major to gather ten men for a firing party. Some of the men objected, and the sergeant-major asked Witton if he would speak to Morant.

Morant wouldn't budge. 'You didn't know Captain Hunt,' Morant exclaimed, 'and he was my best friend; if the men make any fuss, I will shoot the prisoner myself.' After a little delay, men volunteered – 'to get a bit of our own back,' one remarked. Lieutenant Henry Picton, an Englishman, was placed in command of a four-man firing squad, and Visser was shot.[71] Picton finished Visser off with a revolver bullet to the head.

Chapter 18

NOVEMBER 1901, ROTTINGDEAN, BRIGHTON, SOUTHERN ENGLAND

Kipling and I piled into the back of the car, with the great man as excited as a child with a new toy. Out we went, scattering tourists right and left, and away over the Sussex downs.

BANJO PATERSON ON HIS AUTOMOBILE JAUNT WITH ONE OF HISTORY'S GREAT LITERARY FIGURES[1]

THE SUNDRENCHED deck of the *Changsha* was the place to be as the grand vessel glided through the deep blue waters off North Queensland. Banjo found it a much more pleasant place than the South African veldt, and he enjoyed all the trappings of a first-class passenger as he lazed about in the winter warmth and worked on his impressive tan. Not that he was completely relaxed – like many of his fellow Australians at the time, he couldn't hide his fears that this new nation would soon be swamped by invaders.

Back in 1888, Henry Lawson's old boss from *The Worker*, William Lane, had published a serialised dystopian novel, *White or Yellow?: A Story of the Race War of A.D. 1908*,[2] set in a time when hordes of Chinese took over white society and its industries. The politician Kenneth Mackay had kept banging the drum with his warning in *The Yellow Wave*. As the Chinese ship sailed north, Banjo wrote from Thursday Island, on 10 August, that while there were few Asians in Brisbane or among the cane farms south of Rockhampton where South Sea Islanders toiled on the plantations, 'north of Rockhampton the coast towns are already hotbeds of Oriental fecundity'.[3]

Banjo's writings were awash with xenophobia:

> As one goes northward the size of the 'Eastern quarter' of the town increases, till at Thursday Island and Port Darwin it becomes the 'Eastern three-quarters' of the town. In these towns the little Chinese children play about in the streets dressed in their outlandish Chinese costumes; the little black piccaninnies of the Kanaka roll about in the dust, happy as sandboys, side by side with the saddle-coloured offspring of the Malay and Manila man. The fact that a few thousands of these people have settled on our coasts does not trouble us much. They can do little harm in our time. But the same was said of the first few pairs of rabbits let loose in Australia ... We know what troubles the Americans are having over the black question, and these Asiatics will assuredly be all over Northern Australia within the next few years.[4]

As a first-class passenger rather than 'a pauper immigrant', Banjo was allowed to go ashore when the *Changsha* reached Manila on 21 August 1901. Hustle and bustle was going on everywhere, and Banjo thought 'some of the little bronze-black women were very fresh and attractive looking'.[5] While in Manila, Banjo called on the Ohio-born General Adna Chaffee, a decorated veteran of the American Civil War, who was about to become the military governor of the Philippines.

ON 23 AUGUST 1901, near Fort Edward, Breaker Morant led a small patrol to intercept a group of eight bedraggled and battered prisoners who were being brought in under guard from the Elim Hospital in Valdezia. Morant had them detained. Four of them were Dutch schoolteachers who had not taken part in the fighting.

By coincidence, the South African-born Reverend Heese,[6] of the Berlin Missionary Society, was returning from the hospital after taking a soldier there on behalf of Major de Bertodano. The reverend saw the prisoners by the side of the road shaking with fear; he spoke to them briefly and assured them they would be all right, before riding on. When he was out of sight, Morant ordered that all be taken to the side of the road and shot along with three native witnesses.

Startled by the gunshots, Reverend Heese returned to see the corpses by the side of the road. He protested loudly to Morant, who detained him for a week at Fort Edward but then let him and his young native driver leave in their trap. There were rumours that Lieutenant Handcock followed close behind with a rifle.[7]

About a week later, reports began to circulate that Reverend Heese and his driver had been found shot along the Pietersburg road about twenty-four kilometres from the fort.

ON 2 SEPTEMBER 1901, Banjo's ship was in gloom because 'a very old man, a second-class passenger, jumped overboard during the night'. He was in the tea trade and had suffered financial ruin. The man had come out to Manila to go into the timber business, only to find that most of the timber land belonged to the Church. 'So he gave up the struggle and jumped overboard. His married daughter and her husband were on board. The scrap of a note said: "I have decided not to be a burden on the young people."'[8]

Banjo sailed on to 'Hongkong': 'a fine city, with big solid stone buildings' but which would not suit an Australian 'as it is a horseless city ... All traffic is done by Chinese coolies. You can be carried in a chair or dragged in a rickshaw at about half the price of a cab.' At the mouth of the Yangtze, the muddy water was being ploughed by Chinese junks and German, Russian, English and Japanese steamers 'coming and going as busily as possible'. There were too many nations 'shouldering each' other in the area for peace to last.[9]

On 5 September the *Changsha* arrived in Shanghai, and the muddy waters of the Huangpu River reminded Banjo of the Lachlan after a flood. The delta of the Yangtze was one of the richest lands he'd ever set eyes on; as far as he could see there was a vast alluvial plain intersected by creeks and canals, with green crops and fat buffalo and hump-shouldered cattle. Every inch of the land was under cultivation, and it was equal in richness to the best Hunter River or Gippsland flats, with much more water.

The next day Banjo stepped off the ship, and all along the river were moored British, American, Russian, Japanese and German vessels, 'watching each other day and night, each nation determined to prevent the other getting any rights over this splendid territory.'[10]

On Saturday, 7 September 1901, Banjo descended on the Shanghai racetrack at daylight to watch the 'mahfoos' – Chinese grooms – working the horses in a way that would make the hair of any Australian trainer stand on end.

> They are brought down from the north of China usually at the age of 10 or 12 years at the youngest, and they are then broken in and trained for racing. None have ever been known to die. The method of training is as follows: – A mercantile man just out from England, where he has never had anything to do with horses except in omnibuses, buys a China pony at auction and starts to train him … The day after the pony is purchased he is tried for a mile gallop against the watch, and well flogged to encourage him. Every day after that he is galloped from one to two miles against the watch, and invariably well warmed with the whip. And yet, such is their constitution that they thrive on this treatment, and they really race very well.[11]

That evening Banjo went with a detective around the town visiting Chinese gambling dens and theatres, similar to English music halls but where the audiences sat about and drank tea. Next on Banjo's tour were the opium dens, which were 'very terrible – the wan figures of Chinamen seen through an evil-smelling mist'.[12]

From Banjo's perspective, the Chinese looked at him with a mixture of amusement and suspicion. He concluded that they regarded foreigners as 'some kind of unfortunate accident that time will mercifully remove'.[13]

FROM SHANGHAI, BANJO travelled north for nine hundred kilometres on a Russian-owned, British-built ship crewed by Chinese, arriving at Chefoo (now called Yantai) on 15 September 1901. He planned it to be his last stop before catching the train from Vladivostok to St Petersburg.

The wharves in Chefoo were choked with merchandise, and the junks so thick in the harbour that their masts were like a vast forest. Alongside the wharves were dozens of foreign vessels all busy loading raw materials and unloading manufactured goods in exchange. 'The Chinese are beginning to use European goods – clothes, kerosene lamps, vehicles, furniture, and what not,' Banjo reported. 'The possibilities of the market are enormous.' But around Chefoo, espionage was rife among consuls. The tension was just like the eve of the Boxer Rebellion, when 'The Powers were sitting round China like crows round a dying bullock, each anxious to be first to dig its beak in.'[14] 'In addition to the natural desire for trade expansion and colonisation which possesses such countries as England and Germany,' Banjo wrote, 'there are two nations who have special reasons for wanting to get an opening in China. These are the Russians and the Japanese. Japan is heavily taxed and is anxious to get room to extend herself. Russia is China's neighbour in the north, and is anxious to get as big a slice as she can of the fertile Chinese country, with its excellent climate and open ports.'[15] He felt that the people of Chefoo hated foreigners like him with 'a cold intensity that surpasses any hatred ever heard of'.[16]

On Monday, 16 September, Banjo called in to see Chefoo's Russian consul to arrange his trip to St Petersburg but was told that the line from Vladivostok was flooded.

Banjo asked the consul for a guide so he could meet the Australian adventurer and journalist 'Chinese' Morrison,[17] who for the past four years had been the Peking correspondent for the London *Times*. Banjo knew Morrison's record fairly well; a qualified doctor, he had forsaken medicine for life as a traveller and explorer. As a young man, he had trekked through New Guinea and northern Australia. 'The blacks put a spear into him,' Banjo wrote. 'He got his black boy to cut off the shaft of the spear, but never had the head of the spear taken out till he got to Melbourne. A man like that takes some stopping.'[18]

Banjo found Morrison at a watering hole outside Chefoo and paid him no favours, writing that 'in person, he was a tall ungainly man with a dour Scotch face and a curious droop at the corner of his mouth – a characteristic I had noticed in various other freaks, including Olive Schreiner'.

> Of the three great men of affairs that I had met up to that time – Morrison, Cecil Rhodes, and Winston Churchill – Morrison had perhaps the best record. Cecil Rhodes, with enormous capital at his back had battled with Boers and Basutos; Churchill, with his father's prestige and his mother's money to help him, had sailed on life's voyage with the wind strongly behind him; but Morrison had gone into China on a small salary for the *Times* and had outclassed the smartest political agents of the world – men with untold money at the back of them.[19]

Because of the threatened bad weather Banjo took a steamer that returned him to Hong Kong, and he then boarded a P & O liner bound for London via the Suez Canal. Before he left Weihai Harbour, he jotted down in his diary: 'Saw the warships of all nations at anchor using their searchlights like great pencils of flame ... Might, majesty, dominion, and glory – we have them all in our British warships; and the sight of the British flag in a foreign port is never without its thrill to the wandering colonial.'[20]

IN SOUTH AFRICA, Major De Bertodano began compiling as much evidence as he could over the murderous activities of the Bushveldt Carbineers. He had undercover scouts search for information, though witnesses kept disappearing.

Finally, on 4 October 1901, fifteen members of the BVC garrison at Fort Edward signed a letter that was secretly dispatched to Colonel F.H. Hall, the British army officer commanding at Pietersburg. The letter was witnessed by BVC Trooper Robert Mitchell Cochrane, a former justice of the peace from Coolgardie, Western Australia. The letter writers declared: 'Sir, many of us are Australians who have fought throughout nearly the whole war ... We cannot return home with the stigma of these crimes attached to our names. Therefore, we humbly pray that a full and exhaustive inquiry be made by Imperial officers in order that the truth be elicited and justice done. Also we beg that all witnesses may be kept in camp at Pietersburg till the inquiry is finished.' Cochrane listed numerous civilian witnesses who could confirm the allegations.

The letter writers outlined six 'disgraceful incidents' involving men from Fort Edward. These were the shooting at Valdezia of six Afrikaner men and boys who had surrendered and the theft of their money and livestock; the shooting of BVC trooper B.J. van Buuren who had been upset over the Valdezia killings; Morant's execution of Visser; the shooting of the four surrendered Afrikaners and four Dutch schoolteachers, as well as the shooting of the Reverend Heese; the deaths of two boys, aged five and thirteen, and the wounding of a nine-year-old girl after BVC lieutenant Charles H.G. Hannam ordered his men to open fire on a wagon train containing Afrikaner women and children who were coming in to Ford Edward to surrender; and the shooting of Roelf van Staden and his sons Roelf and Christiaan, who were coming in to Fort Edward to surrender. It was alleged that Morant made the father and sons dig their own graves before they were shot.

The letter also accused the field commander of the BVC, Major Robert Lenehan, of being 'privy to these misdemeanours'. 'It is for this reason,' the writers asserted to Cochrane, 'that we have taken the liberty of addressing this communication direct to you.' [21]

ON BOARD BANJO'S LUXURY LINER from China was Sir Assheton Gore Curzon-Howe,[22] who was about to be promoted to rear admiral. He was an old sea-dog, 'always polite' but when riled capable of a 'rugged eloquence' that would make a bullocky blush.[23]

Of much more interest to Banjo was the bawdy music hall singer and comedian Marie Lloyd,[24] a larger-than-life Cockney who boarded the ship at Singapore with her entourage in mid-October. She was 'a very virile lady, this, if one may use the word; a Juno of a woman, with the physique of a ploughman, a great broad face, and eyes very wide apart. She walks into a room as a dreadnought steams into a harbour, followed by a fleet of smaller vessels in the shape of sycophants and hangers on.'[25] Learning that Banjo was 'some sort of literary person', Marie asked him to write a song or two for her, and told him that she had paid 'as much as a pound and thirty bob for some of her song hits in London'. She told him he just needed a good 'ketch-line' for his tune, but he was more amused than flattered, as her conversation was invariably dotted with innuendo, nudges and winks.

AT FORD EDWARD, A SERIES OF ARRESTS were made between 16 and 23 October as all officers and non-commissioned officers were summoned to Pietersburg.

The Breaker had just spent two weeks at the Transvaal Hotel in Pretoria, where he signed himself in as 'Captain Morant'. He said he was there sorting out the affairs of his beloved Captain Hunt.

At Pietersburg, Morant, Handcock, Picton, Witton, Taylor and Lenehan were held in confinement as Major de Bertodano gathered evidence for the deputy judge advocate general, Colonel James St Clair, who was considering the case. St Clair decided that Morant should be charged with four murders, Handcock with five, and Witton with one as well as being an accessory to another.

NEAR THE END OF OCTOBER Banjo's ship berthed in Marseilles, where he watched one of Marie Lloyd's entourage wrestling with a gendarme 'about the size of a weevil' in a comical fracas at the local races. Then in November he arrived in London and found it shrouded in thick fog. He thought the British full of themselves, with a 'beautiful serene self-complacency … that one can never sufficiently admire', and was amused that they even boasted about their weather despite the fact that 'this awful yellow shroud' choked everything.[26] An English bus driver told Banjo with the greatest pride, 'Ah! You don't see fogs like that in no other part of the world.' As the man boasted of the skill of London drivers navigating through the fog, Banjo thought of the remarkable driving he'd seen by some of Cobb & Co's men 'on dark nights with unbroken horses in very broken country; but I didn't try to tell the busman about them'.[27]

Banjo initially ignored the pro-Boer meetings in London. But they attracted Henry Lawson, who had now returned with his wife, Bertha, and their two small children. They were living together in a sad and gloomy little flat up five flights of stairs – all ninety steps – in Paradise Row, London. Bertha had spent ten months in care and was still fragile; Henry was still depressed. Mass protests in London, Zurich and Berlin throughout November denounced the British for Kitchener's barbaric tactics against soldiers and civilians, and especially against women and children. At an anti-Semitic rally in Berlin, university students urged Boer sympathisers to assassinate Joseph Chamberlain.[28]

Lawson wrote 'As Far as Your Rifles Cover'[29] in response to the daily reports of Kitchener's atrocities.

> Do you think, you slaves of a thousand years to poverty, wealth and
> pride,
> You can crush the spirit that has been free in a land that's new and
> wide?
> When you've scattered the last of the farmer bands, and the war for a
> while is over,
> You will hold the land – ay, you'll hold the land – the land that your
> rifles cover.[30]

Banjo, however, thought the Londoners rather apathetic in the main. Redvers Buller, the first commander of the British forces in South Africa, had been pushed aside to make way for Lord Roberts in January 1900, and he was then called back to Britain that October. When *Times* journalist Leo Amery criticised Buller's command, on 10 October 1901 the old soldier hit back publicly in a speech at a luncheon thrown in his honour by the Queen's Westminster Volunteers. His bad temper got the better of him and, breaching army protocol, he quoted from confidential telegrams.[31] Buller's enemies demanded his resignation; he refused and was dismissed on half-pay on 22 October. Banjo was surprised that little news about the affair was released. He talked about the case with an 'English gentleman interested in political matters and having considerable knowledge of affairs'.

> 'Well,' I said, 'in Australia if anything as important as this occurred, there would be a dozen members of Parliament who would go and demand the papers, and would tell their constituents what was the truth. There would be a member on every step of the War Office stairs waiting till it opened in the morning and a howling crowd of their constituents outside.'[32]

Banjo's membership of the Australian Club earned him reciprocal rights at the Junior Carlton Club, an establishment at 30 Pall Mall closely aligned with the Conservative Party. But he had friends who were anything but conservative, and in November 1901 he met up again with Phil May, his old friend from *The Bulletin*, who way back in 1888 had returned to London to test more boundaries. Banjo found May living in St John's Wood and firmly established as one of the leading artists on London *Punch*: 'Phil welcomed me with open arms, mainly because he had bought a horse which he hadn't seen for a year, and he wanted somebody to ride it. Phil was forever buying things that he did not want; and he would have bought (on credit) anything from an elephant to an old master when properly approached.'[33]

May introduced the Bard of the Bush to London's bohemian society and to the West End theatres, where the eccentric artist was regarded 'as a sort of Aladdin' who only had to rub a lamp to get acting work for his friends: 'So they flooded his Sunday nights and asked him to see producers, managers, concert promoters, etc., for them. It appeared that half the leg-shows in London were run by wealthy men, who had nothing to do with the theatre business but who put up their money for female rather than financial reasons.'[34]

On another night, Banjo and May went to the National Sporting Club: 'a somewhat faded institution, where Phil was in great demand; and it was hard to keep the booze hounds off him. Vacant faces loomed through the tobacco smoke and heavy jowls hung over long drinks. A big Lancashire manufacturer joined our party; a fine, fresh-complexioned, burly man, who seemed a good sort. He said that he had a concession (meaning a contract) to install electric tram-cars in Perth and Ballarat, and that he would make fifty thousand pounds out of it. This seemed terrific, but I believed him.'[35]

May was dead less than two years later, aged just thirty-nine. He left nothing for his widow, 'but the *Punch* people gave her all his original drawings. As Phil May did not leave an enemy in the world, people rushed in to buy the drawings, and the widow cleared something like three thousand pounds by the sale. The bohemians of London may have had their weak points, but they were prepared to pay their tribute to the greatest bohemian of them all.'[36]

BANJO WROTE THAT AUSTRALIA was sadly 'the last known place in the world'[37] as far as England was concerned, even though Prince George and his wife Princess Mary had recently visited Australia for the opening of the first national Parliament in Melbourne.[38] If the London papers ever ran anything about his country, Banjo said, it was never more than a few lines at most. But he had a plan to remedy that.

Banjo approached *The Times* asking to be their man Down Under. On 26 November 1901 he endured the 'very severe ordeal' of an interview with the paper's managing director, Moberly Bell,[39] that was prefaced by a haughty junior giving Banjo a long and unwelcome tour of the whole building 'because apparently the rules did not allow anyone to go straight up the stairs'.

On 28 November 1901, Banjo wrote to George Robertson in Sydney from 1 King Street, St James Square, with the news.

> This will give me a good position to try and put some new ideas about Australia into the heads of these English who are quite in the dark about us and our ideas.[40]

The *Times* did not accept his invitation.

Instead, he sold his satire of the Boer War, 'Now Listen to Me and I'll Tell You My Views', to another newspaper, *Reynolds' News*.[41] He also wrote some verses for John Corlett's *Sporting Times*,[42] which everyone called the *Pink 'Un* because it was printed on salmon-coloured paper. It was the same paper that in 1882 had printed a mock obituary for English cricket – after an Australian victory inspired by 'The Demon' Spofforth – and said the 'ashes' would be taken to Australia.[43] This 'obituary' gave rise to cricket's most famous trophy.

AT PIETERSBURG, Morant and his co-accused were kept in isolation, often in solitary confinement. A Tenterfield solicitor, Major James Francis Thomas, would represent all six defendants. The defence would centre on the claim that Kitchener had handed down orders not to take prisoners.

Morant appeared gloomy and irritable; close confinement in his small cell had 'greatly impaired his health, physically and mentally, and he looked upon current events from a very pessimistic standpoint'.[44] Handcock was worried and dejected. George Witton wrote that Handcock was staggered by the charges laid against him. He told the authorities that he 'had a very poor education' and that he 'never cared much about being an officer; all I know is about horses, though I like to fight'.

> He [Handcock] was advised to make a clean breast of everything, as the responsibility would rest solely on Lieutenant Morant. He declined to make any statement whatsoever, and was sent again for a considerable time into close confinement, even the military chaplain not being allowed to see him.[45]

The Reverend Joshua Brough was the Church of England military chaplain at Pietersburg, and he later complained about 'the harsh treatment' Morant and his co-accused received. He said they were kept 'in close arrest' and that, as chaplain, even he was requested not to visit them. He said the case was 'prejudged from the statements of bad men, and by the utterly false accounts which were inserted in English and, I believe, Australian papers'. Handcock, he said, had only 'acted under the orders of Lieutenant Morant, a man of strong feelings and eager to avenge the savage murder of his friend Captain Hunt'.[46]

MOTORING IN THE EARLY DAYS of the twentieth century was, according to Banjo, just in the stage when the betting was about even on whether the car would get its passengers home – or whether the wife would sit and knit by the roadside while the husband lay on his back under the car, smothered in dust and oil.[47]

Having made a friend of Rudyard Kipling during their time in Bloemfontein, Banjo arrived at the owlish writer's Sussex home as the cold Christmas of 1901 loomed. Kipling had a new car, one of the newly invented Lanchesters.[48] It was powered by what was considered a whopping two-cylinder, twelve-horsepower engine and steered by a man in overalls who looked like a 'superior sort of mechanic'. The driver's name was Laurence and he operated the vehicle with a side lever rather than a wheel. Kipling and Banjo piled into the back of the machine, with its owner beaming like a child at Christmas with a new toy. Out they went across the Sussex downs, sending frightened tourists ducking for cover. On and on they chugged along quaint English lanes, where the leaves swirled after the car, and Banjo expected to see 'Puck of Pook's Hill[49] peering out from behind a tree'.[50]

Kipling was sitting in the back seat. As they were in the midst of climbing an absurdly steep hill, with nothing much below them but the Channel, he posed a dangerous question to the driver: 'What would happen if she stopped here, Laurence?'[51] The driver stopped the engine to find out – and let the car, with its two illustrious passengers, roll back towards a terrifying drop. Banjo looked over his shoulder aghast and was preparing to leap to safety, when Laurence hit the brakes and pulled up just short of the precipice. Then he hit the accelerator and away they went.

Banjo was still trying to catch his breath when he turned to Kipling and said, 'Weren't you frightened? I was nearly jumping out.'

'Yes,' Kipling replied, 'I was frightened. But I thought what a bad advertisement it would be for the Lanchester company if they killed me, so I sat tight.'

They drove on until Kipling asked Laurence to pull up outside a butcher's shop. Pointing at a lamb carcass hanging in the window, Kipling asked Banjo to guess its weight. 'Not being altogether inexperienced in the weight of lambs, I had a guess,' Banjo said later. To this guess, Kipling replied, 'I'll go in and buy that lamb, and we'll see if you're right; and we'll see where this butcher is getting his mutton.' It turned out that Banjo was within two pounds of the lamb's weight. This seemed to astonish Kipling, and he said to the butcher, 'This gentleman comes from Australia, where they do nothing but weigh lambs all day long. You must buy all the Australian lamb you can get, and keep the money in the Empire.' The butcher, not knowing in the least who Kipling was, said, 'The Empire. Ha! My customers don't bother about the Empire, sir. It's their guts they think about!'[52]

Banjo came to realise in time that the English looked upon Kipling as one of 'these infernal know-all fellows, who wanted to do all sorts of queer things'.[53] Banjo reckoned they thought he was especially odd for warning them that there could be a great war against Germany before long: 'Fancy advocating that we should give more time to drill, and less time to sports! ... Kipling, out of his own pocket, bought enough land for a rifle-range, and paid the wages of a retired sergeant-major to teach the yokels drill and musketry. Was he applauded by his neighbours? Not that you would notice it.'[54]

Kipling was not at all what Banjo had expected, though he hadn't been exactly sure what to expect. 'When I went to stay with Kipling in England, I was prepared for literally anything,' Banjo wrote later.

> Kipling was remarkable in that his life was so very unremarkable. He hated publicity as his Satanic Majesty is supposed to hate holy water; and in private life he was just a hard-working, common-sense, level-headed man, without any redeeming vices that I could discover. A pity too, perhaps; for there is nothing so interesting as scandals about great geniuses. Though he was a very rich man, I found him living in an unpretentious house ... The only thing that marked it as the lair of a literary lion was the crowd of tourists (mostly Americans) who hung about from daylight till dark trying

> to look over the wall, or waiting to intercept his two little children when they went out for a walk. By having his car brought into the garden and getting into it from his own doorstep, Kipling was able to dash out through the ranks of autograph hunters even as a tiger dashes out when surrounded by savages.[55]

Kipling had houses in Vermont[56] and Cape Town, but he told Banjo he'd like to live in Australia for a while – though he thought it was high time Australians grew up. 'You think the Melbourne Cup is the most important thing in the world,' he said.[57]

AT A BOHEMIAN WATERING HOLE, the Yorick Club in Bedford Street, Covent Garden, Banjo was a guest at a 'smoke night' concert. One reporter wrote that he was hailed as the 'Poet Laureate of Australia', though he was now known as 'Fed Up'.[58] The weather was getting to him. He recited some new lines of doggerel called 'Lay of the Motor Car',[59] about the perils of driving, which he submitted to the *Pink 'Un*: 'We annihilate chickens and time, And policemen and space'.

But Banjo was ready to go home. He booked his passage on the *Duke of Argyll*, leaving London on 7 December 1901.[60]

On 4 December, he wound up his trip by reporting on a rowdy and violent public meeting and march in Hyde Park. It was held in support of the sacked General Buller. Temperance societies were conspicuous with their banners, though Banjo remarked that Buller was no advocate for temperance. The crowd streamed along, pausing occasionally to cheer for Buller and to hoot Lord Roberts.

Banjo wrote a farewell verse to England that was published in 1902:

> The London lights are far abeam
> Behind a bank of cloud.
> Along the shore the gaslights gleam.
> The gale is piping loud;
> And down the Channel, groping blind.
> We drive her through the haze
> Towards the land we left behind –
> The good old land of 'never mind',
> And old Australian ways.[61]

THE FIRST COURT-MARTIAL for the Bushveldt Carbineers opened on 16 January 1901, with Lieutenant Colonel H.C. Denny presiding over a panel of six judges. Denny asked whether the 'trial' Morant had organised before having Floris Visser shot had been constituted like a court-martial, and whether the King's Regulations had been observed.

'Was it like this? No; it was not quite so handsome,' The Breaker famously replied. 'We were out fighting the Boers, not sitting comfortably behind barb-wire entanglements; we got them and shot them under Rule 303!' Kitchener's military secretary, Colonel Hubert Hamilton,[62] emphatically denied any instruction to not take prisoners.

The trial was interrupted on 22 January when Boer General Christiaan Beyers[63] led a raid on Pietersburg. Breaker and the other officers facing death sentences were given rifles to fight off the attack. After Beyers and his men were repulsed, the prisoners handed back their weapons and were returned to their cells. Three days later, Morant was found guilty of Visser's murder and sentenced to death with a recommendation of mercy because of the way he had fought against Beyers and his men. Handcock, Witton and Picton were convicted of manslaughter.

After the legal expert supervising proceedings, Colonel A.R. Pemberton, had observed the trial, he wrote to the War Office to say Morant was properly convicted and Visser's killing was 'a consultation between four officers which ended in a party of subordinates being ordered to commit murder'.[64]

In another court-martial, Morant, Handcock and Witton were found guilty of murder over the killing of the four Afrikaners and four Dutch schoolteachers, and all three were sentenced to death. Morant and Handcock were then sentenced to death for the killing of Roelf van Staden and his two sons. But in the case of the killing of Reverend Heese, two women gave Morant and Handcock alibis, saying that the Australians were each at different farms at the time. Both men were found not guilty. But, in total, Morant was convicted of murder three times and sentenced to death three times, Handcock twice and Witton once. Lenehan was only found guilty of failing to report Handcock's shooting of his comrade, Trooper van Buuren, because he wanted to avoid a scandal. The Englishman, Captain Taylor, known far and wide as a sadistic brute, was exonerated.

WHILE HIS OLD POLO-PLAYING MATE was awaiting a grim fate in South Africa, Banjo was cruising home to Sydney in relaxed style. He had sailed on the *Duke of Argyll* as far as Thursday Island.[65]

There he went sailing in a Japanese pearling lugger and swam to the bottom of the sea in a diving suit. He met Billy Makeela, a South Sea Islander arrayed in a loincloth, who commanded his own lugger 'with all the assurance of Alexander the Great'.[66] Banjo heard about the death of a Japanese diver whose air-pipe became blocked and whose body was torn apart by a shark; this tale inspired his ballad 'The Pearl Diver'.

> Down in the ooze and the coral, down where earth's wonders are
> spread,
> Helmeted, ghastly, and swollen, Kanzo Makame lies dead:
> ...
> Wearer of pearls in your necklace, comfort yourself if you can,
> These are the risks of the pearling – these are the ways of Japan ...[67]

Banjo came to the conclusion that as divers, compared with Malays and Islanders 'for sheer hard work on the open bottom, the Japanese will outlast any of them'.

By 8 February 1902, Banjo was in the North Queensland town of Cairns, where the local paper said the popular verse-writer and war lecturer 'is looking really well ... in fact ... "in first-rate nick." It is understood the solicitor-poet has strong intentions of entering the theatrical profession shortly.'[68]

Banjo finally arrived home to Sydney on the Eastern & Australian steamer *Australian* on 21 February 1902.[69]

That very day, Morant, Handcock, Witton and Picton were on the move too. They had arrived in Pretoria in irons, after being taken from Pietersburg by rail under heavy guard surrounded by soldiers with fixed bayonets. Major Lenehan had been reprimanded, relieved of his command, and sent to Cape Town to be returned to Australia.

The papers from the courts-martial had been sent to Kitchener, who studied them on 22 to 23 February and decided the fate of the men. Picton was to be cashiered out of the army and sent home. Witton was sentenced to death, but the sentence was to be commuted to life in prison. Kitchener confirmed the death sentences of Morant and Handcock; their executions were set for dawn on Thursday, 27 February 1902.

Witton recalled that on the preceding afternoon, two warders were in the workshop, not far from the cells, noisily making two rough coffins. The coffins were then placed just outside the workshop door, in plain sight of the men. At 4 p.m. Witton was informed that he would be leaving the prison at five the following morning. He later wrote that at 6 p.m. a hamper was sent containing a 'nicely got-up dinner for four. We laid it out in my cell, but it was scarcely touched.' It was the last meal for two of them, and Morant remarked, 'Not to be blasphemous, lads; but this is "The Last Supper".'[70] Morant was allowed to share a cell with Handcock for their last night on earth. 'Good-bye, Witton,' Morant said, 'tell the *Bulletin* people The Breaker will write no more verse for them …'

Morant spent most of his last night writing his farewell poem:

In prison cell I sadly sit,
A damned crestfallen chappy,
And own to you I feel a bit –
A little bit – unhappy.

It really ain't the place nor time
To reel off rhyming diction;
But yet we'll write a final rhyme
While waiting crucifixion.

No matter what 'end' they decide –
Quick-lime? or 'b'iling ile' sir?
We'll do our best when crucified
To finish off in style, sir!

But we bequeath a parting tip
For sound advice of such men
Who come across in transport ship
To polish off the Dutchmen.

If you encounter any Boers
You really must not loot 'em,

And, if you wish to leave these shores,
For pity's sake, don't shoot 'em.

And if you'd earn a D.S.O.,
Why every British sinner
Should know the proper way to go
Is: Ask the Boer to dinner.

Let's toss a bumper down our throat
Before we pass to heaven,
And toast: 'The trim-set petticoat
We leave behind in Devon.'

At 5 a.m. Witton was roused by a warder and told he was being taken to Cape Town. He was only allowed to clasp the hands of Morant and Handcock for the last time through a small grate in the cell door, scarcely able to stammer a goodbye. 'I was more unnerved at the thought of their hateful death than they were themselves,' he said. 'They were calmly prepared to meet their death, as they often had been before at times during the war.' At the prison gate Witton passed a squad of Cameron Highlanders – the firing squad – waiting to be admitted.[71] He would always maintain that the pair were being made scapegoats for Britain's combined crimes in the war.

At 6 a.m. the warders opened the door of the doomed men's cell. 'Are you ready?'

'Yes!' replied The Breaker. 'Where is your firing party?'

Then, in the grey light of the dawn, Morant and Handcock held hands as they took their places in a pair of chairs in front of the riflemen. Morant refused a blindfold but he must have been wishing he had a steeplechaser with him to leap over the prison wall. With Handcock sitting beside him, The Breaker folded his arms across his waist and looked the firing squad straight in the eye as they levelled their guns at his heart, ready to apply their version of Rule 303.

'Shoot straight ya bastards, don't make a mess of it,' he said, just as they pulled their triggers.[72] Banjo's old mate, Breaker Morant, died with his arms folded defiantly, and with his eyes wide open.[73]

Chapter 19

25 MARCH 1902, THE AUSTRALIAN CLUB, MACQUARIE STREET, SYDNEY

He was the most sophisticated man who ever attempted to woo me sexually.
Author Stella Miles Franklin describing Banjo Paterson[1]

BANJO WAS HARDLY BACK in Sydney when he received a note from the vivacious and ambitious Stella Miles Franklin, asking for help.

Miles had made an impression on just about every man she met, and Banjo was no different. *The Bulletin*'s Norman Lindsay would raise eyebrows and temperatures around Australia for his daring paintings of nude women, and he had an eye for detail. He described Miles as being 'very short but pleasingly plump … Her mass of dark hair reached her pert rump, which matched her pert nose. She had fine eyes, arched eyebrows and an alluring pair of lips.'[2] And Banjo was still quite the catch, described in a recent account of the war in South Africa as 'a correspondent for the great Australian dailies – one of the keenest of sportsmen, a dashing cross-country rider, thin, wiry and hard as nails' and 'of whose literary works … every Australian may justly feel proud'.[3]

Miles wanted Banjo to help her with the legal agreement for her second book, which she was planning to call *On the Outside Track*.[4] Despite the endorsement of Henry Lawson, sales of her debut novel *My Brilliant Career* had been painfully slow in the first year: just 387 copies in England, and 1012 in Australia and New Zealand. When her first royalty cheque arrived in 1902, it was for just £16 5s 6d, 'about what Miles might have earned as an unskilled hand in the clothing trade for the year'.[5] The 23-year-old was living with her family at Stillwater, a small, struggling property near Goulburn.

Miles relied heavily on Lawson for advice, but with him still gloomy in London she asked Banjo to oversee an agreement with Angus & Robertson for the new book. William Blackwood had published *My Brilliant Career*, and she did not want to give him her second manuscript. Banjo wrote to her in his flowing script from the Australian Club to say that, yes indeed, he was something of an expert when it came to drafting publishing agreements and would be happy to advise her on contractual matters, free of charge. A week later he wrote to Miles again, urging her to come to Sydney soon, otherwise she might miss him as he would soon be travelling on another adventure. He volunteered to read anything she wrote and to see if he could find a publisher. He warned her not to sign anything until she had spoken to him.[6]

Miles caught the train north to Redfern Station, probably at the expense of her mother, and likely stayed at a boarding house in Cleveland Street run by a friend of an aunt. On Monday, 7 April 1902, Banjo wrote to Miles again from the Australian Club, inviting her to lunch the following Wednesday. 'You can tell me what you have done re agreements,' he wrote, adding that he would be waiting at the door and she would easily recognise him as 'a sad-looking person with a very hard face'.[7] Miles had already met one sad-looking writer in Lawson, but Banjo was cut from a different cloth: aristocratic, handsome and athletic. And single. She was a young country girl meeting a famous and sophisticated celebrity who was used to chatting up some of the most eligible women in Sydney. But Miles was undaunted and welcomed Banjo's advances as they chatted over lunch. Banjo thought she was 'free as air' when it came to breaking her agreement with Blackwood and Lawson's English literary agent J. B. Pinker, but the British deal was tighter than he had supposed. Still, he was keen to promote her in any way he could; he read her sketches and told her that parts were 'like Lawson' and that they 'had human interest', while making her bristle when he said some bits were 'sheer drivel'.[8] He was busy 'pen pushing', he said, but promised to let George Robertson look at the manuscript.[9] Soon after lunch with Banjo, Miles met *The Bulletin*'s A. G. Stephens, who gave her a signed copy of his book *Oblation* –

signed also by the artist Norman Lindsay – and a book of poems by the young Scot Will Ogilvie, *Fair Girls and Gray Horses*, published a few years earlier.

Nothing came of Banjo's approach to George Robertson, despite him telling the publisher that her manuscript was 'among the best things I have read'.[10] There was further disappointment when Alfred Rowlandson, publisher of *Rowlandson's Commonwealth Annual* and owner of the prestigious NSW Book Stall Company, did not take her 'How Dead Man's Gap Was Named', which Banjo had described as 'splendid'.

Miles returned to Stillwater disappointed with the reaction to her work but buzzing over the possibilities Banjo presented. She told him she wished she had a recording of his voice, while he wished she were back at his flat with him, reading his poetry and singing to him while playing the piano.[11] He said he was working around the clock, cranking out seven thousand words a day, on a racing manuscript and a piece of comedy, and that he would like her opinion on them when she visited him in Sydney again.[12] Miles wrote back to ask him had he 'been doing anything desperate lately?' and then flirted with him by saying: 'I nearly married since my return. Was so sick of myself & everything about ink that I nearly gave in at last. The man who thinks I am the one woman to whom all servants shall refer as "Missus" … doesn't know one tune … from another … has no appreciation of blank verse poetry and I think would wither me in a fortnight, and as I feel a gamer flip now, have determined to hang out a bit longer.'[13]

They continued their flirtations. On 31 May 1902, Banjo sent Miles his racing story and told her he wanted her to come with him to paradise in the South Pacific[14] as he was leaving that night on an assignment for the *Sydney Morning Herald* to the New Hebrides (now called Vanuatu). Banjo was accompanying a group of new settlers who planned to farm there under the auspices of the Burns Philp company. He gave her such short notice for the trip that he was obviously just flirting; she flirted back and said she had fantasised about dressing up as his valet. She teased him about whether he would be a good boss. Banjo told her that George Robertson wanted her to help him with some 'blood and tears' on 'a sporting yarn' that needed human interest. She asked him to help her with her poems, by adding 'a little more grammar and rhythm'. He was so clever, she said, that later they might work on a dictionary together.[15]

Although there was no basis for this, Miles' sister Linda warned her that if she worked with Banjo he might steal all the credit for her contributions.[16] Fred Maudsley of the *Book Lover* monthly magazine agreed, telling Miles 'you simply must not entertain the idea'.[17] Years later she said that she found Banjo too cynical.[18]

AS BANJO SAILED OUT OF SYDNEY on the Burns Philp steamer *Mambare*, Henry Lawson was heading home to even more troubles. He had seen Bertha and their two children off from London with the writer Mary Gilmore[19] and her family, after the Gilmores had been involved in William Lane's failed Utopian project in Paraguay. Lawson met Bertha and the children in Colombo, but it was hardly a happy reunion; the cracks in his marriage seemed irreparable. In July 1902 he arrived in Melbourne hoping to see the love of his life, Hannah Thornburn, who had moved there to work in her parents' music shop. Lawson's mental state was fragile as it was – and then he discovered, to his horror, that Hannah had died at the Melbourne Hospital six weeks before his arrival. The cause of death was an infection, which may have been caused by a botched abortion.[20] She was just twenty-five.[21] Lawson was inconsolable. He wrote moving verses in her memory.

Spirit girl to whom 'twas given
To revisit scenes of pain,
From the hell I thought was Heaven
You have lifted me again;
Through the world that I inherit,
Where I loved her ere she died,
I am walking with the spirit
Of a dead girl by my side.[22]

Lawson would spend some time being treated for 'his nerves' in a private hospital beside the sea in the Sydney suburb of Manly. He then moved back in with Bertha and the children, into rented cottages called Beauchamp Terrace and Marlow in Whistler Street, a few blocks back from the beach. A reporter who interviewed the 'bush idyllist' at the time described Marlow as 'a little snuggery edging on to the ocean beach'.[23]

But Bertha felt anything but snug. Soon her furniture was seized in lieu of rent. Having spent months in English psychiatric hospitals, she now faced life with two small children and a hard-drinking, unstable, perpetually broke husband who was in love with a dead woman. Soon she was pregnant again. What could possibly go wrong?

BANJO, MEANWHILE, revelled in his new life as an adventurer reporting on exotic locations around the world. The money wasn't great, but the experiences were far more exciting than sitting at his Street & Paterson desk. His baby brother, Hamilton 'Boy' Paterson, had shown the way years earlier – and in many regards was Banjo's hero.

Twelve years younger than Banjo, Boy had followed him into Sydney Grammar. He was part of the rowing crew that won the schools championship, and he was the stroke when Grammar scored a memorable victory over Saint Ignatius College. He had gone to the West Australian goldfields as a teenager to find his fortune but couldn't locate it. However, he became rich in admirers for the way he saved the lives of several miners; they were plummeting down a shaft when he caught the handle of a flying windlass and managed to hold on, even though he was struck a severe blow to the face. He was known far and wide as a young man 'with a particularly fearless disposition'.[24]

Boy moved from the goldfields to the waters of New Britain and New Guinea to look after the engines on a series of trading vessels. On 27 June 1902 he was working on the cutter *Endeavour* off Samarai in New Guinea. The boat had recently been fitted with oil engines to supplement its sails. It was coming down the wide Kumusi River when a naked flame ignited a leak from the fuel tanks; Boy was working on the engines, and the blast knocked him cold. One of the *Endeavour*'s owners was badly burnt, as were seven New Guineans. All those on board the *Endeavour* were dragged off the vessel just before the fuel tanks exploded, destroying the craft. Boy and the rest of the injured men were rushed to the government hospital in Samarai, but Boy never recovered.

Banjo's only brother was dead on 30 June 1902,[25] aged twenty-five.

BANJO'S TRIP TO THE NEW HEBRIDES came during a busy time when he was the most sought-after journalist in Australia. He was also compiling a list of poems for a new book that Angus & Robertson was publishing. Banjo submitted fifty poems, with forty-six making the cut.

The book would be titled *Rio Grande's Last Race and Other Verses.*[26] Banjo's love of horses came through not just in the title poem, but also in 'The Last Parade', his homage to the gallant mounts who had gone to South Africa and never come home.

With never a sound of trumpet,
With never a flag displayed,
The last of the old campaigners
Lined up for the last parade.

Weary they were and battered,
Shoeless, and knocked about;
From under their ragged forelocks
Their hungry eyes looked out.

And they watched as the old commander
Read out, to the cheering men,
The Nation's thanks and the orders
To carry them home again.

And the last of the old campaigners,
Sinewy, lean, and spare –
He spoke for his hungry comrades:
'Have we not done our share?

'Starving and tired and thirsty
We limped on the blazing plain;
And after a long night's picket
You saddled us up again.

'We froze on the wind-swept kopjes
When the frost lay snowy-white.
Never a halt in the daytime,
Never a rest at night!'[27]

Banjo wrote a profile piece for the *Sydney Morning Herald*[28] on the British General Lord Methuen,[29] who had been captured by the Boers. He also wrote chapters about the war for inclusion in *The Story of South Africa Vol II.*[30] And he profiled 'The Late Lieutenant Morant' for the *Sydney Mail.*[31] Reports out of South Africa at the time were still vague about Morant's crimes, and Banjo tried to scotch any notion that he was a bandit or that he would have killed anyone for money. Banjo described his old riding companion as a devotee of all sports, from fox-hunting to performing at shows; a man 'always popular for his dash and courage', who revelled in 'excitement and boon companionship', although Banjo found him untidy in his dress. 'In character he was kind-hearted and good natured to the last degree, an enemy of no man but himself, a spendthrift and an idler, quick to borrow and slow to pay … His death was consistent with his life, for though he died as a criminal he died a brave man facing the rifles with his eyes unbandaged.'[32]

Banjo also wrote of his experiences on the Thursday Island pearl lugger for the *Sydney Mail.* He thrilled readers with his description of walking on the sea floor, sixteen metres below the surface, despite the fears of his guide, Billy Makeela, who told him, 'I frighten let you down. S'posing anything go wrong; you die queek.'[33]

The New Hebrides assignment for the *Sydney Morning Herald* came about at the instigation of the cavalry officer Sir James Burns, who had appeared on stage with Banjo at his Parramatta war lectures eighteen months earlier. The chairman of Burns Philp was 'a thin and austere Scotsman of the old son-of-the-manse type' and 'as near to the Empire builder as we ever saw in these parts … an outstanding financial genius'.[34]

Burns Philp had a scheme to settle British farmers on the New Hebrides with the backing of the new Australian federal government: 'a sort of Pilgrim Fathers affair … the settlers going down to live among wild savages in the land of the golden coconut'.[35] Both the United Kingdom and France were wrestling for control of the islands, and Burns told Banjo that his firm had bought thousands of acres there from an old Scottish company that had gone bust. 'Other areas we bought from native chiefs, traders, and so on,' Burns said. 'Now the French have gone down there, and we may have to fight for our land ... where we bought, say, a thousand acres from a native chief the French are now claiming that they bought the same land from the same chief or that they bought the same land from another chief who had a better right to it.'[36]

The steamer *Mambare* 'was not a bad ship, except that at some time or other she had tried to shift a coral reef and had got a sort of kink in her keel. The captain, a gigantic New Zealander, said she was inclined to steer a bit north by south unless carefully watched.'[37] Banjo was sailing with fourteen prospective settlers and a group of missionaries. The *Mambare* was fitted 'like a regular Robinson Crusoe ship' with sheep, fowls, pigeons, canaries, a cockatoo, a ram and a dog, and a monkey that wouldn't answer to his name of Kruger.[38] Banjo made friends with the settlers and found 'they were the genuine article – hard-handed, anxious-faced men, miners, farmers, shearers, mechanics – all off to tackle a job of which they knew little in a land of which they knew less. Many of them were born adventurers who would start off anywhere at the drop of a hat, just for the sake of seeing something new.'[39] Each of them had a stake of £200.

Banjo gave Australia a glimpse of the nation's near neighbours that most of his readers had never seen. Lord Howe Island, the *Mambare*'s first destination, was 'a boomerang shaped piece of real estate dumped down in the Pacific Ocean without any relation to any other piece of land whatever. It is two days' steam from the nearest other piece.'[40] The settlers there had a 'restful look, born of the fact that they only got newspapers once a month. They had heard of the [Boer] war, but had lost interest in it, and they never asked about the Australian Eleven.'[41] There was no town, 'nor any shop, nor hotel of any kind, nor any street; no doctor and no newspaper'. There was also no anxiety and no people with greater hospitality, anywhere. Banjo was asked to stay for breakfast everywhere he went.[42]

Leaving Lord Howe Island, the settlers 'hit the real tropics and began to have adventure'. As the *Mambare* arrived at the old penal colony of Norfolk Island, a figure came down the steps to welcome the boat. He was a bearded 'semi-aquatic giant' who asked the passengers, 'Bout ye goan?' – meaning, 'Whereabouts are you going to?'.

Banjo wrote that the Norfolk Islanders were descendants of the mutineers from Captain Bligh's *Bounty* and their Tahitian wives. He said that the building of a cable station on Norfolk had changed the old order of things, putting thousands of pounds into circulation there.

> Nowadays the islanders are all making money, landing goods and material for the cable station, carting them over to the station, doing labourers and painters and carpenters' work on the station. Everybody is making money now, and there is quite a boom in Norfolk Island, they are importing jewellery and fancy shirts, and tinned sheep's tongues and potted meats, and articles of luxury, and an era of prosperity has set in. Norfolk Island is facing the dawn bye-and-bye, when the cable station is finished, the prosperity will vanish, and the people will have to go back to the yams and bananas again.[43]

Banjo, being Banjo, was drawn to the unique Norfolk Island horses.

> They are not like any other kind of horse that the world has ever seen. They began by being draught horses, but a mountaineering existence has altered their shape altogether and given them many of the characteristics of the chamois. They can feed on the perpendicular faces of the hills without falling into the sea; and they could, if required, climb up the side of a wall pulling a trap after them. Their heads are large and hairy, with roman noses and long upper lips – like rudimentary elephants' trunks. Perhaps this development arises from having to root among short grass for a living. They look like spring-cart horses but move with the activity – and a good deal of the action – of a kangaroo. They are hardy, useful animals, with plenty of strength.[44]

Given that Norfolk Island was so closely identified with the *Bounty* mutineers, Banjo said that readers were apt to forget it had once been a convict settlement, a place of unimaginable savagery straight from the pages of Marcus Clarke's *For the Term of His Natural Life*.

The *Mambare* pilgrims began to explore Norfolk and marvelled at the richness of the soil. Each homestead was smothered in banana trees and orange groves. Guavas and lemons grew wild everywhere. The land was said to be even better in the New Hebrides.

Their journey was certainly full of surprises: 'A lady passenger came aboard at Norfolk Island and went almost straight to the ladies' bathroom. The ship had been fumigated for cockroaches before leaving Sydney, and the cockroaches, opposing instinct to science, had crawled into the tap of the bath. When she turned on the water she got a stream of cockroaches, all in the highest health and spirits. They fled in various directions, drying their whiskers as they went. It was just a first taste of the tropics, a prelude to the performances of the tree-climbing crab and the coconut-eating rat ...'[45]

From Norfolk the *Mambare* steamed along to the port of Thio,[46] the centre of nickel mining on New Caledonia. French convicts and ex-convicts, Arabs, Italians, and hundreds of Japanese labourers slogged away in the vast open-cut mine with a 'great tumbled mass of volcanic hills in the background'.[47] Banjo and the pilgrims spent three days there watching the local population, with their 'frizzy hair and loin-cloths', toiling over the scoured hills like so many ants, carting ore for the ships in port to ferry it as far off as Glasgow. The farmland was underdeveloped, though. In cattle country as good as anything in Queensland, the pilgrims had to make do with tinned Queensland beef rather than fresh steaks.[48]

All sorts of little shanties were allowed to sell liquor 'so that disputes and shooting-matches' happened 'now and again'. Banjo met a man who was keeping a little wayside restaurant and who told him, in quite a casual way, that two shots had been fired through his house the day before. 'I went out and had a shot at him,' the restaurant owner told Banjo, 'but he dodged too quick. Next time I will get him.' Life on New Caledonia, Banjo remarked, was not quite as uneventful as that in an Australian backblock town.

The one regret among the Australian pilgrims on leaving Noumea was that they had ever let the French get hold of such good country.[49]

By mid-June they were on the island of Aneityum, besotted with the possibilities, and Banjo watched as each man's instinct set to work. An old railway-sleeper cutter, from the Johnstone River in Far North Queensland, 'made for the scrub like a wallaby, with his eyes on the trees, and measured them critically, estimating how many feet he could get out of each'.[50] Someone mentioned the humidity, to which he quickly retorted: 'I ain't afraid of the humidity. I stood the Johnstone River for two years. We used to wrap our matches in flannel and put them in a little bottle. Then we'd wrap that bottle in flannel and put it in a pickle bottle. Then we'd put the pickle bottle inside our coats, and then the matches would be wet. Bring on your humidity!'[51] They were an eclectic bunch.

> One man has a grazing property in New South Wales, another was a stock and station agent, and these two, disregarding everything else, made straight for a small mob of cattle that were coming along the track that came down from the mountain. 'Not too bad, not too bad,' said the grazier. 'Real good, I call 'em,' said the stock and station agent ... A gardener was kicking up the soil and examining some tomatoes that were growing at an old settlement, and the rest of the settlers were gazing in open-mouthed astonishment at the thickness of the scrub. It was an eye-opener to them, that scrub! 'It'd cost four quid an acre to get rid of that in Australia, anyhow,' said a farmer from the Richmond River. 'Aye, and another pound at the back o' that,' said a Camden dairyman. It rather staggered them at first, because after having talked for weeks about clearing scrub and what they would do after it was cleared it was a shock to come face to face with the enemy and find how very far from being cleared it was. The wonderful growth of everything cheered them up a bit, and as a settler from Fiji told them that it was equal to any Fiji land, they were soon comforted.[52]

Around Vila, 'the metropolis of the Hebrides', with its six wood-and-iron stores for the outlying farms and settlers' houses, the pilgrims got the first 'bona-fide sight of the life of a planter'. They were taken to three or four French plantations, where they saw gangs of local workers clearing the jungle with tomahawks and bush knives to the accompaniment of cheers and yells. They saw the first struggling maize crops fighting their way through the clearings; the first young coconut palms. They asked questions galore and were told that the land would grow any tropical product: maize (three crops a year), bananas, cocoa, copra, coffee, vanilla, beans, sugar. The first crop of maize would cover the expense of clearing the land. 'It certainly would seem that to a young man with a little capital there is a practical certainty of making a good property here in ten years,' Banjo told his readers, 'whereas he might work ten years in an office and not be much further ahead than when he started.'[53]

On 20 June 1902, the Australians arrived on the island of Espiritu Santo, the largest of the group. The landscape reminded Banjo of Java and the Philippines, with its volcanic hills, dense jungle and 'magnificent' soil.[54] The rainfall on the coast was as much as 2500 millimetres annually. The settlers set off to inspect the land, tramping Indian file over the black, rich, slippery countryside, heavy with the smell of decaying vegetable matter, 'whilst overhead there was a tangle of vines, tall palms with big leaves, and convolvulus creepers shutting out the sun'.

Eleven settlers decided to remain. They drew lots for choice of sites, areas of two hundred hectares each being roughly marked out.[55] They were wary, though, of the original inhabitants, especially those from the dense jungle where each little village was as removed from the next as countries at war. 'The rule among the villages appears to have been, if you meet a stranger, kill him,' Banjo wrote. 'They are always more or less at war, and until the missionaries came they used invariably to eat the dead and the prisoners.'[56]

The perils of the jungle ended up giving Banjo a good laugh: 'We walked along the path for a couple of miles, and then suddenly round a curve in the little narrow track, we came plump on to a naked savage with a painted face, hair plaited in strips, and rifle on his shoulder. It was our first cannibal ...'[57] The settlers nearly fell over each other trying to get behind the ship's cargo manager, who was a small man and who offered little protection.

> For a while no one spoke. Then in a hoarse voice the cannibal said, 'What name you?' Then he fumbled in his belt, which was his sole clothing and produced a five-franc piece. 'Four sillin,' he said persuasively, meaning that he wanted someone to change the coin for him. Then as no one seemed to jump at the chance, he added in an explanatory and condescending tone, 'That all right, that French money!'

> This was our man-eater! One of the settlers, a Queenslander, looked at him for a while and said, 'Why, he's a kanaka. I believe he's a returned labour boy!' It seemed preposterous that this painted feathered savage should have been a kanaka labourer ... but the Queenslander chanced it. 'You been longa Queensland?' he said. The savage's face lit up.
>
> 'Yiss,' he said. 'I bin longa Kaweenslan' Mackay! Five year!'
>
> 'You savvy Homebush plantation?'
>
> 'Yiss, I savvy. I work longa Homebush. Spose go Mackay, Homebush plantation, how many pubs? Two! Two pubs!
>
> Thus by his knowledge of pubs, did he prove his civilisation. Other armed and painted savages gathered round, some having also been to Queensland. A settler from Sydney had brought ashore an old pocket-knife to barter for curios. He expected to get a full collection of South Sea weapons for it, but after the interview with the savage he didn't feel quite so sure. Anyhow, he produced his knife.
>
> 'How much?' said the savage.
>
> 'Five shillings,' said the settler, thinking he might as well be hung for a sheep as a lamb.
>
> 'I think more like trippence,' said the cannibal.
>
> This ended any idea of getting curios on the cheap. All we got we had to pay for at more than Sydney prices. The noble savage was a delusion and so we found him all through the group.[58]

Life was actually very safe among the island people now, Banjo said. They had given up the spear and the war club and taken to the rifle, though most could not hit the side of a barn with a bullet unless they were inside the barn. They even filed the sights off their old Snider–Enfield rifles so as not to 'spoil the nice smooth look of the barrel'.[59]

Banjo also reported on the work of both the missionaries and the pirates in the area, telling his readers that the 'missionary does not nowadays habitually have to run for his life from savages nor does he go in daily fear of the cooking pot'.[60] The Anglicans, Catholics and Presbyterians were all competing for Melanesian souls while keeping a wary eye on the labour recruiters and their unscrupulous methods; they were known for 'blackbirding' – the kidnapping of slave labour for the Queensland canefields. Sometimes the indigenous people were 'coaxed on board recruiting vessels and, it is alleged, are often taken away without fully understanding what they are going to do. Actual flagrant kidnapping is also charged against some of these dealers in human commodities. A native will come in and explain to the missionary that a lot of "boys" and perhaps a "Mary" or two went on board a recruiting vessel to hear a musical box play and then the vessel suddenly put to sea, taking the lot off to be sold as labour in some other islands or in Fiji.'[61]

BANJO RETURNED TO SYDNEY IN JULY. On the twenty-fifth he wrote to Miles Franklin to tell her of the sad news about his brother Boy – and to describe Alfred Rowlandson as an 'ass' for not publishing her work. Banjo said it was 'a blessing' to read her writing; that it was 'queer' she should let her head go in her letters, and yet be so shy and 'guarded' in her conversation when they were face to face.[62]

They discussed working on a play together. Banjo was excited about it, telling Miles, 'I feel certain we can do well at the drama – you can do the thrill & tears & I can do the villainy & the fighting.' He said that they needed to dispense with anything like Oscar Wilde's 'clever dialogues' and instead include plenty of rants, curses, sweat and tears. There had to be a minimum of talk and a maximum of action to draw the crowds, along with a villain 'so black that charcoal wouldn't leave a mark on him'. There could be an erring daughter trapped by vice and a down-on-his-luck hero whose triumph would be dazzling. He needed to see Miles to talk it over – he volunteered to travel down to Goulburn way but suggested it would be better if she came to Sydney. He offered to lend her any money she needed for the trip. It would be even better if she knew some place they could meet in the country without distractions, perhaps even a friend of her mother's willing to put them up for a couple of guineas a week. He told her they would have to be totally honest with each other in the collaboration, as after dealing with Henry Lawson: 'I found that in his eyes I was either one of the worst rogues in Sydney or one of the whitest men in Australia – as the fit took him'.[63]

Banjo was soon off on assignment for the *Sydney Morning Herald* to report on the devastating drought in New South Wales,[64] so his sister Jessie sent Miles his four-page sketch of an Arthurian drama involving a plot to poison King Arthur and frame Queen Guinevere.[65] Jessie was rapt with the idea and told Miles so, though Miles was guarded with her reply; she stated that she was still carefully considering the idea of working with Banjo.

On 18 August 1902, Banjo wrote to Miles to say that in eight days he was leaving for a lecture tour in Fiji. Miles said that she wanted to go too, but Banjo told her that he wanted to take his younger sister Gwen, and the ship's manager had objected to 'lugging two women around'. He would send Miles £5, and he asked her to come to Sydney for three days to talk over their plans. Miles asked her sister Linda's fiancé, Charles Graham, to ask around Banjo's old friends in the Yass area whether he was 'a cad or a man'.[66]

The meeting of the minds was delayed when Banjo suddenly dashed off to Coonamble for the *Sydney Morning Herald*. He was to report on the shearing strike at Wingadee Station on the Castlereagh.[67] After Miles arrived in Sydney and discovered that Banjo had gone bush, she sent him a telegram to say that she was staying with the suffragist Rose Scott[68] at Edgecliff. Banjo replied by telegram on 25 August that he would be back next Friday and that the Fiji trip was off. So too, it seemed, was any budding romance between him and his young admirer. Jessie Paterson thought it a shame,[69] while Miles's sister Linda wrote to Miles to express her surprise, remarking, 'I always thought you might have him.'[70]

It had been a depressing year for Banjo. His brother's death had come around the same time as that of his uncle and mentor Frank Barton, aged just forty-nine, after he contracted a chill that developed into pneumonia. He was a great loss to his aged mother Emily, still holding court at Rockend. Banjo wrote Frank's obituary for the *Herald*.[71] Then there were smaller concerns. Banjo's writing assignments did not give him the same income that he had made as a solicitor. Jessie was suffering jaundice like their mother had, and Banjo's other Barton uncles – Robert, Charles and Arthur – were struggling in the drought.

Late in the year, Banjo was nervous about the reception he would receive for *Rio Grande's Last Race and Other Verses*, which was due to hit bookshops on 24 November 1902.

On the eve of publication George Robertson wrote from Halstead, his weekend home at Blackheath, that Banjo wanted 'independent judgment' on the proofs of the book and to be sure that among the poems 'nothing below the standard of *Snowy River* goes in'. Robertson asked Dick Thomson from Angus & Robertson to contact Hugh Maccallum, a publishing executive who knew 'the *Snowy* book well' and knew 'what the reviews praised and blamed'. Robertson said Maccallum had 'a good idea of what the general public approved'. He asked that Maccallum look at the proofs of *Rio Grande* and 'size up the various pieces with reference to the *Snowy* standard ... if he will only remember that Paterson isn't, never will be and isn't wanted (by either the Public to whom he appeals or his Publishers) to be a Keats or a Milton he'll do it all right'.[72] Robertson insisted that the only question Maccallum had to answer about each 'pome' was: 'Is it as good as the poorest piece of the same sort in *Snowy River*.' He added that both A.W. Jose and Maccallum 'thought very little of *Snowy* when it was passing through to the press. Jose preferred Dyson! But they were wrong because ABP has gained not only cash but fame by the book. You have to think of the people you are appealing to – and it isn't the Keats crowd.'

Banjo's worries were groundless and *Rio Grande* was another hit – though not to the same level as his first book. Writing in the English journal *Athenaeum*, Jose said: 'The majority of the pieces are vigorous bits of verse journalism, transcripts of racecourse humour, episodes of life in the backwoods.'[73] Two of Banjo's most loved characters, Salt Bush Bill and Mulga Bill, returned for the book, which included verses written during and just after the war such as 'With French to Kimberley', 'The Scottish Engineer', 'By the Grey Gulf-Water', 'The Pearl Diver', 'The Old Australian Ways' and 'Song of the Artesian Water'. Kipling had liked the line 'Till I drink artesian water from a thousand feet below' in 'A Bushman's Song'.

The *Sydney Morning Herald* wrote that Paterson's verses had 'more of Australia in them than any others that this generation knows' but that 'the war has of course changed Mr Paterson somewhat, as it has changed us all'.[74]Amid the humour and the rollicking yarns was a touch of despair in poems such as 'He Giveth His Beloved Sleep',[75] words on the grave of Banjo's father.

IN THAT SAME ISSUE of the *Herald*, a few pages over, Banjo began a series of reports entitled 'Our Good Districts'. They would run for the next six weeks and had been sparked by the Bill for Closer Settlement, then being canvassed as a reform to the old Land Acts. Way back in 1889, Banjo had written of the futility of locking up large tracts of land; he believed his investigation around the country would now prove it. He began:

> It may surprise the reader to learn that there are any good districts left in New South Wales, and that they have any prospects – except the prospects of bankruptcy – before them. There is no doubt that the West is in a bad way, especially for small settlers, but then small settlers have no business out in the West. There are plenty of districts in the colony suited for the small man, and these districts are not half developed. All over the West one can hear of settlers abandoning their holdings and coming into the townships with their few belongings on a cart, drawn by starving horses, and sitting themselves down to see what the Government will do for them; and all over the colony round every country town in the good districts one can hear of miles of good land lying idle while the settler ruins himself out in the West.[76]

Between Gundagai and Tumut, Banjo saw mob after mob of starving stock – 'walking skeletons in sheep's clothing' – totter up the mountain track, making for the hill country with the stock routes eaten bare of grass. The paddocks were all fenced off, and the sheep trudged hopelessly along. It was like following the march of dying horses back in Africa. 'They die in dozens, dropping down in their tracks, and the drovers just pull them off the road and cut their throats to put a speedy end to their miseries. Wherever the mob camps for the night there is a stench of carcases that is overpowering. The few selectors that live along the road are complaining bitterly of the polluted air. One selector said that it was an open question whether it was better to move his house or to move the dead sheep.'[77]

Banjo reckoned the state of New South Wales should have erected a statue to the small settler, rather than celebrate some of the sporting greats of the time.

BANJO WROTE TO MILES FRANKLIN to say that he was 'weary to death' of travelling and tired of 'sleeping in railway trains and bush public houses'.[78] But the idea for a collaboration with her on a play fizzled into nothing. She decided to concentrate on her own brilliant career. While Charles Graham had declined to do detective work on Banjo, he later told Miles she was right to back off from their partnership.[79]

Miles confided in her old friends the Lawsons about her involvement with Banjo. They had moved from Marlow to another unhappy home in the same Whistler Street; this house was called Ladywood but its vibe was the same. Bertha was at her wits' end with Lawson's drinking. Still, she gave Miles a sympathetic ear and told her that the problem with Banjo would have been his fault, and that 'he did not want your love but your brains'.[80] Miles repaid the £5 Banjo had lent her for her fare to Sydney, with interest.

On 4 December 1902, the police wrote to Lawson to say that his wife 'was compelled under reasonable apprehension of danger to her person, [to] leave the residence of you, her husband, and she therefor [sic] prays that she may be deemed to have been deserted by you without reasonable cause. That she is now at Manly aforesaid without means of support. That you are well able to support her but neglect to do.'[81] He was compelled to appear before a magistrate on 10 December to answer the complaint.

He didn't. On 6 December 1902, Lawson was found in a crumpled heap at the bottom of a thirty-metre cliff at Manly. He was not dead, which was perhaps a disappointment to him. He would later give a light-hearted inventory of the damage: 'coat and waist-coat all right, pants torn a little near the knee and foot of one leg, one boot "bust". Landed between jagged rocks on bed of sand – or sand and rubble. Broke ankle and lost one eyebrow. (Pipe, tobacco and matches safe).'[82] A newspaper report compounded Lawson's woes, though, letting everyone know that he 'was in a low state of health lately, and was rather inclined to wander around the cliffs'.[83] 'Ever since his arrival from England Lawson has lived at Manly,' the report continued, 'where, as he himself says, "the swells of the sea assuage sorrow".' Lawson had been brought to Sydney Hospital in Macquarie Street, 'and as it was considered that the state of his health demanded it, he was placed under the control of responsible officials'.[84]

Knowing of her friendship with the Lawsons, Banjo wrote to Miles and asked her how Henry's 'wife and kids' were faring after the suicide attempt. He wanted to know if he could help. He knew Lawson and Bertha were at loggerheads, but two months later when Miles asked him about the rumours that Lawson was mistreating his wife, Banjo leapt to the defence of his old rival to say he had not heard about anything like that. 'Poor wretch,' he wrote, 'he has enough genuine drawbacks without being saddled with imaginary ones.'[85] Lawson's marriage had been a disaster, and Banjo feared that without his wife he would become 'a lost soul altogether'.

Banjo had a much better future mapped out for himself. He'd been offered a new job that promised endless possibilities – and, more importantly, he had found the love of his life.

He was about to wed the sweetest woman he'd ever met.

Chapter 20

8 APRIL 1903, ST STEPHEN'S, A SMALL WOODEN PRESBYTERIAN CHURCH IN TENTERFIELD, NORTHERN NEW SOUTH WALES

I want my children to grow up loving the country and the horses like I did and Alice is only too happy about it.

BANJO PATERSON MOVING HIS YOUNG FAMILY TO HIS OWN SHEEP STATION IN THE MOUNTAINS NEAR ILLALONG[1]

BANJO WAS AN EXPERT ON drafting publishing agreements, but the contract he signed in a small NSW town in 1903 brought him more satisfaction than any other deal that came his way. He had known the lovely Alice Walker for eight years and since then had taken every opportunity to see her, whenever he travelled north or she visited her relatives in Sydney, where she had attended school. Banjo was a fast man on a horse and slow with commitment; his fortieth year seemed as good a time as any to finally marry and settle down.

Alice was a kind and level-headed young woman who shared Banjo's love for tennis, horses and the bush. Like Banjo, she was part of the Scottish-Australian squattocracy. Her grandfather[2] owned the magnificent Castlesteads Station at Burrowa, in 'Banjo' country near Illalong; her father, William Henry Walker,[3] was born at Castlesteads just before the family sold it to the brother[4] of explorer Hamilton Hume. William was educated in Edinburgh before returning to Australia at the age of seventeen to go bush. He worked with the pioneering Archers around Rockhampton and at other Queensland stations, then settled at Tenterfield Station to manage the property for his wealthy cousin

Thomas Walker.[5] He eventually managed the many Walker family properties and was a trustee of the Thomas Walker Convalescent Hospital at Concord (up the Parramatta River from Rockend), a vice-president of the Pastoralists' Union of New South Wales, which was opposed to the shearers' unions, and a director of the Brisbane Newspaper Company.[6] His brother James Walker became president of the Bank of New South Wales. William was fifty-three in 1900 when he hurriedly mounted a horse at Tenterfield and was thrown; at first his injuries were not thought to be serious, but the shock and his internal trauma proved fatal.[7] Three years later, in February 1903,[8] the engagement of his daughter to the famous writer was announced.

The marriage, before the Reverend Richard Dill Macky, caused so much interest in Tenterfield that 'nearly all the town people' turned out for the occasion.[9] Tenterfield's little wooden Presbyterian church was surrounded by well-wishers on the afternoon of Wednesday, 8 April.[10] Alice's family and friends swamped the building, which was decorated with flowers, ferns, pot plants, and arches covered with white chrysanthemums and white dahlias. She looked radiant as she arrived on the arm of her brother Tom, while a small choir sang 'The Voice that Breathed o'er Eden'.[11] Alice wore a sizzling smile and an exquisite gown of crepe de chine, pleated chiffon and Brussels lace. She carried a bouquet of white roses. The wedding itself was a simple affair, with only two attendants: Alice's sister Bessie Palmer Walker as bridesmaid, and Banjo's friend Willie Kelly as best man.[12] Kelly was a young bastion of Sydney conservatism who was about to begin a long run representing the blue-ribbon seat of Wentworth[13] in Sydney's eastern suburbs.

Only close relatives and friends could fit inside the church, but there were hearty cheers from the well-wishers as Mr and Mrs Paterson left it to the sound of Mendelssohn's 'Wedding March'. The reception was held at Tenterfield Station, where the gifts – including a silver salver from the station workers and silver trinket boxes from the ladies of the Presbyterian Church – were on display. It was a private family affair, and Banjo gave a 'few well-chosen words'[14] to return thanks and say how happy he was. That night, Mr and Mrs Paterson left on the evening mail train for Cooma before travelling on to Bombala, in the foothills of the Snowy Mountains, for their honeymoon.

The wedding was covered by many papers around Australia and was given a good run in the pages of Sydney's afternoon paper, the *Evening News*.[15] This was understandable, given that Banjo was now the paper's boss.

He had been appointed editor in January 1903,[16] taking the reins of a lively publication that twenty years earlier had campaigned vigorously against Mr Justice Windeyer, Emily Barton's old friend. The *Evening News* had risen from the ashes of *The Empire,* a Sydney morning paper founded and edited by Henry Parkes, the grand old statesman Banjo had first met as a young solicitor. Cornishman Samuel Bennett,[17] the printing chief for the Fairfax family's *Sydney Morning Herald*, had bought *The Empire* in 1859 with business partner William Hanson, and sixteen years later Bennett merged it with the *Evening News*, which he had founded in 1867 to mirror developments with afternoon newspapers in England. Three years later, Bennett added the weekly *Australian Town and Country Journal* to his stable. When Bennett died at his Coogee home from tetanus after a minor accident in 1878, his sons continued to run his media business from the *Evening News* office in Market Street, now the site of Sydney's State Theatre.[18]

The *News* had been operating for thirty-six years when Banjo became just the fourth editor. He formed a strong friendship with Walter Jeffery,[19] the English-born historian who was editor of the *Town and Country*, and Banjo followed some impressive newspapermen into the editor's office. Samuel Bennett had been succeeded by James Hogue,[20] who became a NSW government minister and colonial secretary. Banjo took over from Englishman Charles Dekker,[21] who had received his early journalistic training in the London office of the American Press Association and become associate editor of the Sunday edition of the *New York Herald* in Paris. Dekker's health declined, and in 1895 he came to the better climate of Sydney to succeed Hogue,[22] taking charge of an editorial staff of five. He worked 'himself almost blind'[23] and died of a heart attack aged just fifty on 3 November 1901.[24]

The paper's chief subeditor filled in for a year until a new editor could be found. While Banjo had never worked full-time in a newspaper office, he ticked a lot of boxes for the Bennett family. He was the most popular writer in the country, *Snowy River* was the most successful book of verse ever published in Australia, and *Rio Grande* was now off and racing – even if Banjo had made enemies at the *Catholic Press*, which headlined its review as 'The Failure of Banjo Paterson'.[25] Banjo had written sterling reports from the Boer War and was a world traveller, an early foreign correspondent who had interviewed all manner of men from drovers to dignitaries. He knew more than most about the world's political affairs and had seen trouble spots, flashpoints and brutal fighting firsthand.

The racy style of the paper suited him too. Page four or five had a regular column called 'To-day's Divorce' with all the seamy details, and in the month when Banjo took over, the eight-page penny newspaper ran headlines gleaned from disasters around Australia and the wider world: 'Shot Himself at 77 – Died to Escape Fleas', 'Priest Murders His Sweetheart Then Commits Suicide', 'Tram and Butcher's Cart: Collision in Oxford Street', 'Youth's Horrible Death', 'Beat His Wife with a Shovel', 'Garrotted in Erskine St.', 'Hanged Himself in a Stable' and 'Madman in Chains'. The masthead boasted that the *Evening News* had 'double the circulation of any other Sydney paper'.

The writing was lurid and captivating. Banjo stressed accuracy and colour.

So it was that Australia's famous action-man adventurer came to find himself sitting in an office six days a week, reviewing news bulletins from around the world and taking the red pencil to contributions. He told Miles Franklin that his new job was 'a prosaic billet' and that it involved reading 'tons of copy and gallons of verse daily'.[26] Banjo also wrote plenty, too, about the big events of the time. A day before 'Chinese' Morrison visited Sydney, Banjo penned a 'special' for page four, telling *Evening News* readers:

> Not only is there trade development to carry on, but there are in China undreamed of sources of wealth – fertile lands that will grow anything, mines of fabulous richness, water rights for irrigation to be snapped up, permits to be obtained to make railways that will soon be carrying their millions of passengers annually ... There are officials to be bribed or bullied into granting concessions – officials whose oath their dearest friends would not believe, and whose written promise is a mere piece

> of waste paper. There are political adventurers, pulling all sorts of hidden strings and producing all sorts of amazing gyrations among the puppets of Chinese politics.[27]

Amid all this tumult and intrigue, there moves one man, Banjo wrote, 'to whose knowledge all white men – Russian, American, German, and Jew alike – defer, Morrison, the Australian, who represents the *Times* in China ...'[28]

Banjo now had one of the most prestigious jobs in Australian journalism, at the same time as two bestselling books on the shelves. Then, in March 1903, newspapers began advertising the nine-pence sheet music for the 'New Song, "Waltzing Matilda," words by "Banjo" Paterson, music arranged by Cowan', which was 'all the rage now in Sydney'. He had sold the rights, but it touched his heart that people around the country were singing the tune he and Christina Macpherson had put together during that turbulent time at Dagworth.

As Banjo honeymooned with the new Mrs Alice Paterson at beautiful Bombala, he was having the time of his life.

IT WAS A VERY DIFFERENT STORY for Henry and Bertha Lawson. More sorrow had come to them, 'and difficulties'.[29] In the very week that Banjo and Alice left for their honeymoon, Bertha wrote out an affidavit that was duly lodged in the Divorce Court. She did not mention Henry's preoccupation with Lizzie Humphrey or Hannah Thornburn, likely because it would have been too humiliating, but instead claimed:

> My husband has during three years and upwards been a habitual drunkard and habitually been guilty of cruelty towardsme.[sic] ... My affidavit consists of the acts and matters following. That my husband during the last three years struck me in the face and about the body and blacked my eye and hit me with a bottle and attempted to stab me and pulled me out of bed when I was ill and purposely made a noise in my room when I was ill and pulled my hair and repeatedly used abusive language and insulting language to me and was guilty of divers [sic] other acts of cruelty to me whereby my health and safety are endangered.[30]

Lawson had tried to laugh off his fall over the Manly cliffs and, recovering in Sydney Hospital eleven days later, wrote to George Robertson on 17 December 1902 to say, 'I wasn't a success as a flying machine, was I?' Robertson annotated the letter with the words 'Henry Lawson fell over a cliff at Manly – drunk, of course.'[31] Only Lawson knew the demons which had driven him over the edge that morning, but he later wrote:

> Twas the white clouds flying over, or the crawling sea below,—
> Or the torture of the present or the dreams of long ago,
> Or the horror of the future born of black-days, fate – or all –
> Never mind! the gods who saw it know the cause of Lawson's fall.[32]

Bertha and Lawson reconciled for a while, and she again fell pregnant. Soon, though, she was telling Lawson that she was sick of the abuse. Bertram Stevens, an art critic, was a mutual friend of husband and wife, even though Lawson once attacked him with a walking stick; he had advised Bertha to see a solicitor and apply for a judicial separation. 'It was clear to me,' he wrote, 'that Lawson was very fond of his wife and loath to lose her, yet it was impossible for them to be happy together.'[33] Bertha told Lawson she was willing to separate if that was what he wanted. 'I have suffered,' Bertha told him. 'God alone knows.'

> You never understood me and never will … Of course when you are drunk, you are not responsible for what you say. But your cursed relatives go and verify your drunken statements. If you wish us to come together again it is on the understanding not a relative of yours darkens our door. I will never speak to Peter or your Mother as long as I live. She can go where you can see her and shed her crocodile tears and make a blessed fuss, but she would not put her hand in her pocket and give your children a sixpence. I hate her.[34]

On 24 April, Bertha told Lawson that unless he gave her some money she would be forced to place the children in the Benevolent Asylum. 'I don't care about myself but I cannot see my children starve,' she said. 'I think it is dreadfully cruel for any Mother to have to part with her children let alone be placed in the position I am in.'[35] Two days later, Lawson was in Prince Alfred Hospital receiving more treatment when he again wrote to George Robertson, to say: 'Dear R, I am here remanded for medical treatment – drunk. She (Mrs. L) has taken out a legal separation, but will forgive me. [H.L]'[36] It was wishful thinking.

On 15 June 1903, Bertha, now four months pregnant, wrote to Lawson from the lodging room she shared with her two children at 397½ Dowling Street, Moore Park.

> Harry,
> … Re the children. I will not consent to let them go. Not through any paltry feelings of revenge, but as a matter of duty. You see, you left me, with these two little children. I was turned into the world, with [1 shilling sixpence] and not a shelter or food for them. I had to pawn my wedding ring to pay for a room. And then had to leave the little children shut up in the room, while I sought for work. And when I got work to do I had to leave them all day, rush home to give them their meals. And back to work again. And mind you, I was suffering torture all the time with toothache, and had to tramp the cold wet streets all day, knowing unless I earnt some money that day the children would go hungry to bed. (I was a fortnight working before Robertson gave Miss [Rose] Scott that money.) I had no money to pay a dentist. I wrote to you at P.A. Hospital telling you, you were forcing me to place the children in the Benevolent Asylum and you took no notice of the letter. I went to the Dental Hospital and had a tooth extracted. They have broken part of the jaw bone. And I go into hospital on Wednesday and go under an operation to have the dead bone removed … You know my condition and I am certainly not fit at the present moment to struggle for a living. As far as the case goes, the sooner it is over the better. You alone have forced this step. God alone knows how often I have forgiven you and how hard I struggled for you. And how have you treated me. Harry there is no power on the earth will ever reunite us. You are dead to me as far as affection goes. The suffering I have been through lately has killed any thought of feeling I may have had for you. When you have proved yourself a better man and not a low drunkard you shall see

> your children as often as you like. Until then, I will not let you see them. They have nearly forgotten the home scenes when you were drinking – and I will not let them see you drinking again. I train them to have the same love for you as they have for me. And if baby's prayers are heard in heaven, you should surely be different, to what you have been. They will have to decide the right and wrong between us, when they are old enough to understand. I think you are very cruel to make the statements you do about me. You know Harry as well I do they are absolutely false. Why don't you be a man? And if you want to talk to people of your troubles, tell them drink is the sole cause … I am so weary of struggling against pain and sorrow that I do not give a tinkers curse for anything – or anybody. Bertha.

Lawson said his wife was mentally unstable and prone to dramatics. He always denied her accusations of cruelty and abuse, and they were never tested in court. Late in 1903, a few months after their legal separation, their baby was stillborn.

BANJO AND ALICE MOVED into the palatial West Hall in Queen Street, Woollahra. Banjo went to work in an 'office lean and dingy', with a roll-top desk taking up most of the space in it, 'the pigeon-holes crammed with odds and ends of letters and clippings … the writing surface of his desk littered high with old proof sheets, out of date newspapers opened and unopened leaving him little elbow-room at his near-submerged writing blotter-pad'.[37]

Jessie Paterson wrote to Miles Franklin to say that Banjo had rarely been happier. The big brother she adored was enjoying the challenge of his new job and was delighted to be 'married and settled down'. He was not so enamoured with sitting at a desk all day when his heart was with the great outdoors, but married life had assuaged his wanderlust. Jessie said Alice was 'very nice' and a 'very good housekeeper'.[38] She was also a terrific mother, and the Patersons' first child, Grace, was born on 11 February 1904.

The *Evening News* was not a broken product, so Banjo had no intention of doing major repair work, though he did tinker with the format. Tom Spencer,[39] the star reporter, was almost always assigned to the day's biggest yarn. Banjo revamped the Saturday supplement, introducing a series of articles on the Australian wildlife that had intrigued him since he watched the great mobs of kangaroos on Buckinbah. He also brought in a regular feature, 'Tales of Far Countries by Men Who Have Been There', and regular military news under the title 'Khaki Column'. Banjo even made an appearance as 'The Amateur Gardener' under his old pseudonym Cincinnatus.[40] He hired Lionel Lindsay as the paper's political cartoonist, and he gave over page two for sport, but with a heavy emphasis on racing. He ran a campaign to help the farmers crippled by drought and raised £10,000 for them. He penned 'The Duties of Racing Stewards'[41] and 'The Death of Gilbert the Bushranger',[42] with reminiscences about Binalong.

One of the contributors to the paper was Charles Bean,[43] an Oxford graduate and the son of the headmaster of All Saints' College, Bathurst.[44] Bean became a junior master at Sydney Grammar, and on Banjo's advice joined the *Sydney Morning Herald* as a junior reporter in January 1908 after he had spent eight hours a day for four months learning shorthand.[45]

Another contributor was the ambitious youngster Claude McKay.[46] He had started out in the newspaper business at the *Kilmore Advertiser* in country Victoria, where he wrote articles, helped to set them in type and print them, and distributed copies on horseback.[47] McKay went on to establish the popular newspaper *Smith's Weekly*, and he reckoned Banjo was unlike most of the harried and stressed newspaper bosses he'd seen rushing about to publish the next scoop. Banjo's approach to the bustle of the big city paper was more like a languid river. 'If the paper had waited for "Banjo" it would have had to be an annual,' he wrote. 'However, in a leisurely sort of way the sub-editor persuaded three, sometimes four, editions to reach the streets each day.'[48] Banjo hated being in that little cluttered office by himself. He was confident and comfortable with the fact that his paper had a big lead in sales and advertising over the competition, and whoever went to his office was welcomed like a long-lost brother. Banjo would lean back comfortably in his chair, time no object, and settle himself down for a long chat. McKay reckoned that if a man from the bush came in with a cattle dog, it wasn't long before the dog 'sensing the situation curled itself up and was asleep'.[49]

Walter Jeffery, the *Town and Country Journal* editor, became general manager of the *Evening News* and was also writing novels about the sea. He had the look of a man who was at home on a schooner, and at peak times on the editorial floor he and Banjo would ignore deadlines and stay in deep conversation about their travels to sunlit plains extended or the palm-fringed islands of the South Seas. Banjo knew that the drover's life had pleasures that the townsfolk never know.

The staff loved Banjo – especially the casual contributors, such as McKay – because he was a generous boss who paid a guinea a column and was always ready to offer a word of encouragement or to have a laugh.

Banjo still found time to write verse and comic stories as well, though none of it matched 'Clancy', 'Snowy River' or 'Matilda'. Much of it was political satire, as with good nature he lampooned politicians of the day in 'The Seven Ages of Wise',[50] 'Macbreath'[51] or his 'Oracle'[52] series. In his short story 'Done for the Double' by 'Knott Gold',[53] he parodied the oeuvre of Nat Gould, the Englishman who made a fortune from racing novels after stints working for the Brisbane *Telegraph*, the *Evening News* and the *Bathurst Times*.

But the bush still held Banjo's heart. He ran 'Saltbush Bill on the Patriarchs'[54] in the 1903 Christmas supplement of the *Evening News*, along with 'Christmas at the Zoo' by Ethel Turner,[55] author of the classic novel *Seven Little Australians*; Lionel Lindsay illustrated both pieces. For the next Christmas, Banjo wrote 'The Man from Goondiwindi',[56] and he got to thinking about seeing a bit more of the bush.

A FEW WEEKS LATER, Banjo gave himself the plum assignment of covering the Dunlop Motor Reliability Trial, the first such event from Sydney to Melbourne. Having had some experience with a motor car when he'd bounced around in Kipling's Lanchester two and a bit years earlier, Banjo was keen to see how far mechanical science had progressed in that short time and how vehicles would cope with the harsh Australian roads. The trial took place between 21 and 25 February 1905, and Banjo raced with a friend from the Sydney Hunt Club, J. M. Arnott of the biscuit-making family. They drove Arnott's Australian-built Innes, with a twenty-horsepower engine,[57] and the journey inspired Banjo's illustrated short story 'Three Elephant Power',[58] which later became the title of a book of stories and sketches.[59]

The only objection to the cars in Australia, Banjo said, was that they frightened horses; but a race was a 'sacred thing' in this country, so much so that the mayor of Albury was planning a public function to entertain the motorists.

At 5.30 a.m. on 21 February, a large crowd turned out to see the twenty-three cars and twelve motorbikes take off from the Sydney Town Hall at three-minute intervals. All sorts and conditions of cars competed; as for the drivers, Banjo said they had to be seen to be believed.[60] 'By common consent, breeches and gaiters similar to those used for riding, seem to be adopted as the correct motor costume. Add to these a high-peaked cap, a white macintosh, a pair of awful goggles, and possibly a mask with a false leather nose …'[61]

The motorcycles left first, 'spluttering and shaking their way along at a great pace, each rider's head nodding over the handles like the head of a Chinese Mandarin'.[62] They were followed by the cars. All along Parramatta Road to the suburb of Ashfield, people congregated to cheer the 'haste waggons' – especially the little five-horsepower Beeston Humberette, driven by Mrs Florence Thomson from Adelaide. Other drivers included the retail king Mark Foy; Charley Kellow, who would later own the champion racehorse Heroic; and Harry Skinner, a leading theatrical entrepreneur. To help motorists from interstate and overseas, a trail of paper was laid through Sydney in order that the right course could be followed. The overall distance of the contest was 572 miles (920 kilometres), with the course comprising '343 miles of good road, 140 of second rate, and 89 miles of bad'.[63]

It was not so much a race but a test of attrition for man, woman and machine on roads that were often little more than bush tracks. Banjo wrote that one elderly motor enthusiast was driving 'a little one-cylinder rubby-dubby, of which he knew so little that his only accessories for the trip were a tack-hammer and a pair of pincers. Failing to get anyone with experience to accompany him, he had picked up a Sydney larrikin for company; but after the first day's drive (from Sydney to Goulburn) this miscreant deserted him, saying that he preferred dishonour to death, or words to that effect. The elderly driver thereafter spent most of his time on his back under the car, and finally threw in the towel at Gundagai.'

The hot favourite for the event was the little French racing driver E. B. Maillard, going faster at the wheel of a Richard-Brasier than any horse Banjo had ever seen. He beat everyone to Goulburn, covering two hundred kilometres in less than six hours; on leaving there he went past the other cars like an 'express train'.[64] Unfortunately he had no knowledge of Australian roads and couldn't speak English. Blissfully unconscious of the many gullies and gutters across the roads around there, he hit one at top speed, 'sending his car up in the air like a hurdle horse which has hit a jump. Parts of the car were scattered all over the road.'[65]

Banjo sent back lively, detailed dispatches to *Evening News* readers, making them feel as though they were rocking along in the cars too, smelling that unfamiliar air of exhaust fumes among the gum trees. He also wrote a series of feature articles accompanied by Lionel Lindsay cartoons.

Roads became increasingly narrow and treacherous the further the cars went from Sydney. By the time the drivers reached Albury, they were 'all pretty tired of it, half blinded with dust, and bruised and shaken by being jolted about in the cars like a pea in a pod … Mrs Thomson, the South Australian lady, had an awful time. Her car is one of the slow but sure order, and her great ambition is to do the run irrespective of what points she gets. All hope that her pluck will be rewarded. Her car stuck in the sand, and was towed out by "yokels," who seemed to spring up out of the ground. She arrived in Albury a lot late, but undaunted.' Everyone was so exhausted that nobody wanted to attend the mayor's reception. One of Maillard's crew had almost been thrown out of the car, and he told Banjo that in European races the passengers were usually tied to their seats.[66] Banjo said the motor car was like an 'untiring horse, that breasts the hills gallantly and then flies away again as fresh as ever on each stretch of smooth road'.[67]

A wheel on Banjo's car had been shattered when Arnott made a cross-country detour near Tarcutta. It needed some flour-mill mechanics at Albury to bolt stout timber supports onto either side of the wheel, in order for them to make it to Melbourne just before the victory speeches were over.[68]

Mrs Thomson finally made it to Melbourne as well, to great adulation, and her car was laden with floral tributes. Seventeen cars had completed the trial from twenty-three starters, and the fastest time was set by a young American, H. L. Stevens, driving a fourteen-horsepower Darracq: twenty-three hours forty-two minutes spread out over four days,[69] though eight teams claimed equal points for reliability.

Pieces of cars and dashed hopes littered the road between Sydney and Melbourne, but the horse was on its way out of everyday Australian life.

THREE MONTHS AFTER THE TRIAL, Banjo wrote to George Robertson[70] to say he would take a week's holiday and finish the novel based on *In No Man's Land*, which had been published serially in Melbourne's *Leader* six years earlier.

> Soon after, Robertson released Banjo's *The Old Bush Songs*,[71] a collection of fifty-five works including two Aboriginal songs. Banjo had spent a decade gleaning this collection from all over Australia, and he said most of the songs were 'composed and sung in the bushranging, digging and overlanding days'.[72] In the preface, he wrote: 'The object is to gather together all the old bush songs that are worth remembering … there will be no more bush ballads composed and sung, as these were composed and sung'.[73]

Among the best-known songs were 'Paddy Malone', 'The Beautiful Land of Australia', 'The Wild Colonial Boy', 'The Squatter's Man' and 'The Eumerella Shore'. He was preserving them, Banjo said, to stop vital links to Australia's past from being lost forever. When the book appeared in shops in January 1906, it featured a bullocky like those Banjo knew in his boyhood, singing as he led his team along a quiet bush track. It sold five thousand copies in the first year.

Banjo had become hooked on the motor car. He and Arnott travelled all over New South Wales in it, once rocking around the Buckinbah region of Banjo's boyhood.[74] They also toured his old Illalong haunts on a trout-fishing excursion up to Wee Jasper on the Goodradigbee River. They rumbled along to Jindabyne and

Queanbeyan, to the site for the Burrinjuck Dam. They took an old pioneering route to Jugiong but needed a steam engine and draughthorse to get them across the Jugiong Creek. Banjo made few friends in Tumut when he told them he much preferred Yass as the site for the proposed national capital.[75]

In May 1906, Banjo became a father for the second time when Alice delivered their son, Hugh Barton Paterson,[76] at home in West Hall. Like Banjo, Hugh would grow to have a great love for bush life and a sense of duty when war called. Banjo celebrated at a dinner in the Australia Hotel attended by Prime Minister Alfred Deakin.[77]

Fifteen days after his son's birth,[78] Banjo wrote to George Robertson to say he had finished his novel. But he wasn't so sure of it, and on 19 June he wrote again from Woollahra to say, 'I send at last the long-promised novel. I am very frightened about it and if you think it will be a frost for goodness sake say so and I will try the racing yarn [later released as "The Shearer's Colt"].'

In No Man's Land was renamed *An Outback Marriage*.[79] The novel was very much Banjo's baby; he had been working on the idea since 1898, writing and rewriting it all the way to South Africa and all the way home. He'd taken it to China with him and to London, and he finally saw it in print in November 1906, six months after Hugh was born.

He based the characters loosely on his own family members. Annette Gordon was inspired by his grandmother Emily Barton and the stories she'd told him about the early days at Boree Nyrang. His Aunt Nora, whose letters had given his mother so much comfort at Illalong, was the model for the governess. The villains were drawn from the tales his uncle Robert Barton had told him, while the sudden death of Illalong's owner Henry Brown gave the novel a twist in the tale of a bush girl who claims to be the secret bride of a recently deceased pastoral millionaire.

Reviewers were kind – especially among his colleagues at the *Evening News*, which described the novel as a 'decidedly excellent, presentment of Australian life and incident'.[80] The *Sydney Morning Herald* called it 'a capital story of Australian life', suggesting that 'the chief interest in the story lies in the fine descriptions of Australian bush life. The author makes every page live when he is telling of those things, or when he introduces his readers to "push" [gang] life in Sydney or to the awe-inspiring proceedings of the Supreme Court ...'[81] Sadly for Banjo, though, readers were not as enthusiastic, and his hopes for another *Snowy River* were dashed. It took him years before he would try again to make it as a writer of prose fiction.

Banjo was so busy with his outside projects that the *Evening News* took a backseat to everything else. As it was, Claude McKay reckoned that 'for news, Paterson had no instinct whatsoever'.[82] In McKay's autobiography, he told the story of how he had offered Banjo a feature on a murderer about to be hanged in Brisbane, but Banjo showed no interest. McKay instead sold the story to the *Sunday Times*, which ran the article big under the headline 'Criminal Monster' and described the killer, James Warton, as one of the most remarkable and perverted personalities to be found in the annals of Australian crime.'[83] Walter Jeffery, aware of what had happened, gave McKay a mock dressing-down in front of Banjo, telling him: 'You contributors are not awake. That murder story in yesterday's *Sunday Times* is the sort of thing we want. We've been scooped badly.'[84]

It wasn't just wounds to Banjo's pride that came with the job. In a rugby report, the *Evening News* described Glebe's star player 'Bull' Joyce as a 'miscreant' and his teammates as 'barbaric'[85] in their battle against South Sydney at Wentworth Park. Two days later, Banjo had to run a grovelling apology headlined 'A Jest That Failed'.[86] Some of the Glebe players had come looking for their editorial assailants but couldn't find them. The rival newspaper *Truth*, languishing in the circulation race, went for Banjo's jugular; the paper asked in its headline if the 'Editor's Abject Apology' would be accepted, and it claimed that Banjo and his team had made a quick dash down the fire escape when the Glebe team burst into the Market Street sanctum of the *Evening* 'Snooze'.[87] Banjo wrote that the article was a joke that had fallen flat and that Bull Joyce was, in fact, 'remarkable for his good temper and fair play'.[88] But *Truth* wasn't, and later that year it jumped on an insulting cartoon Banjo had run by reminding readers of his rugby faux pas. *Truth* declared that since he had taken over the *Evening* 'Snooze', Banjo – or 'The Man from Joey River', as they called him – had failed dismally as a humourist and that 'the pictorial atrocity' he had inflicted on 'our friends and allies the Italians' meant that 'all the Dagos in the metropolitan area are after his scalp ... In Thursday's issue of the "Snooze" Banjoey rises to explain that it was only a joke. "A sense of humour does not seem to be characteristic of the Italian people", claims the plaintive humourist. The famous Banjoey himself is not an Italian. His frozen humour, however, is characteristic of imitation hokey-pokey compounded from the mountain snows amongst which he sought his saddened inspiration.'[89]

The *Catholic Press* was even more hellish towards Banjo. 'Evening journalism has not agreed with the "Banjo's" health,' it sneered. 'When he went to the *Evening News* a few years ago he was a robust looking fellow; today he is thin, stooped and grey, like an old man. One has to be brought up to journalism, in order to be able to withstand the strain, and to leave one's worries in the office. Mr. Paterson is a solicitor by profession, and in journalism he made his reputation as a freelance. Harness and the daily task broke him down, though it is hard to understand how the work of editing one of the Sydney evening papers could be too heavy even for an invalid'.[90]

Banjo had the last word on his jealous critics, though. In October 1906, the *Evening News* informed Sydney that following his tenure there and with a circulation now well above a hundred thousand copies a day,[91] the paper had installed two revolutionary new presses that together could pump out ninety-six thousand newspapers an hour, surging through a river of paper 160 kilometres long every sixty minutes.[92]

But Banjo's work as a daily newspaper editor soon came to an end. With his many other commitments, precious time for Alice and his children was being devoured. Earlier in 1906, Walter Jeffery had suggested they swap work roles; Jeffery could oversee the *Evening News* and Banjo could edit the *Australian Town and Country Journal*, which was more his style and pace. It was now a sixpence weekly that appeared every Wednesday and battled Fairfax's *Sydney Mail* for its audience. *Town and Country* had been at the forefront of Australian journalism since its superb coverage of the capture of Ned Kelly and the destruction of his gang at Glenrowan in 1880.

Banjo's last piece for the *Evening News* was another political satire, 'The Dauntless Three',[93] on 8 December 1906, centred on Australia's third prime minister, Chris Watson. He opened his innings for the *Town and Country* four days later with 'Santa Claus in the Bush'.[94] The *Town and Country*'s usual format of sixty pages included the serialisation of novels and pieces by the likes of Ethel Turner. It also included a 'Ladies Page' with household hints and recipes, and it took the city to the bush, loaded with features on bush life, livestock markets and agricultural shows; each week there was a pictorial feature on a different country town. Banjo also ran articles about the Thomas Walker Convalescent Hospital,[95] named after his wife's uncle, which became home for a while to Henry Lawson.

IN THE CASE OF LAWSON V LAWSON, Bertha was granted her judicial separation,[96] and Henry began stumbling and staggering towards an early grave. Sometimes he waved a tin cup around at Circular Quay, asking for donations so he could buy a drink. His writing was ever more poignant given his circumstances.

> It is down amongst the alleys, in the alleys dull and damp,
> They find kindness in a scoundrel, they find good points in a scamp.
> It is down amongst the alleys, now my star has ceased to shine,
> I find sympathy with sinners and can hide what shame is mine.[97]

A few months later, he wrote:

> Dear Bulletin,
> I'm awfully surprised to find myself sober ... Why does a man get drunk? There seems to be no excuse for it. I get drunk because I'm in trouble, and I get drunk because I've got out of it. I get drunk because I am sick, or have corns, or the toothache: and I get drunk because I'm feeling well and grand. I got drunk because I was rejected; and I got awfully drunk the night I was accepted. And, mind you, I don't like to get drunk at all, because I don't enjoy it much, and suffer hell afterwards. I'm always far better and happier when I'm sober, and tea tastes better than beer. But I get drunk. I get drunk when I feel that I want a drink, and I get drunk when I don't. I get drunk because I had a row last night and made a fool of myself and it worries me, and when things are fixed up I get drunk to celebrate it. And, mind you, I've got no craving for drink. I get drunk because I'm frightened about things, and because I don't care a damn. Because I'm hard up and because I'm flush. And, somehow, I seem to have better luck when I'm drunk. I don't think the mystery of drunkenness will

ever be explained – until all things are explained, and that will be never. A friend says that we don't drink to feel happier, but to feel less miserable. But I don't feel miserable when I'm straight. Perhaps I'm not perfectly sober just now, after all. I'll go and get a drink, and write again later.
HENRY LAWSON

On 27 December 1904, a married woman named Ettie Thrush placed her baby gently on the North Shore wharf and leapt into the water to drown herself – only for Lawson, in a rare moment of clarity, to dive in fully clothed to save her life. Banjo ran a story in the *Evening News*[98] about it. Her baby was taken to an orphanage, and she was asked why she had jumped; she replied, 'I've got my troubles.'[99]

A year later, a desperate Bertha took Lawson to court because he was eight weeks behind in child support. He was ordered to pay £12 5s 6d or spend three weeks and three days in jail, but he didn't have the money. With so many benefactors sick of him and unwilling to help, he was immediately sent to the terrifying Darlinghurst Gaol, a convict-era relic that he called Starvinghurst because of the meagre rations. He recalled the place in 'One Hundred and Three', which was his prison number.

> They shut a man in the four-by-eight, with a six-inch slit for air,
> Twenty-three hours of the twenty-four, to brood on his virtues there.
> And the dead stone walls and the iron door close in as an iron band
> On eyes that followed the distant haze far out on the level land.
> ...
> The clever scoundrels are all outside, and the moneyless mugs in gaol –
> Men do twelve months for a mad wife's lies or Life for a strumpet's tale.
> If the people knew what the warders know, and felt as the prisoners feel –
> If the people knew, they would storm their gaols as they stormed the old
> Bastille.[100]

Between 1905 and 1910, Lawson spent 159 days in Darlinghurst Gaol for offences including wife desertion, failure to pay alimony, and drunk and disorderly.

In April 1907 he sold some manuscripts to the Melbourne publisher Thomas Lothian for £50,[101] but Lothian soon wrote to him to say there was not enough material for the two books Lawson had promised.[102] They exchanged letters for some months as Lawson spent the £50 on libations. On one occasion, the dour Scot Lothian arrived at his office in the morning to find Lawson drunk on the doorstep.[103] By December his patience was spent and, in response to a further postponement, he wrote to Lawson, 'If you can truly think that there has been the slightest pleasure in my doing business with you, that my former experiences should make me anxious or pleased to meet you, then I will apologize.'[104]

THE BUSH KEPT CALLING BANJO as he wearied of city life. The *Town and Country* offered a slower pace than the *News*, but Banjo's immune system was shot, he caught colds and flus, his nerves jangled and he was always so tired. Maybe he really was starting to look like an invalid, as his enemies said.

In the first week of 1908, the *Town and Country*, as well as newspapers and magazines around the country, were advertising the sale of Buckinbah, Banjo's first home, forty-four years after Rose and Andrew Paterson had taken him there. Thomas McCulloch's trustees were auctioning off ten thousand hectares, almost half of it freehold land.[105]

Banjo was already making his move. He loved the country around Illalong, the Upper Murrumbidgee – and he waited for his chance to buy a property there. Then he saw an advertisement in his *Town and Country*. Coodra Vale[106] was a 16,000-hectare mountain kingdom about forty-five kilometres south-west of Yass, at the northern end of the Brindabella Ranges. It was watered by the Goodradigbee River, which was full of trout.

Many years later, Banjo reckoned he'd needed to get back to the country in order to cure 'some sort of nervous breakdown',[107] but this was an exaggeration – even if city life did get on his nerves. 'I want my children to grow up loving the country and the horses like I did,' he said, '… and Alice is only too happy about it.'[108] He reckoned Coodra Vale was closer to Melbourne too – 'easier to get to the Cup' – but above all, it was a vision splendid where 'one could ride for miles and miles in the ranges, seeing nothing but wild horses, wild cattle, wombats and wallaroos, and hearing at night the chatter of the flying squirrels playing among the gum tree blossoms'.[109]

In January 1908 Banjo offered his resignation as editor of the *Town and Country*. He had made £10,000 from *Snowy River* and £3000 from *Rio Grande*, and together with the sale of West Hall in Woollahra he had enough capital to become one of a syndicate of four who bought Coodra Vale in February 1908.[110] Banjo and Charles Lindeman, of the wine-producing family, eventually bought the syndicate out; they registered a brand of a 'P' and 'L' conjoined with the Yass Pastures Protection Board.[111] Not that Banjo ever planned to totally sever ties with the city. On 9 May 1908, he and Alice attended one of the big social events of the month, along with the governor-general and the NSW governor: an interstate tennis match at the NSW Tennis Association's new courts, in Manning Road, Double Bay.[112] The Wimbledon champion Norman Brookes was in slashing form for Victoria.[113]

A little more than a month later, on 15 June 1908, Banjo wrote to George Robertson from the Australian Club to say that he needed to raise as much cash as he could. 'Will you make me an offer for my copyright in *Snowy River* and my other books with you? *Snowy River* has been returning a pretty steady sale for some years so I suppose it has a value for a few years more … If I get into the bush again I hope to get some decent work done. Am always seedy down here. I have about £100 worth of books and pictures I might also put in with the rest; won't want them up there …'[114] Banjo wrote later:

> As a station proposition [Coodra Vale] was best avoided. As a homestead there was nothing better. We had eight miles [thirteen kilometres] of a trout river, which ran all the year round, clear and cold in summer, a fierce snow-fed torrent in winter. As the sun was setting, the lyre-birds came out of their fastnesses and called to each other across the valley, imitating everything that they had ever heard. Gorgeous [lorikeets] came and sat in rows on the spouting that ran round the veranda, protesting shrilly when their tails were pulled by the children. Bower birds with an uncanny scent for fruit would come hurrying up from the end of the garden when the housewife started to peel apples, and would sit on the window-sill of the kitchen, looking expectantly into the room.[115]

The countryside was rough and spectacular, 'left over after the rest of the world was made',[116] but the building work on the new Burrinjuck Dam had opened local waterways for trout-fishing and the promise of a tourism windfall. Riding through the hills and fishing the Goodradigbee River with his family brought Banjo back to his roots, though not everyone wished him a pleasant stay. His old foes at the *Catholic Press* put the boot in yet again, saying that while Henry Lawson's mother was now eking out a living on a small poultry farm and would probably outlast her son, Banjo, the 'horse poet', was 'something of a cocky-grazier in the neighbourhood of Barren Jack'. 'He was never a poet at any time,' the paper spat, 'but in "The Man from Snowy River" he strung together horsey rhymes with pleasing facility. This was the type of verse suited to the backblocker and the stable boy.' Australia's tastes had 'improved' since then, it claimed.

That burning blast couldn't scar Banjo, and neither could the raging bushfire that started on Mount Barren Jack in January 1909. It destroyed twenty-five thousand hectares in the area, razing several homesteads.[117] When the fire hit Coodra Vale on 4 January, at least two fishing parties had to dive into the river to escape, leaving their buggies to burn.[118] Banjo and the family were away at the time, but much of his land and livestock was scorched. Running a big remote station was still not easy. Banjo's grandmother Emily had told him all about the life that she and Robert Barton had led all those years ago on Boree Nyrang.

Banjo had not been at Coodra Vale long when his great link to the pioneering Australian days was broken. Emily, who had left the wine country of France as a delicate young woman for the wilds of Australia, and who had encouraged Banjo's writing all his life, died at Rockend on 24 August 1909, at the age of ninety-one. As she was laid to her rest in St Anne's churchyard beside Banjo's mother, and near her husband, father, and son Frank, the mourners reflected on the doggedness of pioneers like her. The *Evening News* eulogised her as 'the daughter of the late Major Darvall, one of the earliest colonists' and said she had lived at Gladesville for 'upwards of 40 years, and endeared herself to all with whom she came in contact … She was the authoress of many small poems.'[119] Emily's sister Rose Templer had recently passed away in Christchurch, while another sister, Eliza Kater, having also abandoned the bush to live near Emily at Enfield for thirty years, would soon be gone too. A generation that had tamed the Australian wilderness was fading fast, though Banjo's poems and stories remained to remind Australians of their fighting spirit.

Soon the nation would call on that spirit like never before.

Chapter 21

JANUARY 1910, COODRA VALE STATION, NEAR WEE JASPER, NEW SOUTH WALES

And sometimes under sunny skies,
Without an explanation,
The Murrumbidgee used to rise
And overflow the station.
But this was caused (as now I know)
When summer sunshine glowing
Had melted all Kiandra's snow
And set the river going.

BANJO PATERSON ON JUST ONE OF THE PERILS FACED BY MEN AND WOMEN ON THE LAND[1]

THE YEARS LEADING UP to the First World War were not especially kind to Banjo. He had hoped to keep writing for the *Evening News* and *Town and Country* on a freelance basis, but nothing came of it. There was little love from the public for *An Outback Marriage.* The grass had looked so much greener on the other side of New South Wales when he was fantasising about life as a station owner from his editor's office in Market Street, but maintaining Coodra Vale was hard and expensive work.

Banjo largely retreated from the public eye after moving to his mountain property, letting his weary soul and his frail health mend beside the fast-flowing trout-filled streams, the lowing cattle, and the green hills that reached skyward in the cold crisp air. He had nothing published for years, and he visited Sydney only occasionally.

Early in their tenure at Coodra, as they called it, Banjo and Alice were a hit at the 1909 Randwick races, Alice drawing compliments from the press in her 'dark petunia-coloured coat and skirt and hat to match'.[2] A week later they cut a fine figure at Sydney's Government House for a vice-regal ball,[3] and the governor-general's wife, Rachel Ward – Lady Dudley[4] – made a beeline for Banjo. Soon she asked him to visit her again.

Lady Dudley would become the great-grandmother of her namesake, the English-born Australian actress Rachel Ward. Banjo saw her as a complete contrast to the 'swashbuckling Marie Lloyd'.[5] She was 'another woman of finer material, but with, perhaps, even more of steel in her composition. Not that she looked like it; for it was hard to imagine a more beautiful, cultivated, and altogether feminine woman than Rachel – Lady Dudley. But when it came to getting her own way, she displayed a single-minded determination that marked her out as one far above the ordinary level of female humanity.'[6] Not for her the traditional role of vice-regal's wife opening bazaars and shaking hands 'enthusiastically with children who had won prizes for recitation'.[7] Lady Dudley wanted to establish, all over Australia, a chain of bush nurses who would be 'ministering angels to the poor and sick in the back-blocks'. The scheme met with heated opposition from the medical profession in the bush, with one doctor telling Banjo 'we can kill plenty of people ourselves, without having to step in and finish off the nurses' mistakes'.[8]

Still Lady Dudley had a plan, and Banjo was shown into a private parlour at Government House. Since Banjo was so well known among bush people, she asked him to organise a trip for her 'through all the back-blocks towns'. 'I will live in the Governor-General's train,' she said, 'and I will address meetings and ask for subscriptions in every centre, even in the small places. I will get twenty thousand pounds without any trouble. Will you help me to do it?'[9]

Banjo later wrote:

> I had done some back-blocks touring and pictured to myself this delicately-reared woman addressing bush audiences, night after night, in smelly little country halls with the thermometer at a hundred and ten. I knew that the local doctors would warn all the wealthy people to keep their money in their pockets as the

> scheme was sure to fail. But such was my admiration for her pluck that I would have gone with her had it been in any way possible for me to do so. I felt quite ashamed that I had to back out of it, but there was no alternative.[10]

The tour never came off. When Labor won a sweeping federal election, the penny-wise Scot Andrew Fisher[11] was returned to power as prime minister over Alfred Deakin. He had a hostile attitude to Lord Dudley,[12] who had a reputation as a womaniser, maintained expensive government houses in Sydney and Melbourne, and enjoyed travelling around the country in vice-regal pomp. At public expense, Dudley even chartered a steam-yacht to circumnavigate the continent. The governor-general realised he had worn out his welcome and eventually took his wife home to England.[13]

AT COODRA VALE, BANJO set himself the task of writing a book dear to his heart. It would be called *Racehorses and Racing in Australia*, a comprehensive history of the sport and breeding in this country from the earliest days. He felt that Australians loved their racing so much that before the North Pole was discovered, it could have been found easily enough by advertising a race meeting there as a couple of dozen Australians would infallibly have turned up with their horses.[14] Banjo had lengthy correspondence with his publisher over the book's genesis. He said 'of all the thousands who attend races very few have any idea of "the game". People who go to cricket and football mostly know a bit about the games and have played them themselves. But thousands on thousands go racing and bet their money cheerfully on mysterious whispers imparted to them by men without any seat to their pants.'[15]

Banjo went into great detail preparing the book. He studied the works of world authorities on the modern thoroughbred racehorse, and he charted the history of horseracing in England from the time of Emperor Septimus Severus, when Roman soldiers staged races with Arabian horses near York in A.D. 206. He considered the role of the forty Barbary Arabs imported into England by Charles II. He looked at such subjects as 'Buying a Yearling', 'Trainers and Training', 'Handicap Racing' and 'Jockeys'. One of his subjects was 'Punters and Professional Backers', though sadly he couldn't find one for this project.

Robertson regarded the racing book as too specialised, with too narrow an audience, and it would not be published in Banjo's lifetime.[16]

JUST A FEW DAYS AFTER FLAGGING the racing book with Robertson and just a year after fire ravaged their property, Banjo and Alice had another taste of their land of fire and flooding rain.

They were in a buggy with Alice's brother Douglas Walker trying to cross the Murrumbidgee when a great wave of water roared towards them, fully eight feet (2.4 metres) high. The force of the torrent hurled the buggy downstream with the horses still attached. Alice screamed; she and Douglas grabbed on to overhanging branches and clung on for dear life as the water surged under them. Banjo, still agile as his forty-sixth birthday approached, bravely jumped onto the backs of the drowning horses and cut them free from the buggy. It was swept down the river, end over end, as though it weighed no more than a paper boat. Banjo and the animals struggled out of the water to safety, and he helped Alice and her brother down from the trees. He had quite a story to tell the children, Grace and Hugh.[17]

A FEW WEEKS AFTER Banjo's escape from the river, Henry Lawson was released from Darlinghurst Gaol after another short stint when unable to make maintenance payments. His landlady, Mrs Isabel Byers, arranged his release having raised the necessary money; she later recalled, 'They called his "crime" the disobeying of an order of the court, but as he was not allowed to write in jail, how was he to earn money? He had been put on ration No.1 or in plain Australian, "starved"… How Henry Lawson lived through it all and kept his reason I know not.'[18] 'When Lawson got out of jail his bones almost rattled. This is no exaggeration. He was a skeleton. I am not one who is inclined ordinarily to show great emotion but this time I cried when I saw him.'[19]

Lawson's friend Ted Brady took him to have a rest in the East Gippsland bush at Mallacoota for a few weeks. 'The truth about Lawson is that he was the life-long victim of sordid circumstances. With greater leisure and better payment for his output he would have gone further,' Brady wrote. 'Outsiders have said that he liked the life of the hard-up and the drinker, which is a damned lie. He enjoyed it no more than a skylark enjoys a cage.'[20]

EARLY IN HIS WRITING CAREER Banjo had 'versified' about the many perils of a mountain property, where cattle would fall off the steep ridges and where dingoes ate the sheep.[21] So it came to pass at Coodra Vale. Part of his property was enclosed by what he called 'a dingo-proof fence of thirteen wires, with a strand of barbed wire at top and bottom'.

Just like so many of the squatters Banjo had written about – and just like his own father – he had to offload a property that looked beautiful but had a savage bite. Coodra Vale was leaking money, so Banjo sold his share to his partner Charles Lindeman and looked for something smaller and more manageable.

Late in 1911, Banjo and his family moved two hundred kilometres north-west to a smaller but more established property, Glen Esk,[22] outside the village of Bimbi, in the wheat district between Grenfell and Young. The property was in the foothills of the Weddin Mountains,[23] where Ben Hall had once had his base, but it lacked the mountain grandeur of Coodra Vale. It was 550 hectares 'of the best sandy clay country, with rich alluvial soil washed down from the slopes of the mountain'. Most of it was under wheat, and the rabbits had been all but wiped out.

There were pastures of sheep at Glen Esk, too, and the purebred Clydesdale stallion Rob Roy, recently imported from New Zealand, was standing a season there with a fee of £3 3s per mare.[24] There were vines, fruit trees and a flower garden that attracted all manner of colourful and musical birds, and a lagoon in front of a 'picturesque old homestead',[25] though drought sometimes made it less of a vista.

Not that the Patersons were always there to enjoy it. They still maintained their strong social ties in Sydney and were among the crowd of twenty thousand that braved a wet and cold Randwick for the April races of 1912.[26] A couple of weeks later they were at the Forbes Town Hall for the local Picnic Race Club Ball, 'one of the social events of the season' in country New South Wales. Then there was the Governor's Children's Party for two hundred little ones at the Cranbrook mansion in Sydney's Rose Bay,[27] and the lavish ball on the promenade deck of the P & O liner SS *Medina* where Banjo and Alice tripped the light fantastic in a gala event of multicoloured electric lights, palms and bunting.[28] They were also honoured guests at the 'plain and fancy dress ball' at Bimbi in August 1912 to aid the local Roman Catholic Church, with Banjo showing that he held no ill feeling over the scathing reviews in the *Catholic Press*. The little Bimbi Bakery served up a supper of 'a very high standard' and the costume that really 'took the cake' was the half man/half woman.[29]

Farming was rarely fun and games, though. Four years after fire had threatened the homestead at Coodra Vale it came snarling towards Glen Esk, down from the Weddin Mountains thanks to some careless picnickers.[30] As the fire burnt for days, more than a hundred men were called in to make a firebreak for miles around Bimbi to protect the village.[31]

Banjo's stay at Glen Esk was brief. He and the family holidayed at Camden, south-west of Sydney, in October 1913.[32] At the end of the month they were guests at the ostentatious Halloween party of Alice's millionaire relative Dame Eadith Walker,[33] a philanthropist who had inherited the fortune of Thomas Walker, the former owner of Tenterfield Station. Eadith ferried sixty guests, including Banjo and Alice, down the Parramatta River past Rockend to her mansion, Yaralla, at Concord, where a dozen costumed witches stirred a cauldron and a fortune teller was stationed on the lawn. Many of Sydney's wealthiest businesspeople were there, including Geoffrey Fairfax[34] from the *Sydney Morning Herald*.

Banjo's fame had spread beyond Australia with *The Man from Snowy River and Other Verses*, which by now had been in print for almost twenty years. Kipling was not Banjo's only world-famous admirer: the former US president and great outdoorsman Theodore Roosevelt wrote to Claude McKay telling him how much he enjoyed the 'speed and gusto' of Banjo's ballads.[35] In 1913, Roosevelt wrote to the Ballarat lawyer and author Newton Wanliss[36] to say he was an 'old admirer' of Adam Lindsay Gordon's poems, and: 'By the way we also admire a more recent poet of yours, Paterson, very much.'[37]

Banjo settled his family back in Sydney at The Grove in Woollahra, just up Queen Street from their first house there, West Hall. It was a happy home and that wry smile rarely left his suntanned, weather-beaten face. Among his most treasured mementoes of Grace and Hugh growing up were photos taken one Christmas of them hamming it up with boxing gloves. He penned a couple of verses, 'The Road to Hogan's Gap' and 'Song of the Wheat', for *Lone Hand*, the monthly magazine that Jules Archibald and Frank Fox[38] had started in 1907 as a sister publication to *The Bulletin*. He also pressed on with his great history of horseracing, even though there was scant interest from publishers.

Soon, however, there would be a long pause in his research. Events far away in Bosnia would shatter world affairs like nothing before. Banjo would be on the move again for the greatest adventure of his life.

Chapter 22

28 JUNE 1914, THE APPEL QUAY, A WIDE AVENUE IN THE BOSNIAN CAPITAL OF SARAJEVO

It is with a thrill of pride that one sees all those lines of steamships manned and equipped by one's own country, going to do what we can to help our kindred in the great Armageddon … let us pray that success may attend our venture, and that we may manfully do our share towards bringing about victory, followed by an honourable and lasting peace.

Banjo Paterson sailing with the first convoy of Australian troops to the First World War[1]

IN 1914 BANJO WAS FIFTY YEARS OLD and feeling it when on the other side of the world six suicide terrorists and their handler targeted another fifty-year-old in the middle of the Bosnian capital. They loitered along Sarajevo's Appel Quay waiting for a meeting with Archduke Franz Ferdinand, the heir to the Austro-Hungarian throne.

Two decades earlier on a hunting trip to New South Wales, the Archduke had gone deep into Boree Nyrang territory at Narromine[2] and Mullengudgery,[3] shooting any animals that moved: kangaroos, emus, pelicans, turkeys, koalas, a platypus, brolgas and a pair of black swans. He killed more than three hundred birds and animals, making his personal taxidermist – who was travelling with him – work around the clock.

Now, on the bright Sunday morning of 28 June 1914, Franz Ferdinand was about to experience a role reversal.

The assassins were a motley crew of sad misfits from the Black Hand terror group. Five were teenagers, three had tuberculosis, and all said they were ready to sacrifice themselves to free the Bosnian Serbs from the oppressive Austro-Hungarian yoke. Each had a cyanide tablet to end his life when their mission was accomplished. They mingled uneasily among a festive crowd cheering Franz Ferdinand and Sophie, his wife of fourteen years.

Europe was on the precipice of war. For years England and Germany had jostled in an arms race that could only end explosively. All it would take was a single spark to ignite a firestorm.

After a brief review of the troops, at 10 a.m. the Archduke's six-car motorcade headed along the Appel Quay towards Sarajevo's town hall. He and Sophie were seated in the back of an open-top 1910 Gräf & Stift Double Phaeton limousine.

As the Archduke's car approached them, the first two assassins hesitated and kept their grenades in their pockets. Further along, the third assassin, Nedeljko Cabrinovic, drew his grenade from a long black coat, smashed the detonator against a lamppost and tossed it at the Archduke.[4] The grenade bounced off the folded-back hood of the limousine and exploded underneath the car behind, injuring two of the Archduke's officers and more than a dozen bystanders. Cabrinovic swallowed his suicide pill and dived into the Miljacka River, but the cyanide mix only made him vomit and the water was only a few inches deep. He was dragged out, severely beaten and arrested.

Bizarrely, Franz Ferdinand decided to continue his tour. The Double Phaeton raced to the Sarajevo Town Hall, passing three other assassins who either had second thoughts or were unsighted.[5]

One of them, Gavrilo Princip, trudged off to console himself at Moritz Schiller's food store near Sarajevo's Latin Bridge as the Archduke's car screeched to a halt at the town hall.

The Archduke asked to visit the garrison hospital to see the soldiers who had been wounded by the grenade. He and Sophie set off for the hospital, but the chauffeur took a wrong turn into the narrow Franz Joseph Street, stopped in front of Schiller's food store and, realising his mistake, slowly began to reverse. Gavrilo Princip, the sickly 19-year-old with TB and a death wish, couldn't believe his luck. He managed to still his trembling heart for a moment, drew his pistol from his suit-coat and opened fire from five feet. Princip's first bullet struck the Archduke in the jugular and lodged in his spine. As Sophie dived to shield her husband, Princip's second bullet went through the side of the car, her corset and her right side, lodging in her abdomen.

Princip bit into his cyanide capsule, but a policeman swung a baton at his head and knocked it from his mouth. As the boy assassin placed the muzzle of his pistol against his own head, the gun was wrestled off him before he could pull the trigger.

Within an hour the Archduke and his wife were both dead.

After a month of riots and diplomatic threats, Austria, with Germany's backing, declared war on Serbia on 28 July 1914, setting off a chain reaction around the globe. The Tsar mobilised Russia's massive forces to defend Serbia, and France agreed to support Russia. Germany declared war on Russia, France mobilised against Germany, and Germany declared war on Belgium to get at France. Britain, having guaranteed Belgium's neutrality, declared war on Germany on 4 August.

Just a few hours later, Australia had joined what had become the first war that involved the whole Western world, firing the Allies' first shot at Fort Nepean in Victoria and forcing the German cargo steamer SS *Pfalz* to surrender as it was leaving Port Phillip Bay.

Recruiting for the war began immediately in Australia, with promises that the whole thing would be over by December after Germany's Kaiser was put back in his place. As Australia was increasingly gripped by nationalism, Henry Lawson's poem 'The Flag of Eureka' highlighted the way the Southern Cross flag at the Eureka Stockade had inspired Australians to stand up for a fair go.

Few, and taken by surprise,
Oh! the mist that hid the skies –
And the steel in diggers' eyes –
Sunday morning in December long ago;
And they grapple and they strike –
With the pick-handle and pike –
Twenty minutes freed Australia at Eureka long ago.[6]

Australian propaganda highlighted the merits of British imperialism, and the value of frontiersmen who could ride and shoot. There was a stampede to enlist, while a stigma quickly surrounded those men not in uniform. Men motivated by unemployment, jingoism and a sense of adventure clamoured for a chance to fight the Hun. Recruiting officers rejected boys in short pants and bare feet as young as thirteen and men as old as seventy-one. From the Federal Parliament in Melbourne, Prime Minister Andrew Fisher offered Britain twenty thousand troops – but by the end of 1914, 52,561 Australian men had enlisted.[7]

Banjo was off and racing. It was as though he was back on the veldt reporting on battle. He immediately volunteered to reprise the role he had taken up in the Boer War, asking to be the *Sydney Morning Herald*'s correspondent. Bureaucracy had changed, though: with Australia now a nation, the Commonwealth was appointing its own official war correspondents. The best the *Herald* could do was see that Banjo was allowed to travel with the first Australian troops as an honorary veterinarian and report back on the progress of the convoy.

Banjo would have plenty of company in England as the *Herald*'s 'Special Correspondent'. His sister – now Mrs Grace Taylor, aged thirty-seven – was in London with her cousins Dorothea and Ruth Murray-Prior, the daughters of Aunt Nora. They had been holidaying on the Continent but got out of there fast as the floodgates of war began to break. Their half-sister, the novelist Rosa Campbell-Praed was living in Torquay, in Devon. Banjo hoped to find his way to the front from London, though he wasn't sure how that would pan out.

Within two weeks of Australia joining the war, Banjo visited four military camps set up at racetracks around Sydney to report on the 'wonderful progress' being made in the 'task of enrolling, officering, equipping, and instructing a lot of untrained civilians'.[8]

Four battalions were in training. The Light Horseman at Rosebery had a 'very fair lot of horses in camp, many of them gifts from patriotic citizens'. The Waler horses looked a little on the light side, but Banjo reckoned they'd grow strong with proper feed and care. 'Next will come the instruction in marching and musketry drill, and this will be pushed on at once. Arrangements have to be made for shipping the men and horses to the other side of the world, feeding them while on the way, and enrolling, equipping, and officering a new contingent.'[9]

On the same page of the *Herald*, next to one of Banjo's reports, was a small single-column item with the heading 'Lady Dudley's

Appeal'. Now back in England and estranged from the former governor-general, Lady Dudley was raising funds for the Australian Voluntary Hospital to aid the war effort, with Eadith Walker leading her list of donors along with the Narrandera Polo Club, thanks to the influence of Banjo's former partner at Coodra Vale, Charles Lindeman.[10] In an open letter to the *Herald*, Banjo asked the public to support the appeal.[11] He had already asked the Australian people to give the troops 'tobacco, sweets, clothing, and sundries ... and the sooner that help is extended the better'.[12]

By 1 September 1914, Banjo's former contributor Charles Bean had been appointed Australia's official war correspondent by the Australian Journalists' Association. And Germany had begun the conquest of Belgium, treating the entire population as potential guerrillas and executing thousands of civilians while burning buildings across the landscape.

In Brisbane, workmen were refitting the 15,000-tonne ocean liner SS *Euripides* as a troop transport vessel. The ship had just completed her maiden voyage from London to Brisbane, and two days after arriving was requisitioned for the war effort. When the refit was finished on 18 September, the Aberdeen White Star liner had berths for 136 officers and 2204 other ranks, as well as stalls for twenty horses.[13]

In October 1914[14] there was still time for Banjo and Alice to watch Mountain Knight win the AJC Derby at Randwick, and for them to attend the vice-regal function there. It was hosted by the new governor-general, Sir Ronald Craufurd Munro Ferguson,[15] who spent much of the function deep in conversation with Andrew Fisher about the war.[16]

WITH ADVENTURE AND THE great unknown calling, Banjo said goodbye to his wife and children and set sail on the *Euripides* from Woolloomooloo on 20 October 1914.[17] On board were the headquarters of the 1st Infantry Brigade, the 3rd and 4th Battalions, and the 1st Field Ambulance. No one yet knew exactly where they were headed, but never before had so many Australian soldiers sailed on the one vessel. Soon they would be joined by thousands more men.

Banjo was thrilled to be part of 'the greatest national undertaking yet attempted by Australia'.[18] The soldiers on board, most about to have their first bitter taste of war, were writing 'many hundred letters, each addressed to some home that seems so far away now'. Most of the soldiers were young men, and more letters went out to sweethearts and mothers than to wives.

> It may be a long time before they got back, but at any rate they are starting in good heart, and with every belief in themselves and their comrades. The old folks at home will look anxiously for those letters.[19]

As the ship drew near to its rendezvous point for the other transports at Albany, Western Australia, wet weather set in. Banjo and the others peered through the driving mist as they tried to make out what vessels were before them. Steadily they passed down the long line of ships until they came abreast of General William Bridges'[20] flagship HMAT *Orvieto*.

The men, most of them landlubbers like Banjo, struggled down the side of their rolling ship on ten-metre rope ladders. They then plonked themselves into tugboats that were leaping and plunging alongside. As soon as General Bridges' ship moored, Banjo went off to interview him, travelling in a little powerboat that rocked around in the heavy sea like a wild brumby. On board were the red collars of high-ranking officers, and among them two Frenchmen acting as interpreters for headquarters. Banjo reported that between 4500 and 5000 trained and fully equipped doctors and nurses would be with the convoy. General Bridges had his headquarters fitted up in a big reading room, and from it orders were semaphore flagged or flashed to all the vessels of the fleet. They would eventually number thirty-eight, a far cry from the little *Kent* that had carried Banjo on her solo voyage to the Boer War. The horses on this ship were treated like royalty in padded stalls, and there was even a cinematograph operator on board ready to film the great convoy heading to fight for king and country.

The *Euripides* anchored in King George Sound off Albany for five days while other transports arrived and water and coal were taken on board. Finally, as a bright red dawn broke on 1 November, the Anzacs left in the huge convoy of troop ships, with smoke billowing from their funnels and with fire in the bellies of the men. By the time the full convoy came together in the open seas, thirty thousand Australian and New Zealand men were on the water along with 7800 Waler horses. The line of ships stretched for twelve kilometres, with the Japanese cruiser *Ibuki* leading the way as one of the warships enlisted to give the transports safe escort, along with HMAS *Sydney*, HMAS *Melbourne* and a British ship, HMS *Minotaur.* There was a full alert on for the raider *Emden*, part of the German East Asia Squadron, which was wreaking havoc in the Indian Ocean and had just sunk Russian and French cruisers in the Battle of Penang.

Banjo could only gasp at the awesome power Australia could muster as he surveyed the great line of vessels and men in the expanse of still, grey water – 'the most wonderful sight that an Australian ever saw'.[21] 'Sunday, November 1, was a red-letter day in the history of Australia,' he wrote, 'for on that day our big fleet of transports put out from Albany for the long trip across half the world ... Thirty thousand fighting men, representing Australasia, are under way for the great war.'[22]

Two battalions of infantry were on board the *Euripides*, and Banjo reckoned it was a 'topsy-turvy' force. The brigadier, Colonel Henry MacLaurin,[23] a Sydney barrister, had never seen any active service and was killed at Gallipoli two days after the landing there. The ranks were full of English ex-servicemen 'wearing as many ribbons as prize bulls': Yorkshiremen, Cockneys and 'Cousin Jacks' all keen to clear out and rejoin their old regiment as soon as they got to England.[24] Banjo also befriended the 'gigantic' Lieutenant Jack Massie,[25] a great all-round athlete who was as 'strong and rugged as an iron-bark tree' and was a champion at rugby union, boxing, rowing and the 120-yard hurdles. He was a crack rifle shot, too – and, most famously, a left-arm fast bowler for the NSW team, knocking on the door for Australian selection.[26]

Banjo kept a diary for readers back home. Tuesday, 3 November 1914 was Melbourne Cup Day, a 'sacred' time for Australians. He wrote: 'Not much chance of hearing what won it here [Kingsburgh at 20 to 1].'[27]

By Thursday, 5 November, some of the horses were becoming leg weary. Banjo had to put one big stallion in a canvas sling sixty centimetres wide under his belly, and he made a breast band out of two old racing bandages: one laid across the stallion's chest, the other over his neck. The horse went to sleep, lay on the sling, and nearly pitched out of it.

An American sailor on board had been in the Philippines war and in China. He told Banjo he had five medals and had fought with five different nations. He got into the stalls and was hustling a tricky pony about; Banjo said, 'Look out, man, that horse will kill you', and the sailor drawled back, 'Sir, me and this horse is vurry well acquainted.'[28]

On the evening of 7 November, a night alarm sounded. All hands were sent to the boat stations, and the order was given: 'All lights out; all lifebelts on.'

On 8 November a strapping young recruit, Private Varley Haddon Kendal, from Sydney by way of Narrandera, died on board from pneumonia. He was twenty-one, a former policeman with a young wife: 'He was a very fine young fellow. He was nearly well, and supposed to be out of danger and asked for a drink of water, and then fell back dead. The funeral was very impressive. The Dean and the Salvation Army brigadier took turns at prayers and responses. The Dean wished to deliver a sermon, but the great heat made it necessary to cut the service short. The body was committed to the sea. Many of the men cried, and I saw one of the ship's officers with tears running down his face.'[29]

Queues formed for inoculations against typhoid, but it was much more pleasant in the canteen where eight hundred pints of beer were consumed an hour – this was 'good going and would surprise a public barman, I think'. One old soldier played up on the beer question, threatening to see Lord Kitchener 'about this one pint-a-day business', but he was promptly made a prisoner, and Banjo said beer would not trouble him for a time.

On 10 November, Banjo recorded: 'News came last night from the *Sydney* that she had captured the [*Emden*'s] collier and that other vessels in the vicinity had surrendered.'

By a very hot Thursday, 12 November, the ship's band was playing waltzes in the afternoon, and men danced on the afterdeck. Some were in striped football jerseys, some in Canadian bathing costumes, and the sailors with bare feet were all waltzing in pairs 'in the middle of a dense and appreciative crowd'.[30] The next day a heavy rain fell, but a holiday was granted to celebrate crossing the equator.

Then, late on Saturday, 14 November, a message from General Bridges' flagship was read out to the officers on the *Euripides*. It said that the *Sydney* would pass through the transport fleet early the next morning and that there was to be no demonstration, owing to the presence of the badly wounded Germans on board; as she passed, all ranks were to stand at attention. The idea that they might see the *Sydney* close up brought all hands on deck.

The *Euripides* arrived in Colombo on 15 November. Banjo saw Japanese, Russian and British warships, and merchantmen everywhere. All the Australians were 'in a wild state of excitement' over the sinking of the *Emden*. It was almost beyond belief, Banjo said, that Australia's first naval engagement could have been such a sensational win, 'for our people are not sea-going people and our navy … was never taken very seriously. And now we have actually sunk a German ship!'[31]

On 9 November the *Emden* had sailed into the Cocos Islands, where a landing party disembarked to destroy the wireless station on Direction Island. The station managed to send a signal, 'Unidentified ship off entrance', and the *Sydney*'s British captain John Glossop[32] was ordered to investigate. In the fierce battle that followed, the *Sydney* fired 670 cannon blasts at the German ship, scoring about a hundred hits.[33] Out of the *Emden*'s crew of 376 officers and enlisted men, 133 died. Most of her surviving crew were taken prisoner, including skipper Karl von Müller,[34] and the second torpedo officer, Franz Joseph, Prince of Hohenzollern, who was the nephew of the Kaiser; like most of the prisoners he was suffering badly with shellshock.[35] Three of the *Sydney*'s crew were killed and another man died from injuries.

In Colombo, Jack Massie offered to take Banjo to interview Glossop, so he would 'get some stuff that the other correspondents wouldn't get'.[36] Massie's family were 'of considerable importance in Sydney' and had entertained Glossop at their home. As a result Banjo scored one of the big scoops of the year. Glossop was in civilian clothes, having a drink by himself, 'a typical English sailor-man, not a bit excited by the fact that he has "woke up to find himself famous". To him the whole affair was a matter of calculations – range of guns, weight of metal, speed of ship, and of course a good deal of luck.'

Glossop told Banjo that the *Emden* crew had had no idea there was any vessel of her own power in that part of the Pacific.

> She came out looking for a fight – and she got it. She must have got a surprise when she found she had to fight the *Sydney*; and I got a surprise, too, I can tell you ... The whole thing didn't last forty minutes, but it was a busy forty minutes. She tried to get near enough to torpedo us, but she could only do seventeen knots and we could do twenty-seven, so we scuttled out of range. The *Emden* had a captured collier called the *Buresk* hanging about, trying to get near enough to ram us, and I had to keep a couple of guns trained on this collier all the time. We hit the *Emden* about a hundred times in forty minutes, and fourteen of her shells struck us but most of them were fired beyond her range and the shells hit the side and dropped into the water.[37]

In his exclusive report, Banjo told readers back home that the *Emden*'s crew thought that they were coming to meet the *Newcastle*, 'a British ship that somewhat resembles the *Sydney*, but is not quite so heavily armed'.

The two vessels steamed along beside each other exchanging broadsides from ten thousand yards. The first salvo from the *Sydney* killed several sailors on the *Emden* and destroyed her steering gear. Totally outgunned, Captain Müller swung the *Emden* around and headed for the uninhabited coral atoll called North Keeling Island, in order to beach the ship and save his crew. The *Emden* crashed upon the shore 'on fire in several places, her funnels and one mast shot away, her decks a shambles'.[38] The crewmen who were still alive were so shattered that no one had the presence of mind to haul down the German flag, which still flew on her remaining mast. Seeing that the *Emden* had not struck her colours, Glossop fired one or two salvoes at her; and then, seeing that she was 'beached and done for', he headed after the collier, *Buresk*, an English vessel that had been captured by the *Emden* and was being used for refuelling: 'The *Sydney* soon overtook the collier, and made her heave to, and sent a boarding party on board hoping to save her, but the Germans had opened the seacocks; and by the time that the boat's crew from the *Sydney* got on board there was no hope of saving the *Buresk*. The *Sydney* took the crew off and then fired one broadside into the *Buresk* at 600 yards, a beautiful shot, which took her on the water line and sent her to the bottom. So ended Australia's first naval engagement ...'[39]

Reflecting after the battle, Captain Glossop told Banjo and Jack Massie ruefully, 'I have seen my first naval engagement ... and all I can say is thank God we didn't start the war.'[40]

Chapter 23

28 NOVEMBER 1914, APPROACHING THE SUEZ CANAL, EGYPT

In this war we're always moving, moving on,
When we make a friend, another friend has gone.
Should a woman's kindly face
Make us welcome for a space
Then it's boot and saddle, boys, we're moving on.

BANJO PATERSON ON THE LIFE OF THE SOLDIERS WHO SURVIVED THE FIGHTING[1]

THE NEWS SPREAD AROUND the *Euripides* like lightning. The troops would not be travelling to England to prepare for war against the Hun in Europe, as most had imagined, but instead would be disembarking in Egypt[2] for a fight with the Turks. This did not sit well with all the Englishmen, Scots and Irishmen, who had been hoping for a free passage home.

Sun helmets were at a premium among officers days before the *Euripides* led the transports into the Suez Canal on the bright moonlit night of 1 December 1914. The camps of the Indian regiments were clearly visible on the banks; they had built a fort of sandbags secured with wire entanglements and 'were a fine looking lot of men with very soldierly bearing'.[3] As the sun rose, the Diggers had their first taste of a desert mirage: a 'ghostly desert town' with 'spires and big buildings' rose from the sand and gave everyone on the *Euripides* an uncanny feeling, making more of an impression on them than anything else they saw.

On 2 December the transports prepared to moor at Port Said, but there were so many ships they moved on to Alexandria the next day.

The Australians began making their camp at Mena, near Cairo.

Banjo's job was done for both the *Herald* and the horses, so he caught the first transport he could to London, hoping to pull some strings that could help him and his notepad reach the war zone. Despite his reputation, though, there weren't a lot of strings he could pull. He arrived in London in mid-December, and while this created great excitement for his sister Grace and his cousins, he couldn't rustle up any action in France or Belgium. London was in a state of chaos, almost as shell-shocked as the crew on the *Emden*: 'a stricken city, cut off from all reliable news, with everybody working feverishly to organize an army overnight. Where we had one machine-gun the Germans had twenty.'[4]

On 14 December Banjo went to the War Office to push his claims to be a correspondent. He found the waiting rooms and passages 'absolutely blocked by old generals, old colonels, young and old civilians, who all want to do something, or to give something'. They all wanted to get to the front, too.

> I wrote to [General] Sir Archibald Hunter[5] with whom I had been friendly in South Africa to ask if he could get me to the front in any capacity. He said he couldn't get there himself.[6]

The next day Banjo went to see Sir Timothy Coghlan,[7] the agent-general for New South Wales, 'as unemotional as a professional billiard player, and as self-reliant as a sea captain'.[8] Coghlan had battled his way to the top from a minor civil service position and felt 'rather superior to the trammels of red tape'. After considering the matter for a while, he told Banjo:

> I can get you over to France. But if you write one word for a newspaper, or if you tell anybody that you've ever been inside a newspaper office, you'll deserve all that's coming to you. If you go over there and lie low for a while they may let the correspondents go to the front later on. There's an Australian hospital over there, Lady Dudley's hospital they call it, and we have a man there in charge of a government ambulance. He wants to come home; so you can go over and take his place. You'll see something too, let me tell you; for of all the troubled outfits that I ever had to handle,

> this hospital beats the lot. It's a first-class hospital, don't make any mistake about that, but its adventures would make a book.[9]

At the outbreak of war Lady Dudley had put her bush hospital plan into place with a different setting, staffing it from the large numbers of Australian doctors and nurses training or working in the United Kingdom. She discussed her ideas first with King George V then with Lord Kitchener, now England's Secretary of State for War. The British Army's Director General of Army Medical Services, Sir Arthur Sloggett, gave her the go-ahead. Lady Dudley wanted her personal doctor from Melbourne in charge of the hospital, but the War Office would consent to the scheme only if an experienced battlefield medical officer had that role. And so it was that William Eames[10] became its commander.[11] Eames and his family had been holidaying in England when war broke out, and even at fifty-one he was keen to enlist. Banjo had met the tall and dignified doctor in South Africa. On 5 September the hospital opened at St Nazaire, but because of the German advance it moved to Wimereux just outside Boulogne-sur-Mer.

Coghlan told Banjo that everybody wanted a job on the hospital so that they could say they had been over to the front; some of the richest men in London were over there washing out bedpans, carrying coal and washing dishes.

Robert Lucas Tooth, the seventy-year-old Australian beer baron who lived in England, promised £10,000 to the hospital but only if a lady friend, a Mrs Josephine Popplewell, a former singer, was made hospital secretary. No lady friend, no £10,000. Mrs Popplewell turned out to be a godsend: a commonsense, capable woman who ran the hospital administration brilliantly, without a penny wasted.

WHILE WAITING TO TAKE up his new job at the wheel of an ambulance in France, Banjo made a quick trip to the grand Straffan Station Stud, a property owned by his Irish cousins, the Bartons, in County Kildare.

Straffan was the base of the celebrated horse breeder Edward 'Cub' Kennedy:[12] 'racing man, hunting man, and breeder of that great racehorse The Tetrarch … possibly the fastest horse that ever lived'.[13] Kennedy was a pretty fast worker, too. In 1905, at the age of forty-four, he had married Banjo's eighteen-year-old niece Dorie Lumsdaine[14] after meeting her while she was on the Grand Tour at her ancestral home. On 16 December 1914, Kennedy – 'sturdy, square, stiff-built and full of energy' – gave Banjo the guided tour. Banjo had studied Irish horse breeding going back nine centuries, but this was still an education. Although Ireland was full of political strife with police everywhere, on this stud farm Banjo was at peace with the world in the middle of a sea of green grass.

BANJO ARRIVED AT Lady Dudley's hospital in Wimereux two days before Christmas 1914. The hospital was divided between two buildings: a large château and a golf club on the edge of the Wimereux links, where the doctors relaxed between shifts accompanied by small French caddies who counted the years until they were old enough to join the war. Banjo found Colonel Eames 'going on his tranquil, unhurried way' and renewed his friendship with the Scottish-born Alexander MacCormick,[15] with whom he had once lived for some time 'under a Cape cart' on the veldt. 'Others of the staff were Dr Thring, a leading Sydney surgeon; Dr Herschell Harris,[16] an X-ray specialist; Colonel Horne of Melbourne; Dr Dick, an authority on hospital sanitation; and several young doctors. All these young men had been taking post-graduate courses in England when the war broke out and there was no ailment known to the human body but somebody on the staff was a specialist at it.'[17]

The Australians were still in Egypt preparing to fight the Turks, but wounded Englishmen began pouring into the hospital from the fighting at Mons. Banjo began driving an ambulance donated from Australia; he would meet the patients at the railway station and, recalling his time on the Dunlop Reliability Trial, would drive them as fast as he could over 'those infernal cobbled roads, bumping and jolting their wounds and shattered bones'. There was never a whine out of the British Tommies, he said. 'If we apologized for the roughness of the trip they said: "It doesn't matter, sir, so long as you get us there."'

Soon all the beds were taken. Herschell Harris was making full use of his own 'private X-ray outfit',[18] and Banjo recalled that the hospital had a 'wonderful reputation, so much so that the wounded at the front would ask doctors patching them up if they could be sent to the "Australian 'ospital"'.[19] '[M]en at the last stage of exhaustion, hovering on the edge of death from their wounds, had to lie on stretchers in the hall-ways and passages till something could be arranged for them. Patiently, unhurriedly, everybody worked double tides for the credit of their country; and as the hospital could buy whatever supplies it liked and was not tied down to routine issue of rations, etc. the Tommies passed the word back up the line that if there was a home from home in France it was at the Australian hospital.'[20]

Once Banjo watched Alexander MacCormick saving the life of a German prisoner who was very badly wounded, his legs having been 'all blown up' by a shell. The German was very grateful and asked Banjo about the man who had brought him back from the brink of death. 'I told him MacCormick was making seven or eight thousand a year in his own country, but had given it up to come over as a volunteer. He could hardly believe it.'[21]

Lady Dudley's hospital was the busiest and most important private hospital on the Boulogne front, 'a sort of rendezvous for all the great consultants of the military medical world'. Very few women – or men either, Banjo remarked – could have created such a hospital. He thought Lady Dudley a 'wonderful woman' who could have been a general, 'for no doubts assailed her and no difficulties appalled her'.[22] She saved so many lives, but in the end could not save her own – she drowned not long after.[23] Banjo's final memory of her was at her hospital, dressed in white like a vision, surrounded by 'men smothered in mud and at the very last gasp of their vitality, with bad wounds and shell shock and trench fever'. An orderly carried a bucket of hot water behind Lady Dudley as she 'walked the wards like a duchess and insisted on washing the faces of the dirtiest men'.[24]

BANJO SPENT CHRISTMAS DAY 1914 in the hospital mess with some of the world's finest medical specialists, among them the celebrated immunologist Sir Almroth Wright,[25] 'a big, spectacled Irishman with a fine leonine head ... He was a lecturer at the University of Sydney; but they let him go because they didn't think he was worth a salary of (I think) six hundred a year. He now makes ten thousand a year in London.'[26]

On New Year's Day 1915, Banjo sat down to lunch with a wandering English member of parliament and his wife. 'Having worked it to get over to France for the day the lady was very military and wore ammunition boots and puttees over her stockings … and when she got back she would doubtless make the other women sick with envy at her tales of "What I saw in France." She might even write a book about it.'[27]

The special guest at the hospital – 'the star boarder', Banjo called him – was Captain Beachcroft Towse VC,[28] who had lost the sight in both eyes from a bullet in the head during the Boer War. His bravery is said to have reduced Queen Victoria to tears when she pinned the medal on his chest.[29] He was seated next to the visiting politician and his wife.

> … but he happened to be late and when he came in he had not the faintest idea of the identity of his neighbour. For some reason or other he started to talk about the interference by politicians in military affairs, a standing topic with every soldier. We all sat and listened with horror. He had a very fine voice, and though everybody tried to drown him out with talk, clear and strong over the tumult came:
>
> 'There is no honour in politics, no morality, nothing but hunting for votes. Any politician coming near an army ought to be sent away at once.'
>
> We tried to get his orderly to give him a hint, but the orderly was too paralysed with terror to attempt any such thing. When things were explained to [Towse] afterwards he was utterly unregenerate.[30]

BANJO'S HOPES OF BECOMING a war correspondent vanished. He took a ship back to Australia, hoping to try a different tack. By the time he arrived home, the Australian and New Zealand troops he had sailed with to Egypt were at Gallipoli, bogged down in what looked like an unwinnable war of attrition. A desert campaign against the Turks was looming around the Suez Canal, and Banjo knew his experience with horses had to be worth something to the war effort. He was enveloped in patriotism and penned an open letter to the troops in the Dardanelles, 'We're All Australians Now'.[31]

It was printed on a card bearing the crossed flags of Australia and the International Red Cross, and distributed to the troops.

Australia takes her pen in hand,
To write a line to you,
To let you fellows understand,
How proud we are of you.

From shearing shed and cattle run,
From Broome to Hobson's Bay,
Each native-born Australian son,
Stands straighter up today
...
Fight on, fight on, unflinchingly,
Till right and justice reign.
Fight on, fight on, till Victory
Shall send you home again.

And with Australia's flag shall fly
A spray of wattle bough,
To symbolise our unity,
We're all Australians now.

In a similar vein, he would soon write 'Australia Today 1916'.

Banjo now wanted to enlist. The remount units, responsible for training war horses and mules, seemed like his best bet, but at fifty-one he was a year too old even for them. So Banjo did what so many men of a similar age did at recruiting stations: he wound the clock back two years.

Banjo filled out an application on 24 September. He outlined his experience as a dispatch rider in South Africa and ambulance driver in France, and wrote that he had charge of horses to Egypt as an honorary veterinary officer, and that he had taken horses to Africa and China. His postal address was the Australian Club Sydney, while his home address, where his wife resided, was Cooper Street, Edgecliff. He had never been operated on for hernia and was capable of bearing the fatigue 'incident to the performance of military duty'. His eyesight was good.

A. B. Paterson was made a lieutenant in the Australian Military Forces on 13 October 1915, and he joined the sixth squadron in the second of two remount units. His squadron was better known as the 'Methusaliers', the 'Horsehold Cavalry', or the 'Horse-dung Hussars'. He said they made up for their 'un-military appearance' with all the efficiency of Lady Dudley's hospital. All the officers were over-age or unable to pass the doctor for fighting units. 'Not more than two or three of us knew anything about drill; the rest did not even know a sergeant-major from any other major ...'[32]

> ... it was discovered that about a quarter of the Light Horse regiments who were fighting on Gallipoli had been left behind in Egypt to look after the horses; and it was decided to organize a couple of hundred rough-riders, possibly the best lot of men that ever were got together to deal with rough horses. Horse-breakers from the back-blocks; steeplechase riders; men who had got their living by riding outlaw horses in shows – a lot of them had hung back from enlisting for fear that they would never be able to learn the drill. But when they heard that they only had to ride buck-jumpers they decided 'to give the war a fly.'[33]

The 1st Australian Remount Unit was formed of riders from Victoria, South Australia, Western Australia and Tasmania. Banjo's unit, the 2nd, was formed of men from New South Wales and Queensland. Even at fifty-one, Banjo was still as good a rider as any of the recruits, and with his family background of East India servicemen and his private school education he was perfect officer material. By 9 November he was promoted to captain.

The next day, having said his farewells to Alice and the children, he sailed on the 12,000-ton Orient Steam Navigation Company's liner *Orsova*, rebranded as *Transport A67* for the war. The ship arrived at Port Melbourne on the morning of 12 November to collect the men of the 1st Remount Unit based at Maribyrnong, and she set off for the war that afternoon with a large number of nurses on board as well as artillery men.[34] Three days later they were in Fremantle and then began the long journey without stops before loading more coal in Aden.

Some of the men were old but they didn't know it, and some still hoped to fight. Banjo recalled a conversation with a grizzled veteran from the cattle country, who saluted like a man brushing away a fly and leant his elbows on Banjo's desk.

> 'I was jest thinkin',' he says, 'that when we git over there I'd like to exchange into one of them fightin' regiments. I was thinkin' I'd like to go into the flyin' corps. I never been up in an airyplane but if a man can sit a horse I suppose he could sit one of them things.'
>
> I say: 'They only take young men in the flying corps. You want nerves like a goat to go flying. I suppose you want to go as an observer. What would happen to you if the pilot got killed.'
>
> 'Cripes, yes, it'd be pretty tough if he got killed and I was left up there and couldn't come down. I reckon I'd better go for the artillery.'[35]

Banjo was back at the Suez Canal by 8 December, twelve months after his previous visit, and the men disembarked on 9 December, taking the train to the military base at Zeitoun where they set up camp. Three days after Christmas they were shaking the dust off their feet at Maadi al Khabiri. Britain's Director of Remounts, Brigadier-General Loftus Bates,[36] was a highly decorated cavalry officer who had been severely wounded in the Boer War and was a man after Banjo's own heart. He later became chairman of England's Race Course Owners Association. Banjo explained that the work of the Remount Depot was to

> … take over the rough uncivilized horses that were bought all over the world by the army buyers; to quieten them and condition them and get them accustomed to being heel-roped; and finally to issue them in such a state of efficiency that a heavily-accoutred trooper can get on and off them under fire if need be. We had 50,000 horses and about 10,000 mules through the depot, in lots of a couple of thousand at a time. All these horses and mules had to be fed three times and watered twice every day; groomed thoroughly; the manure carted away and burnt, and each animal had to be exercised every day including Sundays and holidays. His Majesty's Methusaliers had a perpetual motion job.[37]

They also had to deal with generals such as 'Hell-Fire Jack' Royston,[38] who was always coming around to demand the best horse. Royston was 'by instinct a bandit chief and by temperament a hero'. Banjo reckoned that while it was 'altogether an admirable thing for a general to set his troops a good example by showing a contempt for danger, it must be admitted that Royston rather overdid it'. Whenever he got anywhere near a fight, 'a sort of exaltation seemed to seize him, and he took no more account of bullets than of so many house flies'. Royston would ride up behind a row of dismounted men firing for their lives and exhort them, 'That's it boys. Pump it into 'em!' – as his men shouted back at him in chorus, 'Get out of that you old bastard. You're drawing the fire on us!'[39]

After leading the 3rd Light Horse Brigade in the first and second battles of Gaza, Royston abruptly left the war on the eve of the battle for Beersheba in October 1917. According to the official history, his departure was 'for urgent personal business'. But Banjo had a different take: he wrote that, despite repeated warnings, Royston took a big gulp of the new poison gas the Germans were using so that he could recognise it instantly and warn his men. Banjo said he later found Royston 'in a hospital, a badly shaken man, passing green urine, and ordered away for long leave'.[40]

THE REMOUNT DEPOT WAS on the edge of the desert with the waters of the Nile in the background, and beyond the river the Pyramids stood clear against the skyline. Flies were everywhere. Sergeant-Major Dempsey, a six-foot-two Australian, 'straight as a stringy-bark sapling and equally as tough',[41] took charge of the roughriders. Their uniform consisted of a shirt and riding breeches, with their socks pulled up outside the ends of the breeches. They wore elastic-sided boots specially made in Australia, with smooth tops so that there would be nothing to catch a rider's foot in his stirrup. Their saddles had high pommels and cantles with big knee and thigh pads. Watching them tame the horses was like a daily rodeo show. 'In a moment the compound was full of trouble,' Banjo wrote after one day's work.

> Horses were bucking all over the place. A big chestnut horse, as soon as he was mounted, threw himself straight over backwards

> and narrowly missed pinning his rider to the ground. A waspish little bay mare refused to move at all when mounted, and crouched right down till her chest nearly touched the ground. It appeared that she was going to roll over, and her rider kicked his feet out of the stirrups. As he did so, she unleashed a terrible spring that shot him out of the saddle and sent him soaring in the air, high enough to see over the pyramids – or at any rate so he said.

Some of the horses bolted back into the compound and fell over the ropes, while others set sail into the desert as though they were racing back to Australia.

Before the Allied Forces could make their push through Palestine, the cavalry had to be strengthened. On 27 March 1916 the commander of Britain's Egyptian Expeditionary Force, General Archibald Murray,[42] had Brigadier Bates merge the two remount units into one: the Australian Remount Depot at Heliopolis. Banjo wrote to his niece Dorie at Straffan to say that he felt as though anyone 'who had an incorrigible [horse] in his possession sold it to the army' but 'I only ride horses intended for generals and thus I get the pick of the mounts'.[43]

Captain A. B. Paterson was given command of a squadron. On 21 October 1916 Major General Harry Chauvel, his old schoolmate from Sydney Grammar, recommended his promotion to major as the remount men moved to the new Moascar base near Ismailia, on the west bank of the Suez. Banjo made the remount men famous with rough-riding displays that drew large crowds of spectators, including Lady McMahon, wife of the High Commissioner of Egypt.[44] He wrote home to George Robertson:

> All joking apart, the work is hard, monotonous, and dangerous, and the men deserve every credit. I don't think the world ever saw such a lot of horsemen got together as I have in my squadron – Queensland horsebreakers and buckjumping-show riders from New South Wales. It is queer to note the difference in the various States – the other squadron are Victorian, Tasmanian and South Australian farmers and they are quite a different type from my lot – far easier to handle not having had the real rough

> horses to deal with they cannot touch my men at horse work. We (my squadron) won five out of seven events open to all troops in Egypt at a show the other day. In the wrestling on horseback one of my Queenslanders, a big half caste named Nev Kelly, pulled the English Tommies off their horses like picking apples off a tree. You say what does this do towards winning the war? Well, it shows that we are up in our work and are doing it and it is not too easy. At the present moment I have two men with broken legs, one with a fractured shoulder blade, two with badly crushed ankles, and about seven others more or less disabled, in hospital at one time out of about 100 riders.[45]

Banjo never had to tell a man twice to get on a horse 'no matter how hostile the animal appeared'. He could only scoff at most of the English generals in Cairo, though. He reckoned there must have been ninety of them living at the plush Shepheard's Hotel, 'where they either just existed beautifully or they made themselves busy about such jobs as reporting upon the waste of jam tins'. The rank and file, he said, were forbidden to enter the hotel even to buy a drink or to meet a friend, 'lest they should come between the wind and the nobility of the staff officers'.[46] Banjo recalled that one night a riot of protest took place outside the hotel. Two Australian officers had just bought a motor car and were having a good dinner in Shepheard's 'with a view to, later on driving their new acquisition out to the pyramids with some female youth and beauty on board … Belonging to a non-combatant unit, they easily persuaded themselves that they were not called upon to go out and quell riots; so they sat tight and wound up a satisfactory dinner with some excellent cognac. Then, the riot having subsided, they went out and found that out of three hundred motor-cars the troops had burnt just one – and that was their new car!'[47]

All that changed with the 27 June 1917 arrival of big, beefy General 'Bull' Allenby[48] to command the Egyptian Expeditionary Force. He weeded out the non-performers one by one. Allenby had been a major when Banjo knew him in South Africa, but Banjo said it was a changed Allenby who took command now. He had been through the disaster of fighting at Mons when the English were devastated by German forces; Allenby had dismounted his cavalry and thrown them into the fighting line in a vain effort to stop the German charge. Being a big man, he was affected by the heat of Egypt – but nowhere near as by much as the telegram he received from his wife on 31 July that said their only son Michael, a lieutenant who had received the Military Cross, had been killed in action in France. 'The Chief' was utterly bowled over, and no one who knew him as Bull would have recognised him. His staff said he was a pitiable figure for two weeks until he pulled himself together. Banjo sensed that the grief only made Allenby tougher: 'Where he had been granite before he was steel now.'[49]

Banjo had been knocked around, too. Though his recollections were always flavoured with the same good humour his mother had shown in times of distress at Illalong, the heat and the dust wore him down. Insomnia was a killer – literally. A few months earlier[50] one of his comrades, Captain Daniel Hay Machattie of the New Zealand Veterinary Corps, had shot himself at the depot, and the only reason anyone could think of was the lack of sleep.[51] Banjo was admitted to the 14th Australian General Hospital at Abbasia in Cairo on 11 July 1917, suffering from 'debility'.[52] He complained to the doctors that he had been sleeping 'very badly' and 'had not been feeling well for some time'.[53] After spending the next three weeks in hospital, he rejoined his unit at Moascar.

Allenby came to inspect the horse depot on 20 September 1917.[54] He appeared as 'a great lonely figure of a man, riding silently in front of an obviously terrified staff. He seemed quite glad to recognize a friend in me.' 'I am afraid I am becoming very hard to get on with,' Allenby told Banjo. 'I want to get this war over and if anything goes wrong I lose my temper and cut loose on them.'[55]

It was about this time that the American war correspondent and adventurer Kermit Roosevelt,[56] son of Teddy, visited Moascar. Roosevelt was twenty-seven at the time and would soon be awarded a Military Cross. As a boy he had thrilled to the verses of 'The Man from Snowy River', and he still admired its author as he related in his book of the war:

> When I left Mesopotamia I made up my mind that there was one man in Palestine whom I would use every effort to see if I were held over waiting for a sailing. As soon as I landed I asked

> every Australian officer that I met where Major Paterson was, for locating an individual member of an expeditionary force, no matter how well known he may be, is not always easy. Everyone knew him. I remember well when I enquired at the Australian headquarters in Cairo how the man I asked turned to a comrade and said, 'Say, where's Banjo now? He's at Moascar, isn't he?' Whether they had ever met him personally or not, he was 'Banjo' to one and all ... At Moascar ... I found him. He was a man of about 60 with long moustaches and strong aquiline features very like the type of American plainsman that Frederic Remington so well portrayed. He has lived everything that he has written. At different periods of his life he has dived for pearls in the islands, herded sheep, broken broncos and known every chance and change of Australian station life. The Australians told me that when he was at his prime he was regarded as the best rider in Australia ... He told me that among American writers he cared most for the works of Joel Chandler Harris and O. Henry ...[57]

Roosevelt wrote of Banjo driving three hundred mules straight through Cairo without losing a single animal, and late in 1917 Banjo again reverted to the droving days of his youth as Allenby ordered a field remount station at Rafa for the push on towards the coastal port of Gaza in Palestine. On 19 October 1917, Banjo and forty other men were dispatched fifty kilometres north to Kantara,[58] taking 130 horses and twenty mules by rail. They then rode on for another two hundred kilometres until they reached Rafa ten days later, with the animals 'in a very satisfactory condition'. The Official War Diary recorded the 'above particulars of the conducting of animals to Rafa are entered in the Diary to show that the distance and heavy nature of the route really did no harm whatever to them rather the reverse as the animals actually improved'.[59]

FORTY KILOMETRES EAST, on 31 October, Harry Chauvel – now a lieutenant general in command of the Desert Mounted Corps – climbed to a vantage point outside the little market town of Beersheba. The town was situated at the foot of the Judean Hills, and its main road linked it with Gaza, then controlled by the Turks.

German and Turkish troops used Beersheba as a base for raids into British occupied territory.

Chauvel had distinguished himself during the heavy fighting at Gallipoli in 1915, but this was to be his masterpiece. After an assault on Beersheba by British infantry in the morning, Chauvel's 4th Light Horse Brigade charged, the dust rising all around them as they headed towards Beersheba's mosque, gleaming white in the setting sun. The Light Horsemen had their rifles slung over their backs and bayonets in their hands like swords. They galloped into the town and captured almost two thousand Turkish soldiers.

The victory propelled British and Anzac troops to break the Ottoman line near Gaza the following week. There were thirty-one Light Horsemen killed that day, including Tibby Cotter, a celebrated Australian Test cricketer; in the closing stages of the battle at Beersheba, a Turkish soldier shot Cotter dead at close range. Years later Banjo would claim that he visited Beersheba soon after the charge and saw a man blown apart by a booby trap.[60]

Soon the Allies overran Jaffa and Lod. On 11 December, Allenby walked through the gates of Jerusalem.

Banjo never got to see the frontline fighting as he had done in the Boer War. Instead he stayed in Palestine for ten more months. He continued to organise buckjumping shows and wrote some verses for the military magazine *Kia-Ora Coo-ee*. He was much more excited by the arrival of Alice, who volunteered as 'Hospital Helper' at the Ismailia English Red Cross Hospital.[61] In January 1918, newspapers reported that Alice had gone to Egypt to join her husband 'who is engaged in special war work'[62] and that she would on arrival 'immediately engage' in the Voluntary Aid Detachment (VAD) as a civilian providing nursing care.

Banjo having been away from home for more than two years, it was a touching reunion between husband and wife. But there was a war to win and soldiers to comfort. Alice signed on to the hospital on 25 March 1918 and served there until 18 March the next year. She also set up a canteen with some other women volunteers. Her Red Cross certificate said her character was 'good'. Banjo thought so too.

Grace and Hugh lived with Alice's widowed mother, Georgina Walker, in New South Head Road, Edgecliff, while their parents were in Egypt.[63] Among their most treasured possessions was a poem,

'A Grain of Desert Sand', that Banjo sent them in a letter. A couple of his other poems, 'Boots' and 'The Old Tin Hat', would be published when he returned home. Banjo also took to writing a short novel, *The Cook's Dog*, set in a sheep station like Coodra.

A much more gripping drama continued, though, out in the desert, and Banjo wished he could ride roughshod into some of the desert towns at the head of the conquering troops as he had done at Bloemfontein. Instead, every day he turned out more and more horses to be cut down by the enemy or to be discarded as refuse when their work was done. With the end of the war in sight, everything was being hurried up.

> The big English flying school near our camp has been ordered to turn out as many pilots as quickly as possible and there is an average of eighteen planes in the air all day long, just over our heads. The din is indescribable, but the horses never look up, or otherwise take the slightest notice of the planes. The life of a pilot, computed in flying hours, is pitifully short; many of them are killed while learning. My wife is working as voluntary aid at a hospital in Ismailia, and she and her associates are constantly making shrouds for these boys.[64]

Part of the training for young pilots was to get them to buzz close by fixed objects – sometimes too close.

> One boy who had the natural gift for flying swooped down on an Egyptian fisherman in the canal and went so close that he hit him with the undercarriage and killed him. Then the boy lost his head and after landing his plane by the side of the canal he set off to walk blindly across the desert. The flying people had a nice problem on their hands – an abandoned plane by the side of the canal, a fisherman with his head smashed to pieces in a boat, and beyond that, nothing. Sherlock Holmes would have been puzzled. Later, the boy, hardly knowing what he was doing, walked into a camp some miles up the line and the whole thing was explained. The Royal Air Force had their own system of courts martial: this youngster was sentenced to confinement to a camp where he could go on with his flying. One life doesn't

matter much in a war, and the army couldn't afford to lose the services of a pilot with the big move just ahead.[65]

On 16 September 1918, with the Allies about to take Nazareth, the home town of Jesus, Banjo's B Squadron was moved a hundred kilometres to Lod.[66] Ten days later they returned to Moascar, and Banjo's chance to see fighting was over. On 31 October 1918 the Turks signed an armistice, eleven days before the Germans did the same in France.

Alice and Banjo stayed in Egypt for five more months as work at the hospital continued and repatriation to Australia was being organised. They would be going home, but none of Banjo's horses would see Australia again.

Early in 1919, orders were issued that because of strict quarantine laws now in place, none of the thirty thousand Australian horses would return except one, Sandy, the horse of General Bridges who had been killed by a sniper at Gallipoli. Some horses were sold on to the British Army for use in the Indian cavalry. But many of the Australians, fearing that their trusted mount would become a mistreated workhorse in Egypt or dinner for someone's dog, decided to save them from an ignoble end. More than two thousand Waler horses were shot dead.[67] Banjo was sickened.

But he was not nearly as troubled as Alice. Just a few weeks before the ceasefire in France, her brother Corporal Douglas Walker – who had clung to the tree branches with her above the flooded Murrumbidgee at Coodra – was killed by a bomb while working a machine gun in France. Their brother Harold was with him but could do nothing to save his life. Douglas was, according to one tribute, 'handsome, brown as a berry, hard as nails, with an air of elasticity about him that fascinated. He was splendid. Excelling at rugger, tennis, cricket, he was perhaps at his best on horseback, and rode as he lived, straight as a die, scoffing at danger.'[68] He was buried at Maricourt.

As an old man, Banjo told Australian radio audiences that he had been 'a sort of looker on in four wars one way and another, never in danger you understand'[69] – though he was being extremely modest about his experiences in South Africa, his reporting from Manila and China, and his more than three years of important service in the Great War.

South Africa had taught Banjo that the enemy, the Boer, was usually not much different from the soldier who was trying to kill him. It had been the same story in Palestine. Banjo was once with a force that gathered up a battalion of demoralised Turks in the Jordan Valley: poor ragged men with cheap, shoddy uniforms and worn-out boots. Battalions that had had no food for three days came in as prisoners in military formation, 'not a man out of the ranks', and sat silently down to take whatever fate had in store for them. The Turkish colonel in command refused food until his troops were fed.

Banjo was anxious to find out something about these Turks. Selecting one man at random, he asked him in English, 'What do you do for a living in Turkey?' In perfect English, the prisoner replied, 'I'm a linotype operator.' So there was Banjo, in the newspaper business himself, and the first captured Turk he interviewed was a linotype operator.[70]

Chapter 24

5 OCTOBER 1924, THE RUNNING OF THE AJC DERBY, RANDWICK RACECOURSE, SYDNEY

Are big punters a help or a hindrance to honest racing? This question is just now in the minds of all well-wishers of the sport, for within the last few days we have seen very unfortunate happenings on the turf.

BANJO PATERSON, AS EDITOR OF THE NEWSPAPER ***SYDNEY SPORTSMAN***, WRITING ABOUT ONE OF HIS LIFELONG PASSIONS[1]

BANJO AND ALICE PATERSON left Egypt's Port Said on 1 April 1919 aboard the *Kildonian Castle*. After the ship docked at Woolloomooloo on the afternoon of 9 May, they were met by Grace, now fifteen, and Hugh, who was about to have his thirteenth birthday party. Grace was already in the A team for tennis in just her second year at the Ascham non-denominational private school in Edgecliff.[2]

Twenty-three years after he had spoken with Bernard Espinasse for *Table Talk* in his first major interview, Banjo spoke with another reporter from the newspaper – this time, though, the reporter was more interested in 'Mrs Banjo' and her nursing work.[3]

The Australian papers devoted much more ink to another passenger: Charles Bean, Banjo's one-time contributor, who would now begin the monumental task of publishing his meticulous accounts of the war, focusing as much on the experiences of individual soldiers as on the big themes of the conflict. Banjo had wished all along that he could trade places with the tall, austere bespectacled Bean and pen the big yarns, but instead he was now fifty-five and frustrated that he could not rekindle the spark that had burnt so brightly with 'Clancy' and 'Snowy River'.

He set up home once more in Sydney's eastern suburbs, where he would live out his days at a variety of addresses: first at a house called Rockwell on New South Head Road, Woollahra, then Edgecliff, and then at Redbank in Darling Point, before moving eventually to 19 South Street, Double Bay, where his phone number was 2877.

Banjo was back from the war only a day when he was out at Double Bay watching tennis. The sporting newspaper *Referee* reminded its readers that Banjo was once in the 'first flight of players', playing right- and left-handed 'alternately with equal skill'. As honorary treasurer of the Sydney Lawn Tennis Club, it said, 'he was a great worker for the game till he went on the land'.[4]

While Banjo was in Egypt, Angus & Robertson had published two of his books. There was a collection of short stories and sketches edited by A.W. Jose that included 'Concerning a Dog-fight', 'The Cast-iron Canvasser', 'His Masterpiece' and 'Done for the Double', along with 'Three Elephant Power', which provided the book's title.[5] A third volume of Banjo's ballads, *Saltbush Bill J.P. and Other Verses*,[6] appeared at the same time, but only because he kept his advance to a modest £150 by using earlier works for which he still owned the copyright. The quality of the ballads was uneven, as Robertson had needed a few fillers to stretch the book to 137 pages.

Among the forty-three works, Robertson had included some ballads from early in Banjo's career, such as 'Song of the Pen' and 'Mulligan's Mare', and some new critically acclaimed works, such as 'A Ballad of Ducks' and 'The Gundaroo Bullock'. There was also a more modest effort, 'A Singer of the Bush'. 'Waltzing Matilda' was given a start as well; although the Inglis Tea Company owned the rights to a new version, Robertson used Banjo's early version and had it polished by Jose.

Banjo was producing very little new poetry and not much to match the song of his pen when he'd ridden high as Australia's favourite writer. The two new books set no records.

He initially had high hopes for his novel *The Cook's Dog*, too, but then began to have doubts. Banjo wrote to Robertson to seek his opinion, half knowing what the answer would be. 'I am very dissatisfied with the thing; and am afraid I will have to do it over again to make it readable. The style is so stiff.'[7]

Robertson was even more critical. Three weeks later he wrote back to give Banjo the damning advice that he could 'rewrite it till hell's blue' and it still wouldn't pass muster: 'I am sure you will never make anything of the [manuscript] ... It has hardly a redeeming feature ... You lack the ability to construct a novel ... Your forte is verse – descriptive, humorous, pathetic. But just because it's your forte, you want to do something else.'[8]

CLAUDE MCKAY HAD JUST started a bold new magazine that was named *Smith's Weekly* after the man bankrolling it, Sydney's Lord Mayor Sir Joynton Smith.[9] Clyde Packer (father of Sir Frank and grandfather of Kerry) was manager. The magazine was an instant hit in much the same way as *The Bulletin* had been for Jules Archibald, *Smith's Weekly*'s new literary editor. It found a big audience by concentrating heavily on the exploits of the laconic Digger. Archibald commissioned Banjo and Henry Lawson to write some verses.

Banjo went off half-cocked, eulogising the great Australian airman Harry Hawker, who had disappeared in an attempt to be the first man to fly across the Atlantic. 'Hawker the Standard Bearer' appeared in *Smith's Weekly* on 24 May 1919 and included this final verse:

> Though Hawker perished, he overcame
> The risks of the storm and the sea,
> And his name shall be written in stars of flame,
> On the topmost walls of the Temple of Fame,
> For the rest of the world to see.

Hawker and his co-pilot Kenneth Mackenzie Grieve had actually survived and were plucked out of the ocean by a Danish freighter that had no radio. They finally made it to land, 'back from the dead', two days after the publication of Banjo's poetic obituary.

Lawson wrote 'The Township'[10] for *Smith's Weekly.* He was back in Sydney, under the care of his former landlady Mrs Byers. In 1916, they had set up house together in the bush town of Leeton when Henry accepted a government-funded position: it involved writing a few pieces to attract settlers to the fertile lands of the Murrumbidgee

Irrigation Area. He'd also hoped that a change of scene would change his fortunes. But although prohibition existed in Leeton, Lawson still frequented hotels in Narrandera and Whitton, where he renewed his old friendship with Jim Gordon who now went by the pseudonym Grahame. The job petered out in 1917, and Lawson went back to the big city and all its dangers.

Banjo predicted the tough life ahead for the returned servicemen in 'Gilded Brick, The Hard, Hard Road',[11] one of many features he wrote for the magazine. But Jules Archibald died in 1919, and Lawson and Banjo's involvement in the magazine dropped off too.

Banjo had other interests. In collaboration with Angus & Robertson, he had sold the film rights of 'The Man from Snowy River' for £100 to the director and producer Beau Smith,[12] who announced that he would use the film to try to break into the US market. He planned to shoot the movie there. Smith left for America in November 1919, but his plans went awry and he returned to Sydney in the middle of 1920. Shooting began almost immediately, west of Sydney around the Nepean River at Mulgoa,[13] Wallacia and Luddenham, where Smith invited horsemen from the local area to participate in a race day at the local showground for the cameras and to recreate the chase for the colt from old Regret.[14] Smith brought new characters into the story, including Saltbush Bill, Stingey Smith, and Jim and Kitty Carewe. One newspaper critic said the film was a 'convincing picture of Australian life … pure in its Australian sentiment, and a better dramatic story has never been put on the Australian screen'.[15] Banjo didn't think so – his most-remembered summary of the big event was 'What a pity they murdered the picture as they did.'[16]

Banjo assisted Robertson to bring out the first collected edition of his verse, which was published in 1921.[17] He then began pouring his energies into a new job, back as a newspaper editor for a ten-page weekly, the *Sydney Sportsman*, a publication owned by the heirs of the John Norton estate and eventually by Norton's disinherited son Ezra.[18] It billed itself as 'The Most Authoritative Sporting Newspaper in Australia'. John Norton,[19] a bullying, drunken domestic abuser, had started the *Sportsman* in 1900 during one of the most colourful careers of any Australian newspaperman. His ironically titled Sunday flagship, *Truth*, poked its nose at every possible authority figure, calling Queen Victoria a 'German woman who sits on the throne of England … flabby, fat, and flatulent'[20] and accusing Lord Dudley of 'libidinous lecheries and lascivious lapses'.[21]

Banjo eventually joined the board of Truth and Sportsman Ltd. He used the pages of the *Sportsman* to write a tribute to Archibald in January 1922[22] – not just to thank him for the support he had given him and Henry Lawson over the years, but also as a way of promoting the new Archibald Prize for portraiture, which Billy McInnes[23] had just collected along with a cheque for £400.[24]

Banjo stayed in the job for eight of the happiest years of his life. He headed trackside every chance he got. His son, Hugh, who was contemplating a career as an outback station manager, said Banjo was 'a tremendous racing enthusiast. He had a very good knowledge of breeding and of everything to do with racing and he was a very, very good judge of horses. He actually purchased yearlings for a lot of his friends. They would ask him to select yearlings for them at the yearling sales and with fairly cheap purchases he had quite a lot of success for some of his friends. They won quite a lot of races.'[25]

Banjo filled his newspaper pages with not just racing but also all the latest news and views from around Australia and the globe – on cricket, football, boxing, athletics, tennis and any other sport that could draw a reader. Early in his tenure he hired the Test cricketer and artist Arthur Mailey, a man with a similarly dry sense of humour, as a special correspondent.[26] In addition to editing the *Sportsman*, Banjo covered the races each week for *Truth*, heading to Randwick, Rosehill and Flemington, and setting the standard for coverage of the sport at a time of intense competition from rival sporting papers such as *The Referee*. He was able to move easily between all facets of the racing game, having been a champion amateur jockey himself, having ridden horses in the heat of battle, having tamed so many buckjumpers he couldn't keep count, and having mixed with lords, ladies and gentlemen. Banjo was still a formidable player on the tennis court, even well into his fifties; his daughter, Grace, at seventeen, received a mention in the papers for her promising form on court,[27] before going on to win the NSW schoolgirls championship in 1922.[28] The *Sydney Mail*, which had once run many of Banjo's poems, ran an action shot of Grace in full flight and said 'her play was much admired'.[29] She had been captain of the Ascham school's team since her third year of high school.

Banjo had rarely felt so alive.

HENRY LAWSON WAS DEAD. He died in his sleep on 2 September 1922 in the small Abbotsford cottage where he lived with Mrs Byers on Great North Road. The consequences of a hard life had caught up with him at last.

Two years earlier, Lawson had been stricken by ill health and the Commonwealth Literary Fund had granted him a £1-a-week pension. But the largesse did not last long. Lawson had stared at the bottom of a bottle and at the ceiling of a prison cell so many times that the final cerebral haemorrhage was just one more of life's cruel blows. He died destitute at fifty-five, his estate not much more than two suits, an overcoat, a tie, a collar-stud, a pipe, spectacles, a tin matchbox, a walking stick, a pencil and two packets of tobacco. Mrs Byers distributed most of his belongings among his close friends.

There were tributes from Prime Minister Billy Hughes, and at the end of a long obituary the *Sydney Morning Herald* remarked: 'To the end of his life Lawson was exceptionally shy among strangers and always oddly sensitive. In those earlier unfruitful days of poverty and repression – isolated and driven in upon himself by deafness, and out of tune with his environment – his shyness was almost a disease. He became embittered in mind, aloof, and sombre in bearing, retreating in habit. A widow and a son and daughter survive him. The son, Mr. James Lawson, is on the land, and Miss Lawson a graduate in arts at Sydney University, is one of the officials at the Public Library.'[30]

Later that day, thousands of Sydneysiders turned out to say goodbye to Lawson at a state funeral in St Andrew's Cathedral. Billy Hughes took a front pew surrounded by government ministers, both federal and state. When the casket was carried out to the waiting hearse, so dense was the crowd in George Street that it was some time before all the mourners could find their way to their carriages. Traffic was held up to allow the funeral to pass through Paddington and Bondi Junction as people lined both sides of the route to Waverley Cemetery overlooking the blue ocean.[31] Newspapers from around the country sent representatives.

Banjo always had a great regard for Lawson, but he did not attend the funeral. He told fellow journalist Vince Kelly[32] that he regretted ever calling his old rival 'the melancholy poet with a graveyard of his own'.[33] Bertha Lawson suggested that Sydney erect a statue of her late husband opposite the one of Robert Burns in the Domain; she pointed out that both poets 'wrote of the sufferings of the people'.[34]

A MONTH AFTER LAWSON'S FUNERAL, Banjo and Alice were among a crowd of eighty thousand at Randwick to see Rivoli win the AJC Derby. They dined at a luncheon party with the new governor's wife, Dame Margaret Anderson. The Melbourne *Argus* reported:

> … [the] passing of Lawson and the widespread demonstration of interest in him has naturally stimulated additional thought of the poets or writers of popular verse who are with us … It is hardly necessary to say that, of these none is better known or more widely appreciated than 'Banjo' Paterson whose books have had extraordinary sales for Australia, or, indeed, any other part of the world … Mr. Paterson wrote a novel that did not have much of a run, though it ought to be read by sport-loving Australians for, the description of buffalo-hunting in the Northern Territory. The title is *An Outback Marriage.* At this date it can presumably be had only at some of the libraries.[35]

Banjo remained a dignified presence at the track, either in the members' enclosure at Randwick or swapping yarns with the jockeys and strappers. Vince Kelly remembered him as being 'tranquil, slow in walk and movement, as unflurried in his conversation as he was quick in mind', with a down-to-earth 'bullock-driver's assessment' of men and situations, 'enlivened by a mischievous humour'.[36] Kelly would sometimes watch hurdle races with Banjo, and whenever a horse stumbled Banjo would murmur the title of one of his ballads from the Boer War: 'There's another blessed horse fell down!'[37]

He was at full gallop most of the time. He produced a column called 'General Turf Notes' and was always looking for an opportunity to entertain with his sardonic humour. He reported on the horse owner and king of rorts, James 'Grafter' Kingsley, and on 23 August 1923 was trackside at Rosehill to see Grafter's horse Dreblah win the Rosehill Handicap at long odds with a slashing run after suspiciously poor form in the lead up. In an article called 'A Ned Kelly System to Beat the Tote', he mocked rival paper the *Sun* for featuring the 'mathematical system of betting' being touted by a racecourse spruiker. Banjo wrote that 'it is a deplorable fact that in spite of our civilization, education and scientific knowledge, there are still hundreds of thousands of people who believe in fortune tellers, the divining rod, the rich uncle in Fiji, the philosopher's stone, perpetual motion and betting systems … Why should this inventor, who is making all this easy money, suddenly seek the limelight of newspaper publicity? Most people with a money-making invention of this sort in their exclusive possession would be dumb as oysters about it.'[38]

Banjo always wanted to be impartial as a reporter. In 1924, George Robertson asked him to write the foreword for an American book called *Piebald* about a wild horse, but Banjo did not want to be a 'recommendation for hire', replying: 'I will be sixty years old in a few days and I don't want to forfeit my self-respect by writing against my convictions and I know you would be the last man to ask me to do so.'[39]

BANJO ALSO USED THE PAGES of the *Sportsman* to feature some more of his amusing verses: 'That Half-Crown Sweep: A Tale of the Territory',[40] 'Jimmy Dooley's Army, A Political Ballad by Our Bolshevik Bard',[41] 'Typographical: A Ballad of Burdens'[42] and 'A Job for McGuinness'.[43] Many times, when Banjo had his own reports to file for *Truth*, he would work extra hours to help out if a fellow reporter was away sick or was in difficulties producing copy. He was held in great regard by others on staff: a jovial elder statesman of writing with a ready smile, especially for young reporters and copy boys who would buy second-hand copies of his poems and ask him to autograph them.[44]

Banjo kept his private life private, and Hugh Paterson remarked that 'he did not talk very much about himself'.[45] He was still a member of the Australian Club and played bridge there at all hours.[46]

His economic concerns were heightened after Black Tuesday, 24 October 1929, when share prices at the New York Stock Exchange fell through the floor, precipitating the Great Depression and years of financial hardship around the world. The next year, at the age of sixty-six, Banjo retired from day-to-day work; he handed in his notice at the *Sportsman* in 1930 in return for four months' salary. Given his family history of respiratory problems, he was glad to take it easy in the twilight of his life. His newspaper articles would now largely be confined to freelance work for the *Sydney Mail*.

Sales of his *Collected Verse* had exceeded twenty thousand, and Robertson tried to interest Banjo in writing a book with a similar theme to that of *The Sentimental Bloke* by C. J. Dennis, which was a roaring success. Robertson hoped for a novel that would tell the adventures of a bush battler, in contrast to Dennis's city larrikin. But when Robertson sent Banjo a cheque for £100 to encourage his interest, Banjo sent it back and told his publisher that he felt too flat to try.[47]

On 12 December 1931 Banjo's daughter, Grace married naval officer Lieutenant Kenneth Harvie from HMAS *Australia*. The wedding took place under the big trees in Dame Eadith Walker's Yaralla, one of Sydney's most magnificent gardens, the brilliant blue sky competing with the blue of the peaceful Parramatta River to create an ideally romantic setting. Dame Eadith gave Grace her bridal frock of ivory satin with a Limerick lace veil. Grace's proud mother, Alice, wore a gown of blue floral chiffon with a navy hat, and carried a posy of delphiniums. The Fairfaxes and Walkers were prominent among the friends and relatives, who watched the ceremony take place beneath a large bell-shaped canopy of roses that hung from a vast ancient Moreton Bay fig tree. Banjo was showing his age but he looked like the proudest man in Australia as he gave the beautiful bride away, his suntanned face creased with a smile of satisfaction.

NOW APPROACHING THE FINAL TURN towards the home straight of his life, Banjo was more eager than ever to share his knowledge of horses and horsemen with the Australian public. Following the victory of the mighty racehorse Phar Lap in the 1930 Melbourne Cup, the *Sydney Mail* asked Banjo to compare the 'Red Terror' with Carbine, Australia's great stayer of forty years earlier. Banjo outlined the thoughts of the late Harry MacKellar, one-time starter for the Australian Jockey Club:

> Carbine the greatest horse that Australia ever saw? It's only the old fellows that talk like that. They've got it on the young fellows because the young fellows never saw Carbine, so the old 'uns can bluff them into believing that Carbine had wings. Since I have been A.J.C. starter I have started at least ten better all-round horses than Carbine. Limerick and Eurythmic, for instance, would have beaten his head off, and up to a mile and a quarter he wouldn't have had Buckley's chance against Beauford, or Gloaming, or Amounis … No; all this Carbine worship is hot air. It's just a sign of old age.[48]

Phar Lap would achieve mythical status in Australian culture, just like the colt from old Regret – and the Man from Snowy River and Clancy, who both chased after him.

Banjo and his ballads had risen from an era when the horse was an integral part of Australian daily life as the chief mode of transport. He had started work as a solicitor in an age when the captains of industry and great legal minds still travelled to work in traps pulled by animals that were kept in livery stables in the city. Now the stables had made way for skyscrapers. Motor cars were clogging the great new bridge across Sydney Harbour. Australia was a very different place from the one that had nurtured Banjo's romantic view of bush life and its characters. But his stories about a fading way of life still resonated with the public – and he was about to start telling the stories again in a new way, through the most modern medium of communication then known: radio.

Chapter 25

JULY 1935, ELIZABETH BAY HOUSE, A GRAND COLONIAL MANSION, SYDNEY

He was terribly fond of Australia, naturally, but he did not make a very great parade of that. But you could sense it the whole time – that he loved Australia and he loved the bush of Australia, and anything to do with the Australian way of life.

HUGH PATERSON ON HIS FATHER'S ABIDING AFFECTION FOR ALL THINGS AUSTRALIAN.[1]

IT WAS ONCE THE FINEST home in Australia, built on an extravagant scale with a 'wilderness of rooms'.[2] But by 1935, Elizabeth Bay House, with its cedar fittings and the majestic staircase winding around a great oval hall, had been converted into studios for artists. They found the soft light and sublime outlook towards Sydney Harbour inspiring.

Banjo did too, as he sat inside a studio there transfixed by another great Australian: bush-bred and, also like Banjo, grey-haired, moustachioed, wiry and energetic. Sir John Longstaff flitted about, rarely standing still despite his advancing years, with paintbrush in hand and a gleam in his eye. Born just a few weeks after Banjo in the old mining town of Clunes outside Ballarat, Longstaff was among the finest artists of his era. He had set up a studio in Elizabeth House in pursuit of another Archibald Prize, having won four of them in the preceding decade. Banjo knew his work well. In decades past, had often gazed upon Longstaff's painting *Breaking the News* in Archibald's *Bulletin* office; it depicted, in sombre colours, a man visiting a humble worker's cottage to tell a poor housewife that her husband had been killed in a mining accident. Archibald had been so impressed with the pathos and realism that he commissioned Longstaff for a portrait of Henry Lawson that now hangs in the NSW Art Gallery. Now Banjo was the subject for the master, presenting an image of 'a modest, grizzled, tough-looking old man, not very ready to talk about himself'.[3]

Banjo's health had been failing. The sittings had been suspended while he had a short stay in hospital with heart trouble,[4] and he was always amused when he met an admirer surprised to discover that he was still alive. To those who knew him at the time, it seemed Banjo had very little sense of the place he had in his country's affections. Longstaff was well aware of it, though, and he had Banjo adopt the pose of a contented man from the landed gentry during a time of good seasons.

Longstaff told Paterson that he thought Australian landscape painters had great opportunities in the inland country. He suggested that the great Australian picture of the future might be painted far out on the Western Plains, something that endeared him to Banjo even more.

This portrait had been commissioned by the English writer and adventurer J. H. Curle,[5] a fan of Banjo's who had met him at the Australian Club. Curle was an expert on South African goldmines and had written several international bestsellers on his travels, during which he had been mightily impressed by the dash of a young American mining engineer he had met in Western Australia: the future President Herbert Hoover.

The portrait of Banjo was completed in October 1935.[6] Three months later, Longstaff had his fifth Archibald Prize and a winner's cheque for £430.[7] Banjo would use his experiences of sitting for the painter and of meeting Curle for a series of radio talks he was preparing for the three-year-old Australian Broadcasting Commission.

BY 1935, BANJO HAD BEEN WORKING in radio for four years, trying to parlay his popularity as a balladeer into a career behind the microphone. Staying in the job, though, was tougher than staying on a Barcoo buckjumper.

Back on 7 October 1931 he had prepared his first broadcast for a private entity, the Australian Broadcasting Company, run by a consortium headed by the theatrical producers J. C. Williamson Ltd and J & N Tait. The business sold programming to the Sydney radio stations 2FC[8] and 2BL,[9] which were operated by the Postmaster-General's Department. At the time Banjo was writing his weekly 'Turf' column for the *Sydney Mail* about the upcoming Melbourne Cup. On 7 October the newspaper reported that 'the original "Banjo" Paterson himself' would be heard on 2BL Sydney, 5CL Adelaide and 3LO Melbourne that night, and he would be 'reading many of his classics, "Clancy of the Overflow", "The Man from Snowy River", "Rio Grande's Last Race", etc.'.

A month later, Banjo recited 'In the Droving Days' and 'The Man from Snowy River'[10] on 2BL, and on 28 November he gave his recollections of Archibald for 2FC.[11] His drawl with all its Australian inflections was out of place among the plummy tones of 1930s broadcasters, but he pressed on.

On 25 March 1932, he sat down at the 2FC studio to give another talk on his war experiences, telling his audience around Australia about the extraordinary sense of duty shown by the doctors and nurses at the front. He said he had known highly paid Sydney dentists to leave their lucrative practices in order to work on soldiers day after day in a tent in the desert with the thermometer at 120 degrees Fahrenheit and a dust storm blowing. He recalled a foggy morning when the surgeon Dr Thomas Fiaschi was out looking for wounded men and walked right up to a Boer trench. 'The Boers gaped at him,' Banjo said, and Fiaschi commanded them, 'Come out of that trench, you men, and give me your rifles. You have no chance.' Banjo told his audience, 'They thought he had the whole British Army with him the way he talked and handed over their rifles and Dr Fiaschi brought the Boers in. Dr Fiaschi got a DSO for this – the first Australian to get the decoration at that time.'[12] In a letter to the *Sydney Morning Herald* two years later, Banjo wrote that Fiaschi and his handful of stretcher-bearers had 'bluffed' 209 armed Boers into surrendering in the belief that they were outnumbered.[13]

Banjo became a prolific letter writer too, on any crisis confronting the bush. He sent in missives to the *Sydney Morning Herald* on such topics as water conservation, wildlife protection, irrigation and land management.

In May 1932, Banjo told his radio audience about 'Australian Literature'[14] and 'Blackbirding in the South Seas'.[15] He remarked that it was time for the great Australian historical novel, and that there was plenty of material to draw upon with the explorers' diaries available and the collection of books put together by David Mitchell[16] in his Sydney library.[17] If Banjo had designs on writing that great novel, he was too busy with the turf and his happy family life to devote much time to the project. For his 'Blackbirding' talk he drew on letters he had received from his brother Hamilton forty years earlier.

Three days later he called on that correspondence again for 'Go West Young Man'[18] on 2BL, recalling his brother's days as a prospector on the West Australian goldfields, and his days as a budding travel writer when he reviewed a voyage on the Hawkesbury as 'Four Hours in Hell for Four Shillings'.[19] Banjo's son, Hugh, with the dark good looks and the aquiline nose of the Patersons, had a similarly adventurous spirit. He was embarking on the life that so many of the Bartons and Patersons had undertaken, working sheep and cattle on vast runs in New South Wales and Queensland.

Banjo finished his 2BL tenure on 7 June with 'In a Reminiscent Mood'.[20] For a series of six radio talks, he charged 5 guineas each.

LATE IN 1932 GEORGE ROBERTSON fell in the bathroom of his flat above the Castlereagh Street headquarters of Angus & Robertson, suffering a severe head injury. He never really recovered and died in Sydney on 27 August 1933.[21]

Banjo was now being courted by another publisher, who while more flamboyant than Robertson was far less reputable and less stable. 'Inky' Stephensen[22] was a young maverick from Maryborough, Queensland, who had joined the Communist Party – and then shocked his family, friends and especially himself when he won Queensland's Rhodes scholarship in 1924. In England, Inky befriended D. H. Lawrence and helped him produce a secret edition of *Lady Chatterley's Lover* to beat the British censors. Together with Norman Lindsay's son Jack, who provided the saucy illustrations, Inky published a series of underground books for private circulation in Britain. He arrived back in Australia in 1932 with a plan to start his own publishing house, Endeavour Press, financed by the Bulletin Newspaper Company. He met with Banjo and Norman Lindsay, and the result was a children's book, *The Animals That Noah Forgot*, based on poems and characters Banjo had created for his own children years earlier. Inky also published other Australian authors including Norman Lindsay, Miles Franklin, Eleanor Dark and Charles Chauvel, who recounted the story behind the filming of his movie *In the Wake of the Bounty* starring Errol Flynn.

Inky trumpeted Banjo's book with a blurb on the inside cover of its brown jacket: 'After a silence of many years, Australia's great national poet Banjo Patterson now issues another book of verses, dealing mainly with unique and lovable Australian animals.' Banjo wrote of the many and varied creatures of the Australian bush, and Lindsay drew them, each astonishing in its own way – from Baggy-beak the Pelican to Billy the Porcupine to Weary Willie the Wombat King:

> He digs his homestead underground,
> He's neither shrewd nor clever;
> For kangaroos can leap and bound
> But wombats dig forever.[23]

There are the emus, white cockatoos, army mules, bullocks, and the thousand ornery critters of 'The Billy-Goat Overland' and the uniquely Australian 'Old Man Platypus':

> Far from the trouble and toil of town
> Where the reed-beds sweep and shiver
> Look at a fragment of velvet brown –
> Old Man Platypus drifting down,
> Drifting along the river ...[24]

Inky, however, was beset with under-capitalisation and over-expectations. Banjo's verses were of mixed quality, and Endeavour Press suffered from uneven distribution. The book had a cover price of 2s 6d and sold three thousand copies in the first few months of publication,[25] making it the company's best performer – but it was still not a success. Inky admitted in his disappointing manager's report for the half-year that sales at that rate would barely pay the cost of printing. In 1935, Endeavour Press went down like the ship it was named after.

FROM AS FAR BACK AS THE BOER WAR, Banjo had kept notes on all the extraordinary characters he had met, with an eye to one day publishing the account of his travels. In 1901 he had written to George Robertson from London to say, 'I have kept very full diaries and think I can give you a rather amusing book of travel – something new in that line – will talk it over with you.'[26] Now, as Banjo found himself in the final chapter of his life, Norman Lindsay told him that while giving radio chats was fine, the words were not permanent and Banjo should get all his memories down on paper before it was too late. 'This stuff is too good to throw away in talk,' Lindsay told him. 'Why don't you write it?'[27]

Banjo sparked the interest of the new chairman at Angus & Robertson, the mild-mannered Walter Cousins, who would often sit in Hyde Park with authors discussing their work. Banjo preferred to discuss the details of his new book by mail – and he had some bright marketing ideas.

Prince Henry, the Duke of Gloucester, had agreed to open Melbourne's centenary celebrations, as well as dedicate John Monash's Shrine of Remembrance in October 1934 and Sydney's Anzac memorial in November. Banjo had known Prince Henry's uncle, the Duke of Teck, in South Africa during the Boer War, when the Duke was Director of Remounts, 'a carefree sportsman who knew quite a lot about horses, but was a bit casual as to details and organization'.[28] Banjo wanted to curry favour with the royals in the hope they might endorse his book in England. He added in a postscript, 'If I played up the Teck princes and called it "Princes and Potentates" we might get Royalty interested.'[29]

Thirteen days later, Banjo told Cousins he wanted to make the book 'as English as possible in hopes of catching an English sale'. He had some alternative titles in mind: *Famous Folk at Close Range*, *All Nurses Swear*, *Princes in Private*, *Princes and Privates*, *Notes on the Notables* and *From Prince to Puppet — I met 'em all.*

'Of these,' he wrote, 'I think *Happy Despatches* is the best.' Then, as an afterthought: 'How would *Strictly Private* go as a name?'[30]

On 14 March he added: 'How would this go for a title and subtitle – *GIANTS IN OUR DAY* or *GIANTS I HAVE MET* (and as a subtitle) *RACY RECOLLECTIONS OF WORLD FAMOUS PEOPLE*. Then we might add in quotation marks "Some were so big and some were so small; but it was every man for himself as the elephant said when he danced among the chickens."'[31]

Banjo had waited twenty years too long to write what became *Happy Dispatches*. By the time the book appeared in 1934 during the Great Depression, many of the principal characters were consigned to dulled memories and scant regard. Lord French, Kitchener, Haig, 'Chinese' Morrison, Glossop and Allenby were no longer household names, and Churchill had not yet risen to prominence as a saviour of the free world. The book was competing against a variety of lavishly illustrated works by world travellers – and it floundered on an uncertain foundation. Banjo would have most likely fared much better with an autobiography rather than vignettes of other people's stories. His weakening heart was almost broken by the disappointment.

BANJO STILL HAD MANY STORIES to tell, though, and he was mulling over a novel about a shearer's colt. There were still opportunities aplenty in radio, too. On 1 July 1932, the newly instituted Australian Broadcasting Commission had taken over the role of Australia's national broadcaster, and Banjo again saw a chance to monetise his memories. On 16 November 1934 at a luncheon in the city, he chatted with Major Walter Conder:[32] Gallipoli veteran, former Pentridge Gaol governor and now general manager of the ABC. Banjo wrote to Conder the next day:

> I meet all sorts of people from Field Marshals to buffalo shooters and I would like to try getting interviews with them and working in as much information as possible about their lives, the people they meet, and so on.[33]

Conder knew that Banjo's voice was not suited to the airwaves, and so with all manner of diplomacy he suggested 'there can be little doubt that matter which is put on the air as literary matter is more widely appreciated than even the best of "talks", lectures, addresses, interviews in person and all the other things which would naturally appear to be better suited for radio presentation … so what I should like you to consider would be to write us a series of these interviews and let us read them in the different States, not as "talks" by you but as your "literary" work. I trust that this idea will appeal to one who understands public psychology as well as you obviously do.'[34]

Banjo's hand was becoming shaky as he neared his seventy-first birthday, so he bought a typewriter with which he slowly tapped out a reply. The most famous writer in Australia was hardly one to pump himself up, telling Conder on 12 December 1934: 'This appeals to me very much, the only trouble being to write the stuff well enough. As an experiment I have written the enclosed matter, and would like you to consider it.'[35] Banjo sent in a script called 'Australian Local Colour', which referred to Australia's preference for overseas writers to books of 'local colour … by this I mean books descriptive of Australian life'. He gave brief critiques of Marcus Clarke, using 'local colour lavishly, daubing it on in great lumps',[36] and of Adam Lindsay Gordon. Whereas the English Romantic poet Percy Bysshe Shelley 'wrote the song of the skylark', Banjo ventured, 'our poets have written the wail of the curlew'.[37]

Conder's staff suggested some judicious publicity before the program ran, since it was suspected that most Australians thought Banjo was long dead. There was also a suggestion that *Happy Dispatches* could be read over the air, but Banjo wanted to wait until he had heard from his English publishers. In the event, listeners did not get to hear any of *Happy Dispatches* and the book did not receive the vital publicity that could have pushed sales.

The ABC decided on a series of fifteen talks by Banjo read by a different ABC announcer in each state. Banjo asked for twelve guineas per talk (£12 12s), figuring that each of the six states could throw in £2. But the ABC's Lancashire-born federal controller of talks, Charles Moses,[38] a former discus-thrower and Victorian amateur heavyweight boxing champion, blanched at the demand. He told Conder it was 'far too much to pay', and that he had heard that in the past Banjo had been willing to give radio talks for three guineas. Moses wanted Banjo to give the talks himself because he was such a 'well known personality'.[39] Conder still preferred the idea of someone reading Banjo's work but liked Moses's suggestion of offering Banjo five guineas per script.[40] Banjo managed to wangle a little more cash; Conder wrote to him on 3 April offering him £100 for fifteen talks to run on Sundays. The first broadcast went to air on 12 May 1935[41] and was titled 'Land of Adventures', in which Banjo outlined the great unfulfilled potential of the Northern Territory. The next week it was 'New Guinea Gold'[42] about the discovery of the precious metal there, and the engineering feats and airlift of machinery to exploit it. 'Old Letters'[43] followed, as Banjo related the adventures of his long-lost baby brother, first in journalism, then on the goldfields of the west, and then working boats in the South Seas and New Guinea. In June he related, over two weeks, the stories of his pioneering grandparents at Boree Nyrang and consulted the diary of his wife's relative Thomas Walker for anecdotes.

In subsequent talks he wrote about his experiences with the New Hebrides settlers in 1902 and of the great rowing events on the Parramatta River. In 'Bush Life', he wrote of beds with strips of green-hide in the place of springs, and the eerie loneliness of the Western Plains.

He wrote 'Pearl Fishing' and 'Sheep' and 'Thoroughbred Horses'. In 'An English View', he reported on the eugenics theories of J. H. Curle, who saw Australia as the perfect environment to create Caucasian supermen. He also wrote of some of the great athletes he had met, especially the cricketers old and new. He had been in a Sydney sports store once when a wiry little sunburnt kid from the bush came in and started looking over the wares on display. Banjo said to the salesman, 'That's a hard looking young fellow and he's very light on his feet. I should say he had done some boxing or was accustomed to riding rough horses.' The salesman laughed and told Banjo, 'that's Don Bradman, the new boy wonder cricketer they have just discovered'. The salesman brought the boy over, and Banjo and Bradman shook hands. The salesman told Banjo that the secret to Bradman's success was that he watched the ball to the very last moment before he hit it. His timing was so great, his eye so sharp and his movements so quick that he could hit the ball to the fence without any swing at all.[44]

On 18 August, Banjo recounted his recent experiences sitting for John Longstaff. The following week the series concluded with Banjo writing in 'News' of the great work done by 'Chinese' Morrison in his world-exclusive reports.

BANJO KEPT WRITING SMALL SCRIPTS and sketches, and he occasionally spoke at various clubs, but time was running out for him to write the great Australian novel. *Happy Dispatches* and *The Animals Noah Forgot* had both stalled on the shelves and the great writer was now on the wrong side of seventy-one.

Sarah Riley, the great love of his youth, had died aged seventy-two at a private hospital in Camberwell, Melbourne,[45] during the run of Banjo's radio talks. She had never married and had spent much of her life in Scotland and holidaying in Europe,[46] returning permanently to Melbourne only in 1930. In a household of elderly spinsters, she lived with her younger sister Annie and their friend Maud Rattray, organising charity events and, during the Great War, assisting the Red Cross from Annie's large farmhouse at Panton Hill, on Melbourne's north-eastern outskirts. Sarah was buried with her parents, James and Harriet Riley, in Geelong. Eight months later, Chris Macpherson – Sarah's friend and Banjo's collaborator on 'Waltzing Matilda' at Dagworth Station – died at seventy-one after living much of her life alone in South Yarra, Melbourne. She was buried at St Kilda Cemetery after a small private funeral,[47] and her grave remained unmarked until a headstone was placed there in 1994.

Banjo knew his race was just about run, too. He completed his novel *The Shearer's Colt*, but the mid-1930s was not the time for a horse novel from a bygone era.

Banjo had once been contemptuous of the success of the racing journalist turned author Nat Gould, parodying him as Knott Gold in his farce 'Done for the Double' while he was editing the *Evening News*. From 1905 he had been turning over the idea for a racing novel of his own, and now in the home straight of his life he had the time and still possessed the recall to do it.

The novel begins when a Breaker Morant-style rogue, Hilton Fitzroy, the son of a moneyed English family, gets into strife at Oxford and is sent down to Australia so his rough edges can be knocked off. He joins the Queensland Mounted Police and makes the mistake of arresting a shearer turned wealthy squatter, Fred Carstairs. The two become friends, though, and attend a race meeting at

Randwick where Fred is enthralled by a magnificent colt called Sensation, which he buys for the astonishing sum of ten thousand guineas. Sensation wins the A.J.C. St Leger, and Fred takes the great horse to England. On board the ship Fred meets the brassy, bawdy music hall star Lady Seawood, 'a peroxide blonde with the face of a Roman emperor'[48] who could have been Marie Lloyd in a different story. Sensation is entered in a Grand International Stakes, a race for the champions of four countries with 'the hoofs drumming on the turf'.[49] The huge crowd includes a gang of American criminals, members of the 'International League of Dopers' and an Aussie villain bent on revenge.

There is tension and turmoil and some wonderfully descriptive prose. But the book, competitively priced at six shillings, was decried by some critics as a Victorian melodrama forty years out of place.[50] The *Sydney Morning Herald* was kind to its former star correspondent, saying 'Nat Gould never wrote anything quite so good as this',[51] but the *Weekly Times* was more measured, saying while 'the author has a graphic pen, his characters in themselves will seem unreal to the modern reader'; '... undoubtedly many will find it a readable yarn, entertaining and breezy. To the critical, however, it is somewhat rambling and weak in construction and style.'[52]

The book was serialised weekly in Melbourne's *Australasian* newspaper, but sales were again disappointing. Banjo had never made a fortune from his writing and now he was making a pittance. He and his family were never likely to struggle, though, and in 1937 Alice inherited £10,000 from the estate of Dame Eadith Walker, which was sworn for probate at £265,340.[53]

Banjo's four-year-old granddaughter, Eadith Rosamund Harvie,[54] collected £3000, enough to buy ten new motor cars if she were old enough to drive. Two years later Grace presented Alice and Banjo with her second daughter, Phillipa Grace Harvie.[55] It was for his granddaughters that Banjo eventually wrote the stories of his own childhood in the bush, after four-year-old Rosamund asked him 'tell me about when you were a little boy'.[56] He called the evocative and compelling stories of his family's early days 'Illalong Children'.[57] Rosamund remembered him as a 'splendid grandfather' who was able to devote more time to his grandchildren than he had been able to give to his own children. He took great pleasure in reading to the little ones and jogging his own memories about his boyhood. For the last few years of Banjo's life, he and Alice lived next door to the Harvies, and he would play with and read to his grandchildren every day.

In late February 1938 Banjo and Alice took a holiday in Tasmania.[58] They stayed at the Bush Hotel in New Norfolk at Hobart and visited the hamlet of Ouse in the Central Highlands. At Hobart's Hutchins School, he spoke of 'what were in his opinion the best book, the best men, and the best woman he had known'. 'First among books came Thomas Carlyle's *Past and Present*, a difficult book, he said, but one that repaid all the trouble taken to master it. Among men, two whom he had known stood out – Lord Roberts, the hard-headed practical man of action, and Rudyard Kipling, the imaginative dreamer. Of women, Madame Curie he placed first. In her work associated with the discovery of radium, she had set an example of courageous endeavour.'[59]

As Banjo left the stage, the schoolboys stood to attention and gave a rousing rendition of 'Waltzing Matilda', by now long regarded as Australia's national song. Later that year Banjo penned 'Looking Backward' for the *Sydney Mail* and outlined the background of his best-known works, adding that he considered himself 'fortunate to have seen so much of the changes and developments in a new country'.[60]

A few days after that reminiscence appeared, Banjo became a Commander of the British Empire in the 1939 New Year's honours list, along with Jeannie Gunn,[61] who wrote *We of the Never Never*. Banjo was reluctant to talk about his honour, 'although the twinkle in his eye showed that he was appreciative'.[62] He told a reporter that he was now too old to write verse, but he found satisfaction that his verses were still selling steadily, decades after he had written them. 'By some Mr. Paterson has been referred to as the famous Australian poet, but he modestly says that what he wrote were merely "jingles", and that he wrote them just because it was in his blood.'[63]

His 'Looking Backward' article prompted far more detailed recollections, complete with assorted embellishments and errors, in a five-part series for the *Sydney Morning Herald* between 4 February and 4 March 1939. As he neared seventy-five, Banjo's memory was in worse shape than his failing heart; still, he could make words dance.

In his first piece, 'In the Days of the Gold Escorts', he told about his Scottish forebears and his time on Buckinbah and Illalong, his father's tribulations on the land, the bullockies and the bushrangers, and his first forays into the sport of kings at a bush race meeting.

At the time the articles appeared, Banjo was on holiday with Alice again, visiting Melbourne before arriving in Launceston on the *Taroona* on 11 February. There, he chatted for a long time with journalists about his love for racing, and how he had owned and raced some good ones but frustratingly never a real champion.[64] Banjo and Alice celebrated his seventy-fifth birthday in Hobart and then revisited the mountain village of Ouse where the *Mercury* newspaper photographed him fishing.[65]

Meanwhile, his series of recollections continued in the *Herald.* Part II, 'Giants of the Paddle, Pen and Pencil', recalled his days on the Parramatta River as a Sydney Grammar schoolboy, his early days as a lawyer and the grand time he had as one of the best polo players in New South Wales. He explained his early involvement with Archibald and Lawson. Part III covered the great Motor Reliability Trial and Banjo's time on Coodra, where he reckoned he lived as a 'hillbilly' recovering from 'some sort of nervous breakdown'.[66] He gave no insights into his work as the editor of the *Evening News* except to hint that it almost drove him mad. Part IV, 'An Execution and a Royal Pardon', related the stories of Breaker Morant and the old convict Edmund Galley, and Part V told of the political giants he had met – Henry Parkes and John Robertson, George Reid and Edmund Barton – and the statesman-like James Burns and his plan to colonise the New Hebrides.

Banjo's memory was called into question by Bertha Lawson, and his recall of the events surrounding Morant from almost forty years earlier was also awry. He wrote that Morant's lawyer J. F. Thomas had died years ago, and that Morant's crimes were committed by a man drunk with his one day of power; a man who had always seen himself as the underdog and who was 'now up in the stirrups. It went to his head like wine.' J. F. Thomas, though, was still very much alive, and Banjo had many details of the crimes jumbled up. The war historian and journalist Fred Cutlack, who claimed he had known Morant as a boy in South Australia and was fresh from editing *War Letters of General Monash*, wrote an angry letter to the *Herald* saying that while Morant had 'perhaps deceived some people, and left them angry', he was known 'in all the back country from Queensland to the Lower Murray, and great numbers of other people of careless habits – or even of some scrupulous rectitude – loved him despite his faults'.[67]

AUSTRALIA HAD MUCH MORE to worry about in 1939, though, than Breaker Morant's reputation. Germany invaded Czechoslovakia in March, and on 1 September Adolf Hitler ordered the invasion of Poland. Two nights later, at 9.15 p.m., the radios that had once delivered Banjo's recitations and reminiscences now delivered the melancholy message of Prime Minister Bob Menzies, who told the nation that as a consequence of Germany's aggression, Great Britain had declared war upon her 'and that as a result, Australia is also at war'. Banjo knew what that meant. He had seen men killed in South Africa, and he had seen them die in France and Egypt. *Smith's Weekly* declared that 'Waltzing Matilda' should be Australia's national marching song, as 'it is chanted in every hut in Australia, and is one of the most popular camp-fire songs'.[68] Banjo's son-in-law Kenneth Harvie, now a lieutenant commander, was recalled to active service in the navy.

By June 1940, the Germans had repeated their charge of the First World War, roaring through Belgium and into France. The British troops were evacuated from Dunkirk. 'Waltzing Matilda', though, was boosting the Australian troops and had become 'particularly popular at camp concerts'. London's largest firm of music publishers was turning out thousands of copies of the sheet music, with a cover that featured a photograph of the second AIF marching through Sydney.[69] Hugh Paterson, now thirty-three, returned to Sydney from Dunumbrel Station, which he had been happily running at Collarenebri in northern New South Wales. At Martin Place on 7 June 1940, Hugh signed on for the 20th Infantry Anti-Tank Company, and he would soon become one of the legendary Rats of Tobruk.[70]

Banjo tried writing a few more patriotic verses. 'The Dry Canteen' was published as sheet music on 26 March 1940. That September, as Hugh prepared to ship out for northern Africa,[71] Banjo wrote 'Song of Murray's Brigade' about soldiers thinking of home. But the work was unremarkable, as was a small piece for the *AIF News* on his time at Moascar.[72]

The 510-word article was being prepared for publication as Banjo sat in an armchair at the Denholm Private Hospital in Darling Point, not far from his home, on 5 February 1941. He had tried to remain energetic and enthusiastic right until this point, even though he was nearly seventy-seven and his heart had been giving him trouble for a long time. His arteries were thickening and he was having difficulty walking. His doctor had admitted him to the hospital in January for a rest. On 5 February, there had been heavy showers overnight and it rained for most of the day. Banjo sat in the hospital listening to the way the rain fell all around, thinking of the way it had fallen on the roof at Buckinbah and Illalong, and the way the farmers had cried out for it in the dry season and cursed it in the floods.

The newspapers that day were full of reports from the war. Australian troops in Singapore were gearing up on the off-chance the Japanese might attack, and Bob Menzies was planning a visit to Libya, where Hugh Paterson was stationed. Often, as his life grew more sedentary, Banjo had thought about how he'd still like one more chance to change places with Clancy, 'like to take a turn at droving where the seasons come and go' or chase the breakaways down by Kosciuszko's side where 'the air is clear as crystal, and the white stars fairly blaze'.

As Banjo sat in the hospital, waiting for Alice to collect him, with the rain falling and the clock ticking, the golden bowl of his mind was still brimful with beautiful memories of Australia. His eyes had dulled but they still had a perfect vision of the countryside he loved: the windows to the soul of his nation. As he sat there quietly waiting for his wife, Banjo closed those eyes and died.

THERE WAS NO STATE FUNERAL FOR HIM, no great fanfare. Australians much younger and with much more life ahead were dying every day in yet another sickening war. Banjo had never courted publicity and in death it remained so. A stranger – 'no relation' – gave the details of his life to the 'Registrar-General' and got most of them wrong, stating that Banjo had been born at Wellington and that he had only one child, Grace.[73]

His funeral the next day was a private affair: a Presbyterian service followed by cremation at the Northern Suburbs Crematorium in North Ryde. At the time of his death he had £221 17s 1d in the bank and liabilities of £46. He owned a block of land at Eden on the South Coast, valued at £26, and with some personal effects including jewellery, the total estate of the balladist who had sold more books than any Australian at the time came to £303 3s 1d.[74] His doctor certified the cause of death as syncope, myocardial degeneration and arteriosclerosis.[75]

One obituary writer said that Banjo 'was one of those fortunate men who, dying, are yet never dead, since the work they have done in life, the forces they have been instrumental in inspiring and releasing, continue after they have gone as part of the national life'.[76]

> With Henry Lawson, Paterson awoke a young people to the potentialities of native-born writers, whose nationality was evident in their manner and their viewpoint. There had been finer poets than either Lawson or Paterson, writers of prose fiction that, in the eyes of the literary critic, might excel the stories of either, but it was left to these men to capture the imagination of a continent. Each in his own style, they wrote of the life of the ordinary man … Banjo Paterson's ballads were passed from hand to hand when they appeared in the *Bulletin* and other journals; in book form, they sold in huge editions; they were recited around camp fires, in the shearing shed, and wherever bushmen and city men got together. Unconsciously, we have adopted them as part of our picture of ourselves …[77]

Epilogue

20 DECEMBER 1947, NARRAMBLA, JUST OUTSIDE ORANGE, NEW SOUTH WALES

I would fain go back to the old grey river,
To the old bush days when our hearts were light,
But, alas! those days they have fled forever,
They are like the swans that have swept from sight.
BANJO PATERSON, 'BLACK SWANS'[1]

NOT LONG AFTER BANJO'S DEATH, an Australian army official scratched out his name on the papers of his son, Hugh, and wrote in the name of a new 'next of kin': Alice Emily Paterson of 95 Byng St, Orange. Alice moved to a house not far from Banjo's birthplace, and it was just outside Orange, on the old Narrambla property, that she unveiled an obelisk to Australia's most famous writer in 1947. It was a simple ceremony beside the Ophir Road attended by a few hundred people.[2] The Templers' homestead was long gone but the crumbling Templer's Mill would remain a local attraction for another thirty years, until it was demolished as a safety hazard. Three years later, Alice travelled to Yass for the unveiling of a bust to her husband at the renamed Banjo Paterson Park.

Calls for a monument in Banjo's honour began the day after he died, though as the journalist Alec Chisholm immediately suggested in the Melbourne *Herald*, the work of the 'most recited rhymster in Australian history' would be an everlasting memorial.[3] *The Worker* said that Banjo's ballads and stories would live on as long as Australia lived.[4] There were calls to restore Banjo's childhood home at Illalong as a permanent monument, but what remained of the old place was falling apart – the house had been rundown even when Banjo lived there – and it eventually had to be demolished. A wisteria Rose planted remains as an outdoor shade area for the Grogan family, the current owners.

Banjo's writings were much more enduring than his old home. 'Waltzing Matilda' became a rallying cry for Australian servicemen and women in times of distress, when this country faced its great crises during the Second World War.

On 20 January 1942, in the last major battle of the Malayan campaign, Australian soldiers of the 2/29th Battalion were fighting near Parit Sulong along the Muar Road. Japanese soldiers with six heavy machine guns had pinned down 'C' Company of the 2/19th. With a platoon from the 2/29th, Lieutenant William Picken Carr led a forward attack through a swamp. Under orders to divert gunfire from their comrades who were being massacred, Carr's platoon was ordered to charge. It was an impossible task, but Carr and his men rose as one and rushed at the enemy, 'bayonets fixed, guns blazing'[5] while singing 'Waltzing Matilda' at the top of their voices. They, too, were mown down. Japanese soldiers would speak in awe of the Australians who had advanced on them singing an Australian song even though they knew they were facing certain death.[6]

Three days after that battle, a group of thirteen nurses and a planter's wife were taken prisoner by the Japanese in Rabaul. They were later loaded onto a truck and shipped out. They sang 'Waltzing Matilda' as they were carted away to what they expected would be certain death. Instead, they became slave labour, building roads, digging trenches and carting water. One of the nurses, Sister Jean McLellan of Weranga, near Dalby in Queensland, spent three and a half years as a prisoner of the Japanese. 'When we marched out in work we shouted "Waltzing Matilda",' she recalled on her arrival back in Australia. 'We remained cheerful. They were so nonplussed at our refusal to be licked that we were let off lightly.'[7]

'Waltzing Matilda' was played at the 1952 Olympic Games in Helsinki when Australian champions such as Shirley Strickland and Marjorie Jackson stepped onto the dais to take gold, and it was played at the closing ceremony of the 1956 Olympics. The victorious sailors aboard *Australia II* sang it after winning the America's Cup yacht race in 1983. Slim Dusty sang it at the finale of the closing ceremony of the 2000 Olympics, nineteen years after astronauts Bob Crippen and John Young played Slim's rendition of Banjo's song from the space shuttle *Columbia* as it passed over Australia.

In 1974, 'Waltzing Matilda' finished second to 'Advance Australia Fair' in a poll to choose a new national anthem – not bad for a song about a suicidal hobo who steals a sheep.

In 1968, Banjo's portrait was used for a five-cent stamp. In 2014, 'Clancy', 'Mulga Bill', 'Waltzing Matilda' and 'Snowy River' were the subjects for a series of four seventy-cent stamps. In 1993, Banjo's portrait, as well as images and words from 'Snowy River', were used on the new polymer $10 banknote; Banjo usurped Henry Lawson, who had graced the paper note for twenty-seven years.

HUGH PATERSON WAS COMMISSIONED as a lieutenant in 1943 and married Rhona White the next year. While fighting in Tobruk, Hugh penned at least two poems that had his father's verve in the verses. In August 1941, Australian newspapers printed 'This Place They Call Tobruk':

> There's a place that I've been in
> I didn't like too well,
> New England's far too blooming cold,
> And Winton's hot as Hell;
> The Walgett beer is always warm,
> In each there's something crook;
> But each and all are 'perfect' to
> This place they call Tobruk.[8]

In November there was 'The Stately Homes of Tobruk':

> The dugout of a private
> Is unlike all of these;
> It's like a wombat burrow
> He enters on his knees;
> Wherein with drawn bayonet
> He braves the rats and fleas.[9]

Back in Australia after war's end, Hugh and Rhona ran the 35,000-hectare Collymongle Station in northern New South Wales for twenty-five years. They retired to a flat in Ocean Street, Woollahra, not far from where Hugh was born. Hugh died in 1977. His sister, Grace Harvie, died at Rose Bay six years later, leaving her daughters Rosamund Campbell and Phillipa Harvie to preserve Banjo's memory in two volumes of his collected works, *Singer in the Bush* and *Song of the Pen*, released in 1983.

In the years since there has been the establishment of the Banjo Paterson Museum at Yeoval, just down the road from Buckinbah, the opening of the Waltzing Matilda Centre in Winton, and the release of the 1982 hit motion picture *The Man from Snowy River* and the arena spectacular that followed.

Of course, Banjo's legacy is not so much in the physical monuments and performances that honour him, but in the enduring words and evocative images that promoted a love for the heart of Australia, its land, rivers and mountains, and the mateship of his country.

Perhaps nothing illustrates the power of his words better than what happened at 4.10 on the morning of 14 May 1943, just before dawn, off Queensland's Moreton Island.

The Australian Hospital Ship *Centaur* was ablaze with lights that shone brightly on the vivid Red Cross markings along its white hull as it headed north along the coast. Then two Japanese torpedoes blew holes in its side.

Thirty-year-old nursing sister Lieutenant Ellen Savage, from Quirindi, New South Wales,[10] was asleep in her bunk when the 96-metre, 3200-tonne vessel began to fold in around her. Sister Savage was sucked down into a whirlpool of thrashing wood and metal. Her ribs, nose and palate were broken, her eardrums perforated. Bruised all over, she surfaced in the middle of an oil slick and somehow found her way to a raft. She was the only one of twelve nurses to survive. A lump of wood had hit her friend Merle Morton in the head and killed her.

As the *Centaur* sank like a stone, Seaman Matty Morris found himself alone in the cold, dark water, his eyes full of salt and oil. He struggled aboard a small raft and then spotted his mate Bobbie Teenie, and hauled him aboard. In their loneliness and fear they hugged each other even as the raft started sinking.[11]

Light began to shine over the horizon, and they spotted a bigger raft in the distance. Sister Savage was already on board.

Over the next thirty-four hours, the other survivors all made their way to the bigger raft as bull sharks circled. Matty Morris encouraged everyone not to give in to fear. All morning, he led them in vigorous renditions of 'Waltzing Matilda'.

Morris was pressed against badly burnt Private Jack Walder from Orange, NSW, the place of Banjo's birth. Jack remained silent. He died and his burnt flesh stuck to Morris's arm. Morris took Jack's identification disc off him and gave it to Sister Savage. She said the Rosary, and Morris answered it, and they buried Jack at sea.

As the survivors continued to sing Banjo Paterson's homage to the little Aussie battler, an Avro Anson was flying patrol at about three hundred metres off the Queensland coast, doing an anti-submarine sweep with no idea the *Centaur* had been hit. It was to be the last patrol for days.

In the distance the crew saw a discolouration in the water well to the south, and turned back for a look. They caught sight of a raft and people in the water, and a white sign with one word painted in black: *Centaur.*

Of the 322 on board the *Centaur*, only sixty-four survived.[12] Banjo's 'Waltzing Matilda' had kept their spirits afloat.

Acknowledgements

Sometimes, as Banjo Paterson's great-grandson looks out from the veranda of his bush property at Young, New South Wales, he reflects on the life of Australia's favourite poet and the country he wrote about.

Alistair Caird Campbell heard the stories his mother Rosamund told about Banjo and how her questions encouraged him to write down his earliest recollections of life in the bush for his grandchildren.

Rosamund remembered Banjo as a kind and loving grandpa.

Australia now remembers him as a national voice, a man who created characters and stories that remain part of our national identity more than 150 years after Banjo's birth.

Every time a new baby is named Banjo or Clancy or Matilda, Paterson's work lives on just as it does every time 'Waltzing Matilda' is sung, every time the excitement of 'The Man from Snowy River' is recalled and every time 'Clancy of the Overflow' stirs the passion for a free life in the bush under the wond'rous glory of the everlasting stars.

Banjo had many great passions in life. Foremost was his family but close behind was the great outdoors – rowing at Balmain, playing tennis on the Sydney Cricket Ground, riding at Rosehill and Randwick and helping to run the Kiandra Snow Shoe Club as its vice-president.

As a writer, he met so many important historical figures of his time and was on hand for many of the monumental events around Australia's formation.

It was a privilege to write Banjo's biography and there were many people who helped me.

Thanks to Alistair, who by coincidence has a property on Henry Lawson Way at Young, for his valuable insights and his family photos of Banjo. Thanks, also, to Orange historian Elizabeth Griffin, whose father Thomas Leslie Griffin drove Banjo and J.M. Arnott on many excursions through the bush before helping to form the electrical firm O'Donnell Griffin.

A big thank you also to Alf and Sharon Cantrell for their hospitality and fascinating tour of their superb Banjo Paterson Museum, at Yeoval, NSW, not far from Banjo's childhood home.

Thanks to the great journalist Mike Colman for his information about his distant relatives the Patersons and their Scottish background, and thank you to my editors Kevin McDonald and Kate Goldsworthy for shaping my words.

I am also indebted to the state libraries of New South Wales, Queensland and Victoria.

A book of this size and scope is not possible without enormous support from my publishers and the team at HarperCollins/ABC Books: Jude McGee, Lachlan McLaine, Brigitta Doyle, Matt Howard, Georgia Williams and Nicolette Houben.

Thanks so much for the honour of writing the story of Banjo's life.

Bibliography

Debra Adelaide (ed), *A Bright and Fiery Troop: Australian Women Writers of the Nineteenth Century*, Penguin, 1988.

Robert D Barton, *Reminiscences of an Australian Pioneer*, Tyrrell's Limited, 1917.

Thomas Carlyle, *The Life of John Sterling* (Second Edition), Chapman & Hall, 1852.

Marcus Clarke, For the Term of *His Natural Life,* George Robertson, 1874.

Edmund Clingan, *Century of Revolution: A World History, 1770–1870,* iUniverse, 2013.

J. H. L. Cumpston, *Thomas Mitchell, Surveyor General and Explorer*, Oxford University Press, 1955.

Arthur Davey, *Breaker Morant and the Bushveldt Carbineers*, Van Riebeeck Society, 1987.

Kerrie Davies, *A Wife's Heart: The Untold Story of Bertha and Henry Lawson*, University of Queensland Press, 2017.

William Eastmead, *Historia rievallensis: containing the history of Kirby Moorside, and an account of the most important places in its vicinity*, R. Peat, Thirsk, 1824,

Encyclopaedia Britannica, Eleventh Edition, University Press, Cambridge, 1911.

C. Brad Faught, *Gordon: Victorian Hero*, Potomac Books, 2008.

Andrew Forrester, *The Man Who Saw the Future*, Thomson/Texere, 2004.

Sir Philip Francis, *The Francis Letters, Volume 2*, E.P. Dutton and Co., 1901.

Jennifer Gall, *Looking for Rose Paterson*, National Library of Australia, 2017.

John Blackwood Greenshields, *Annals of the Parish of Lesmahagow*, Caledonian Press, 1864.

John Hood, *Australia and the East: Being a Journal Narrative of a Voyage to New South Wales in an Emigrant Ship*, John Murray, 1843.

Arthur Wilberforce Jose, *The Romantic Nineties*, Angus & Robertson, 1933.

Henry Lawson, *A Camp-fire Yarn: Henry Lawson Complete Works 1885–1900,* Lansdowne, 1984.

Henry Lawson, *Henry Lawson: Collected Verse: Vol. I 1885–1900*, Angus & Robertson, 1967.

Henry Lawson, *In the Days When the World was Wide and Other Verses*, Angus & Robertson, 1896.

Henry Lawson, *While the Billy Boils*, Angus & Robertson, 1896.

Henry Lawson, Colin Roderick (ed), *Collected Prose: Autobiographical and other writings, 1887–1922*, Angus & Robertson, 1922.

Norman Lindsay, *Bohemians of the Bulletin*, Angus & Robertson, 1965.

Jeremy Long, *Strugglers and Settlers: Darvall Family Letters (1839–1849),* Evolve Studios, 2005.

Kenneth Mackay, *The Yellow Wave: A Romance of the Asiatic Invasion Of Australia,* Bentley, 1895.

Richard Magoffin, *Waltzing Matilda, Song of Australia*, Mimosa Press, 1983.

A. L. May, *Sydney Rows: A Centennial History of the Sydney Rowing Club*, Sydney Rowing Club, 1970.

Godfrey Charles Mundy, *Our Antipodes*, Richard Bentley, 1857.

Dennis O'Keeffe, *Waltzing Matilda: The Secret History of Australia's Favourite Song*, Allen & Unwin, 2012.

Vance Palmer, *The Legend of the Nineties*, Melbourne University Press, 1954.

Geoffrey Partington, *The Australian Nation: It's British and Irish roots,* Australian Scholarly Publishing, 1994.

A. B. Paterson, *The Animals Noah Forgot* (Illustrated by Norman Lindsay), The Endeavour Press, 1933.

A. B. Paterson, *Happy Dispatches*, Angus & Robertson, 1934.

A. B. Paterson, *Rio Grande's Last Race and Other Verses*, Angus & Robertson, 1902.

A. B. Paterson, *Singer of the Bush*, Lansdowne Press, 1983.

A. B. Paterson, *Song of the Pen*, Lansdowne Press, 1983.

A. B. Paterson, *The Man from Snowy River and Other Verses*, Angus & Robertson, 1896.

A. B. Paterson, *Three Elephant Power and Other Stories*, Angus & Robertson, Sydney, 1917.

James Perry, *Arrogant Armies: Great Military Disasters and the Generals Behind Them,* Edison: Castle Books, 2005.

Roland Perry, *Monash and Chauvel*, Allen & Unwin, 2017.

John Prebble, *The Darien Disaster: A Scots Colony in the New World, 1698–1700,* Holt, Rinehart and Winston, 1969.

Denton Prout, *Henry Lawson: The Grey Dreamer*, Rigby, 1963.

Joseph Wilson Raven, *Reminiscences of a Western Queensland Pioneer*, Mitchell Library, State Library of New South Wales, collected 1909 (unpublished)

W. F. Refshauge, *Searching for The Man from Snowy River*, Arcadia, 2012.

Colin Roderick, *Banjo Paterson: Poet by Accident*, Allen & Unwin, 1993.

Colin Roderick, *Rose Paterson's Illalong Letters, 1873–1888*, Kangaroo Press, 2000.

Jill Roe, *Stella Miles Franklin: A Biography,* HarperCollins Australia, 2010.

Costa Rolfe, *Winners of the Melbourne Cup: Stories that Stopped a Nation*, Red Dog Books, 2009.

Kermit Roosevelt, *War in the Garden of Eden*, Charles Scribner's Sons, 1919.

Clement Semmler, *The Banjo of the Bush* (Second Edition), University of Queensland Press, 1974.

Paul Terry, *Banjo*, Allen & Unwin, 2014.

Robert Trow-Smith, *A History of British Livestock Husbandry, 1700–1900*, Routledge, 2013.

John Winckworth, *A popular treatise on the teeth and gums and diseases attendant on them*, Renshaw and Rush, 1831.

George Witton, *Scapegoats of the Empire*, Angus & Robertson, 1907.

INTERNET RESOURCES

adb.anu.edu.au
adc.library.usyd.edu.au/data-2/barstra.pdf
aiatsis.gov.au
alldownunder.com
ancestry.com.au
angloboerwar.com
angusrobertson.com.au
anzacportal.dva.gov.au/multimedia/publications/sinking-centaur/survivors
aogu.ascham.nsw.edu.au
australiangeographic.com.au
austlit.edu.au
barton101.com
bartondatabase.com
bdm.nsw.gov.au
bdm.vic.gov.au
budbloom.blogspot.com.au/2006/09/top-20-greatest-banjo-paterson-poems.
centralnswmuseums.orangemuseum.com.au
dictionaryofsydney.org/entry/west_ryde
familypedia.wikia.com
folklore-network.folkaustralia.com
grapevine.com.au
griffithreview.com
gutenberg.net.au
heritageaustralia.com.au
independentaustralia.net
lieutpjhandcock.com
nationalanzaccentre.com.au
navy.gov.au
nla.gov.au
nma.gov.au
northpinebushpoets.com
oa.anu.edu.au/obituary/barton-charles-hampden-1162
orange-nsw.com/BanjoPatterson.html

parliament.nsw.gov.au
pioneerwomen.com.au/collection/herstory-archive/darvall
pittwateronlinenews
poetrylibrary.edu.au/poets/barton-emily-mary
rowinghistory-aus.info
stpauls.edu.au
sydgram.nsw.edu.au
trove.nla.gov.au
tolarnostation.com.au
tumuthistory.com
wallisandmatilda.com.au
waltzingmatilda.com.au
westerndistrictfamilies.com

Endnotes

Prologue

1 A. B. Paterson, 'Clancy of the Overflow', first published in *The Bulletin*, 21 December 1889, p. 17. Under the tagline 'Banjo'.
2 A. B. Paterson, *Song of the Pen*, Lansdowne Press, 1983, p. 563. Originally from a wireless talk, 'Singers Among Savages', for the ABC.
3 In metric: height 179 centimetres, weight seventy-five kilograms, chest ninety-five centimetres.
4 'The Transports', *Sydney Morning Herald*, 8 December 1914, p. 8.
5 A. B. Paterson, 'Clancy of the Overflow', first published in *The Bulletin*, 21 December 1889, p. 17. Under the tagline 'Banjo'.
6 'An Australian Poet: "The Banjo" Interviewed', *Table Talk* (Melbourne), 31 January 1896, p. 6.
7 A. B. Paterson, 'Clancy of the Overflow', first published in *The Bulletin*, 21 December 1889, p. 17. Under the tagline 'Banjo'.
8 'Waltzing Matilda', written by Banjo Paterson and Christina Macpherson in 1895, first published by James Inglis & Co. Ltd, with an advertisement for Billy Tea on the back cover, 1903.
9 In 1981, astronauts Bob Crippen and John Young played Slim Dusty's rendition of 'Waltzing Matilda' from the space shuttle *Columbia* as it passed over Australia.
10 Timothy Hall, *New Guinea 1942–44*, Routledge, p. 172.
11 'Defence Forces: More Troops to be Mobilised', *Sydney Morning Herald*, 6 August 1914, p. 8.
12 Sir Ernest Daryl Lindsay, born 31 December 1889, Creswick, Victoria; died 25 December 1976, Mornington, Victoria.

Chapter 1

1 A. B. Paterson, *Singer of the Bush*, Lansdowne Press, 1983, p. ix.
2 Emily Mary Barton (nee Darvall) born 12 November 1817, York, England; died 24 August 1909, at her home, Rockend, in Gladesville, Sydney.
3 Rose Paterson to Nora Murray-Prior, March–April 1882, National Library of Australia, MS 9423.
4 'Shipping Intelligence: Arrivals', *Sydney Gazette and New South Wales Advertiser*, 9 January 1840, p. 2.
5 Built in India in 1818 and weighing 650 tons.
6 January 7 1840, *Alfred*, from New South Wales Government *Inward passenger lists*. Series 13278, Reels 399–560, 2001–2122, 2751. State Records Authority of New South Wales, Kingswood, New South Wales.
7 Emily Mary Barton, *Straws on the Stream*, W. E. Smith, 1910, preface.
8 Robert Johnston (sometimes reported as Johnstone) Barton, born 30 June 1809, died 4 October 1863 at the Australian Club, Sydney.
9 From Emily Mary Darvall at Roseneath Cottage, Parramatta to Miss Bessy Francis, Regent's Park, London, 14 June 1840, reprinted in Jeremy Long, *Strugglers and Settlers: Darvall Family Letters (1839–1849)*, Evolve Studios, 2005, p. 125.
10 *Diary of Miss Emily Darvall: Kept during the voyage of the 'Alfred' from England to Australia in 1839/1840*, Friday, 25 October 1839. From State Library of New South Wales. M A920.7/ B293.2/ 1.

11 John Thomas Edward Flint, born 21 May 1786 in Scotland, died 9 February 1855 at Douglas, Isle of Man.
12 *Diary of Miss Emily Darvall: Kept during the voyage of the 'Alfred' from England to Australia in 1839/1840*, Friday, 25 October 1839.
13 'To J. T. E. Flint, Esq, H. C. S, Commander of the ship Alfred', *Sydney Gazette and New South Wales Advertiser*, 27 January 1838, p. 3.
14 *Diary of Miss Emily Darvall: Kept during the voyage of the 'Alfred' from England to Australia in 1839/1840*, Friday, 25 October 1839.
15 Born 10 May 1775 Masulipatam, India; died 16 May 1869 at his home, Ryedale, in Ryde, Sydney.
16 localhistories.org. Some estimates of the time put life expectancy for men in the 1830s at just thirty-seven years.
17 'The Population of Sydney', *Sydney Morning Herald*, 8 May 1841, p. 2. The population was listed as 29,973.
18 'Town and Country', *Sydney Mail*, 22 May 1869, p. 5.
19 Edmund Clingan, *Century of Revolution: A World History, 1770–1870*, iUniverse, 2013, p. 152.
20 Sir Philip Francis, *The Francis Letters, Volume 2*, E.P. Dutton and Co., 1901, p. 613.
21 Emily Godschall Johnson, born 2 November 1788 in Bloomsbury, England; married 26 June 1805, St Martin in the Fields, Westminster; died 12 May 1841 in Sydney.
22 Seven survived infancy.
23 William Eastmead, *Historia rievallensis: containing the history of Kirby Moorside, and an account of the most important places in its vicinity*, R. Peat, Thirsk, 1824, p. 182.
24 On 3 December 1817.
25 Sir John Bayley Darvall, born 19 November 1809 at Felixkirk, Yorkshire; died 28 December 1883 in London.
26 On board were Emily's sisters Eliza and Rose and brothers Frederick and Horace.
27 Charles Barton, born 20 April 1760 in Dublin; died 11 June 1819.
28 Thomas Carlyle, John Sterling, *The Life of John Sterling* (second edition), Chapman & Hall, 1852, p. 83.
29 Robert D. Barton, *Reminiscences of an Australian Pioneer*, Tyrrell's Limited, 1917, p. 1.
30 He first set sail in February 1825 on the ship *Kellie Castle* to Bombay and China, later serving as an officer on similar voyages on the *Bridgewater* and *Lowther Castle*.
31 barton101.com.
32 Dated 1839, it was published posthumously in 1910.
33 *Diary of Miss Emily Darvall: Kept during the voyage of the 'Alfred' from England to Australia in 1839/1840*, 19 September 1839.
34 *Ibid.*, 8 October 1839.
35 Frederick Orme Darvall, born 27 February 1816 in Saint Michael-Le-Belfry, York; died 10 September 1886. He was Auditor-General of Queensland 1860–77.
36 Rosamond Mary Darvall, born 1822 in England; died 1909 in Christchurch, New Zealand. Married Arthur Templer in 1844 at Hunters Hill, Sydney.
37 *Diary of Miss Emily Darvall: Kept during the voyage of the 'Alfred' from England to Australia in 1839/1840*, 15 October 1839.
38 *Ibid.*, 20 October.
39 *Ibid.*
40 'Wellington District', *Sydney Morning Herald*, 30 September 1848, p. 2. (Sixty thousand acres.)
41 A new thirty-room homestead built by the Bartons' in-laws, the Katers, is now on the property at 154 Peabody Road, Molong.
42 'Family Notices', *Sydney Monitor and Commercial Advertiser*, 19 May 1841, p. 3.
43 Emily's inheritance was later used to buy out her father's share, and eventually Fred Darvall sold his third.
44 William Grant Broughton (1788–1853).
45 'Family Notices', *Colonist* (Sydney), 1 August 1840, p. 3. The wedding took place on 30 July 1840.
46 A. B. Paterson, *Song of the Pen*, Lansdowne Press, 1983, p. 549. Originally a wireless talk 'Pioneers and Places' for the ABC.

47 Henry Herman Kater (born 1813, England, died 28 June 1881, at Canterbury, Sydney). He bought the property Bungarribee near Blacktown but after eighteen months faced bankruptcy and had to sell his stock. He moved his family to Caleula, near Orange, started a flour mill and then a woollen mill and made enough money to retire to Sydney. He and Eliza (born 1820 in London, died 12 October 1909 in Burwood, Sydney) are buried together at the St Thomas' Anglican Cemetery, Enfield, along with their daughter Alice, wife of Banjo Paterson's first boss in a Sydney legal office.

48 'Domestic Intelligence', *Sydney Gazette and New South Wales Advertiser*, 9 February 1841, p. 2.

49 A. B. Paterson, *Song of the Pen*, Lansdowne Press, 1983, p. 527. From wireless talk 'The Northern Territory'.

50 J. E. Paterson, 'Pioneers of the South, Memories of the Yass District', *Sydney Mail*, 23 February 1921, p. 17.

51 Emily Barton at Boree Nyrang to Bessy Francis, 30 September 1840, Papers of the Murray-Prior Family, 1810–1945, National Library of Australia, MS 7801. Reprinted in Jeremy Long, *Strugglers and Settlers: Darvall Family Letters (1839–1849),* Evolve Studios, 2005, p. 150.

52 Emily Barton at Boree Nyrang to Bessy Francis, 1 January 1841, Papers of the Murray-Prior Family, 1810–1945, National Library of Australia, MS 7801. Reprinted in Jeremy Long, *Strugglers and Settlers: Darvall Family Letters (1839–1849)*, Evolve Studios, 2005, p. 181.

53 'Family Notices', *Sydney Morning Herald*, 18 May 1841, p. 3.

54 Emily Barton at Boree Nyrang to Bessy Francis at Albury Heath, Albury, Guildford, 12–21 May 1842, Papers of the Murray-Prior Family, 1810–1945, National Library of Australia, MS 7801, Box 6, Folder 22/45.

55 Emily Barton at Boree Nyrang to Bessy Francis at Hurley House, Hurley, near Marlow, 26 January 1845, Papers of the Murray-Prior Family, 1810–1945, National Library of Australia, MS 7801, Box 6, Folder 22/53.

56 Jane McCullough (1825–1899).

57 'Death of Mrs Darvall', *Queensland Times, Ipswich Herald and General Advertiser*, 4 May 1899, p. 4.

58 Emily Susanna Barton, born 2 June 1841, Hunters Hill, Sydney, died 29 March 1917, Drummoyne, Sydney.

59 Emily Barton at Boree Nyrang to Bessy Francis, 30 September 1840, Papers of the Murray-Prior Family, 1810–1945, National Library of Australia, MS 7801. Reprinted in Jeremy Long, *Strugglers and Settlers: Darvall Family Letters (1839–1849)*, Evolve Studios, 2005, p. 154.

60 barton101.com.

61 Emily Barton at Boree Nyrang to Catherine (Catey) Francis at Hampstead, 18 April 1842, Papers of the Murray-Prior Family, 1810–1945, National Library of Australia, MS 7801, Box 6, Folder 22/44.

62 Emily Barton at Boree Nyrang to Bessie Francis at Albury Heath, in Albury, Guildford, 12–21 May 1842, Papers of the Murray-Prior Family, 1810–1945, National Library of Australia, MS 7801, Box 6, Folder 22/45.

63 Robert D. Barton, *Reminiscences of an Australian Pioneer*, Tyrrell's Limited, 1917, p. 1.

64 *Ibid.*, p. 5.

65 *Ibid.*

66 George Essex Evans, born 18 June 1863 in London; died 10 November 1909 in Toowoomba.

67 First published *Argus*, 7 September 1901, p. 4.

68 John Hood, *Australia and the East: Being a Journal Narrative of a Voyage to New South Wales in an Emigrant Ship*, John Murray, 1843, p. 150.

69 *Ibid.*, p. 150.

70 *Ibid.*

71 *Ibid.*, p. 226.

72 *Ibid.*, p. 231.

73 *Ibid.*, p. 151.

74 He said he was born in 1842, but the record shows it was 16 April 1843 at Boree Nyrang. He died on 16 August 1924 in Roseville, Sydney.

75 Robert D. Barton, Reminiscences of an Australian Pioneer, Tyrrell's Limited, 1917, p. 5.

76 *Ibid.*, p. 51.

77 Emily Susanna Barton (1841–1917); Robert Darvall Barton (1843–1924); Mary Eliza Barton (1844–1845); Rose Isabella Barton (1844–1893); Nora Clarina Barton (1846–1931); Charles Hampden Barton (1848–1912); Edward Hugh Barton (1850–1891); Georgina Lucy Barton (1852–1936); Henry Francis 'Frank' Barton (1853–1902); Arthur Stirling Barton (1856–1916).
78 Robert D. Barton, Reminiscences of an Australian Pioneer, Tyrrell's Limited, 1917, p. vii.
79 Emily Mary Barton, *Straws on the Stream*, W. E. Smith, 1910.
80 Rose Isabella Barton (married name Paterson), born 30 December 1844, baptised in Kelso, NSW, died 24 February 1893.
81 Emily Mary Barton at Boree Nyrang to Bessy Francis at Wentworth House, Hampstead, 26 January 1845, Papers of the Murray-Prior Family, 1810–1945, National Library of Australia, MS 7801. Reprinted in Jeremy Long, *Strugglers and Settlers: Darvall Family Letters (1839– 1849)*, Evolve Studios, 2005, p. 273.
82 *Ibid.*
83 Emily Mary Barton at Boree Nyrang to Bessy Francis, 30 November 1845, Papers of the Murray-Prior Family, 1810–1945, National Library of Australia, MS 7801. Reprinted in Long, *Strugglers and Settlers*, p. 277.
84 Emily Mary Barton at Boree Nyrang to Bessy Francis, 20 January 1846, Papers of the Murray-Prior Family, 1810–1945, National Library of Australia, MS 7801, Box 6, Folder 22/55.
85 *Ibid.*
86 J.H.L. Cumpston, *Thomas Mitchell, Surveyor General and Explorer*, Oxford University Press, 1955, p. 174.
87 Robert D. Barton, Reminiscences of an Australian Pioneer, Tyrrell's Limited, 1917, p. 6.
88 Emily Barton at Boree Nyrang to Bessy Francis at Albury Heath, Albury, Guildford, 12–21 May 1842, Papers of the Murray-Prior Family, 1810–1945, National Library of Australia, MS 7801, Box 6, Folder 22/45.
89 Godfrey Charles Mundy, *Our Antipodes*, Richard Bentley, 1857, p. 72.
90 Nora Barton (married name Murray-Prior), born 3 December 1846, baptised in Carcoar, NSW, died 12 May 1931 in London.
91 Rosamond Mary Templer (nee Darvall), born 1822, died 19 May 1909, Christchurch, New Zealand.
92 John Arthur Templer (known as Arthur by his family), born Cullompton, Devon, 29 July 1817, died Christchurch, New Zealand, 7 October 1885.
93 Originally known as Nyrambla.
94 Emily Barton at Boree Nyrang to Bessy Francis at Hurley House, Hurley, near Marlow, 26 January 1845, Papers of the Murray-Prior Family, 1810–1945, National Library of Australia, MS 7801, Box 6, Folder 22/53.
95 Emily Barton at Boree Nyrang to Catherine (Catey) Francis at Hampstead, 18 April 1842, Papers of the Murray-Prior Family, 1810–1945, National Library of Australia, MS 7801, Box 6, Folder 22/44.
96 Robert D. Barton, Reminiscences of an Australian Pioneer, Tyrrell's Limited, 1917, p. 5.
97 'Hargraves' Story: Discovery of Gold', *Sydney Morning Herald*, 28 December 1923, p. 8.
98 'The Gold Fever', *Bathurst Free Press*, 17 May 1851, p. 4.
99 Barton, *Reminiscences*, p.12.
100 *Ibid.*, p. 11.
101 *Ibid.*, p. 10.
102 'An Australian Pioneer: Death of Mrs. E. M. Barton', *Wellington Times* (NSW), 26 August 1909, p. 5.
103 'Aboriginal Warfare', *Bathurst Free Press*, 7 December 1850, p. 3.
104 Frederic Barker (1808–1882).
105 Emily Mary Barton, *Straws on the Stream*, W. E. Smith, 1910, preface.
106 Robert D. Barton, *Reminiscences*, p.13.
107 John Smith's daughter Fanny Blanche (born 15 July 1851 at Molong; died 15 December 1935 at Parramatta) married Robert Darvall Barton. Another daughter, Annie (born 2 August 1855 at Molong; died 9 December 1938 at Wellington, New South Wales), married Emily's son Charles Hampden Barton (born 8 July 1848 at Boree Nyrang; died 21 December 1912 in Darlinghurst,

Sydney). Emily's youngest son, Arthur Stirling Barton (born 13 July 1856 at Boree Nyrang; died 19 July 1916 at Homebush, Sydney) married Smith's niece, Lucy Jane Smith (born 16 January 1861 at Vale Head, Molong; died Strathfield, Sydney, 4 June 1918).

108 John Paterson, born 8 December, 1831 at Clyde Vale, Scotland (from *Aberdeen Journal*, Wednesday, 14 December); married Emily Susanna Barton in 1859 at Boree Nyrang; died 1871.

109 Andrew Bogle Paterson, born 1833 in Lesmahagow, Lanarkshire, Scotland, to John Paterson (1783–1850) and Ann Howison (1793–1838). Died 7 June 1889 at Illalong Station, near Binalong, NSW.

110 188 centimetres.

111 Christine Haddow (1640–1679).

112 Sir William Paterson (April 1658 – 22 January 1719).

113 '"Banjo" Paterson Tells His Own Story: In The Days of the Gold Escorts', *Sydney Morning Herald*, 4 February 1939, p. 21.

114 John Prebble, *The Darien Disaster: A Scots Colony in the New World, 1698–1700*, Holt, Rinehart and Winston, 1969, p. 269.

115 Andrew Forrester, *The Man Who Saw the Future*, Thomson/Texere, 2004, p. 303.

116 John Paterson of Lochlyoch.

117 Robert Wallace and [Sir] J. A. Scott Watson, *Farm Live Stock of Great Britain* (5th edition), Oliver and Boyd, p. 447.

118 '"Banjo" Paterson Tells His Own Story: In The Days of the Gold Escorts', *Sydney Morning Herald*, 4 February 1939, p. 21.

119 Robert Trow-Smith, *A History of British Livestock Husbandry, 1700–1900*, Routledge, 2013, p. 160.

120 *Ibid.*

121 John Blackwood Greenshields, *Annals of the Parish of Lesmahagow*, Caledonian Press, 1864, p. 39.

122 *Ibid.*, p. 40.

123 *Ibid.*

124 '"Banjo" Paterson Tells His Own Story: In The Days of the Gold Escorts', *Sydney Morning Herald*, 4 February 1939, p. 21.

125 James Paterson, born 2 December 1829 in Edinburgh, Scotland; died 16 September 1893 in Melbourne. Buried in Coburg Cemetery with his wife Anne Moffat Paterson and youngest daughter Barbara Wilson Pascoe (died 28 January 1932, aged 64).

126 Janet Howison 'Jessie' Paterson, born 6 October 1834 in Lanarkshire, Scotland; died 4 September 1880 in Newcastle, New South Wales. Married Dr Cosby Morgan on 5 July 1860 at St James' Church, Sydney.

127 The Western Bank opened 101 branches and sub-branches throughout Scotland between 1832 and its collapse in 1857.

128 Andrew B. Paterson, Illalong, Yass, to Alex. Anderson Esq, Western Bank, Lanark, Scotland, 22 December 1854. Letter in possession of Alf and Sharon Cantrell of the Banjo Paterson Museum in Yeoval.

129 John travelled to Melbourne and became the Australian agent for English Colonial Coal and Coke with offices at 125 Flinders Street.

130 James Paterson, 'Illalong, Yass, NS Wales' to Alex. Anderson Esq, Western Bank, Lanark, Scotland. Letter in possession of Alf and Sharon Cantrell of the Banjo Paterson Museum in Yeoval.

131 Robert D. Barton, *Reminiscences*, p. 68.

132 'New Church of England, Orange', *Australian Town and Country Journal* (Sydney), 6 January 1877, p. 21.

133 'Family Notices', *Bathurst Free Press and Mining Journal*, 28 December 1859, p. 2.

134 'Sudden Death of Mr. John Paterson, of Illalong', *Wagga Wagga Advertiser and Riverine Reporter*, 16 August 1871, p. 3.

135 'Persons Advertised For', *Sydney Morning Herald*, 16 November 1860, p. 1.

136 Now the town of Young, NSW.

137 The banner is on display at the Lambing Flat Folk Museum in Young.

138 'The Burrangong Riot', *Empire* (Sydney), 9 July 1861, p. 8.

139 *Ibid.*, 6 July 1861, p. 5.

140 *Ibid.*, 9 July 1861, p. 8.
141 Ben Hall, born 9 May 1837 at Maitland; died 5 May 1865 at Billabong Creek, near Forbes.
142 Robert D. Barton, *Reminiscences*, p. 40.
143 'News from the Interior: Mail Robbery', *Sydney Morning Herald*, 8 December 1845, p. 2.
144 *Ibid.*
145 Johnny Gilbert, born in Hamilton, Ontario, Canada, in 1842; shot dead by police on 13 May 1865 near Binalong, NSW.
146 'The Late Escort Robbery', *Sydney Mail*, 28 June 1862, p. 5.
147 'Execution of Henry Manns', *Empire* (Sydney), 27 March 1863, p. 5.
148 'Marriages', *Sydney Morning Herald*, 13 April 1863, p. 1.
149 'Stock, Station and Produce Reports', *Sydney Morning Herald*, 4 July 1863, p. 8.
150 J. E. Paterson, 'Pioneers of the South, Memories of the Yass District', *Sydney Mail*, 23 February 1921, p. 17.
151 'Family Notices', *Sydney Mail*, 17 October 1863, p. 9.
152 'In the Supreme Court of NSW', *Sydney Morning Herald*, 26 October 1863, p. 1.
153 On 19 November 1863.
154 'Telegraphic Intelligence', *Maitland Mercury and Hunter River General Advertiser*, 24 November 1863, p. 2.
155 'The shooting of John Gilbert', *Mercury* (Hobart), 27 May 1865, p. 4.
156 *J. E. Paterson,* 'Pioneers of the South, Memories of the Yass District', *Sydney Mail*, 23 February 1921, p. 17.
157 Clement Semmler, *The Banjo of the Bush*, University of Queensland Press, (Second Edition), 1974, p. 33.
158 'Debate reignited over Paterson's birthplace', *Wellington Times*, 17 May 2013. There is speculation in Orange that Paterson may have been born in Emmaville Cottage, a building now at the Botanic Gardens. The cottage had been brought to Narrambla as a redwood kit home from California. However, Paterson's granddaughter Rosamund Campbell, when shown the cottage by local historian Elizabeth Griffin, said it was definitely *not* the house where her grandfather was born.
159 'Anniversary of "Banjo" Paterson's Baptism', *Glen Innes Examiner*, 19 March 1946, p. 6.

Chapter 2

1 A. B. Paterson, *Singer of the Bush*, Lansdowne Press, 1983, p. 4. His granddaughters were Rosamund Campbell and Philippa Harvie.
2 Rose Florence Paterson, born 18 October 1865, Orange, NSW; married Reverend Edwin Sandys Lumsdaine 5 July 1884; died 8 May 1931, Bulli, NSW.
3 Emily Jessie Paterson, born 1867 Molong, NSW; died 14 October 1908 at Hunters Hill, NSW.
4 Also known as Gorothong.
5 Then called Currah Creek.
6 'Advertising', *Sydney Morning Herald*, 22 May 1869, p. 11.
7 Rose Paterson to her younger sister, Nora Murray-Prior, 9 April 1873, National Library of Australia, MS 9423.
8 A. B. Paterson, *Singer of the Bush*, Lansdowne Press, 1983, p. 7.
9 *Ibid.*, p. 6.
10 Edward Hugh Barton (1850–1891).
11 A. B. Paterson, *Singer of the Bush*, Lansdowne Press, 1983, p. 6.
12 'Summary', *Sydney Mail*, 9 July 1864, p. 4. Gardiner served ten years before being pardoned on the condition he leave Australia. He became a saloon keeper in San Francisco.
13 On 28 May 1864.
14 Henry Francis Barton, born 5 November 1853; died 26 October 1902.
15 *J. E. Paterson,* 'Pioneers of the South, Memories of the Yass District', *Sydney Mail*, 23 February 1921, p. 17.
16 'Canowindra and Ben Hall', *Leader* (Orange, NSW), 30 May 1917, p. 5.
17 'Another Robbery by Ben Hall's Gang', *Bell's Life in Sydney and Sporting Chronicle*, 4 June 1864, p. 3.

18 *J. E. Paterson*, 'Pioneers of the South, Memories of the Yass District', *Sydney Mail*, 23 February 1921, p. 17.
19 'Ben Hall's Gang at Bang Bang!', *Sydney Morning Herald*, 3 June 1864, p. 5.
20 'Topics of the week', *South Australian Weekly Chronicle* (Adelaide), 13 May 1865, p. 1.
21 John Dunn, born 14 December 1846; hanged 19 March 1866.
22 J. E. Paterson, 'Pioneers of the South, Memories of the Yass District', *Sydney Mail*, 23 February 1921, p. 17.
23 Born John Fuller, 30 April 1830 in Appin, NSW; died 9 April 1865 at Peechelba Station, near Wangaratta, Victoria.
24 Christina Rutherford Moreton Macpherson, born 18 June 1864 at Peechelba, Victoria; died 27 March, 1936 at St Kilda, Victoria.
25 'Alice Keenan', *Ovens and Murray Advertiser* (Beechworth), 13 May 1865, p. 3.
26 'Morgan, The Bushranger', *Argus* (Melbourne), 14 April 1865, p. 6.
27 Craig Cormick, *Ned Kelly: Under the Microscope*, CSIRO Publishing, 2014, p. 124.
28 'Morgan, The Bushranger', *Argus*, 14 April, 1865, p. 6.
29 'Items of news', *Mount Alexander Mail*, 16 May 1865, p. 2.
30 'Melbourne', *Sydney Morning Herald*, 17 April 1865, p. 5.
31 'Government Advertisements', *Brisbane Courier*, 12 October 1865, p. 5.
32 Joseph Wilson Raven, born 10 February 1832 in Workington, England; died 5 May 1925 at his residence, Stainburn, in Bourke Street, Dubbo.
33 The area was listed at forty-two square miles or 26,800 acres. From *Rockhampton Bulletin and Central Queensland Advertiser*, 23 April 1867, p. 3.
34 Paterson and others recalled it as 'Stainbourne Downs'.
35 'Obituary', *Dubbo Liberal and Macquarie Advocate*, 8 May 1925, p. 4.
36 Joseph Wilson Raven, 'Reminiscences of a Western Queensland pioneer', Mitchell Library, State Library of New South Wales, Collected 1909 (unpublished), p. 3.
37 *Ibid.*, p. 5.
38 A. B. Paterson, *Singer of the Bush*, Lansdowne Press, 1983, p. ix.
39 '"Banjo" Paterson Tells His Own Story: In The Days of the Gold Escorts', *Sydney Morning Herald*, 4 February 1939, p. 21.
40 A. B. Paterson, *Singer of the Bush*, Lansdowne Press, 1983, p. xi.
41 'Obituary: Death of Dr R Rygate, Snr', *Wellington Times* (NSW), 5 August 1907, p. 2.
42 'Distressing Accident', *Empire* (Sydney), 3 October 1865, p. 5.
43 Jennifer Gall, *Looking for Rose Paterson*, National Library of Australia, 2017, p. 100.
44 A. B. Paterson, *Singer of the Bush*, Lansdowne Press, 1983, p. 15.
45 *British Dental Journal*, Published online: 14 July 2001, nature.com.
46 John Winckworth, *A popular treatise on the teeth and gums and diseases attendant on them*, Renshaw and Rush, 1831, p. 7.
47 Rose to Nora, 20 February [1874], National Library of Australia, MS 9423.
48 *Ibid.*
49 A. B. Paterson, *Singer of the Bush*, Lansdowne Press, 1983, p. 4.
50 *Ibid.*
51 *Ibid.*
52 *Ibid.*
53 '"Banjo" Paterson Tells His Own Story: In The Days of the Gold Escorts', *Sydney Morning Herald*, 4 February 1939, p. 21.
54 *Ibid.*, p. 6.
55 *Ibid.*, p. 7.
56 A. B. Paterson, *Song of the Pen*, Lansdowne Press, 1983, p. 558. Originally from a wireless talk, 'Sheep', for the ABC.
57 A. B. Paterson, *Singer of the Bush*, Lansdowne Press, 1983, p. 7.
58 *Ibid.*
59 'Death of Mr A. B. Paterson', *Burrowa News* (NSW), 17 June 1889, p. 2.
60 Rose to Nora, 14 December 1873, National Library of Australia, MS 9423.
61 A. B. Paterson, *Singer of the Bush*, Lansdowne Press, 1983, p. 5.

62 *Ibid.*, p. 8.
63 *Ibid.*
64 'Rockend Cottage', environment.nsw.gov.au.
65 Now known as Victoria Road.
66 'Advertising', *Sydney Morning Herald*, 2 January 1864, p. 7.
67 Colin Roderick, *Rose Paterson's Illalong Letters, 1873–1888*, Kangaroo Press, 2000, pp. 204–5.
68 Rose to Nora, 9 April 1873, National Library of Australia, MS 9423.
69 John McEvitt, aka Mick McEvitt.
70 'Execution in Bathurst Jail, Terrible Scene', *Queanbeyan Age*, 6 June 1868, p. 3.
71 Also reported as Munday or Mundy.
72 'Atrocious Murders at Conroy's Gap', *Maitland Mercury and Hunter River General Advertiser*, 24 March 1868, p. 3.
73 *Ibid.*
74 'The Conroy's Gap Murders', *Hamilton Spectator and Grange District Advertiser* (South Melbourne), 25 April 1868, p. 4.
75 *Ibid.*
76 'Execution of Munday Alias Collins', *Goulburn Herald and Chronicle*, 3 June 1868, p. 2.
77 'The Conroy's Gap Murders', *Hamilton Spectator and Grange District Advertiser* (South Melbourne), 25 April 1868, p. 4.
78 'The wool industry – looking back and forward', *Year Book Australia*, 2003, abs.gov.au.
79 'The Fall in Wool', *Goulburn Herald and Chronicle*, 20 January 1869, p. 4.
80 'The Financial Crisis in Queensland', *Sydney Morning Herald*, 24 July 1866, p. 5.
81 Joseph Wilson Raven, *Reminiscences of a Western Queensland pioneer*, Mitchell Library, State Library of New South Wales, Collected 1909 (unpublished), p. 24.
82 'Central Police Court', *Sydney Mail*, 5 May 1866, p. 11.
83 '"Banjo" Paterson Tells His Own Story: In The Days of the Gold Escorts', *Sydney Morning Herald*, 4 February 1939, p. 21.
84 Robert D. Barton, *Reminiscences of an Australian Pioneer*, Tyrrell's Limited, 1917, p. 90.
85 'Advertising', *Sydney Morning Herald*, 22 May 1869, p. 11.
86 'Stock, Station, and Produce Reports', *Empire* (Sydney), 16 June 1869, p. 3.
87 'Mercantile and Money Article', *Sydney Morning Herald*, 7 August 1869, p. 8.
88 Thomas McCulloch, born Glasgow, 1818; died 13 April 1889, Newtown, Sydney.
89 'Mercantile and Money Article', *Sydney Morning Herald*, 7 August 1869, p. 8.
90 'Lists of Runs and Rents for the Year 1871', *Australian Town and Country Journal* (Sydney), 28 January 1871, p. 11.
91 Suzanne Edgar, 'Laidlaw, Thomas (1813–1876)', *Australian Dictionary of Biography*, Volume 5, MUP, 1974.
92 'List of Runs and Rents for the Year 1871', *Empire* (Sydney), 12 January 1871, p. 4.
93 'Transfer of runs', *Rockhampton Bulletin and Central Queensland Advertiser*, 12 April 1870, p. 2.
94 'Death of Mr A. B. Paterson', *Burrowa News* (NSW), 17 June 1889, p. 2.
95 'Jottings by the Way, The Murrumbidgee and Yass', *Australian Town and Country Journal* (Sydney), 26 February 1870, p. 23.
96 *Ibid.*
97 A. B. Paterson, *Singer of the Bush*, Lansdowne Press, 1983, p. 8.
98 A. B. Paterson [The Banjo], *The Animals Noah Forgot* (illustrated by Norman Lindsay), The Endeavour Press, 1933, prologue, 'The Plains'.
99 A. B. Paterson, *Singer of the Bush*, Lansdowne Press, 1983, p. 8.

Chapter 3

1 '"Banjo" Paterson Tells His Own Story: In The Days of the Gold Escorts', *Sydney Morning Herald*, 4 February 1939, p. 21.
2 A. B. Paterson, *Singer of the Bush*, Lansdowne Press, 1983, p. 8.
3 *Ibid.*, p. ix.
4 J. E. Paterson, 'Pioneers of the South, Memories of the Yass District', *Sydney Mail*, 23 February 1921, p. 17.

5 A. B. Paterson, *Singer of the Bush*, Lansdowne Press, 1983, p. 8.
6 '"Banjo" Paterson Tells His Own Story: In The Days of the Gold Escorts', *Sydney Morning Herald*, 4 February 1939, p. 21.
7 'Destructive Flood at Yass', *Maitland Mercury and Hunter River General Advertiser*, 30 April 1870, p. 2.
8 A. B. Paterson, *Song of the Pen*, Lansdowne Press, 1983, p. 493. Originally from a wireless talk, 'Floods in Queensland', for the ABC.
9 J. E. Paterson, 'Pioneers of the South, Memories of the Yass District', *Sydney Mail*, 23 February 1921, p. 17.
10 *Ibid.*
11 Thomas Lodge Murray-Prior (1819–1892).
12 Rose Paterson to her younger sister, Nora Murray-Prior, 9 April 1873, National Library of Australia, MS 9423.
13 '"Banjo" Paterson Tells His Own Story: In The Days of the Gold Escorts', *Sydney Morning Herald*, 4 February 1939, p. 21.
14 *Ibid.*
15 'Advertising', *Sydney Morning Herald*, 22 May 1869, p. 11.
16 A. B. Paterson, *Singer of the Bush*, Lansdowne Press, 1983, p. 24.
17 'Advertising', *Sydney Morning Herald*, 22 May 1869, p. 11.
18 A. B. Paterson, *Singer of the Bush*, Lansdowne Press, 1983, p. 25.
19 Emily Darvall 'Madam' Paterson (1864–1945) suffered from an eye disease and was blind by her teens. She became a well-known composer and set music to the words of her cousin Banjo. In 1907 she set up the After Care Association in Gladesville to help former psychiatric patients at a time when there were no mental health support services available to integrate those with a mental illness back into the community. The other children of John and Emmy Paterson were Jack (1862–1941), Hester Beata Paterson (1867–1952) and Robert Paterson (1869–1918).
20 'Advertising', *Sydney Morning Herald*, 22 May 1869, p. 11.
21 'Sudden Death of Mr. John Paterson, of Illalong', *Wagga Wagga Advertiser and Riverine Reporter*, 16 August 1871, p. 3. Reprinted from *Yass Courier*.
22 On 9 August 1871.
23 J. E. Paterson, 'Pioneers of the South, Memories of the Yass District', *Sydney Mail*, 23 February 1921, p. 17.
24 'Sudden Death of Mr. John Paterson, of Illalong', *Wagga Wagga Advertiser and Riverine Reporter*, 16 August 1871, p. 3. Reprinted from *Yass Courier*.
25 *Ibid.*
26 Rose to Nora, 9 April 1873, National Library of Australia, MS 9423.
27 *Ibid.*
28 blackswanbinalong.com.au.
29 Rose to Nora, 11 June 1878, National Library of Australia, MS 9423.
30 'A. B. Paterson: A Memoir', *The Burrowa News*, 10 June 1949.
31 A. B. Paterson, *Singer of the Bush*, Lansdowne Press, 1983, p. 9.
32 *Ibid.*
33 A. B. Paterson, *Singer of the Bush*, Lansdowne Press, 1983, p. 10.
34 Mary Edith Paterson (1872–1950), married Guy Huntley, 1900.
35 Rose to Nora, 9 April 1873, National Library of Australia, MS 9423.
36 Hamilton Howison 'Boy' Paterson, born 5 September 1876, Gladesville, Sydney; died 30 June 1902 at Samarai, New Guinea. The remaining children were Grace Sterling 'Gracie' Paterson (1877–1969); married Frederick Taylor 1897; and Gwendoline Alexa 'Gwen' Paterson (1881–1946).
37 Rose to Nora, 9 April 1873, National Library of Australia, MS 9423.
38 A. B. Paterson, *Singer of the Bush*, Lansdowne Press, 1983, p. 10.
39 *Ibid.*
40 '"Banjo" Paterson Tells His Own Story: In The Days of the Gold Escorts', *Sydney Morning Herald*, 4 February 1939, p. 21.
41 *Ibid.*

42 Opened in 1861.
43 '"Banjo" Paterson Tells His Own Story: In The Days of the Gold Escorts', *Sydney Morning Herald*, 4 February 1939, p. 21.
44 A. B. Paterson, *Singer of the Bush*, Lansdowne Press, 1983, p. 21.
45 '"Banjo" Paterson Tells His Own Story: In The Days of the Gold Escorts', *Sydney Morning Herald*, 4 February 1939, p. 21.
46 A. B. Paterson, *Singer of the Bush*, Lansdowne Press, 1983, p. 21.
47 *Ibid.*
48 'Dunn, Gilbert, and Ben Hall', *Evening News* (Sydney), 11 April 1903, p. 3.
49 A. B. Paterson, *The Old Bush Songs*, Angus & Robertson, 1905.
50 *Ibid.*, Introduction.
51 Rose to Nora, 9 April 1873, National Library of Australia, MS 9423.
52 J. E. Paterson, 'Pioneers of the South, Memories of the Yass District', *Sydney Mail*, 23 February 1921, p. 17.
53 'My Various Schools – No. 2', *Sydneian: A Magazine Edited by Members of the Sydney Grammar School*, June 1890, p. 4.
54 A. B. Paterson, *Singer of the Bush*, Lansdowne Press, 1983, p. 27.
55 *Ibid.*, p. 29.
56 *Ibid.*
57 'My Various Schools – No. 1', *Sydneian: A Magazine Edited by Members of the Sydney Grammar School*, May 1880, p. 7.
58 '"Banjo" Paterson Tells His Own Story: In The Days of the Gold Escorts', *Sydney Morning Herald*, 4 February 1939, p. 21.
59 'My Various Schools – No. 2', *Sydneian: A Magazine Edited by Members of the Sydney Grammar School*, June 1890, p. 4.
60 *Ibid.*
61 *Ibid.*
62 A. B. Paterson, *Singer of the Bush*, Lansdowne Press, 1983, p. 21.
63 The Prince survived the assassination attempt on 12 March 1868. O'Farrell was hanged the following month.
64 '"Banjo" Paterson Tells His Own Story: In The Days of the Gold Escorts', *Sydney Morning Herald*, 4 February 1939, p. 21.
65 A. B. Paterson, *Singer of the Bush*, Lansdowne Press, 1983, p. 21.
66 'My Various Schools – No. 2', *Sydneian: A Magazine Edited by Members of the Sydney Grammar School*, June 1890, p. 4.
67 '"Banjo" Paterson Tells His Own Story: In The Days of the Gold Escorts', *Sydney Morning Herald*, 4 February 1939, p. 21.
68 *Ibid.*
69 *Ibid.*
70 'My Various Schools – No. 2', *Sydneian: A Magazine Edited by Members of the Sydney Grammar School*, June 1890, p. 4.
71 *Ibid.*
72 A. B. Paterson, *Singer of the Bush*, Lansdowne Press, 1983, p. 21.
73 *Ibid.*, p. 22.
74 *Ibid.*
75 *Ibid.*
76 'Gardiner and His Gang Near Yass', *Empire* (Sydney), 12 May 1863, p. 4.
77 A. B. Paterson, *Singer of the Bush*, Lansdowne Press, 1983, p. 22.
78 *Ibid.*
79 *Ibid.*, p. 23.
80 Paterson, *Singer of the Bush*, Lansdowne Press, 1983, p. 23.
81 Rose to Nora, 12 August 1875.
82 'Bowning to Binalong', *Australian Town and Country Journal* (Sydney), 9 Feb 1878, p. 17.
83 'Laurence J. Dargan', *Freeman's Journal* (Sydney), 30 March 1922, p. 31.
84 A. B. Paterson, *Singer of the Bush*, Lansdowne Press, 1983, p. 16.

85 *Ibid.*, p. 15.
86 Rose to Nora Murray-Prior, 20 February 1874, National Library of Australia, MS 9423.
87 Edmund Galley, born 15 November 1810 in Surrey; died 6 November 1885 at Binalong, NSW.
88 'Edmund Galley', *Australian Town and Country Journal* (Sydney), 18 October 1879, p. 17.
89 '"Banjo" Paterson Tells His Own Story: An Execution and a Royal Pardon', *Sydney Morning Herald*, 25 February 1939, p. 21.
90 A. B. Paterson, *Singer of the Bush*, Lansdowne Press, 1983, p. 16.
91 *Ibid.*
92 '"Farmer's Friend" and "Painkiller"', *Daily News* (Perth), 9 March 1905, p. 1.
93 '"Banjo" Paterson Tells His Own Story: An Execution and a Royal Pardon', *Sydney Morning Herald*, 25 February 1939, p. 21.
94 *Ibid.*
95 A. B. Paterson, *Singer of the Bush*, Lansdowne Press, 1983, p. 27.
96 *Ibid.*, p. 26.
97 Edward Hiram Howard (1840–1874).
98 '"Banjo" Paterson Tells His Own Story: An Execution and a Royal Pardon', *Sydney Morning Herald*, 25 February 1939, p. 21.
99 'Death in the Bush', *Sydney Morning Herald*, 23 February 1874, p. 5.
100 Jane Howard (nee Barker), 1842–1888.
101 *Yass Courier*, 18 June 1875.
102 William Joseph Galley (9 October 1875–1960).
103 In 1879.
104 '"Banjo" Paterson Tells His Own Story: An Execution and a Royal Pardon', *Sydney Morning Herald*, 25 February 1939, p. 21.
105 'The Case of Edmund Galley', *Queenslander*, 3 September 1881, p. 310.
106 '"Banjo" Paterson Tells His Own Story: An Execution and a Royal Pardon', *Sydney Morning Herald*, 25 February 1939, p. 21.
107 A. B. Paterson, *Singer of the Bush*, Lansdowne Press, 1983, p. 27.
108 Rose to Nora, 9 April 1873, National Library of Australia, MS 9423.
109 *Ibid.*, 20 February [1874].
110 Amelia Margaret Campbell (nee Breillat), born 26 May 1835 in Sydney, married David Campbell 19 February 1856; died 28 May 1870 at Cunningham Plains near Murrumburrah, NSW.
111 'Family Notices', *Sydney Morning Herald*, 31 May 1870, p. 1.
112 Louise Campbell (nee Powell), born October 1841 at Lake George, NSW; married David Campbell 2 April 1872; died 25 April 1892 at Bungendore, NSW.
113 Rose to Nora, 9 April 1873, National Library of Australia, MS 9423.
114 A. B. Paterson, *Singer of the Bush*, Lansdowne Press, 1983, p. 14.
115 *Ibid.*
116 *Ibid.*
117 Now on display at the National Museum of Australia in Canberra.
118 J. E. Paterson, 'Pioneers of the South, Memories of the Yass District', *Sydney Mail*, 23 February 1921, p. 17.
119 Thomas Alexander Browne, aka Rolf Boldrewood, born 6 August 1826 in London; died 11 March 1915, South Yarra, Melbourne.
120 From Banjo Paterson's poem, 'In the Stable', featured in *Rio Grande's Last Race and Other Verses*, Angus & Robertson, 1902.
121 A. B. Paterson, *Singer of the Bush*, Lansdowne Press, 1983, p. 14.

Chapter 4

1 '"Banjo" Paterson Tells His Own Story: In The Days of the Gold Escorts', *Sydney Morning Herald*, 4 February 1939, p. 21.
2 *Ibid.*
3 J. E. Paterson, 'Pioneers of the South, Memories of the Yass District', *Sydney Mail*, 23 February 1921, p. 17.

4 '"Banjo" Paterson Tells His Own Story: Giants of the Paddle, Pen, and Pencil', *Sydney Morning Herald*, 11 February 1939, p. 21.

5 J. E. Paterson, 'Pioneers of the South, Memories of the Yass District', *Sydney Mail*, 23 February 1921, p. 17.

6 'The V.R.C. Spring Meeting', *Advocate* (Melbourne), 9 November 1872, p. 9.

7 Costa Rolfe, *Winners of the Melbourne Cup: Stories that Stopped a Nation*, Red Dog Books, 2009, p. 24.

8 In June 1843 Tait became the licensee of the Albion Inn, Hartley, and in 1847 took over the Black Bull Inn at Bathurst.

9 Also known as Lobb's Hole. Along the Yarrangobilly River in what is now the northern wilderness of Kosciuszko National Park.

10 '"Banjo" Paterson Tells His Own Story: In The Days of the Gold Escorts', *Sydney Morning Herald*, 4 February 1939, p. 21.

11 A. B. Paterson, *Song of the Pen*, Lansdowne Press, 1983, p. 558. Originally from a wireless talk, 'Sheep', for the ABC.

12 '"Banjo" Paterson Tells His Own Story: In The Days of the Gold Escorts', *Sydney Morning Herald*, 4 February 1939, p. 21.

13 *Ibid.*

14 J. E. Paterson, 'Pioneers of the South, Memories of the Yass District', *Sydney Mail*, 23 February 1921, p. 17.

15 '"Banjo" Paterson Tells His Own Story: In The Days of the Gold Escorts', *Sydney Morning Herald*, 4 February 1939, p. 21.

16 'Looking Backward', *Sydney Mail*, 28 December 1938, p. 7. In this version, Paterson explained the origins of 'Pardon, the Son of Reprieve' in this way: 'My father's cousin known as 'Blenty' because he wore spectacles, and Blenty is, I believe, the Scotch for a man who wears spectacles – owned a bush horse called Pardon in the days when they ran mile races in three heats. Pardon was left in a stable at a bush pub on a very rigid diet awaiting his race on the morrow; but being gifted with brains and resource Mr Pardon managed to knock down the rails of his stall and to get at a bale of lucerne. Tradition goes that by the time daylight came he had eaten most of it … he seemed in no shape for racing. In these circumstances his victory was, to say the least of it, creditable, and earned the tribute of a set of verses.'

17 'My Various Schools', *Sydneian: A Magazine Edited by Members of the Sydney Grammar School*, May 1890, p. 7.

18 *Ibid.*

19 *Ibid.*

20 *Ibid.*

21 'My Various Schools – No. 2', *Sydneian: A Magazine Edited by Members of the Sydney Grammar School*, June 1890, p. 4.

22 *Ibid.*

23 H. J. Gibbney, 'Murray-Prior, Thomas Lodge (1819–1892)', *Australian Dictionary of Biography*, published first in hardcopy 1974.

24 'In The Steps of Rosa Praed and Tasma: Biographical Trails', a lecture by Patricia Clarke, Harold White Fellow, at the National Library of Australia, Canberra, 1993.

25 Rosa Caroline Praed (1851–1935).

26 'In The Steps of Rosa Praed and Tasma: Biographical Trails', a lecture by Patricia Clarke, Harold White Fellow, at the National Library of Australia, Canberra, 1993.

27 Rose Paterson to Nora Murray-Prior, 28 March 1880, National Library of Australia, MS 9423.

28 *Ibid.*, 19 September 1875.

29 *Ibid.*, 12 August 1875.

30 *Ibid.*, 15 December 1873.

31 *Ibid.*

32 *Ibid.*, 14 December 1873.

33 Annie Brown (nee Friend), born 8 February 1837; married Henry Brown in 1856 at St James's Church, Sydney; died 1883 in Hunter's Hill.

34 J. E. Paterson, 'Pioneers of the South, Memories of the Yass District', *Sydney Mail*, 23 February 1921, p. 17.
35 *Ibid.*
36 Rose to Nora, 12 August 1875, National Library of Australia, MS 9423.
37 *Ibid.*
38 Richard Hall, *Banjo Paterson: His Poetry and Prose*, Allen & Unwin, 1993.
39 A. B. Paterson, *Singer of the Bush*, Lansdowne Press, 1983, p. 24.
40 *Ibid.*, p. 15.
41 Paterson called it 'an eaglehawk'.
42 Paterson, *Singer of the Bush*, Lansdowne Press, 1983, p. 18.
43 *Ibid.*, p. 29.
44 *Ibid.*, p. 38.
45 *Ibid.*, p. 40.
46 *Ibid.*, p. 19.
47 *Ibid.*
48 *Ibid.*, p. 20.
49 'Looking Backward', *Sydney Mail*, 28 December 1938, p. 7.
50 Sidney Blaxland (1854–1932).
51 Paterson, *Singer of the Bush*, Lansdowne Press, 1983, p. 15.
52 *Ibid.*
53 *Ibid.*, p. 16.
54 *Ibid.*, p. 27.
55 Paterson, *Singer of the Bush*, Lansdowne Press, 1983, p. 27.
56 *Ibid.*, p. 11.
57 *Ibid.*
58 *Ibid.*
59 *Ibid.*, p. 12.
60 J. E. Paterson, 'Pioneers of the South, Memories of the Yass District', *Sydney Mail*, 23 February 1921, p. 17.
61 Rose to Nora, 20 February [1875], National Library of Australia, MS 9423.
62 Paterson, *Singer of the Bush*, Lansdowne Press, 1983, p. 11.
63 *Ibid.*
64 James 'Blenty' Paterson, born 1 October 1840, Douglas, Lanarkshire, Scotland; died 4 March 1888, McHenry's Creek, Young, NSW.
65 Rose to Nora, 20 February [1875], National Library of Australia, MS 9423.
66 *Ibid.*
67 *Ibid.*
68 *Ibid.*, 12 August 1875.
69 *Ibid.*, 11 June 1878.
70 *Ibid.*, 28 March 1880.
71 J. E. Paterson, 'Pioneers of the South, Memories of the Yass District', *Sydney Mail*, 23 February 1921, p. 17.
72 *Ibid.*
73 Paterson, *Singer of the Bush*, Lansdowne Press, 1983, p. 31.
74 As recounted by artist Norman Lindsay in an ABC radio documentary broadcast on 17 April 1964. From Clement Semmler, *The Banjo of the Bush* (second edition), Queensland University Press, 1974, p. 18.
75 Paterson, *Singer of the Bush*, Lansdowne Press, 1983, p. 33.
76 *Ibid.*, p. 35.
77 Paterson, *Singer of the Bush*, Lansdowne Press, 1983, p. 17.
78 *Ibid.*
79 *Ibid.*, p. 18.
80 *Ibid.*, p. 31.
81 *Ibid.*, p. 36.

82 J. E. Paterson, 'Pioneers of the South, Memories of the Yass District', *Sydney Mail*, 23 February 1921, p. 17.
83 Paterson, *Singer of the Bush*, Lansdowne Press, 1983, p. xi.
84 Sir Edward Knox (6 June 1819 – 7 January 1901).
85 Clement Semmler, *The Banjo of the Bush* (second edition), Queensland University Press, 1974, p. 42.
86 Paterson, *Singer of the Bush*, Lansdowne Press, 1983, p. xi.
87 Rose to Nora, 20 February [1875], National Library of Australia, MS 9423.
88 'My Various Schools – No. 2', *Sydneian: A Magazine Edited by Members of the Sydney Grammar School*, June 1890, p. 4.

Chapter 5

1 A. B. Paterson, *Singer of the Bush*, Lansdowne Press, 1983, p. ix.
2 '"Banjo" Paterson Tells His Own Story: Giants of the Paddle, Pen, and Pencil', *Sydney Morning Herald*, 11 February 1939, p. 21.
3 A. B. Paterson, 'Clancy of the Overflow', first published in *The Bulletin*, 21 December 1889, p. 17.
4 'Opening of the Railway to Binalong', *Evening News* (Sydney), 7 November 1876, p. 2.
5 Then known as Sutton Forest.
6 Marcus Clarke, *His Natural Life,* George Robertson, 1874.
7 Marcus Andrew Hislop Clarke, born 11 Leonard Place, Kensington, London, 24 April 1846; died 2 August 1881 at his home in Inkerman St, St Kilda, Melbourne.
8 It ceased publication in 1962.
9 From the debut issue of *The Australian Journal*, 2 September 1865.
10 Alfred Henry Massina, born 3 November 1834 at Stepney, London; died 4 February 1917, Richmond, Melbourne. He was also a director of The Herald and Weekly Times Ltd.
11 'Master Printer Retires', *Weekly Times,* Melbourne, 6 March 1909, p. 40.
12 *Ibid.* In reality Clarke was editor for about eighteen months (from Ronald G Campbell, *The First Ninety Years: The Printing House of Massina, Melbourne, 1859–1949*, A.H. Massina, 1949).
13 Paterson, *Song of the Pen*, Lansdowne Press, 1983, p. 476. Originally from a wireless talk, 'Australian Local Colour'.
14 'My Various Schools – No. 2', *Sydneian: A Magazine Edited by Members of the Sydney Grammar School*, June 1890, p. 4.
15 *Diary of Miss Emily Darvall: Kept during the voyage of the 'Alfred' from England to Australia in 1839/1840*, 29 September.
16 visitsydneyaustralia.com.au/looking-glass-bay.html.
17 Paterson, *Song of the Pen*, Lansdowne Press, 1983, p. 539. Originally from a wireless talk 'On the River'.
18 Sir William Charles Windeyer (29 September 1834 – 11 September 1897).
19 Edward Marsden Betts (1839–1922).
20 Later known as Gladesville Mental Hospital and originally called the Tarban Creek Lunatic Asylum.
21 Paterson, *Song of the Pen*, Lansdowne Press, 1983, p. 530. Originally from a wireless talk, 'Old Cricketers'.
22 *Ibid.*
23 *Ibid.*
24 *Ibid.*, p. 532.
25 George John Bonnor (25 February 1855 – 27 June 1912).
26 Paterson, *Song of the Pen*, Lansdowne Press, 1983, p. 530. Originally from a wireless talk, 'Old Cricketers'.
27 George Eugene 'Joey' Palmer (22 February 1859 – 22 August 1910).
28 Paterson, *Song of the Pen*, Lansdowne Press, 1983, p. 532. Originally from a wireless talk, 'Old Cricketers'.
29 George Giffen (27 March 1859 – 29 November 1927).
30 Paterson, *Song of the Pen*, Lansdowne Press, 1983, p. 532. Originally from a wireless talk, 'Old Cricketers'.

31 *Ibid.*, p. 539. Originally from a wireless talk, 'On the River'.
32 '"Banjo" Paterson Tells His Own Story: Giants of the Paddle, Pen, and Pencil', *Sydney Morning Herald*, 11 February 1939, p. 21.
33 Sir Henry Parkes, born 27 May 1815, Canley, Coventry, United Kingdom; died 27 April 1896, Annandale, Sydney.
34 Albert Bythesea Weigall, born 16 February 1840 in Nantes, France; died 20 February 1912, Darlinghurst, Sydney.
35 Albert Bythesea Weigall, 'The School', *Sydneian*, August 1907, p. 1.
36 *Sydneian*, No 1, September 1875, p. 3.
37 General Sir Henry George Chauvel, born 16 April 1865 at Tabulam, New South Wales; died 4 March 1945 in Melbourne.
38 Roland Perry, *Monash and Chauvel*, Allen & Unwin, 2017.
39 Clement Semmler, *The Banjo of the Bush* (second edition), Queensland University Press, 1974, p. 42
40 'Sydney Grammar School', *Sydney Morning Herald*, 17 December 1875, p. 6.
41 Sir George Edward Rich, born 3 May 1863, Braidwood; died 14 May 1956.
42 '"Banjo" Paterson Tells His Own Story: Giants of the Paddle, Pen, and Pencil', *Sydney Morning Herald*, 11 February 1939, p. 21.
43 Sir Alfred Stephen (20 August 1802 – 15 October 1894).
44 John Dunmore Lang (25 August 1799 – 8 August 1878).
45 'Sydney Grammar School', *Sydney Morning Herald*, 17 December 1875, p. 6.
46 A. B. Paterson, *Singer of the Bush*, Lansdowne Press, 1983, p. xi.
47 'Sydney Grammar School', *Sydney Morning Herald*, 17 December 1875, p. 6.
48 Rose Paterson to Nora Murray-Prior, 20 February 1874, National Library of Australia, MS 9423.
49 *Ibid.*, 12 August 1875.
50 *Ibid.*, April–May 1875.
51 *Ibid.*
52 *Ibid.*, May 1875.
53 *Ibid.*
54 *Ibid.*
55 Mary Wilson, born 21 February 1842, Douglas, Lanarkshire; married Blenty Paterson, 27 March 1875, St Philip's Church, Sydney.
56 Rose to Nora, 14 May 1875, National Library of Australia, MS 9423.
57 *Ibid.*, 12 August 1875.
58 *Ibid.* 11 January 1877.
59 *Ibid.*
60 *Ibid.*
61 Paterson, *Song of the Pen*, Lansdowne Press, 1983, p. 539. Originally from a wireless talk, 'On the River'.
62 '"Banjo" Paterson Tells His Own Story: Giants of the Paddle, Pen, and Pencil', *Sydney Morning Herald*, 11 February 1939, p. 21.
63 Henry Ernest Searle (1866–1889).
64 He was in reality only 178 centimetres. He rowed at seventy-four kilograms but weighed eighty-four kilograms when out of training. His measurements were chest 105 centimetres, biceps thirty-four centimetres, forearm twenty-eight centimetres, thigh fifty-six centimetres and calf forty-one centimetres. From Scott Bennett, 'Searle, Henry Ernest (1866–1889)', *Australian Dictionary of Biography*, Volume 6, MUP, 1976.
65 '"Banjo" Paterson Tells His Own Story: Giants of the Paddle, Pen, and Pencil', *Sydney Morning Herald*, 11 February 1939, p. 21.
66 *Sydneian*, No 1, September 1875, p. 29.
67 Edward 'Ned' Trickett, born 12 September 1851 in Greenwich, Sydney; died 28 November 1916 in Uralla, New South Wales from injuries sustained when the walls of a mine shaft collapsed on him.
68 Joseph Henry Sadler (1839–1889).

69 The Championship Course is 6779 metres.
70 191 centimetre and 72 kilograms.
71 'Race for The Scullers' Championship of the World', *Warwick Argus and Tenterfield Chronicle*, 31 August 1876, p. 1.
72 '"Banjo" Paterson Tells His Own Story: Giants of the Paddle, Pen, and Pencil', *Sydney Morning Herald*, 11 February 1939, p. 21.
73 'Chronicle of The Month', *Australasian Sketcher with Pen and Pencil* (Melbourne), 23 December 1876, p. 146.
74 Edward 'Ned' Hanlan (12 July 1855 – 4 January 1908).
75 Paterson, *Song of the Pen*, Lansdowne Press, 1983, p. 541. Originally from a wireless talk, 'On the River'.
76 William Beach, born 6 September 1850 in Chertsey, Surrey, England; died 28 January 1935 at Brownsville, Wollongong, New South Wales.
77 Paterson, *Song of the Pen*, Lansdowne Press, 1983, p. 539. Originally from a wireless talk, 'On the River'.
78 '"Banjo" Paterson Tells His Own Story: Giants of the Paddle, Pen, and Pencil', *Sydney Morning Herald*, 11 February 1939, p. 21.
79 On 16 August 1884.
80 Paterson, *Song of the Pen*, Lansdowne Press, 1983, p. 539. Originally from a wireless talk, 'On the River'.
81 *Ibid.*, p. 571. Originally from a wireless talk, 'Sydney in the Seventies'.
82 *Encyclopaedia Britannica*, eleventh edition, University Press, Cambridge, 1911.
83 James Inglis, *Our Australian Cousins*, Macmillan, 1880, p. 145.
84 'Family Notices', *Sydney Morning Herald*, 30 September 1876, p. 8. Hamilton's birth has often been misreported as being in 1875.
85 *Ibid.*
86 Jennifer Gall, *Looking for Rose Paterson*, NLA Publishing, 2017, p. 71.
87 Rose to Nora, 14 May 1876, National Library of Australia, MS 9423.
88 *Ibid.*, 19 September 1876.
89 *Ibid.*, 5 October 1881.
90 *Ibid.*, 19 September 1876.
91 *Ibid.*, 11 June 1878.
92 *Ibid.*, 19 September 1876.
93 'University of Sydney', *Australian Town and Country Journal*, 28 December 1878, p. 13.
94 The land on which the Albert Ground sat is now occupied by public housing near Redfern Park. It is bounded by Elizabeth, Redfern, Kettle and Moorehead Streets.
95 Paterson, *Song of the Pen*, Lansdowne Press, 1983, p. 568. Originally from a wireless talk, 'The Sydney Ground'.
96 Frederick Robert Spofforth (9 September 1853 – 4 June 1926), also known as 'The Demon Bowler'.
97 Charles Bannerman (3 July 1851 – 20 August 1930).
98 First Test, England tour of Australia, Melbourne Cricket Ground, 15–19 March 1877. Australia won by 45 runs, the score identical to that in the Centenary Test at the same venue a hundred years later.
99 Paterson, *Song of the Pen*, Lansdowne Press, 1983, p. 568. Originally from a wireless talk, 'The Sydney Ground'.
100 'Sporting. The English Eleven v. Eleven of New South Wales', *Sydney Morning Herald*, 10 February 1879, p. 6.
101 Colonel George Robert Canning Harris, 4th Baron Harris (3 February 1851 – 24 March 1932).
102 Paterson, *Song of the Pen*, Lansdowne Press, 1983, p. 569. Originally from a wireless talk, 'The Sydney Ground'.
103 barton101.com.
104 George Coulthard (1 August 1856 – 22 October 1883). After surviving the shark attack, he died of tuberculosis aged just 27.

105 'Sporting. The English Eleven v. Eleven of New South Wales', *Sydney Morning Herald*, 8 February 1879, p. 6.
106 *Ibid.*
107 Sir Hercules George Robert Robinson, 1st Baron Rosmead (1824–1897).
108 Paterson, *Song of the Pen*, Lansdowne Press, 1983, p. 569. Originally from a wireless talk, 'The Sydney Ground'.
109 'Sporting. The English Eleven v. Eleven of New South Wales', *Sydney Morning Herald*, 10 February 1879, p. 6.
110 *Ibid.*
111 Paterson, *Song of the Pen*, Lansdowne Press, 1983, p. 569. Originally from a wireless talk, 'The Sydney Ground'.
112 'Sporting. The English Eleven v. Eleven of New South Wales', *Sydney Morning Herald*, 8 February 1879, p. 6.
113 Albert Neilson Hornby, commonly designated A. N. Hornby, nicknamed Monkey Hornby, born 10 February 1847 in Blackburn, Lancashire; died 17 December 1925 in Nantwich, Cheshire.
114 George 'Happy Jack' Ulyett; born in 21 October 1851; died in Sheffield, 18 June 1898.
115 Paterson, *Song of the Pen*, Lansdowne Press, 1983, p. 569. Originally from a wireless talk, 'The Sydney Ground'.
116 'Sporting. The English Eleven v. Eleven of New South Wales', *Sydney Morning Herald*, 8 February 1879, p. 6.
117 Paterson, *Song of the Pen*, Lansdowne Press, 1983, p. 569. Originally from a wireless talk, 'The Sydney Ground'.
118 *Ibid.*, p. 531, From a wireless talk 'Old Cricketers'.
119 'Bushrangers', *Sydneian*, February 1879, p. 13.

Chapter 6

1 'An Australian Poet: "The Banjo" Interviewed', *Table Talk* (Melbourne), 31 January 1896, p. 6.
2 Grace Sterling Paterson (1877–1969).
3 'School Notices', *Sydneian*, August 1879, p. 15.
4 'School Holidays', *Sydney Morning Herald*, 20 December 1879, p. 3.
5 Albert Bathurst Piddington (9 September 1862 – 5 June 1945).
6 'The Acting Governor: Sir Alfred Stephen Sworn in', *Newcastle Morning Herald and Miners' Advocate*, 4 November 1890, p. 4.
7 'History of the Sydney Exhibition', *Sydney Daily Telegraph*, 18 September 1879, p. 6.
8 It ran from 17 September 1879 to 20 April 1880.
9 Thomas Henry Kendall (1839–1882).
10 'The Prize Poem', *Sydney Morning Herald*, 17 September 1879, p. 5.
11 'Burning of The Garden Palace', *Illustrated Sydney News*, 25 October 1882, p. 1.
12 'Destruction of the Garden Palace by Fire', *Sydney Morning Herald*, 23 September 1882, p. 7.
13 As the oddly titled Master in Equity and Lunacy. The Lunacy Act of 1878 made provision for the appointment of a Master of Lunacy to 'undertake the general care, protection and management or supervision of the management of estates of all insane persons and patients in New South Wales.' From records.nsw.gov.au.
14 'Government Gazette', *Sydney Mail and New South Wales Advertiser*, 8 April 1882, p. 549.
15 Albert Bythesea Weigall, 'The School', *Sydneian*, August 1907, p. 1.
16 'More Reminisces', *Sydneian*, August 1890, p. 7.
17 'Enigma', *Sydneian*, August 1879, p. 16.
18 Going to see the Governor', *Sydneian*, August 1879, p. 6.
19 'A Day on the Murrumbidgee', *Sydneian*, August 1879, p. 4.
20 *Ibid.*
21 'Shooting on the Parramatta River', *Sydneian*, September 1879, pp. 2–3.
22 Colin Roderick, *Banjo Paterson: Poet by Accident*, Allen & Unwin, 1993, p. 42.
23 Rose Paterson to Nora Murray-Prior, 11 January 1877, National Library of Australia, MS 9423.
24 *Ibid.*, 28 March 1880.
25 *Ibid.*, 11 June 1878.

26 'The Bell-Coleman Meat Preserving Process', *Maitland Mercury and Hunter River General Advertiser*, 11 December 1879, p. 3.
27 *Ibid.*
28 'Technology in Australia 1788–1988: Refrigeration and the Export of Meat', austehc.unimelb.edu.au, 1988.
29 Rose Paterson to Nora Murray-Prior, September–October 1880, National Library of Australia, MS 9423.
30 *Ibid.*, 28 March 1880.
31 'A Matter of Public Concern', *Bulletin*, No. 1, 31 January 1880, p. 1.
32 waverley.nsw.gov.au.
33 J. F. Archibald, born 14 January 1856 in Kildare, Victoria (now Geelong West); died 10 September 1919 at St Vincent's Hospital, Sydney.
34 'Great Australian Journalist, J. F. Archibald', *Sydney Sportsman*, 25 January 1922, p. 9.
35 *Ibid.*
36 *Bulletin*, 28 May 1887, as quoted in Patricia Rolfe, *The Journalistic Javelin: An Illustrated History of The Bulletin*, Wildcat Press, 1979.
37 Rosa Frankenstein, born London, 1853; died Darling Point, Sydney, 1911.
38 'Cricket', *Sydneian*, February 1880, p. 13.
39 *Ibid.*
40 Rose Paterson to Nora Murray-Prior, 28 March 1880, National Library of Australia, MS 9423.
41 A. B. Paterson, *Song of the Pen*, Lansdowne Press, 1983, p. 584, originally from a wireless talk called 'Wild Horses'.
42 *Ibid.*
43 *Ibid.*
44 Rose Paterson to Nora Murray-Prior, 10 August 1880, National Library of Australia, MS 9423.
45 *Ibid.*, September–October 1880.
46 *Ibid.*
47 'Last Quarter's Births and Deaths in Sydney', *Sydney Morning Herald*, 29 May 1880, p. 7.
48 'European and Colonial Items', *Grafton Argus and Clarence River General Advertiser*, 28 May 1880, p. 4.
49 Edith Jane Blaxland, nee Betts, born 13 July 1855 at Riverstone, NSW; died 22 April 1943 at Gladesville. The home, Cleves, was built in the 1850s by her husband's uncle Charles Blaxland and his wife Elizabeth. It was located in the wedge between Charles Street and Waterview Street, Putney. A house of the same name built by Emily Barton's brother John Bayley Darvall had existed on the site previously. Cleves was demolished in 1926. From ryde.nsw.gov.au.
50 Dr Herbert Blaxland (1852–1904). He was another grandson of the explorer Gregory Blaxland. His brother was Sid Blaxland, a frequent visitor to Illalong with Paterson's uncle Frank Barton.
51 Rose Paterson to Nora Murray-Prior, 3 October 1880, National Library of Australia, MS 9423.
52 *Ibid.*
53 'Death of Mr Henry Brown, JP, of Bendenine, Near Yass', *Goulburn Herald and Chronicle*, 5 January 1881, p. 2. Originally published in the *Yass Courier*.
54 'Family Notices', *Sydney Morning Herald*, 17 January 1881, p. 8.
55 Sir George Wigram Allen (16 May 1824 – 23 July 1885).
56 Rose Paterson to Nora Murray-Prior, October–November 1880, National Library of Australia, MS 9423.
57 Rose Paterson to her mother, Emily Mary Barton, November–December 1880, National Library of Australia, MS 9423.
58 Rose describes Robert Barton as 'Uncle Tye' in the letter to her mother.
59 Rose Paterson to Nora Murray-Prior, 11 February 1881, National Library of Australia, MS 9423.
60 *Ibid.*
61 *Ibid.*, 25 January 1882.
62 *Ibid.*, 18 November 1883.
63 'Old Sydneians', *Sydneian*, June 1888, p. 5.
64 Rose Paterson to Nora Murray-Prior, July 1881, National Library of Australia, MS 9423.

65 '"Banjo" Paterson Tells His Own Story: Giants of the Paddle, Pen, and Pencil', *Sydney Morning Herald*, 11 February 1939, p. 21.
66 Rose Paterson to Nora Murray-Prior, 3 October 1880, National Library of Australia, MS 9423.
67 *Ibid.*, 10 April 1884.
68 *Ibid.*
69 *Ibid.*, 3 October 1880.
70 'The Late Miss M. A. Flower', *Sydney Morning Herald*, 14 November 1900, p. 7.
71 Mary Ann Flower, born 24 March 1811 in London; arrived in Sydney 1847; died at her home in Victoria St, Darlinghurst, 11 November 1900.
72 Rose Paterson to Nora Murray-Prior, 11 February 1881, National Library of Australia, MS 9423.
73 *Ibid.*, 29 January 1882.
74 *Ibid.*, 22 January 1881.
75 Walter William Friend, born in Totnes, Devon, England 8 March 1836; died 20 October 1895 at his home in Burwood, Sydney.
76 Owen Friend, born in Sydney on 5 September 1847; died at his home at Newtown, Sydney on 14 July 1894.
77 William Smale Friend (1812–1896). From 'Personal', *Daily Telegraph* (Sydney), 29 October 1895, p. 5. His headquarters was in York St, Sydney.
78 Rose Paterson to Nora Murray-Prior, 29 January 1882, National Library of Australia, MS 9423.
79 'Death of Mr Walter Friend', *National Advocate* (Bathurst), 29 October 1895, p. 3.
80 Rose Paterson to Nora Murray-Prior, 22 May 1881, National Library of Australia, MS 9423.
81 'Advertising', *Sydney Mail and New South Wales Advertiser*, 1 October 1881, p. 562.
82 They were sons of Rose's aunt Eliza Darvall, who had married Henry Kater in the double ceremony of 1840 when Rose's mother had married Robert Barton.
83 Alice Eliza Kater (1861–1907). Known in her family as Leila.
84 Herbert Salwey (born 1852). They were married on 31 July 1882, at St Paul's Church in Burwood, Sydney.
85 Staunton Spain, born 4 November 1833 in Hampshire, England; died 15 May 1888 in Neutral Bay, Sydney.
86 Rose Paterson to Nora Murray-Prior, 10 April 1884, National Library of Australia, MS 9423.
87 Annie Brown (nee Friend), born 8 February 1837; married Henry Brown, 1856 at St James's Church, Sydney; died 1883 at Hunter's Hill.
88 Rose Paterson to Nora Murray-Prior, 29 January 1882, National Library of Australia, MS 9423.
89 Rose Paterson to Nora Murray-Prior, 5 October 1881.
90 *Ibid.*, 4 September 1881.
91 *Ibid.*
92 *Ibid.*, 29 January 1882.
93 *Ibid.*
94 'Medical', *Goulburn Herald*, 13 May 1882, p. 3.
95 Rose Paterson to Nora Murray-Prior, 29 January 1882, National Library of Australia, MS 9423.
96 Gwendoline Alexa Paterson, born 24 December 1881 in Yass; died 18 December 1946 at her home in Roslyndale Avenue, Woollahra, Sydney.
97 *Ibid.*

Chapter 7

1 A. B. Paterson writing about J.F. Archibald, from 'Great Australian Journalist, J. F. Archibald', *Sydney Sportsman*, 25 January 1922, p. 9.
2 Recollections of Banjo's cousin Mrs Sylvia Palmer, daughter of Frank Barton, from Clement Semmler, *The Banjo of the Bush* (second edition), University of Queensland Press, 1974, p. 51.
3 'Kellymania', *Ovens and Murray Advertiser*, 10 July 1880, p. 1.
4 T. Inglis Moore, 'Browne, Thomas Alexander (1826–1915)', *Australian Dictionary of Biography*, Volume 3, MUP, 1969.
5 183 centimetres and eighty-two kilograms.
6 'Fiction: Robbery Under Arms', *Sydney Mail and New South Wales Advertiser*, 1 July 1882, p. 6.

7 Rose Paterson to Nora Murray-Prior, 11 February 1881, National Library of Australia, MS 9423.
8 *Sydney Daily Telegraph*, 1 July 1881, p. 2.
9 '"Banjo" Paterson Tells His Own Story: Giants of the Paddle, Pen, and Pencil', *Sydney Morning Herald*, 11 February 1939, p. 21.
10 Mrs Campbell Praed, *An Australian Heroine*, Chapman & Hall Ltd, 1880.
11 Chris Tiffin, 'Praed, Rosa Caroline (1851–1935)', *Australian Dictionary of Biography*, Volume 11, MUP, 1988.
12 Henry Kendall, *Songs from the Mountains*, William Maddock, 1880.
13 Rose Paterson to Nora Murray-Prior, 6 June 1882, National Library of Australia, MS 9423.
14 Mary Anne Friend, nee Stockham (1841–1917).
15 Matilda Aimee (Meta) Murray-Prior (1873–1939).
16 Rose Paterson to Nora Murray-Prior, 29 January 1882, National Library of Australia, MS 9423.
17 *Ibid.*, 5 October 1881.
18 Ann Dyne Morgan (1863–1965). She was the daughter of Andrew Paterson's late sister Jessie and Dr Cosby Morgan. Jessie died on 4 September 1880 in Newcastle, NSW. Morgan married Hattie Scott (1830–1907) two years later.
19 Rose Paterson to Nora Murray-Prior, 17 September 1882, National Library of Australia, MS 9423.
20 She died at Katoomba in the Blue Mountains in 1965. From worldconnect.rootsweb.ancestry.com
21 Rose Paterson to Nora Murray-Prior, 6 January 1883, National Library of Australia, MS 9423.
22 *Ibid.*, March–April 1882.
23 *Ibid.*, 17 September 1882.
24 Chris Tiffin, 'Praed, Rosa Caroline (1851–1935)', *Australian Dictionary of Biography*, Volume 11, MUP, 1988.
25 Dale Spender, 'Rosa Praed: Original Australian Writer' in *A Bright and Fiery Troop: Australian Women Writers of the Nineteenth Century* (ed. Debra Adelaide), Penguin, 1988, p. 210.
26 Campbell Praed & Co Ltd of Wellingborough was absorbed by Phipps Northampton Brewery Company Ltd in 1954.
27 Rose Paterson to Nora Murray-Prior, 6 June 1882, National Library of Australia, MS 9423.
28 *Ibid.*
29 *Ibid.*, 5 October 1881.
30 'Obituary', *Australian Town and Country Journal*, 19 May 1888, p. 13.
31 'Vice-Admiralty Court', *Sydney Morning Herald*, 23 March 1881, p. 7.
32 'Law Report', *Sydney Morning Herald*, 21 May 1881, p. 11.
33 *Ibid.*, 13 August 1881, p. 7.
34 Edwin Sandys Lumsdaine, born 18 July 1857 in Balmain; died 26 March 1931 at Nepean District Hospital, Kingswood, New South Wales.
35 On 5 July 1884.
36 'The Late Rev. William Lumsdaine', *Sydney Morning Herald*, 11 April 1902, p. 4.
37 Rose Paterson to Nora Murray-Prior, 10 April 1884, National Library of Australia, MS 9423.
38 In 1881 the Sydney University Senate unanimously decided to allow the admission of women, and the passing of the *University Amendment Act in 1884* secured the legal rights of women at Sydney University.
39 Major-General Charles George Gordon (28 January 1833 – 26 January 1885).
40 Isma'il Pasha (31 December 1830 – 2 March 1895).
41 Muhammad Ahmad bin Abd Allah (12 August 1844 – 22 June 1885). Five months after the capture of Khartoum, El Mahdi died of typhus.
42 James Perry, *Arrogant Armies: Great Military Disasters and the Generals Behind Them*, Edison: Castle Books, 2005, p. 189.
43 C. Brad Faught, *Gordon: Victorian Hero*, Potomac Books, 2008, p. x.
44 'General Gordon', *Sydney Morning Herald*, 12 February 1885, p. 5.
45 'The Embarkation of the New South Wales Troops for the Soudan', *Maitland Mercury and Hunter River General Advertiser*, 5 March 1885, p. 2.

46 'Departure of New South Wales Troops for Egypt', *Illustrated Sydney News*, 14 March 1885, p. 11.
47 'Pastoral News', *Wagga Wagga Advertiser*, 28 February 1885, p. 3.
48 A. B. Paterson, *Singer of the Bush*, Lansdowne Press, 1983, p. xi.
49 *Ibid.*, p. xii.
50 Algernon Charles Swinburne (1837–1909).
51 *Song of the Pen, Lansdowne Press, 1983, p.* 563. Originally from a wireless talk, 'Singers Among Savages', for the ABC.
52 'Departure of New South Wales Troops for Egypt', *Illustrated Sydney News*, 14 March 1885, p. 11.
53 'The Contingent', *Sydney Morning Herald*, 24 June 1885, p. 7.
54 'A Splendid Business', *Bulletin*, 28 February 1885, p. 1.
55 'Departure of New South Wales Troops for Egypt', *Illustrated Sydney News*, 14 March 1885, p. 11.
56 Rose Paterson to Nora Murray-Prior, 13 February 1885, National Library of Australia, MS 9423.
57 Colin Roderick, *Banjo Paterson: Poet by Accident*, Allen & Unwin, 1993, p. 54.
58 A. B. Paterson, 'Concerning a Dog-fight', *Bulletin*, 18 May 1895, p. 24.
59 *Ibid.*
60 *Ibid.*
61 '"Banjo" Paterson Tells His Own Story: Giants of the Paddle, Pen, and Pencil', *Sydney Morning Herald*, 11 February 1939, p. 21.
62 Finally published by Gordon & Gotch, 1889.
63 A. B. Paterson, 'Australia for the Australians: A Political Pamphlet Showing the Necessity for Land Reform Combined with Protection', Gordon & Gotch, 1889.
64 *Ibid.*
65 Thomas Robert Malthaus (1766–1834).
66 A. B. Paterson, 'Australia for the Australians: A Political Pamphlet Showing the Necessity for Land Reform Combined with Protection', Gordon & Gotch, 1889.
67 *Ibid.*
68 '"Banjo" Paterson Tells His Own Story: Giants of the Paddle, Pen, and Pencil', *Sydney Morning Herald*, 11 February 1939, p. 21.
69 *Ibid.*
70 *Ibid.*
71 A. B. Paterson, *Singer of the Bush*, Lansdowne Press, 1983, p. xii.
72 Cincinnatus Heine Miller (September 8, 1837 – February 17, 1913). He wrote under the pen name Joaquin Miller.
73 A. B. Paterson, *Singer of the Bush*, Lansdowne Press, 1983, p. xii.
74 '"Banjo" Paterson Tells His Own Story: Giants of the Paddle, Pen, and Pencil', *Sydney Morning Herald*, 11 February 1939, p. 21.
75 'Local Land Board', *Burrowa News*, 27 November 1885, p. 2.
76 Clement Semmler, 'Paterson, Andrew Barton (Banjo) (1864–1941)', *Australian Dictionary of Biography*, Volume 11, MUP, 1988.
77 Florence Earle Hooper, 'Biography of A. B. Paterson (Part 3)', *Yass Tribune Courier*, 20 June 1949.
78 J. F. Archibald to Banjo Paterson, 22 August 1886, from A. B. 'Banjo' Paterson, *Singer of the Bush*, Lansdowne Press, 1983, p. xii.
79 *Ibid.*
80 '"Banjo" Paterson Tells His Own Story: Giants of the Paddle, Pen, and Pencil', *Sydney Morning Herald*, 11 February 1939, p. 21.
81 A. B. Paterson writing about J.F. Archibald, from 'Great Australian Journalist, J. F. Archibald', *Sydney Sportsman*, 25 January 1922, p. 9.
82 *Ibid.*
83 *Ibid.*
84 Wilfred Blacket (1859–1937).
85 '"Banjo" Paterson Tells His Own Story: Giants of the Paddle, Pen, and Pencil', *Sydney Morning Herald*, 11 February 1939, p. 21.

86 *Ibid.*
87 Claude McKay, 'J. F. Archibald was a Living Legend', *Sunday Herald* (Sydney), 23 November 1952, p. 12.
88 *Ibid.*
89 *Ibid.*
90 John Haynes (1850–1917).
91 Sylvia Lawson, 'Archibald, Jules François (1856–1919)', *Australian Dictionary of Biography*, Volume 3, MUP, 1969.
92 'A Matter of Public Concern', *Bulletin*, No. 1, 31 January 1880, p. 1.
93 'Marriages', *Sydney Morning Herald*, 10 December 1885, p. 1.
94 William Henry Traill (7 May 1842 – 21 May 1902).
95 '"Banjo" Paterson Tells His Own Story: Giants of the Paddle, Pen, and Pencil', *Sydney Morning Herald*, 11 February 1939, p. 21.

Chapter 8

1 '"Banjo" Paterson Tells His Own Story: Giants of the Paddle, Pen, and Pencil', *Sydney Morning Herald*, 11 February 1939, p. 21.
2 Adam Lindsay Gordon (1833–1870).
3 From State Library of New South Wales, MLMSS 4937/Box 24/Item 4.
4 He won 12 of his 13 starts as a three-year-old including the VRC Champion Stakes. He won the Randwick Derby by 10 lengths in record time, and in beating Trenton for the VRC Canterbury Plate he broke the Australia–New Zealand record. The only race he did not win was the Melbourne Cup where he finished fourth.
5 'Melbourne Cup', *Evening News* (Sydney), 3 November 1886, p. 6.
6 *Ibid.*
7 Donelly Fisher (1850–1919).
8 'Partnerships', *Daily Telegraph* (Sydney), 2 November 1886, p. 8.
9 'Well-Known Solicitor's Death', *Sydney Morning Herald*, 21 August 1919, p. 7.
10 Andrew Walter Irby Macansh (1863–1933).
11 Hester Beata Paterson (1867–1952).
12 On 19 March 1891.
13 'An Australian Poet: "The Banjo" Interviewed', *Table Talk* (Melbourne), 31 January 1896, p. 6.
14 '"Banjo" Paterson Tells His Own Story: Giants of the Paddle, Pen, and Pencil', *Sydney Morning Herald*, 11 February 1939, p. 21.
15 *Ibid.*
16 A. B. Paterson, *Song of the Pen*, Lansdowne Press, 1983, p. 558. Originally from a wireless talk, in the 1930s titled 'Sheep'.
17 A. B. Paterson (The Banjo), 'The Man from Snowy River', *Bulletin*, 26 April 1890, p. 13.
18 A. B. Paterson writing about J. F. Archibald, from 'Great Australian Journalist, J. F. Archibald', *Sydney Sportsman*, 25 January 1922, p. 9.
19 *Ibid.*
20 A. B. Paterson (The Banjo), 'The Mylora Elopement', *Bulletin* (Christmas edition) 25 December 1886, p. 12.
21 From State Library of New South Wales, MLMSS 4937/Box 24/Item 4.
22 Livingston York Yourtee 'Hop' Hopkins, born 7 July 1846 in Bellefontaine, Ohio; died 21 August 1927 in Mosman, Sydney.
23 Philip William May, born 22 April 1864 in Wortley, Leeds; died 5 August 1903 in London.
24 '"Banjo" Paterson Tells His Own Story: Giants of the Paddle, Pen, and Pencil', *Sydney Morning Herald*, 11 February 1939, p. 21.
25 *Ibid.*
26 Vance Palmer, *The Legend of the Nineties*, Melbourne University Press, 1954, p. 101.
27 H. P. Heseltine, 'May, Philip William (Phil) (1864–1903)', *Australian Dictionary of Biography*, Volume 5, MUP, 1974.
28 A. B. Paterson, *Happy Dispatches*, Angus & Robertson, 1934, Chapter X: Phil May.
29 A. B. Paterson (The Banjo), 'Only a Jockey', *Bulletin*, 26 February 1887, p. 12.

30 'In the Wind', *Melbourne Punch,* 5 May 1887, p. 1.
31 Fergusson Wright Hume (8 July 1859 – 12 July 1932).
32 Sir John Robertson, born 15 October 1816 in Bow, London; died 8 May 1891 in Watsons Bay, Sydney.
33 A. B. Paterson, *Song of the Pen*, Lansdowne Press, 1983, p. 554. Originally from a wireless talk, in the 1930s titled 'Political Giants'.
34 *Ibid.*
35 Sir Henry Parkes, born 27 May 1815 in Canley, Coventry, England; died 27 April 1896 in Annandale, Sydney.
36 A. B. Paterson, *Song of the Pen*, Lansdowne Press, 1983, p. 554. Originally from a wireless talk, in the 1930s titled 'Political Giants'.
37 A. B. Paterson, 'The Deficit Demon', *Bulletin*, 5 March 1887, p. 12.
38 The rape of a young girl at Mount Rennie in what is now the Sydney suburb of Waterloo resulted in Justice Windeyer sentencing nine young men to death. Four eventually hanged and five served long prison sentences.
39 A. L. May, *Sydney Rows: A Centennial History of the Sydney Rowing Club*, Sydney Rowing Club, 1970.
40 Balmain Regatta: A Successful Event, *Sydney Morning Herald,* 10 November 1896, p. 3.
41 A. L. May, *Sydney Rows: A Centennial History of the Sydney Rowing Club*, Sydney Rowing Club, 1970.
42 huntershilltennisclub.com.au.
43 'Ambidextrous Players', *Sydney Morning Herald,* 26 January 1911, p. 10.
44 A. B. Paterson, *Song of the Pen*, Lansdowne Press, 1983, p. 569. Originally from a wireless talk, in the 1930s titled 'The Sydney Ground'.
45 Henry Lawson, born 17 June 1867 in Grenfell, New South Wales; died 2 September 1922 in Abbotsford, Sydney.
46 Niels Hertzberg Larsen, born 12 September 1832 in Tromøya, Norway; died 31 December 1888 in Mount Victoria, New South Wales.
47 Louisa Lawson, nee Albury, born 17 February 1848 on Guntawang Station, near Mudgee; died 12 August 1920 in the Hospital for the Insane, Gladesville.
48 'Local News', *Grenfell Record and Lachlan District Advertiser,* 24 October 1908, p. 2.
49 Now called Eurunderee.
50 'A Mudgee Man's Life Story: Henry Lawson's Early Days', *Mudgee Guardian and North-Western Representative,* 2 April 1908, p. 8. Reprinted from *Lone Hand.*
51 'Henry Lawson Australia's Gifted Bush Poet', *Gundagai Independent,* 3 June 1937, p. 6.
52 'A Mudgee Man's Life Story: Henry Lawson's Early Days', *Mudgee Guardian and North-Western Representative,* 2 April 1908, p. 8. Reprinted from *Lone Hand.*
53 *Ibid.*
54 *Ibid.*
55 Philip Whistler Street (1863–1938), 8th Chief Justice of NSW and 13th Lieutenant Governor of New South Wales. Both his son Sir Kenneth (married to the human rights campaigner Lady Jessie Street) and his grandson Sir Laurence Street served the two roles of Chief Justice and Lieutenant Governor.
56 John William Street, born 11 January 1862 in Sydney; died 26 July 1943 in Elizabeth Bay, Sydney.
57 Susanna Caroline Lawson (1836–1872).
58 'Law Report. Supreme Court, Re Herbert Salwey, Solicitor', *Sydney Morning Herald,* 11 May 1894, p. 3.
59 Alban Joseph Riley (1844–1914).
60 'News of the Day', *Sydney Morning Herald,* 4 June 1887, p. 11.
61 'Celebration of the Queen's Jubilee', *Sydney Morning Herald,* 11 June 1887, p. 8.
62 Heather Radi, 'Lawson, Louisa (1848–1920)', *Australian Dictionary of Biography,* Volume 10, MUP, 1986.
63 'The Jubilee Celebration', *Sydney Morning Herald,* 16 June 1887, p. 5.
64 *Ibid.*

65 *Ibid.*
66 'Correspondence', *Bulletin*, 18 June 1887, p. 15.
67 'A Mudgee Man's Life Story: Henry Lawson's Early Days', *Mudgee Guardian and North-Western Representative,* 2 April 1908, p. 8. Reprinted from *Lone Hand.*
68 Henry Lawson, *Letters: 1890–1922,* Angus & Robertson, 1970, p. 88.
69 *Bulletin*, 2 July 1887.
70 *Bulletin*, 19 November 1887, p. 4.
71 *Bulletin*, 2 July 1887.
72 *Ibid.*
73 Henry Lawson, *Letters: 1890–1922,* Angus & Robertson, 1970, p. 88.
74 'Correspondence', *Bulletin*, 23 July 1887, p. 6.
75 *Bulletin*, 23 July 1887, p. 7.
76 Henry Lawson, *A Camp-fire Yarn: Henry Lawson Complete Works 1885–1900,* Lansdowne, 1984, p. 44.
77 Henry Lawson, (ed Colin Roderick), *Collected Prose: Autobiographical and Other Writings, 1887–1922,* Angus & Robertson, 1922, p. 757.
78 Henry Lawson, 'A Song of the Republic', *Bulletin*, 1 October 1887, p. 5.
79 Denton Prout, *Henry Lawson: The Grey Dreamer,* Rigby, 1963, p. 68.
80 Henry Lawson, *A Camp-fire Yarn: Henry Lawson Complete Works 1885–1900,* Lansdowne, 1984, p. 673.
81 Henry Lawson, 'The Wreck of the Derry Castle', *Bulletin*, 24 December 1887, p. 12.
82 'The Day We Were Lagged', *Bulletin*, 21 January 1888, p. 4.
83 'The Day We Ought to Celebrate', *Bulletin*, 21 January 1888, p. 5.
84 Norman Lindsay, *Bohemians of the Bulletin,* Angus & Robertson, 1965, p. 82.
85 From Street & Paterson to Angus & Robertson, 14 July 1899.

Chapter 9

1 'Looking Backward', *Sydney Mail,* 28 December 1938, p. 7.
2 'Advertising', *Sydney Morning Herald*, 4 April 1888, p. 16.
3 *Ibid.*, 20 April 1888, p. 9.
4 *Ibid.*, 12 February 1890, p. 2.
5 Roderick, *Banjo Paterson: Poet by Accident,* Allen & Unwin, 1993.
6 '"Banjo" Paterson Tells His Own Story: Giants of the Paddle, Pen, and Pencil', *Sydney Morning Herald*, 11 February 1939, p. 21.
7 A. B. Paterson, 'Uncle Bill', *Bulletin*, 9 June 1888, p. 8.
8 Semmler, *The Banjo of the Bush* (second edition), Queensland University Press, 1974, p. 210.
9 'Our Derby Candidates', *Leader* (Melbourne), 29 September 1877, p. 10. The breeding was by Yattendon from Gazelle.
10 'V.R.C. Spring Meeting. The Oaks Day', *Argus*, 9 November 1877, p. 7.
11 'Randwick Autumn Meeting', *Hay Standard and Advertiser*, 30 April 1873, p. 4. Dagworth then won a run-off by a neck to decide the issue.
12 Sarah Ann Riley, born 29 May 1863 in Indented Head, Victoria; died 31 July 1935 in Camberwell, Victoria.
13 Sarah's aunt Sarah Maria Smith had married John Rendell Street in 1883. Two boys from his first marriage were Banjo's business partner John Street and his brother Philip. Sarah's uncle Thomas Whistler Smith had also married Sarah Maria Street.
14 'Town Talk', *Geelong Advertiser*, 25 May 1892, p. 2.
15 James Brook Riley, born 1847 in Gloucestershire, England; died 5 October 1889 in Winton, Queensland; and Frederick Whistler Riley, born 7 December 1856 in Gheringap, Victoria; died 9 November 1914 in Winton, Queensland.
16 'Sales of stations', *Queenslander*, 28 July 1923, p. 32.
17 'Obituary, Mrs M. G. Riley', *Longreach Leader*, 2 May 1942, p. 12.
18 Madame Elise Pfund (1833–1921). Oberwyl was established in the former Etloe Hall at 35 Burnett Street, St Kilda.
19 St Kilda Historical Society (skhs.org.au).
20 Emily Mary Barton to Nora Murray-Prior, 18 October 1888.

21 A. B. Paterson, 'As Long as Your Eyes are Blue', *Bulletin*, 7 November 1891, p. 24.
22 propertyobserver.com.au.
23 Henry Shubrick Martin, born 1839.
24 Rose Paterson to Nora Murray-Prior, 6 August 1888, National Library of Australia, MS 9423.
25 *Ibid.*
26 'Death of Mr A. B. Paterson', *Burrowa News*, 14 June 1889, p. 2.
27 Emily Mary Barton to Nora Murray-Prior, 18 October 1888.
28 *Ibid.*
29 'Publications Received', *Sydney Morning Herald*, 29 January 1889, p. 11.
30 A. B. Paterson, 'The Corner Man', *Bulletin*, 26 January 1889, p. 7.
31 A. B. Paterson, 'The Sausage Candidate', *Bulletin*, 9 February 1889, p. 5.
32 Sir George Richard Dibbs (12 October 1834 – 5 August 1904).
33 A. B. Paterson, 'Who is Kater Anyhow?', *Bulletin*, 2 March 1889, p. 6.
34 Richard Edward O'Connor (1851–1912), Member of the NSW Legislative Council, 1887–98, Senator, NSW, 1901–03.
35 The town is now called Boorowa.
36 Philip Thornton Thane (1859–1944).
37 Andrew Bogle Paterson, death registration 7465/1889.
38 'Death of Mr A. B. Paterson', *Burrowa News*, 14 June 1889, p. 2.
39 Psalm 127:2, King James version of the Holy Bible.
40 Nora to T. L. Murray-Prior, 5 August 1889. National Library of Australia. MSS 1578.
41 A. B. Paterson, 'Tar and Feathers', *Bulletin*, 21 September, p. 8.
42 A. B. Paterson, 'Hughey's Dog: A Station Sketch', *Bulletin*, 2 November 1889, p. 8.
43 *Ibid.*
44 A. B. Paterson, 'Mulligan's Mare', *Bulletin*, 23 November 1889, p. 19.
45 *Ibid.*
46 Arthur Wilberforce Jose, *The Romantic Nineties*, Angus & Robertson, 1933, p. 15.
47 Henry Lawson, 'The Roaring Days', *Bulletin*, 21 December 1889, p. 26.
48 Henry Lawson, 'The Legend of Mammon Castle', *Bulletin*, 21 December 1889, p. 26.
49 Henry Lawson, 'The Teams', *Australian Town and Country Journal*, 21 December 1889, p. 16.
50 Henry Lawson, 'Brighten's Sister-in-Law', *Australian Town and Country Journal*, 21 December 1889, p. 25.
51 Henry Lawson., 'Mount Bukaroo', *Australian Town and Country Journal*, 21 December 1889, p. 32.
52 A. B. Paterson, 'An Idyll of Dandaloo', *Bulletin*, 21 December 1889, p. 14.
53 A. B. Paterson, 'The Scapegoat', *Bulletin*, 21 December 1889, p. 15.
54 Originally published as 'The Bard That Is to Be', *Bulletin*, 21 December 1889, p. 30, under the byline 'J.W.'. Reprinted as 'Song of the Future' in A. B. (Banjo) Paterson, *Rio Grande's Last Race*, Angus & Robertson, 1902.
55 Francis William Lauderdale Adams (1862–1893).
56 A. B. Paterson, *Song of the Pen*, Lansdowne Press, 1983, Lansdowne Press, 1983, p. 563. Originally from a wireless talk 'Singers Among Savages' for the ABC.
57 'Looking Backward', *Sydney Mail*, 28 December 1938, p. 7.
58 *Ibid.*
59 '"Banjo" Paterson Tells His Own Story: Giants of the Paddle, Pen, and Pencil', *Sydney Morning Herald*, 11 February 1939, p. 21.
60 A. B. Paterson, 'Clancy of the Overflow', *Bulletin*, 21 December 1889, p. 17.
61 *Ibid.*
62 'Old Stockriders', *Australasian*, 8 February 1890.
63 'Personal Items', *Bulletin*, 8 March 1890, p. 9.
64 'Golden Shanty', *Bulletin*, 27 September 1890, p. 26.
65 Review, *Daily Telegraph* (Sydney), 13 September 1890, p. 9.
66 A. B. Paterson to George Robertson, 18 January 1913, in reply to a letter from Angus & Robertson asking him to explain whether 'Overflow' referred to an old station of that name; George Paterson Papers, State Library of NSW.

67 Thomas Gerald Clancy, born 21 December 1835 in Castletownroche, County Cork, Ireland; died 4 September 1914 in North Carlton, Melbourne.
68 'An Old Melbourne Citizen', *Advocate* (Melbourne), 26 February 1910, p. 16.
69 The will was signed in 1899. From Michael Cathcart, 'Was Clancy of the Overflow a real person?', abc.net.au, 28 February 2014.
70 *Port Phillip Patriot and Melbourne Advertiser.*
71 'An Old Melbourne Citizen', *Advocate* (Melbourne), 26 February 1910, p. 16.
72 'Clancy of the Overflow', *Age*, 11 December 1943, p. 7.
73 Michael Cathcart, 'Was Clancy of the Overflow a real person?', abc.net.au, 28 February 2014.
74 T. G. Clancy, 'Clancy of the Overflow – the Reply', *Freeman's Journal* (Sydney), 7 November 1907, p. 12. The poem was written in 1897. Clancy wrote a number of poems under the byline 'Clangerald'.
75 Alexander Hugh Chisholm (1890–1977).
76 'All Thought They Knew "Clancy"', *Sunday Herald* (Sydney), 4 December 1949, p. 8.
77 'Clancy of the Overflow', *Age*, 11 December 1943, p. 7.
78 Michael Cathcart, 'Was Clancy of the Overflow a real person?', abc.net.au, 28 February 2014.
79 Louise Southerden, 'Clancy's Overflow', *Outback*, No. 9, February–March 2000, p. 39.
80 'Supreme Court. In Equity. (Before his Honor Judge Owen).', *Evening News* (Sydney), 1 February 1890, p. 6.

Chapter 10

1 'Looking Backward', *Sydney Mail,* 28 December 1938, p. 7.
2 *Ballarat Star*, 15 June 1886, p. 2.
3 'Shearers' Union, Blackall', *Queensland Figaro and Punch* (Brisbane), 5 March 1887, p. 3.
4 'The Shearers' Strike', *South Australian Advertiser* (Adelaide), 1 August 1887, p. 6.
5 'The Shearers' Conference', *Sydney Morning Herald*, 15 February 1890, p. 9.
6 'The Shearers' Dispute in Queensland', *Sydney Morning Herald*, 13 May 1890, p. 5.
7 'Maritime Difficulties', *Sydney Morning Herald*, 19 August 1890, p. 5.
8 Peter Stuckey Mitchell (1854–1921).
9 Walter Edward Mitchell (1863–1917).
10 Thomas Mitchell (1818–1887).
11 *Wodonga and Towong Sentinel*, 7 October 1887, p. 2.
12 'Death of Mr. Walter E. Mitchell', *Albury Banner and Wodonga Express*, 21 September 1917, p. 27.
13 In 1909.
14 A. B. Paterson, 'The Snow-Line', *Sydney Mail*, 24 August 1932, p. 4.
15 A. B. Paterson, *Song of the Pen*, Lansdowne Press, 1983, Lansdowne, p. 511, Originally from a wireless talk, 'Men and Horses'.
16 The rules of the competition stated that 'women competitors must be unmarried and under the age of 30. Youths must be under the age of 21.' They had to be British subjects and bona-fide residents of the Commonwealth of Australia, of a white race, and not the offspring of first cousins. They had to have good physical health, be able to swim, and ride a horse 'reasonably well', and have a knowledge of the geography, climates, and primary products of Australia. They had to know something about the history of the British Empire. A knowledge of elementary anatomy and physiology and the main functions of the human body and of first-aid was required. 'The main test that women candidates must pass is: "Practical and theoretic knowledge of the nursing in sickness and health, handling, management, training, care, and rearing to perfect health and strength of babies and young children." They will also be judged on the soundness of their "knowledge of practical housekeeping and domestic economy, and the necessity for clean and sanitary surroundings and conditions." An extra requirement for male candidates is that they must be able to shoot "reasonably well." They must also have "honourably fulfilled all military obligations imposed upon them by the laws of the Commonwealth of Australia." Male applicants will be tested also on their knowledge of the British Constitution and on the Constitution of the Commonwealth of Australia and of their own State. In addition, both male and female applicants must have a "knowledge and understanding" of the Protestant Bible'. From 'Peter Mitchell Will Quest', *Australian Women's Weekly*, 25 September 1957, p. 16.

17 'The Remarkable Will of Peter Mitchell', *Age*, 9 February 1921, p. 9. Mitchell's eugenics plan was tied up in legal argument over his will for thirty years but was finally sponsored by the *Australian Women's Weekly*. The organisers eventually awarded £10,000 in prizes between 1955 and 1959.

18 From the Aboriginal word for the local water spiders, 'ton-a-roggin', from Frank Clune, *Journey to Kosciusko by Road from Sydney*, Angus & Robertson, 1965, p. 333.

19 John Riley, born 1841 in Castlebar, Ireland; died 15 July 1914 near Corryong, Victoria. Arrived in Sydney 13 March 1854, aboard the *Rodney*. From State Records Authority of New South Wales, Kingswood New South Wales. 'Persons on bounty ships to Sydney, Newcastle, and Moreton Bay (Board's Immigrant Lists)'; Series: 5317; Reel: 2467; Item: [4/4940].

20 'Omeo', *Gippsland Guardian*, 7 February 1862, p. 3.

21 Omeo Cause Lists 1873 and 1876, quoted in W. F. Refshauge, *Searching for The Man from Snowy River*, Arcadia, 2012, p. 94.

22 uppermurraybusinessdirectory.com.au.

23 W. F. Refshauge, *Searching for The Man from Snowy River*, Arcadia, 2012, p. 94

24 *Ibid.*, p. 97.

25 'Castlebar man – Australian Folk hero', castlebar.ie, 18 April 2005.

26 John Pierce (1870–1930). 'A Mountain Tragedy', *Corryong Courier*, 23 July 1914, p. 3.

27 Recollections of John Pierce's daughter Peg Gersinic, quoted in W. F. Refshauge, *Searching for The Man from Snowy River*, Arcadia, 2012, p. 106.

28 Recollections of Walter Mitchell's daughter-in-law Elyne Mitchell (nee Chauvel), from 'Castlebar man – Australian Folk hero', castlebar.ie, 18 April 2005.

29 Gordon Williams, 'There Was a "Man from Snowy River"', *Argus Week-End Magazine*, 15 January 1949, p. 3.

30 *Ibid.*

31 *Ibid.*

32 *Ibid.*

33 A. B. Paterson, 'How I Shot the Policeman', *Bulletin*, 4 January 1890, p. 8.

34 Edward Dyson, 'The Tiredest Man', *Bulletin*, 21 December 1889, p. 22.

35 A. B. Paterson, 'Our New Horse', *Bulletin*, 22 March 1890, p. 8.

36 'Looking Backward', *Sydney Mail*, 28 December 1938, p. 7.

37 *Ibid.*

38 A. B. Paterson, 'The Man from Snowy River', *Bulletin*, 26 April 1890, p. 8.

39 *Ibid.*

40 A. B. Paterson, 'How Wild Horses Are Yarded', *Sydney Morning Herald*, 12 September 1891, p. 4. Under the byline A.B.P.

41 A. B. Paterson, 'The Man from Snowy River', *Bulletin*, 26 April 1890, p. 8.

42 *Ibid.*

43 A. B. Paterson, 'How Wild Horses Are Yarded', *Sydney Morning Herald*, 12 September 1891, p. 4. Under the byline A.B.P.

44 W. F. Refshauge, *Searching for The Man from Snowy River*, Arcadia, 2012, p. 13.

45 A. B. Paterson, *Song of the Pen*, Lansdowne Press, 1983, p. 584, originally from a wireless talk called 'Wild Horses'.

46 A. B. Paterson, 'How Wild Horses Are Yarded', *Sydney Morning Herald*, 12 September 1891, p. 4. Under the byline A.B.P.

47 'Personal Items', *Bulletin*, 8 March 1890, p. 9.

48 'Intercolonial Lawn Tennis Tournament', *Sydney Morning Herald*, 14 May 1890, p. 8.

49 A. B. Paterson, 'The Hypnotist', *Bulletin*, 19 July 1890, p. 5.

50 A. B. Paterson, 'Gilhooley's Estate', *Bulletin*, 23 August 1890, p. 14.

51 *Ibid.*

52 'The Newcastle Colliery Strike', *Sydney Morning Herald*, 21 September 1888, p. 8.

53 'The Colliery Strike', *Brisbane Courier*, 29 September 1888, p. 8.

54 *Argus*, 1 September 1890, p. 4.

55 'Colonel Price's Address to the Mounted Rifles', *Argus*, 24 October 1890, p. 10.

56 A. B. Paterson, 'Those Names', *Bulletin*, 20 September 1890, p. 11. Also known as 'The Fearsome Names Out Back'.
57 *Ibid.*
58 A. B. Paterson, 'The Maori Pig Market', *Bulletin*, 22 November 1890, p. 6.
59 *Ibid.*
60 'V.R.C. Spring Meeting', *Riverine Grazier* (Hay), 7 November 1890, p. 3.
61 *Ibid.*
62 'The Cup Winner', *Age*, 5 November 1890, p. 6.
63 *Ibid.*
64 A. B. Paterson, *Song of the Pen*, Lansdowne Press, 1983, p. 348.
65 A. B. Paterson, 'On Kiley's Run', *Bulletin*, 20 December 1890, p. 6.
66 'Looking Backward', *Sydney Mail*, 28 December 1938, p. 7.
67 A. B. Paterson, 'The Story of Conroy's Gap', *Bulletin*, 20 December 1890, p. 13. Later known simply as 'Conroy's Gap'.
68 *The Man from Snowy River*, 1920. Produced and directed by Beaumont Smith.
69 *Ibid.*, 1982. Produced by Geoff Burrowes, Michael Edgley and Simon Wincer; directed by George T. Miller.
70 'Stockman of Whom Poet Sang', *Courier-Mail* (Brisbane), 21 December 1938, p. 2.
71 W. F. Refshauge, *Searching for The Man from Snowy River*, Arcadia, 2012, p. 140.
72 Barcroft Henry Thomas Boake (26 March 1866 – 2 May 1892).
73 Barcroft Boake, 'On The Range', *Bulletin*, 30 May 1891, p. 24.
74 'The Man from Snowy River', *Age*, 17 July 1948, p. 6
75 'A Mountain Tragedy', *Corryong Courier*, 23 July 1914, p. 3.
76 *Ibid.*
77 Patrick Joseph Hartigan (1878–1952).
78 'John O'Brien's' Life Story and Reminiscences – Part II', *Catholic Weekly* (Sydney), 15 May 1952, p. 1.
79 *Ibid.*
80 'A Mountain Tragedy', *Corryong Courier*, 23 July 1914, p. 3.
81 'Man from Snowy River', *Sydney Morning Herald*, 17 July 1914, p. 9.
82 'The Man from Snowy River', *Corryong Courier*, 6 August 1914, p. 3.
83 Walter Thomas Mitchell (1906–1984).
84 W. F. Refshauge, *Searching for The Man from Snowy River*, Arcadia, 2012, p. 113.
85 Sybil Elyne Keith Mitchell (née Chauvel, 30 December 1913 – 4 March 2002).
86 'Conqueror of the colt from Old Regret', *Canberra Times*, 4 July 1993, p. 21.
87 'Looking Backward', *Sydney Mail*, 28 December 1938, p. 7.

Chapter 11

1 'An Australian Poet: "The Banjo" Interviewed', *Table Talk* (Melbourne), 31 January 1896, p. 6.
2 *Ibid.*
3 Recollections of Sylvia Palmer, Banjo's cousin, from Semmler, *The Banjo of the Bush* (second edition), Queensland University Press, 1974, p. 67.
4 *Ibid.*
5 '"Banjo" Paterson Tells His Own Story: Giants of the Paddle, Pen, and Pencil', *Sydney Morning Herald*, 11 February 1939, p. 21.
6 'Central Criminal Court', *Sydney Morning Herald*, 2 December 1890, p. 3. Burnett's surname was first recorded as 'Barnett'.
7 *Ibid.*
8 'Legislative Assembly', *Sydney Morning Herald*, 10 September 1891, p. 5.
9 *Ibid.*
10 'Quarter Sessions', *Daily Telegraph*, 9 October 1891, p. 3.
11 'The Assaulter of Females', *Australian Star*, 14 October 1891, p. 3.
12 'Amateur Athletics', *Referee* (Sydney), 2 September 1891, p. 3.
13 'Sporting Intelligence', *Sydney Morning Herald*, 22 May 1893, p. 3.
14 'An Australian Poet: "The Banjo" Interviewed', *Table Talk* (Melbourne), 31 January 1896, p. 6.

15 'Queensland Government Loan of 1891', *Brisbane Courier*, 14 October 1891, p. 6.
16 '"Banjo" Paterson Tells His Own Story: Giants of the Paddle, Pen, and Pencil', *Sydney Morning Herald*, 11 February 1939, p. 21.
17 *Ibid.*
18 'Tasma's Letter', *Clarence and Richmond Examiner* (Grafton), 18 June 1898, p. 4.
19 'Sydney Social Items, Etc', *Illustrated Sydney News*, 5 December 1891, p. 5.
20 'Events of the Week', *Sydney Mail and New South Wales Advertiser*, 28 November 1891, p. 1191.
21 'Polo Contest', *Daily Telegraph* (Sydney), 30 March 1893, p. 6.
22 Recollections of Edie Paterson (Mrs Guy Huntley) to Florence Earle Hooper, from Semmler, *The Banjo of the Bush (second edition)*, Queensland University Press, 1974, p. 67.
23 A. B. Paterson, 'The Downfall of Mulligan's', *Bulletin*, 28 February 1891, p. 19.
24 A. B. Paterson, 'His Masterpiece', *Bulletin*, 4 April 1891, p. 22.
25 *Ibid.*
26 A. B. Paterson, 'In the Droving Days', *Bulletin*, 20 June 1891, p. 24.
27 A. B. Paterson, 'The Flying Gang: A Railway Song', *Bulletin*, 18 July 1891, p. 10.
28 A. B. Paterson, 'The Lost Drink', *Bulletin*, 1 August 1891, p. 24. Under the byline 'B.'
29 A. B. Paterson, 'An Evening in Dandaloo', *Bulletin*, 29 August 1891, p. 23.
30 A. B. Paterson, 'History of a Jackaroo in Five Letters', *Bulletin*, 5 September 1891, p. 23.
31 *Ibid.*
32 A. B. Paterson, 'Victor Second', *Bulletin*, 31 October 1891, p. 21.
33 *Ibid.*
34 A. B. Paterson, 'A Mountain Station', *Bulletin*, 19 December 1891, p. 19.
35 A. B. Paterson, 'The Cast Iron Canvasser', *Bulletin*, 19 December 1891, p. 7.
36 *Ibid.*
37 *Ibid.*
38 A. B. Paterson, 'The Ace, from Snowy River', *Bulletin*, 19 December 1891, p. 6.
39 *Ibid.*
40 'Lawn Tennis', *Sydney Morning Herald*, 12 March 1891, p. 8.
41 'Programme Intercolonial Match', *Illustrated Sydney News*, 11 April 1891, p. 2.
42 'Lawn Tennis', *Illustrated Sydney News*, 25 April 1891, p. 16.
43 'Lawn Tennis. The Intercolonial Tournament. Last Day', *Daily Telegraph* (Sydney), 18 May 1891, p. 6.
44 *Ibid.*
45 Henry Lawson, 'Andy's Gone with Cattle', *Australian Town and Country Journal*, 13 October 1888, p. 29.
46 *Ibid.*
47 Henry Lawson, 'Eureka!', *Bulletin*, 2 March 1889, p. 12.
48 Written in 1887, from *Henry Lawson: Collected Verse: Vol. I 1885–1900*, Angus & Robertson, 1967, pp. 8–9.
49 Henry Lawson letter to Lancelot Lindley-Cowen, 20 May 1890. From *Henry Lawson Letters* (edited by Colin Roderick), Angus & Robertson, 1972, p. 47.
50 Gresley Lukin, born 21 November 1840 in Launceston, Tasmania; died 12 September 1916 Wellington, New Zealand.
51 'The *Boomerang*, Conducted by Gresley Lukin', *Week* (Brisbane), 6 December 1890, p. 18.
52 William Lane, born 6 September 1861 in Bristol, England; died 26 August 1917 in Auckland, New Zealand.
53 Ann Nugent, 'The Queensland Shearers Strike in the 1890s', *National Library Magazine*, June 2012, p. 19.
54 'The Shearing Dispute', *Brisbane Courier*, 3 February 1891, p. 5.
55 *Ibid.*
56 'The Queensland Shearers', *Express and Telegraph* (Adelaide), 19 February 1891, p. 3.
57 John (Julian) Alexander Salmon Stuart, born 18 December 1866 in Eagleton, New South Wales; died 3 July 1929 in Perth, Western Australia.
58 *Brisbane Courier*, 21 February 1891, p. 4.
59 'The Shearers' Dispute', *Queensland Times, Ipswich Herald and General Advertiser*, 21 February 1891, p. 5.

60 'The Shearers' Trouble', *Bathurst Free Press and Mining Journal*, 23 February 1891, p. 3.
61 'The Shearers' Dispute', *Brisbane Courier*, 21 February 1891, p. 5.
62 'The Labor Crisis', *Western Star and Roma Advertiser*, 25 March 1891, p. 2.
63 'Shearers Troubles', *Australian Town and Country Journal*, 28 March 1891, p. 13.
64 'Bread or Blood', *National Advocate* (Bathurst), 24 April 1891, p. 2.
65 'The Shearing Strike', *Morning Bulletin* (Rockhampton), 8 April 1891, p. 5.
66 'The Editorial Mill', *Worker* (Brisbane), 21 March 1891, p. 2.
67 'Legislative Assembly', *Queenslander* (Brisbane), 11 July 1891, p. 1.
68 'The Labor Crisis', *Western Star and Roma Advertiser* (Toowoomba), 6 May 1891, p. 2.
69 Henry Lawson, 'Freedom on the Wallaby', *Worker*, 16 May 1891, p. 8.
70 *Ibid.*
71 'The Vote of Thanks Debate', *Worker*, 25 July 1891, p. 3.
72 *Ibid.*
73 'The Late Shearing Strike', *Brisbane Courier*, 16 June 1891, p. 5.
74 Myles Sinnamon, '125th Anniversary of the Manifesto of the Queensland Labour Party', John Oxley Library, http://blogs.slq.qld.gov.au.
75 Andrew Dawson (16 July 1863 – 20 July 1910), also known as Anderson Dawson.
76 'Events of the Week', *Sydney Mail and New South Wales Advertiser*, 28 November 1891, p. 1191.
77 'Polo', *Sydney Mail and New South Wales Advertiser*, 16 January 1892, p. 152.
78 'Polo Match at Scone', *Sydney Morning Herald*, 7 January 1892, p. 6.
79 'Rosehill Tournament', *Australian Star* (Sydney), 23 January 1892, p. 3.
80 George Joachim Goschen, 2nd Viscount Goschen (15 October 1866 – 24 July 1952).
81 'Rosehill Tournament', *Australian Star* (Sydney), 23 January 1892, p. 3.
82 Semmler, *The Banjo of the Bush* (second edition), Queensland University Press, 1974, p. 67.
83 'The "*Boomerang*"', *Maryborough Chronicle, Wide Bay and Burnett Advertiser*, 12 December 1891, p. 6.
84 Henry Lawson, 'The Shame of Going Back', *Bulletin*, 10 October 1891, p. 22.
85 *Ibid.*

Chapter 12

1 A. B. Paterson, 'In Answer To Various Bards', *Bulletin*, 1 October 1892, p. 2.
2 '"Banjo" Paterson Tells His Own Story: Giants of the Paddle, Pen, and Pencil', *Sydney Morning Herald*, 11 February 1939, p. 21.
3 Later Sir Francis Bathurst Suttor (1839–1915).
4 'Polo Contest', *Australian Star* (Sydney), 28 April 1892, p. 8.
5 Henry Lawson, 'A Song of Southern Writers', *Bulletin*, 28 May 1892, p. 24.
6 Arthur Wilberforce Jose, born 4 September 1863 in Bristol, England; died 22 January 1934 in Brisbane.
7 John Farrell, born 18 December 1851 in Buenos Aires, Argentina; died 8 January 1904 in Sydney.
8 Farrell was appointed editor in June 1890 but the pressure got to him and he resigned three months later.
9 Henry George, *Progress and Poverty*, Appleton and Company, 1879.
10 William Henry Ogilvie, born 21 August 1869 in Kelso, Scotland; died 30 January 1963 in Ashkirk, Scotland.
11 Will H Ogilvie, *Fair Girls and Gray Horses: With Other Verses*, Bulletin Newspaper Company, 1898.
12 Edward George Dyson, born 4 March 1865 in Ballarat, Victoria; died, 22 August 1931 in Elwood, Melbourne. He was the third of the *Bulletin*'s Paterdylaw trio – Paterson-Dyson-Lawson.
13 Edwin James Brady, born 7 August 1869 in Carcoar, New South Wales; died 22 July 1952 in Pambula, New South Wales.
14 Barcroft Henry Thomas Boake, born 26 March 1866 in Balmain, Sydney; died 2 May 1892 in Middle Harbour, Sydney.
15 Barcroft Boake, 'On the Range', *Bulletin*, 30 May 1891, p. 24.

16 *Ibid.*
17 'Suicide of Mr. B. H. Boake', *Wagga Wagga Express*, 17 May 1892, p. 2.
18 A. B. Paterson, 'The Tug-of-War', *Bulletin,* 20 February 1892, p. 20.
19 'The Tug of War', *Daily Telegraph* (Sydney), 13 February 1892, p. 6.
20 A. B. Paterson, 'The Pannikin Poet', *Bulletin,* 28 May 1892, p. 22.
21 Henry Lawson, 'Borderland', *Bulletin,* 9 July 1892, p. 21. Renamed 'Up the Country' in Lawson's *Poetical Works* in 1917.
22 A. W. Jose, *The Romantic Nineties,* Angus & Robertson, 1933, p. 18.
23 Henry Lawson, 'Borderland', *Bulletin,* 9 July 1892, p. 21.
24 A. B. Paterson, 'In Defence of the Bush', *Bulletin,* 23 July 1892, p. 17.
25 *Ibid.*
26 *Ibid.*
27 Henry Lawson, 'The Drover's Wife', *Bulletin,* 23 July 1892, pp. 21–21.
28 *Ibid.*
29 *Ibid.*
30 Henry Lawson, 'In Answer to "Banjo" and Otherwise', *Bulletin,* 6 August 1892, p. 5.
31 *Ibid.*
32 Henry Lawson, 'Grog- An'- Grumble Steeplechase', *Bulletin,* 10 September 1892, p. 20.
33 A. B. Paterson, 'In Answer To Various Bards', *Bulletin,* 1 October 1892, p. 2.
34 *Ibid.*
35 *Ibid.*
36 Henry Lawson, 'The Poets of the Tomb', *Bulletin,* 8 October 1892, p. 20.
37 *Ibid.*
38 A. B. Paterson, 'The Man from Ironbark', *Bulletin,* 17 December 1892, p. 5. Although listed as page 5, the page was regarded as the front of the magazine, the preceding pages being advertising wraparounds.
39 Henry Lawson, 'The Man from Waterloo', *Truth* (Sydney), 28 June 1896, p. 1.
40 A. B. Paterson, 'A Voice from the Town', *Bulletin,* 20 October 1894, p. 24.
41 *Ibid.*
42 'Mostly about the "Breaker"', *Windsor and Richmond Gazette,* 18 June 1898, p. 5.
43 '"Banjo" Paterson Tells His Own Story: Giants of the Paddle, Pen, and Pencil', *Sydney Morning Herald,* 11 February 1939, p. 21.
44 'Henry Lawson. To The Editor of the Herald', *Sydney Morning Herald,* 13 February 1939, p. 7.
45 Angus & Robertson to A. B. Paterson, 3 September 1895, State Library of NSW. Reference code: 1232021.
46 A. B. Paterson to George Robertson, 15 July 1899, State Library of NSW. Reference code: 1232021.
47 Henry Lawson, 'In The Height of Fashion', *Newsletter,* 7 July 1906, p. 2.
48 *Ibid.*
49 Rose Paterson to Nora Murray-Prior, 4 September 1881, National Library of Australia, MS 9423.
50 'Family Notices', *Sydney Morning Herald,* 28 February 1893, p. 1. Rose Paterson was 48.
51 A. B. Paterson, *The Man from Snowy River and Other Verses,* Angus & Robertson, 1895.

Chapter 13

1 'Letters from Harry Morant', *Bulletin,* 10 May 1902, p. 36.
2 'Personal Items', *Bulletin,* 17 June 1953, p. 10.
3 A. B. Paterson, 'The Geebung Polo Club', *Antipodean,* 1893, pp. 4–7.
4 '"Banjo" Paterson Tells His Own Story: Giants of the Paddle, Pen, and Pencil', *Sydney Morning Herald,* 11 February 1939, p. 21.
5 'Polo', *Sydney Mail and New South Wales Advertiser,* 13 May 1893, p. 985.
6 'Polo', *Goulburn Herald,* 8 May 1893, p. 3.
7 'Polo', *Manaro Mercury, and Cooma and Bombala Advertiser,* 6 May 1893, p. 5.
8 A. B. Paterson, 'Polo', *Australian Magazine,* 6 July 1899.
9 'Polo', *Goulburn Evening Penny Post,* 11 May 1893, p. 3.

10 *Ibid.*
11 '"Banjo" Paterson Tells His Own Story: Giants of the Paddle, Pen, and Pencil', *Sydney Morning Herald*, 11 February 1939, p. 21.
12 'Polo', *Sydney Mail and New South Wales Advertiser*, 13 May 1893, p. 985.
13 'Notes from The City', *Wingham Chronicle and Manning River Observer* (NSW), 2 June 1953, p. 1
14 Sir Granville de Laune Ryrie (1865–1937).
15 'The Banquet', *Manaro Mercury, and Cooma and Bombala Advertiser*, 9 May 1893, p. 8.
16 'Personal Items', *Bulletin*, 17 June 1953, p. 10.
17 *Ibid.*
18 *Ibid.*
19 'Notes from The City', *Wingham Chronicle and Manning River Observer* (NSW), 2 June 1953, p. 1
20 George Robertson, born 5 July 1825 in Glasgow; died 28 March 1898 in St Kilda, Melbourne.
21 George Robertson, born 14 April 1860 in Gosfield, Essex, England; died 27 August 1933 in Sydney.
22 David Mackenzie Angus, born 12 July 1855 in Thurso, Scotland; died 21 February 1901 in Edinburgh.
23 'Polo', *Sydney Mail and New South Wales Advertiser*, 13 May 1893, p. 985.
24 A. B. Paterson, 'Polo', *Australian Magazine*, 6 July 1899.
25 *Ibid.*
26 *Ibid.*
27 *Bulletin*, 22 January 1925.
28 John Norton, born 25 January 1858 in Brighton, England; died 9 April 1916 in Melbourne.
29 *Bulletin*, 22 January 1925.
30 *Ibid.*
31 *Ibid.*
32 Bruce Elder, 'In Lawson's tracks', griffithreview.com.
33 Alfred George Stephens, born 28 August 1865 in Toowoomba; died 15 April 1933 in Darlinghurst, Sydney.
34 Henry Lawson, 'A Stranger on the Darling', *Western Herald*, 1 October 1892.
35 John Barnes, 'The Making of a Legend: Henry Lawson at Bourke', *La Trobe Journal*, No. 99, March 2017, p. 43.
36 Henry Lawson to his aunt, Emma Brooks, 21 September 1892, from Colin Roderick (ed.), *Henry Lawson Letters 1890–1922*, Angus & Robertson, 1970, p. 49.
37 *Ibid.*
38 Henry Lawson to Emma Brooks, 27 September 1892, in Roderick, *Henry Lawson Letters* (edited by Colin Roderick), Angus & Robertson, 1972, p. 50.
39 Donald Macdonell (1862–1911).
40 'Polo', *Sydney Morning Herald*, 8 October 1892, p. 10.
41 *Ibid.*, 24 October 1892, p. 3.
42 A. B. Paterson, 'The Boss of the "Admiral Lynch"', *Bulletin*, 10 December 1892, p. 21.
43 Henry Lawson, 'In a Dry Season', *Bulletin*, 5 November 1892, p. 20.
44 *Ibid.*
45 *James William Gordon*, born, Creswick, Victoria, 23 October 1874; died, Leeton, N.S.W., 12 August 1949.
46 James Gordon (who wrote under the name 'Jim Grahame'), Cyril Goode Papers, PA 271/Box 7, State Library Victoria.
47 *Ibid.*
48 *Ibid.*
49 Henry Lawson, 'Pursuing Literature in Australia', *Bulletin*, 21 January 1899.
50 '"Banjo" Paterson Tells His Own Story: Giants of the Paddle, Pen, and Pencil', *Sydney Morning Herald*, 11 February 1939, p. 21.
51 Denton Prout, *Henry Lawson: The Grey Dreamer*, Angus & Robertson, 1963, p. 106.
52 Henry Lawson, 'Out Back', *Bulletin*, 30 September 1893, p. 19.
53 Lawson to Emma Brooks, 16 January 1893, in Roderick (ed.), *Henry Lawson Letters 1890–1922*, Angus & Robertson, 1970, p. 53.

54 *Ibid.*
55 John Barnes, 'The Making of a Legend: Henry Lawson at Bourke', *La Trobe Journal*, No. 99, March 2017, p. 44.
56 Henry Lawson, 'Hungerford', from *While the Billy Boils*, Angus & Robertson, 1896, pp. 40–44.
57 Henry Lawson to Emma Brooks, 16 January 1893, in Roderick (ed.), *Henry Lawson Letters 1890–1922*, p. 53.
58 *Ibid.*
59 *Ibid.*
60 *Ibid.*
61 Henry Lawson, '"Pursuing literature" in Australia', *Bulletin*, 21 January 1899.
62 *Ibid.*
63 'Lawn Tennis', *Evening News* (Sydney), 26 September 1893, p. 2.
64 Henry Lawson, 'In a Wet Season', *Bulletin*, 2 December 1893, p. 20.
65 '"Banjo Paterson Tells His Own Story – An Execution and Royal Pardon', *Sydney Morning Herald*, 25 February 1939, p. 21.
66 Harry 'Breaker' Harbord Morant, born 9 December 1864 in Bridgewater, England; executed by firing squad 27 February 1902 in Pretoria, South Africa.
67 '"Banjo Paterson Tells His Own Story – An Execution and Royal Pardon', *Sydney Morning Herald*, 25 February 1939, p. 21.
68 Daisy May O'Dwyer, later Daisy Bates, born 16 October 1863 in Tipperary, Ireland; died 18 April 1951 in Prospect, Adelaide.
69 'Who was "Morant"', *Northern Miner* (Charters Towers), 14 April 1902, p. 3.
70 *Ibid.*
71 Harry 'Breaker' Morant, 'A Night Thought', *Bulletin*, 5 September 1891.
72 'Letters from Harry Morant', *Bulletin*, 10 May 1902, p. 36.
73 '"Banjo Paterson Tells His Own Story – An Execution and Royal Pardon', *Sydney Morning Herald*, 25 February 1939, p. 21.
74 *Ibid.*
75 A. B. Paterson, 'Tommy Corrigan: Died 13 August 1894', *Bulletin*, 18 August 1894, p. 16.
76 A. B. Paterson, 'Saltbush Bill', *Bulletin* (Christmas edition), 15 December 1894, p. 18.
77 Henry Lawson, *Short Stories in Prose and Verse*, L. Lawson (publisher), 1894.
78 *Ibid.*
79 'The Sydney Polo Club's Gymkhana. A Comic Race Meeting', *Daily Telegraph* (Sydney), 29 October 1894, p. 3.
80 'Australian Jockey Club Summer Meeting', *Sydney Morning Herald*, 31 December 1894, p. 3.
81 *Sydney Morning Herald*, 29 May 1895, p. 8.

Chapter 14

1 A. B. Paterson, *Song of the Pen*, Lansdowne Press, 1983, p. 500. From a 1930 wireless talk 'Golden Water'.
2 A. B. Paterson, *Singer of the Bush*, Lansdowne Press, 1983, p. xxiii.
3 A. B. Paterson, 'The Man Who Was Away', *Bulletin* (Christmas edition), 15 December 1894, p. 5.
4 *Ibid.*
5 A. B. Paterson, 'Reconstruction: From a Farmer's Point of View', *Bulletin*, 17 June 1893, p. 5.
6 *Ibid.*
7 Anthony Barker, 'Robertson, George (1860–1933)', *Australian Dictionary of Biography*, Volume 11, MUP, 1988.
8 *Ibid.*
9 angusrobertson.com.au.
10 Henry Lawson, *While the Billy Boils*, Angus & Robertson, 1896.
11 Henry Lawson, *In the Days When the World was Wide and Other Verses*, Angus & Robertson, 1896.
12 A. B. Paterson, 'Looking Backward', *Sydney Mail*, 28 December 1938, p. 7.
13 Peter Airey (1865–1950).
14 David Henry Souter (1862–1935).
15 A. B. Paterson, 'Jim Carew', *The Man from Snowy River and Other Verses*, Angus & Robertson, 1895.

16 Alice Emily Walker, born 15 September 1877 in Toowoomba, Queensland; died 23 June 1963 in Chatswood, Sydney.
17 Roderick, *Banjo Paterson: Poet by Accident,* Allen & Unwin, 1993, p. 65.
18 Semmler, *The Banjo of the Bush* (second edition), Queensland University Press, 1974, p. 251; recollections of Peter MacGregor.
19 *Ibid.*, recollections of Sir Edward Knox.
20 'Spring Dances', *Sydney Mail and New South Wales Advertiser,* 28 September 1895, p. 636.
21 'Social', *Sydney Morning Herald,* 21 September 1895, p. 7.
22 'The French Ball', *Sydney Mail and New South Wales Advertiser,* 19 October 1895, p. 792.
23 woollahra.nsw.gov.au.
24 'Social', *Sydney Morning Herald,* 5 October 1895, p. 6.
25 'A Tenterfield Debutante in Sydney', *Queenslander,* 19 October 1895, p. 765.
26 Christina Rutherford Moreton Macpherson, born 18 June 1864 in Peechelba, Victoria; died 27 March 1936 in St Kilda, Victoria.
27 'Woman's World', *Brisbane Courier,* 28 May 1895, p. 6.
28 'Social Gossip', *Queenslander,* 6 July 1895, p. 6.
29 Ewen Cluny Macpherson (1821–1896).
30 Jane 'Jean' Macpherson (1859–1927).
31 The wedding took place in April 1896; from 'Winton', *Queenslander,* 9 May 1896, p. 869.
32 Robert 'Bob' Macpherson (1855–1930), John Macpherson (1862–1903), Gideon Macpherson (1848–1930) and Angus Macpherson (1851–1930).
33 'Obituary: Robert Rutherford Macpherson', *Longreach Leader,* 8 August 1930, p. 15.
34 Margaret Macpherson (nee Rutherford) died 5 December 1894 at Armadale, Melbourne.
35 The song was first published in 1818, with words by Scottish poet Robert Tannahill and music by James Barr. Godfrey Parker converted the music into a marching tune in 1894.
36 The works included were an Introductory Prelude, 'The Man from Snowy River'; 'Old Pardon, the Son of Reprieve'; 'Clancy of The Overflow'; 'Conroy's Gap'; 'Our New Horse'; 'An Idyll of Dandaloo'; 'The Geebung Polo Club'; 'The Travelling Post Office'; 'Saltbush Bill'; 'A Mountain Station'; 'Been There Before'; 'The Man who was Away'; 'The Man from Ironbark'; 'The Open Steeplechase'; 'The Amateur Rider'; 'On Kiley's Run'; 'Frying Pan's Theology'; 'The Two Devines'; 'In The Droving Days'; 'Lost'; 'Over the Range'; 'Only a Jockey'; 'How McGinnis went Missing'; 'A Voice from the Town'; 'A Bunch of Roses'; 'Black Swans'; 'The All Right 'Un'; 'The Boss of the Admiral Lynch'; 'A Bushman's Song'; 'How Gilbert Died'; 'The Flying Gang'; 'Shearing at Castlereagh'; 'The Wind's Message'; 'Johnson's Antidote'; 'Ambition and Art'; 'The Daylight is Dying'; 'In Defence of the Bush'; 'Last Week'; 'Those Names'; 'A Bush Christening'; 'How the Favourite Beat Us'; 'The Great Calamity'; 'Come by Chance'; 'Under the Shadow of Kiley's Hill'; 'Jim Carew' and 'The Swagman's Rest'.
37 A. B. Paterson, *The Man from Snowy River,* Angus & Robertson, 1895, Preface.
38 Clement Semmler, *The Banjo of the Bush* (second edition), Queensland University Press, 1974, p. 73.
39 'The Banjo's Book', *Bulletin,* 26 October 1895.
40 'Second Edition Now Ready', *Bulletin,* 23 November 1895.
41 A. B. Paterson to Nora Murray-Prior, 27 April 1896, National Library of Australia, MS 9251.
42 Quoted in *Bulletin,* 27 June 1896.
43 *Ibid.*
44 Rudyard Kipling to Robertson, 10 December 1895. A & R papers, State Library of New South Wales, ML MSS 314/43/357.
45 Clement Semmler, *The Banjo of the Bush* (second edition), Queensland University Press, 1974, xi.
46 There is conjecture over the date of Banjo's visit, but tracking Banjo's sporting activities in Sydney and the travel path of the two young ladies it was most likely in August 1895 or January 1896 when a Mr A. B. Paterson travelled by a mail train from New South Wales into Queensland, crossing the border at Wallangarra on 3 January 1896 and returned five weeks later on 8 February. Sarah Riley and Chris Macpherson were still there at the same time.
47 Roderick, *Banjo Paterson: Poet by Accident,* Allen & Unwin, 1993, p. 65.

48 tolarnostation.com.au
49 'How the Rodney was Burnt', *Glen Innes Examiner and General Advertiser*, 26 October 1894, p. 3.
50 'Burning of the Rodney', *Armidale Express and New England General Advertiser*, 5 March 1895, p. 2.
51 In October 1894, eight men were acquitted in Broken Hill over the fire but in February 1895, shearer Thomas Bonner was sentenced to seven years in prison.
52 One of the men, Billy McLean, was sentenced to three years' imprisonment in Goulburn jail but developed tuberculosis from the bullet wound to his lung. He was released from prison but died a few weeks later.
53 'Two Unionists Shot', *Queenslander*, 1 September 1894, p. 425.
54 'The Shearing Dispute', *Brisbane Courier*, 5 July 1894, p. 5.
55 'Burning of Dagworth Shed', *Western Champion and General Advertiser for the Central-Western Districts* (Barcaldine), 4 September 1894, p. 7.
56 'Burning Of Dagworth Woolshed. Ayrshire Downs', *Queensland Times, Ipswich Herald and General Advertiser*, 4 September 1894, p. 5.
57 'Magisterial inquiry before E. Eglinton re. The burning of the Dagworth wool-shed on September 2 1894', Department of Justice, Queensland, 6 September 1894.
58 'The Shearing Dispute', *Brisbane Courier*, 15 September 1894, p. 5. Tierney was later acquitted of the charge.
59 Samuel Hoffmeister (1862–1894).
60 'The Shearing Dispute', *Brisbane Courier*, 5 September 1894, p. 5.
61 'Waltzing Matilda', written by Banjo Paterson and Christina Macpherson in 1895, first published in the *Hughenden Observer* and then by James Inglis & Co. Ltd, with an advertisement for Billy Tea on the back cover, 1903.
62 'Magisterial inquiry before E. Eglinton re. The burning of the Dagworth wool-shed on 2 September 1894', Department of Justice, Queensland, 6 September 1894.
63 'The Shearing Dispute', *Brisbane Courier*, 4 September 1894, p. 5.
64 'The Wild West. A Mysterious Death', *The Northern Miner* (Charters Towers), 4 September 1894, p. 4.
65 'The Shearing Strike', *Morning Bulletin* (Rockhampton), 5 September 1894, p. 5.
66 The exact date of Banjo's visit remains uncertain. Tracking Banjo's sporting and social activities in Sydney alongside the travels of Sarah and Chris, it was most likely in August 1895 or January 1896. Travel records show that a Mr A. B. Paterson travelled by mail train from New South Wales into Queensland, crossing the border at Wallangarra on 3 January 1896, and returned five weeks later on 8 February. Sarah Riley and Chris Macpherson were still in western Queensland at the same time.
67 A. B. Paterson, *Song of the Pen*, Lansdowne Press, 1983, p. 498. From a talk 'Golden Water'.
68 *Ibid.*
69 Richard Magoffin, *Waltzing Matilda, Song of Australia*, Mimosa Press, 1983, p. 51.
70 Letter from Christina Macpherson to Dr Thomas Wood (author of *Cobbers*, 1934); National Library of Australia, MS 9065 – Papers relating to the song 'Waltzing Matilda'.
71 *Ibid.*
72 Henry Lawson, 'Some Popular Australian Mistakes', *Bulletin*, 18 November 1893, p. 20.
73 'Who'll Come a Waltzing Matilda With Me', pandora.nla.gov.au.
74 Henry George Lamond (1885–1969).
75 Clement Semmler, *The Banjo of the Bush* (second edition), Queensland University Press, 1974, p. 90.
76 Some early versions used the word 'billabongs' but Chris Macpherson's earliest manuscript makes it singular.
77 'Waltzing Matilda', written by Banjo Paterson and Christina Macpherson in 1895, first published in the *Hughenden Observer* and then by James Inglis & Co. Ltd, with an advertisement for Billy Tea on the back cover, 1903.
78 *Ibid.*
79 'Waltzing Matilda', written by Banjo Paterson and Christina Macpherson in 1895.
80 A. B. Paterson, 'Bushfires: Dangers and Difficulties', *Sydney Morning Herald*, 9 January 1932, p. 7.

81 Sir Herbert Ramsay (1832–1924).
82 Both are now at the National Library of Australia.
83 Letter from Christina Macpherson to Dr Thomas Wood (author of *Cobbers*, 1934); National Library of Australia, MS 9065 – Papers relating to the song 'Waltzing Matilda'.
84 Dianna Baillieu interview with Dennis O'Keeffe, 22 August 1995, from folklore-network. folkaustralia.com.
85 *Ibid.*
86 Diana Baillieu interviewed by Robyn Holmes. Located at National Library of Australia Oral History Collection ORAL TRC 5713, Manuscript reference no.: MS Acc10.183.
87 Roderick, Banjo Paterson: *Poet by Accident*, Allen & Unwin, 1993, p. 88. Letter written by Ethel Vivienne Riley (born 1900) on 29 August 1983.
88 Letter from Christina Macpherson to Dr. Thomas Wood (author of *Cobbers*, 1934); National Library of Australia, MS 9065-Papers relating to the song 'Waltzing Matilda'.
89 A. B. Paterson, *Song of the Pen*, Lansdowne Press, 1983, p. 500. From a 1930 talk 'Golden Water'.
90 Clement Semmler, *The Banjo of the Bush* (second edition), Queensland University Press, 1974, p. 89.
91 'Waltzing Matilda', *Longreach Leader*, 15 December 1943, p. 19.
92 Richard Magoffin, *Waltzing Matilda, Song of Australia*, Mimosa Press, 1983, p. 51.
93 Sale of the book's copyright to Banjo's publisher was registered in New South Wales on 12 January 1903 as No. 03/1725.
94 Billy tea advertisement 1903, National Library of Australia, MUS NL mba 783.24215990994 C874.
95 Clement Semmler, *The Banjo of the Bush* (second edition), Queensland University Press, 1974, p. 91.
96 Letter from Christina Macpherson to Dr Thomas Wood (author of *Cobbers*, 1934); National Library of Australia, MS 9065 – Papers relating to the song 'Waltzing Matilda'.
97 Clement Semmler, *The Banjo of the Bush* (second edition), Queensland University Press, 1974, p. 100.
98 'Polo Players', *Windsor and Richmond Gazette*, 15 January 1898, p. 6.

Chapter 15

1 'The Banjo', 'Buffalo Shooting in Australia', *Sydney Mail and New South Wales Advertiser*, 7 January 1899, pp. 23–25.
2 Published from 26 June 1885 until 1939.
3 Bernard Espinasse, born 5 December 1868 in Gravesend, England.
4 Bernard Espinasse, 'An Australian Poet: "The Banjo" Interviewed', *Table Talk* (Melbourne), 31 January 1896, p. 6.
5 'The New Opera – "Club Life"', *Sydney Morning Herald*, 16 December 1895, p. 3.
6 Ernest Edwin Philip Truman (1869–1948). Appointed city organist in 1909, he presided over the Sydney Town Hall organ for twenty-six years.
7 Francis (Frank) Mahony (1862–1916).
8 Bernard Espinasse. 'An Australian Poet: "The Banjo" Interviewed', *Table Talk* (Melbourne), 31 January 1896, p. 6.
9 *Ibid.*
10 *Ibid.*
11 *Ibid.*
12 'Brevities', *Cumberland Argus and Fruitgrowers Advocate* (Parramatta), 15 February 1896, p. 1.
13 Roderick, *Banjo Paterson: Poet by Accident*, Allen & Unwin, 1993, p. 92.
14 Bertha Marie Louise Bredt (1876–1957). The marriage took place on 15 April 1896.
15 Hannah Forrester Thornburn (1877–1902). She was a model for sculptor Nelson Illingworth in Sydney.
16 Henry Lawson, 'Hannah Thornburn', *For Australia and Other Poems*, Standard Publishing, 1913, pp. 217–223.
17 Jim Lawson was born in 1898 and Bertha Lawson in 1900.
18 'Rosehill Races', *Sunday Times* (Sydney), 29 March 1896, p. 6.

19 'Mulga Bill's Bicycle', *Sydney Mail and New South Wales Advertiser*, 25 July 1896, p. 183.
20 A. B. Paterson to Editor, *Town and Country Journal*, 8 July 1896. Letter in possession of Banjo Paterson Museum, Yeoval.
21 A. B. Paterson, 'Pioneers', *Australian Town and Country Journal*, 19 December 1896, p. 17.
22 A. B. Paterson, 'Saltbush Bill's Second Fight', *Antipodean*, Christmas 1897, pp. 29–37.
23 A. B. Paterson, 'Ballad of the Calliope', *Antipodean*, Christmas 1897, pp. 102–104.
24 *Australian Magazine*, 6 July 1899.
25 A. B. Paterson, *Song of the Pen*, Lansdowne Press, 1983, from a talk 'Floods in Queensland'.
26 'Mostly About the Breaker', *Windsor and Richmond Gazette*, 18 June 1898, p. 5.
27 George Washington Thomas Lambert (1873–1930).
28 'The Banjo', 'Buffalo Shooting in Australia', *Sydney Mail and New South Wales Advertiser*, 7 January 1899, pp. 23–25.
29 *Ibid.*
30 '"Banjo" as Buffalo Hunter', *Northern Territory Times and Gazette*, 14 October 1898, p. 3.
31 *Ibid.*
32 'Notes of the Week', *Northern Territory Times and Gazette*, 28 October 1898, p. 2.
33 *Ibid.*
34 A. B. Paterson, 'Father Riley's Horse', *Bulletin* (Christmas edition), 9 December 1899, p. 14.
35 A. B. Paterson, 'Johnny Riley's Cow', *Singer of the Bush*, Lansdowne Press, 1983, p. 306. Written in 1908 and published posthumously.
36 'Queensland News', *Capricornian*, 15 July 1899, p. 24.
37 'The New South Wales Lancers', *Newcastle Morning Herald and Miners' Advocate*, 4 October 1899, p. 5.
38 Morant, enlisted on 27 December 1899.
39 A. B. Paterson, *Singer of the Bush*, Lansdowne Press, 1983, xiv.
40 Donald Alaster Macdonald (1859–1932).
41 The siege lasted from 2 November 1899 until 28 February 1900 at Ladysmith, Natal.
42 'Departure of N.S.W. Contingent', *Sunday Times* (Sydney), 29 Oct 1899, p. 7.
43 'Happy Dispatches', *Western Mail* (Perth), 19 September 1935, p. 6.

Chapter 16

1 A. B. Paterson, *Happy Dispatches*, Angus & Robertson, 1934, Chapter III: Lord Roberts, French, Haig, and Others.
2 'Mr. A. B. Paterson', *Sydney Mail and New South Wales Advertiser*, 28 October 1899, p. 1049.
3 'Mr. A. B. Paterson', *Sydney Morning Herald*, 28 October 1899, p. 9.
4 'On Board the Kent', *Sydney Mail and New South Wales Advertiser*, 4 November 1899, p. 1108.
5 A. B. Paterson, *Happy Dispatches*, Angus & Robertson, 1934, Chapter 1: Sir Alfred Milner.
6 *Ibid.*
7 'The N.S.W. Contingent at Albany: A Rough Passage Across the Australian Bight', *Sydney Morning Herald*, 15 November 1899, p. 7.
8 A. B. Paterson, *Happy Dispatches*, Angus & Robertson, 1934, Chapter 1: Sir Alfred Milner.
9 A. B. Paterson to George Robertson, 5 November 1899, State Library of NSW, MLMSS 8404.
10 *Ibid.*, 3 August 1899.
11 *Ibid.*, 8 August 1899.
12 *Ibid.*, September 1899.
13 A. B. Paterson, 'Life on Board the S.S. Kent', *Sydney Morning Herald*, 29 December 1899, p. 7.
14 *Ibid.*
15 Thomas Henry Fiaschi (1853–1927).
16 *Ibid.*
17 A. B. Paterson, 'Life on Board the S.S. Kent', *Sydney Morning Herald*, 29 December 1899, p. 7.
18 'On Board the Kent', *Nepean Times* (Penrith), 30 December 1899, p. 3.
19 A. B. Paterson, 'Life on Board the S.S. Kent', *Sydney Morning Herald*, 29 December 1899, p. 7.
20 A. B. Paterson, 'With the S.S. Kent Contingent', *Sydney Morning Herald*, 28 December 1899, p. 5.
21 A. B. Paterson, 'Capetown – Arrival and landing', *Sydney Morning Herald*, 28 December 1899, p. 5.

22 *Ibid.*
23 A. B. Paterson, *Happy Dispatches*, Angus & Robertson, 1934, Chapter 1: Sir Alfred Milner.
24 A. B. Paterson, 'With the S.S. Kent Contingent', *Sydney Morning Herald*, 28 December 1899, p. 5.
25 *Ibid.*
26 'Formal Landing of the Kent Contingent', *Sydney Morning Herald*, 28 December 1899, p. 5.
27 A. B. Paterson, *Happy Dispatches*, Angus & Robertson, 1934, Chapter 1: Sir Alfred Milner.
28 *Ibid.*
29 Alfred Milner, 1st Viscount Milner (23 March 1854 – 13 May 1925).
30 A. B. Paterson, *Happy Dispatches*, Angus & Robertson, 1934, Chapter 1: Sir Alfred Milner.
31 *Ibid.*
32 *Ibid.*
33 *Ibid.*
34 *Ibid.*
35 'Formal Landing of the Kent Contingent', *Sydney Morning Herald*, 28 December 1899, p. 5.
36 A. B. Paterson, 'The Reveille', *Sydney Mail and New South Wales Advertiser*, 6 January 1900, p. 30.
37 A. B. Paterson, *Happy Dispatches*, Angus & Robertson, 1934.
38 A. B. Paterson, 'Capetown – Arrival and landing', *Sydney Morning Herald*, 28 December 1899, p. 5.
39 Later Field Marshal Douglas Haig, 1st Earl Haig (19 June 1861 – 29 January 1928).
40 A. B. Paterson, *Happy Dispatches*, Angus & Robertson, 1934, Chapter III: Lord Roberts, French, Haig, and Others.
41 *Ibid.*
42 A. B. Paterson, 'From the Seat of War', *Sydney Morning Herald*, 12 January 1900, p. 5.
43 A. B. Paterson, 'From the Seat of War', *Sydney Morning Herald*, 30 January 1900, p. 5.
44 Now called Noupoort.
45 A. B. Paterson, 'From the Seat of War', *Sydney Morning Herald*, 12 January 1900, p. 5.
46 Later Sir John French, Viscount French and Field Marshal John Denton Pinkstone French, 1st Earl of Ypres (28 September 1852 – 22 May 1925).
47 A. B. Paterson, *Happy Dispatches*, Angus & Robertson, 1934, Chapter II: Winston Churchill.
48 *Ibid.*, Chapter III: Lord Roberts, French, Haig, and Others.
49 A. B. Paterson, 'From the Seat of War', *Sydney Morning Herald*, 12 January 1900, p. 5.
50 *Ibid.*
51 *Ibid.*
52 *Ibid.*
53 *Ibid.*
54 Field Marshal Frederick Sleigh Roberts, 1st Earl Roberts (30 September 1832 – 14 November 1914).
55 Field Marshal Horatio Herbert Kitchener, 1st Earl Kitchener (24 June 1850 – 5 June 1916).
56 General Sir Redvers Henry Buller (7 December 1839 – 2 June 1908).
57 Olive Schreiner (24 March 1855 – 11 December 1920).
58 A. B. Paterson, 'From the Boer Side', *Sydney Morning Herald*, 17 February 1900, p. 9.
59 *Ibid.*
60 *Ibid.*
61 *Ibid.*, p. 10.
62 Heather Kennett, 'Link to "Breaker" under threat', couriermail.com.au, 20 November 2011.
63 William John Lambie (1860–1900).
64 'A Prisoner of War', *Leader* (Melbourne), 12 May 1900, p. 25.
65 *Ibid.*
66 'Mr A. B. Paterson', *Sydney Morning Herald*, 12 September 1900, p. 5.
67 *Ibid.*
68 A. B. Paterson, 'At the Front', *Sydney Morning Herald*, 24 March 1900, p. 9.
69 'Mr Paterson's Lecture', *Newcastle Morning Herald and Miners' Advocate*, 9 October 1900, p. 5.
70 A. B. Paterson, 'At the Front. Incidents in the Relief of Kimberley', *Sydney Morning Herald*, 31 March 1900, p. 9; 'At the Front', *Sydney Morning Herald*, 24 March 1900, p. 9.
71 Cecil John Rhodes PC (5 July 1853 – 26 March 1902).

72 A. B. Paterson, 'At the Front', *Sydney Morning Herald*, 24 March 1900, p. 9.
73 Howell Arthur Keir Gwynne (1865–1950).
74 Editor from 1911 to 1937.
75 Pieter Arnoldus Cronjé, commonly known as Piet Cronjé (4 October 1836 – 4 February 1911).
76 A. B. Paterson, 'At the Front. Position of General Cronje's Laager', *Sydney Morning Herald*, 4 April 1900, p. 7.
77 A. B. Paterson, *Happy Dispatches*, Angus & Robertson, 1934, Chapter III: Lord Roberts, French, Haig, and Others.
78 A. B. Paterson, 'At the Front', *Sydney Morning Herald*, 21 April 1900, p. 9.
79 *Sydney Morning Herald*, 2 April 1900, p. 6.
80 A. B. Paterson, 'At the Front. To Bloemfontein', *Sydney Morning Herald*, 20 April 1900, p. 6.
81 A. B. Paterson, 'At the Front', *Sydney Morning Herald*, 21 April 1900, p. 9.
82 *Ibid.*
83 'Mr Paterson's Letters from the Front', *Sydney Mail and New South Wales Advertiser*, 19 May 1900, p. 1193.
84 A. B. Paterson, *Happy Dispatches*, Angus & Robertson, 1934, Chapter III: Lord Roberts, French, Haig, and Others.
85 *Ibid.*
86 *Ibid.*
87 Julian Ralph, *War's Brighter Side*, C. Arthur Pearson, 1901, Chapter XII.
88 Sir Neville Francis Fitzgerald Chamberlain (13 January 1856 – 28 May 1944). He is sometimes confused with Arthur Neville Chamberlain (8 March 1869 – 9 November 1940), who was British Prime Minister at the outbreak of the Second World War.
89 General Sir Hector Archibald MacDonald (4 March 1853 – 25 March 1903).
90 A. B. Paterson, *Happy Dispatches*, Angus & Robertson, 1934, Chapter III: Lord Roberts, French, Haig, and Others.
91 *Ibid.*
92 *Ibid.*
93 Paterson, *Singer in the Bush*, p. xiv.
94 A. B. Paterson, *Happy Dispatches*, Angus & Robertson, 1934, Chapter III: Lord Roberts, French, Haig, and Others.
95 Published from 1772 to 1937.
96 A. B. Paterson, *Happy Dispatches*, Angus & Robertson, 1934, Chapter II: Winston Churchill.
97 *Ibid.*
98 *Ibid.*
99 A. B. Paterson, 'At the Front', *Sydney Morning Herald*, 14 July 1900, p. 5.
100 Francis William Lauderdale Adams (1862–1893).
101 Jason Steger, 'How Lawson drove his wife to misery', theage.com.au, 17 February 2007.
102 Henry Lawson, 'The Triangles of Life', *Triangles of Life and Other Stories*, Standard Publishing Co., 1913.
103 Henry Lawson, 'The Lily of St Leonards', *Bulletin*, 4 April 1907, p. 32.
104 Henry Lawson, 'The Last Review', *Bulletin*, 29 September 1904, p. 35.
105 Christiaan Rudolf de Wet (7 October 1854 – 3 February 1922).
106 A. B. Paterson, 'At the Front', *Sydney Morning Herald*, 11 May 1900, p. 5.
107 A. B. Paterson, 'At the Front', *Sydney Morning Herald*, 13 June 1900, p. 7.
108 A. B. Paterson, 'At the Front', *Sydney Morning Herald*, 14 July 1900, p. 9.
109 A. B. Paterson, *Happy Dispatches*, Angus & Robertson, 1934, Chapter III: Lord Roberts, French, Haig, and Others.
110 A. B. Paterson, 'At the Front', *Sydney Morning Herald*, 3 August 1900, p. 5.
111 General Sir Ian Standish Monteith Hamilton (16 January 1853 – 12 October 1947).
112 Louis Botha (27 September 1862 – 27 August 1919). First Prime Minister of the Union of South Africa.
113 Lieutenant William Rupert Harriott (1876–1900).
114 Percy William Chanter Drage (1867–1900).
115 'At The Front. Pretoria', *Sydney Morning Herald*, 28 July 1900, p. 11.

116 'At The Front. Pretoria', *Sydney Morning Herald,* 1 August 1900, p. 7.
117 'At The Front. Pretoria', *Sydney Morning Herald,* 7 September 1900, p. 5.
118 On 16 June 1900, Roberts made the following proclamation, No. 5/1900: 'Whereas small parties of raiders have recently been doing wanton damage to public property in the Orange River Colony and South African Republic by destroying railway bridges and culverts and cutting the telegraph wires, and whereas such damage cannot be done without the knowledge and connivance of the neighbouring inhabitants and the principal civil residents in the districts concerned; Now, therefore, I, Frederick Sleigh, Baron Roberts, of Kandahar and Waterford, K.P., G.C.B., G.C.S.I., G.C.I.E., Field-Marshal, Commander-in-Chief of Her Majesty's Troops in South Africa, warn the said inhabitants and principal civil residents that, whenever public property is destroyed or injured in the manner specified above, they will be held responsible for aiding and abetting the offenders. The houses in the vicinity of the place where the damage is done will be burnt and the principal civil residents will be made prisoners of war.' Pretoria, 16 June 1900. From 'British "scorched earth policy" during Second Boer War', southafricatoday.net, 17 June 2015.
119 'Mr. Paterson's Letters from The Front', *Sydney Mail and New South Wales Advertiser,* 18 August 1900, p. 422.
120 A. B. Paterson, 'On the Trek', *Rio Grande's Last Race and Other Verses*, Angus & Robertson, 1902. (Written 1900.)
121 *Ibid.*
122 A. B. Paterson, 'Basutoland', *Sydney Morning Herald*, 6 October 1900, p. 7.
123 *Ibid.*
124 Prince Francis of Teck (Francis Joseph Leopold Frederick; 9 January 1870 – 22 October 1910). His sister would become Queen Mary, wife of King George V.
125 'Mr A. B. Paterson', *Sydney Morning Herald*, 12 September 1900, p. 5.
126 A. B. Paterson, 'The Last Parade', *Rio Grande's Last Race and Other Verses*, Angus & Robertson, 1902. (Written 1900.)
127 A. B. Paterson, 'A Day Under Fire, A Battlefield Sketch', *Sydney Morning Herald*, 11 August 1900, p. 7.

Chapter 17

1 A. B. Paterson, 'Now Listen to Me and I'll Tell You My Views', *Bulletin*, 29 March 1902, p. 15. First printed in the British newspaper *Reynolds' News.*
2 'More Returned Soldiers', *Evening News* (Sydney), 8 September 1900, p. 4.
3 'Return of Mr. A. B. Paterson', *Sydney Morning Herald*, 8 September 1900, p. 11.
4 'Mr A. B. Paterson', *Sydney Morning Herald*, 12 September 1900, p. 5.
5 *Ibid.*
6 Australia and the Boer War, 1899–1902, awm.gov.au. Six Australians received the Victoria Cross in South Africa.
7 Stephanus Johannes Paulus 'Paul' Kruger (10 October 1825 – 14 July 1904), President of the South African Republic.
8 Joseph Chamberlain (8 July 1836 – 2 July 1914). His son Arthur Neville Chamberlain (8 March 1869 – 9 November 1940) was British Prime Minister at the outbreak of the Second World War.
9 A. B. Paterson, 'Now Listen to Me and I'll Tell You My Views', *Bulletin*, 29 March 1902, p. 15.
10 *Ibid.*
11 'Proclamation Uniting the People of New South Wales, Victoria, South Australia, Queensland, Tasmania, And Western Australia in a Federal Commonwealth' (Imperial Statutory Rules And Orders, Revised 1948, Vol. II., Australia, p. 1027), 1900, No. 722.
12 A. B. Paterson, 'Our Own Flag', *Singer in the Bush*, p. 686. (Written 1900.)
13 *Ibid.*
14 'War Correspondents', *Truth*, 30 September 1900, p. 6.
15 'Mr A. B. Paterson's Lectures', *Sydney Morning Herald*, 22 September 1900, p. 9.
16 *Ibid.*
17 *Ibid.*

18 Later Major General John Macquarie Antill, Jr (26 January 1866 – 1 March 1937).
19 A. B. Paterson, 'The Offer of Troops' in George Burnett Barton & Frank Wilkinson, *The Story of South Africa Vol II,* World Publishing Co, 1902.
20 'War Correspondents', *Truth*, 30 September 1900, p. 6.
21 *Ibid.*
22 Later Field Marshal Douglas Haig, 1st Earl Haig (19 June 1861 – 29 January 1928).
23 A. B. Paterson, *Happy Dispatches*, Angus & Robertson, 1934, Chapter III: Lord Roberts, French, Haig, and Others.
24 *Ibid.*
25 *Ibid.*
26 William Lygon, 7th Earl Beauchamp (20 February 1872 – 14 November 1938).
27 'At The Front. The Hon. Edward Lygon. A Gallant Officer', *Sydney Morning Herald*, 3 May 1900, p. 7.
28 General Sir Archibald Hunter (6 September 1856 – 28 June 1936).
29 Lieutenant-General Robert Stephenson Smyth Baden-Powell, 1st Baron Baden-Powell (22 February 1857 – 8 January 1941).
30 'Mr A. B. Paterson's Lectures', *Sydney Morning Herald*, 27 September 1900, p. 6.
31 A. B. Paterson, 'Horses in Warfare', from George Burnett Barton, Frank Wilkinson, *The Story of South Africa Vol II*, World Publishing Co., 1902.
32 *Ibid.*
33 *Ibid.*
34 Later Sir James Burns (1846–1923).
35 A. B. Paterson to George Robertson, 30 October 1900, State Library of NSW, MLMSS 8404.
36 'From Near and Far', *Warwick Argus*, 2 July 1901, p. 3.
37 Bennet Graham Burley (1840–1914). He later changed his surname to Burleigh.
38 Percy Frederick Hunt (1873–1901).
39 'The Bushveldt Carbineers', from lighthorse.org.au.
40 Peter Joseph Handcock (1868–1902). Commissioned 28 February 1901.
41 Henry Lawson to George Robertson, 15 May 1901.
42 Bertha Lawson to her mother, 30 July 1900, Lawson family papers, Mitchell Library, ML MSS 7692.
43 Henry Lawson, *The Country I Come From*, William Blackwood and Sons, 1901.
44 Miles Franklin, *My Brilliant Career*, William Blackwood and Sons, 1901.
45 Stella Maria Sarah Miles Franklin, born 14 October 1879 in Talbingo, New South Wales; died 19 September 1954 in Drummoyne, Sydney.
46 Henry Lawson to George Robertson, April 1900.
47 Miles Franklin to Henry Lawson, 19 November 1899.
48 Henry Lawson to Miles Franklin, 29 December 1899.
49 James Alexander Kenneth Mackay (1859–1935).
50 Kenneth Mackay, *The Yellow Wave: A Romance of the Asiatic Invasion Of Australia*, Bentley, 1895.
51 *Bulletin*, 30 May 1901.
52 Norman Alfred Williams Lindsay (1879–1969).
53 Sir Lionel Arthur Lindsay (1874–1961).
54 Bernard Smith, 'Lindsay, Norman Alfred (1879–1969)', *Australian Dictionary of Biography*, Volume 10, MUP, 1986.
55 From an ABC radio documentary, broadcast in 1964, quoted in Semmler, *The Banjo of the Bush* (second edition), *Queensland University Press, 1974, p.* 251.
56 *Steele Rudd* was the pen name of Arthur Hoey Davis (14 November 1868 – 11 October 1935).
57 In an ABC radio commentary on Banjo compiled by his friend, Peter Macgregor, Semmler, *The Banjo of the Bush* (second edition), Queensland University Press, 1974, p. 147.
58 Norman Lindsay, *Bohemians of the Bulletin*, Angus & Robertson, 1965, p. 78.
59 Victor James William Patrick Daley (1858–1905).
60 Launched in April 1903.
61 'War Correspondents', *Truth*, 30 September 1900, p. 6.
62 A. B. Paterson, 'Our Federal Army and its Cost', *Sydney Morning Herald*, 13 July 1901, p. 4.

63 'Letters from the East', *Sydney Morning Herald*, 27 July 1901, p. 11.
64 A. B. Paterson, 'Our Eastern Neighbours', *Sydney Morning Herald*, 17 August 1901, p. 7.
65 George Witton, *Scapegoats of the Empire*, Angus & Robertson, 1907.
66 George Ramsdale Witton (1874–1942).
67 Now called Polokwane.
68 Frederick Ramon Lopez de Bertodano (1871–1955).
69 Witton, *Scapegoats of the Empire*, Angus & Robertson, 1907. Witton wrote that Hunt's 'legs had been slashed with a knife'. It is suspected that that was a polite expression for genital mutilation.
70 *Ibid.*
71 *Ibid.*

Chapter 18

1 A. B. Paterson, *Happy Dispatches*, Angus & Robertson, 1934, Chapter XI: Rudyard Kipling.
2 William Lane, 'White or Yellow? A Story of the Race-war of A.D. 1908', serialised in *Boomerang*, 18 February – 5 May 1888.
3 A. B. Paterson, 'Going North', *Sydney Morning Herald*, 31 August 1901, p. 7.
4 *Ibid.*
5 *Ibid.*
6 Carl August Daniel Heese (1867–1901).
7 In 1929, George Witton wrote to James Francis Thomas, the major who represented Morant, Handcock and Witton at their courts-martial. Witton wrote: 'I saw Handcock shortly afterwards and asked him about the Heese business, he said 'why wasn't you standing beside Morant when he asked me if I was game to follow the missionary and wipe him out'.
8 A. B. Paterson, *Happy Dispatches*, Angus & Robertson, 1934, Chapter VII: Chinese Morrison.
9 A. B. Paterson, 'Hongkong and the China Coast', *Sydney Morning Herald*, 26 October 1901, p. 6.
10 *Ibid.*
11 A. B. Paterson, 'A Diary in China', *Sydney Morning Herald*, 2 November 1901, p. 7.
12 *Ibid.*
13 *Ibid.*
14 A. B. Paterson, 'China and the East', *Sydney Morning Herald*, 9 November 1901, p. 7.
15 *Ibid.*
16 *Ibid.*
17 Dr George Ernest (Chinese) Morrison (1862–1920).
18 A. B. Paterson, *Happy Dispatches*, Angus & Robertson, 1934, Chapter VII: Chinese Morrison.
19 *Ibid.*
20 *Ibid.*
21 Colonial secretary, Pretoria: CS 1092, Letterbook II, pp. 37–46, in Arthur Davey, *Breaker Morant and the Bushveldt Carbineers*, Van Riebeeck Society, 1987.
22 Admiral the Honourable Sir Assheton Gore Curzon-Howe (10 August 1850 – 1 March 1911).
23 A. B. Paterson, *Happy Dispatches*, Angus & Robertson, 1934, Chapter IX: Marie Lloyd.
24 Matilda Alice Victoria Wood (12 February 1870 – 7 October 1922), professionally known as Marie Lloyd.
25 A. B. Paterson, *Happy Dispatches*, Angus & Robertson, 1934, Chapter IX: Marie Lloyd.
26 A. B. Paterson, 'An Informal Letter from London', *Sydney Morning Herald*, 11 January 1902, p. 7.
27 *Ibid.*
28 'The Boer War', *Argus*, 21 November 1901, p. 5.
29 Henry Lawson, 'As Far as Your Rifles Cover', from *Children of the Bush*, Methuen, 1902, p. 258.
30 *Ibid.*
31 Peter Donaldson, *Remembering the South African War*, Oxford University Press, 2013, p. 115.
32 A. B. Paterson, 'An Informal Letter from London', *Sydney Morning Herald*, 11 January 1902.
33 A. B. Paterson, *Happy Dispatches*, Angus & Robertson, 1934, Chapter X: Phil May.
34 *Ibid.*
35 *Ibid.*
36 A. B. Paterson, *Happy Dispatches*, Angus & Robertson, 1934, Chapter X: Phil May.
37 A. B. Paterson, 'An Informal Letter from London', *Sydney Morning Herald*, 11 January 1902.

38 On 9 May 1901 at the Exhibition Building, Melbourne.
39 Charles Frederic Moberly Bell (2 April 1847 – 5 April 1911).
40 A. B. Paterson to George Robertson, 28 November 1901, State Library of NSW, MLMSS 8404.
41 A popular Sunday newspaper that appeared under different names from 1850 until 1967.
42 Published 1865–1932.
43 *Sporting Times*, September 2 1882.
44 George Witton, *Scapegoats of the Empire*, Angus & Robertson, 1907.
45 *Ibid.*
46 'Those Bushveldt Scapegoats', *Bathurst Free Press and Mining Journal*, 3 January 1903, p. 3.
47 A. B. Paterson, *Happy Dispatches*, Angus & Robertson, 1934, Chapter XI: Rudyard Kipling.
48 Their first horseless carriage appeared in 1896 and the company built automobiles until 1955.
49 The title of a fantasy book by Kipling, published in 1906.
50 A. B. Paterson, *Happy Dispatches*, Angus & Robertson, 1934, Chapter XI: Rudyard Kipling.
51 *Ibid.*
52 *Ibid.*
53 *Ibid.*
54 *Ibid.*
55 *Ibid.*
56 Anne Lawrence Guyon, 'Where Kipling Reared Mowgli (In Vermont)', nytimes.com, 18 March 2010.
57 A. B. Paterson, *Happy Dispatches*, Angus & Robertson, 1934, Chapter XI: Rudyard Kipling.
58 'Personal Notes from England', *Register* (Adelaide), 6 January 1902, p. 6.
59 A. B. Paterson, 'Overland to Melbourne', *Evening News* (Sydney), 20 February 1905, p. 3.
60 Shipping, *Queenslander* (Brisbane), 15 February 1902, p. 384.
61 A. B. Paterson, 'The Old Australian Ways', from *Rio Grande's Last Race and Other Verses*, Angus & Robertson, 1902.
62 Later Major General Hubert Ion Wetherall Hamilton (27 June 1861 – 14 October 1914).
63 Christian Frederick Beyers (1869–1914).
64 Arthur Davey, *Breaker Morant and the Bushveldt Carbineers*, Van Riebeeck Society, 1987, pp. 139–141.
65 Shipping, *Queenslander* (Brisbane), 15 February 1902, p. 384.
66 A. B. Paterson, *Song of the Pen*, Lansdowne Press, 1983, p. 545, from a talk 'Pearl Fishing'.
67 A. B. Paterson, 'The Pearl Diver', from *Rio Grande's Last Race and Other Verses*, Angus & Robertson, 1902.
68 'Banjo', *Morning Post* (Cairns), 11 February 1902, p. 5.
69 'Odds and Ends', *Northern Star* (Lismore), 26 February 1902, p. 5.
70 George Witton, *Scapegoats of the Empire*, Angus & Robertson, 1907.
71 *Ibid.*
72 'Letter from a Pretoria Warder. An Account of the Execution', *Sydney Morning Herald,* 3 April 1902, p. 7. Morant was quoted in the newspaper as saying, 'Be sure and make a good job of it', though the more strident expression became legend and the word 'bastards' was unlikely to appear in publications of the time.
73 'Letter from a Pretoria Warder. An Account of the Execution', *Sydney Morning Herald,* 3 April 1902, p. 7.

Chapter 19

1 Jill Roe, *Stella Miles Franklin: A Biography,* HarperCollins Australia, 2010.
2 Norman Lindsay, *Bohemians of the Bulletin*, Angus & Robertson, 1965, p. 144.
3 From a description by Colonel W.D.C. Williams and Major A. E. Perkins of the Medical Corps in George Burnett Barton & Frank Wilkinson, *The Story of South Africa Vol II,* World Publishing Co., 1902, p. 368.
4 It was unpublished.
5 Jill Roe, *Stella Miles Franklin: A Biography,* HarperCollins Australia, 2010.
6 A. B. Paterson to Stella Miles Franklin, 25 March 1902 and 2 April 1902, Franklin Papers, vol. 7, Mitchell Library, State Library of New South Wales.

7 *Ibid.*, 7 April 1902 and 12 April 1902.
8 *Ibid.*, 29 April 1902.
9 A. B. Paterson to George Robertson, 14 April 1902.
10 *Ibid.*
11 A. B. Paterson to Miles Franklin, 2 May 1902, Franklin Papers, vol. 7, Mitchell Library, State Library of NSW.
12 *Ibid.*
13 Miles Franklin to 'Dear Sir', Franklin Papers, vol. 6, p. 405 (d).
14 A. B. Paterson to Miles Franklin, 31 May 1902, Franklin Papers, vol. 7.
15 Miles Franklin to A. B. Paterson, Franklin Papers, vol. 7, p. 295.
16 Linda Franklin to Miles, 30 June 1902, Franklin Papers, vol. 49.
17 Fred Maudsley to Miles, 8 June 1902, Franklin Papers, vol. 7.
18 Jill Roe, *Stella Miles Franklin: A Biography,* HarperCollins Australia, 2010.
19 Dame Mary Jean Gilmore (née Cameron; 16 August 1865 – 3 December 1962).
20 K.M. Davies, *Mrs L, a work of literary journalism, and exegesis: The poetics of literary journalism and illuminating absent voices in memoir and biography*, Department of Media and Communication, University of Sydney, September 2017.
21 'Family Notices', *Sydney Mail and New South Wales Advertiser*, 21 June 1902, p. 1593.
22 Henry Lawson, 'To Hannah', *Bulletin*, 1 September 1904, p. 3.
23 'Grimy Old Babylon', *Young Chronicle*, 6 August 1902, p. 4.
24 'Death of Mr H. H. Paterson', *Sydney Morning Herald*, 25 July 1902, p. 5.
25 *Ibid.*
26 A. B. Paterson, *Rio Grande's Last Race and Other Verses*, Angus & Robertson, 1902.
27 A. B. Paterson, 'The Last Parade', *Rio Grande's Last Race and Other Verses*, Angus & Robertson, 1902.
28 A. B. Paterson, 'A Fighting General', *Sydney Morning Herald*, 12 March 1902, p. 9.
29 Later Field Marshal Paul Sanford Methuen, 3rd Baron Methuen (1 September 1845 – 30 October 1932).
30 George Burnett Barton & Frank Wilkinson, *The Story of South Africa Vol II,* World Publishing Co., 1902.
31 A. B. Paterson, 'The Late Lieutenant Morant. A Personal Sketch', *Sydney Mail and New South Wales Advertiser*, 12 April 1902, p. 898.
32 *Ibid.*
33 'Pearling Industry at Thursday Island: A Day on a Lugger', *Sydney Mail and New South Wales Advertiser*, 17 May 1902, p. 1240.
34 '"Banjo" Paterson Ends His Story: Political Giants and "Pilgrim Fathers"', *Sydney Morning Herald*, 4 March 1939, p. 21.
35 *Ibid.*
36 *Ibid.*
37 *Ibid.*
38 A. B. Paterson, 'The New Hebrides. Voyage of The Pilgrims. No. I', *Sydney Morning Herald*, 1 July 1902, p. 5.
39 '"Banjo" Paterson Ends His Story: Political Giants and "Pilgrim Fathers"', *Sydney Morning Herald*, 4 March 1939, p. 21.
40 A. B. Paterson, 'The New Hebrides. Voyage of The Pilgrims. No. II', *Sydney Morning Herald*, 5 July 1902, p. 5.
41 *Ibid.*
42 *Ibid.*
43 *Ibid.*
44 *Ibid.*
45 '"Banjo" Paterson Ends His Story: Political Giants and "Pilgrim Fathers"', *Sydney Morning Herald*, 4 March 1939, p. 21.
46 Banjo recorded the place name as 'Tchiou'.
47 A. B. Paterson, 'The New Hebrides. Voyage of The Pilgrims. No. IV', *Sydney Morning Herald*, 19 July 1902, p. 7.

48 *Ibid.*
49 *Ibid.*
50 A. B. Paterson, 'The New Hebrides. Voyage of The Pilgrims. No. V', *Sydney Morning Herald*, 24 July 1902, p. 5.
51 '"Banjo" Paterson Ends His Story: Political Giants and "Pilgrim Fathers"', *Sydney Morning Herald*, 4 March 1939, p. 21.
52 A. B. Paterson, 'The New Hebrides. Voyage of The Pilgrims. No. V', *Sydney Morning Herald*, 24 July 1902, p. 5.
53 *Ibid.*
54 A. B. Paterson, 'The New Hebrides', *Sydney Morning Herald*, 21 July 1902, p. 7.
55 *Ibid.*
56 A. B. Paterson, 'The New Hebrides. Cannibals and Traders', *Sydney Morning Herald*, 26 July 1902, p. 12.
57 *Ibid.*
58 *Ibid.*
59 *Ibid.*
60 A. B. Paterson, 'The New Hebrides, Missionaries and Pirates', *Sydney Morning Herald*, 30 July 1902, p. 7.
61 *Ibid.*
62 A. B. Paterson to Miles Franklin, 7 August 1902, Franklin Papers, vol. 8.
63 *Ibid.*
64 A. B. Paterson, 'A Visit to Drought Land', *Sydney Morning Herald*, 23 August 1902, p. 7.
65 Jessie Paterson to Miles Franklin, 2 August 1902, Franklin Papers, vol. 8.
66 Charles Graham to Miles Franklin 2 September 1902, Franklin Papers, vol. 49.
67 'Trouble at Wingadee Station', *Sydney Morning Herald*, 29 August 1902, p. 5.
68 Rose Scott (1847–1925).
69 Jessie Paterson to Miles Franklin, 17 October 1902, 14 November 1902.
70 Linda Franklin to Miles Franklin, 16 May 1903, Franklin Papers, vol. 49.
71 'Death of Mr H. F. Barton', *Sydney Morning Herald*, 27 October 1902, p. 7.
72 George Robertson to Dick Thomson, undated, Robertson papers, Mitchell Library, State Library of New South Wales.
73 *Athenaeum*, 9 April 1903.
74 'Rio Grande's Last Race', *Sydney Morning Herald*, 6 December 1902, p. 4.
75 A. B. Paterson, 'He Giveth His Beloved Sleep', *Rio Grande's Last Race and Other Verses*, Angus & Robertson, 1902.
76 A. B. Paterson, 'Our Good Districts. And Their Prospects', *Sydney Morning Herald*, 6 December 1902, p. 11.
77 A. B. Paterson, 'Our Good Districts. The Southern Mountains' *Sydney Morning Herald*, 20 December 1902, p. 8.
78 Roderick, *Banjo Paterson: Poet by Accident*, Allen & Unwin, 1993, p. 178.
79 Charles Graham to Miles Franklin, 2 September 1902, Franklin Papers, vol. 49.
80 Bertha Lawson to Miles Franklin (undated) from Ladywood, Manly, Franklin Papers, vol. 6, p. 417.
81 Summons to Henry Lawson, 1902, in Lothian Publishing Company Records, 1895–1950, MS 6026, Box XX1A, State Library Victoria.
82 Henry Lawson, Letter to *The Bulletin*, c. 1903, in *Henry Lawson: A Campfire Yarn*, Lansdowne, 1984, p. 168.
83 'Henry Lawson: Found at Bottom of Cliffs', *Australian Star*, 8 December 1902, p. 6.
84 *Ibid.*
85 A. B. Paterson to Miles Franklin, 4 February 1903, Franklin Papers.

Chapter 20

1 Semmler, *The Banjo of the Bush* (second edition), Queensland University Press, 1974, p. 160; quoting the reminiscences of Mrs B MacSmith of Orange.
2 John William Walker (1799–1875).

3 William Henry Walker, born 24 May 1846, Castlesteads, Burrowa, New South Wales; died 27 March 1900, Tenterfield, New South Wales.
4 Francis Rawdon Hume (1803–1888).
5 Thomas Walker (1804–1886).
6 'The Late Mr W. H. Walker', *Australasian Pastoralists' Review*, 14 April 1900, p. 85.
7 *Ibid.*
8 'Social News', *Australian Town and Country Journal* (Sydney), 18 February 1903, p. 44.
9 'Orange Blossoms', *Queensland Figaro* (Brisbane), 16 April 1903, p. 14.
10 'Fashionable Wedding', *Tenterfield Intercolonial Courier and Fairfield and Wallangarra Advocate*, 10 April 1903, p. 2.
11 *Ibid.*
12 William Henry Kelly (1877–1960). He was the member for Wentworth from 16 December 1903 until 3 November 1919.
13 In more recent years, Wentworth has been represented by such Liberal figures as John Hewson and Malcolm Turnbull.
14 'Wedding', *Evening News*, 10 April 1903, p. 5.
15 *Ibid.*
16 'Interesting Items', *Tumut and Adelong Times*, 30 January 1903, p. 2.
17 Samuel Bennett (1815–1878).
18 Claude McKay, 'When a Poet Edited a Sydney Daily', *Sunday Herald* (Sydney), 9 November 1952, p. 11.
19 Walter James Jeffery (1861–1922).
20 James Alexander Hogue (2 September 1846 – 2 August 1920).
21 Charles Edward Dekker (1851–1901).
22 'Death of Mr C. E. Dekker', *Daily Telegraph* (Sydney), 4 November 1901, p. 4.
23 *Bulletin*, 7 April 1900.
24 'Death of Mr C. E. Dekker', *Daily Telegraph* (Sydney), 4 November 1901, p. 4.
25 'The Failure of "Banjo" Paterson', *Catholic Press*, 31 December 1902, p. 16.
26 A. B. Paterson to Miles Franklin, 4 February 1903.
27 'Dr Morrison', *Evening News*, 21 January 1903, p. 4.
28 *Ibid.*
29 Bertha Lawson, 'Memories', in *Henry Lawson by His Mates*, ed. Bertha Lawson [Jago] and John Le Gay Brereton, Angus & Robertson, 1931, p. 117.
30 In the Supreme Court of New South Wales Matrimonial Causes Jurisdiction, 3 April 1903.
31 Henry Lawson to George Robertson, 17 December Letters, published in Colin Roderick, ed., *Henry Lawson. Letters 1890–1922*, Angus & Robertson, 1970, Letter no. 119, pp. 137, 444.
32 'Lawson's Fall', Lothian Papers, Lothian Publishing Company Records, 1895–1950, MS 6026, Box XX1A, State Library Victoria. There is also an incomplete story which hints at a suicide attempt.
33 Bertram Stevens, *Henry Lawson* [1917]. Unpublished manuscript 1889, Angus & Robertson Publishing Manuscripts, Mitchell Library, State Library of NSW.
34 Bertha Lawson to Henry Lawson, believed to be written February 1903, Lothian Publishing Company records, 1895–1950, MS 6026, Box XX1A, State Library Victoria.
35 Bertha Lawson, Letter to Henry Lawson, April 1903, in Lothian Publishing Company Records, 1895–1950, MS 6026, Box XX1A, State Library Victoria.
36 Henry Lawson to George Robertson, 26 April 1903, in Roderick, *Henry Lawson Letters: 1890–1922*, Angus & Robertson, 1972, p. 140.
37 Claude McKay, 'When a Poet Edited a Sydney Daily', *Sunday Herald* (Sydney), 9 November 1952, p. 11.
38 Roderick, *Banjo Paterson, Poet by Accident*, Allen & Unwin, 1993, p. 182.
39 Tom was the son of Thomas E. Spencer who wrote the poem 'How MacDougall Topped the Score' for the *Bulletin* in 1901. The poem became the foundation for the 1906 book *How McDougall Topped the Score and other Verses and Sketches*.
40 'The Amateur Gardener', *Evening News*, 19 December 1903, p. 8.
41 'Duties of Racing Stewards', *Evening News*, 3 February 1903, p. 6.

42 'The Death of Gilbert the Bushranger', *Evening News*, 20 June 1903, p. 2.
43 Charles Edwin Woodrow Bean (1879–1968).
44 K. S. Inglis, 'Bean, Charles Edwin (1879–1968)', *Australian Dictionary of Biography*, Volume 7, MUP, 1979.
45 *Ibid.*
46 Claude Eric Fergusson McKay (1878–1972).
47 V. J. Carroll, 'McKay, Claude Eric Fergusson (1878–1972)', *Australian Dictionary of Biography*, Volume 15, MUP, 2000.
48 Claude McKay, 'When a Poet Edited a Sydney Daily', *Sunday Herald* (Sydney), 9 November 1952, p. 11.
49 *Ibid.*
50 'The Seven Ages of Wise', *Evening News*, 11 April 1904, p. 7.
51 'Macbreath', *Evening News*, 25 January 1904, p. 4.
52 The 'Oracle' series ran between January and December 1904.
53 'Done For The Double', *Evening News*, 16 December 1905, p. 10.
54 'Saltbush Bill on the Patriarchs', *Evening News*, 19 December 1903, p. 3 (Christmas Supplement).
55 Ethel Mary Turner (1870–1958).
56 'The Man from Goondiwindi', *Evening News*, 17 December 1904, p. 12.
57 'The Dunlop Motor Contest', *Sydney Morning Herald*, 10 February 1905, p. 4.
58 A. B. Paterson, 'Three Elephant Power', *Australian Town and Country Journal*, 11 December 1907, pp. 45–46.
59 A. B. Paterson, *Three Elephant Power and Other Stories*, Angus & Robertson, 1917.
60 A. B. Paterson, '"Banjo" Paterson Tells His Own Story. A "Reliability" Drive to Melbourne', *Sydney Morning Herald*, 18 Feb 1939, p. 21.
61 'Motoring to Melbourne', *Evening News*, 23 February 1905, p. 6.
62 *Ibid.*
63 'Overland to Melbourne', *Evening News*, 21 February 1905, p. 6.
64 A. B. Paterson, '"Banjo" Paterson Tells His Own Story. A "Reliability" Drive to Melbourne', *Sydney Morning Herald*, 18 February 1939, p. 21.
65 *Ibid.*
66 'Motoring to Melbourne', *Evening News*, 25 February 1905, p. 4.
67 'Motoring to Melbourne', *Evening News*, 23 February 1905, p. 6.
68 A. B. Paterson, '"Banjo" Paterson Tells His Own Story. A "Reliability" Drive to Melbourne', *Sydney Morning Herald*, 18 February 1939, p. 21.
69 'The Dunlop Reliability Motor Contest', *Sydney Mail and New South Wales Advertiser*, 1 March 1905, p. 545.
70 On 25 May 1905.
71 A. B. Paterson (editor), *The Old Bush Songs*, Angus & Robertson, 1905.
72 *Ibid.*
73 *Ibid.*
74 'Local Jottings', *Wellington Times* (NSW), 20 August 1906, p. 2.
75 'General', *Tumut Advocate and Farmers and Settler's Adviser,* 20 February 1906, p. 2.
76 Hugh Barton Paterson, born Woollahra, Sydney 14 May 1906; died Woollahra, Sydney, 14 November 1977.
77 'An Official Dinner', *Sydney Morning Herald*, 18 May 1906, p. 8.
78 On 29 May 1906.
79 A. B. Paterson, *An Outback Marriage*, Angus & Robertson, 1906.
80 'Books and Publications', *Evening News,* 24 November 1906, p. 9.
81 'Current Literature', *Sydney Morning Herald*, 17 November 1906, p. 4.
82 Claude McKay, *This is the Life: the autobiography of a newspaperman*, Angus & Robertson, 1961, p. 58.
83 'Criminal Monster', *Sunday Times,* 16 July 1905, p. 5.
84 Claude McKay, *This is the Life: the autobiography of a newspaperman*, Angus & Robertson, 1961, p. 58.

85 'A Football Match. Brutality in Sydney', *Evening News*, 19 May 1903, p. 8.
86 'A Jest That Failed', *Evening News*, 21 May 1903, p. 4.
87 'A Prognathous-Jawed Joke', *Truth* (Sydney), 24 May 1903, p. 2.
88 'A Jest That Failed', *Evening News*, 21 May 1903, p. 4.
89 'The Ban-Joey Bloke', *Truth*, 29 November 1903, p. 2.
90 'All About People', *Catholic Press* (Sydney), 17 May 1906, p. 14.
91 'The Week's Work', *Evening News*, 27 August 1908, p. 4.
92 'Progress of the Evening News', *Evening News*, 11 October 1906, p. 6.
93 A. B. Paterson, 'The Dauntless Three', *Evening News*, 8 December 1906, p. 4.
94 A. B. Paterson, 'Santa Claus in the Bush', *Australian Town and Country Journal* (Sydney), 12 December 1906, p. 34.
95 'Thomas Walker Convalescent Hospital', *Australian Town and Country Journal*, 18 December 1907, p. 50.
96 'Divorce Court', *Sydney Morning Herald*, 5 June 1903, p. 8.
97 Henry Lawson, 'The Alleys', *Bulletin*, 24 September 1903.
98 'Woman in the Water', *Evening News*, 27 December 1904, p. 5.
99 *Ibid.*
100 Henry Lawson, 'One Hundred and Three', *Bulletin*, 26 November 1908, p. 39.
101 Thomas Carlyle Lothian (1884–1974), proprietor and founder of the Lothian Publishing Company.
102 T. C. Lothian to Henry Lawson, 7 March 1907. Lothian Papers.
103 T. C. Lothian to Harry F. Chaplin, 12 September 1961.
104 T. C. Lothian to Henry Lawson, 5 December 1907. Lothian Papers.
105 'Advertising', *Sydney Wool and Stock Journal*, 3 January 1908, p. 7.
106 Now called Coodravale.
107 A. B. Paterson, '"Banjo" Paterson Tells His Own Story. A "Reliability" Drive to Melbourne', *Sydney Morning Herald*, 18 February 1939, p. 21.
108 Semmler, *The Banjo of the Bush* (second edition), Queensland University Press, 1974, p. 160.
109 A. B. Paterson, '"Banjo" Paterson Tells His Own Story. A "Reliability" Drive to Melbourne', *Sydney Morning Herald*, 18 February 1939, p. 21.
110 'Advertising', *Yass Courier*, 4 February 1908, p. 2.
111 Dated 20 October 1908.
112 'Social Items', *Evening News*, 16 May 1908, p. 14.
113 'Lawn Tennis', *Sunday Times* (Sydney), 10 May 1908, p. 11.
114 A. B. Paterson to George Robertson, 15 June 1908, George Robertson papers, Mitchell Library, State Library of NSW.
115 A. B. Paterson, '"Banjo" Paterson Tells His Own Story. A "Reliability" Drive to Melbourne', *Sydney Morning Herald*, 18 February 1939, p. 21.
116 *Ibid.*
117 'Bush Fires', *Northern Miner* (Charters Towers), 5 January 1909, p. 5.
118 'Bush Fires in The Yass District', *Goulburn Evening Penny Post*, 5 January 1909, p. 3.
119 'An Australian Pioneer', *Evening News*, 25 August 1909, p. 8.

Chapter 21

1 *A. B. Paterson*, 'A Mountain Station', *Bulletin*, 19 December 1891, p. 19.
2 'Dresses and Attendance', *Sydney Morning Herald*, 15 April 1909, p. 8.
3 'Vice-Regal Ball. A Magnificent Scene', *Sydney Morning Herald*, 21 April 1909, p. 10.
4 Born Rachel Gurney (1868–1920). Her great-granddaughter is the actress Rachel Ward, wife of Australian actor Bryan Brown.
5 A. B. Paterson, *Happy Dispatches*, Angus & Robertson, 1934, Chapter XIII: Lady Dudley.
6 *Ibid.*
7 *Ibid.*
8 *Ibid.*
9 *Ibid.*
10 *Ibid.*

11 Andrew Fisher (29 August 1862 – 22 October 1928).
12 William Ward, 2nd Earl of Dudley (25 May 1867 – 29 June 1932).
13 On 31 July 1911.
14 In an ABC script 'News' written in a series 'The Land of Adventure' (1935).
15 A. B. Paterson to George Robertson, State Library of NSW, MLMSS 8404.
16 It was finally published in its entirety in 1983, inside Banjo's collected works.
17 'Concentrates', *Cobar Herald*, 28 January 1910, p. 4.
18 'Reminiscences of Henry Lawson by Isabel Byers' (1925), edited by Aubrey C. Curtis, in Lawson Family Papers, MLMSS 3694/Box 2/Folder 2, State Library of NSW.
19 *Ibid.*
20 Edwin J. Brady, from J.K. Moir Collection (Box 23/5) of the State Library of Victoria, 1938; Moir, 'Notes on Henry Lawson' by E.J. Brady. Originally written in *Books by Lawson*, J. K. Moir, from *La Trobe Journal*, No. 70, Spring 2002, p. 86.
21 A. B. Paterson, 'A Mountain Station', *Bulletin*, 19 December 1891, p. 19.
22 Now better known as 'Glenesk'.
23 'Glen Esk', *Grenfell Record and Lachlan District Advertiser*, 10 July 1914, p. 6.
24 'Advertising', *Grenfell Record and Lachlan District Advertiser*, 7 October 1911, p. 7.
25 *Ibid.*
26 'At the Races', *Evening News*, 11 April 1912, p. 12.
27 'Social Chat of the Day', *The Newsletter*, 6 July 1912, p. 9.
28 'Ball on the Medina', *Sydney Morning Herald*, 22 August 1912, p. 10.
29 'Plain and Fancy Dress Ball at Bimbi', *Grenfell Record and Lachlan District Advertiser*, 27 August 1912, p. 2.
30 'Bushfire', *Sydney Morning Herald*, 29 January 1913, p. 14.
31 *Riverine Grazier* (Hay, New South Wales) 4 February 1913, p. 4.
32 'Social Chat of the Day', *The Newsletter*, 11 October 1913, p. 11.
33 Dame Eadith Campbell Walker (1861–1937).
34 Geoffrey Evan Fairfax (1861–1930).
35 Claude McKay, *This is the Life: the autobiography of a newspaperman*, Angus & Robertson, 1961.
36 John Newton Wellesley Wanliss (1861–1950), the chairman of the Gordon Memorial Committee.
37 The letter is dated 28 August 1913.
38 Sir Frank James Fox (1874–1960).

Chapter 22

1 A. B. Paterson, 'With Our Troops', *Sydney Morning Herald*, 20 November 1914, p. 8.
2 *Sydney Morning Herald*, 22 May 1893, p. 6.
3 Shane Maloney and Chris Grosz, 'Archduke Franz Ferdinand & the Platypus', *Monthly*, May 2011.
4 Luigi Albertini, *The Origins of the War of 1914*, vol. 2, Oxford University Press, 1953.
5 Morton, *Thunder at Twilight*, Da Capo Press, 2014.
6 Henry Lawson, 'Australia's Forgotten Flag' (aka 'The Flag of Eureka'), in *A Fantasy of Man: Henry Lawson Complete Works 1901–1922*, Leonard Cronin (editor), Lansdowne, 1984, pp. 508–509.
7 Anthony MacDougall, *Australians at War: A Pictorial History*, The Five Mile Press, 1995.
8 A. B. Paterson, 'Making an Army', *Sydney Morning Herald*, 4 September 1914, p. 6.
9 *Ibid.*
10 'Lady Dudley's Appeal', *Sydney Morning Herald*, 4 September 1914, p. 6.
11 A. B. Paterson, 'Red Cross Work', *Sydney Morning Herald*, 15 September 1914, p. 8.
12 A. B. Paterson, 'Application of the Funds', *Sydney Morning Herald*, 22 August 1914, p. 6.
13 Dr David Stevens, 'Australian Sea Transport 1914', navy.gov.au.
14 On 3 October 1914.
15 Sir Ronald Craufurd Munro Ferguson, Viscount Novar of Raith (1860–1934).
16 'On The Lawn', *Sydney Morning Herald*, 5 October 1914, p. 3.
17 nationalanzaccentre.com.au.

18 *Ibid.*
19 *Ibid.*
20 Major General Sir William Throsby Bridges (18 February 1861 – 18 May 1915).
21 A. B. Paterson, 'The Transports', *Sydney Morning Herald*, 8 December 1914, p. 8.
22 *Ibid.*
23 Brigadier General Henry Normand MacLaurin (31 October 1878 – 27 April 1915). He was promoted to Brigadier posthumously.
24 A. B. Paterson, *Happy Dispatches*, Angus & Robertson, 1934, Chapter XII: Captain Glossop.
25 Robert John 'Jack' Allwright Massie (8 July 1890 – 14 February 1966).
26 His father Hugh Massie played nine Tests for Australia.
27 A. B. Paterson, 'With The Troops', *Sydney Morning Herald*, 1 January 1915, p. 3.
28 *Ibid.*
29 *Ibid.*
30 *Ibid.*
31 A. B. Paterson, *Happy Dispatches*, Angus & Robertson, 1934, Chapter XII: Captain Glossop.
32 John Collings Taswell Glossop (1871–1934).
33 'Narrative of the Proceedings of H.M.A.S. Sydney', *Naval Review*, The Naval Society, 1915, pp. 448–459.
34 Karl Friedrich Max von Müller (16 June 1873 – 11 March 1923).
35 'Result of Emden's Capture. German Prince Goes Mad', *Queensland Times* (Ipswich), 20 March 1915, p. 3.
36 A. B. Paterson, *Happy Dispatches*, Angus & Robertson, 1934, Chapter XII: Captain Glossop.
37 *Ibid.*
38 *Ibid.*
39 *Ibid.*
40 *Ibid.*

Chapter 23

1 A. B. Paterson, 'Moving On', *Kia-ora Coo-ee* (= monthly magazine for Australian and New Zealand troops in the Middle East), May 1918. According to an early Paterson biographer, Florence Earle Hooper, it was written as a farewell to Major Weir of Yass, who visited Paterson at Moascar, in Egypt, during the First World War.
2 A. B. Paterson, 'The First Force: End of the Voyage', *Sydney Morning Herald*, 12 January 1915, p. 9.
3 *Ibid.*
4 A. B. Paterson, *Happy Dispatches*, Angus & Robertson, 1934, Chapter XIII: Lady Dudley.
5 General Sir Archibald Hunter (6 September 1856 – 28 June 1936).
6 A. B. Paterson, *Happy Dispatches*, Angus & Robertson, 1934, Chapter XIII: Lady Dudley.
7 Sir Timothy Augustine Coghlan (1855–1926).
8 A. B. Paterson, *Happy Dispatches*, Angus & Robertson, 1934, Chapter XIII: Lady Dudley.
9 *Ibid.*
10 William L'Estrange Eames (1863–1956).
11 David Horner, 'Eames, William L'Estrange (1863–1956)', *Australian Dictionary of Biography*, Volume 8, MUP, 1981.
12 Edward 'Cub' Kennedy (1860–1925).
13 A. B. Paterson, *Happy Dispatches*, Angus & Robertson, 1934, Chapter XIII: Lord Derby.
14 Beryl Doris Lumsdaine (1886–1988), daughter of Edwin Lumsdaine and Banjo's sister Flo Paterson.
15 Sir Alexander MacCormick (1856–1947).
16 Lawrence Herschel Levi Harris (1871–1920).
17 A. B. Paterson, *Happy Dispatches*, Angus & Robertson, 1934, Chapter XIII: Lady Dudley.
18 A. B. Paterson, *Song of the Pen, Lansdowne Press, 1983, p.* 579, Originally from a wireless talk, 'War'.
19 *Ibid.*
20 A. B. Paterson, *Happy Dispatches*, Angus & Robertson, 1934, Chapter XIII: Lady Dudley.

21 A. B. Paterson, *Song of the Pen, Lansdowne Press, 1983, p.* 579, from a Wireless Talk entitled 'War'.
22 A. B. Paterson, *Happy Dispatches*, Angus & Robertson, 1934, Chapter XIII: Lady Dudley.
23 'Countess of Dudley Drowned While Bathing. Gifted and Popular Lady', *Sydney Morning Herald*, 29 June 1920, p. 8. An excellent swimmer, she went to bathe with her maid while staying in Ireland in 1920, and drowned while in the sight of that maid, who was powerless to assist.
24 A. B. Paterson, *Happy Dispatches*, Angus & Robertson, 1934, Chapter XIII: Lady Dudley.
25 Sir Almroth Edward Wright (10 August 1861 – 30 April 1947).
26 A. B. Paterson, *Happy Dispatches*, Angus & Robertson, 1934, Chapter XIII: Lady Dudley.
27 *Ibid.*
28 Sir Ernest Beachcroft Beckwith Towse (23 April 1864 – 21 June 1948).
29 Arthur Lincoln Haydon, *The Book of the V.C.*, Dutton, 1907, p. 248.
30 A. B. Paterson, *Happy Dispatches*, Angus & Robertson, 1934, Chapter XIV: Captain Towse, VC.
31 A. B. Paterson, 'We're All Australians Now', written in 1915 for Australian troops, first published 'To Aid Recruiting', *Warwick Examiner and Times* (Qld) 16 July 1917, p. 1.
32 A. B. Paterson, *Happy Dispatches*, Angus & Robertson, 1934, Chapter XV: Hell-Fire Jack.
33 *Ibid.*
34 Australian Imperial Force unit war diaries, 1914–18 War – AWM4 Subclass 28/1 – Australian Remount Depot.
35 A. B. Paterson, *Happy Dispatches*, Angus & Robertson, 1934, Chapter XV: Hell-Fire Jack.
36 Brigadier Sir Charles Loftus Bates (1863–1951).
37 A. B. Paterson, *Happy Dispatches*, Angus & Robertson, 1934, Chapter XV: Hell-Fire Jack.
38 Brigadier-General John Robinson Royston (29 April 1860 – 25 April 1942).
39 A. B. Paterson, *Happy Dispatches*, Angus & Robertson, 1934, Chapter XV: Hell-Fire Jack.
40 *Ibid.*
41 *Ibid.*
42 General Sir Archibald James Murray (23 April 1860 – 21 January 1945).
43 A. B. Paterson in Heliopolis, Egypt, to Doris Lumsdaine, 8 May 1916, National Library of Australia, NLA MS 9226.
44 On 10 November 1916, from Australian Imperial Force unit war diaries, 1914–18 War – AWM4 Subclass 28/1 – Australian Remount Depot.
45 A. B. Paterson, *Happy Dispatches*, Angus & Robertson, 1934, Chapter XVI: Lord Allenby.
46 *Ibid.*
47 A. B. Paterson, *Happy Dispatches*, Angus & Robertson, 1934, Chapter XVI: Lord Allenby.
48 Later Field Marshal Edmund Henry Hynman Allenby, 1st Viscount Allenby (23 April 1861 – 14 May 1936).
49 A. B. Paterson, *Happy Dispatches*, Angus & Robertson, 1934, Chapter XVI: Lord Allenby.
50 On 20 December 1916.
51 Australian Imperial Force unit war diaries, 1914–18 War – AWM4 Subclass 28/1 – Australian Remount Depot.
52 Paterson, Andrew Barton (Banjo), National Archives of Australia, Series number: B2455.
53 *Ibid.*
54 Australian Imperial Force unit war diaries, 1914–18 War – AWM4 Subclass 28/1 – Australian Remount Depot.
55 A. B. Paterson, *Happy Dispatches*, Angus & Robertson, 1934, Chapter XVI: Lord Allenby.
56 Kermit Roosevelt (10 October 1889 – 4 June 1943).
57 Kermit Roosevelt, *War in the Garden of Eden*, Charles Scribner's Sons, 1919, pp. 199–200.
58 Better known now as El Qantara.
59 Australian Imperial Force unit war diaries, 1914–18 War – AWM4 Subclass 28/1 – Australian Remount Depot.
60 A. B. Paterson, *Happy Dispatches*, Angus & Robertson, 1934, Chapter XVII: Lord Allenby.
61 Information supplied by the British Red Cross, London.
62 'Gone to Egypt', *Moree Gwydir Examiner and General Advertiser*, 18 January 1918, p. 2.
63 'Through the Eyes of a Woman', *Mirror* (Sydney), 27 April 1919, p. 6.
64 A. B. Paterson, *Happy Dispatches*, Angus & Robertson, 1934, Chapter XVII: Lord Allenby.
65 *Ibid.*

66 Australian Imperial Force unit war diaries, 1914–18 War – AWM4 28/1/6 PART 2 – August–September 1918 – Australian Remount Depot.
67 From Captain Adele Catts, Museum Manager, Army Museum South Queensland, Victoria Barracks, Petrie Terrace, Brisbane, blogs.slq.qld.gov.au.
68 'Late Douglas Walker', *Darling Downs Gazette* (Qld), 23 August 1920, p. 2.
69 A. B. Paterson, *Song of the Pen*, Lansdowne Press, 1983, p. 510, originally from a wireless talk, 'Men and Horses'.
70 A. B. Paterson, *Happy Dispatches*, Angus & Robertson, 1934, Chapter XVII: Lord Allenby.

Chapter 24

1 'A Menace to the Turf', *Sydney Sportsman*, 7 October 1924, p. 3.
2 Andrew Powell, head of school, 'Sport at Ascham plays an integral role in the girls' education', *Ascham Old Girls' Magazine*, Winter 2017.
3 'Sydney Week by Week', *Table Talk* (Melbourne), 22 May 1919, p. 2.
4 'Personals in Sport', *Referee* (Sydney), 14 May 1919, p. 1.
5 A. B. Paterson, *Three Elephant Power and Other Stories*, Angus & Robertson, Sydney, 1917.
6 A. B. Paterson, *Saltbush Bill J.P. and Other Verses*, Angus & Robertson, Sydney, 1917.
7 A. B. Paterson to George Robertson, 15 December 1919.
8 George Robertson to A. B. Paterson, 6 January 1920.
9 Sir James John Joynton Smith (October 1858 – 10 October 1943).
10 Henry Lawson, 'The Township', *Smith's Weekly*, 7 June 1919.
11 A. B. Paterson, 'Gilded Brick', *Smith's Weekly*, 12 July 1919, p. 3.
12 Frank Beaumont 'Beau' Smith (15 August 1885 – 2 January 1950).
13 'The Man from Snowy River', *Mail* (Adelaide), 6 November 1920, p. 7.
14 'The Man from Snowy River', *Mail* (Adelaide), 20 November 1920, p. 11.
15 *Ibid.*
16 Semmler, *The Banjo of the Bush* (second edition), Queensland University Press, 1974, p. 178.
17 A. B. Paterson, *The Collected Verse of A. B. Paterson*, Angus & Robertson, 1921.
18 Ezra Norton (1897–1967).
19 John Norton (1858–1916).
20 'God Save the Queen', *Truth* (Sydney), 27 September 1896, p. 4.
21 'Dudley Dementia', *Truth* (Brisbane), 18 September 1910, p. 1.
22 'Great Australian Journalist, J. F. Archibald', *Sydney Sportsman*, 25 January 1922, p. 9.
23 William Beckwith (Billy) McInnes (1889–1939). He won the prize seven times.
24 'First Archibald Art Prize', *Truth* (Sydney), 22 January 1922, p. 1.
25 Semmler, *The Banjo of the Bush* (second edition), Queensland University Press, 1974, p. 206.
26 'Arthur Mailey: Bowler and Artist, His Views on Cricket', *Sportsman*, 19 January 1921, p. 1.
27 'Lawn Tennis', *Sydney Morning Herald*, 27 August 1921, p. 14.
28 'Lawn Tennis', *West Australian* (Perth), 11 May 1922, p. 9.
29 'Sydney's Tennis Carnival: The New South Wales Championships', *Sydney Mail*, 17 May 1922, p. 20.
30 *Ibid.*
31 'Henry Lawson, State Funeral', *Sydney Morning Herald*, 5 September 1922, p. 10.
32 Vincent Gatton Kelly (1898–1976). A prolific author, he worked for *Smith's Weekly* and the *Sun*.
33 Roderick, *Banjo Paterson, Poet by Accident*, Allen & Unwin, 1993, p. 219.
34 'Henry Lawson', *Sydney Morning Herald*, 16 September 1922, p. 14.
35 'Sydney Day by Day', *Argus*, 4 October 1922, p. 10.
36 Semmler, *The Banjo of the Bush* (second edition), Queensland University Press, 1974, p. 184.
37 *Ibid.*
38 'A Ned Kelly System', *Sydney Sportsman*, 8 August 1922, p. 1.
39 A. B. Paterson to George Robertson, 2 February 1924, State Library of NSW.
40 A. B. Paterson, 'That Half-Crown Sweep: A Tale of The Territory', *Sportsman*, 11 January 1922.
41 A. B. Paterson, 'Jimmy Dooley's Army, A Political Ballad by Our Bolshevik Bard', *Sydney Sportsman*, 16 January 1923.
42 A. B. Paterson, 'Typographical: A Ballad of Burdens', *Sydney Sportsman*, 24 April 1923.